SEEING RACE BEFORE RACE

VISUAL CULTURE AND THE RACIAL MATRIX IN THE PREMODERN WORLD

SEEING RACE BEFORE RACE

VISUAL CULTURE AND THE RACIAL MATRIX IN THE PREMODERN WORLD

EDITED BY

NOÉMIE NDIAYE

AND **LIA MARKEY**

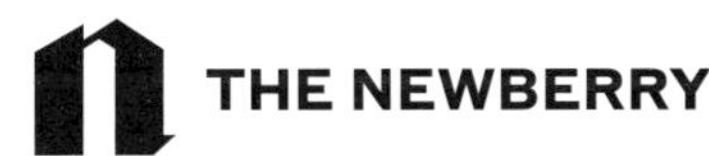

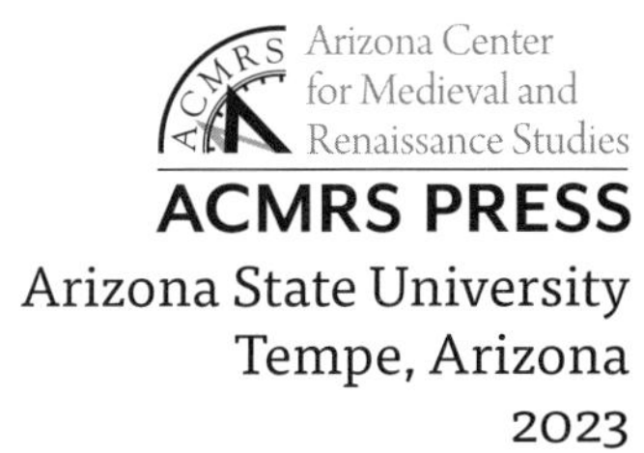

Arizona State University
Tempe, Arizona
2023

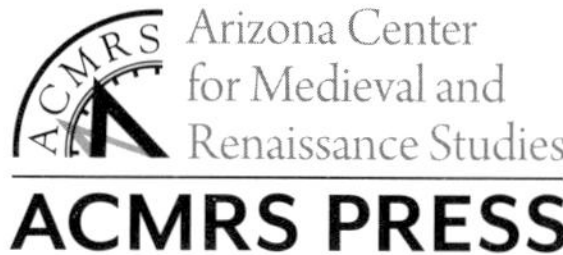

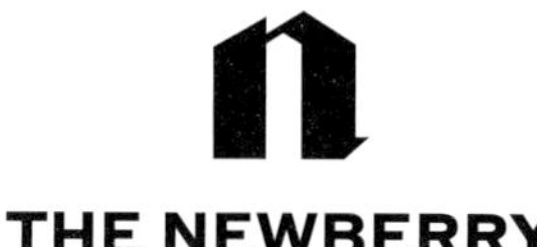

Seeing Race Before Race: Visual Culture and the Racial Matrix in the Premodern World was published in 2023 by ACMRS Press at Arizona State University in Tempe, Arizona in cooperation with The Newberry Library.

This book is available online at https://asu.pressbooks.pub/seeing-race-before-race/

Library of Congress Cataloging-in-Publication Data
Names: Ndiaye, Noémie, editor. | Markey, Lia, editor.
Title: Seeing race before race : visual culture and the racial matrix in the premodern world / edited by Noémie Ndiaye and Lia Markey.
Description: Tempe, Arizona : ACMRS Press, Arizona State University, 2023. | Includes bibliographical references and index. | Summary: "Explores the deployment of racial thinking and racial formations in the visual culture of the pre-modern world"-- Provided by publisher.
Identifiers: LCCN 2023009258 (print) | LCCN 2023009259 (ebook) | ISBN 9780866988414 (hardcover) | ISBN 9780866988421 (paperback) | ISBN 9780866988438 (ebook)
Subjects: LCSH: Race awareness in art. | Arts and society. | BISAC: PHILOSOPHY / Movements / Critical Theory | ART / History / Renaissance
Classification: LCC NX650.R34 S44 2023 (print) | LCC NX650.R34 (ebook) | DDC 701.03--dc23/eng/20230331
LC record available at https://lccn.loc.gov/2023009258
LC ebook record available at https://lccn.loc.gov/2023009259

Printed in the United States of America.

CONTENTS

xi *Foreword*
Ayanna Thompson and Daniel Greene

xiii *Introduction*
Noémie Ndiaye and Lia Markey

Part 1: FIGURING

3 **Essay 1**
Manuscripts and Printed Books: Book History and Race
Brandi K. Adams and Carissa M. Harris

21 **Essay 2**
Fashioning Racial Materiality in Nicolas de Nicolay's Representations of Jews
M. Lindsay Kaplan and Dana E. Katz

41 **Note From the Field 1**
"Touching each book":
Demystifying Special Collections in Community
Analú María López

51 **Exhibition Catalogue: "Seeing Race Before Race"**
Part 1: *Figuring*. Entries 1–14.

Part 2: MAPPING

83 **Essay 3**
Geographies of Race: Constructions of Constantinople/Istanbul in the Western European Imaginary
Roland Betancourt and Ambereen Dadabhoy

CONTENTS

107 **Essay 4**
Race, Empire, and Cartography
Ricardo Padrón and Risa Puleo

129 **Note From the Field 2**
Displaying Black Art in the Medieval Galleries at The Met Museum
Andrea Myers Achi

135 **Exhibition Catalogue: "Seeing Race Before Race"**
Part 2: *Mapping*. Entries 15-26

Part 3: PERFORMING

161 **Essay 5**
Back Bending Labor, Savage Dances, Pious Stances: Race in Motion between Africa and the Americas
Elena FitzPatrick Sifford and Cécile Fromont

183 **Note From the Field 3**
Bringing Premodern Critical Race Consciousness to Shakespeare's Globe Theatre.
Farah Karim-Cooper

189 **Exhibition Catalogue: "Seeing Race Before Race."**
Part 3: *Performing*. Entries 27–42.

217 ***Interview***
On Early Modern Critical Race Studies and Critical Indigenous Studies
Kim F. Hall, Scott Manning Stevens, L. Lehua Yim

229 ***Glossary***

235 ***Bibliography***

257 ***Acknowledgments***

259 ***Biographies of Contributors***

267 ***Index***

LIST OF ILLUSTRATIONS

Introduction

1 Nikolaus Rugendas the Elder, *Figure Clock with an African Man*, ca. 1620 11 ½ × 6 × 5 ¼ in. (29.21 × 15.24 × 13.34 cm), gilt brass, gilt copper, iron, blued iron, and polychrome decoration, Milwaukee Museum of Art, Gift of Gabriele Flagg Pfeiffer M1995.670. Photo credit: Larry Sanders

Part 1: Figuring

1.1 *A collection of serious, humorous and affectionate poems,* early 18th century, manuscript, Newberry Library, VAULT Case MS Y 184 .18

1.2 *A LETTER from a Merchant at JAMAICA TO A Member of Parliament in LONDON, Touching the AFRICAN TRADE. To which is added, A SPEECH made by a BLACK of Gardaloupe, at the Funeral of a Fellow-Negro*, London, 1709, Newberry Library, Ayer 1000.5 .J25 L65 1709

1.3 Anonymous Artist, *Double portrait of two women with face patches*, oil on canvas, circa 1650, location unknown

2.1 Nicolas de Nicolay, "Jewish Physician" (170r), *Les navigations pérégrinations et voyages, faicts en la Turquie*, Antwerp, 1576, Newberry Library, Wing ZP 5465 .S587

2.2 Nicolas de Nicolay, "Jewish Merchant" (249r), *Les navigations pérégrinations et voyages, faicts en la Turquie*, Antwerp, 1576, Newberry Library, Wing ZP 5465 .S587

2.3 Pietro Bertelli, "Jewish Peddler" (Plate 15), *Diversarum nationum habitus* (1594–1596), Folger Library, GT513 B4 Cage copy 1 vol. 1

2.4 Nicolas de Nicolay, "Jewish woman of Andrinople" (276r), *Les navigations pérégrinations et voyages, faicts en la Turquie*, Antwerp, 1576, Newberry Library, Wing ZP 5465 .S587

2.5 Nicolas de Nicolay, "Christian gentlewoman of Pera" (123r), *Les navigations pérégrinations et voyages, faicts en la Turquie*, Antwerp, 1576, Newberry Library, Wing ZP 5465 .S587

2.6 Nicolas de Nicolay, "Young Jewish woman of Andrinople" (277r), *Les navigations pérégrinations et voyages, faicts en la Turquie*, Antwerp, 1576, Newberry Library, Wing ZP 5465 .S587

2.7 Nicolas de Nicolay, "Christian gentlewoman of Andrinople" (268r), *Les navigations pérégrinations et voyages, faicts en la Turquie*, Antwerp, 1576, Newberry Library, Wing ZP 5465 .S587

Note 1

1 Nahua youth from the Cuentepec community viewing the facsimile copy of a 1524 map of Tenochtitlan, Cuentepec, Morelos, Mexico, 2022 (Photo: Victorino Torres Nava (Nahua)

Part 2: Mapping

3.1 Hartmann Schedel, "Constantinople" in *Liber chronicarum*. Nuremberg, 1493, Newberry Library, VAULT oversize Inc. 2084

3.2 Henry Holcroft, Frontispiece of *The history of the warres of the Emperour Justinian*, London, 1653, Newberry Library, Case Y 642 .P82

3.3 Nicolas de Nicolay, "Grand Dame Turque" (98r), *Les navigations pérégrinations et voyages, faicts en la Turquie*, Antwerp, 1576, Newberry Library, Wing ZP 5465 .S587

3.4 Nicolas de Nicolay, "Fille de Ioye Turque" (270r), *Les navigations pérégrinations et voyages, faicts en la Turquie*, Antwerp, 1576, Newberry Library, Wing ZP 5465 .S587

4.1 Nicolas de Fer, "L'Amérique, Divisée Selon l'étendue Ses Principales Parties," 1698, Newberry Library, Novacco 8F 02 01

4.2 Map of lands in the Tultepec and Jaltocán regions adjacent to the Hacienda de Santa Inés (Mexico), 1569, Pen-and-ink and watercolor (red, green, brown, yellow); mounted on amatl paper, Newberry Library, VAULT drawer Ayer MS 1801 map 1

4.3 Detail from Nicolas de Fer, "L'Europe Divisée Selon l'étendue de Ses Principales Parties," Paris, 1696, Bibliothèque Nationale de France

4.4 Detail from Nicolas de Fer, "L'Europe Ou Tous Les Points Principaux." Paris, 1695, Bibliothèque Nationale de France

4.5 Detail from Nicolas de Fer, "L'Asie Divisée Selon l'étendue de Ses Principales Parties...," 1696. Bibliothèque Nationale de France

4.6 MS. Arch. Selden. A. 1, fol 2r, *Codex Mendoza*, Viceroyalty of New Spain, c. 1541–1542, pigment on paper, © Bodleian Libraries, University of Oxford

4.7 *Codex Reese*, sixteenth-century Mexico, Yale Collection of Western Americana, Beinecke Rare Book & Manuscript Library

4.8 Toponyms for Tultepec, Wikipedia

Note 2

1 Crossroads Installation 2020 (left: *Male Figure with Raised Arms*, 14th–17th Century, Dogon peoples, The Michael C. Rockefeller Memorial Collection, Gift of Nelson A. Rockefeller, 1969 (1978.412.322) and right: *African Magus, one of the Three Kings from an Adoration Group*, before 1489, German, The Cloisters Collection (1952. 52.83.2)

2 *Terracotta vase with janiform heads*, 4th century B.C.E., Metropolitan Museum of Art, Rogers Fund, 1906, 06.1021.204

Part 3: Performing

5.1 Christoph Weiditz, "African with a wineskin" in *Trachtenbuch*,1529, Germanisches Nationalmuseum, Nuremberg, Germany

5.2 Theodor de Bry, "Nigritae exhaustis venis metallicis consiciendo saccharo operam dare debent," in *America. Pt. 5*, Frankfurt am Main, 1590, Newberry Library, VAULT Ayer 110 .B9 1590b v. 5

5.3 Michel Wolgemut, "Dance of Death" in Hartmann Schedel, *Liber chronicarum*. Nuremberg, 1493, Newberry Library, VAULT oversize Inc. 2084

5.4 Hans Burgkmair, "Natives of Guinea and Algoa," 1508, handcolored woodcut (28.5 × 42.4 cm), Freiherrlich von Welsersche Familienstiftung, Neunhof (Photo credit: copyright Freiherrlich v. Welsersche Familienstiftung)

5.5 Theodor de Bry, "Virginiensium saltandi ratio solennibus festis," in *America. Pt. 1*, Frankfurt am Main, 1590, Newberry Library, VAULT Ayer 110 .B9 1590b v. 1

5.6 Theodor de Bry, "Prestigiator," in *America. Pt. 1*, Frankfurt am Main, 1590, Newberry Library, VAULT Ayer 110 .B9 1590b v. 1

5.7 Paolo da Lorena (attr.), Plate 23 in Giovanni Antonio Cavazzi and Fortunato Alamandini, *Istorica descrizione de' tre' regni Congo, Matamba, et Angola,* Bologna, 1687, Newberry Library, Ayer 263 .C211 C2 1687

5.8 Paolo da Lorena (attr.), Plate 25 in Giovanni Antonio Cavazzi and Fortunato Alamandini, *Istorica descrizione de' tre' regni Congo, Matamba, et Angola,* Bologna, 1687, Newberry Library, Ayer 263 .C211 C2 1687

5.9 Unidentified Artist, *Saint Luis Beltrán Baptizing an African Slave*, 39 ½ x 30 ⅛ in, oil on canvas, Ecuador, 1750, Thoma Foundation

5.10 Klauber Workshop. *St. Francis Xavier Baptizing a Native*, engraving, 18th century. Trento, Museo Diocesano Tridentino

5.11 Unknown Capuchin artist, *Black Lord or Prince in the Countryside,* watercolor on paper, 34 ×24 cm, late seventeenth century, Parma Watercolors, folio 27, Virgili Collection, Photograph: C. Fromont

5.12 Tenerani and Voigt, *Bolivar Freeing the Slaves Statue Inauguration*, silver medal, 48.58 mm.; 57.96 gms, 1846, Colonial Williamsburg Foundation, accession #2002–28

5.13 Copy of Thomas Ball, *Emancipation Memorial*, bronze, 1876, Boston

5.14 Paul Colin, *Josephine Baker*, crayon and gouache on paper, 1930, Framed H x W x D: 111.8 × 82.6 × 3.8 cm (44 in. × 32 ½ in. × 1 ½ in.), The Collection of Richard H. Driehaus, Chicago, inv. 49.2016.3

FOREWORD

"It's about time," as Lia Markey and Noémie Ndiaye explain in their introduction to this groundbreaking book, to see anew—or perhaps, for some readers, to see for the first time—the many ways that race and racial thinking are represented in the visual culture of premodern times. This volume, accompanying an exhibition opening at the Newberry Library in September 2023, explores multiple expressions of racial formation in the visual culture of the premodern world (1300–1800). The visual archive brought to light here in words and images includes annotated and illuminated manuscripts, Renaissance costume books and travel books, maps and cartographic volumes produced by both Europeans and Indigenous peoples, mass-printed pamphlets, decorative arts, religious iconography, paintings, ceremonial objects, festival books, and play texts intended for live performance, among others. This expansive exploration is one of the greatest strengths of *Seeing Race Before Race;* indeed, we can see expressions of what co-editor Noémie Ndiaye calls "the racial matrix" across the medieval/early modern chronological divide and across vast transnational and multilingual geographies. The product of a remarkable collaboration between the Newberry Library and RaceB4Race®—an ongoing conference series and professional network community by and for scholars of color working on issues of race in premodern literature, history, and culture—the book intends to serve as a starting point for fresh and ambitious conversations among scholars of premodern race studies, art history, performance studies, and book history.

This shared commitment to multidisciplinarity and collaboration brought the Newberry and RaceB4Race® together more than three years ago to envision this project. In addition to the catalogue and exhibition, *Seeing Race Before Race* includes enduring resources for scholars, school teachers, and the public. As this project encourages both scholarly and public audiences to see race and expressions of racial thinking across the vast visual archive from centuries ago, we hope it will lead to deeper understandings not only of the past, but also of present and future expressions of race and racism.

The *Seeing Race Before Race* project has relied on contributions from staff at the Newberry Library and the RaceB4Race® collective. Noémie Ndiaye, Assistant Professor of Renaissance and Early Modern English Literature at the University of Chicago and Executive Board Member of RaceB4Race®, has been an essential collaborator with Newberry co-curators, Lia Markey, Christopher Fletcher, and Rebecca Fall, in providing curatorial vision for this exhibition and accompanying publication. Noémie and Lia brought together a dedicated community through this project, including both colleagues and students in their research process. Here, they have collected contributions from 39 individuals, including undergraduate and graduate students who helped write catalog entries. The book also highlights collaborative essays written by senior and early career scholars in diverse disciplines.

The *Seeing Race Before Race* book received generous funding from the Kress Foundation to defray the costs of publication. We're also grateful to the University of Chicago Quad Undergraduate Research Scholars Program, which supported research by graduate assistant Vivian Lei. ACMRS Press, the publications division of the Arizona Center for Medieval and Renaissance Studies at Arizona State University, has been an essential partner in the production process of *Seeing Race Before Race*. And the stunning images of Newberry collection items included here are the work of staff photographer Catherine Gass.

It is our hope that this volume will inspire further collaborative, multidisciplinary projects. The co-editors, our institutions, and the RaceB4Race® collective have all benefited from seeing and thinking about the racial matrix anew. While this volume is innovative in its scope and focus, it is also intended to inspire other scholars, teachers, students, and artists to see and interpret archival materials in new ways. What have we not seen? How do we continue to challenge ourselves to see anew?

— Ayanna Thompson
Regents Professor of English and Director of the Arizona Center for Medieval & Renaissance Studies, Arizona State University

— Daniel Greene
President and Librarian, Newberry Library

INTRODUCTION

By Noémie Ndiaye and Lia Markey

The work of Augsburg-based clockmaker Nikolaus Rugendas the Elder is on display in major museums around the world: equinoctial dials, compass dials, sundials, moondials, stack-freed watches at the British Museum, finely carved egg-type watches at the Art Institute in Chicago, ruby-studded pocket watches, and watches made of lapis-lazuli, gemstones, and gilt metal at the Metropolitan Museum of Art all astound visitors with their carefully contrived baroque designs.[1] The Milwaukee Art Museum, however, owns a particularly rich collection of German Renaissance timepieces, among which you might encounter the astonishing "Figure Clock with an African Man" that Rugendas crafted circa 1620 CE. Made of gilt brass, copper, colored iron, and polychrome decorations, this small automaton clock (29.21 × 15.24 × 13.34 cm) features a Black-skinned Moorish man holding a long rod, halfway between a wand and a spear, which directs our attention to a rotating sphere. When the hour strikes, the sphere rotates and the Black man's head turns sideways to look at us (Figure 1).[2] At his feet, a static monkey faces him, holding up an unidentified object to mimic his pose while looking at us. The derogatory association

1. On the role of early modern automata in European culture, see *Making Marvels: Science and Splendor at the Courts of Europe*, ed. Wolfram Koeppe (New Haven: Metropolitan Museum of Art, New York, 2019); Jessica Keating, *Animating Empire: Automata, the Holy Roman Empire, and the Early Modern World* (University Park: Penn State University Press, 2018); Maurice Klaus and Otto Mayr, eds., *Clockwork Universe: German Clocks and Automata, 1550–1650* (New York: N. Watson Academic Publications, 1980).

2. "Collection: Milwaukee Art Museum," Milwaukee Art Museum, accessed March 31, 2022, https://collection.mam.org/details.php?id=7927.

of Black men with apes and monkeys was pervasive in early modern European culture; so were sexual anxieties about the size of their threatening phallic wands, and of course, the automation of this figure resonates with the mass enslavement of Afro-diasporic people on both sides of the Atlantic that started in the mid-fifteenth century.[3] Indeed, there were many enslaved people of sub-Saharan descent in Rugendas's Germany: just like those figure clocks produced for the open market in Augsburg, they were increasingly accessible to the upper middle-class, and one can hardly think of a better materialization than this automaton figure clock for the Aristotelian idea that the slave is merely "an instrument which takes precedence of all other instruments."[4]

Notice the man's outfit: while his hat resembles some of the Moorish headpieces featured in Renaissance costume books, his dress is unambiguously Roman, which aligns this figure with Saint Maurice, the African patron saint and martyr enlisted in the Roman army who died in 287 CE and whose cult was particularly strong in premodern* Germanic regions. This gives a new meaning to the Black man's spear, for Saint Maurice's lance was associated in Catholic cultural imagination with the Holy lance that had pierced Jesus's side on the cross.[5] In a culture where Christ's death had literally warranted the re-start of time and marked the beginning of a new era, the Maurice-like figure's Holy lance pointing towards the Roman numbers on a rotating sphere that conspicuously looks like an earthly globe evokes the origins of Christian time and turns him into a witness to its worldwide marching towards the end of times. In the same mechanical gesture, however, the automated Black figure signals the start of a new age, a new era of increased commodification of Blackness in the context of rising capitalism and consumerism—in other words, the beginning of a new racial era worldwide. Across a 400-year divide, an enslaved automated Saint Maurice turns his mechanical head to hail us and impart silent lessons about premodern racial times. The present volume aims to unpack those lessons. It is about time.

Racially charged automata overtly confront viewers in today's museums, forcing us to think about the role of enslaved Africans and Turkish soldiers in European courts as well as other power relations across the premodern globe. Yet one lesson we wish to impart here is that race is also visually represented and invented in the pages of books, that is, in the printed woodcuts* and engraved images often hidden in storerooms and vaults within museum and library collections today. Many of these images and texts, like Rugendas's automaton itself, have not made their way into scholarship on race in the medieval and Renaissance periods, and many remain unknown or little studied. For instance, in plain sight within Albrecht Dürer's renowned *Four Books on Human Proportion* (Cat. No. 5), first published in 1528 but then reprinted and translated for centuries, are African heads measured in comparison with European heads in a mode that seems to anticipate racial profiling today. In similarly explicit imagery, an early seventeenth-century etching* documenting festivities at the Medici court, French engraver Jacques Callot (Cat. No. 36) depicted costumed aristocrats performing race through the streets of Florence. At the end of the seventeenth-century, a Black eunuch in Turkish dress represented on the frontispiece* of Jean Racine's play *Bajazet* (1697) (Cat. No. 34), in the very crease of the book, makes visible a pivotal figure that the play text itself invisibilizes. Finally, an eighteenth-century antisemitic colored print (Cat. No. 41) blatantly satirizes Jews as part of a "University of Big Noses." Replete with premodern

3. On the association between African people and apes, see Kim F. Hall, "'Troubling Doubles': Apes, Africans, and Blackface in Mr. Moore's Revels," in *Race, Ethnicity, and Power in the Renaissance*, ed. Joyce Green MacDonald (Madison and Teaneck: Fairleigh Dickinson Press, 1997), 120–144, 125–26; Noémie Ndiaye, *Scripts of Blackness: Early Modern Performance Culture and the Making of Race* (Philadelphia: University of Pennsylvania Press, 2022), 205–14.

4. Paul H. D. Kaplan, "The Calenberg Altarpiece: Black African Christians in Renaissance Germany," in *Germany and the Black Diaspora: Points of Contact, 1250–1914*, ed. Mischa Honeck, Martin Klimke, and Anne Kuhlmann-Smirnov (New York: Berghahn Books, 2013), 21–37; Aristotle, *Aristotle's Politics*, trans. Benjamin Jowett (Oxford: Clarendon Press, 1905), 31.

5. Karen Blough, "The Lance of St Maurice as a Component of the Early Ottonian Campaign against Paganism," *Early Medieval Europe* 24, issue 3 (2016): 338–61.

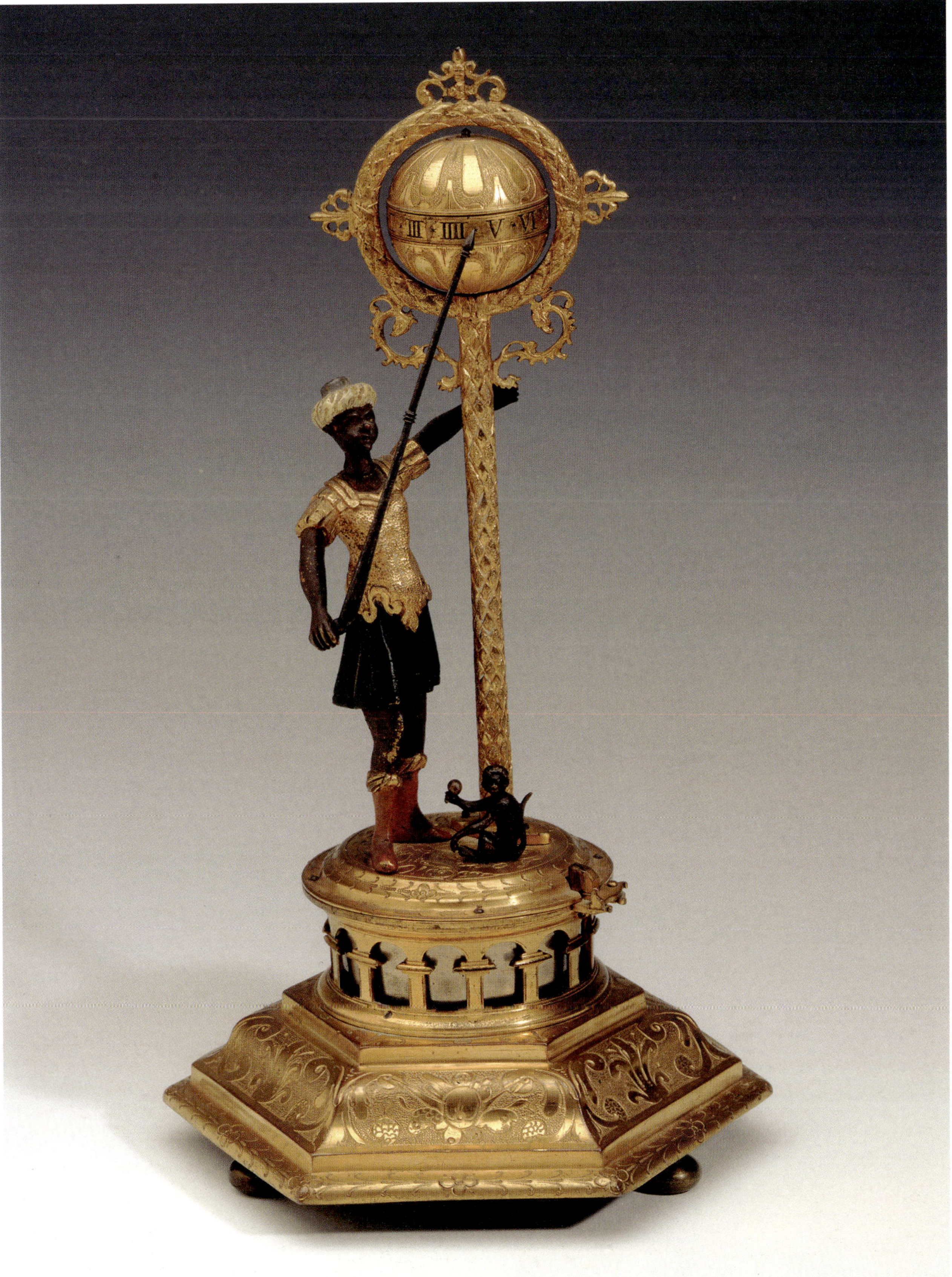

Figure 1
Nikolaus Rugendas the Elder, *Figure Clock with an African Man*, ca. 1620
11½ × 6 × 5¼ in. (29.21 × 15.24 × 13.34 cm), Gilt brass, gilt copper, iron, blued iron, and polychrome decoration, Milwaukee Museum of Art, Gift of Gabriele Flagg Pfeiffer M1995.670
Photo credit: Larry Sanders

racial tensions, the Newberry's archive functions as an ideal case study for this project.

There is a double meaning to the title of this volume. *Seeing Race Before Race* plays on the name of the RaceB4Race® interdisciplinary research collaborative and conference series, an initiative of the Arizona Center for Medieval and Renaissance Studies, focused on Premodern Critical Race Studies (henceforth PCRS)*, with which the Newberry Library is partnering in 2023 to organize an exhibition of the same name. But this book's title also explicitly rejects the logic that allows scholars and entire disciplines, such as art history among others, to claim that they "do not see race" when they focus on time periods that precede the Enlightenment. Indeed, as co-editor Noémie Ndiaye puts it elsewhere,

> While race is a system of power falsely and strategically packaged as a system of knowledge mobilizing the dominant epistemic* fields at any given point in time, scholars often privilege specific epistemic fields in their own investigations. Taking parts of the system for its totality, race historians often tend to think synecdochically* and ignore periods in which the system of race drew on different epistemic fields. Thus eighteenth-century specialists often see the invention of race as coterminous with the invention of scientific racism. For Ivan Hannaford, for instance, "it is unhistorical to perceive the concept of race before the appearance of physiological anthropology proper" [...]: prior to Bacon, "attempts to establish anatomical, physiological, geographical, and astrological relationships between man and man, and man and beast, did not produce a fully developed idea of race, since there was no proper anthropology, natural history, or biology to support it."[6]

In premodernity*, the epistemic fields grounding emerging racial categorizations were religion, class, physiognomy*, culture, and sexuality. Scholars — primarily in English studies but also in Middle Eastern, Colonial, Atlantic, and African Studies, have explored premodern racial formations within those epistemic frameworks — and within their own disciplines — for the last thirty years, but these methods have yet to obtain transdisciplinarity, and have often met with hostility both within and across disciplines*. Claims that "race did not exist" prior to the Enlightenment impoverish our understanding of premodern visual cultures and allow us to ignore the various forms of prejudice that have shaped our archives as well as our methodologies*, thereby reinforcing the status quo. Race can be seen, literally, in vast visual archives spanning centuries, and it *must* be seen too, if we want to understand the long-lasting effects of that social construct across time and space. Eighteenth-century and nineteenth-century scientific racism were not made out of thin air: just like color-based slavery, Indigenous dispossession and genocide, colonization, Islamophobia, and the Holocaust, they have deep roots in a historical terrain whose many sedimented layers rest on premodernity and its racial thinking. We must see race in the archives, and see it for what it is, in order to dismantle the regimes of contemporary white supremacy, which Charles Mills defines as "a political system, a particular power structure of formal or informal rule, socioeconomic privilege, and norms for the differential distribution of material wealth and opportunities, benefits and burdens, rights and duties."[7] The task is urgent, for, as PCRS scholars like Dorothy Kim have shown, that system often finds its own justification in the cultural archives of Western premodernity.[8]

In order to see race then, this volume explores the visual manifestations of what co-editor Noémie

6. Noémie Ndiaye, "Rewriting the *Grand Siècle*: Blackface in Early Modern France and the Historiography of Race," *Literature Compass* 18, no 10 (2021): 3, e12603, https://doi.org/10.1111/lic3.12603. Ivan Hannaford, *Race: The History of an Idea in the West* (Washington, DC: Woodrow Wilson Center Press, 1996), 147, 183.

7. Charles W. Mills, *The Racial Contract* (Ithaca, NY: Cornell University Press, 1997), 3.

8. Dorothy Kim, "White Supremacists Have Weaponized an Imaginary Viking Past. It's Time to Reclaim the Real History," *Time*, April 12, 2019, https://time.com/5569399/viking-history-white-nationalists/

Ndiaye calls "the racial matrix" across the medieval/early modern chronological divide and across vast transnational and multilingual geographies.[9] Ania Loomba and Jonathan Burton accurately remarked fifteen years ago that "whereas in other respects the 'darkness' of the Middle Ages is routinely contrasted to the 'enlightenment' of the Renaissance, with respect to race, there is often a fascinating conflation of the two to mark a premodern time before race. Thus the study of race interrogates the principles of conventional periodization."[10] But once we reject the idea that race did not exist in premodernity — and there is now a critical consensus around that rejection in our field — interrogating the principles of conventional periodization* means examining with greater granularity the continuities and evolutions of racial thinking between the Middle Ages and early modernity. Thus, in this volume, we embrace Margo Hendricks's eloquent statement that "Premodern Critical Race Studies begins with a rejection of the periodization of the past and its implication for the study of race. PCRS's refusal to employ 'medieval' or 'renaissance' as markers signals a step away from a post-Enlightenment tendency to carve time, place, and human lives into discrete boxes."[11] It is precisely because early modernists working on race heard for so long from scholars of eighteenth-century Europe that their work was "anachronistic" that they must refuse to do that to medievalists today.[12]

The racial matrix is a metaphor used to articulate the relations between concepts that twenty-first-century readers tend to think of as separate, but which, in premodern times, were part and parcel of the same conceptual whole called race. Those concepts are, namely, religion, class, and phenotype*. Indeed, race in premodernity referred to any type of difference that was strategically selected and essentialized in order to justify the specific positioning of different demographic groups in uneven social hierarchies. The critical lexicon of PCRS is built upon key definitions articulated over a decade ago by Geraldine Heng ("Race is a structural relationship for the articulation and management of human differences, rather than a substantive content"),[13] and it embraces Stuart Hall's idea that the "structural relationship of race" is an interested mechanism affecting "the distribution of symbolic and material resources between different groups and the establishment of racial hierarchies."[14] When sixteenth-century French aristocrats looked for a way to contest the king's efficacious ability to turn his bourgeois protégés and supporters into aristocrats themselves, they used the vocabulary of race.[15] When the Spanish Inquisition imagined Judaism or Islam as being transmittable through blood and strong enough to void the idea of sincere and efficacious conversion to Christianity, they thought of religion in racial terms. While phenotype has become synonymous with race for modern readers, in premodern times, it was only one paradigm* in the racial matrix, one that developed rather late and always operated in relation or in tension with the older paradigms of class and religion. The metaphor of the racial matrix speaks to race's

9. Ndiaye, *Scripts of Blackness*, 4–8.

10. Ania Loomba and Jonathan Burton, *Race in Early Modern England: A Documentary Companion* (New York: Palgrave Macmillan, 2007), 2.

11. Margo Hendricks, "Coloring the Past, Considerations on Our Future: RaceB4Race," *New Literary History* 52, no. 3/4 (2021): 381, https://doi.org/10.1353/nlh.2021.0018

12. While the Newberry exhibition and this volume focus on the 1300–1800 time period, the RaceB4Race® interdisciplinary research collaborative also comprises classicists and actively cultivates the inclusion of Antiquity within the scope of PCRS.

13. Geraldine Heng, "The Invention of Race in the European Middle Ages: Locations of Medieval Race II," *Literature Compass* 8, no. 5 (2011): 332–350, https://doi.org/10.1111/j.1741-4113.2011.00795.x

14. Stuart Hall, "Subjects in History: Making Diasporic Identities," in *The House that Race Built*, ed. Wahneema Lubiano (New York: Pantheon Books, 1997), 290.

15. "The term [race] was popularised during the [early modern] crisis of the French aristocracy, when the old aristocracy – la noblesse d' épée, the military elite, whose noble origins were medieval – felt threatened in its prerogatives by the emergence of an educated, wealthy, and ambitious bourgeois class (la noblesse de robe). Members of that bourgeois class could buy aristocratic status by purchasing the expensive administrative offices offered for sale by an increasingly domineering crown. In reaction, a discourse developed that endowed the old nobility with supposedly hereditary superior qualities – physical, moral, and intellectual, transmitted through blood, and thus non-vendible." Noémie Ndiaye, "The African Ambassadors' Travels: Playing Black in Late Seventeenth Century France and Spain," in *Transnational Connections in Early Modern Theatre*, eds. M.A. Katritzky and Pavel Drábek, (Manchester University Press, 2020), 74–75.

ability to produce new paradigms without abandoning old ones, and to the profound kinship that indissolubly binds class, religion, and phenotype together within the racial logic in premodern times. In this volume, we endeavor to explore — or rather *see* — premodern racial formations as they deployed themselves across time through the entire racial matrix.

The visual archives studied in this volume include a trove of materials: annotated and illuminated manuscripts, Renaissance costume books and travel books, maps and cartographic volumes produced by Europeans as well as Indigenous peoples, mass-printed pamphlets*, jewelry, decorative arts, religious iconography*, paintings from around the world, playing cards, ceremonial objects, festival books, automata, play texts intended for live performance, and more. This volume heeds Kim F. Hall and Peter Erickson's 2015 call for the field of Early Modern Critical Race studies to include visual culture in pursuit of "historically specific definitions of race" — and it does so in the most expansive way possible.[16] More than a catalog, this volume uses the items of the Fall 2023 exhibition "Seeing Race Before Race" — a collaboration between RaceB4Race and the Newberry Library co-curated by the co-editors of this volume and the Newberry Library's Center for Renaissance staff members Rebecca Fall and Christopher Fletcher — as a starting point for the fresh and ambitious theoretical conversations between PCRS, art history, performance studies, book history, and Critical Race Theory*.

Historiography* and State-of-the Field

In a recent interview celebrating the twenty-fifth anniversary of the landmark publication of *Things of Darkness* hosted by the Newberry Library, PCRS pioneer and volume contributor Kim F. Hall was asked what she would change to the book that launched the field of Early Modern Critical Race Studies if she were to rewrite it today.[17] She answered that she would change its internal structure to open the book with her chapter on Blackness in the visual and material culture of early modern England. Hall's answer confirmed the premise of the present volume: that visual culture is a foundational regime of racialization* that may not be elided in the racial historiographies of premodern Europe. Twenty years ago, Peter Erickson and Clark Hulse co-edited an important collection meant to "explore the social contexts in which [English] paintings, statues, textiles, maps and other artefacts are produced and consumed" and "also explore how these artefacts and the acts of creating, collecting, and admiring them are themselves mechanisms for fashioning the body and identity, situating the self within a social order, defining the visual otherness of race, ethnicity and gender, and establishing relationships of power based on exploration, surveillance, and insight."[18] Yet to a large extent, Hall's, Erickson's, and Hulse's visual examples have not been followed by race scholars working at the intersection of English studies and cultural studies in a framework informed by Critical Race Theory. In other words, within the study of race, while literary scholars influenced by Critical Race Theory have started bridging the traditional periodization gap that exists between medieval and early modern studies (due to no small extent to the RaceB4Race® conference series), disciplinary gaps, especially the gap between literary studies and art history, endure.[19]

Although vast, early art historical readings of race in the visual and material culture of the medieval and

16. Peter Erickson and Kim F. Hall, "'A New Scholarly Song': Rereading Early Modern Race," *Shakespeare Quarterly* 67, no. 1 (Spring 2016): 5, https://doi.org/10.1353/shq.2016.0002.

17. Kim F. Hall and Noémie Ndiaye, "Race in Dialogue: Kim Hall and Noémie Ndiaye," Newberry Center for Renaissance Studies, interview streamed November 13, 2020, on YouTube video, 1:05:10, https://youtu.be/Ys2VBTgpyNs.

18. *Early Modern Visual Culture: Representation, Race, and Empire in Renaissance England*, eds. Clark Hulse and Peter Erickson (Philadelphia: University of Pennsylvania Press, 2000), 3.

19. Under the leadership of scholars like Geraldine Heng, Jonathan Hsy, Cord Whitaker, and Dorothy Kim, the field of medieval critical race studies has been rapidly expanding of late. For a suggestive bibliography, see https://docs.google.com/document/d/18JClsma1BMKYCxvgeWqwPej3ZSCrQXlAlXbL0CdqWmE/edit. This online

early modern periods alike have long been characterized by a certain reparative naivete.[20] In general, the scholarship can be defined as Premodern Race Studies (PRS) but not as Premodern *Critical* Race Studies (PCRS), and here is the difference, as Margo Hendricks luminously puts it: "as part of the larger critical race theory practice and practices, PCRS actively pursues not only the study of race in the premodern, not only the way in which periods helped to define, demarcate, tear apart, and bring together the study of race in the premodern era, but the way that outcome, the way those studies can effect a transformation of the academy and its relationship to our world."[21] In other words, the "critical" in PCRS involves a set of concepts, tools, and keywords produced within the field of Critical Race Theory (which originated in legal studies yet has always aspired to interdisciplinary dissemination),[22] but it also involves, just as importantly, an ethical mandate for scholars to consider their own implication in the racial histories that they study.

For an example of *non*-critical premodern race studies in art history, consider the collection and sumptuous series of edited volumes *The Image of the Black in Western Art*, which, launched in the 1960s during the push for the Civil Rights movement, were powered by Dominique de Menil's nostalgia for "a time when 'ideals of fraternity blossomed' between Europeans and Africans, a time before the start of the African slave trade to Europe and the New World, a time when race-based slavery and Jim Crow segregation were not the basis of the dominant socioeconomic relationship between them or the ways in which black people were 'seen' and represented in Western culture."[23] Nostalgia is a limiting critical affect. Rare are art historians who probed power dynamics like Paul Kaplan did in *The Rise of the Black Magus in Western Art* (1985) and in his prolific output of articles over the past decades.[24] The development of Critical Race Theory (henceforth CRT) in the 1990s has yet to find its way into art historical methodologies.

Indeed, the 2012 exhibition "Revealing the African Presence in Renaissance Europe" and its catalog, edited by Joaneath Spicer, subscribe to the same reparatively-driven argumentative grammar, highlighting the ways in which the Renaissance "allowed (within the constraints of ingrained prejudice) for a gradually more nuanced view of blackness and of persons of African ancestry," focusing on "the immensity, voluptuous strangeness, and seeming unknowability" of the African continent.[25] None of the essays by art historians included in the widely influential and groundbreaking *Black Africans in Renaissance Europe* volume edited by T.F. Earle and Kate Lowe in 2012 use the word "race."[26] The same affectively-tipped argumentative grammar is manifest in recent scholarship published in early modern Hispanic studies that attend to visual

bibliography was inspired by the following online crowdsourced bibliography maintained by Kim F. Hall: https://docs.google.com/document/d/1AaMp1al8y-715FklUq1x5scqBHYS9QpzvMzgYU_ZyFow/edit Exciting exceptions to disciplinary partitioning include Geraldine Heng, who explores visual materials and cites art historians in the introduction to her landmark *The Invention of Race in the European Middle Ages* (Cambridge, UK: Cambridge University Press, 2018).

20. For the large output of art historical writing on race and representation compiled by Patricia Simons, see https://docs.google.com/document/d/1aPgPgXUVTWel8aXe1lzUrgmS4t30Xiye/edit?usp=sharing&ouid=117723222805979041146&rtpof=true&sd=true

21. Margo Hendricks, "Coloring the Past, Rewriting Our Future: Raceb4Race," lecture, Folger Shakespeare Library, July 8, 2020, transcript and audio, 23:31, https://www.folger.edu/institute/scholarly-programs/race-periodization/margo-hendricks.

22. CRT pioneer Kimberlé Crenshaw theorizes those aspirations to interdisciplinary dissemination in "Unmasking Colorblindness in the Law: Lessons from the Formation of Critical Race Theory," in *Seeing Race Again: Countering Colorblindness Across the Disciplines* (Oakland, California: University of California Press, 2019), 52–84. Moreover, the importance of literature, music, and African-American cultural life in the formation of key texts in legal CRT is palpable in various essays collected in Richard Delgado and Jean Stefancic, eds., *Critical Race Theory: An Introduction*, 2nd ed. (New York: New York University Press, 2012).

23. David Bindman, Henry Louis Gates, Jr, and Karen C. C. Dalton, eds., *The Image of the Black in Western Art*, new edition, (Cambridge, MA: Belknap Press of Harvard University Press in collaboration with the W.E.B. Du Bois Institute for African and African American Research and the Menil Collection, 2010), viii. The 2010 re-edition of the series volumes includes new critical essays moving in the right direction, yet the price of the series has limited its circulation for the most part.

24. Paul H. D. Kaplan, *The Rise of the Black Magus in Western Art* (Ann Arbor, MI: UMI Research Press, 1985).

25. Joaneath Spicer, ed., *Revealing the African Presence in Renaissance Europe*, (Baltimore: Walters Art Museum, 2012), 10–11.

26. Kate Lowe, ed., *Black Africans in Renaissance Europe*, (Cambridge, UK: Cambridge University Press, 2005).

culture. For instance, in *Black Saints in Early Modern Global Catholicism* (2019), Erin Rowe explores the rich iconography of Black Saints only to argue that it produced "discourses of universal humanity in ways that decentered race as an exclusive lens through which to view Africans and their descendants";[27] and in *Black but Human: Slavery and Visual Art in Hapsburg Spain, 1480–1700* (2019), Carmen Fracchia primarily seeks to foreground the ways in which early modern visual representations "provide material for critical and emancipatory practices by Afro-Hispanic slaves and ex-slaves in imperial Spain."[28]

Studies of art historians of colonial Latin America and Africa, led by the pioneering work of Thomas B.F. Cummins and more recently by volume contributor Cécile Fromont and Ananda Cohen Suarez, have made headway in thinking about the power dynamics of colonial racial images.[29] This volume expands their approach to a wider set of materials, deliberately embracing a capacious understanding of visual culture whose study requires interdisciplinary collaboration. *Seeing Race Before Race* intervenes in the field of PCRS by asking art historians and literary scholars steeped in cultural studies of premodernity to think together across disciplinary formations about the racializing regimes operative in premodern visual culture through the lens of Critical Race Theory. All essays in the present volume share the previously mentioned CRT-infused critical ethos as well as some fundamental conceptual premises: they all think about race as a system of power falsely packaged as a system of knowledge, about racism as systemic and institutionally upheld, and about whiteness as manufactured property whose manufacturing took centuries. They all aspire to think intersectionally* about race, gender, and sexuality; and they are all attentive to the ways in which white privilege has shaped the various disciplinary historiographies that they have inherited.

Museum Interventions and the Newberry Collections

Our project responds to the interdisciplinary historiographic challenges described above but we also aim, with the Fall 2023 "Seeing Race Before Race" Newberry exhibition and the exhibition catalog included in this volume, to follow in the footsteps of groundbreaking museum interventions. The most renowned example of such interventions is Fred Wilson's 1992 *Mining the Museum* at The Contemporary in Baltimore, curated by Lisa Graziose Currin.[30] Part contemporary gallery show, part history museum lesson, and part institutional critique, Wilson's *Mining* unearthed objects and works of art at the Maryland Historical Society and placed them in contexts (often ironic) that made clear the racist power dynamics at play in the materials. For instance, an eighteenth-century portrait of a boy with his slave wearing a dog collar was paired with audio of a child's voice asking: "Am I your brother? Am I your friend? Am I your pet?" Artist and writer Howard Halle wrote of the exhibition: "Mining the Museum succeeds in circumventing its own polemical potential; although it is a devastating indictment of racism, it is also — and chiefly — an optimistic act of consciousness-raising, and this hopeful note sets it apart from other, similar, works."[31] Indeed *Seeing Race* also aims to inspire awareness and incite scholarly activism by unearthing materials in the Newberry Library's collection and thinking about them in novel ways.

27. Erin Rowe, *Black Saints in Early Modern Global Catholicism* (Cambridge, UK: Cambridge University Press, 2019), 10.

28. Carmen Fracchia, *'Black but Human': Slavery and Visual Arts in Hapsburg Spain, 1480–1700* (Oxford: Oxford University Press, 2019), 1.

29. Representative work from each of these authors includes Thomas B.F. Cummins, "Three Gentlemen from Esmeraldas; A Portrait for a King," in *Slave portraiture in the Atlantic world*, eds. Agnes Lugo-Ortiz and Angela Rosenthal (Cambridge, UK: Cambridge University Press, 2013), 118–45; Cécile Fromont, *The Art of Conversion: Christian Visual Culture in the Kingdom of Kongo* (Chapel Hill: University of North Carolina Press, 2014); Ananda Cohen-Aponte, "Making Race Visible in the Colonial Andes," in *Envisioning Others: Race, Color, and the Visual in Iberia and Latin America*, ed. Pamela Patton (Leiden: Brill, 2015), 187–212.

30. See Fred Wilson, *Mining the Museum: An Installation* (Baltimore: Contemporary, 1994).

31. Fred Wilson and Howard Halle, "Mining the Museum," *Grand Street* 44 (1993): 151–72.

Recent exhibitions and projects have similarly begun to illuminate the representations of enslaved, Indigenous, and other subjugated peoples of the premodern world in traditional museum exhibitions. The craftsmanship and ingenuity of Indigenous Americans have been celebrated in numerous exhibitions over the last decades starting with *Circa 1492* at the National Gallery in Washington D.C. that juxtaposed pre-conquest Mixtec codices* and other objects alongside Renaissance works. Joaneath Spicer's aforementioned *Revealing the African Presence in Renaissance Europe* (2012) at the Baltimore Museum of Art, Sylviane A. Diouf's *Africans in India from Slaves to Generals to Rulers* (2013) at the New York Public Library, and Awam Akpa's *ReSignifications: European Blackamoors, Africana Readings* (2016) in multiple museums in Florence, each brought to light the role of Africans in European iconography. In contrast to these exhibitions that focused on images of Africans, *Caravans of Gold, Fragments of Time: Art, Culture, and Exchange across Medieval Saharan Africa* (2019) attended to Africans' economic agency in the medieval world. Furthermore, several more recent exhibitions, such as *Balthazar: A Black African King in Medieval and Renaissance Art* (2019–2020) at the Getty Center, *Afro-Atlantic Histories* (2018–2022) at Museu de Arte de São Paulo and the Instituto Tomie Ohtake in Brazil and the National Gallery, Washington D.C. (2022), *Slavery* at the Rijksmuseum (2022), *La voce delle ombre: Presenze africane nell'arte dell'Italia settrionale* (XVI-XIX) (2022) at the Museo delle Culture in Milan, and *European Art on First Nations Land* at the Art Gallery of Ontario (ongoing) tackle issues of slavery, the African diaspora, and violence. Those exhibitions, their related publications, and in some cases complementary online resources are all significant contributions to race studies: our project simultaneously builds upon them and departs from them by working closely with the tenets of premodern critical race studies.[32]

Inside and outside museums today, curators and artists are approaching displays and developing projects that confront audiences with issues surrounding race. For instance, volume contributor Andrea Myers Achi has taken the lead in questioning race and intersectionality in the medieval galleries of the Metropolitan Museum of Art. Artist Justin Randolph Thompson, the force behind "Florence Black History Month," has found that the Uffizi's collection is ripe for racial analysis. Thompson has compiled entries by scholars about paintings and developed a video series on the Uffizi collection entitled "African Presence" that contextualizes the African figures in their social contexts.[33] These entries and videos deal with issues related to status, class, and slavery, probing representations and questioning the past narratives surrounding them.

While the Newberry is not a museum, its archive is similarly well suited for critical analysis of racial depictions from the medieval and early modern period due to the sheer magnitude and diversity of its manuscripts, printed books, and maps. The heart of its collection developed in the final years of the nineteenth-century and first decades of the twentieth-century when Newberry presidents, curators, librarians, and donors actively purchased books throughout Europe and the Americas. The Newberry was founded in 1887, and its first librarian, William F. Poole, acquired some 120,000 books and 44,000 pamphlets. Following a 1917 bequest from John M. Wing, who founded a history of printing collection, curators have built a collection of books by nearly every printer working in early modern Europe and Britain.[34]

More than half of the objects catalogued in this book and displayed in the related exhibition derive from the Newberry's Ayer collection. It is worth

32. See for instance the significant recent edited volumes connected to the Balthazar exhibition at the Getty and *La voce delle ombre* exhibition in Milan: Bryan Keene and Kristen Collins, eds., *Balthazar: A Black African King in Medieval and Renaissance Art* (Los Angeles: J. Paul Getty Museum, 2023) and Carolina Orsini, Sara Rizzo, Luca Tosi, eds., *La voce delle ombre: Presenze africane nell'arte dell'Italia settrionale* (XVI–XIX) (Milan: Silvana editoriale, 2022).

33. "Black Presence: Uffizi Galleries," Gallerie degli Uffizi, accessed March 31, 2022, https://www.uffizi.it/en/video-stories/black-presence.

34. Joel L. Samuels, "The John M. Wing Foundation on the History of Printing at the Newberry Library," *The Library Quarterly* 58, no. 2 (April 1988): 164–89.

expanding here a bit on the complexity of Edward Ayer (1841–1927) as a collector and on today's Ayer collection, in order to demonstrate why the Newberry serves as such a rich archive for this study.[35] Current Indigenous Studies Librarian and Ayer Curator Analú María López's note in this volume further illuminates the importance of this collection. A self-made midwesterner who had a passion for collecting books and objects related to the Americas, Ayer helped to found Chicago's Field Museum and donated a significant collection of anthropological materials to the museum. As a benefactor, Ayer gave the Newberry 20,000 books and manuscripts, 6,000 maps, 3,000 paintings, drawings, prints, engravings* and lithographs*, and over 9,000 photographs.

Ayer is a complex figure: he recalls collectors of the early modern period, as he simultaneously sought to conserve the records and materiality of Indigenous populations while he was also subsumed in the very network involved in the process of their obliteration. In her analysis of Ayer, Carolyn Kastner uses Renato Rosaldo's concept of "imperialist nostalgia" to define Ayer as a collector who has "longing" for "what [he] is complicit in destroying or altering."[36] Kastner goes on to state: "as a chronicler of Indian history, Ayer stands to speak for the Native Americans but writes them out of authorship."[37] Indeed it is often difficult to find the Indigenous voice in Ayer's manuscripts and books. The diverse rarities highlighted in the catalog from Ayer such as Columbus's 1494 printed letter to the King of Spain (Cat. No 22), an Ottoman manuscript about the Americas (Cat. No 21), a Dutch world atlas* (Cat. No. 26), and an Indigenous map of a region of Mexico (Figure. 3.2) all serve to represent the western response to or control over the Americas or other regions of the world. These materials cannot help but tell multiple stories here in the context of this project. They represent the power dynamics of their original time and place of production, evoke Ayer's fraught collecting interests in Americana from the late nineteenth-century, and at the same time serve to mirror racial conflicts today.

Book Description

This book is organized thematically, following the same tripartite structure as the Newberry's "Seeing Race Before Race" exhibition itself, around the practices of "Figuring," "Mapping," and "Performing" as techniques and epistemologies* of premodern race-making. Each of those three thematic parts contains essays, notes, and catalog entries. The five long-form essays of *Seeing Race Before Race* take items from the Newberry Library's holdings as catalysts for inquiries into the workings of the racial matrix in premodernity. All are co-authored by scholars working across disciplinary lines, and, often, across traditional lines of periodization, thereby modeling the kind of collaborations necessary for opening new directions in Premodern Critical Race Studies today. Envisioning visual culture as a capacious domain cutting across fine arts, material culture, and books of all types, those five essays explore the involvement of visual culture in the shaping of premodern racial formations: they foreground the lines of communication and influence that exist between visual culture, instantiated in individual items, and various institutions such as the law, justice systems, chattel slavery, and aggressively proselytizing Christianity. While visual culture is not an institution, it is a system, and the essays in this volume reckon with that system while attending to the uniqueness of each item by studying both the affordances of specific media for the purposes of race-making and the ways in which individual items

35. On Ayer, see Frederick Hoxie, "Businessman, Bibliophile, and Patron: Edward E. Ayer and his Collection of American Indian Art," *Great Plains Quarterly* 9, no. 2 (Spring 1989): 78–88; Carolyn Kastner, "Collecting Mr. Ayer's Narrative," in *Acts of Possession: Collecting in America*, ed. Leah Dilworth (New Brunswick, NJ: Rutgers University Press, 2003): 138–62.

36. Kastner, "Collecting Mr. Ayer's Narrative," 149.

37. Kastner, 154.

can sometimes resist the white supremacist agenda that conjured them up.

Seeing Race Before Race is meant to showcase original and cutting-edge scholarship, but it is also meant to offer a reflection on the circulation of PCRS beyond academia and its mobilization within the larger framework of anti-racist activism. Thus, in combination with those five long-form essays, the volume offers three "Notes from the Field": shorter essays written by PCRS and Critical Indigenous scholars about their experiences working in public-facing institutions adjacent to academia such as museums, libraries, and theaters. These essays and notes will shed a new light on the third kind of writing contained in this volume, the catalog entries for the items on display during the exhibition of the same name at the Newberry Library in Fall 2023. Those forty-two catalog entries are authored by brilliant graduate students, early career scholars, and Newberry staff members who are part of the extended RaceB4Race community: Beatrice Bradley, Katherine Chacon, Cecilio Cooper, Aylin Corona, Caitlin DiMartino, Olivia Dill, Alana Edmondson, Rebecca Fall, Christopher Fletcher, Jamie Keener, Andrés Irigoyen, Edward Johnson, Emily Kang, Suzanne Karr Schmidt, Stephanie Lee, Vivian Lei, Sarah-Gray Lesley, Julia Marsan, Earnestine Qiu, Arianna Ray, Melani Shahin, Daniela Gutiérrez Flores, Elizabeth Neary, and the book's co-editors.

The first part of this book, exploring the practices and affordances of "Figuring" for the purposes of premodern race-making, opens with the essay "Manuscripts and Printed Books: Book History and Race," where book historian Brandi K. Adams and English literary scholar Carissa M. Harris focus on the phenotypical paradigm of the premodern racial matrix, reading two items from the Newberry Library's archives through a Black feminist lens in an attempt to undo the intersectional violence of gendered racism. Adams examines the deployment of what digital humanities scholar Moya Bailey calls misogynoir in English print culture by bringing to light the plight of Black women whose artificial images were circulated without their consent in early modern English literature. She focuses on the case study of Henry Rainolds's and Henry King's manuscript poems "A Black-moor Maid wooing a fair Boy" (1630s–1650s) and "The Boy's Answer to the Blackmoor" (1630s–1650s)—mid-seventeenth-century avatars of the "Aethiopissa poems" launched by George Herbert, a genre based on literary blackface that often ridiculed the very idea of Black women as erotic subjects. In Adams's view, those two poems' ultimate circulation in print without authorial consent mirrors the violent act of writing and distributing poems about Black women and their personhood without their consent.

Carissa M. Harris closely reads *A Letter from a Merchant at Jamaica* (1709), a mass-produced London pamphlet advocating for slavery reform that features scenes where Englishmen abuse enslaved Black women in the British West Indies. Paying minute attention to the various slurs used to frame Black women as simultaneously made for labor yet always insufficiently laboring, and to the philological* history of those terms from the twelfth-century onwards, Harris practices what she calls "intersectional material philology" in order to produce an account of lexical power and marginalization dynamics that still informs Black women's lives today. Moreover, focusing on the visual dimension of the typographic* choices made in the production of this pamphlet to dehumanize Black women while calling for their "improved" continual enslavement, Harris locates in the mass printed medium techniques of racialization that invite readers' participation in what Saidiya Hartman would call scenes of subjection. Those techniques, Harris notes, often have their roots in older forms of manuscript publication. Adams and Harris ultimately remind us that book history "occupies a special place in visual culture as both constituted by its appearance on the page and inflected by philological and literary histories," and they give us new ways of seeing gendered racism in that crucial interstitial field of inquiry.

The following essay of this section extends the focus on book history by investigating its intersections with material culture. Indeed, in "Fashioning Racial

Materiality in Nicolas de Nicolay's Images of Jews," English literary scholar M. Lindsay Kaplan and art historian Dana E. Katz see early modern material culture, and clothing in particular, as crucial sites comparable to somatic* constructions for the formation of racial identity. Since the Middle Ages, clothing had, via discriminatory sumptuary laws, facilitated the racialization of European Jews and Muslims for whom somatic difference often fails as a stable weaponizable visual marker. Early modern maps and costume books proclaim the power of clothing to fix racialized and gendered identities. Nicolas de Nicolay's visual treatment of clothing in his 1567 *Les Quatre Premiers Livres des navigations et pérégrinations orientales* (*The Nauigations, Peregrinations and Voyages, made into Turkie*), half a travel narrative and half a costume book, strategically plays on similarities and distinctions between Jewish and Muslim clothing in the Ottoman world. Indeed, Nicolay participated in the European tradition that had, since the Middle Ages, mobilized the Muslim world and faith to uphold ideas of Jewish inferiority, either by framing Jews and Muslims as allies in their perceived attempts at overthrowing Christianity, or by highlighting the subjugation of Jews in Muslim cultures. Kaplan and Katz explore the sartorial* manifestations of that coordination of Jews and Muslims in Christian visual imagination, which strategically accommodated contradictory fantasies of amity and enmity among "infidels" as the need arose.

Kaplan and Katz offer a detailed analysis of the interplay between text and image in Nicolay's widely circulated account of the Ottoman world, showing how, among its sixty black and white woodcuts, images of Jewish men and women are caught in a compensatory relation with the accompanying text. That compensatory relation allows the book as a whole to advance a racial theology systematically framing Jews as inferior, even when the images or the text struggle to do so on their own due to the radical leveling that the *zimmi* status performed between Christians and Jews in Ottoman lands. Kaplan and Katz show how "the conflicting evidence of image and word reveals the counterfactual labor of race construction, the effort that goes into bending empirical evidence of the Ottoman Jewish experience to fit the imperatives of Christian triumphalism." Focusing on the religious paradigm of the premodern racial matrix, Kaplan and Katz take us through a complex and fascination exploration of the strategic machinations of antisemitism and Christian supremacy.

In her "Note from the Field," Analú María López shares her experience working as Ayer Librarian and Assistant Curator of American Indian and Indigenous Studies at the Newberry Library and thus "*figuring* out" her relation to a primarily white institution with a historically fraught relationship with Indigenous communities, as she discusses what a meaningful decolonization of archives and institutions might look like. "Without continuous commitment to serve as accomplices to Indigenous people, institutional gestures of acknowledgement risk reconciling 'settler guilt and complicity' and rescuing 'settler futurity,'" López warns us. The key to true reconciliation, she suggests, is for libraries and cultural institutions to think proactively about how to best serve a primarily Indigenous audience and how to bring in Indigenous community members both as collaborators and project leaders. While this first part concludes with the catalog entries for the exhibition items listed under the "Figuring" heading (1–14), we take liberties here in that we are using the catalog as a platform to highlight, even more than the exhibition itself does, two particularly salient heuristics* in our project: Blackness and gender. Indeed, the "Figuring" section of this catalog, playing on the double meaning of the word as a way of figuring *out* race through visualization of the human body, proposes two thematic itineraries: the invention of racial Blackness from a 1250 Franciscan Bible to a 1638 government document attesting to Black and Indigenous alliances against white supremacy in Barbados, and the gendering of the racial analytic* in a broad generic cluster showcasing the racialization of Black, white, Ottoman, South-Asian, and Indigenous women.

The second part of this book, which explores the logic and racializing effects of early modern "mapping" technologies and geographical thinking, starts with the essay "Geographies of Race: Constructions of Constantinople/Istanbul in the Western European Imaginary," in which art historian Roland Betancourt and English literary scholar Ambereen Dadabhoy examine the descriptions of Constantinople/Istanbul in the writings of medieval and early modern Western* Europeans. Their essay "highlight[s] the ways in which the city was either othered or embraced by the West throughout its medieval and early modern history," and show how such othering and embrace were always strategic in nature, following the needs of a specific cultural moment in a continuous history of imperial competition and religious opposition between Constantinople/Istanbul and Western Europe. Betancourt first examines early medieval documents by Western authors that sought to erase the Roman identity of the Byzantines, emphasize their Greekness, and exoticize their customs and physical appearance. By contrast, Crusader narratives framed the Byzantines as Christian kin crucial to Western interests against the Turks, and the long-standing Western-Byzantine antagonism was rewritten along those lines in the wake of the fall of Constantinople in 1453 (often framed as the result of the Byzantine schism). Starting in the mid-fifteenth-century and throughout the craze for early modern antiquarianism*, Western historiographic interest in Byzantium solidified as a desire to learn how to resist Ottoman expansion, turned Byzantium into a Christianized object lesson, and whitened its inhabitants, using them as strategic floating signifiers in the process.

In turn, Dadabhoy shows how the city and its inhabitants were further racialized by early modern Western travelers in the Ottoman age. In those accounts, while the religious, social, political, and cultural habits of Ottoman Istanbul inhabitants were othered, the city's geography was Europeanized: this representational strategy fantasized about the easily sexualizable vulnerability of a European city fallen into Muslim hands. Dadabhoy shows how sexualized tropes* of white vulnerability were increasingly mobilized to frame the harem and the hammam as sites of radical alterity in Nicolas de Nicolay's *The Navigations, Pérégrinations and Voyages Made into Turkie* (1585) and Sir Paul Rycaut's *The Present State of the Ottoman Empire* (1668). Those two texts and their images "attest to the longue durée of both racial formation and Orientalism* and the strategic ways in which these discourses intersect in order to advance relations of epistemic power in situations where material power is often lacking." Asking how geographies can be racialized, Betancourt and Dadabhoy show that, across centuries, European authors wielded tropes of religious, cultural, and sexual difference against the inhabitants of Constantinople/Istanbul in futile attempts at reifying, through the strength of racial discourse, an East/West binary that the glorious Eurasian city always already resisted.

In the second essay of this section, "Race, Empire, and Cartography," Hispanic studies scholar Ricardo Padrón and art historian Risa Puleo explore the premodern racial politics of cartography as a spectrum by pairing two case studies that sit at the opposite end of that spectrum: gigantic wall maps of the four continents made by French cartographer* Nicolas de Fer in the 1690s and an Indigenous 1569 map known as the *Farmers vs. Covarrubias* map made in colonial Mexico. While the de Fer maps illustrate the complicity of global cartographic geography in the development of Western ideas about race and colonization, the *Farmers vs. Covarrubias* map shows how maps could become tools in the effort to resist the racialized notions of property ownership that colonialism unleashed in the Americas.

Medieval theories of difference inherited from Antiquity, such as climate theory, proved inadequate to shore up Eurocentric notions of absolute human differences and hierarchies in the age of colonial travel: Padrón shows that early modern theories of essential continental difference emerged as a solution to that problem, working in synergy with medieval discursive tropes of race that were repurposed to accommodate colonial developments. The de Fer maps illustrate the shift from climatic to continental thinking, reserving civility to Europe while framing Asia in proto-Orientalist terms and Africa and America in primitive terms. However, the America map stands out in that, by representing Indigenous peoples in the same space as enslaved Africans and Spanish conquistadors, the American map signals that their identities remained intact despite migrations, simultaneously underlining the limitations of continental logic and laying the groundwork for Enlightenment developments in racial theories.

For her case study, Risa Puleo goes back to the roots of Critical Race Theory: court cases. In 1569, the Indigenous farmers in the Tultepec area sought to protect their land and its capacity to produce food supplies (guaranteeing Indigenous food autonomy) against the encroachment of overgrazing sheep owned by Spanish colonials such as Covarrubias. Puleo shows how the *Farmers of Tultepec vs. Spanish Rancher Juan Antonio Covarrubias* map that was produced to supplement that property claim court case in colonial Mexico over a hundred years before de Fer created his Parisian maps used the affordances of Nahuatl pictography* to speak a double language: one recognizable to the Spanish court using Nahuatl maps as admissible evidence (the language of property rights), and one recognizable to Indigenous viewers (the language of sovereignty*). By uncovering symbols such as the *altepetl* glyph*, which read as a church to Spaniards but as a sovereign city-state in pre-Conquest Nahuatl political theory, Puleo shows how fifty years after the military conquest of the Aztec empire, "the Tultepecans existed in a state of double-consciousness, much like the map itself." Read together, Puleo's and Padrón's case studies evidence the involvement of cartographic culture in ideological production and the ways in which the medium itself could pressure the ideological project of white supremacy that necessitated it in the first place.

Focusing on museums' spatial politics of display, Andrea Myers Achi shows in her "Note from the Field" how curatorial* practices have accompanied the global turn in medieval studies by sharing her experiences incorporating medieval African (especially Ethiopian) art into the medieval galleries at the Metropolitan Museum in New York. She explores the implications of curating "Black art in white spaces," for "museums are the first entry point to the medieval world for many people, and these spaces have the opportunity to share the multifaceted perspectives of the medieval period." Myers Achi's reflection is followed by the second segment of the exhibition catalog, "Mapping," which traces a path through the rich cartographic archives of the Newberry Library by putting medieval and early modern maps in conversation with supplementary documents revealing the various acts of concrete racial violence authorized by the epistemes* in which those maps participated. This collection of entries demonstrates how cartography, from the bound portolan* charts of the fifteenth-century to large-scale wall maps of the eighteenth-century, functioned to delimit space based on race and to define power and control. Many of the items highlighted in this section also demonstrate how commonly premodern cartography displays racialized bodies on maps.

The third section of this book, "Performing," focuses on the participation of premodern performance culture (capaciously defined) in the emergence of new racial formations. In their essay "Back Bending Labor, Savage Dances, Pious Stances: Race in Motion between Africa and the Americas," early modern art historians Elena FitzPatrick Sifford and Cécile Fromont further explore the premodern manifestations of antiblack racism, yet they locate it in a visual discourse centering not skin color but civility and its manifestations in comportment and motion. Those, they argue, could sometimes supersede complexion and physiognomy as indicators of racial taxonomies*. Renaissance culture, drawing on rhetorical traditions with roots in Antiquity, read bodily posture and movement as reflections of the soul. FitzPatrick Sifford and Fromont explore the ascription of bent and wayward postures to enslaved Africans whose depiction is not phenotypically marked in a wide array of visual sources including costume books, travel writings, map cartouches, illustrations in printed travelogues, and other artworks from Germany, Italy, England, France, and the Low Countries.

European visual representations of African and Indigenous American dances repurposed older choreographies* of incivility, such as the medieval dance of death, to racialize their subjects. Inversely, early modern representations of the harmonious postures of Christianized Africans expressed early modern beliefs in the civilizing power of conversion. That is particularly visible in the religious paintings of colonial South America, where, for instance, the cross-armed stance pervasive in late medieval representations of the Passion became a standard feature of the *bozal** baptizand. Every medium has its own affordances for the purposes of race-making. FitzPatrick Sifford and Fromont's essay suggests that one major affordance of motion as a racializing medium is its particularly strong ability to repurpose older tropes for new contexts by de-emphasizing the phenotypical differences that might hinder such repurposing. In the medium of motion, an Indigenous American can be made to look like a pre-*Reconquista** Muslim/"Moor" particularly easily. Studying the deployment of motion in visual sources can help us track with great acuity the series of strategic repurposings that animated the racial matrix. At the same time, the essay unambiguously concludes on the idea that the kinetic discourse of racialization has, over time, crystallized primarily around afro-descendants and fueled global antiblackness in ways that can be felt to this day.

Zooming in on theatrical culture more specifically in her "Note from the Field," Farah Karim-Cooper charts the curatorial process that she has developed over 17 years as Head of Research and now Co-Director Education and Research at Shakespeare's Globe Theatre, especially since 2017. She comments that "cultural organizations have the power to integrate scholarly conversations into their programming [in modes] that can influence and even alter the public discourse in impactful ways." Persisting in the face of racist and traditionalist backlash, Karim-Cooper reminds us, however, that institutions can only instigate meaningful public conversations around PCRS if they start by taking steps to align their own structures and practices with the values of PCRS. Like Myers Achi, Karim-Cooper emphasizes the importance of using one's platform to materially help create a student pipeline in PCRS. The last section of the exhibition catalog, "Performing," moves from literary dramatic canon, masques, carnival performances, and theatricality of all stripes that fashion racial difference, Otherness, and hierarchy to striking instances of what we call "performances of the racial self." Those include a number of individual performances of whiteness requiring props conserved in visual archives today.

This book concludes with an exclusive tri-interview featuring Kim F. Hall (PCRS and Africana studies), Scott Manning Stevens (Critical Indigenous Studies and early modern studies), and L. Lehua Yim (Critical Indigenous Studies and early modern studies), who discuss the complex relation between PCRS and Native Studies/Critical Indigenous Studies* and underline the importance of joint Native/Indigenous and Black critical interventions into early modern studies. Lucidly analyzing the structural factors that have hitherto hindered meaningful conversations between those fields, especially in Western scholarship on early modern periods, Hall, Stevens, and Yim discuss potential collaborations and mutual support between the fields. They identify promising convergences around the critique of unchallenged tropes and truisms from history and anthropology and of premodern "histories of white settler colonial* fear or pleasure." There is potential for issue-driven "coalescence" between these fields. Hall, Stevens, and Yim define the conditions of possibility for mutual recognition and respectful, non-extractive knowledge-sharing, and they imagine how research institutions such as the Newberry Library might facilitate such necessary sharing. In relation to the theme of this volume, Hall, Stevens, and Yim also note that early modern visual culture and modern scholarship on it can be particularly potent sites of epistemological violence against Black lives and liberation and Native/Indigenous lifeways and sovereignties, thereby alerting us to the fact that ethically studying those images requires particularly thoughtful methodological and historiographic engagements.

Conclusion

It is our hope that the wealth of insights, analyses, provocations, and critical frameworks offered by the contributors to this book will illuminate our readers' encounter with the objects presented in the catalog entries and encourage them to search the Newberry Library holdings for more. From Sir John Mandeville's marvelous journeys en route to Jerusalem (Cat. No. 15) to Aphra Behn's 1688 *Oroonoko* (Cat. No. 30) and its subsequent adaptations for the stage, via Wolfram von Eschenbach 1477 romance *Parsival* (Cat. No. 3) and Mary Wroth's 1621 *The Countess of Montgomery's Urania* (Cat. No. 11); from Spanish patents of nobility proving one "purity of blood" (Cat. No. 40) to Nahuatl translations for the word "Blackness" in an annotated edition of Antonio de Nebrija's *Dictionarium* (Cat. No. 6), via royal *cedulas** from sixteenth-century Guatemala (Cat. No. 23); from Shakespeare's *Othello* (Cat. No. 27) to its 1794 French adaptation written in the wake of the Haitian Revolution (Cat. No. 29), via Ben Jonson's *Masque of Blacknesse* (Cat. No. 35) and the mysterious frontispiece of Thomas Kyd's *The Spanish Tragedy* (Cat. No. 33)–the possibilities for interdisciplinary critical engagement are endless. From the "map of monstrous races" in the 1493 *Nuremberg Chronicle* (Cat. No. 17) to Joan Blaeu's 1663 atlas (Cat. No. 25) and its representation of animalized Chinese people via the 1550 *Manuscript portolan atlas of the world* (Cat. No. 20) which isolates Sultan Suleiman the Magnificent from other European monarchs, and the only known portrait from life of Pocahontas (Cat. No. 12),we want readers to forge their own paths through the thick visual archives produced by the premodern racial matrix. Examine Jan Huygen van Linschoten's depiction of Hindu *sati* rituals in his 1596 *Itinerario* (Cat. No.9). Muse over the grisaille* rendering of the Queen of Sheba in the 1455 *miroir de humaine saluation* (Cat. No. 2). The items featured in this exhibition include Crusade chronicles, conversion narratives, travel writings, ethnographic scrapbooks, maps, maps, maps and more maps, treatises on cosmetics, costume books, missionary writings, colonial administration documents, antisemitic caricatures, and emblem books, but there is more where they come from, and readers are invited to join the effort and help us further open the archives of the Newberry Library so we may finally face our past.

Many of the items discussed in this volume defy categorization and encompass more than one of the themes mentioned above. For instance, the sixteenth-century playing cards hung prominently on the wall of the exhibition (Cat. No. 39) map out figures in space on a page and would have been used in a performative manner for play. Analysis of the paper and style of figures has linked the cards to a specific printmaker in Germany. At first glance, this tattered sheet of playing cards is difficult to even comprehend and in fact, their recent discovery within the files of the Newberry archive inspired a variety of initial questions: What does this sheet represent? How did it function? Where are they from? To begin to answer these questions, one must first imagine cutting out each figure and pasting it onto a card or heavier paper as reinforcement. Then one must imagine a community of players holding these diverse figures of soldiers from around the world in hand in a lively game of exchange across a table, which, like any card game, demands from participants a vigorous sense of competition and the deployment of keen strategic thinking — two key elements underlying processes of racial formation across the ages. Imagine this community of players literally playing the race card. In our exhibition and in the present volume, the uncut playing cards symbolically encapsulate a premodern world in which race functioned as a powerful sleight of hand across cultures, class, and locations. While the Newberry archive is necessarily constrained by the limits of its holdings, which are largely Western reflections of its early twentieth-century collectors' tastes, its objects can be used in creative ways to make links across time and space and to question the power plays of a past that lingers.

Seeing Race Before Race will be of interest to a variety of readers from academics to high school students and the general public. Beyond historians of the book, art, performance, and literature, the volume will speak to scholars in the more specialized fields of gender, Black, Jewish, Islamic, Indigenous, and colonial studies. Museum and library curators, hopefully, will feel hailed too. The volume's essays will serve well on syllabi that teach PCRS to undergraduate students alongside Kim F. Hall's *Things of Darkness* and Peter Erickson and Clark Hulse's *Early Modern Visual Culture*. The catalog entries will help high school instructors teaching medieval and Renaissance studies holistically ground their teaching with visual aids. To that end, we have also included a Glossary of specialized and technical terms with which readers may not yet be familiar. As these terms appear in the book, they are followed by an asterisk. Available in open access, this volume is meant to showcase pathbreaking new PCRS scholarship, to reflect upon and encourage the deployment of PCRS outside of academia, and to help inspire and foster future PCRS scholarship. As Rugendas's 1620 automated Saint Maurice would say if he could speak: it is time. We hope that you will find this book a useful tool. We dedicate *Seeing Race Before Race* to the diverse publics seeking to understand the long history of today's racial thinking, from teachers to community organizers, activists, and — last but not least — visual artists.

PART 1
FIGURING

MANUSCRIPTS AND PRINTED BOOKS: BOOK HISTORY AND RACE

By Brandi K. Adams and Carissa M. Harris

How can scholars *see* the intersections between race and gender in premodern manuscripts and printed books in ways that are "rooted in an ethical commitment to undoing gendered domination," to use Imani Perry's evocative charge?[1] Our coauthored essay explores the nexus between book history and premodern critical race studies in two objects from the Newberry Library's collection. Brandi K. Adams analyzes Henry Rainolds's and Henry King's manuscript poems entitled "A Blackmoor Maid wooing a fair Boy" (1630s–1650s) and "The Boy's Answer to the Blackmoor" (1630s–1650s) (Figure 1.1) and she reveals that these poems, which eventually appeared in print without authorial consent, mirror the act of writing and distributing poems about Black women and their personhood without their consent. Carissa M. Harris examines *A Letter from a Merchant at Jamaica* (1709) (Figure 1.2), a mass-produced anonymous London pamphlet that features explicit scenes of Englishmen abusing enslaved Black women in the British West Indies. Together focusing on representations of Black women in premodern English textual culture, we show how material choices by book owners, copyists*, and typesetters* helped readers visualize race on the page. In the printed pamphlet, this visualization of race takes the form of gendered racial

1. Imani Perry, *Vexy Thing: On Gender and Liberation* (Durham, NC: Duke University Press, 2018), 7.

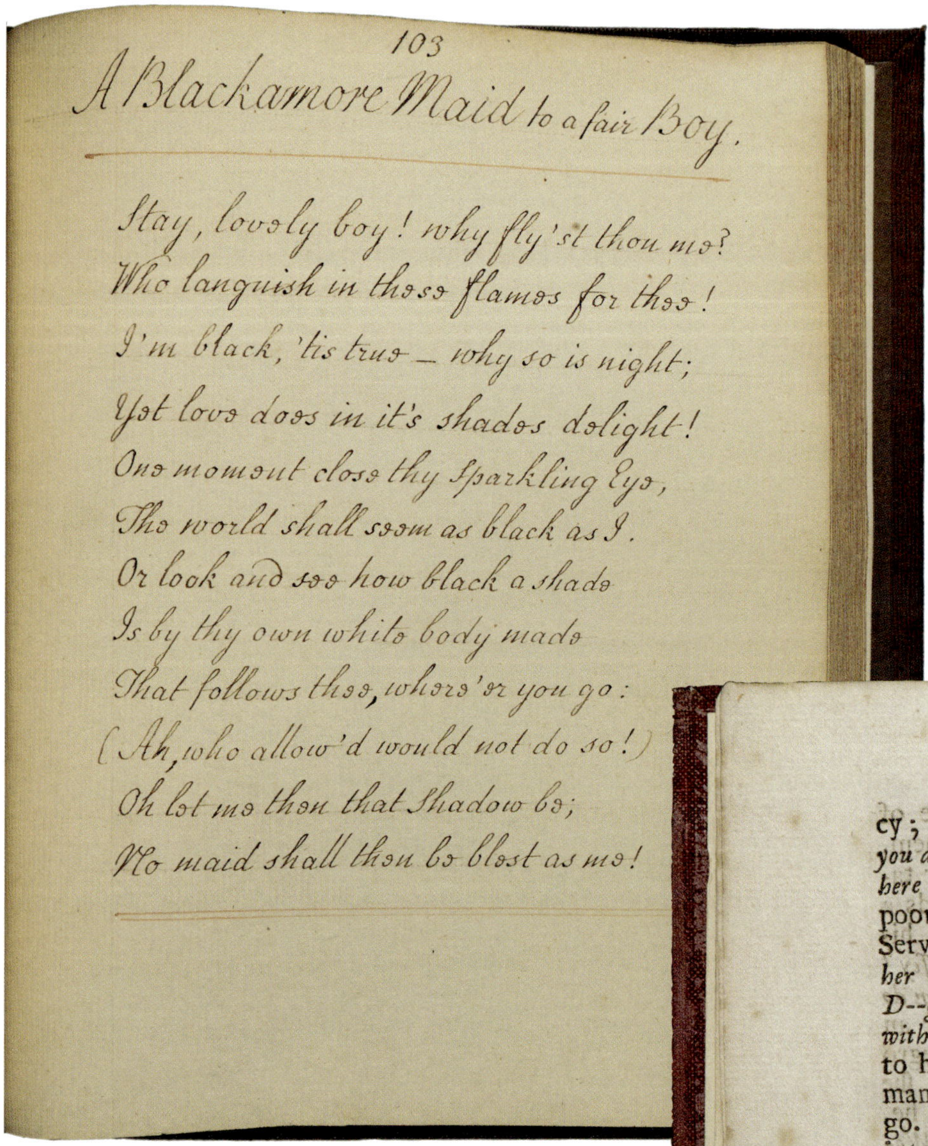

103

A Blackamore Maid to a fair Boy.

Stay, lovely boy! why fly'st thou me?
Who languish in these flames for thee!
I'm black, 'tis true — why so is night;
Yet love does in it's shades delight!
One moment close thy Sparkling Eye,
The world shall seem as black as I.
Or look and see how black a shade
Is by thy own white body made
That follows thee, where'er you go:
(Ah, who allow'd would not do so!)
Oh let me then that Shadow be;
No maid shall then be blest as me!

Figure 1.1
A collection of serious, humorous and affectionate poems,
early 18th century, manuscript,
Newberry Library,
VAULT Case MS Y 184 .18

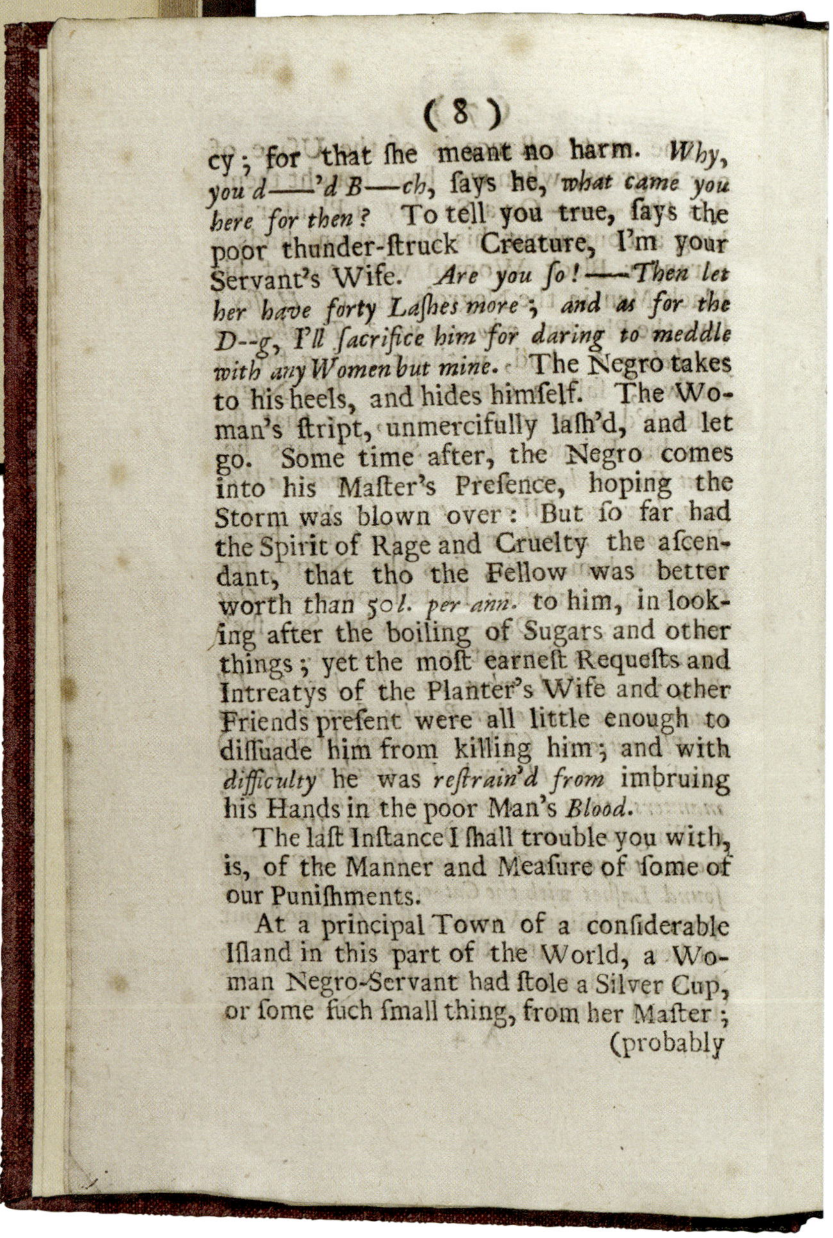

(8)

cy; for that ſhe meant no harm. *Why, you d——'d B——ch,* ſays he, *what came you here for then?* To tell you true, ſays the poor thunder-ſtruck Creature, I'm your Servant's Wife. *Are you ſo!——Then let her have forty Laſhes more; and as for the D--g, I'll ſacrifice him for daring to meddle with any Women but mine.* The Negro takes to his heels, and hides himſelf. The Woman's ſtript, unmercifully laſh'd, and let go. Some time after, the Negro comes into his Maſter's Preſence, hoping the Storm was blown over: But ſo far had the Spirit of Rage and Cruelty the aſcendant, that tho the Fellow was better worth than 50*l. per ann.* to him, in looking after the boiling of Sugars and other things; yet the moſt earneſt Requeſts and Intreatys of the Planter's Wife and other Friends preſent were all little enough to diſſuade him from killing him; and with *difficulty* he was *reſtrain'd from* imbruing his Hands in the poor Man's *Blood.*

The laſt Inſtance I ſhall trouble you with, is, of the Manner and Meaſure of ſome of our Puniſhments.

At a principal Town of a conſiderable Iſland in this part of the World, a Woman Negro-Servant had ſtole a Silver Cup, or ſome ſuch ſmall thing, from her Maſter;

(probably

Figure 1.2
A LETTER from a Merchant at JAMAICA TO A Member of Parliament in LONDON, Touching the AFRICAN TRADE. To which is added, A SPEECH made by a BLACK of Gardaloupe, at the Funeral of a Fellow-Negro,
9 London, 1709,
Newberry Library, Ayer 1000.5 .J25 L65 1709

slurs rendered with typographical conventions that emphasize and reenact their intersectional violence, demonstrating how typography's visual dimensions can give us new ways of seeing race in book history that often have a genesis in the handwritten material forms of manuscript publication. Meanwhile, examinations and visualizations of race in manuscripts have a history that both precedes and provides an analog to print. Through a display of early English handwriting, it is possible to visualize the ways that white English writers constructed and shared their conceptions of race to particular communities.

Part 1.
"We had not thus trespassed against your consent": The Blackamoor Poems by Henry Rainolds and Henry King (1630s–1650s)

By Brandi K. Adams

Located in the Newberry Library is a presentation copy of an eighteenth-century manuscript miscellany* entitled *A Collection of Serious, Humorous, and Affectionate Poems* (Figure 1.1).[2] The 135-page manuscript is recorded in black ink in a clear italic hand. In a subsection of the book called "A Collection of Affectionate Poems", there is an unattributed entry of twelve-line in rhyming couplets entitled "A Blackamore Maid to a fair Boy":

Stay, lovely boy! Why fly'st thou me?
Who languish in these flames for thee!
I'm black, 'tis true _ why so is night;
Yet love does in it's shades delight!
One moment close thy sparkling Eye,
The world shall seem as black as I.
Or look and see how black a shade
Is by thy own white body made
That follows thee, where'er you go:
(Ah, who allow'd would not do so!)
Oh let me then that Shadow be;
No maid shall then be blest as me! (103)

Written from the perspective of a young black woman, this poem entreats a "fair" or white young man to remain by her side and not to "fly" from her. In order to theorize her affection, the narrator constructs a symbiotic relationship between herself and "black" materials in nature: the night sky, shadows, and shades. She then implores the fair boy to become his "Shadow," which would allow her to remain connected and "blest" — an extension of his white body. A companion to this poem entitled "The Boy's answer," appears on the subsequent page of the manuscript. Here, the narrator rebukes the Black maid and enumerates the reasons it remains impossible for him to accept her affection:

Black maid, complain not that I fly,
When fate commands Antipathy!
How monstrous would that union prove
Where night and day should mingled move?
And the Conjunction of our lips
Not kisses make, but an Eclipse?
In which the black shading the white
Portend more terror than delight!
Yet if my shadow thou will be,
Enjoy my shadow's property;
Which tho' attendant on my Eye,
Yet hasts away as I come nigh.
Else stay till death has struck me blind,
And then at will thou may'st be kind. (104)

2. Anonymous, *A Collection of serious humorous and affectionate poems,* (n.p., n.d.), Case MS Y 184.18, Newberry Library, Chicago. The transcriptions are my own. Because of the Covid-19 worldwide pandemic, I was unable to see this manuscript in person. Thank you to Lia Markey and Rebecca Fall for providing me with images of the manuscript.

The response poem employs similar tropes of shadows and shades, yet also uses scientific discourse to emphasize the "monstrous" nature of any connection between them. For the white male speaker, only death would be the moment in which he would consent to their union. While these poems are unattributed in this particular eighteenth-century manuscript miscellany, at the time they were first recorded in this volume, they likely would have been recognized as variations of "The Blackamoor Poems," a popular pair of verses by Henry Rainolds (1564–1632) ("A Black-moor maid wooing a fair boy") and Henry King (1592–1669) ("The Boyes answer to the Blackmoor"), which King first published in manuscript in the 1630s.[3] The poems and their derivatives remain extant in several manuscript collections held in libraries in the United Kingdom, United States, and several countries in Europe. They vary slightly, but maintain the general form of the originals (which I cite below). The preservation and distribution of these specific poems invite both questions and speculation about the reason for their existence and their enduring popularity. What was it that was so compelling about these diptych-like portrait poems of a Black woman and her unrequited love for a white man?

The frequent inclusion of these poems in manuscript collections suggests that the verses and their subject matter remained fascinating for certain communities of mid-seventeenth century English readers of manuscript poems. After their initial scribal publication, readers continued to copy and share these poems and others with their larger social networks. New readers would then alter the poems to change words, meter, or rhyme to suit their individual style and taste. "Their passage from community to community," Harold Love writes, "was marked by deletions and interpolations* to suit the tastes of their new readerships."[4] As these popular verses moved among even larger networks of readers, they recorded a small piece of the history and relationship between race and manuscript culture. Through the Blackamoor poems, it is also possible to see the ways that early modern readers in England employed handwritten poems to construct cultural imaginings about race and desire —ones that they might not necessarily commit to print. These poems also record the sentiment of a network of seventeenth-century English writers (who in this case were white and male) who felt compelled to write in the voice of Black women speakers or to use their bodies — as well as Black men's bodies — as various metaphors of darkness, displacement, pseudoscientific inquiry, and absurdity within poems.

Through the "Blackamoor" poems in particular, Henry King, Henry Rainolds, and their networks of transcribers and readers have contributed to unsolicited, uninformed, and nonconsensual narratives about Black women that continue to persist. Much needed interventions by Kim F. Hall and Mary Hobbs have drawn attention to the popularity of this genre of poems and the negative tropes perpetuated by them.[5] Additional work is now needed to consider the role these poems had in constructing mid-to-late seventeenth-century English ideas about race in the community of readers in which these manuscripts were circulating freely. In what follows, I employ the work of Premodern Critical Race studies scholars to trace the history of the "Blackamoor" poems closely related to those found in the manuscript miscellany in the Newberry Library. I then demonstrate the ways in which white male early modern English poets freely

3. For a comprehensive introduction to the circulation of poems in manuscript and print in early modern England, see Arthur Marotti, *Manuscript, Print, and The English Renaissance Lyric* (Ithaca, NY, Cornell University Press, 1995); see also Harold Love, *The Culture and Commerce of Texts: Scribal Publication in Seventeenth-Century England,* (Amherst, University of Massachusetts Press, 1993); for work on earlier miscellanies see Megan Heffernan, *Making The Miscellany: Poetry Print, and the History of the Book in Early Modern England* (Philadelphia: University of Pennsylvania Press, 2021).

4. Love, *Commerce of Texts,* 181.

5. In order to see the breadth of poems of this type, see Kim F. Hall, *Things of Darkness: Economies of Race and Gender in Early Modern England* (Ithaca, NY: Cornell University Press, 1995). In the index, Hall has gathered several poems by well-known and lesser-known poets from England in the Seventeenth Century on this topic. See Mary Hobbs, "An Edition of the Stoughton Manuscript (an Early Seventeenth-Century Poetry Collection in Private Hands, Connected with Henry King and Oxford) Seen in Relation to Other Contemporary Poetry and Song Collections," (PhD thesis, London University, 1973). See also Werner Sollors, *An Anthology of Interracial Literature: Black-White Contacts in the Old World and the New* (New York: New York University Press, 2004).

interpreted and envisaged the voices and bodies of early modern Black women in the "Blackamoor" manuscript poems using classical, contemporary, and burgeoning scientific sources to create a consensus on how Black women should be read and considered. Finally, I demonstrate how the pervasive acceptance of nonconsensual behavior around these poems led to their eventual printing and widespread publication against the original authors' wishes.

It is a manifestly obvious statement that the original "Blackamoor" poems are not about historical Black women; these poems are distorted representations. Joyce Green MacDonald explains that as the Black woman's racialized body was represented in early modern England, it was both "curiously subject to abstraction and displacement [and] it was also simultaneously endowed with a stubborn materiality."[6] These manuscript poems exemplify MacDonald's observations as they are textual abstractions of Black womanhood, but also real, material objects that seemingly provide answers to the types of questions scholars such as Saidiya Hartman, Imtiaz Habib, and Marisa J. Fuentes ask of other archival materials.[7] Until the elusive autobiographical poem written by a Black woman in early modern England is recovered, the "Blackmore/Blackmoor/Blackamoor" manuscript and printed poems must be read and reexamined to elicit answers to the question concerning historical Black women in England that Fuentes raises about enslaved women in the Caribbean: "How do we construct a coherent historical accounting out of that which defies coherence and representability?"[8] To this question I add: How did these manuscripts compel readers to visualize Black women in a collective manner?

For now, part of this accounting for Black women in England comes from these fictional poetic constructions in manuscript. They allow literary critics and historians to understand how white early modern writers conceived (or failed to conceive) of the personhood of Black women while also locating and historicizing modes of popular conversation encompassing Blackness and race. Rainold's and King's poems may be grouped with several others from the sixteenth and seventeenth centuries in which poets constructed portraits of Black women (and in some cases Black men) to love — or at least to admire — to ridicule, or to impersonate through versification*. From encomia* and blazons* praising her beauty, to textual portraits in which a Black woman's love is summarily rebuffed, there is variety and subtlety to this genre, which is part of a lineage that may have its genesis in a Latin poem about a Black woman by well-known seventeenth-century poet George Herbert.

Several works that attempt to materialize and visualize Black women, including Rainold's, King's and those in the Newberry Library manuscript, may have started with Herbert's poem "Aethiopissa ambit Cestum Diversi Coloris Virum" [A Black woman desires Cestus, a man of a different color]. Herbert's poem was composed in Latin sometime between 1612–26, and certainly before the 1630s, when Rainolds's translated/adapted version of the poem appeared in manuscript.[9] Herbert conscripts the body and voice of a Black woman to espouse the developing rhetoric of an "Africanist presence" and "tropes of blackness" in language and culture that Kim F. Hall locates in early

6. Joyce Green MacDonald, *Women and Race in Early Modern Texts* (New York: Cambridge University Press, 2002)

7. Marisa J. Fuentes, *Dispossessed Lives: Enslaved Women, Violence, and the Archive* (Philadelphia: University of Pennsylvania Press, 2016). See also Imtiaz Habib, *Black Lives in the English Archives, 1500–1677: Imprints of the Invisible* (New York: Routledge, 2020); Saidiya Hartman, "Venus in Two Acts," *Small Axe* 12, no. 2 (2008): 1–14. https://www.muse.jhu.edu/article/241115.

8. Fuentes, *Dispossessed Lives,* 1–12.

9. John T. Gilmore, "Æthiopissæ: The Classical Tradition, Neo-Latin Verse and Images of Race in George Herbert and Vincent Bourne," *Classical Receptions Journal* 1, Issue 1 (2009): 73–86, https://doi.org/10.1093/crj/clp007; see also V. M. Braganza, "The Shadow Casts a Body: Racial Dialogue in Two Neo-Latin Lyrics Attributed to George Herbert," *Studies in Philology* 117, no. 1 (2020): 108–28, https://doi.org/10.1353/sip.2020.0003; G. P. Meyer, "The Blackamoor and Her Love," *Philological Quarterly*, 17 (1938): 371–76.

modern England at that time and earlier.[10] "Aethiopissa" remains extant in many manuscript collections including one version (located at Yale University) which contains a Latin response much in the spirit of Henry King's. In Herbert's original poem, the speaker, an Ethiopian woman, asks "Quid mihi si facies nigra est? [What if my face is Black?]"[11] The speaker then continues by emphasizing that her darkness makes her a perfect shadow to a potential lover. His use of Latin implies that Herbert imagines a Classical past for Black women steeped in disappointment, which is also perhaps an allusion to Queen Persinna in Heliodorus's *Aethiopica* (220–370 CE; first English translation 1569), a tale in which a Black Ethiopian queen gives birth to a pale, white daughter.[12] Herbert's composition of the neo-Latin "Aethiopissa" may also be related to his use of Blackamoors as a metaphor for incomplete or unsatisfactory work in early poems set in his contemporary London.

John T. Gilmore also notices the relationship between Herbert's Latin poem and the untitled one that Herbert dedicated to Francis Bacon (who at the time was Lord Chancellor of England). As Herbert's speaker compares gifts of literary works that they have exchanged, he describes Bacon's work a "diamond" in comparison to his own. The speaker insists that his own manuscript is a "Blackamoor," seemingly in order to contrast both the supposedly inferior state of his work and his position as a scholar with Bacon's. The gift-text itself, a "Blackamoor" literary production, is the polar opposite of a clear, valuable diamond, the type of "shining and sharp" work that Francis Bacon supposedly produces. Nevertheless, the speaker requests that Bacon accept this gift:

> Only, most noble Lord, shut not the door
> Against this mean and humble Blackamoor.
> Perhaps some other subject I had tried
> But that my ink was factious for this side.[13]

Despite what he categorizes as the meanness of his work, Herbert's speaker still wishes to forward it, blaming the "Blackamoor" nature of his writing on ink that is unruly or disputative — not unlike criticism of Blackness in various printed forms.[14] The language of disparagement and false modesty is evocative of Herbert's "Aethiopissa" poem in which she belittles her own physicality as if to ensure that, for her potential lover, her existence and desire — like the Blackamoor gift-text from Herbert's speaker — will always remain tributary. In the poem to Francis Bacon, however, the structure suggests that there remains hope that the speaker's gift will be accepted, whereas "Aethiopissa's" argument is framed from a defensive position in which the speaker must immediately and continually justify her existence. Gilmore suggests that the "Aethiopissa" poem can be read within the grim realities of sugar plantations and England's expanding colonial violence, which would have conditioned English and European readers of the poem to react to any Black woman's perspective as "manifestly absurd."[15] By displacing desire for Black women that Englishmen may have experienced back onto the speaker, the poem forces Aethiopissa's actions and desires to become the focus of the verse, a reinforcement of the futility of her mistaken feelings of love. In turn, this uneven desire makes her culpable for any relationship that develops. This act of continual rejection of Aethopissa and other Black women becomes a popular trope that

10. Hall, *Things of Darkness,* 6–14.

11. May also be translated as "What is it *to me* if my face is Black?"

12. On the popularity of Aethiopica, see Jonathan Crewe, "Drawn in Color: Aethiopika in European Painting," *Word & Image* 25, no. 2 (2009): 129–42, https://doi.org/10.1080/02666280802047729; for insight into stage versions of Aethiopica see Noémie Ndiaye "'Everyone Breeds in His Own Image': Staging the Aethiopica across the Channel," *Renaissance Drama* 44, no. 2 (2016): 157–86, https://doi.org/10.1086/688684; see also Margo J. Hendricks, *Race and Romance: Coloring the Past* (Tempe, AZ: ACMRS Press, 2022), 15–34.

13. F. E. Hutchinson, ed., *The Works of George Herbert* (Oxford: Clarendon Press, 1972, first published 1941).

14. See Miles Parks Grier, "Inkface: The Slave Stigma in England's Early Imperial Imagination," in *Scripturalizing the Human: The Written as the Political,* ed. Vincent L. Wimpish (New York: Routledge, 2015): 193–218.

15. Gilmore, "Æthiopissæ," 74.

found itself translated into English for a wider group of readers when Rainolds introduces his version of the poem in the 1630s. As a result, Herbert's classically inspired, yet historically inaccurate, presentation of Black women and their emotions becomes codified by a larger and more influential coterie of readers, for it is Rainold's translation of Herbert's poem that inspires Henry King to compose what becomes a very well-read response.

It is necessary to note that what may appear as intellectual exercises in fact tell a microhistory of white English writers attempting to contextualize Blackness and delineate the worth of Black women's bodies. While these poems are characterized by Arthur Marotti as "witty trivia," and identified as a benign translations (with additions) of Herbert's "Aethiopissa," Rainolds's poem unquestioningly translates and adapts the neo-Latin work promulgating a rather unflattering portrait of a "blackmoor maid" into a quippy rondeau prime (a twelve-line poem that usually contains seven lines (called a septet) followed by five additional lines (called a cinquain).[16] Following the historically-inspired spirit of Herbert's "Aethiopissa" and using what he imagines as the voice of a Black maid, Rainolds's speaker entreats the fair boy to allow her to follow him as she attempts to validate her existence:

> *A Black-moor Maid wooing a fair Boy:*
> *sent to the Author* by Mr. Hen. (s).
> STay lovely Boy, why fly'st thou mee
> That languish in these flames for thee?
> I'm black 'tis true: why so is Night,
> And Love doth in dark Shades delight.
> The whole World, do but close thine eye,
> Will seem to thee as black as I;
> Or op't, and see what a black shade
> Is by thine own fair body made,
> That follows thee where e're thou go;
> (O who allow'd would not do so?)
> Let me for ever dwell so nigh,
> And thou shalt need no other shade than I.[17]
>
> Mr. Hen.*Rainold(s).*

As she "languish[es] in these flames" of love, the speaker capitulates to the boy's implied denial and further claims that she shares a color with Night. Like Aethiopissa, this unnamed Black woman speaker aligns her color with the evening, a time in which sexual activities can take place, to evoke and enflame the fair boy's desire. The speaker uses her color, nature, and sexuality to invent value for the object and addressee of her affections. To further persuade him, she insists that if he only "close[s] thine eye," night becomes a default setting for the world, a filter through which she normalizes her body and coloring, to "seem to thee as Black as I." For the speaker, her existing proximally to the fair boy is enough; she only wishes to perform her role as a shadow, like Aethiopissa: "Hoc saltem officio fungar amore tui," [This, at least, is a duty I can perform for you, beloved].[18] Along with this invocation of shadows is an implied servitude both in the speaker's voice of supplication, and in the title of the poem as she and her shadow are always subordinate to the sun of the fair boy.

An analogue may be found in a recently auctioned "English School Double Portrait" (1650) (Figure 1.3) in which two women, one white and one Black, are seated together, their faces painted with astrological symbols. Although the women are seated next to one another, rather equally, the Black woman's features fade into the darkness and shadows of the background of the painting. Her equality is diminished because of the luminescence of the white woman's hair and skin. Peter Erickson notes that in paintings of this type that equanimity is illusory. He writes about Black servants in particular: "Inclusion of the Black servant does not

16. Marotti, *Manuscript*, 131.

17. Henry King, *Poems, elegies, paradoxes, and sonnets* (London, 1657), B3v. I have lightly edited each poem by standardizing the long *s*, but I have made no other changes to spelling or punctuation.

18. Line 8 translation is mine. Gilmore translates line 8 in the spirit of early modern poetry as, "To be thy shadow is mine only prayer," and Braganza translates it as, "This office, at least, I will perform out of love for you."

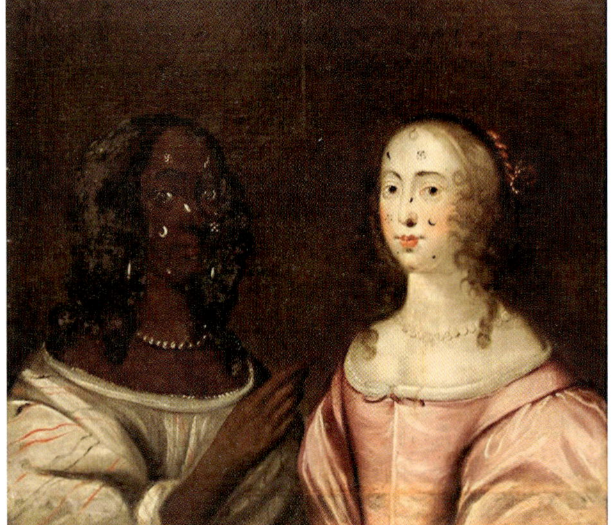

Figure 1.3
Anonymous Artist,
Double portrait of two women with face patches,
oil on canvas, circa 1650, location unknown

represent benign inclusiveness but is rather keyed to incorporation into a visual regime structured in white dominance. Artistic sophistication in no way guarantees complexity in the sense of humanly sensitive, enlightened images of black [people]."[19] Blackness in this painting replicates that which is found in the portraitlike manuscripts. It is a response to whiteness and maleness—a shadow of the primary figure. The Black woman figure in this double portrait could easily become the "Blackamoor" of Herbert's, King's, and Rainolds's imaginations.

Rainolds's (and by extension, Herbert's) use of the trope of the "Blackamoor" is also perhaps indicative of what Ella Shohat recognizes in visual material and historical representations of this imagined people:

> A figure of simultaneous Blackness and Moorishness, the Blackamoor offers an exemplum of the continuities between various Eurocentric representations, which include the racialization and Orientalization of various others. The Blackamoor can be seen as a fluid mélange of paradoxes; its Blackness is embedded in Orientalism, just as its Moorishness is embedded in the racialization of Africa.[20]

Located in the term "Blackamoor" and in the poem itself is a power dynamic that forever structures a white, English (possibly colonial) voice and discourse at the center of the speaker's words. As other scholars have pointed out, poems such as this engage in a rhetorical blackface, which affirms white English readers' perceptions about Black women, Blackness, and imagined relationships between Black women and white Englishmen.[21] In this narrative, the attraction can only be unidirectional, which provides an impetus for Henry King's response in sonnet form.

The Rainolds and King poems are usually paired together, much like a diptych painting, in which King's response serves as a rejoinder, and mimics the dynamics of power that are evident in the Rainolds poem. King offers a response in the voice of the fair boy:

> *The Boyes answer to the Blackmoor.*
> Black Maid, complain not that I fly,
> When Fate commands Antipathy:
> Prodigious might that union prove,
> Where Night and Day together move,
> And the conduction of our lips
> Not kisses make, but an Eclipse;
> In which the mixed Black and white

19. Peter Erickson, "Invisibility Speaks: Servants and Portraits in Early Modern Visual Culture." *Journal for Early Modern Cultural Studies* 9, no. 1 (2009): 23–61. http://www.jstor.org/stable/40339610.

20. Ella Shohat, "The Specter of the Blackamoor: Figuring Africa and the Orient," *The Comparatist* 42, no. 1 (2018): 158–88, https://doi.org/10.1353/com.2018.0008.

21. See Braganza, "Shadow Casts a Body," and Gilmore, "Æthiopissæ."

Portends more terror than delight.
Yet if my shadow thou wilt be,
Enjoy thy dearest wish: But see
Thou take my shadowes property,
That hastes away when I come nigh:
Else stay till death hath blinded mee,
And then I will bequeath my self to thee[22]

In his sonnet response (in the form of rhyming couplets) to Rainold's adaptation of Herbert's poem, King has the fair speaker further normalize the hierarchical relationship between himself and the Black maid. By invoking Fate, the speaker simultaneously yokes timelessness and historical precedence to their incompatibility. The speaker articulates Kim F. Hall's notion that whiteness remains in polarity to Blackness in early modern English discursive contexts.[23] For English readers — for whom this kind of relationship seemed nothing short of impossible — it provides them with assurance that this Black maid, however fictive, has no place in the Copernican universe where day and night must remain separate. The fear of the phenomenon and the terror associated with the overturn of the universe in the form of an eclipse — or the speaker's "kiss" with the Black maid — was indeed palpable at the time. Anthony Grafton records a history of early responses to the scientific phenomenon and includes Caspar Peucer's vivid response to the notion of eclipses in 1533: "We can see with our own eyes what vicissitudes eclipses of the sun and moon, especially that of the sun, have caused for the empire, what disturbances they have provoked, what changes and quarrels they have portended for the realm of religion."[24] King's speaker then invokes the terror of celestial disturbance to articulate the impossibility and the apocalyptic nature of this pairing. He reads the eclipse as many early modern Englishmen and Europeans did, "as signs of victory or disaster, portents of a future that made them tremble with joy, horror, or both."[25] In this case, the eclipse or kiss is nothing but sheer terror.

To the speaker, the mixing of Blackness with whiteness remains the antithesis of an ordered universe. He does offer the Black maid a type of solace in which he invites her to become the shadow that she requests in the initial poem, as her skin remains in striking contrast to his. Instead, she is to embody the properties of an actual shadow, one that "hastes away," as he approaches, keeping the Black maid and fair boy at distance from each other. His last offering to her is that of death, which will blind him to the world, and allow her to finally embrace him. This rebuff stands in stark contrast to other poems of the period including one by T. R. entitled, "In Praise of Black Women," published in 1654 in a printed miscellany called *The Harmony of the Muses*.[26] Here, in the first six lines of the forty-four lined poem, the speaker inverts several of the metaphors invoked by King's fair speaker:

IF shadows be a Pictures excellence,
And makes the shew more glorious to the sense;
If Stars in the bright day be hid from sight,
And shine more glorious in Masque of night,
Why should you think rare creature that you lack
Perfections, cause your hair and eyes be Black;[27]

Despite being called "creatures," the Black women of T.R.'s poem are "excellent" and full of "perfections," as the speaker constructs an extended blazon of an entire group of women. The perspective is clearly

22. King, *Poems, elegies, paradoxes, and sonnet,* B4r.

23. Hall, *Things of Darkness,* 9.

24. Anthony Grafton, "Some Uses of Eclipses in Early Modern Chronology," *Journal of the History of Ideas* 64, no. 2 (2003): 213–29, https://doi.org/10.2307/3654126. Grafton translates Caspar Peucers's text from Latin.

25. Grafton, "Uses," 214.

26. R.C., ed. *The harmony of the muses, or, the gentlemans and ladies choisest recreation full of various, pure and transcendent wit : Containing severall excellent poems, some fancies of love, some of disdain, and all the subjects incident to the passionate affections either of men or women / heretofore written by those unimitable masters of learning and invention, dr. joh. donn, dr. hen. king, dr. W. stroad* (London, 1654).

27. R.C., *harmony of the muses,* B3r-B4v.

that of a white, male speaker. There are, of course, moments of objectification and colonialist constructions, but to the speaker's credit, the poem takes time to reverse tropes that make Blackness negative. The polarity is switched and if this poem is read without irony, it is a much more generous notion of Blackness for the time. This particular poem was published in print three years before Rainolds and King's poems, so it is likely that they could all be read together to construct a spectrum of opinions regarding the position of Black women in early modern English society, although King may not have wanted to advertise his own creative work on the subject as publicly as it was in 1657.

While the "Blackamoor" poems were in circulation, they originated with the author and traveled through King's social circles. Very much like Katherine Philips and his friend John Donne, King supervised the circulation of his works. Therefore, it is likely that most manuscript copies of his poem were circulated without hindrance from King, as he was a "scribal publisher of miscellanies, presenting his own poems intermixed with those of friends."[28] As the son of the Bishop of London and a graduate of Christ Church, Oxford (B. A. 1611 and M. A. 1614), his social circle was substantial and included playwright Ben Jonson, along with his aforementioned fellow poet and clergyman John Donne. Mary Hobbs traces the itinerary of Henry King's poems through scribes* at Christ Church, to other colleges in Oxford, to attorneys at Inns of Court and then to groups of musicians in London.[29] As they were circulated and recirculated, the "Blackamoor" poems remained popular within these groups of readers and perhaps solidified white cultural ways of thinking about Blackness and Black women.[30] For the readers of these works, particularly as the manuscripts were read, copied, and reread, the Black Maid speakers from Rainolds's poem as well as the Black Maid addressees from King's may have become for them the literal voices — ironic or not — of actual Black women living in and around London. To these coteries of readers, the identity and worth of Black women may have been solidified without their knowledge and certainly without their consent. In 1657, King experienced a modicum* of their experience as he had his work, which included the "Blackamoor" poems, printed and circulated outside of his control.

Somehow, King's poems were acquired by publishers Richard Marriott and Henry Herringman, who then printed and sold them in St. Dunstans Churchyard Fleet-street, and at the New-Exchange (also called Britain's Bourse) on the Strand. There, fashionable shoppers could purchase expensive clothing and furniture as well as books, including King's. If King's manuscript was indeed conscripted for publication (or sold by someone in possession of his manuscript), it suffered a somewhat similar fate to the Black woman in his poem. The poems and the words that he carefully governed in manuscript became available to a much larger reading public than those in his network of manuscript readers. At this point in his life, King had been removed from his position of Bishop of Chichester (as a part of the Interregnum*) and was awaiting reinstatement — his own position unsteady and mutable, yet not as uncomfortable as the Black maid of his poem. The seizure and publication of his poetry mimics his own actions as well as those of George Herbert and Henry Rainolds as they took possession of an identity that did not belong to them. Like the women of the poems, his manuscript became a commodity that could be handled, controlled, and interpreted by people outside of familiar readers and communities. Both the Black women subjects of the poems and the poems themselves became something worth exploiting for profit, whether this revenue manifested itself as fame or as monetary capital.

Unlike Herbert, Rainolds, or even King, the publishers of King's work attempted to justify their actions. In a highly unusual paratextual move, Marriott and

28. Love, *Commerce of Texts,* 5–50.

29. Hobbs cited in Love, *Commerce of Texts,* 181.

30. Hobbs, "Stoughton Manuscript."

Herringman chose to write a prefatory* letter to King (instead of the usual letter to readers) to publicly admit that they took it upon themselves to publish these poems. And to add to the injury, the publishers blame King for not committing these poems to print:

> The Lord Verulam comparing ingenious Authors to those who had Orchards ill neighbored, advised them to publish their own labors, lest others might steal the fruit: Had you followed his example, or liked the advice, we had not thus trespassed against your consent, or been forced to an Apology, which cannot but imply a fault committed.[31]

The publishers assure him that they have saved him from further injury and "added violence," because they prevented "false copies of these Poems from being pushed into the marketplace."[32] They assure him that his "Juvenalia" is more than acceptable with several readers waiting to enjoy his words. They take the blame for the person who shared the work with them, as they are "persons at a distance," which allows them freedom to enact this grievance without many repercussions.[33] Unlike the Black women subjects in the above poems, King at least received an apology — however disingenuous — as his work was converted from the manuscripts over which he exhibited at least some control to the wider reading public. The "added violence" of print remains the taking of a Black woman's likeness and distributing it to the point where it was able to be read, characterized, undervalued, and likely misunderstood by so many individual readers who never encountered or comprehended her existence in England. The Rainolds and King poems, while perhaps never really about Black women, nevertheless promulgated modes of thought and textual portraits about them that continued throughout the century well into the present.

Part 2:
Misogynoir in Print: *A Letter from a Merchant at Jamaica* (1709)[34]

By Carissa M. Harris

A vivid account of an Englishman abusing an enslaved Black woman in colonial Jamaica unfolds in a political pamphlet advocating for slavery's reform. While touring his plantation one Sunday, a planter discovers a Black man in bed with a woman he does not recognize: "*Hussey!* says the Planter, *who are you? To whom do you belong?*"[35] Without waiting for an answer, he beats her, unleashes a barrage of racist gendered insults, and orders her to be stripped and whipped. The pamphlet's London typesetter highlights the

31. King, *Poems, elegies, paradoxes, and sonnet,* A3r.

32. King, A3r

33. King, A4v.

34. I am grateful to Kinohi Nishikawa and Rebbeca Tesfai for sharing helpful feedback on earlier versions of this piece; to Becky Fall for alerting me to the existence of the Letter; to Jill Gage for her generosity in sharing typography and punctuation sources with me; to Lia Markey and Noémie Ndiaye for their editorial flexibility and understanding during Omicron January; to my foremothers Rhoda, Madinda, Jane, Eliza, and many others who survived slavery's horrors; and to Margery the cat, who kept company with me in her dying days as I wrote this.

35. *A LETTER from a Merchant at JAMAICA TO A Member of Parliament in LONDON, Touching the AFRICAN TRADE. To which is added, A SPEECH made by a BLACK of Gardaloupe, at the Funeral of a Fellow-Negro* (London, Printed for A. Baldwin, 1709), 7; see Chicago, Newberry Library, Ayer 1000.5 .J25 L65 1709. All references are to page numbers in this edition. The pamphlet's full text is printed in Jack P. Greene, "'A Plain and Natural Right to Life and Liberty': An Early Natural Rights Attack on the Excesses of the Slave System in Colonial British America," *William and Mary Quarterly* 57, no. 4 (2000): 799–808, https://doi.org/10.2307/2674156; and analyzed in Dallin Lewis, "Domesticating the Plantation: The Politics and Tragedy of Slave Kinship in the British Atlantic World," *The Eighteenth Century* 60, no. 3 (2019): 311–30, https://doi.org/10.1353/ecy.2019.0020.

planter's slurs — *"Hussey," "D—'d B—ch," "W—re"* — by setting them in italics to designate them as direct speech and censoring many of them with long dashes due to their obscenity (Figure 1.2). The typesetter's visual emphasis on these terms, which accrued powerful overlapping meanings of femininity, youth, excessive sexuality, and low social status over time, illuminates their shared structural role in what Imani Perry calls "a complicated architecture of relations of domination."[36] The anonymous author who chose them, and the typesetter who decided how they would look on the printed page, together call attention to Black women's dehumanization in a text that argues for their continued enslavement.

This narrative comes from *A Letter from a Merchant at Jamaica*, an anonymous thirty-one-page pamphlet printed in London in 1709 and held in the Newberry Library as well as Brown University's John Carter Brown Library. The pamphlet, its price of two pence advertised on the title page, consists of two parts. The first, a thirteen-page section dated October 10, 1708, is titled "A LETTER *from a Merchant at* Jamaica *to a Member of Parliament in* London, *touching the* AFRICAN TRADE." In it, an English merchant living in Jamaica addresses an unnamed MP with whom he claims "the honor" of "Acquaintance . . . whilst I was in *England*" (4). Stating he has "HEAR[D] from *England*, that there's like to be a Struggle next Session of Parliament between the *African* Company and the other Traders thither" (3), the merchant purports to tell the unvarnished truth about the "Cruelty" of the slave trade in the British West Indies that neither "the Planters or Merchants, the Company or Traders" will disclose during the upcoming session (4).[37] He argues for slavery's reform by narrating three incidents of Englishmen's violence against enslaved African women: a planter who tries to separate a Black couple because he wishes to purchase the man but not the woman; the episode I discussed briefly above, in which a planter abuses a Black woman for her sexual choices because she "*belong*[*s*]" to someone else; and an enslaver ordering a heavily pregnant woman to be stripped naked and publicly whipped for petty theft (3–15).[38] The merchant-narrator urges that enslaved Black people "be treated with Humanity and Reason; [and] if they are ill us'd, that the Law should give them . . . Protection or Redress" (14). But his solution to slavery's cruelty does *not* entail abolition. Rather, he details these graphic spectacular "scenes of subjection," using Saidiya Hartman's term for this phenomenon, to contend that the institution should be reformed so it can be "preserve[d] and increase[d]" (13) for the benefit of men like him.[39]

I analyze the Letter using Moya Bailey's concept of misogynoir, a term she defines as "the uniquely co-constitutive racialized and sexist violence that befalls Black women as a result of their simultaneous and interlocking oppression at the intersection of racial and gender marginalization."[40] Bailey focuses on the media's central role in perpetuating misogynoir because of how it shapes popular perceptions of Black women that in turn influence law, policy, and public health outcomes. She contends that "[r]epresentations of Black women in popular culture help support and perhaps even bolster the harm they experience."[41] We can read this mass-produced pamphlet — printed, cheap, widely available to a London audience — as a form of media misogynoir asserting the hypersexuality, animality, and, as I shall shortly show,

36. Perry, *Vexy Thing*, 9.

37. This letter "appears to refer to a bill considered in the Commons in March 1710," which did not pass; see Ruth Paley, Cristina Malcolmson, and Michael Hunter, "Parliament and Slavery, 1660–c.1710," *Slavery and Abolition* 31, no. 2 (2010): 265, https://doi.org/10.1080/01440391003711107.

38. For more on gender, violence, and labor on British Caribbean plantations in the eighteenth century, see Nicholas Radburn, "'[M]anaged at First as if They Were Beasts': The Seasoning of Enslaved Africans in Eighteenth-Century Jamaica," *Journal of Global Slavery* 6 (2021): 11–30, https://doi.org/10.1163/2405836X-00601008; Justin Roberts, "The Whip and the Hoe: Violence, Work and Productivity on Anglo-American Plantations," *Journal of Global Slavery* 6 (2021): 108–30, https://doi.org/10.1163/2405836X-00601005; Stella Dadzie, *A Kick in the Belly: Women, Slavery and Resistance* (New York: Verso, 2020).

39. Saidiya V. Hartman, *Scenes of Subjection: Terror, Slavery, and Self-Making in Nineteenth-Century America* (Oxford: Oxford University Press, 1997). I am grateful to Kinohi Nishikawa for directing me to this reference.

40. Moya Bailey, *Misogynoir Transformed: Black Women's Digital Resistance* (New York: New York University Press, 2021), 1.

41. Bailey, *Misogynoir Transformed*, 13.

intrinsically laboring nature of Black women's bodies to support the author's argument for their necessary domination. The pamphlet's misogynoir operates through its libidinally-charged descriptions of violence inflicted on Black women's naked bodies, its gendered slurs carrying long histories of intersecting vulnerabilities and structural disempowerment, and its typesetter's choices to censor some of these insults with dashes, enabling readers to experience the thrill of reconstructing the obscenities and rendering them more visually prominent on the page. These dashes are so powerful because they are inherently participatory, compelling readers to interact with them to supply the missing letters. The dashes' interactivity is reinforced by the brutality of these scenes' violence: Saidiya Hartman declares that "[w]hat interests me are the ways we are called upon to participate in such scenes," and this pamphlet's typographical choices call upon readers to participate in its misogynoir.[42]

Asserting slavery's benefit to men like "Us," the merchant writes, "It must be own'd our Plantations are of great Consequence to both Us and *England.* They are work'd and cultivated mostly by the hands of Negroes, and it would be hard to do it by any others" (14). Central to the Letter's constellation of insults for enslaved Black women — "Cow," *"ill-thriven Jade," "Hussey," "B—ch," "W—re"* — is their signification of exploitable feminine bodies, for they conflate female animals, lower-status women, sex workers, and Black women and insist that they are built for "Labour" in all its senses — domestic, sexual, physical, reproductive — to benefit any man who can afford their hire. Emphasized on the printed page through capitalization, italics, and dashes, the merchant's lexicon of misogynoir affirms his argument that Black people must remain enslaved because they are "Negroes . . . by whose Labour we are enrich'd" (14). His use of the term "Labour" is significant: for centuries, the language of physical toil overlapped with the vernacular of sexual activity in words such as "swink," "labour," and "werk," causing this capacious sense of "Labour" to resonate with the Letter's misogynoirist slurs insisting on the inherent exploitability of Black women's bodily exertion.[43] Leaving aside "whore" because its rich history lies outside the scope of this short chapter section, I trace these terms' development in England and Scotland during the twelfth through seventeenth centuries to show how they accrued sedimented meanings of disadvantage rooted in class, race, labor, gender, and sexuality, an accretion which enabled them to function as powerful tools of misogynoir by the early eighteenth century.[44] Following Perry's exhortation to "think of feminism as a critical reading practice in which one 'reads through these layers' of gendered forms of domination," I "seek deep understanding" of how these constellated terms amassed the figurative freight to anchor the merchant's argument for Black women's continued enslavement.[45] I call this methodology "intersectional material philology," and I enlist it in service of providing an account of lexical power and marginalization that continues to shape Black women's lives today.[46]

In the Letter's first anecdote, an English planter attempts to purchase "a stout jolly young Fellow" on a slave ship (5). The ship's captain warns, "Sir . . . he has a Wife; if you have him, you must take the Cow too." The planter reacts indignantly: "*D—n her,* says the Planter, *she's an ill-thriven Jade; I'll not meddle with her: Prithee let me have the Fellow alone.*" Here, the dashes that the typesetter uses to replace the obscene word's core letters for propriety's sake, as he does elsewhere with "*W—re*," "*d—'d B—ch*," "*D—g*," and "D—l," draw

42. Hartman, *Scenes of Subjection,* 6.

43. *Middle English Dictionary* (hereafter *MED*), s.v. "labouren" (v.), 1(a): "To perform manual or physical work, work hard, toil; also copulate"; "swinken" (v.), 1(a), 2(e); "werken" (v.[1]), 5(a), 6. On enslaved Black women's labor in all its senses, see Jennifer L. Morgan, *Laboring Women: Reproduction and Gender in New World Slavery* (Philadelphia: University of Pennsylvania Press, 2004).

44. I use this methodology elsewhere with "wench"; see Carissa Harris, "A History of the Wench," *Electric Literature,* June 3, 2019, https://electricliterature.com/a-history-of-the-wench/; "Chaucer's Wenches," *Studies in the Age of Chaucer* 45 (2023), forthcoming.

45. Perry, *Vexy Thing,* 9.

46. I am grateful to co-editor Noémie Ndiaye for helping me to arrive at this methodological terminology.

visual attention to the planter's curse. Anne Toner has traced how printers used dashes to censor objectionable content beginning in sixteenth-century dramatic texts, noting that "the dash marks the suppression of lewdness, while at the same time making it more evident."[47] She discusses "the visual dimension of the ellipsis," or the fact that "the associative nature of reading . . . brings punctuation's graphic dimensions to life," modeling ways we can read the Letter's long horizontal dashes: as an arm stretching taut to deliver a blow, as the propulsive forward movement of a fist hurtling to meet flesh, as a body knocked prone to the ground by the words' violent force.[48]

The enslavers use animal epithets — "Cow" and "*ill-thriven Jade*" — to name the woman on the slave ship, both signifying bodies whose value inheres in their capacity to benefit men with their labor.[49] The typesetter capitalizes both "Cow" and "*Jade*," as he does with nearly all nouns in the pamphlet.[50] Edward Phillips's 1696 English dictionary defines "Cow" as "A Tame Beast with Horns, a Female to a Bull, that brings forth Calves, and gives Milk. The Emblem of . . . a Lazy, Dronish, Beastly woman, who is likened to a Cow."[51] Phillips, like the slave ship's captain, defines the "Cow" by her status as a female "Beast" counterpart to a male animal. Phillips's "Cow" is a reproductive body that "brings forth" offspring and "gives Milk"; when applied to women, paradoxically, it carries derogatory connotations of animality and unproductivity. The slave ship captain's use of "Cow" casts the Black woman as a feminized body that is expected to labor both physically and reproductively, but whose labor is not sufficient for those who wish to profit from it.

"*Jade*," the planter's insult for the Black woman that echoes the ship captain's in its gendered animal connotations, originally signified a horse whose body was broken down by labor.[52] In Geoffrey Chaucer's *Nun's Priest's Prologue* (1390s), the Canterbury pilgrimage's host encourages a priest to tell a story while gently mocking his decrepit horse:

> Be blithe, though thou ryde upon a jade.
> What thogh thyn hors be bothe foul and lene?
> If he wol serve thee, rekke nat a bene.
>
> [Be merry, even though you ride upon a broken-down horse. Who cares if your horse is both emaciated and in poor physical condition? If he will serve you, it doesn't matter.][53]

Harry Bailly uses "jade" to name a "hors . . . bothe foul and lene," a work-exhausted body existing solely to "serve" the man who "ryde[s]" on it.[54] "Jade" initially designated a male or female horse, as attested by Chaucer's use of "he" to name the animal. But it came to signify transgressive feminine sexuality by the sixteenth century, due to its connections to excessive corporeal toil. These connections transferred to women whose bodies were deemed to be worn out by prodigious amounts of sex, like overridden horses exhausted for profit by men who have hired them, in a cluster of terms — "nag," "jade," "hackney," "mare," "stotte" — that carried overlapping meanings of

47. Anne Toner, *Ellipsis in English Literature: Signs of Omission* (Cambridge, UK: Cambridge University Press, 2015), 40; for a broader discussion, see 26, 36–40.

48. Toner, *Ellipsis*, 10.

49. *Oxford English Dictionary* (hereafter *OED*), s.v. "cow" n[1], 4b: "Applied to a coarse or degraded woman. Also, loosely, any woman, used esp. as a coarse form of address."

50. For more on how typographical conventions shifted away from capitalizing all nouns to capitalizing only proper nouns during the eighteenth century, see Richard Wendorf, "Abandoning the Capital in Eighteenth-Century London," in *Reading, Society and Politics in Early Modern England,* eds. Kevin Sharpe and Steven N. Zwicker (Cambridge, UK: Cambridge University Press, 2003), 72–98.

51. Edward Phillips, *The new world of words, or, A universal English dictionary* (London: Printed for R. Bently, J. Phillips, H. Rhodes, and J. Taylor, 1696), s.v. "Cow."

52. *MED,* s.v. "jade" (n.), 1(a): "A cart horse, a hack." This is the only quotation listed under the entry.

53. Geoffrey Chaucer, *The Riverside Chaucer,* 3rd ed., eds. Larry D. Benson et al. (Boston: Houghton Mifflin, 1987), VII.2812–14. References are to fragments and lines in this edition.

54. *MED,* s.v. "foul" (adj.), 4(b); "lene" (adj.[1]), 1(b), 1(c).

excessive equine labor and feminine sexuality.[55] In the anonymous Tudor interlude *The Nice Wanton* (c. 1550), the epithet "jade" is hurled at an outspoken woman who scolds her neighbors: "There is one Xantippe, a curst shrew . . . Such a jade she is, and so curst a quean [whore], / She would out-scold the devil's dame, I ween."[56] Here the "jade" is characterized by her unruly anger and illicit sexuality, aligned with the disruptive "shrew" and the promiscuous "quean." Xantippe's daughter Dalila, a sex worker who dies of syphilis, is denigrated in similar terms: "Gup, whore; do ye hear this jade?" one male character shouts as she exits the stage (104).

In sixteenth- and seventeenth-century Britain, "jade" was so offensive that women went to court to prosecute those who called them jades, as historians Laura Gowing and Kirilka Stavreva have shown.[57] In Banff on Scotland's northern coast, a carpenter's wife named Margaret Gray was imprisoned in 1662 for attacking Isobel Greig by "calling her Jad and queyn and offering to strik her with stones."[58] At this point, "jad" was legally abusive speech connected to other gendered sexual slurs ("queyn") and threats of physical violence. By the time the planter insults an enslaved African woman as *"ill-thriven Jade"* in an eighteenth-century pamphlet, the term bore centuries-old symbolic freight of animality, degraded femininity, and illicit sexuality. Above all, "jade" signified a body worn out and irreparably damaged from men's extraction of its labor.[59]

In the Letter's second "scene of subjection," to use Hartman's term, a planter attacks "a Stranger Black Woman" whom he finds with "one of his Black Men" on his plantation (7). After addressing her as *"Hussey"* and caning her, he berates the man for coupling with a woman who *"belong[s]"* to another plantation patriarch: *"If you want a Woman, have not I Women enou' for you? You Dog you! Sirrah, whose is she?"* he shouts (7). He calls her *"Hussey"* again and tells his servants, *"strip this W—re; tie her to yonder Tree, and let her have forty sound Lashes with the Cat-of-nine-tails"* (7), cursing her as *"you d—'d B—ch"* (8). When she says that she is the man's wife, the planter orders forty more lashes, then attempts to kill the man *"for daring to meddle with any Women but mine"* (8). His rage stems from his thwarted sense of patriarchal domination: believing he has power over the bodies he "owns" and averse to the possibility of "one of his Black Men" (7) impregnating a woman whose reproductive labor would benefit another Englishman, he has her beaten, stripped, and whipped as though she *"belong[s]"* to him.

In both this anecdote and the previous one, the typesetter sets the planter's direct speech in italic type*, visually differentiating it from the rest of the text in roman type. Mark Bland traces how, beginning in the sixteenth century, "the choice of italic marked the otherness of the text and the difference of voice" and thus frequently designated direct speech.[60] Here, italics both draw visual attention to the enslavers' words by differentiating them from the narrator's and enable the narrator to reproduce the slurs while denying ownership of them.

"B[it]ch," designated as obscene by the typesetter's censoring dashes, named a female dog from the early Middle Ages onward and signified a limitless, indiscriminate sexual appetite. Due to these associations, "bitch" was also an insult directed at women, much like it is today. A twelfth-century gloss on one

55. *OED*, s.v. "jade" (n.), 1(a): "A contemptuous name for a horse; a horse of inferior breed, e.g., a cart- or draught-horse as opposed to a riding horse; a roadster, a hack; a sorry, ill-conditioned, wearied, or worn-out horse"; 2: "A term of reprobation applied to a woman." *OED*, s.v. "nag" (n.[1]), 1, 2(b); s.v. "hackney" (n.), 1(b), 3; *MED*, s.v. "mere" (n.[1]), 2(a), 2(c); s.v. "stot" (n.), 1(b), 2(a).

56. *The Nice Wanton*, in *The Dramatic Writings of Richard Wever and Thomas Ingelend*, ed. John S. Farmer (London: Barnes and Noble, 1905), 110. Because there are no scene or line numbers in this edition, references are to page numbers.

57. Laura Gowing, *Domestic Dangers: Women, Words, and Sex in Early Modern London* (Oxford: Oxford University Press, 1996), 59–100; Kirilka Stavreva, *Words Like Daggers: Violent Female Speech in Early Modern England* (Lincoln: University of Nebraska Press, 2015), 17–44.

58. William Cramond, ed., *The Annals of Banff*, 2 vols. (Aberdeen: New Spalding Club, 1891), 1:145.

59. Justin Roberts explores how enslaved people's bodies in Britain's Caribbean colonial plantations were broken down by labor in "The Whip and the Hoe," 114–21.

60. Mark Bland, "The Appearance of the Text in Early Modern England," *Text* 11 (1998): 99.

of Ælfric's Old English sermons reads "fulan horan and byccan" [foul whores and bitches], pointing to the term's longstanding usage as a derogatory term connoting illicit feminine sexuality.[61] In *Handlyng Synne* (c. 1303–17), the monk Robert Mannyng compares a copulating couple to "dog and bych that men on wondre" [a dog and bitch that people stare at] (8952), a line one reader deemed so offensive that they scraped it from the parchment page in a late fourteenth-century manuscript.[62] Mannyng's pairing of "dog and bych" to describe two people caught having illicit sex (in this case, because it occurs on church property) resonates with the planter's use of "*Dog*" and "*B*[*it*]*ch*" to address the enslaved couple. Mannyng underscores the demeaning significance of "bycche" elsewhere by sharing "a tale of a wycche, / That leved no better than a bycche" [A witch that lived no better than a bitch] (499–500). In John Rolland's Middle Scots translation of *The Seven Sages of Rome* (1560), the narrator exclaims of an adulterous empress, "Fy, bitter bitche!" and denigrates her as "this bald [bold] bittre Bitch," linking his repetition of "bitch" to feminine sexual voracity.[63] "Bitch" was a common insult in early modern defamation cases: in 1590, Edith Parsons leaned out of her London house to shout at Sicilia Thornton, "thou art an whore, an arrant whore, a bitche, yea worse than a bitch," and in the Welsh market town of Ruthin, Jane Lloyd was insulted as "proud bitch, lying under every bodyes breech under hedges."[64] By the time that the planter attacks the enslaved Black woman as a "*B*[*it*]*ch*" and the typesetter underscores its offensiveness with a censoring ellipsis, the term's sedimented gendered, sexual, and animal meanings enabled its racialization.[65]

In addition to insulting her as "*B*[*it*]*ch*" and "*W*[*ho*] *re*," the planter twice addresses the Black woman as "*Hussey*." "Hussy" originated as a fifteenth-century Scots abbreviation of "housewife," defined by her gender and domestic labor, before also becoming "a derogatory term for a woman or girl: a woman of low character or of the lower orders, a wanton, a wench."[66] The complimentary phrase "a hwsy that can hows" [a housewife who knows how to run a house], in monastic historian Andrew of Wyntoun's *Original Chronicle* (c. 1420), is its earliest recorded reference in the *Dictionary of the Older Scottish Tongue*.[67] But by the time Edinburgh town officials decreed expulsion for "vagabounds, young fallowis or young husis, haffand na prettik nor service to life upon" [idlers, young fellows or young hussies, having no job nor service to live upon] in 1505, "hussy" was a legally transgressive category of lower-status young woman unable to support herself materially.[68] Another Edinburgh statute in 1530 ordered all landowners and householders to expel "hussis vile personis and vagabundis that wantis housbondis to wyn thar liffing" [hussies, lowly people, and idlers who lack husbands to win their living] from their households.[69] The "hussy" is marked by her multiple disadvantages of youth, femininity, poverty, subjugation, singleness, and lower social status. She is expected to labor for property-owning patriarchs, and she is treated derisively because she

61. *Dictionary of Old English: A to I online,* eds. Angus Cameron, Ashley Crandell Amos, Antonette diPaolo Healey et al. (Toronto: Dictionary of Old English Project, 2018), s.v. "bicce" (n.), 2, https://doe.artsci.utoronto.ca/.

62. Robert Mannyng, *Robert of Brunne's "Handlyng Synne,"* ed. Frederick J. Furnivall, 2 vols., Early English Text Society, o.s., 119, 123 (London: Early English Text Society, 1901, 1903); London, British Library, MS Harley 1701, fol. 59r.

63. John Rolland of Dalkeith, *The Seven Sages: In Scotish Metre* (Edinburgh: Bannatyne Club, 1837), 82, 121.

64. Cited in Gowing, *Domestic Dangers,* 98; Stavreva, *Words Like Daggers,* 25–26.

65. Monique Allewaert's concept of "parahumanity" in Caribbean plantation contexts is a useful way to extend my analysis of the Letter's animal terms such as "Cow," "ill-thriven Jade," "Dog," and "Bitch": Monique Allewaert, *Ariel's Ecology: Plantations, Personhood, and Colonialism in the American Tropics* (Minneapolis: University of Minnesota Press, 2013), 85–113.

66. *Dictionary of the Older Scottish Tongue,* s.v. "hussy" (n.), 1, 3.

67. Andrew of Wyntoun, *The Orygynale Cronykil of Scotland,* ed. David Laing, 3 vols. (Edinburgh: Edmonston and Douglas, 1872–79), 2:36 (book 5, line 5090).

68. J. D. Marwick, ed., *Extracts from the Records of the Burgh of Edinburgh, 1403–1589,* 4 vols. (Edinburgh: Colston and Son for the Scottish Burgh Records Society, 1869–82), 1:107.

69. Marwick, *Extracts,* 2:40.

fails to fulfill those expectations. Like "bitch" and "jade," "hussy" signified illicit sexuality: one 1596 history of Scotland claims that the notoriously dissolute tenth-century King Cuilén "gave him selfe to all filthines, nycht and day to banket, Jug, and drink, with the foullest slutt husies and servandis, and was sa kendlet in lust" [gave himself to all filthiness, night and day to banquet, tipple, and drink to excess with the foulest disreputable hussies and servants, and was so inflamed by lust], linking "hussy" with subservience, filth, drunkenness, and lechery.[70] "Hussy" was not as offensive as "bitch" or "jade," as evidenced by its relative absence from slander cases, but it had a long history as an insulting term signifying lower-status women expected to perform household work and disparaged for not doing enough of it, often with connotations of excessive sexual activity. When the planter's first word upon spying the Black woman is "*Hussey,*" he invokes these numerous structural vulnerabilities: to him, she is an unprofitable, sexually transgressive "*Hussey*" because he is not entitled to exploit her labor under the system of slavery. The term's implications regarding patriarchal ownership and feminine servility are clear in his initial questions, "*To whom do you belong?*" and "*Whose is she?*" He is enraged because the woman is "*here*" "*upon my Plantations*" and yet does not "*belong*" to him (7); instead, another property-owning Englishman profits from her labors.

Intersectional material philology enables us to see how the planter's word choices frame Black women as made for labor yet insufficiently laboring. This vocabulary thus perfectly espouses the pamphlet's agenda to "preserve and increase" slavery by philologically centering the value of Black women's labor to white men and implying that they need to work harder for them. By tracing these terms' sedimented histories, we can see not only how they accrued connotations of intersectional disadvantage, physical toil, and gendered disgust but also how they frequently clustered together as part of a larger constellation of misogyny* that became misogynoir in the context of Britain's trans-Atlantic slave trade. The *Oxford English Dictionary* defines "constellation" as "a number of fixed stars grouped together within the outline of an imaginary figure traced on the face of the sky," rendering it a useful metaphor for reading the Letter's lexicon of misogynoir because it elucidates how these terms, each with its own dynamic lineage, together form "the outline of an imaginary figure" of degraded racialized femininity characterized by sexual availability and exploitable labor.[71] Whereas Henry King uses the eclipse as a misogynoiristic solar metaphor in "The Boyes answer to the Blackmoor," as Adams shows, I turn to the sidereal metaphor of constellation to illuminate how these words operate: as "fixed stars" clustering together that accrete new matter over time as they shape the lives of those who live under their malicious light.

This constellating of the Letter's terms for Black women, like the individual terms themselves, has a rich history that the merchant implicitly leverages in his argument for Black women's necessary subordination due to their corporeal usefulness to "White-men" (31). The late medieval biblical drama *The Woman Caught in Adultery* (c. 1475) stages a group of Pharisees publicly abusing a woman apprehended in her lover's bed as "thou hore and stynkynge bych Clowte [whore and stinking raggedy bitch]", in a scene that resonates with the planter discovering "a Stranger Black Woman" and attacking her as "*d—'d B—ch*" and "*W—re.*"[72] This clustering is most pronounced in legal defamation cases, demonstrating how frequently these terms were used together in everyday life: Laura Gowing recounts a 1638 London incident in which Frances Powell called her neighbor "base jade base whore base queane base bitch," using three of the

70. Rev. Father E. G. Cody and William Murison, eds., *The historie of Scotland wrytten first in Latin by the most reverend and worthy Jhone Leslie, bishop of Rosse, and translated in Scottish by Father James Dalrymple*, 2 vols. (Edinburgh: W. Blackwood and Sons for the Scottish Text Society, 1888–95), 1:290.

71. *OED*, s.v. "constellation" (n.), 3.

72. K. S. Block, ed., *Ludus Coventriæ: or, The plaie called Corpus Christi: Cotton ms. Vespasian D. VIII*, Early English Text Society, e.s. 120 (London: Oxford University Press, 1922), line 147.

Letter's epithets for enslaved Black women; the neighbor responded by calling Frances a "bitch," drawing from the same lexicon of insult.[73] In Strathbogie in northeast Scotland in 1653, Janet Mawer was allegedly drunk on the Sabbath when she called Margret Ogstoune "base whore, drunkard, thieef-faced bitch, English jade, landlooper [vagabond], queane."[74] Margaret retaliated by calling Janet "drunken jade." Again, "whore," "bitch," and "jade" appear together in a tirade of abuse, mutually reinforcing their disparaging gendered, sexual, and animal connotations.

These terms' interconnected histories enable us to see the full misogynoirist import of their usage in this mass-produced pamphlet by an English merchant who deploys the spectacle of the brutalized Black female body to support his case for reforming the slave trade so it can continue to "make us some of the happiest People in the World" (14). The words' layout on the printed page increases their symbolic significance and invites readers' eyes and minds to dwell upon them: there is a libidinal thrill to conjuring the deleted letters of "*D—n her,*" "*you d—'d B—ch,*" and "*strip this W—re*"), all obscenities naming or directed at Black women, their italicization, capitalization, and dashes all drawing visual attention to them. Here, typographical technologies heighten the constellated terms' misogynoir in multiple ways: the redacting* dashes encourage sustained readerly interaction and mental labor to supply the letters that they hide from sight; the capitalization designates all the terms as nouns, reinforcing their constellation; and the italics, with their connection to emphasis and voice as "the typeface of privilege, as the type of quotation, of accuracy, obtrusion, assertion," in the words of Joseph Loewenstein, encourage readers to hear and linger upon the words as they encounter them visually.[75]

The typesetter's choices elucidate these terms' longstanding structural relationship with one another and encourage us to see them as interconnected so that the combined weight of their derogatory intersectional connections can be leveraged to argue for the necessity of Black women's enslavement.

Conclusion: New Directions in Book History and Visual Culture

This chapter maps out ways that we can use book history—which occupies a special place in visual culture as both constituted by its appearance on the page and inflected by philological and literary histories—to gain greater insight into how premodern copyists and printers encouraged their readers to envision the intersections between race and gender and thus laid the groundwork for the misogynoir that continues to be weaponized against Black women today. These methodologies can be employed fruitfully in analyzing other objects from the Newberry Library's collection that lie beyond this chapter's scope: for example, the early eighteenth-century Scottish commonplace book belonging to Jane Pigot, with its treatise on manners and civility and recipe for curing greensickness copied alongside its drawing of a naked man with his genitals vigorously dashed out, can shed light on the construction of white bourgeois femininity during this time.[76] Likewise, the manuscript titled *An Account of the Indians in Virginia and of some remarkable things in that country* (1689), based on an English planter's notes about Indigenous women's "tawny colour" (3), "Imployment" (11), and marital customs, is ripe for exploration of how its visual appearance and contents illuminate histories of racialized misogyny.[77]

73. Gowing, *Domestic Dangers*, 76.

74. John Stuart, ed., *Extracts from the Presbytery Book of Strathbogie, 1631–54* (Aberdeen: Spalding Club, 1843), 231, 233.

75. Joseph F. Loewenstein, "*Idem:* Italics and the Genetics of Authorship," *Journal of Medieval and Renaissance Studies* 20, no. 2 (1990): 224.

76. Jane Pigot, *Commonplace book, containing Rules of civility & good manners, Numeration and miscellanea*, Chicago, Newberry Library, Case MS B 69 .188.

77. John Clayton, *An Account of the Indians in Virginia and of some remarkable things in that country*, Chicago, Newberry Library, Ayer MS 9.

FASHIONING RACIAL MATERIALITY IN NICOLAS DE NICOLAY'S REPRESENTATIONS OF JEWS

By M. Lindsay Kaplan and Dana E. Katz

This essay intervenes in early modern critical race studies by advancing an intersectional argument for racial materiality, that is, the formation of racial identity through material goods, rather than, alongside, or in addition to, physical markers. Kim F. Hall's generative *Things of Darkness* lays the foundation for this exploration, as it has for so many others, in her consideration of material objects serving as signifiers of racial difference through aristocratic acts of display and exchange.[1] While somatic* characteristics appear permanent and intrinsic, in contrast to clothing/accessories that can be alternatively attached to or detached from the body, both function metonymically* to equate materiality with interiority. Furthermore, many of the early texts that underpin Western racism imagine bodies, like clothing, to be as susceptible to change: classical views on the appearance and constitution of the human body understood it as transformed by diet, climate, and age. Christian scripture avers that one may alter external appearance to hide an evil interior (Matt. 23:27–29),

1. Kim F. Hall, *Things of Darkness: Economies of Race and Gender in Early Modern England* (Ithaca, NY: Cornell University Press, 1995), 211–53. Ian Smith has recently advanced this field: "The Textile Black Body: Race and 'Shadowed Livery' in *The Merchant of Venice*," in *The Oxford Handbook of Shakespeare and Embodiment: Gender, Sexuality, and Race*, ed. Valerie Traub (Oxford: Oxford University Press, 2016), 170–85 and "Othello's Black Handkerchief," *Shakespeare Quarterly* 64, no. 1 (2013): 1–25. https://www.jstor.org/stable/24778431

while patristic* associations of Ethiopians with sin and the demonic also assumed the capacity of repentance and redemption to whiten skin. For centuries up through the early modern period, physicians, theologians, and poets affirmed the shaping power of maternal imagination to change the appearance of unborn children. Thus, the receptivity of the body to change, including through its fashioning by clothes, already circulates through early racializing discourses.

Drawing on recent work in premodern racialization of gendered religious others, we focus on a Christian tradition of coordinating Jewish and Muslim racial identities. In particular, we attend to the complex relationship of clothing to medieval and early modern hierarchized identity, ecclesiastical and temporal laws imposing a degrading marking of Jewish and Muslim clothing relative to that of Christians, and early modern representations of male and female Jews. Our analysis considers the visual and textual portrayals of Jews inhabiting Ottoman lands in Nicolas de Nicolay's *Les quatre premiers livres des navigations et pérégrinations orientales* (*The Nauigations, Peregrinations and Voyages, made into Turkie*).[2] The *Navigations*, a widely circulating hybrid costume book and travel narrative, includes four visual representations of Jews.[3] Most of the scholarship on Nicolay to date focuses on the representation of Muslims or offers a partial consideration of the representation of Jews. We contribute to the critical conversation with a systematic analysis of the compensatory interplay of text and image that demonstrates Nicolay's advancement of a racial theology positing an inherent infidel inferiority relative to Christians. The *Navigations* strategically plays on similarities and distinctions in Jewish and Muslim clothing in an attempt to visualize inherent Jewish subordination in an Ottoman context that problematically undermines the divine superiority of Christianity.

Racialized and Gendered Religious Identities in Christian Hierarchy

Our theorization follows the work of Ania Loomba and others in its assumption that all racism results from cultural construction, whether through discourses of bodily composition (which always have social significance and connote inner states) or other authoritative epistemes, especially the theological, given the centrality of religion for forming premodern identity.[4] We define racism as a systemic ascription of inherent inferiority to one people by another.[5] In the West, Christianity provided a powerful logic in the creation of subordinated racial identities, initially for Jews and subsequently for Muslims, coordinating the latter into subjugating tropes established for the former.[6] The Christian belief that God punished the Jews' alleged murder of Jesus with a spiritual enslavement operated as a racializing rationale in ascribing inherent inferiority to Jews. Although the advent of Islam postdated the death of Jesus, medieval Christianity's

2. This is the title of the first French edition (1567–68). We analyze the Newberry Library's copy of Nicolas de Nicolay's *Les navigations et pérégrinations et voyages, faicts en la Turquie . . .* (Antwerp: G. Silvius, 1576). The text follows the original French edition. Our discussion largely relies on the early modern English translation, *The Nauigations, Peregrinations and Voyages, made into Turkie* (London: Thomas Dawson, 1585), with occasional translations of our own to correct imprecise renderings in the early modern English text.

3. Joseph Hacker claims these are the earliest portrayals of Ottoman Jews, "The Sephardi Diaspora in Muslim Lands from the 16th to 18th Century," in *Odyssey of the Exiles: The Sephardi Jews 1492–1992*, eds. Ruth Porter and Sarah Harel-Hoshen (Tel Aviv: Beth Hatefutsoth, Nahum Goldmann Museum of the Jewish Diaspora, 1992), 95–123, 201–4.

4. Some recent influential monographs on early modern critical race theory focusing on cultural constructions of race in the Christian West include Patricia Akhimie, *Shakespeare and the Cultivation of Difference: Race and Conduct in the Early Modern World* (New York: Routledge, 2018); Dennis Austin Britton, *Becoming Christian: Race, Reformation, and Early Modern English Romance* (New York: Fordham University Press, 2014); Geraldine Heng, *The Invention of Race in the European Middle Ages* (Cambridge, UK: Cambridge University Press, 2018); and Ania Loomba, "Race and the Possibilities of Comparative Critique," *New Literary History* 40, no. 3 (2009): 501–22, https://doi.org/10.1353/nlh.0.0103.

5. M. Lindsay Kaplan, *Figuring Racism in Medieval Christianity* (New York: Oxford University Press, 2019), 4.

6. "As the only religious minority the Latin West knew and tolerated during the early Middle Ages, the Jews invariably presented Christendom with a paradigm for the evaluation and classification of the Muslim 'other.'" Jeremy Cohen, *Living Letters of the Law: Ideas of the Jew in Medieval Christianity* (Berkeley: University of California Press, 1999), 161. For Cohen's fuller discussion of Muslim-Jewish coordination, see *Living Letters of the Law*, 158–65, 219. See also Suzanne Conklin Akbari, *Idols in the East: European Representations of Islam and the Orient, 1100–1450* (Ithaca, NY: Cornell University Press, 2009).

correlation of Muslim identity with that of the Jews produced a discourse of hereditary guilt that racialized both groups as inherent inferiors to Christians.[7] This theological doctrine shaped canon* law, which frequently included Muslims in rulings about Jews with the objective of ensuring the legal and social subordination of both groups to Christians.[8] An anxious perception that Jews and Muslims challenge the imagined divine hierarchy situating Christians on top motivates the characterization of "infidel" dominance as a sinful and demonic threat.[9]

Medieval Western Christianity produced ostensibly conflicting accounts of the relationship between Muslims and Jews relative to Christians; however, all shared the aim of subordinating non-Christians to the true faith. On the one hand, the "historical" event of the crucifixion gave rise to an imagined contemporary alliance between Jews and Muslims, in which the latter secretly instigated Muslim violence against or resistance to Christianity. Christians falsely accused Jews of conspiring to betray the city of Toulouse to Muslims or directing the Muslim caliph who ordered the destruction of the Church of the Holy Sepulcher in Jerusalem.[10] Alternatively, medieval authors such as Jacques de Vitry (c.1160–1240) perceived Muslims as enforcing God's subjugating punishment of Jewish sin: "The Saracens [Muslims] among whom . . . [Jews] dwell hate and despise them more than the Christians; . . . [Jews] are the serfs and slaves of the infidels, and are only suffered to dwell among them in the lowest station of life."[11] The Christian coordination of "infidel" faiths, whether stressing Jewish enmity in conspiracies with Muslims or emphasizing subordination perpetrated by Muslims, serves to justify and realize the punishing status of racialized Jewish inferiority.

Even while early modern Christians developed more nuanced attitudes towards both Muslims and Jews arising from increasing contact, changing theological doctrines, and economic imperatives, medieval tropes continued to circulate.[12] Awareness of Muslim military and economic power and assumptions about the Jews' support of these capacities effectively repeated medieval discourses registering anxiety over "infidel" dominance. The familiar fantasy of hostility between Muslims and Jews appears in accounts representing Muslims as violent "barbarians" attacking Jews.[13] Fears of Muslim-Jewish plots similarly continue to motivate false charges that Iberian Jews settling in Ottoman lands provided key arms-producing intelligence to Muslims.[14] Several forgeries advanced the view that Jews took advantage of their relative religious freedom under the Ottomans to conspire with hidden Iberian Jews; one allegation asserted that Ottoman Jews instructed converted Jewish physicians in Iberia to murder their Christian patients. Some early modern authors argued that the Jews' malign influence on the Ottomans contributed to God's providential plan of an apocalyptically decisive Christian

7. In a thirteenth-century ruling, Pope Urban IV explicitly extends guilt for the crucifixion to Muslims: "these same Jews and Muslims, whose proper guilt submitted them to perpetual servitude" (our translation), in Solomon Grayzel and Kenneth R. Stow, *The Church and the Jews in the XIIIth Century*, Vol. 2 (New York: Jewish Theological Seminary in America, 1989), 79; and Kaplan, *Figuring*, chaps. 1 and 5.

8. David M. Freidenreich, "Muslims in Western Canon Law, 1000–1500," in *Christian-Muslim Relations: A Bibliographical History*, 5 vols., eds. David Thomas and Alex Mallett (Leiden: Brill, 2011), 3–42; and Kaplan, *Figuring*.

9. Kaplan, *Figuring*, 5; and Francisco Bethencourt, *Racisms: From the Crusades to the Twentieth Century*, (Princeton, NJ: Princeton University Press, 2013), 7–8.

10. Phyllis G. Jestice, "A Great Jewish Conspiracy? Worsening Jewish-Christian Relations and the Destruction of the Holy Sepulcher," in *Christian Attitudes Toward the Jews in the Middle Age: A Casebook*, ed. Michael Frassetto (New York: Routledge, 2007), 25, 27.

11. Jacques de Vitry, *The History of Jerusalem. A.D. 1180*, trans. Aubrey Stewart (London: Palestine Pilgrims' Text Society, 1896), 87. https://doi.org/10.1007/s10835-017-9266-0

12. Jonathan Ray recently argues that sixteenth-century travel narratives gradually challenged medieval theological views. "Christian (Re)Encounters with Jews in the Sixteenth-Century Mediterranean," *Jewish History* 30, no. 3/4 (2016): 183–206. However, his discussion (188–89) omits Nicolay's theological condemnations of the Jews.

13. José Alberto Rodrigues da Silva Tavim, "The *Grão-Turco* and the Jews: Translation to the West of Two Oriental 'Powers' (XVI–XVII Centuries)," *Mediterranean Historical Review* 28, no. 2 (2013): 167–68, https://doi.org/10.1080/09518967.2013.837645.

14. Gilles Veinstein, "The Ottoman Jews: Between Distorted Realities and Legal Fictions," *Mediterranean Historical Review* 25, no. 1 (2010): 54–55, https://doi.org/10.1080/09518967.2010.494100.

victory over Islam.[15] While these charges advance clearly contradictory views, they all imagined a coordinated degradation, and thus racialization, of Jews and Muslims relative to Christians.

Other medieval and early modern fantasies coordinate Muslim and Jewish racial identities in narratives that portray "infidel" women as "fair," the designation of white beauty for Christian women.[16] This appearance, often taken as an indicator of infidel women's willingness to convert to Christianity, nevertheless renders them problematically indistinguishable from Christian women. While Jewish invisibility can indicate the successful subjugation of Judaism by Christianity through supersessionary* erasure, conversion, or expulsion, it also suggests a continued Jewish threat rendered even more dangerous in its hidden state.[17] Furthermore, a lack of differentiation in representations of Jewish and Christian women effectively erodes the superiority of the latter over the former. The almost invisible appearance of non-Christian women inflects the ways clothing and accessories both mark and unmark their identity, creating hierarchical crises, as we will discuss below.

Clothing, Racial Materiality, and Religious Identity

In analyzing racial materiality through the medium of clothing as depicted in early modern images of Jews, we are indebted to the scholarship of Ann Rosalind Jones and Peter Stallybrass, who demonstrate the constitutive force of clothing for the early modern understanding of identity. Clothes possess agency in that they shape, not merely reflect, the persons of their wearers. Jones and Stallybrass point to the practice of investiture as a profoundly significant social practice "through which the body politic was composed . . . . For it was investiture, the putting on of clothes, that quite literally constituted a person as a monarch or a freeman of a guild or a household servant. Investiture was . . . the means by which a person was given a form, a shape, a social function, a 'depth.'"[18] They argue that in early modernity, "clothes permeate the wearer," materializing a person's essential self. However, this formational function of clothing, like all social constructs, is susceptible to falsification, even as it attempts to stabilize identities and relationships; clothes "are bearers of identity, ritual and social memory, even as they confuse social categories."[19] Furthermore, since garments could be exchanged for money, their economic value increases their power to shape or dissolve identity; hence, clothing paradoxically materialized social standing even as it circulated as a commodity.[20]

While clothing both organizes and disorganizes social status, including gender and class within a nation, it also serves as a lens for understanding other national and religious cultures. Valerie Traub develops a nuanced account of clothes worn by figures represented in early modern maps, which place

> the human form . . . on a conceptual grid, localized not only by the land it inhabits, but by what the early moderns called *habit*. Derived from the

15. Tavim offers a synthesis of these apparently contradictory views, *"Grão-Turco,"* 181.

16. For the coordination of Muslim and Jewish women, see Louise Mirrer, *Women, Jews, and Muslims in the Texts of Reconquest Castile* (Ann Arbor: University of Michigan Press, 1996); and Britton, *Becoming Christian*. For the "fair" Saracen princess, see Jacqueline De Weever, *Sheba's Daughters: Whitening and Demonizing the Saracen Woman in Medieval French Epic* (New York: Garland, 1998); and Sharon Kinoshita, "'Pagans are wrong and Christians are right': Alterity, Gender, and Nation in the *Chanson de Roland*," *Journal of Medieval and Early Modern Studies* 31, no.1 (2001): 79–111, https://doi.org/10.1215/10829636-31-1-79. On Saracen whiteness in general, see Akbari, *Idols*.

17. Adrienne Williams Boyarin has recently argued for the derogating force of sameness, although she omits consideration of race: *The Christian Jew and the Unmarked Jewess: The Polemics of Sameness in Medieval English Anti-Judaism* (Philadelphia: University of Pennsylvania Press, 2021).

18. Ann Rosalind Jones and Peter Stallybrass, *Renaissance Clothing, and the Materials of Memory* (Cambridge, UK: Cambridge University Press, 2000), 2.

19. Jones and Stallybrass, *Renaissance Clothing*, 5. Sumptuary laws offer another example of the social and economic force of clothing. Proscribing "clothing, fashions, fabrics, colors, and jewelry for societal groups in a way that corresponded to their levels on the social scale. . .sumptuary legislation thus functioned as an instrument to maintain and reinforce social barriers," explains Maria Giuseppina Muzzarelli, "Reconciling the Privilege of a Few with the Common Good: Sumptuary Laws in Medieval and Early Modern Europe," *Journal of Medieval and Early Modern Studies* 39, no. 3 (2009): 599, https://doi.org/10.1215/10829636-2009-006.

20. Jones and Stallybrass, *Renaissance Clothing*, 11.

> Latin for 'holding, having, 'havior,' *habit* in the period signified 'the way in which one holds or has oneself . . . a) externally; hence demeanor, outward appearance, fashion of the body, mode of clothing oneself, dress, habitation; [and] b) in mind, character, or life; hence mental constitution, character, disposition, way of acting, comporting oneself.' *Habit* thus synthesizes the separate, yet closely related concepts, *costume* and *custom*, *manners* and *morals*.[21]

Here again, clothing manifests interiority, an essential self.[22] The advent of the costume book in the late sixteenth century served to standardize people of diverse regions of the world and emphasize socio-religious differences, creating an abstracted vision of a world that fostered social stereotypes.[23] However, clothing simultaneously demonstrates the possibility of disrupting the relationship between exterior and interior. As Diane Owen Hughes argues, costume books could also evince a "'bricolage of fashion' that celebrates and encourages the cross-cultural contact of clothes, a 'miscegenation' that mirrors the aesthetic intermingling of clothing styles promoted by the fashion industry itself."[24] Even as changing fashions eluded representation, nevertheless "printed costume books sought to normalize and categorize regional dress according to strictly defined social, political, and gendered classifications."[25] We argue that, like premodern somatic constructions that sought to fix personal or group identities within a social or global order, clothing lends itself to processes of differentiating and organizing cultural hierarchies. However, as we shall see, visual and textual depictions of similarities and distinctions in clothing grapple with shifting signifiers in attempts to fix subordinated racialized and gendered identities.

The history of the racialization of Jewish and Muslim identity in the Christian West operates in part through the medium of clothing.[26] This reflects the difficulty of manifesting the inherent inferiority of sin that leaves no visible indication on "infidel" bodies. The Fourth Lateran Council* (1215) promulgated five canons specifically regulating Jews' behavior, all attempting to prevent "any who blaspheme against Christ [from having] . . . power over Christians," Jews as well as "pagans," i.e., Muslims.[27] As Norman Vincent observes, Canon 68 ordering Jews and "Saracens" to wear distinguishing clothing emerges in the context of attempts to regulate the attire of Christian clergy; strikingly, the law prescribing "infidel" apparel constituted "the first pan-European sartorial legislation."[28] Clothing legislation operates here by imposing signs on otherwise unmarked bodies to create and enforce social stratification; Jewish and Muslim indistinguishability from Christians raises the scandalous

21. Valerie Traub, "Mapping the Global Body," in *Early Modern Visual Culture: Representation, Race, and Empire in Renaissance England*, eds. Peter Erickson and Clark Hulse (Philadelphia: University of Pennsylvania Press, 2000), 51.

22. See Bronwen Wilson, "*Foggie diverse di vestire de' Turchi*: Turkish Costume Illustration and Cultural Translation," *Journal of Medieval and Early Modern Studies* 37, no. 1 (2007): 104, 134n18, https://doi.org/10.1215/10829636-2006-012.

23. Giorgio Riello, "The World in a Book: The Creation of the Global in Sixteenth-Century European Costume Books," *Past and Present* 242, Supplement 14 (2019): 281–317, https://doi.org/10.1093/pastj/gtz047.

24. Quoted in Traub, "Mapping," 51.

25. Margaret F. Rosenthal, "Cultures of Clothing in Later Medieval and Early Modern Europe," *Journal of Medieval and Early Modern Studies* 39, no. 3 (2009): 473, https://doi.org/10.1215/10829636-2009-001.

26. Heng argues that Canon 68 "instantiates racial regime, and racial governance, in the Latin West through the force of law" precisely through the regulation of clothing (*Invention*, 32). Muslim sartorial legislation designating the inferior status of minority religious groups perhaps influences medieval Christian law; see Ilse Lichtenstadter, "The Distinctive Dress of Non-Muslims in Islamic Countries," *Historia Judaica* 5, no. 1 (1943): 35; Naomi Lubrich, "The Wandering Hat: Iterations of the Medieval Jewish Pointed Cap," *Jewish History* 29, no. 3/4 (2015): 226, https://doi.org/10.1007/s10835-015-9250-5; and Flora Cassen, *Marking the Jew in Renaissance Italy: Politics, Religion, and the Power of Symbols* (Cambridge, UK: Cambridge University Press, 2017), 45. Cassen's analysis of the Jewish badge ultimately argues, wrongly in our view, against its racist force (194–98).

27. Solomon Grayzel, *The Church and the Jews in the XIIIth Century*, Rev. ed., Vol. 1 (New York: Hermon Press, 1966), 311. On the Christian designation of Muslims as pagans, see John Victor Tolan, *Saracens: Islam in the Medieval European Imagination* (New York: Columbia University Press, 2002), 105–34.

28. Nicholas Vincent, "Two Papal Letters on the Wearing of the Jewish Badge, 1221 and 1229," *Jewish Historical Studies* 34 (1994): 211; and Lubrich, "The Wandering Hat," 226, http://www.jstor.org/stable/29779960.

possibility of inferiors exercising power over their spiritual and social superiors.[29] The canon accuses Jews and Muslims of using clothing to insult Christians and Christianity during Holy Week: "[infidels] do not blush to go out . . . more than usually ornamented [*ornatius*], and do not fear to poke fun at the Christians who display signs of grief at the memory of the most holy Passion."[30] The term *ornatius*, connoting splendid attire as well as an honored status relative to the mourning Christians, signals the blasphemous hierarchy inversion effected through clothing. Conversely, the degrading force of clothes for racial formation registers in the numbers of Jews across Europe who sought to avoid this decree through paying fines; even popes admitted that the requirement to wear distinctive garments might expose Jews to violent attacks.[31]

Medieval visual imagery also relied on clothing as a means of materializing the racial identity of infidel men and women. In her analysis of the distinctive "Jewish hat," Naomi Lubrich documents "The quantity and complexity of anti-Jewish iconography featuring hatted Jews starting in the twelfth century;" strikingly this artistic convention contributes to subsequent clothing legislation requiring Jews to wear hats as another type of identifying clothing or badge.[32] Medieval artists also employ distinguishing head-coverings to designate Muslim identity.[33] However, some images use a turban to depict both Muslims and Jews; while primarily an indicator of Muslim identity, its appearance on the heads of Jews suggests an allegiance of both groups against Christians.[34] Furthermore, even though Canon 68 applied to both male and female Jews and Muslims, some localities required Jewish women to display additional signs specific to their gender. Diane Owen Hughes's study of medieval and early modern Italian visual representations demonstrates how earrings operated as a gendered Jewish marker that was associated with Eastern and Islamic opulence as well as with the "sartorial splendor" of sex workers.[35] Nicolay's use of clothing and jewelry in images and texts emerges out of a visual tradition relying on material markers to create gendered religious hierarchies.

Nicolay's Jews

While Nicolas de Nicolay's *Navigations* combines the genres of travel narrative and costume book, his images may constitute the more influential aspect of this work, which circulated in multiple subsequent editions and translations.[36] Although the text

29. John Teutonticus' thirteenth-century commentary on the Lateran rulings indicates the canon's intent to subordinate Jews and Muslims by citing other hierarchies effected through differentiated clothing (Vincent, "Two Papal," 214).

30. Grayzel, *Church*, 1:308.

31. Grayzel, *Church*, 1:63–69.

32. Lubrich, "Wandering Hat," 224. Sara Lipton argues for art's power to create rather than reflect anti-Jewish attitudes in *Dark Mirror: The Medieval Origins of Anti-Semitic Iconography* (New York: Metropolitan Books, 2014), 10; she devotes a chapter to the early history of the "Jewish hat" (13–54).

33. Debra Strickland analyzes the *tortil* as one such identifying headwear, *Saracens, Demons and Jews: Making Monsters in Medieval Art* (Princeton, NJ: Princeton University Press, 2003), 161, 174, 177, 181.

34. Strickland explains that this portrayal sometimes appears in images establishing both Muslims and Jews as idolaters, *Saracens*, 106, 137, 157–68. Depictions of turbans that connected and racialized Muslims and Jews in early modern images, such as in Pierre Boiastuau's *Histoires prodigieuses* (1560), continued associations with idolatry and violence against Christians.

35. Diane Owen Hughes, "Distinguishing Signs: Ear-Rings, Jews and Franciscan Rhetoric in the Italian Renaissance City," *Past & Present* 112 (1986): 6, 10–11, http://www.jstor.org/stable/650997.

36. Scholars attesting to the impact of Nicolay's images include David Brafman, "Facing East: The Western View of Islam in Nicolas de Nicolay's 'Travels in Turkey,'" *Getty Research Journal* 1 (2009): 154, https://doi.org/10.1086/grj.1.23005372; Marie-Christine Gomez-Géraud and Stefanos Yerasimos, *Dans l'empire de Soliman le Magnifique* (Paris: Presses du CNRS, 1989), 33–36; Frédéric Hitzel, "Les ambassades occidentales à Constantinople et la diffusion d'une certaine image de l'Orient," *Comptes rendus des séances de l'Académie des Inscriptions et Belles-Lettres*, 154e année, 1 (2010): 279, https://doi.org/10.3406/crai.2010.92806; Chandra Mukerji, "Costume and Character in the Ottoman Empire: Dress as Social Agent in Nicolay's *Navigations*," in *Early Modern Things: Objects and Their Histories, 1500–1800*, ed. Paula Findlen (London: Routledge, 2013), 151; Wilson, "*Foggie diverse*," 110; and Amanda Wunder, "Western Travelers, Eastern Antiquities, and the Image of the Turk in Early Modern Europe," *Journal of Early Modern History* 7, no. 1/2 (2003): 119, https://doi.org/10.1163/157006503322487368. Gomez-Géraud and Yerasimos, *Dans l'empire*, list ten early modern editions of the *Navigations*: three French, two German translations, one English translation, one Dutch translation, and three Italian translations (33). Wilson explains that Nicolay's "figures became archetypes, and their poses and attire were replicated, even traced, in at least eight costume books

purportedly narrates Nicolay's first-hand account of his travel to Istanbul in 1551 as part of a French embassy to the Ottoman empire, his imagery displays greater originality than his descriptions, which iterate views of contemporary authors.[37] Nevertheless, as we will demonstrate, the interplay between text and image supports a larger polemic that advances Christian global domination.[38] Nicolay envisages that the "intrinsically human and political activities" of travel and communication will produce a utopia of global exchange and co-existence under the rule of Christianity.[39] However, contemporary political and theological realities threaten this aspirational Christian superiority; during his travels he encounters first-hand forms of Christian subordination to Muslims, including relegation of Ottoman Christians to the status of non-believer or *zimmi*, a social and political inferior.[40] Nicolay also devotes attention to the troubling hierarchy inversions posed by Jews, insofar as *zimmi* legislation effectively erases the proper gradation by equalizing Christians with inherently inferior Jews. Even more blasphemously, the absence in the Ottoman context of discriminatory regulations such as those enforced in the Christian West enables Jews to thrive and even excel their religious/racial superiors precisely in the essential fields of language and travel.[41]

In order to counter this threat, the *Navigations* deploys racializing discourses of Christian doctrines in concert with ethnographic interest in the Ottoman dress to materialize inherent Jewish inferiority. The illustrations codify the customs and costumes of daily life in sixty woodcuts, from shrouded Turkish women walking to the baths and cavorting men intoxicated by opium to a janissary and Arab merchant in full regalia.[42] Nicolay attempts to impose order through clothing, producing gradations across multiple taxonomies including class, gender, and religion, whether within Islam, between Muslims and *zimmis*, or between Christians and Jews. Nicolay portrays four Jews of different genders, ages, and, in some cases, professions: a Jewish physician, a Jewish merchant, a Jewish woman, and a young Jewish maiden. For the most part, neither the engravings nor woodcuts in the various early modern editions capture the colors of their attire, a significant feature in identifying the quality of the garments and the ethnicity of their respective

that were published by 1601" ("*Foggie diverse,*" 110). Mukerji argues that the multiple translations indicate "printers clearly assumed people wanted to read it as well as look at the pictures. So the text as well as the illustrations mattered" ("Costume," 166).

37. This embassy sought to forge a French alliance with the Ottoman Porte against the Holy Roman Empire; Nicolay's ambivalent view of the "Turk" resonates with that of contemporary French authors, Marcus Keller "Nicolas de Nicolay's 'Navigations' and the Domestic Politics of Travel Writing," *L'Esprit Créateur* 48, no. 1 (2008): 18–31, https://doi:10.1353/esp.2008.0005, and "The Turk of Early Modern France," *L'Esprit Créateur*, 53, no. 4 (2013): 1–8, https://doi:10.1353/esp.2013.0045. Radu G. Păun demonstrates the extent of Nicolay's borrowing: "Sur quelques 'modèles' livresques: les 'Navigations et pérégrinations' de Nicolas de Nicolay," *Revue des études sud-est européennes* 33, no. 1/2 (1995): 171–80. However, Nicolay included some copies of other artists' work alongside his original images (Wilson, "*Foggie diverse,*" 114).

38. Wunder notes the relationship between word and image: "The combination of images and the verbal explanations created a multi-layered ekphrasis that brought to life the peoples of the Levant for the reader/viewer of the *Navigations*." "Western Travelers," 117. See also Mukerji, "Costume and Character," 156; Wilson, "*Foggie diverse*," 110; Păun, "Sur quelques 'modeles,'" 173; and Brafman "Facing East," 153.

39. Keller, "Nicolas," 22. The preface, absent in the English edition, imagines all humans mutually emending their barbarous vices and equally instructing themselves in "the true religion," forging a community of whom God is the great father and Jesus Christ the oldest son, *Navigations* (1576), NP, fourth page of Preface.

40. *Zimmi* is the Turkish form of *dhimmī*, a member of *ahl al-kitāb*, "people of the Book," that included Jews and Christians to whom Islam accorded religious toleration and protection at the price of social and political inferiority. Restrictions on the *zimmi* included payment of a poll tax and wearing distinguishing garments as an "enforced sign of inferiority to the ruling class," Lichtenstadter, "Distinctive Dress," 38, 44. See also Minna Rozen, *A History of the Jewish Community in Istanbul: The Formative Years, 1453–1566* (Leiden: Brill, 2002), 16–17.

41. Păun, in reviewing the common topoi Nicolay repeats from other authors, registers surprise over the avoidance of the well-represented observation that Ottoman Jews own Christian slaves ("Sur quelques 'modèles,'" 175). Given Nicolay's aim to demonstrate Christian superiority over Jews in the Ottoman context, we might assume a deliberate suppression of this topos*.

42. Léon Davent executed sixty copperplate engravings for the original French edition (1567–68) from drawings Nicolay made during his travels in the Levant. In 1576, Willem Silvius published a second French edition of Nicolay's book in Antwerp, as well as translations in Dutch, German, and Italian, with woodcuts by Anton van Leest copied from Davent's engravings. See David Brafman, "Les quatre premiers livres des navigations et pérégrinations Orientales," in *Christian-Muslim Relations 1500–1900*, ed. David Thomas, http://dx.doi.org/10.1163/2451-9537_cmrii_COM_26242.

wearers.[43] Compensating for the lack of chromatic detail in the printed image, the text specifies color in dress, referencing *zimmi* status in order to materialize Jews' inherent subordination.[44] However, Nicolay creates a complex interplay between word and image, supplementing accounts of Levantine Jewish success with degrading visual signs in the illustrations, sometimes adducing verbal evidence of ascribed inherent Jewish inferiority when images insufficiently convey their degradation. In viewing first-hand the thriving Ottoman Jewish community, Nicolay seeks to expose this success as merely apparent by employing a combined verbal and visual representation of clothing that reveals the Jews' true lesser status.

Nicolay's image and text draw on similarities and differences in clothing to assert the Jews' inferior status in Muslim society. However, in his portrayal of the Jewish physician with its accompanying text, he grapples with the problem of Jews excelling Christians and Muslims alike in multilingual fluency. In his chapter "Of the Phisitions of Constantinople," he explains, "the reason wherefore in this Arte . . . [Jews] doe commonly exceede all other nations, is the knowledge which they haue in the language and letters, . . . [in which] haue written the principall Authours of . . . the sciences meete and necessarye for those that study phisick."[45] The Jews' familiarity with multiple languages accounts for their success, to the extent that the physician attending upon the sultan was a Jew: "muche esteemed, aswell for his goods, knowledge, and renowne, as for honour and portlinesse."[46] Nicolay registers Jewish difference here, but this is an elevating, rather than derogating distinction, demonstrating how linguistic fluency privileges them relative even to their Turkish peers.

In order to counter this improper superiority, Nicolay combines text and image to portray the Jew's true inferiority: "As for the dress of Turkish physicians, there is no difference from that of the common people. But there is a difference for those of Jewish physicians: because instead of the yellow turban, belonging to the Jewish nation, they wear a high pointed hat, colored in scarlet red, of the type as one can see in the following portrait"[47] (Figure 2.1). While Muslim physicians resemble the common people in dress, Jewish physicians wear a distinctive red hat. Nicolay's description of it includes a reminder that Jews normally wear the demeaning yellow turban, effectively equating both as signs of Jewish inferior difference, even while suppressing the fact that Islamic law also marked Christian subordination through clothing.[48] The accompanying image shows the Jewish physician outfitted in a long caftan tied at the waist, covered by a robe, and donned in a tall hat, denoting his religion and vocation. In choosing to depict only a Jewish doctor, Nicolay singles him out as different, not by virtue of his skill as physician, but as subordinated in Ottoman society as a social inferior. The text and image portray the red cap as a

43. Some hand-colored volumes of the first edition appear to have been produced, copies of which are held in the Victoria and Albert Museum (https://collections.vam.ac.uk/item/O1463611/les-quatre-premiers-livres-des-book-nicolas-de-nicolay/) and the British Library (Wilson, "*Foggie diverse*," 110). On religious identity and garment color, see Rozen, *History*, 284.

44. Wunder considers Nicolay's use of color in his text to supplement his images: "The author was surprisingly silent about pigmentation and physiology, channeling his energy instead into detailed descriptions of costumes. The print portraits in the book directly communicated what Nicolay had seen abroad, down to the finest details, while the text revealed that which the black-and-white linear images could not communicate (colors, fabrics, and explanations for peculiarities of dress)" ("Western Travelers," 116–17). Wilson observes, "Although Nicolay often describes the colors of the costumes in the text, extant hand-colored editions indicate that illuminators did not read the text or were not interested in accuracy" ("*Foggie diverse*," 110). Kaplan disagrees after consulting the British Library hand-colored 1568 edition (Shelf mark C.18.c.8.); the colors indicated in the text match the coloring of the hat and turban worn by the Jewish physician and merchant respectively. However, the colorist did use shades of gray wash to indicate dark skin on a number of figures, including several images of "Moors."

45. Nicolay, *Navigations* (1585), 93r.

46. Nicolay, *Navigations* (1585), 93r. Early seventeen-century Ottoman records of physicians affirm Jews outnumbering Muslims (Rozen, *History*, 208–9).

47. Nicolay, *Navigations* (1576), 169, our translation. Lale Uluç cites other early modern travel narratives mentioning the yellow turban, "Images of Jews in Ottoman Court Manuscripts," in *A History of Jewish-Muslim Relations: From the Origins to the Present Day*, eds. Abdelwahab Meddeb and Benjamin Stora (Princeton, NJ: Princeton University Press, 2013), 903.

48. Lichtenstadter cautions against approaching Muslim clothing legislation "from an exclusively Jewish angle, for it arose out of the relationship prevailing generally between Muslims and all non-Muslims, whether Christian, Jewish, or of any other non-Muslim faith" ("Distinctive Dress," 35).

sartorial signifier of race that diminishes Jewish bodies through the cut and color of a material object.

However, Nicolay employs another visual strategy of vestimentary* subordination in creating an identification between Jews and Muslims. While Ottoman dress culture constructed class hierarchies, it also homogenized the sartorial practices between Muslims and non-Muslims. Nicolay renders his Jews as nearly indistinguishable from Muslims, in face and in fashion, reiterating how the garments of Jewish men are similar to those of "other nations of Leuant."[49] Nicolay's image of the Jewish physician offers an example of this visual strategy that clothes Jews and Muslims in the same attire to suggest shared enmity to Christians. While this appears to contradict the illustration of distinctive clothing to indicate the Jews' subordinated difference, in fact both methods share the goal of materializing Jewish inferiority. With the exception of his hat, the Jewish physician's long-belted caftan and robe resembles that of his Muslim colleagues as well as the Muslim "common people." The portrayal of an Islamicized Jewish physician visualizes the myth of "infidel" conspiracy that animates charges like the one that Ottoman Jews colluded with hidden Iberian Jewish doctors to murder rather than heal Christian patients. While this falsehood developed in the medieval period, it continued to circulate throughout early modern Europe.[50] The interpellation of Muslims into the category of deicides, expressed in terms of the military threat they posed to Christians that Nicolay himself advances, ramified myths of Jewish-Muslim conspiracies. In representing a Jewish physician in Muslim attire, Nicolay employs a material mark of clothing to imply and reveal a shared threat to Christian life that proves inherent non-Christian inferiority.

In addition to coordinating Jewish-Muslim enmity through cloth, Nicolay reprises the theme of Jewish linguistic facility to disclose its role in strengthening Ottoman military power. In his extended chapter on Jewish merchants, he accuses recently immigrated Iberian Jews,

> who to the great . . . damage of the Christianitie, haue taught the Turkes . . . to make artillerie . . . and other munitions . . .. [T]hey haue also the commoditie & vsage to speake and vnderstand all other sortes of languages vsed in Leuant, which serueth them greatly for the communication and trafique . . . with other strange nations, to whom oftentimes they serue for . . . interpretours.[51]

These Jews allegedly share their expertise in the manufacture of weapons with their Muslim hosts, thereby increasing the military threat against Christianity.[52] This fabricated charge builds upon fears of Jews instigating Muslims to join with them in a conspiracy to kill Christians. Again, the Jews' proficiency in multiple languages assists them in communicating this dangerous information to Muslims. Nicolay limns a double threat here, insofar as Jewish linguistic ability not only renders them superior to Christians but also enables a conspiracy with Muslims against the true Church; taken together these challenges to God's will display Jewish inherent sinful inferiority.

The chapter on merchants also brings into focus the fact that Jews excel Christians at the other necessary action required for the fulfillment of Nicolay's utopian vision, that of global travel. However, Nicolay deploys racial theology to transform the relative advantage of Jewish dispersal into a cursed chastisement. Jews do

49. Nicolay, *Navigations* (1585), 131v.

50. Concerns about indistinguishability fanned fears that converted Jewish physicians in Iberia could hide behind an orthodox appearance while secretly murdering Christians. François Soyer argues that Jewish anti-Christian medical conspiracies inspired charges against Muslim converts, "Antisemitism, Islamophobia and the Conspiracy Theory of Medical Murder in Early Modern Spain and Portugal," in *Antisemitism and Islamophobia in Europe: A Shared Story?*, eds. James Renton and Ben Gidley (London: Palgrave Macmillan, 2017), 51–75, 58, 66. See Tavim, "*Grão-Turco*," 173–76.

51. Nicolay, *Navigations* (1585), 130v–131r.

52. Veinstein proves the fallacy of this accusation; the Turkish innovation in weaponry stemmed from information provided by French army deserters in the late 1490s, "Ottoman Jews," 55. See also Tavim, "*Grão-Turco*," 176–79.

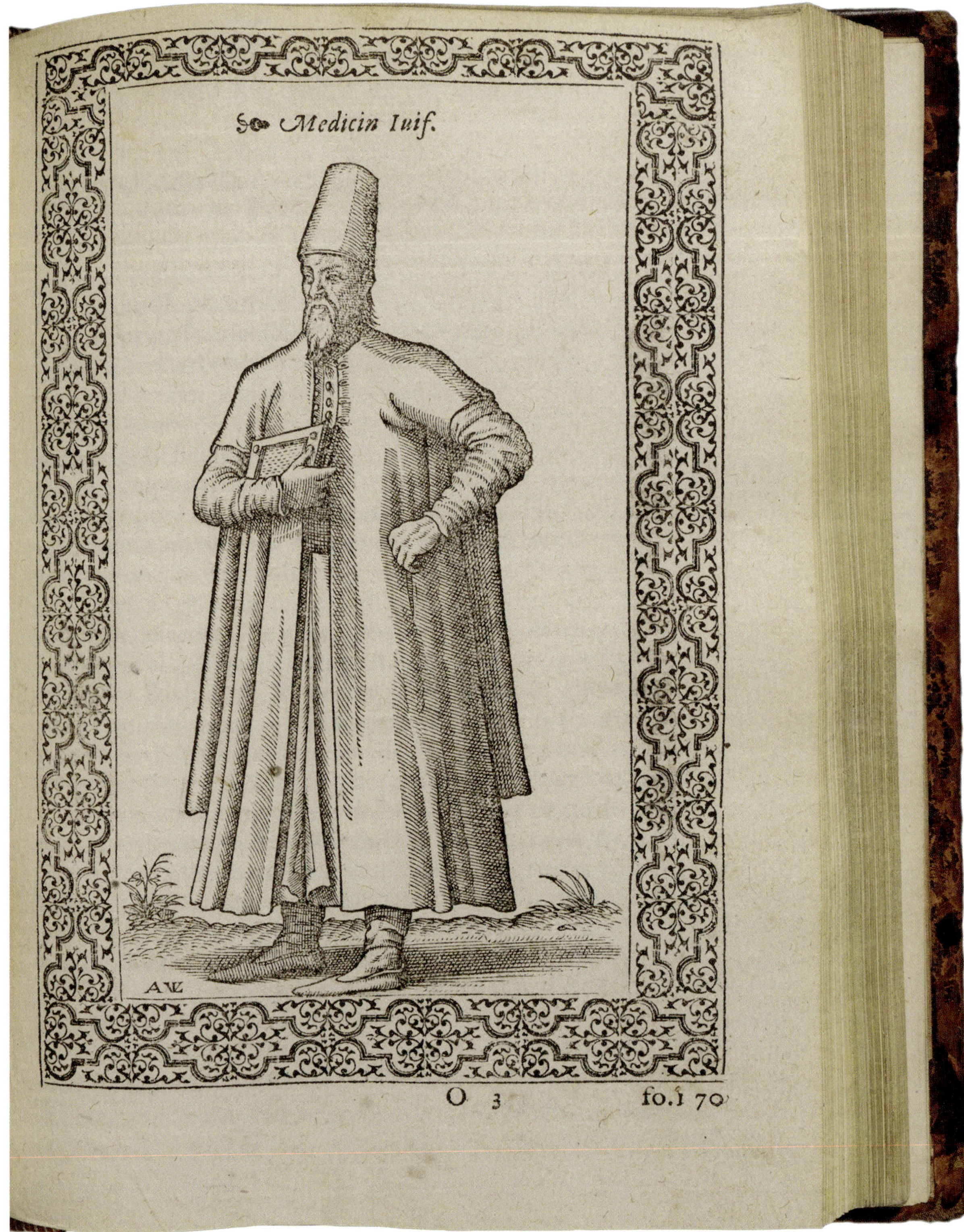

Figure 2.1
Nicolas de Nicolay, "Jewish Physician" (170r),
Les navigations pérégrinations et voyages, faicts en la Turquie,
Antwerp, 1576,
Newberry Library, Wing ZP 5465 .S587

not fulfill the imperative of travel ordained by God to humans, but experience exile as a divinely imposed punishment. He advances the familiar claim that the Jews crucified Jesus:

> and charging themselues with the offence & sinne committed towardes his person, wrote vnto Pilate, hys blood bee vppon vs and our children, [Matt 27:25] and therfore their sinne hath followed them and their successours throughout al generations, . . . for since their extermination and the vengeaunce vpon Ierusalem vnto this present day, they . . . haue alwayes gone straying dispearsed and driuen awaye from Countrie to countrie. And yet euen at this day in what region soeuer they are permitted to dwell vnder tribute, they are abhorred of God and menne.[53]

Nicolay iterates the medieval Christian logic that racializes Jews, citing the verse from Matthew proving Jewish hereditary guilt that elicits a divine curse of repeated expulsions, extending to the contemporary moment. God's hatred, shared by the people of every nation, continues in the punishment of perpetual inferiority, as countries only permit Jews residence "vnder tribute," that is, as permanent inferiors.[54]

However, this poses another disturbing equivalence for Nicolay, insofar as the Ottomans impose a subordinate status of *zimmi* on Christians as well as Jews, effectively reducing both to the same degraded level. By situating the Jews' payment of tribute within the context of hostile Christian discourse of divine punishment, Nicolay attempts to distinguish Jewish tributary status from that of Christians. However, both are subject to a tax imposed on non-Muslims, as Nicolay explains in his discussion of religion of the Armenians: "they are christians, hauing their church and ceremonies a part, as all other not being Turks haue, al which the great Lord doth permit, to liue according to their minde, their lawe and religion, paying vnto him the Carach or tribute of a Ducate for euery head by the yeere."[55] Other conditions imposed on *zimmis* included wearing distinguishing garments of specific colors. In his description of Ottoman Greece, Nicolay writes of Salonica's religious plurality in chromatic terms:

> This citie is as yet most ample & rich, inhabited of thre sundry sorts of people, to wit, Christian Greeks, Iewes, & Turkes: but the number of Iewes (being mercha[n]ts very rich) is the greatest: and there are 80 synagogues: their attire on their head is a yellow Tulbant safroned, that of the Grecian christians is blew, & that of the Turks white, for that through the same diuersitie of colors, they should be known the one from the other, & are all clothed in long gownes as the other Orientals are.[56]

According to Nicolay, the flowing robes of Muslims, Jews, and Christians signified their sartorial sameness. Only the color of turban cloth distinguished between the indiscernible bodies of the Ottoman Empire. While emphasizing similarity and presenting difference neutrally, Nicolay suppressed the fact that the colors permitted to both Christians and Jews signaled their shared subordination to Muslims, the only group who could wear white headgear. These moments where mutual *zimmi* status threatens the hierarchy between Christian and Jew animate Nicolay's strategy in materializing Jewish subordination.

Nicolay's image of a Jewish merchant affords visual and textile signifiers, in addition to text, to represent racialized subordination (Figure 2.2). A compensatory

53. Nicolay, *Navigations* (1585), 131r.

54. In early modern French, *tribut* signifies a contribution imposed by a nation on another, vanquished people; the first definition of *tributaire*, a person or people owing tribute, is the Jews. See Adolphe Hatzfeld, et al., *Dictionnaire général de la langue Française* (Paris: Librairie Charles Delagrave, 1926).

55. Nicolay, *Navigations* (1585), 133v. Lichtenstadter discusses the poll tax, "The Distinctive Dress," 38–39. Nicolay frequently mentions Christian payment of tribute, both in money and through enslavement, *Navigations* (1585), 36v–37v, 45r–45v, 69rff, 95r, 128r, and 160r.

56. Nicolay, *Navigations* (1585), 149v.

degradation appears in his representation of a Jewish merchant dressed in long *shalvar* trousers and a belted caftan topped by a long robe.[57] The text elaborates on this image:

> The Iewes which dwell in Constantinople . . . & other places of the dominion of the great Turke, are all apparrelled with long garments, like vnto the Gretians, and other nations of Leuant, but for their mark and token to be knowen fró[m] others, they weare a yealow Tulbant . . . . This which I haue drawen out is one of those that carie cloath to sell through the citie of Constantinople.[58]

Nicolay's Jewish merchant wears a yellow turban, revealing his ubiquitous subservience to Muslims. However, he shares the rest of his apparel as well as a subordinated *zimmi* status with Christian Greeks, again threatening to destabilize the racial/religious hierarchy.

Nicolay therefore introduces another material subordination in the image of the Jewish merchant, not in the clothes he wears, but in the cloth he carries, draped over his left arm. Although he describes the Jews as virtually monopolizing all trade in Constantinople, he chooses a textile to represent their primary commodity.[59] Jewish merchants living in the Ottoman Empire sold spices, jewels, and clothing accessories, as well as luxurious cloth of wool, silk, brocade, and velvet.[60] However, the depiction undercuts the Ottoman Jews' aforementioned participation in multiple trades by creating a visual resonance with Christian societies, which restricted Jews to a few professions, including the lending of clothes and money.[61] Clothing served as collateral to secure loans on which the creditor could charge interest, and Nicolay's image here may reinforce his repeated textual condemnation of Jewish usury, another racializing degradation.[62] Nicolay's depiction of a Jewish merchant anticipates that of Pietro Bertelli in his *Diversarum nationum habitus* (1594–1596, Figure 2.3), in which a Paduan Jewish peddler* holding swathes of textiles publicly exclaims, "What do you want to give" ("Was welt ihr geben").[63] Nicolay's Jewish merchant does not carry a used garment in his arms, but the depiction and description of him as carrying "cloath to sell through the citie of Constantinople" (131v) undermines the initial account of Jewish trade in the city.[64] In suggesting the more familiar restricted economic status of Jews in early modern European countries, Nicolay's text and image work in concert to import Christian hierarchy and enforce a racializing subordination of Jews not adequately realized by the Ottomans.

Nicolay pursues the strategic interplay of image and text to racialize Jews in his depictions of Levantine Jewish women. Their wardrobe, both modest and magnificent, make them nearly indistinguishable not only from Ottoman Muslim women, but from Christian women as well. However, this study in sartorial sameness incorporates identifying accessories

57. Rozen, *History*, 287.

58. Nicolay, *Navigations* (1585), 131v–132r.

59. Nicolay claims Jews "haue. . .the moste. . .trafique of merchandize and readie money. . . in al Leuant" (*Navigations*, 130v). Nicolay mostly toured Galata, a predominately Jewish area with many warehouses, giving him "the impression that most of the commerce was controlled by Jews" (Rozen, *History*, 239).

60. Rozen, *History*, 233–34.

61. Fynes Morrison's early modern travel narrative (1617) mentions the Christian limitation of Jewish economic activity to lending clothes and money; see Charles Hughes, ed., *Shakespeare's Europe: A Survey of the Condition of Europe at the End of the 16th Century*, 2d ed., (New York: B. Blom, 1967), 487–88. For Jews in the second-hand clothes trade, see Patricia Allerston, "Reconstructing the Second-Hand Clothes Trades in Sixteenth- and Seventeenth-Century Venice," *Costume* 33, no. 1 (1999): 46–56, https://doi.org/10.1179/cos.1999.33.1.46; and Kate Kelsey Staples, "The Significance of the Secondhand Trade in Europe, 1200–1600," *History Compass* 13, no. 6 (2015): 297–309, https://doi.org/10.1111/hic3.12240.

62. Nicolay, *Navigations* (1585), 130v–131r. Canon law condemns a Jewish creditor's exercising power over a Christian debtor (Grayzel, *Church*, 1:307). Jones and Stallybrass discuss the association of pawnbroking, second-hand clothes, and usury (*Renaissance Clothing*, 181–82).

63. Ulinka Rublack argues that Bertelli's Paduan peddler references the racial trope of greedy Jewish usurers in *Dressing Up: Cultural Identity in Renaissance Europe* (Oxford: Oxford University Press, 2010), 221.

64. Jews in Istanbul were not primarily itinerant peddlers: "The most common role for a Jew in Istanbul's commercial sector was that of a small shopkeeper" (Rozen, *History*, 233–34).

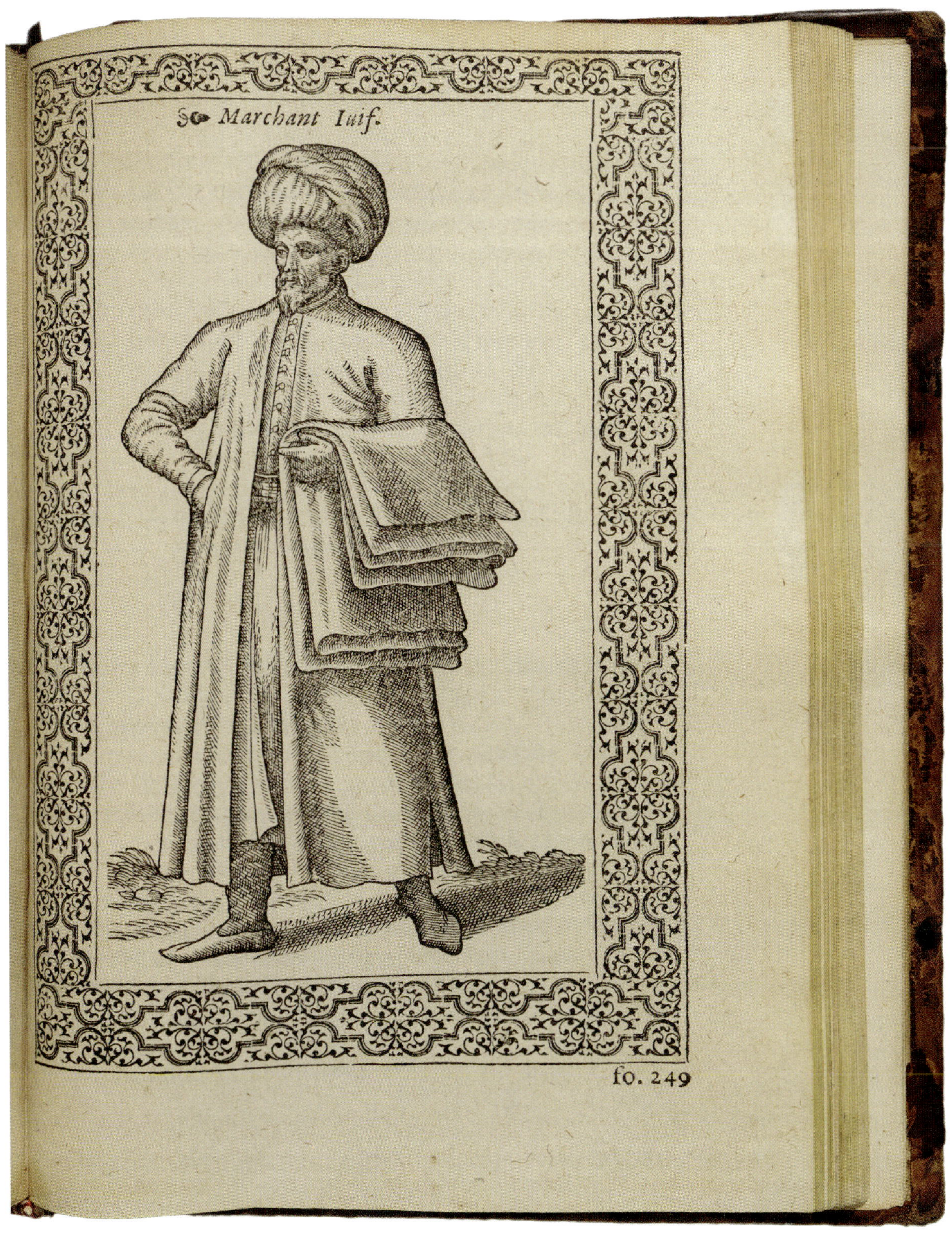

Figure 2.2
Nicolas de Nicolay, "Jewish Merchant" (249r),
Les navigations pérégrinations et voyages, faicts en la Turquie,
Antwerp, 1576,
Newberry Library, Wing ZP 5465 .S587

to materialize racial difference. Nicolay portrays the young Jewish woman of Andrinople wearing a distinctive cup-shaped hat and low-heeled shoes to convey her subordination, in contrast to Muslim women who don veils and high- or medium-heeled shoes to register their higher social status.[65] The shoe embodied the Muslim women's superior social position by the verticality it produced, which physically lifted Muslim women while materially visualizing inferiority by lowering the stature of Jewish women. However, these same rulings apply to Christian women, represented in similar subordinating attire relative to Muslims. The threat that shared *zimmi* status posed to the Christian hierarchy over Jews reappears in this gendered context.

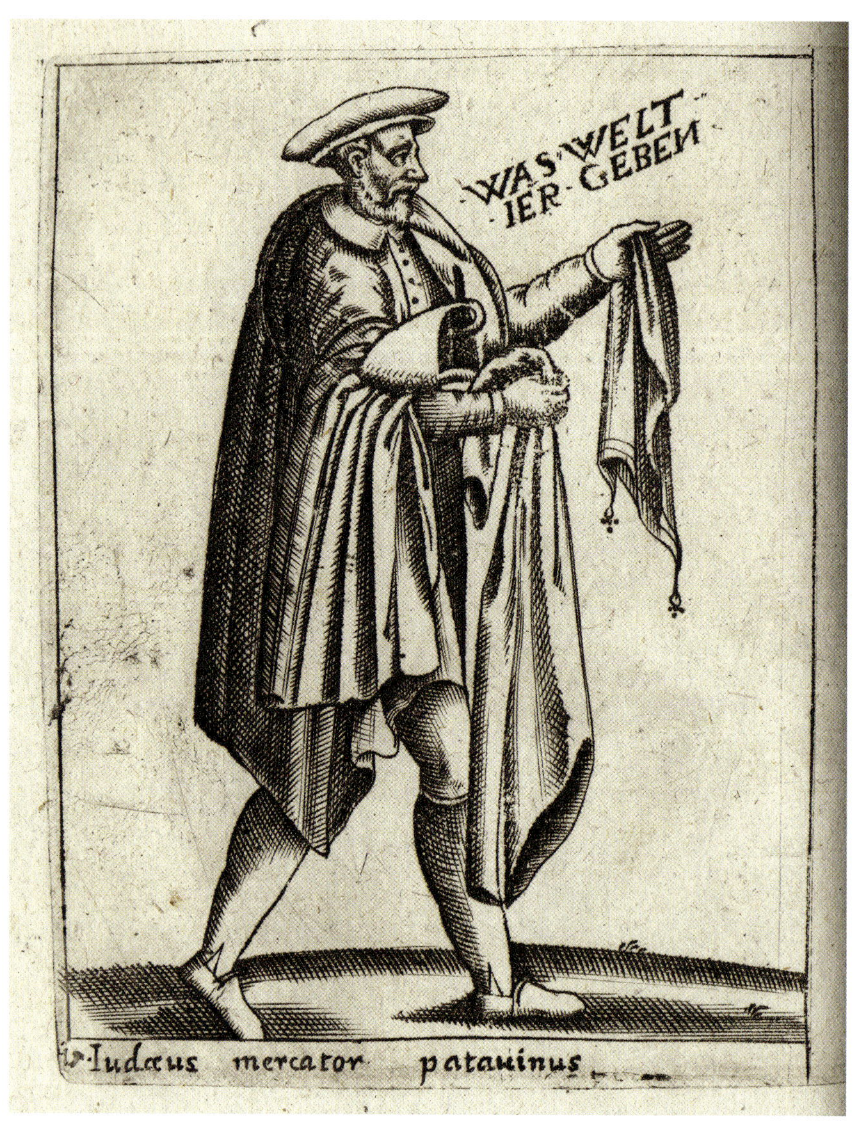

Figure 2.3
Pietro Bertelli, "Jewish Peddler" (Plate 15), *Diversarum nationum habitus* (1594–1596), Folger Library, GT513 B4 Cage copy 1 vol. 1

Furthermore, strategic portrayal of jewelry also suggests the problematic superiority of the wealth and adornments of Jewish women relative to Christian ones. Nicolay clads the older Jewish woman of Andrinople in a simple dress and wrap (Figure 2.4). The modesty of her garments, similar to a Christian gentlewoman of Pera, is offset and elevated by a prominent chain and pendant necklace worn low on her chest (Figure 2.5). Travelers observed that Levantine Jewish women, particularly Spanish émigrées*, wore substantial pieces of jewelry, heirlooms given to daughters from their Sephardic* mothers.[66] Her long chains mark her body with Jewish distinction, the simplicity of her dress further emphasizing the extravagance of her accessories. The adornment of the older Jewish woman's attire is exceeded in the rendering of the young Jewish maiden (Figure 2.6). Nicolay presents the fictional fabric ornamenting the unmarried Jewish woman as a jacquard*, probably damask* velvet, and possibly brocaded*, with flora patterning that exemplified the luxurious silk

65. As Rozen explains, "several items of apparel differentiated between *zimmi* and Muslim women; . . . high heels and the veil, were probably worn to emphasize that the Muslims were of a higher class" (*History*, 287).

66. Mark Mazower, *Salonica, City of Ghosts: Christians, Muslims and Jews, 1430–1950* (New York: Alfred A. Knopf, 2005), 54–55; and Peter Christensen, "'As If She Were Jerusalem': Placemaking in Sephardic Salonica," *Muqarnas* 30, no. 1 (2013): 168n41, https://doi.org/10.1163/22118993-0301P0007a.

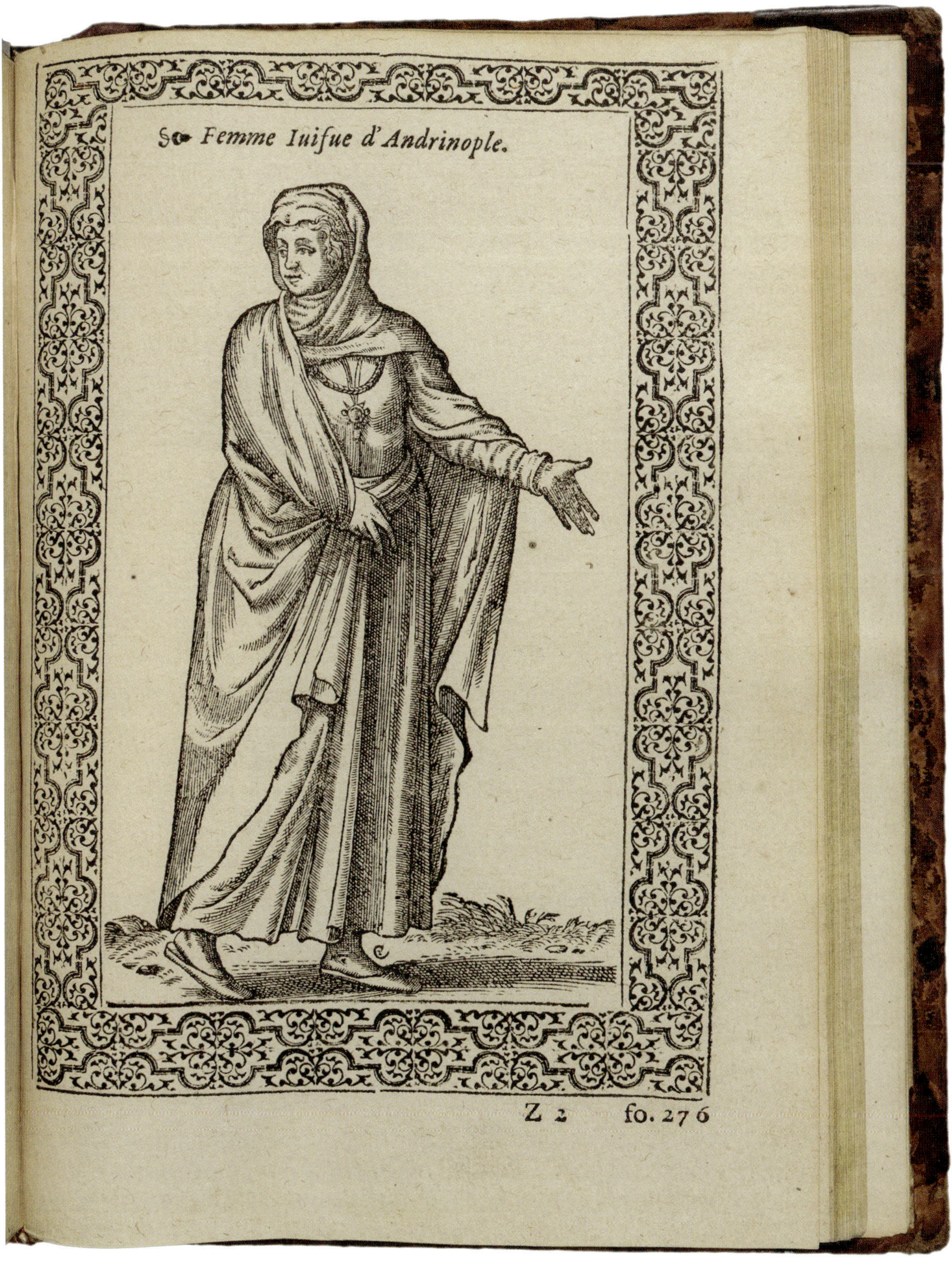

Figure 2.4
Nicolas de Nicolay, "Jewish woman of Andrinople" (276r),
Les navigations pérégrinations et voyages, faicts en la Turquie,
Antwerp, 1576,
Newberry Library, Wing ZP 5465 .S587

garments of the international marketplace.[67] While this fabric also appears in the garment worn by the Christian gentlewoman of Andrinople (Figure 2.7), the young Jewish woman displays an additional long chain around her neck. The conspicuous consumption of sumptuous fabrics and expensive jewelry cladding the Jewish maiden's body presents her with vestimentary prominence that competes with that of Christian women in Ottoman lands and threatens the supposedly inherent superiority of the latter.

Nicolay counters the doubled threat posed by both the indistinguishability and superiority of Jewish women's apparel relative to that of neighboring Christians through strategic use of image and text. Nicolay offers visual and extensive verbal visions of the rich jewelry and apparel worn by other Christian women, such as those on the Ile of Chio, whose beauty he praises while depicting them wearing elaborate necklaces atop gowns and coats of sumptuous fabrics embroidered with gold and pearls.[68] Notably, he provides no textual exegesis related to the garments adorning his portrayals of two Jewish women from Andrinople; only captions identify their religion and their spatial coordinates. However, in the chapter describing the town and inhabitants of Andrinople, he describes a descending gradation in the accompanying illustrations: "As for the manner of the garments of the inhabitaunts, I haue hereafter presented *in order* the liuely drafts of a woman of estate of Graecia, of a Turky woman of [middle] estate, and of a mayden of ioy or a common woman, or strumpet."[69] The order in which he presents these women begins with a Christian gentlewoman, then declines to a middle class Muslim woman, and finally, a sex worker. The images of the two Jewish women of Andrinople follow the woodcut of the sex worker, situating them at the nadir* of the social structure, unworthy of even a mention in the text. If the similarity or superiority of attire threatens that of Christian women, the organizing syntax of the text along with the placement of images relegates Jewish women to their proper inferior place.

However, the *Navigations* considers Jewish women elsewhere in the text to reinforce the racial superiority enjoyed by Christian inhabitants of Ottoman lands relative to Jews. The allegation, advanced in medieval Christian discourses that Turks fulfil God's will in punishing Jews with subordination, appears in the chapter on Jewish merchants.[70] The Jews are, Nicolay claims:

> more persecuted of the Turkes, . . . then of any other nation, who haue them in such disdaine and hatred, that by no meanes they will eate in their companie, and much lesse marry any of their wiues or daughters, notwithstanding that oftentimes they doe marry with Christians, whom they permit too liue according to their lawe, and haue a pleasure too eate and bee conuersant with Christians: and that which is woorse, if a Iewe woulde become a Muselman, he should not bee receiued, except first leauing his Iudaical sect he became a christian.[71]

While universally hated, Jews, alleges Nicolay, suffer even more under Turkish persecution, a point emphasized in the marginal note in the original French text.[72] However, he falsely ascribes a rationale developed from Christian canon law, which forbids Christians to

67. On the Jewish maiden, see Christensen, "'As If She Were Jerusalem,'" 148. On pictorial representations of luxurious textiles, see Rembrandt Duits, *Gold Brocade and Renaissance Painting: A Study in Material Culture* (London: Pindar Press, 2008).

68. Nicolay, *Navigations* (1585), 37r–39r; see especially the portrayal of the young woman of the island of Chio in *Navigations* (1576), 72r. Nicolay depicts Chios as an exemplary Christian polity within the Ottoman context, (Keller, "Nicolas," 25). Păun identifies the beauty of the women of Chios as another topos common among French authors ("Sur quelques 'modèles,'" 172).

69. Nicolay, *Navigations* (1585), 141r, emphasis added. The English edition incorrectly translates the French "moyen estate" as "mean" or low status.

70. See claims by Jacques de Vitry discussed earlier and Tavim, "*Grão-Turco*," 179–81.

71. Nicolay, *Navigations* (1585), 131r–v.

72. "Jews hated by all nations and especially by Turks" and "A Christian woman married to a Turk is permitted to live according to her law, [i.e., continue to practice Christianity]," our translation. Nicolay, *Navigations* (1576), 247.

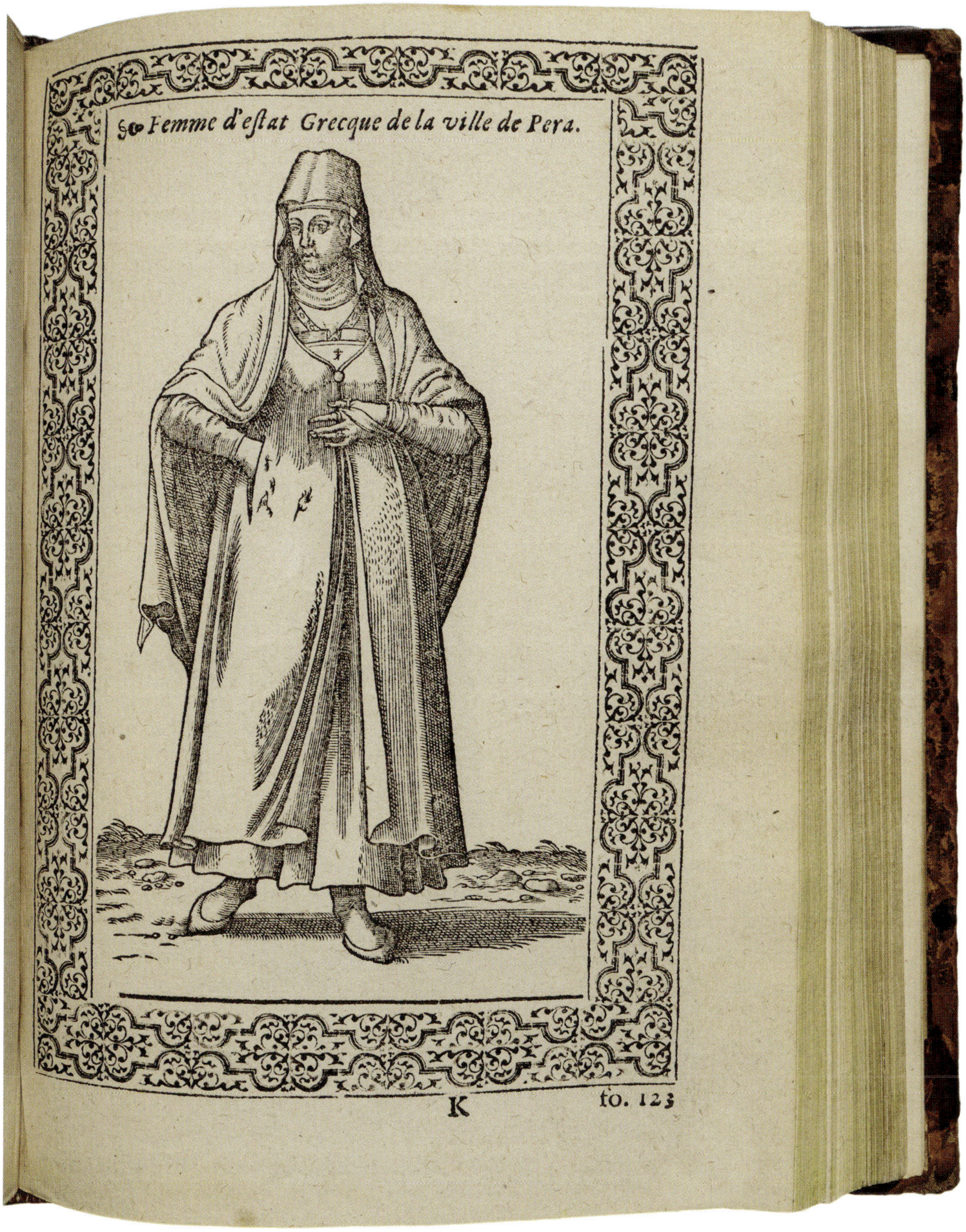

Figure 2.5
Nicolas de Nicolay, "Christian gentlewoman of Pera" (123r), *Les navigations pérégrinations et voyages, faicts en la Turquie*, Antwerp, 1576, Newberry Library, Wing ZP 5465 .S587

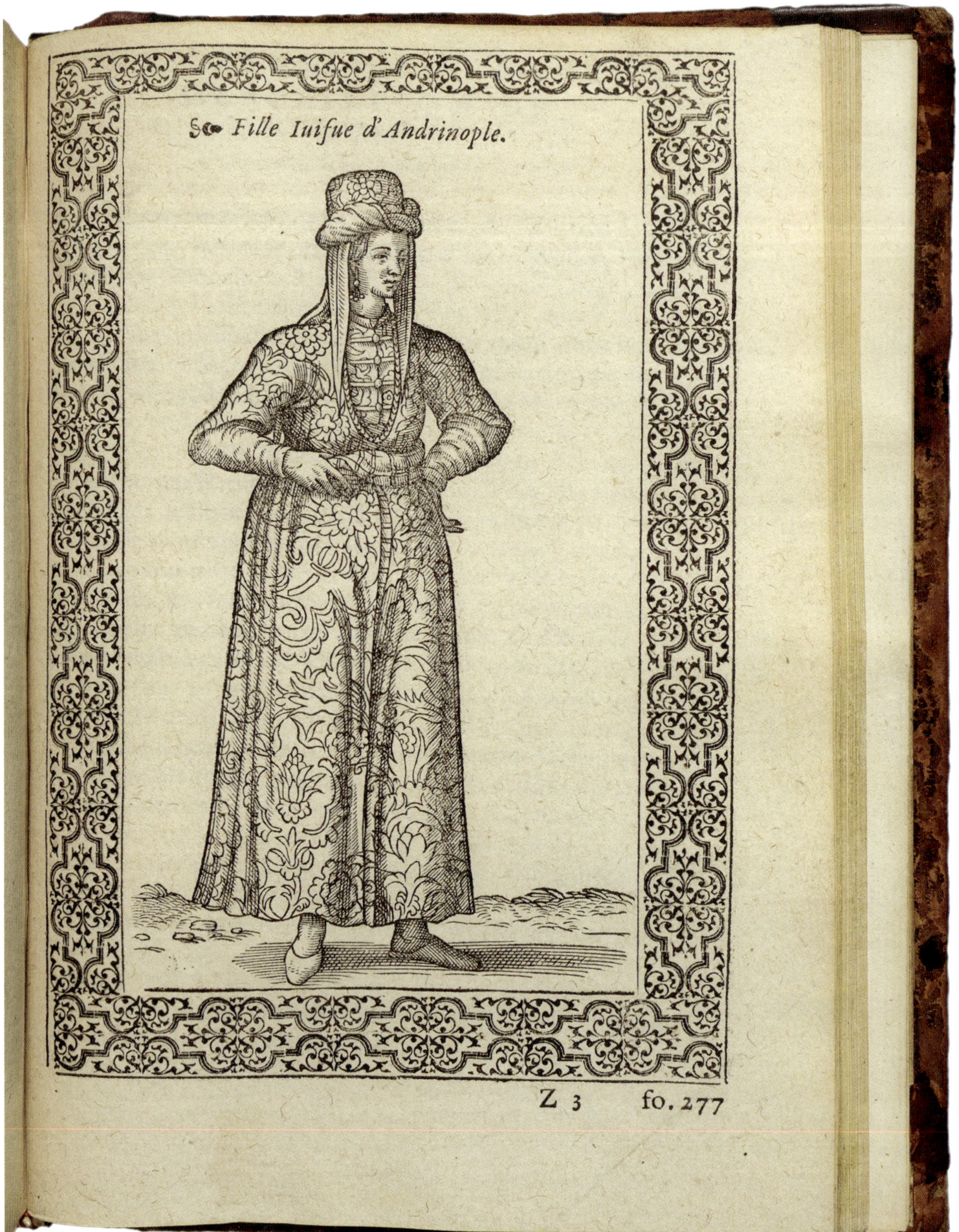

Figure 2.6
Nicolas de Nicolay, "Young Jewish woman of Andrinople" (277r),
Les navigations pérégrinations et voyages, faicts en la Turquie,
Antwerp, 1576,
Newberry Library, Wing ZP 5465 .S587

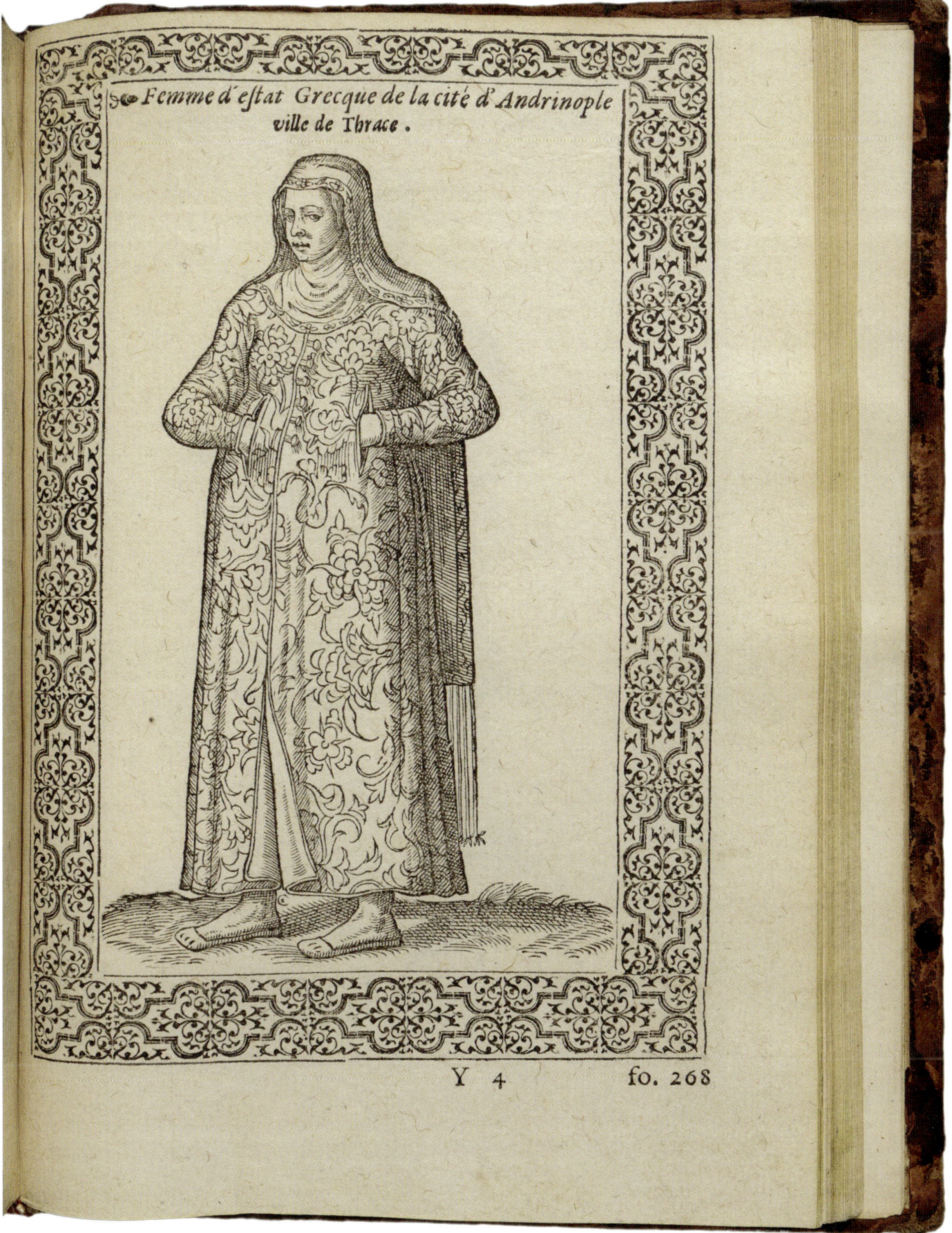

Figure 2.7
Nicolas de Nicolay, "Christian gentlewoman of Andrinople" (268r),
Les navigations pérégrinations et voyages, faicts en la Turquie,
Antwerp, 1576,
Newberry Library, Wing ZP 5465 .S587

eat and intermarry with Jews, to Muslim law, which in fact treats all *zimmis* as equals.[73] He also fabricates a hierarchy in which Christians enjoy privileges over Jews, asserting that Muslims willingly marry and share meals with the former but decline to do so with the latter out of contempt.[74] Here, he specifically alleges the inferiority of Jewish women in the estimation of Muslim men, who refuse to marry them. In contrast, Muslim men contract marriages with Christian women, holding them in esteem by allowing them to continue their religious observance. Nicolay nullifies the implicit threats to Christian hierarchy posed by the images of Jewish women, through either leveling similarity or superior ornamentation, in alleging their relative degradation by Muslims.

The conflicting evidence of image and word reveals the counterfactual labor of race construction, the effort that goes into bending empirical evidence of the Ottoman Jewish experience to fit the imperatives of Christian triumphalism. While Nicolay's preface voices confidence in a glorious future of global Christianity, in contemporary Ottoman lands, the status of both Jews and Muslims often surpasses that of Christians, thwarting rather than fulfilling God's will. The compensatory power of materialized degradation seeks to manifest the actual, essential status of infidel inferiority that Islamic law perniciously occludes.[75] In illustrating an ideality of Christian imperative, the *Navigations* aspires to transform the imperfect terrestrial world, permanently returning recalcitrant religious others to their proper subordinated place in the divine order.

73. David M. Freidenreich, "Jews, Pagans, and Heretics in Early Medieval Canon Law," in *Jews in Early Christian Law: Byzantium and the Latin West, 6th–11th Centuries*, eds. John V. Tolan et. al (Turnhout, Belgium: Brepols, 2014), 73–91, especially 76–79. "Christian authorities . . ., unlike Muslims, found it important to establish laws directed exclusively at Jews" (91).

74. The canard that Muslims prohibit Jews from converting to Islam unless they first become Christian circulates through other early modern texts written by Christians, Ania Loomba and Jonathan Burton, *Race in Early Modern England: A Documentary Companion* (New York: Palgrave Macmillan, 2007), 172, 196.

75. For an example of somatic, rather than material, manifestation of inherent Jewish inferiority, see Kaplan, *Figuring*, 81–102.

Note From the Field 1

"TOUCHING EACH BOOK": DEMYSTIFYING SPECIAL COLLECTIONS IN COMMUNITY

By Analú María López

"When touching each book, it is as if the words were imprinted in each finger and begged to be pronounced so as not to be forgotten. It is really a meeting between words and emotions."[1]

— Victorino Torres Nava
(Nahua Community, Cuentepec, Morelos, Mexico)

First, I would like to express gratitude and love to my kin, and all the Native American, Indigenous, Pueblos Originarios, and First Nation communities, past, present, and future. Wherever you travel across the Americas, you are on Indigenous land. This land is and will always be Indigenous Land.

A Note on Terminology

It's important to acknowledge the diversity of Indigenous Peoples' cultures, traditions, and languages throughout the Western Hemisphere. When teaching about a particular tribe or nation, learning and

1. Original text was in Spanish: "Al tocar cada libro, es como si las palabras se impregnaran en cada dedo y suplicaran pronunciarse para no olvidarnos de ellas. Es realmente un encuentro entre las palabras y las emociones." A dear friend, colleague, and Nahua scholar shared this with me after his first visit to the Newberry Library in 2019. In our respective Indigenous communities, we see these collections as our relatives.

using accurate terms specific to the community can prevent stereotypes and encourage cultural understanding and sensitivity. Throughout this essay, I use the words "Indigenous" and "Native" to be inclusive of all peoples who are the original inhabitants of the land. These words encompass more specific terms like "American Indian," "First Nations," "Naciones Originarias (Original Nations)," and others that refer to Indigenous peoples in specific regions.

Introduction

I have been a longtime admirer of libraries, museums, and cultural institutions worldwide but particularly in Chicago. As a child, I was fortunate to have aunts instilling their love of libraries and museums in me and my siblings. I have many fond memories exploring places such as the Field Museum and the Chicago Public Library with my aunts. My family and I are part of the Indigenous diaspora here in Chicago; we are Chichimeca (specifically Guachichil/Xi'úi) from El Aguaje de Garcia, San Luis Potosi, Mexico but we have been here in Chicago since the 1950s.

I was a precocious child, which often got me into trouble because I constantly asked questions. I often wondered why Indigenous culture, history, and languages were not taught in school. Now as an adult I have developed the language to describe why: white supremacy, indoctrination, assimilation, imperialism, racism, just to name a few. Public schools rarely, if at all, teach Indigenous culture, histories, language, literature and if they do, they are extremely biased. In the city of Chicago alone, there is no curriculum yet within the Chicago Public Schools focusing on Native American or Indigenous experiences.[2] I am a graduate of the Chicago Public School system and I was born, raised, and still reside on the Southwest side of Chicago in the historic neighborhood of La Villita (Little Village). Our community has a strong history of action and coalition building to address the continued oppression our community and other BIPOC communities face in the areas of education, employment, healthcare, gentrification, and environmental racism.

An important historical example related to coalition building in Little Village involves the now defunct Harrison Technical high school. The same high school my mom and aunts also attended at the time. On September 16, 1968, 1,000 of the 3,000 students enrolled at this high school — the only high school at the time serving South Lawndale and Pilsen — protested the absence of African American history courses and the unfavorable conditions throughout the overcrowded school, including ongoing underfunding and a lack of bilingual teachers. While the initial protest was unsuccessful, a month later, 2,500 students participated in a second walkout in which African American students were joined by their Latinx/e counterparts.[3] Inspired by the African American student advocacy group *New Breed*, Latinx/e[4] students created their own manifesto of grievances, which included a protest against the lack of diversity in the curriculum and teaching staff for both communities.[5] You can see a copy of this manifesto along with other ephemeral materials related to this action in an artist book created by Jose Resendiz in 2016, at the Newberry.[6] Although these efforts

2. Since January 2022, House bill Native American Curriculum, HB4548 has been going through the legislature here in Chicago requiring the State Board of Education to develop a curriculum relating to the Native American experience for students in kindergarten through grade 12. It also requires the implementation of the Native American curriculum starting in the 2023–2024 school year.

3. To read more about this historical action, see *Digital Chicago*, "Harrison High Protests of 1968: Demanding Better Education," by Hannah Bradford and Anna Hevrdejs, https://digitalchicagohistory.org/exhibits/show/harrison-high-protests-1968/home.

4. Latinx/e is defined as a person of Latin American origin or descent. The "x" in Latinx is a gender-neutral term for a person of Latin American descent but breaks the linguistic structure of the word in Spanish in an attempt to un-gender the term Latino, yet it still pays deference to a Eurocentric ideology that actively denies the Indigenous and African heritage of the people it claims to represent.

5. Tanner Howard, "Fifty years ago, 35,000 Chicago students walked out of their classrooms in protest. They changed CPS forever," *Chicago Reader*, October 4, 2018, https://www.chicagoreader.com/chicago/student-protests-1968-chicago-public-schools/Content?oid=59097994

6. https://i-share-nby.primo.exlibrisgroup.com/permalink/01CARLI_NBY/i5mcb2/alma999615258805867

brought attention to educational and racial disparities in our neighborhoods, our schools are still lacking in resources and relevant curriculums.

The demographics* of Little Village are 60% Latinx/e, 34% Black non-Latinx, 6% White non-Latinx and of the Latinx/e population a majority of which are foreign born.[7] However, within these demographics, Indigenous identity as it pertains to Indigenous people in Latin America is erased. This is mostly a result of immigrants being classified as "Latinx" even if they are members of a particular Indigenous community in Mexico. This is the first stage in the colonial project to assimilate Indigenous people: it strips you of your identity. The next stage of assimilation is to separate you from your language. The curriculum will be offered in either English or Spanish after a student is enrolled in a public school. When we enroll in the public education system, we are then taught a history that is either biased or unrelated to our experiences. As my friend and Nahua scholar Victorino Torres Nava once wrote:

> In elementary school they forced me to memorize the names of the rivers and capitals of Europe and they forced me to forget the names of the rivers and the names of my town. Something like that happens with our languages. That if you no longer speak any language other than Spanish or another of the whites, it is not because you have entered the category of *mestizo**, but because your grandparents were forced to forget their language and their history, they were named mestizo.[8]

Having attended public schools in Chicago and Texas, I can speak from personal experience regarding the lack of curricula related to Indigenous experiences within most public schools. The opportunity to facilitate and elevate topics and conversations related to Indigenous histories, culture, and language is what I value most about working at the Newberry. The opportunity to host community members worldwide and teach in a Special Collections classroom at an independent research library like the Newberry is unique. In many respects, the numerous, ongoing partnerships aimed at facilitating Native and Indigenous people's access to the Newberry's collection of materials have helped to reunite and reclaim the histories that have been over time separated from these communities.

Indigenous Studies Collection at the Newberry

When Edward E. Ayer donated his library to the Newberry in 1911, he also stipulated his library always have a librarian or curator stewarding the Indigenous Studies collection. The first two Ayer librarians at the Newberry were white women: Clara Smith, who was also Ayer's niece, and Ruth Lapham Butler. White men and a white woman thereafter took their places. Before the 1970s at the earliest, it can be presumed that the majority of users and possibly staff using the American Indian and Indigenous studies collection would be white (or, at least, non-Native). The founding of the D'Arcy McNickle Center for American Indian and Indigenous Studies in 1972 helped shift and improve this way of thinking at the library. Indeed, the McNickle Center was intended to facilitate important topics related to stimulating research and improving scholarship in American Indian and Indigenous studies broadly, but it was built with the Indigenous community—teachers, scholars, and researchers—in mind. It was specifically founded to help facilitate

7. University of Chicago website: https://harris.uchicago.edu/files/little_village.pdf.

8. The original correspondence was in Spanish: "En la primaria me obligaron a memorizar los nombres de los ríos y capitales de Europa y me obligaron a olvidar los nombres de los ríos y nombres de mi pueblo. Algo así pasa con nuestras lenguas. Que si ya no hablas ninguna lengua más que el español u otra de los blancos; no es porque hayas entrado en la categoría de mestizo, sino porque a tus abuelos los obligaron a olvidar su lengua y su historia y lo nombraron mestizo." Facebook message, March 12, 2021.

their work, and to provide a meeting ground for Indigenous people interested in their own histories.

As an Indigenous Librarian working at a Predominantly White Institution (PWI), negotiating my relationship with the Newberry feels different from my everyday life and lived experience as a community member accountable to an inter-tribal Indigenous community here in Chicago and in Latin America. My work does not exist in a vacuum; it is not simply for the institution; it is also for the numerous communities that I come from, with which I work, and with which I stand in solidarity. I am accountable to these communities, above all. It can be a challenge for colleagues not living in the community and not from the community to fully understand this fact. While I have many interests, my passion lies in intentional community collaborations to build points of access to materials within the Newberry Library. An example I provide below is working in collaboration with Nahua community members in Cuentepec, Morelos, Mexico to obtain a facsimile* copy of a historical sixteenth century map of Tenochtitlan. In addition, I have a strong commitment to the preservation and revitalization of Indigenous languages. Despite the challenges, I have committed to this work both within and outside of the library.

As the Indigenous Studies Librarian and Assistant Curator, I help steward the Indigenous studies collection while guiding library users through, connecting them with, and interpreting materials linked to the Indigenous Studies collection. Any time someone has a question about materials within the vast collection, I help them navigate it and connect them with resources for their research. I also lead many in-person instructional sessions and tours to visiting classes and groups. These range from high school and undergraduate students to Newberry-associated consortium groups, community groups, tribal representatives, and families; the list is very long. Aside from my main responsibilities, I am involved in multiple interdepartmental committees related to external and internal initiatives for providing access to materials to various Indigenous communities. For the past two years I have also co-chaired the Diversity, Equity, and Inclusion initiatives at the library. My Instruction practice is informed not only by my lived experience but by international initiatives working towards uplifting historically underrepresented Indigenous communities and their knowledge systems, which have often been dismissed within the libraries and archives fields. Researching collection objects in-depth with relation to provenance and item history is a part of my practice as a librarian. Since the Indigenous studies collection is quite vast, many community members are unaware of the existence of specific materials or related supplementary resources, so part of this work includes reconnecting the community to that knowledge and history. For example, at the moment I am working with my home community in San Luis Potosi, Mexico to gather resources related to the Guachichil language and history.

My career as a librarian started back in 2010 while working for a research library in Chicago. The position I held at this library was a Digital Imaging Assistant and exposed me to many historical documents. In this role, I encountered many documents I had never known to exist, like a full run of Mexican newspapers. I wondered if research topics and assignments in high school would have changed had I known an institution like this existed. Would I have written about these newspapers? After working at this research library for many years I went to work for a contemporary art museum in Chicago. Working for that museum was traumatizing. During my time there I came to understand their blatant disregard for the communities that they and many museums profit from through the use of stolen labor and exploited narratives. Shortly after my time abruptly ended here, I decided to pursue a Master's in Library and Information Science in 2014. Over the years, I kept looking for job openings at the Newberry and finally after thirteen years and thirty-five job applications sent to various cultural institutions in Chicago, the Indigenous Studies Librarian position opened at the Newberry and I applied.[9] This was also shortly after graduating from Dominican University with a Master's in Library and Information Science and a certificate in Archives and Cultural Heritage Resources and Services.

#ArchivesSOWhite

In 2016, I contributed an article titled "#ArchivesSO White: Preparing for the Field," to an online arts publication called *Sixty Inches from Center*. This piece focused on diversity (or the lack thereof) within the library and archives fields. Six years after writing this article, I now work as the Indigenous Studies Librarian and Assistant Curator of American Indian and Indigenous Studies at the Newberry Library, an independent research library focused in the Humanities but also a P.W.I. Statistically, the most common ethnicity of librarians (and only counting credentialed librarians), that is, those with a Master's degree accredited by the American Library Association is: White 89%, Black or African American 5%, Hispanic or Latinx 2%, Native American/Alaskan <1%, Asian/Pacific Islander 3% and two or more 1%.[10] If you consult the U.S. Bureau of Labor Statistics annual report from 2010 for more current information, it is likely to remain the same. It's an overwhelmingly white profession. As librarian Jessamyn Charity West wrote "When confronting the problem of Whiteness in libraries it's good to remember that this isn't just a random thing that happened, but a problem that was built on top of structural racism within the United States. People in librarianship then made choices to make these situations better, or worse, within living memory."[11] I think about this often within the profession and how this connects to broader discussions about U.S. policies aimed towards separating Indigenous peoples from their history, land, culture, and language. These very policies are historically rooted in imperialism and capitalism. For example, how was someone like Edward E. Ayer, a wealthy, white, collector and donor of the Indigenous Studies collection at the Newberry,[12] able to obtain materials from the Philippines at the end of the nineteenth century when he first learned that the United States had "acquired" the islands from Spain under the terms of the treaty that ended the Spanish-American War? How is this connected more broadly to white supremacy and the collections the Newberry has?

In addition to considering the importance of Indigenous languages and the reasons why the Newberry's collection of related materials is crucial for reestablishing ties with the people from which they originate, I also consider the current situation of Indigenous languages. Indigenous languages comprise about 4,000 of the roughly 6,500 to 7,000 languages spoken today. However, the majority of the languages under threat are Indigenous languages. It is estimated that one Indigenous language dies every two weeks. Fluent native speakers of Indigenous languages are becoming less and less common, which is directly due to genocidal, historical (and present), assimilationist, and educational policies that violate the rights of various minority linguistic populations. Although Article 13 of the United Nations Declaration on the Rights of Indigenous Peoples states that "Indigenous peoples have the right to revitalise, use, develop and transmit to future generations their languages, oral traditions, writing

9. My official title is "Ayer Librarian," which honors Edward E. Ayer, the collection's donor and a former Newberry Trustee. This fact alone is problematic, especially in light of what First Nations Librarian Jessie Loyer called "a singular, white man's joy," in that most collections in libraries, archives, and museums were created by them [white men]. Additionally, the majority of these collections bear the names of these same white men. "Collections Are Our Relatives: Disrupting the Singular, White Man's Joy That Shaped Collections," in Megan Browndorf, Erin Pappas, and Anna Arays, eds., *The Collector and the Collected: Decolonizing Area Studies Librarianship* (Library Juice Press, 2021), 3–19. https://mru.arcabc.ca/islandora/object/mru%3A793.

10. The American Library Association's 2000 Census estimates data. See Denise M. Davis and Tracie D. Hall, *Diversity Counts*, (ALA: Office for Research and Statistics, Office for Diversity, 2007), https://www.ala.org/aboutala/sites/ala.org.aboutala/files/content/diversity/diversitycounts/diversitycounts_rev0.pdf

11. Jessamyn Charity West, "Segregation in Library Associations" in Violet B. Fox, *Disorientation Guide to Librarianship*, http://violetbfox.info/disorientation-guide-to-librarianship/. Find more information and formatted/printable versions of the zine at the main page: violetbfox.info/disorientation.

12. Edward E. Ayer was also part of the Newberry's Board of Trustees.

systems and literatures,"[13] public policies continue to lack support for communities to fund, implement, and sustain the learning and use of Indigenous languages. Why is this important? Capitalism (and non-Native languages) is the primary language of the majority of the world's largest polluters. More than 96% of the world's Indigenous languages are currently in danger of extinction or are under threat. It is no coincidence that as speakers of historically marginalised languages pass away, the rest of the world grieves as well, grieving over the loss and threat of the languages (and communities) that have protected the world's most priceless treasures — the earth and the water.[14]

Decolonizing the Archive?

We hear the term "decolonize" quite a bit these days but what does it mean within libraries and archives? Within a colonial construct many often argue it is impossible to "decolonize" an Institution because they perpetuate colonial ideals. Historically libraries and archives have cataloged Indigenous materials in Western ways oftentimes disregarding Indigenous knowledge.[15] As part of a grant-funded initiative at the Newberry, my colleagues and I are currently challenging this framework by updating our internal library practices and protocols as they relate to cataloging and archival standards to make them inclusive of Indigenous knowledge systems.[16] For example, one collaborative project that includes Indigenous community members and staff, includes updating online catalog records, digital resources to address racial slurs, problematic subject headings and discussing options for implementing Traditional Knowledge (TK) labels into catalog records.[17] Traditional Knowledge Labels identify and clarify community-specific rules and responsibilities regarding access and future use of traditional knowledge held within non-Tribal institutions.

Although many archives, libraries, museums, cultural institutions, and the academy as a whole have diversified over the years, this does not mean they have "decolonized." Indigenous people need to have control over their own knowledge, histories, stories, and resources because no matter how experienced a non-Native person thinks they are, they cannot and will not have the lived experience. To me, decolonizing means enough with capitalism, colonialism, and imperialism. We must respect the self-determination and sovereignty of Indigenous communities worldwide. As Eve Tuck and K. Wayne Yang wrote in their essay "Decolonization is not a Metaphor":

> Decolonization brings about the repatriation of Indigenous land and life; it is not a metaphor for other things we want to do to improve our societies and schools. The easy adoption of decolonizing discourse by educational advocacy and scholarship, evidenced by the increasing number of calls to "decolonize our schools," or use "decolonizing methods," or, "decolonize student thinking", turns decolonization into a metaphor.[18]

Hiring Native people and tossing in land acknowledgements alone is not decolonization either. To me, representation alone will not solve the centuries of structural racism, violence, indoctrination, assimilation

13. https://www.ohchr.org/en/indigenous-peoples/un-declaration-rights-indigenous-peoples

14. According to data referenced in Australia's recently issued 2021 State of the Environment report, Indigenous peoples are safeguarding 80% of the world's remaining biodiversity even though they make up just 5% of the world's population

15. The Indigenization Project, University of British Columbia, see Ian Cull; Robert L. A. Hancock, Stephanie McKeown, Michelle Pidgeon, and Adrienne Vedan, "Decolonization and Indigenization," in *Pulling Together: A Guide for Front-Line Staff, Student Services, and Advisors*, (Victoria, BC: BCcampus, 2018), https://opentextbc.ca/indigenization.

16. Read more about this grant project: https://www.newberry.org/news/newberry-library-will-collaborate-with-native-communities-to-expand-access-to-indigenous-studies-collection

17. More information about TK Labels is available at https://localcontexts.org/labels/traditional-knowledge-labels.

18. Eve Tuck and K. Wayne Yang, "Decolonization is not a metaphor," *Decolonization: Indigeneity, Education & Society* 1, no. 1 (2012), 1, https://jps.library.utoronto.ca/index.php/des/article/view/18630.

policies, and continued imperialism Indigenous people are still subjected to. Representation and individuals being involved in processes that historically were created without Indigenous people involved is the minimum starting point. And because Tuck and Yang wrote it best:

> "When metaphor invades decolonization, it kills the very possibility of decolonization; it recenters whiteness, it resettles theory, it extends innocence to the settler, it entertains a settler future . . . The metaphorization of decolonization makes possible a set of evasions, or "settler moves to innocence", that problematically attempt to reconcile settler guilt and complicity, and rescue settler futurity."[19]

In other words, non-tribal institutions stewarding Indigenous collections must do more than simply display gestures of solidarity.[20] Efforts to 'decolonize' institutions are embodied in ritual acts of acknowledging Indigenous presence and claims to territory. We are seeing these acts worldwide. However, these acknowledgements are increasingly—if only recently—understood as prerequisites for demonstrating engagement with Indigenous communities.[21] Performative acts rarely if ever lead to sustainable change within institutions, a continuous commitment to serve as accomplices to Indigenous people is what is necessary. For example, we need to work on prioritizing Indigenous voices (e.g. collecting and purchasing Native-created works), creating opportunities for the hiring of Native people within public facing positions, and supporting and investing in Native-led projects.

Additionally, I have a strong interest in tribal critical theory (TribalCrit). TribalCrit is an offshoot of Critical Race Theory (CRT) and is based on the various, complex, historically and geographically situated epistemologies and ontologies that are present in Indigenous communities all over the world.[22] As Jones Brayboy and Bryan McKinley point out: "The primary tenet of TribalCrit is the notion that colonization is endemic to society. By colonization, I mean that European American thought, knowledge, and power structures dominate present-day society in the United States."[23] And this is the same within the academy and libraries, where these perspectives are prioritized over Indigenous community members or scholars we have been taught to believe "authorities" on particular subjects. For example, during my first years as the Indigenous Studies librarian, I was giving a tour to a community member and they asked me "Why is this white scholar seen as an authority on this topic or community?" The scholar was Charles Dibble and the topic related to translations done in English from Nahuatl. Although Dibble has contributed greatly to the field of Mesoamerican studies and Linguistics, why is he considered an authority in relation to anything Nahua? Why are Indigenous scholars or Indigenous language speakers often studied but rarely given authority within scholarship or the archive?

Community Collaborations: Indigenous Scholars from the Community

I am passionate about working towards building sustainable relationships with communities and community members where materials originate from. For example, it has been very important to me to learn two Indigenous languages once spoken by family members, not only to do the work in the library, but also to understand my belonging within the community.

19. Tuck and Yang, 1–3, .

20. I would also extend this to any institution stewarding Black, Indigenous, Queer, and POC collections.

21. *The Red New Order* artist collective.

22. Jones Brayboy and Bryan McKinley, "Toward a Tribal Critical Race Theory in Education," *The Urban Review* 37, no. 5 (2005): 425–446, https://doi.org/10.1007/s11256-005-0018-y.

23. Bradboy and McKinley, 430.

Through a commitment to learning two languages I am able to get closer to living communities and build reciprocal relationships working against the exploitative and extractive practices museums, libraries, and archives have used to fill their collections. At the library I also work towards demystifying special collections within colonial spaces like the Newberry because these institutions can be intimidating for some community members. And although institutions such as ours are "open to the public" I always ask:

- What mechanisms are in place that will ensure welcoming atmospheres for community members visiting the library and working with the materials?

- Do communities know what is held within our institutions? And if so, what are we doing to connect them with these resources?

- How are we stewarding these collections? Do we consider specific Indigenous protocols for culturally sensitive materials?

Over the years I have had the honor of welcoming a variety of individuals into the library, from Newberry Consortium groups, community groups and tribal representatives to high school students and families. At times, these interactions open up potential collaborative projects with hidden stories about a particular item within the collection. One example of such a collaborative project included me writing an article with a Nahua scholar. Back in 2019 Victorino Torres Nava and I focused on an eighteenth-century Nahuatl play in the Newberry collection. When this item arrived at the library in 2018, the dealer description stated that the play chronicles the story of a grandmother who leaves her grandson to watch over their turkeys while also telling him to keep an eye on a jar filled with a mysterious liquid, *possibly* honey. She tells her grandson not to drink the liquid and warns him that, if he does, he will become sick.

The description provided by the auction house translated the word *"necuitetzahuac"* to mean just honey. Upon further investigation of this term within the manuscript in collaboration with a Nahuatl speaker we came to find that the term used for "honey," necuitetzahuac, was in fact *"aguamiel"* (honey water in English) or the sap from the maguey plant which when fermented becomes the alcoholic drink *pulque*. After the grandmother leaves, her grandson gets very hungry and drinks the necuitetzahuac, becoming drunk. He then believes that he has been transformed into a coyote and begins to howl. When she returns, the grandmother scolds him, and the play concludes with them dancing as they exit. We also transcribed and translated the article into a modern variant of Nahuatl along with English and Spanish versions. The Nahuatl transcription was done by another Nahua scholar, Abelardo de la Cruz. For the published article, we made sure to prioritize the Nahuatl language as well. These and other instances demonstrate how crucial it is to consult and collaborate with Indigenous communities, especially when they speak an Indigenous language as their mother tongue. Similarly, it is crucial to provide community members with leadership opportunities within institutional initiatives.

One of my more recent collaborative project was a blog post titled "The Codex Zempoala: Asserting Indigenous Rights," written last year which is available in English, Spanish, and a Nahuatl translation done by Victorino. Recently, the Newberry donated a facsimile copy of the 1524 map of Tenochtitlan (or so-called Mexico City) to Victorino's community in Cuentepec.[24] (Figure 1) It's important to build these reciprocal relationships, especially within communities that have historically been underrepresented on a social, political, and educational level. Indigenous communities in Latin America, like many other Native communities across the globe, still experience state violence at the hands of its colonial government.

24. For the community of Cuentepec, Morelos, is the last community in the entire state of Morelos that retains its Indigenous language of Nahuatl as their first language.

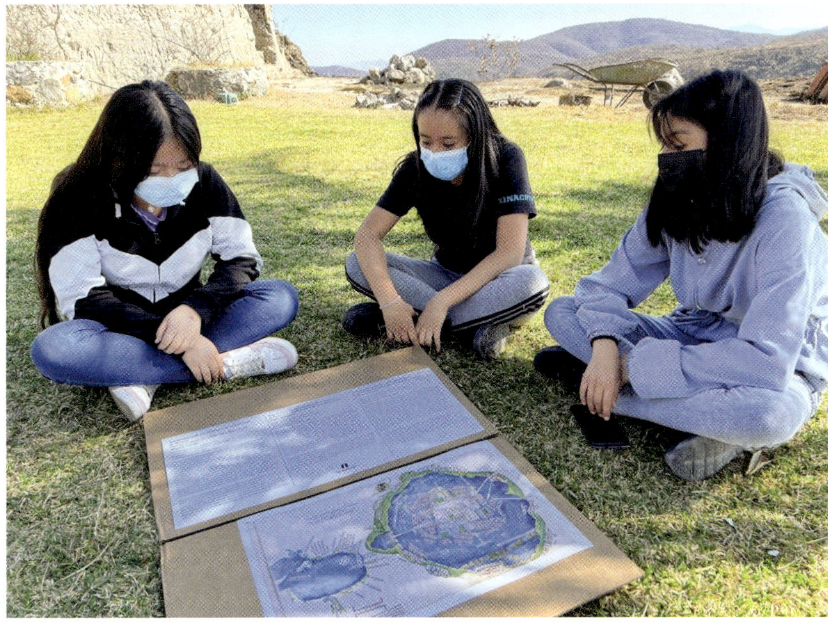

Figure 1
Nahua youth from the Cuentepec community viewing the facsimile copy of a 1524 map of Tenochtitlan, Cuentepec, Morelos, Mexico, 2022 (Photo: Victorino Torres Nava (Nahua)

Although Mexico has public schools for Indigenous people, the curriculum is mostly in Spanish. The public schools rarely, if at all, teach subjects in an Indigenous language even though Mexico has an extraordinary linguistic diversity of seven million speakers of an Indigenous language. It is one of the countries with the most Indigenous languages! A total of sixty-eight native languages are spoken, divided into more than three hundred and fifty linguistic variants.

The Newberry has accomplished and continues to accomplish some admirable reconciliation and reckoning with its very own past as an institution tied to actions of Indigenous knowledge being separated from origin communities, especially within Indigenous communities in Latin-America.[25] As Elizabeth Joffrion and Natalia Fernández wrote:

> When relationships are built on a foundation of trust and mutual respect, the resulting collaborative efforts can create beneficial alliances that produce new understandings of Indigenous cultural history and more sensitive approaches to the stewardship of Native heritage by non-Native cultural institutions."[26]

All these efforts may mark a very small step toward reconciliation between institutions rooted in colonial history and Indigenous communities.

But the work never ends.

25. The recent exhibition, ¡Viva la *Libertad!*, curated by my colleague Will Hansen, included this statement of provenance: "The books, maps, and manuscripts in this exhibition were acquired by the Newberry Library over our 130-year history. Edward E. Ayer, a trustee of the library, donated many of these items to the Newberry in 1911. Some were given to the Newberry by other collectors, and some were purchased as recently as last year. The Newberry acquired these materials in good faith from what were believed to be their proper owners. Yet we also acknowledge the long history of removal of cultural heritage from Latin America, and particularly from Indigenous peoples, to colonizing nations and institutions. Such removals sometimes occurred through pillage, theft, coercion, exploitative purchase, and other inappropriate means. We recognize this historical context and seek to build reciprocal relationships with the communities from which these items and the knowledge that they carry came."

26. Joffrion, Elizabeth and Fernández, Natalia, "Collaboration between Tribal and Non-Tribal Organizations: Sharing Expertise, Knowledge, and Cultural Resources" (2015). Western Libraries Faculty and Staff Publications. https://cedar.wwu.edu/library_facpubs/32

EXHIBITION CATALOG

PART 1. FIGURING

Case Study #1: Imagining Blackness

ENTRY #1 (NO IMAGE)

Franciscan Bible, Paris, c. 1250
Manuscript on parchment* with illuminations*
VAULT Case MS 19

The Bible was the foundation for almost all learning, worship, and art in medieval Europe. As such, the central text of Christianity served as the primary lens through which highly trained intellectuals as well as unlearned peasants visualized everything in their world, including race. The biblical texts include multiple references to people of color, both literary (e.g., the "black yet beautiful" woman in Song of Songs 1:4) and historical (e.g., the Ethiopian eunuch converted by the Apostle Philip in Acts 8: 26–40), which became entrenched in European culture through commentaries, sermons, devotional literature, and visual art. The presence of non-white people in the Christian story was shared more widely starting in the thirteenth century, when Franciscan and Dominican friars used small, complete copies of the Bible to minister to increasingly diverse audiences. The example here was certainly used for this purpose; alongside the full Biblical text, it featured exquisite illuminations and supplementary texts for saying mass and managing devotional practices, all of which helped to bring biblical material to Christians outside the intellectual elite. Over time, laypeople took the biblical content they learned from these encounters to shape their own devotional lives. The cultural significance of the Bible ensured that race was firmly implanted within the European imagination, where it could be employed in a variety of ways to visualize the world, the different peoples within it, and the power dynamics between them.

Further Readings

Light, Laura. "The Thirteenth Century and the Paris Bible." In *The New Cambridge History of the Bible: from 600 to 1450*, edited by Richard Marsden and E. Ann Matter, 380–391. Cambridge: Cambridge University Press, 2012.

Van Engen, John. *Sisters and Brothers of the Common Life: The Devotio Moderna and the World of the Later Middle Ages*. Philadelphia: University of Pennsylvania Press, 2008, esp. 266–304.

Christopher Fletcher

ENTRY #2

Ludolphus de Saxonia (c. 1295–1378), attributed
Le miroir de humaine saluation (Mirror of Human Salvation) 1455
Parchment with ink and gold leaf
VAULT folio* Case MS 40

Illuminated in Flanders by an unknown artist, this French manuscript associates Christian salvation with whiteness. Translated from its Latin original, *Le miroir de humaine saluation* explains salvation through typology—a method of biblical interpretation whereby events drawn from the Hebrew Bible were read as prophetic symbols of the New Testament. This artist used grisaille*, a technique for evoking depth in stone sculpture, in the three prefigurative scenes to convey how, just as colorful realism replaces inanimate stone, what was unrefined in the Hebrew Bible would be fulfilled by the New Testament. Across two pages side by side, the Adoration of the Magi is juxtaposed with a star guiding the Magi to Christ, three Israelite soldiers before King David, and the Queen of Sheba paying homage to Solomon, each prefiguration intended to prophesize the universal mission of Christendom that would draw Gentiles* and Jews towards Christ.

Solomon's ivory and gold throne was understood as a symbol of the Virgin Mary because ivory's "whiteness and coolness," as the text underneath the scene describes, symbolized her virginity. Delicate lines of gold embellishment adorn the white throne, mirroring the pale skin and blonde hair of the Virgin on the opposite page. Noticeably, the African Queen of Sheba and the Magus Balthazar are depicted with light skin and the Queen is seen from behind. European artists increasingly represented both figures with dark skin from the eleventh to the fifteenth centuries, and Balthazar in particular was painted Black in other *Miroirs* produced in Flanders in the mid-1400s. This manuscript perhaps more closely reflects the conventions of medieval French romances* that represented Saracen women who converted to Christianity or aided French armies with pale skin to convey virtue.

Further Readings

Kaplan, Paul. *The Rise of the Black Magus in Western Art*. Ann Arbor: UMI Research Press, 1985.

Weever, Jacqueline de. *Sheba's Daughters: Whitening and Demonizing the Saracen Woman in Medieval French Epic*. East Sussex: Psychology Press, 1998.

Wilson, Adrian, and Joyce Lancaster Wilson. *A Medieval Mirror: Speculum Humanae Salvationis 1324–1500*. Berkeley: University of California Press, 1984.

Caitlin DiMartino

Tres magi adorant xpm munera offerentes

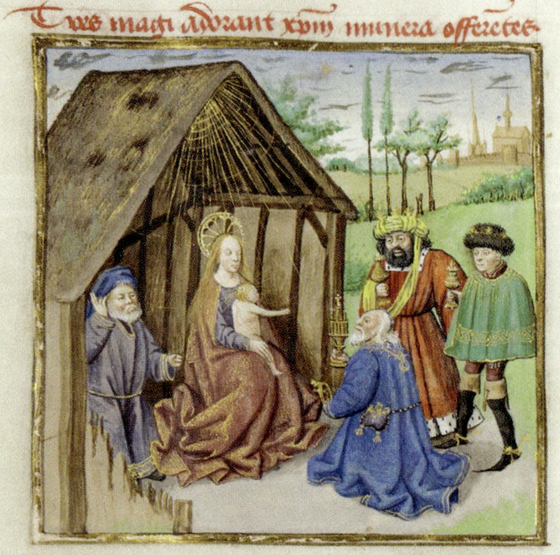

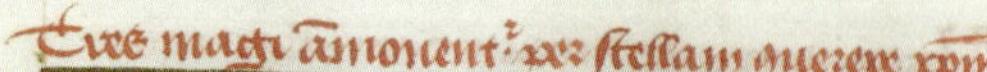

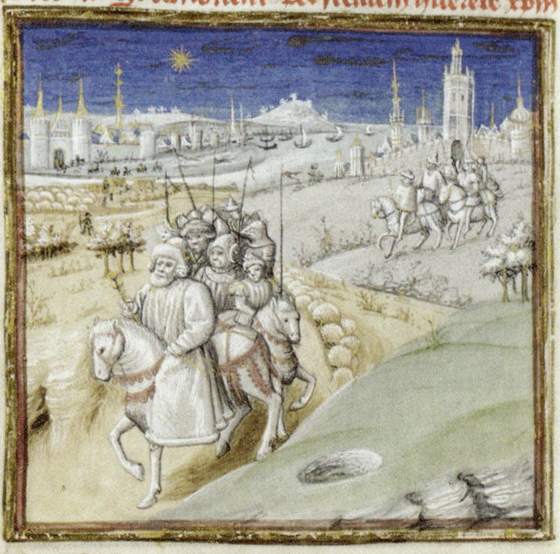

Mathei primo.

Ainsi que dessus est dit fu approuvee la nativite de nostre seigneur. Il est vray que au treizieme jour de la dicte nativite vindrent trois roys adorant en bethleem avecques grande devotion qui adorans icellui luy donnerent offrirent et firent trois dons. Or. Encens. et mirre. lesquelz roys Jaspar melcior et baltasar estoient paiens. Et la nuit de la nativite comme iceulx veissent la nuit clere et seraine. eulx qui souventeffois estudioient es circonstances des estoilles et du soleil. se partirent. et chascun en sa terre se mirent sur trois haultes montaignes de leurs pays. Puis se prindrent a contempler vers le firmament et tantost ilz veirent chascun par soy une estoille clerement reluisant ou moien de laquelle estoit la forme dun enfant de tant haulte facon et beaute quil enluminoit tout le ciel. et portoit une croix sur son chief toute dor resplendissant dont iceulx voians ce signe par grant admiration ne savoient que penser. Sy oyrent une voix par le vouloir divin disant. Vous qui veez ce signe ne vous esmerveilliez point car il vous denotte que le roy de tout le monde est ne en Judee et en la cite de bethleem le trouverez. Alez y et le adorez. laquelle voix oye ilz se mirent a genoulx rendans loanges audit enfant et promptement

In hystoria magorum

se partirent si vindrent comme dessus est dit. Lesquelz trois roys povons nous acomparer a trois hommes robustes et fors que le roy david envoia en bethleem querre de leaue dune cisterne sans craindre lexercite de leurs ennemis. mais hardiement et corageusement passans leurs chasteaulx et forteresses ilz espuisierent et prindrent de leaue de ladicte cisterne et le offrirent en trois vaissiaulx au roy david. par quoy povoit lors estre prophetisie que les trois roys devoient venir querre de leaue de la cisterne. cest assavoir de la fontaine de grace voire sans craindre la puissance de herode qui cuidoit estre souverain roy. car ilz le interroguerent du roy nouvel. lesquelz roys eurent de leaue de la cisterne celestre. et les trois robustes eurent de la terrestre. par quoy david qui tant fors hommes et robustes avoit estoit moult joyeux. comme estoit dieu par la conversion des roys paiens. car par icelle il prefiguroit la conversion des infideles. Et ainsy que david desiroit la vertu de ses hommes. Dieux desiroit le salut de son pueple. Et se aucun demandoit comment les trois roys qui estoient de tant lointain pays avoient peu venir en si brief temps en bethleem On puet respondre que cellui qui mena soudainement abacuc de judee en babilonne pareillement conduisi briefment iceulx trois roys des regions

Entry #2

Tres robusti attulerunt david aquam de cysterna betht

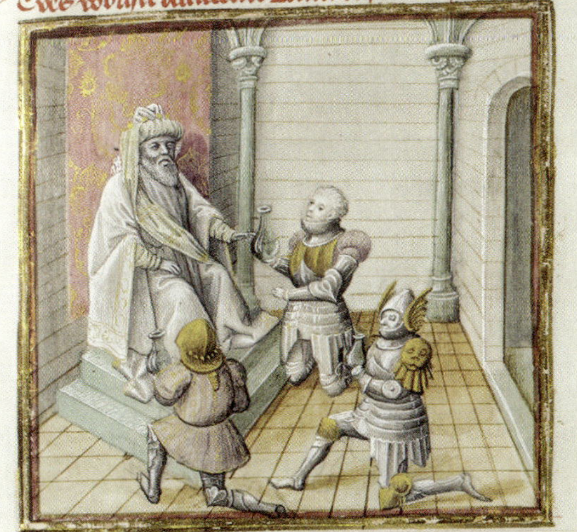

Thronus regis salomonis

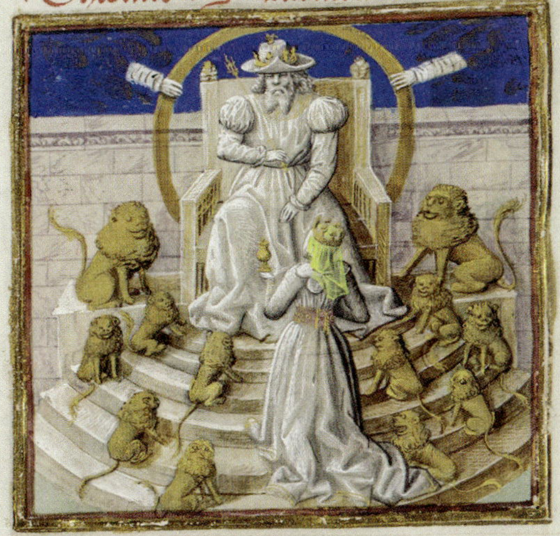

Sedi regum xxiii° Et pⁱmi palipo xi°

Vrient ces marches de Iudee. [C]La figure de
ce nouvel roy Iadis nous fut aucunement
demonstree ou regne du roy salomon. qui des
quil estoit en lestat de Ieunesse estoit tressage
Et dieu ne lestoit point moins en son enfance
que apres. Cestui salomon faisoit sa residence
en vng trosne dyuoire tresnet. et estoit vestu
de precieux et trespur or. si estoient tous les
roys de la terre pour celle preciosite desirans
le veoir et lui portoient plente de precieux dons
mais entre ces roys la royne sabba lui offri
vne fois telz Ioyaulx q̃ paravant en Iherusalem
nulz telz navoient este veus. Lequel throsne
de salomon est la benoite vierge marie. ouquel
estoit le roy vestu dor. cestassavoir ihũs plain
de vraie sagesse. Et estoit ce trosne fait dyuoire
moult noble resplendissant plus que lor. par
lequel noble yuoire pour sa splendeur et froi
deur signifie virginale chastete nette ⁊ pure
Et ainsi que lyuoire ancien prent couleur ver
meille. aussi chastete longue ⁊ de grant duree
est reputee martire. Et lor qui surmonte et
est de plus grant valeur que nulz autres de
metaulx signifie charite. laquelle est mere
principale et souveraine de toutes les autres
vertus. Si povons dire q̃ marie est dyuoire
po^r sa chastete. et pour sa charite vestue dor

Tercii regum x° et sedi paralipo ix°

tresprecieux. car a belle virginite affiert charite
sans laquelle virginite est devant dieu repu
tee de nulle valeur Car comme le larron ne
craint point la chandelle non ardante. aussy
le dyable ne doubte point chastete sans lard^r
de charite. Le throsne de salomon estoit emi
ne sur six degrez. car il avoit este fait apres
les vii. eages du monde. et estoit icellui de
core de xii. lyons beaulx et riches. et la som
mite dicellui throsne estoit rond. et le tenoiet
deux mains. et a brief parler en tous les di
vers royaumes du monde navoit point de
ouvrage tant riche et tant parfait. pourquoy
nous povons entendre par le throsne qui
estoit sur six degrez la vierge marie qui fut
monte six estats. cestassavoir des patriarches
prophetes appostles martirs confes ⁊ vierges
Et par les xii. beaulx lyons sur quoy ce thros
ne estoit assis peuent estre entendus les xii.
appostlez ou les xii. patriarches desqlz la benoite
vierge marie yssi. et par la rondeur du somet
du throsne q̊ estoit nonpareil doit estre entendue
la nettete de ladicte vierge q̊ estoit sans tache
le plus plentureux chief deuvre q̃ Iamais fu
veu entre les faiz de nature. Et po^r ce nous
ne no^s devons pas faindre doffrir a ce precieux
throsne riches Ioyaux attendu ce q̃ en povons avoir.

ENTRY #3 (NO IMAGE)

Wolfram von Eschenbach (c. 1160/80–c. 1220), author
Parsival, 1477
Book with letterpress*
VAULT folio Inc. 216

Although evidence indicates that people of color were physically present throughout Europe during the Middle Ages, white Europeans also "saw" them depicted in literary works. In these contexts, readers and hearers had the opportunity to play with the meaning behind phenomenological* differences like skin color. One of the clearest examples of this approach to seeing race is the character of Feirefiz, a biracial knight who plays a prominent role in *Parsival*, the most popular Arthurian romance in medieval Germany. The son of a white Christian knight and a Black "Saracen" queen, Feirefiz literally embodies the competing natures of his racial heritage: his skin is described as a patchwork of black and white "like a magpie," and he simultaneously displays the qualities white, noble Europeans ascribed to themselves (courage, martial skill, courtesy) and those they ascribed to non-white "Others" (ignorance of Christianity, pride, wealth). Medieval audiences thus understood Feirefiz not as an accurate representation of a biracial person (which many could certainly have seen in person), but as an invitation to playfully envision the social, moral, and biological implications of racial difference. This open-minded approach to seeing race contributed to *Parsival*'s enduring popularity during the Middle Ages (parts of it survive in nearly hundred medieval manuscripts and the 1477 printed edition shown here), but fell out of favor in the early modern period, when the colonial system demanded more stringent legal distinctions between white Europeans and the peoples of color they subjugated and enslaved.

Further Readings

Hahn, Thomas, ed. Special Issue on Race and Ethnicity in the Middle Ages. *Journal of Medieval and Early Modern Studies* 31, no. 1 (2001).

Heng, Geraldine. *The Invention of Race in the European Middle Ages*. Cambridge: Cambridge University Press, 2018, esp. 181–256.

Whitaker, Cord J., *Black Metaphors: How Modern Racism Emerged from Medieval Race-Thinking*. Philadelphia: University of Pennsylvania Press, 2019.

Christopher Fletcher

ENTRY #4

A. Andrea Alciato (1492–1550), author; Jollat(?), artist
Andreae Alciati Emblematum libellus, 1536
Book with letterpress and woodcuts
Case W 1025 .0165

B. Andrea Alciato (1492–1550), author; Barthélemy Aneau (c. 1510–1561), translator and commentator
Emblèmes d'Alciat: en latin et françois vers pour vers: ordonnez en lieux communs auec briefues expositions et figures propres: auec la table d'iceux, mise à la fin, 1561
Book with letterpress and engravings
Wing ZP 539 .M3675

C. George Whitney (1548?–1601?), author
A Choice of Emblemes and other Devises, for the Moste Parte Gathered Out of Sundrie Writers, Englished and Moralized, 1586
Book with letterpress and engravings
Case W 1025 .0165

Emblems were one of the most significant sites for early modern Europeans to think through visual culture. By the middle of the sixteenth century, authors and artists deployed them in a variety of visual media —books, public monuments, household objects, and so on—in order to provide entertainment and instruction for their readers in a range of topics, from religion to politics to primary education. In all these

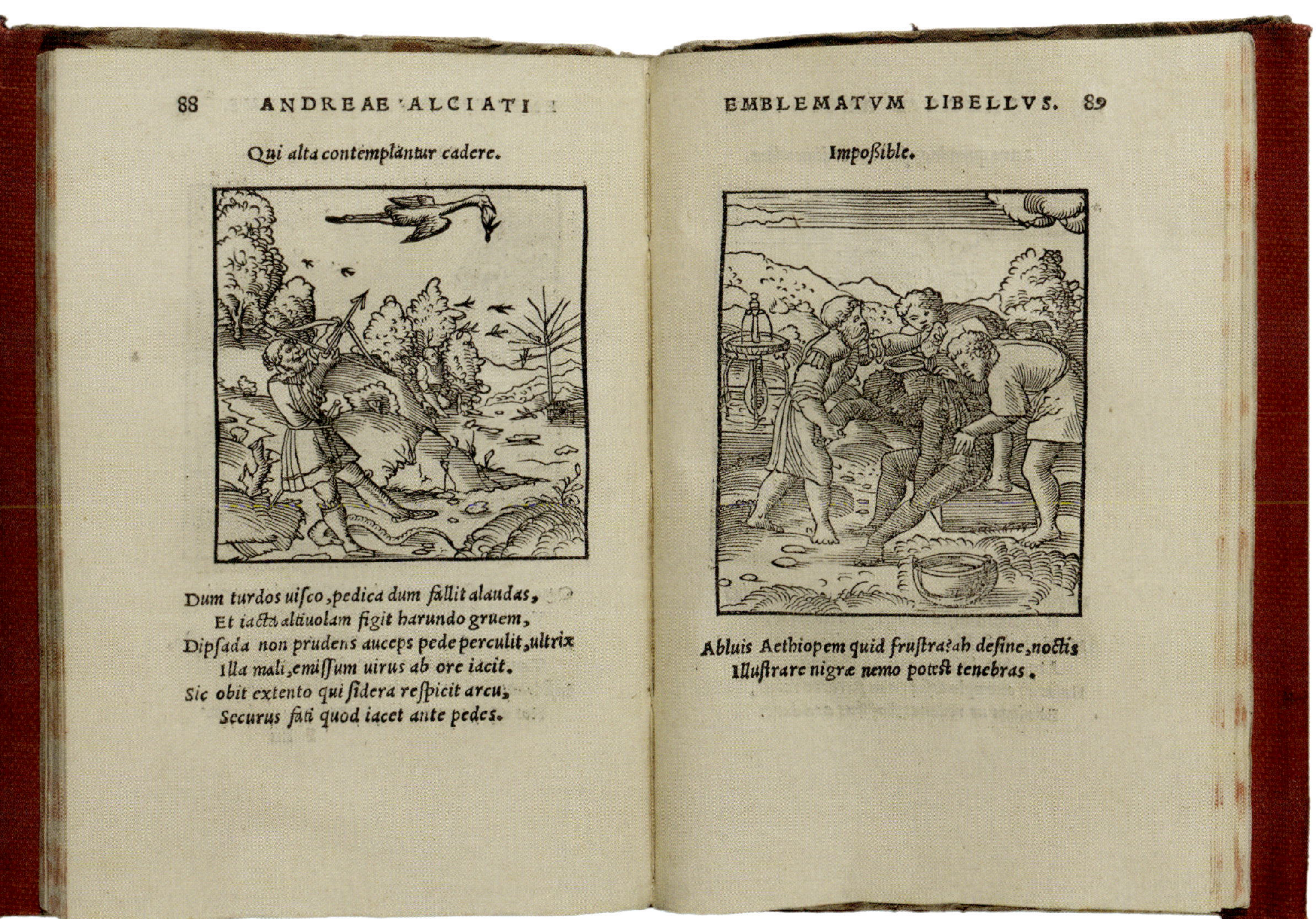
88 ANDREAE ALCIATI

Qui alta contemplantur cadere.

Dum turdos uiſco, pedica dum fallit alaudas,
Et iacta altiuolam figit harundo gruem,
Dipſada non prudens auceps pede perculit, ultrix
Illa mali, emiſſum uirus ab ore iacit.
Sic obit extento qui ſidera reſpicit arcu,
Securus fati quod iacet ante pedes.

EMBLEMATVM LIBELLVS. 89

Impoßible.

Abluis Aethiopem quid fruſtra? ah deſine, noctis
Illuſtrare nigræ nemo poteſt tenebras.

Entry #4A

formats, emblems functioned as literary-visual puzzles that consisted of a titular inscription (*motto*), an image (*pictura*), and a short text (*subscriptio*), which was usually an epigram*. Viewers, often working together in groups, used the different elements of the emblem to interpret and comment on the others in order to decipher or invent some kind of lesson or truth that would help them understand the natural world, human behavior, religious truth, and how all should properly work. In this, emblems played an important role in how European audiences made sense of the rapidly expanding and diversifying world in the sixteenth century. Naturally, then, audiences throughout Europe also used emblems to think about race, which was becoming ever more visually present in their daily lives.

Emblems functioned as another way to implicitly or explicitly categorize physical differences between peoples. One of the clearest examples of this was an emblem depicting the fruitless effort to wash the blackness out of an Ethiopian man, shown here in three different emblem books produced between 1536 and 1586. All three use this image to illustrate an impossible task, thus reinforcing the notion that

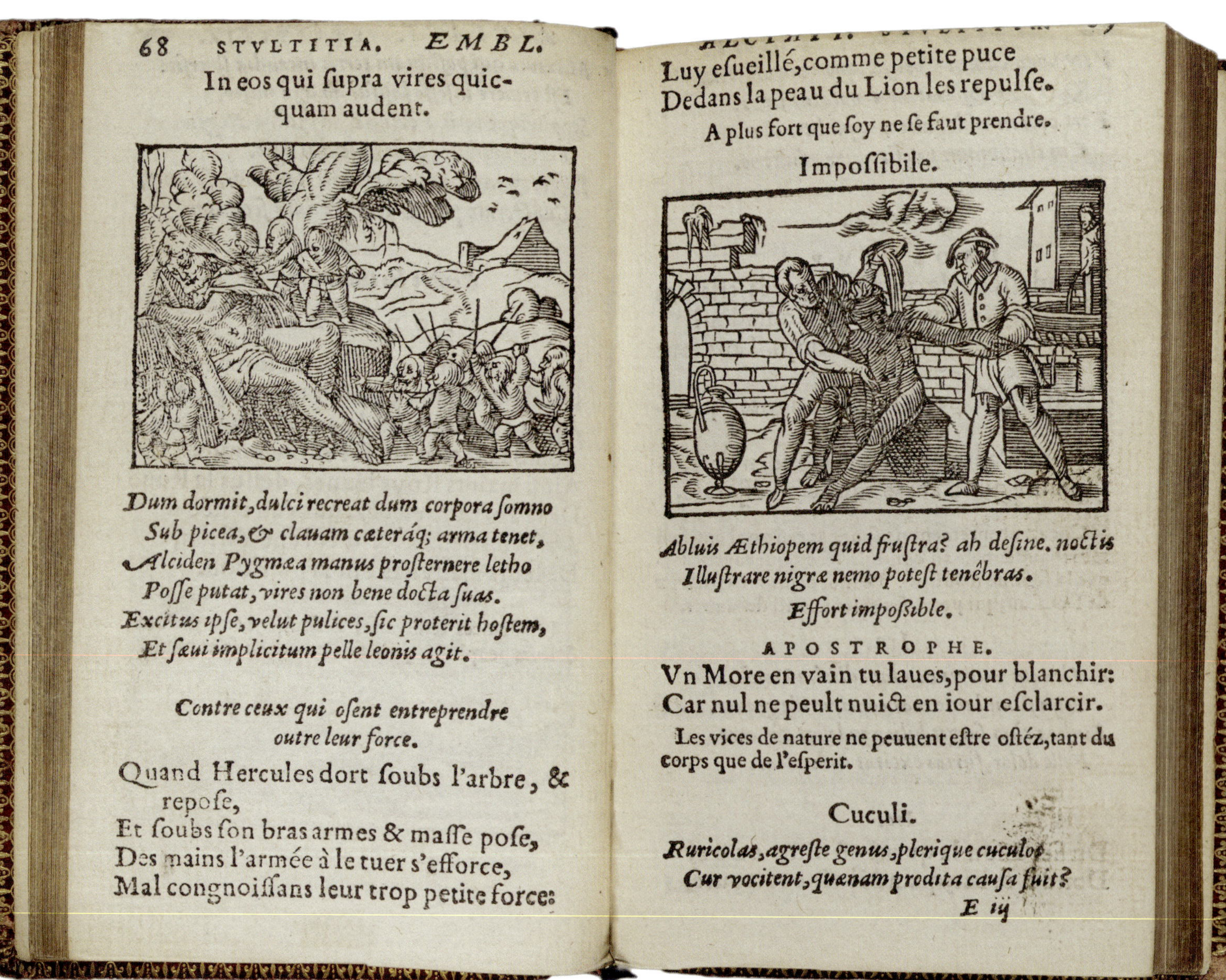

68 STVLTITIA. EMBL.

In eos qui ſupra vires quicquam audent.

Dum dormit, dulci recreat dum corpora ſomno
Sub picea, & clauam cæteráq; arma tenet,
Alciden Pygmæa manus proſternere letho
Poſſe putat, vires non bene docta ſuas.
Excitus ipſe, velut pulices, ſic proterit hoſtem,
Et ſæui implicitum pelle leonis agit.

Contre ceux qui oſent entreprendre outre leur force.

Quand Hercules dort ſoubs l'arbre, & repoſe,
Et ſoubs ſon bras armes & maſſe poſe,
Des mains l'armée à le tuer s'efforce,
Mal congnoiſſans leur trop petite force:
Luy eſueillé, comme petite puce
Dedans la peau du Lion les repulſe.

A plus fort que ſoy ne ſe faut prendre.

Impoſſibile.

Abluis Æthiopem quid fruſtra? ah deſine. noctis
Illuſtrare nigræ nemo poteſt tenebras.

Effort impoſſible.

APOSTROPHE.

Vn More en vain tu laues, pour blanchir:
Car nul ne peult nuict en iour eſclarcir.

Les vices de nature ne peuuent eſtre oſtéz, tant du corps que de l'eſperit.

Cuculi.

Ruricolas, agreſte genus, plerique cuculos
Cur vocitent, quænam prodita cauſa fuit?

E iij

Entry #4B

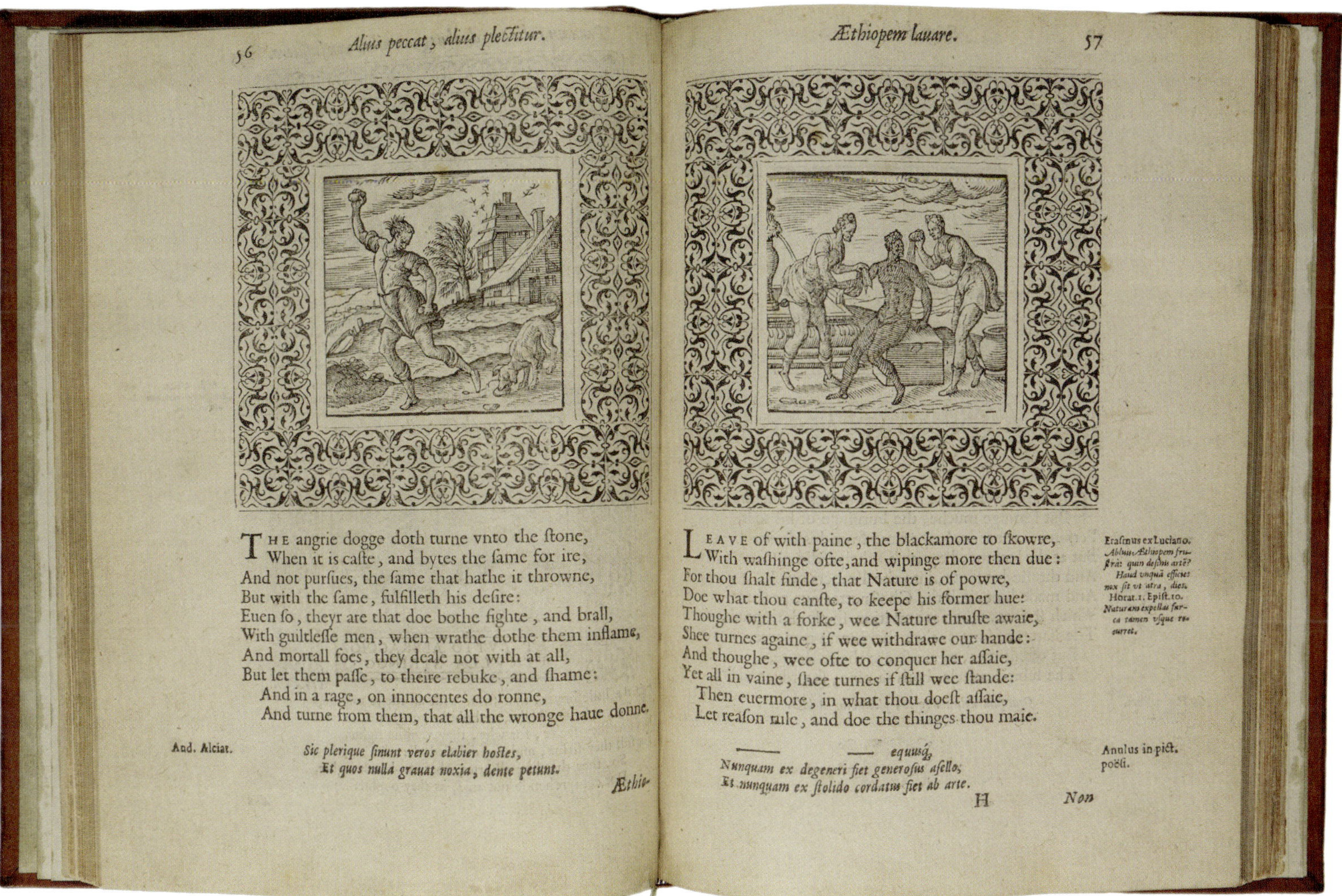

56 *Alius peccat, alius plectitur.*

THE angrie dogge doth turne vnto the ſtone,
When it is caſte, and bytes the ſame for ire,
And not purſues, the ſame that hathe it throwne,
But with the ſame, fulfilleth his deſire:
Euen ſo, theyr are that doe bothe fighte, and brall,
With guiltleſſe men, when wrathe dothe them inflame,
And mortall foes, they deale not with at all,
But let them paſſe, to theire rebuke, and ſhame:
And in a rage, on innocentes do ronne,
And turne from them, that all the wronge haue donne.

And. Alciat.

Sic plerique ſinunt veros elabier hoſtes,
Et quos nulla grauat noxia, dente petunt.

Æthio-

Æthiopem lauare. 57

LEAVE of with paine, the blackamore to ſkowre,
With waſhinge ofte, and wipinge more then due:
For thou ſhalt finde, that Nature is of powre,
Doe what thou canſte, to keepe his former hue:
Thoughe with a forke, wee Nature thruſte awaie,
Shee turnes againe, if wee withdrawe our hande:
And thoughe, wee ofte to conquer her aſſaie,
Yet all in vaine, ſhee turnes if ſtill wee ſtande:
Then euermore, in what thou doeſt aſſaie,
Let reaſon rule, and doe the thinges thou maie.

Eraſmus ex Luciano.
Abluis Æthiopem fruſtra: quin deſinis artē?
Haud vnquā efficies nox ſit vt atra, dies.
Horat. 1. Epiſt. 10.
Naturam expellas furca tamen vſque recurret.

——— ——— *equuſq́,*
Nunquam ex degeneri fiet generoſus aſello;
Et nunquam ex ſtolido cordatus fiet ab arte.

Anulus in pict. poeſi.

H *Non*

Entry #4C

skin color, as it is a product of "Nature," could be used to sharply delineate one people from another. Although the emblem could be used to consider an endless variety of impossible tasks or irreconcilable differences in nearly endless contexts, this particular *pictura*—which appeared in hundreds of emblem books throughout Europe—also served to reinforce the hardening power dynamics between white-skinned Europeans and Black Africans, who were, at the very same time, being enslaved to work in European colonies in ever-growing numbers. The three emblem books considered here, for example, would have first reached audiences in France and England, at a time when colonial aspirations were just becoming economic and political priorities for each kingdom. Within this context, white French and English readers could hardly have missed the "truth" of European supremacy expressed by the image of fully clothed white men forcibly washing the skin of a naked Black man, who seems, in all three cases, resigned to his fate. In this, the emblematic treatment of "washing the Ethiopian white" confirmed the assumed primacy of white Europeans in the new world order, demonstrating how, even when solving puzzles with friends for their own entertainment, Europeans were constantly reminded of their fantasized racial dominance.

Further Readings

Daly, Peter M. *The Emblem in Early Modern Europe: Contributions to the Theory of the Emblem*. New York: Routledge, 2014.

Manning, John. *The Emblem*. London: Reaktion, 2002.

Spicer, Joaneath, ed. *Revealing the African Presence in Renaissance Europe*. Baltimore: Walters Art Museum, 2012, 126. Exhibition catalog.

Christopher Fletcher

ENTRY #5

Albrecht Dürer (1471–1528), author; Charles Perier, Publisher
Les Qvatre livres d'Albert Dvrer, peinctre & geometrien tres excellent, de la proportion des parties & pourtraicts des corps humains (The Four Books on Human Proportion), 1557
Book with letterpress and woodcuts
Wing folio ZP 539.P412

Albrecht Dürer intended the *Four Books on Human Proportion* to aid artists in drawing human figures. The text defines several ideal types of human physiognomy based on the measurements and proportions of different limbs described in classical sources. It then explains how artists can apply mathematical projections to alter these types and generate varied, imagined, human forms like the profiles shown here at left. Dürer also envisioned this system as a means of comparing real, observed physiognomies to these ideal types, believing that deviations from the ideal were linked to a person's race and character. At right, the profile drawn with curly hair compares a Black African sitter drawn from life to an "ideal" profile with particular attention to the sitter's nose. Elsewhere in this text Dürer claimed that African faces, and especially noses, were less "handsome" than Europeans'.

While Dürer's system is ungainly—some sixteenth-century users complained that it was difficult to apply in practice—in this edition, stains splashed on the page at left, may attest to this text's use. The *Four Books on Human Proportion* ultimately became widely

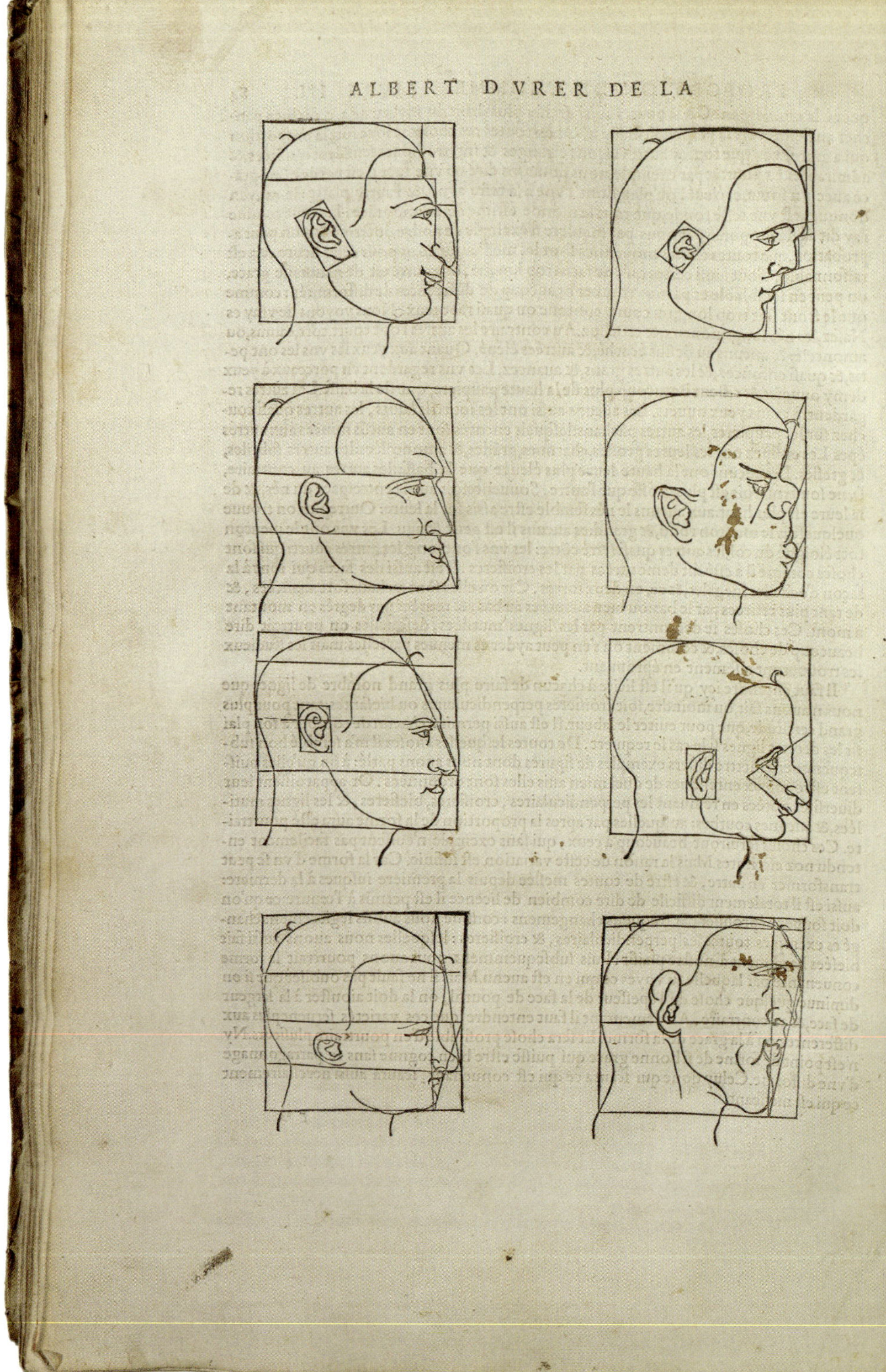

PROPORTION DE L'HOMME. LIVRE III. 85

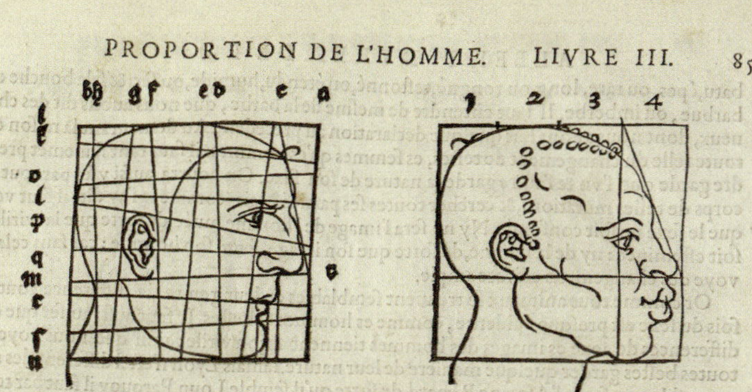

Il reſte que nous parlions du changement des effigies de front, & de leurs variations. Mais pour autant que la raiſon de remuer les croiſieres, de toutes les effigies de pourfil eſt de meſme de celles de front:c'eſt donc pour ceſt heure temps perdu de parler des varietés des croiſieres. Tant ſeulement vous veux ie bien auertir que les croiſieres peuuent eſtre toutes bieſées,ou en partie en celle de front. Les faces de vray ſont auſsi bien torces, comme quand vn coté du quarre eſt raualé, & l'autre eleué. Pourſuyuons donques le propos des perpendiculaires : leſquelles comme ſuyuant noſtre doctrine elles ſoient notées dedans les cotés a.b. des lettres I.g.c.d.e.f.h. k. & qu'elles notent les principales parties, comme le front, les yeux,le nés, les oreilles,la bouche, & le menton,elles peuuent chacune,ou partie, ou bien toutes eſtre remuées de leur lieu: de ſorte que comme plus elles ſeront diſtantes, de tant plus grande ſera la largeur:& plus proches, de tant plus ſera elle moindre: Mais encor ſont elles pourtraites de ſorte, que quaſi elles ſ'aſſemblent par le haut : & ſemblent au deſſous ſ'entrefuir,& au contraire.

On les pourtrait auſsi panchantes,& lors elles ne tirent plus à plomb,eſtans ou bieſantes, ou courbes. Touchant ceſte raiſon tu trouueras en la forme exprimée , le front ſ'elargir,ou reſerrer:& entre les angles des yeux des petis eſpaces grandelets,ou étroits,& entre eux, interualles plus grans, ou plus reſerrés . Les yeux auſsi pourront eſtre notés d'inegale grandeur,& lieu,& les paupieres,& ſourcils. Tu verras auſsi à l'vn le nés aggrandi,à l'autre retiré haut, ou bas:le meſmes encores droit, & auſsi courbe : amoncelé , ou agu : plein, ou noueux, étroit iuſques aux narilles , elles eſtans ouuertes. Ou bien au contraire , au deſſus d'elles fort élargi, elles eſtans fort ſerrées. Nous pourrons dire le ſemblable de l'étendue, ou reſerrement de la bouche, menton, & machoueres. Et de chacune partie qui au deſſus ſera reſerrée & au deſſous étendue, & au contraire. Par ceſte voye donques d'inegaleté les faces ſont pourtraites boſſues,ou torſes,& étranges en pluſieurs ſortes,comme d'vne bouche étroite , ou grande , à leures courbes,groſſes, petites, grandes , ou bien inegales , machoueres amples, reſerrées , agues, mouces , d'vne iointe apparente , ou non . Toutes leſquelles choſes & diuerſités vn ſtudieux lecteur , & experimenté deura exprimer , dont il pourra découurir beaucoup de choſes admirables , qui y ſont cachées. Il n'eſt rien ſi certain, que ceux qui ont la cognoiſſance de la difformité , & laidure , pourront facilement entendre ce qui leur eſt à euiter en vne entreprinſe d'vn ouurage de bonne grace. Il eſt de vray neceſſaire que comme plus quelqu'vn fuira la difformité , de tant plus approchera il de la beauté. Celuy à qui ces choſes ſeront manifeſtes entendra facilement, & appertement comment vne choſe eſt differente d'vne autre , & la raiſon eſt : que non ſeulement auiendra neceſſairement es plates peintures, mais auſsi es ouurages taillés, & burinés.Leſquels celuy qui entreprendra ignorant ceſte raiſon(combien qu'il face quelque choſe proportionnée, & egale:)ce ſera toutesfois d'auanture,& non d'art.

Mais reuenons à noſtre propos. La face apparoit autre aſsiſe ſur vn col long, & greſle, & autre ſur vn court,& gros. Outreplus il faut prendre garde aux lineamens de la face,leſquels aux vns ſont grans, & pleins d'yeux,de nés, & menton, aux autres menus,& preſſés. Les faces auſsi apparoiſſent autres ſi la teſte eſt cheuelue, ou raſe, ou à poil creſpelu,ou ab-

p iij

popular. First published in German in 1528, the book was translated into five languages, and issued in more than 15 different editions over the subsequent 125 years, including three (French, Italian, and German) in the Newberry collection alone. The work's popularity speaks to the appeal in the early modern period of the possibility, whether theoretical or applied, of quantifying human difference on the basis of the repeatable interpretation of visible signifiers.

Further Readings

Koerner, Leo Joseph. "The Epiphany of the Black Magus circa 1500." In *The Image of the Black in Western Art*, edited by David Bindman and Henry Louis Gates, 3:7–92. Cambridge, MA: Belknap Press of Harvard University Press, 2010, 86–89.

Smith, Jeffrey Chipps. *Dürer*. London: Phaidon Press, 2012, 365–69.

Spicer, Joaneath, ed. *Revealing the African Presence in Renaissance Europe*. Baltimore: The Walters Art Museum, 2012, 46. Exhibition catalog.

Olivia Dill

ENTRY #6

Antonio de Nebrija (1444?–1522), author; Anonymous, transcriber
"Negreguear" entry, in *Dictionarium ex Hisniensi in Latinum sermonem*
(also known as *Vocabulario trilingüe*, that is, *Trilingual Vocabulary*), 1540
Manuscript VAULT Ayer MS 1478

Antonio de Nebrija's reputation as an authority on vernacular* languages was solidified after he systematized Castilian grammar with a treatise in 1492 and debuted a Spanish-Latin dictionary three years later. The Newberry's *Dictionarium ex Hisniensi in Latinum sermonem* (1540) is attributed to him as well, since its trilingual body, composed of Latin, Spanish, and manuscript Nahuatl (one of the native languages of modern-day Mexico), is largely based on his dictionary's second edition (1516). Several subsequent versions of this early pair were printed in Salamanca and Seville respectively and circulated throughout New Spain, the East Indies, and elsewhere in Europe, as imperial lexicographical* templates from the sixteenth century onward.

The anonymous scholar who copied by hand entries from Nebrija's printed bilingual dictionary in this manuscript is believed to have been an Indigenous person fluent in Nahuatl. Presumably writing for a Nahua audience, the scribe augmented more than 70 percent of the original Spanish-Latin entries in black ink with nearly 12,000 Nahuatl translations just below them in red ink. The resulting modified manuscript of Ayer 1478 is also comprised of idioms and lengthier explanations for incommensurable terms, including religiously inflected vocabulary predicated on Christian worldviews. The appearance of *"negreguear"* alongside *"nigreo"*—meaning "to blacken" or "become black" in Spanish and Latin—within its pages signals the confluence of cosmological*, chromatic, and racial import. It further gestures towards the occulted role that Black African -derived people would come to play in seemingly bipartisan debates around settler-native encounters in the New World. Though not accompanied by a third translation, the Nahuatl cognate for black *"tlíltic"* is listed above this entry in the same column.

Further Readings

Clayton, Mary L. "Evidence for a Native-Speaking Nahuatl Author in the Ayer *Vocabulario Trilingüe*." *International Journal of Lexicography* 16, no. 2 (2003), 99–119. https://doi.org/10.1093/ijl/16.2.99.

Wynter, Sylvia. "1492: A New World View." In *Race, Discourse, and the Origin of the Americas: A New World View*, edited by Vera Lawrence Hyatt and Rex Nettleford, 1–57. Washington, DC: Smithsonian Institution press, 1995.

Cecilio M. Cooper

Naue o naueta de encensio. acerra.e.
Nauegable cosa. nauigabilis.e. acallica panauiloni
Nauegar o iorro. remulco.as. aui.
Nauegar hasta el cabo. enauigo.as.aui.
Nauegar con velas tendidas. velifico.as. quauhpantire nipano
Nauegar con remos. remigo.as. nitlaneloa
Nauegar como quiera. nauigo.as. lego.is. nacalpano
Nauegar para placer. nauiculor.aris.
Nauegar allende. transfreto.as. nacalmpano
Naues echar al agua. deduco naues. nacallatoctia
Naues sacar del agua. subduco naues. nacalaluacaquictia
Nauidad. natalis christi ang. nō natiuitas. itlacatiliz intotecuio ihu xpo
Nauigacion. nauigatio. onis. etc. acalpanoliztli
Nauigacion allende. transfretatio. anal onpanoliztli
Nauio lo mesmo q naue. nauigiū. ii. castilla acalli
¶ Neboda yerua conocida. nepeta.e.
Neblina o niebla. nebula.e. aiauitl
Neblina o niebla hazer. nebulo.as. naiauhchichioa
Nebli especie de halcō. accipiter colūbarius. tlotli
Necedad. inscicia.e. insipiētia. ignorantia. atlamatiliztli
Necessaria cosa. necessarius.a.ū. cenca monequini
Necessario en genero neutro. necessuz.
Necessaria mente. necessario. necesse.
Necessidad. necessitas. necessitudo.
Necessaria o priuada. latrina. forica. axixcalli

Necio. insciens.a. ignarus.a.ū. amo tlamatini
Neciamente. ignoranter. amotlamatca
Negar. nego.as. inficias eo. amo nicnomachitoca
Negacio en esta manera. negatio amo natlamachitoquiliztli
Negar q no lo hizo. inficior. inficias eo
Negador en esta manera. inficiator. amo motlamachitoani
Negacion en esta manera. inficiatio
Negar cō iuramento. abnego.as. teixiotica amo ninotlamachitoca
Negacion assi. abnegatio. onis.
Negar sacudiendo la cabeça. renuo.is. ninotzontecomiicoa
Negacion assi. abnutus.us. netzontecomiuiuicoliztli
Negar lo pedido. abnego.as.
Negar hasta el cabo. pernego.as.
Neguijon de dientes. scabricia dentius. tlanqualiztli
Negligente cosa desquidada. negligens.tis. cuitlacotlar tlatziuhqui
Negligentia este desquydo. negligentia.e. cuitlacotlaualiztli
Negligentemente. negligenter. tlatziuhca
Negocio cōtrario de ocio. negociū.ii. netlacuitlauiliztli
Negociado llano de negocios. negociosus.a. motlacuitlauiani
Negocial cosa de negocio. negocialis.e.
Negociar. negocior. aris. res ago. ninotlacuitlauia
Negociador. negociator. rerū actor. motlacuitlauiani
Negociacion. negociatio. rerū actio. netlacuitlauiliztli
Negociador en mercaderia. institor. oris. tlanecuiloani

Negra cosa. niger.a.ū. ater.a.ū. tlitic
Negro. pullus.a.ū. aquilus.a.ū. tlitic
Negro vn poco. subniger.a.ū. achitlitic. iaiactic
Negro de guinea. ethiops.pis tlilticatl
Negra de guinea. ethiopissa.e. cioatl tlitic
Negreguear. nigreo.es. nigresco. nitliliui. nitlilihuitia
Negreguear por de fuera. nigrico.as.
Negro hazer. nigrefacio.is. denigro.as. nitlatliloa
Negro hazer de blanco. decoloro.as.
Negror. nigredo. nigricia. nigror. tliliuiliztli
Negror. atritas.atis. atror.oris.
Negromancia diuinacion. necromantia.
Negromantico diuino assi. necromanticus.a.ū.
Nenufar o escudete yerua. nimphea.e.
Neruio de los animales. neruus.i. tlalhuatl
Neruioso cosa rezia por ellos. neruosus.a.ū. tlaluaio
Neruiosidad de neruios. neruositas. atis. tlaluaiotl
Neruiosa cosa de neruios. neruaceus.a.ū.
Neruio espesso & calloso. torus.i.
Neruioso en esta manera. torosus a.ū.
Neruiosidad assi. torositas. atis.
Neruiar trauar cō neruios. neruo. as. nitlalhoaioa
Neuar hazer nieue. ningo.is.xi. nicepaiaui
¶ Ni coniuncion. ne. ne. nec. neq. amono
Ni vno ni otro. neuter.a.um. aicma momenti

Ni a vna parte ni a otra. neutro adv. acan
Ni en vn lugar ni en otro. neutrubi. adverbiū. acampa
Nidal o nido de aues. nidus.i. tapaculli
Nidal hueuo del nido. ouum nidale.
Nido hazer el aue. nidifico.as. ninotapacoltia
Niebla o neblina. nebula.e. aiauitl
Nieruo. lo mesmo es que neruio. texocoquahuitl
Niespero arbol conocido. mespilus.i.
Niespero fruta deste arbol. mespilū. i. texocotl
Nieto tercero. nepos ex filio vl filia. ixhuiuhtli
Nieta. neptis ex filio vel filia. ciua ixhuiuhtli
Nieto dos vezes. pronepos. otis.
Nieta assi. proneptis.
Nieto tercero. abnepos. otis.
Nieta tercera. abneptis. is.
Nietos decendientes abaxo. minores. us. catepantlacatini
Nieue. nix. niuis. grece chion. cepaiahuitl
Ninguna cosa. nil. nihil. nihilū. i. atlei
Ningun hombre o muger. nemo. inis.
Ninguno como quiera. nullus.a.ū. aiac
Niño o niña q aun no habla. infans. tis. conetl
Niño o niña de teta. lactens. tis. cone chichini
Niño o niña pequeños. pupus. pupa. conetl
Niñez edad de aquestos. infantia.e. coconeiotl
Niñerias de aquestos. nimię. ay. pipillotl

Entry #6

ENTRY #7

William Blathwayt (1649–1717), Secretary for Trade and Plantations (1675–1679)
The Short State of Barbados and the Government Thereof: A Remarkably Interesting Manuscript, 1638
Ayer MS 827

This document from 1684 features in the collection of William Blathwayt, who served as assistant secretary of trade and plantations of England from 1675 until he was promoted to full secretary in 1679. The manuscript, whose scribe is unknown, begins with a narrative section logging the "situation," "extent," and "discovery" of the island of Barbados, which the author notes was "found uninhabited and very fit for a plantation" and then documents the English's role in creating and maintaining foundational legal structures to govern the institution of slavery, with slave law codification occurring in Barbados in 1661 and 1688. The document makes clear that Barbadians made racialized distinctions between those who would be indentured* for life, and those who would serve under contract. Inhabitants were sorted into four different categories: "Freeholders, "Freemen," "Servants," and "Slaves." While the former three sorts contain no mention of race, "Slaves" are described specifically as "the Negros brought thither from the coast of Guiny, Cormantine [?], and Madagascar, who live as slaves to their Mastirs."

The population census is divided into "Whites" and "Blacks" with totals of 19,566 and 66,070 respectively. The document refers to the "acquisition" of "St. Lucia, Dominico, St. Vincents, and others," with "St. Vincents" being inhabited by "Negroes which are come thither either out of Ships driven upon the Coast by stormes, or else escaped from their Masters in neighboring Colonies." It is noted that there are several islands which are "uninhabitable" due to the "Native Inhabitants" who "bear soe great hatred to the English, that as they doe continualy annoy them, even in time of Peace with the Neighbouring Colonies." This manuscript largely logs statistical, governmental, and geographic particulars, but the contents additionally offer a narrative of Black and Indigenous resistance to colonization, the author noting that the "Native Inhabitants" are "like to bee most dangerous and pernicious Enemies," and especially so "in conjunction with any Foreign State."

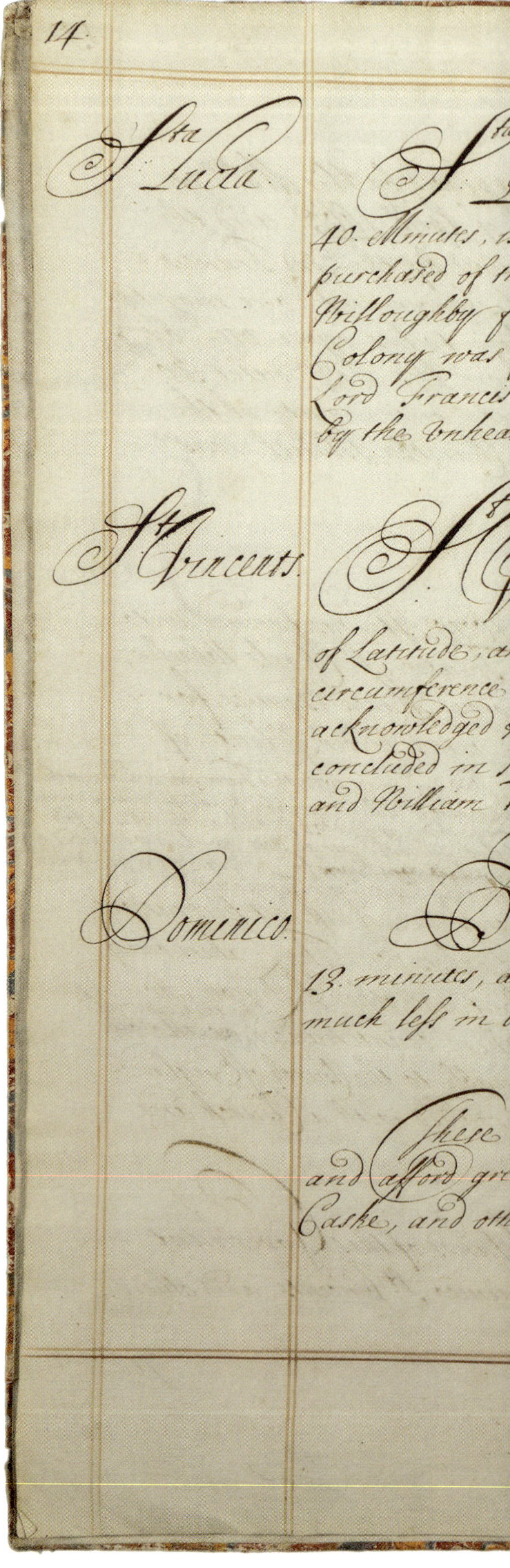

Further Readings

Pettigrew, William A. "Free to Enslave: Politics and the Escalation of Britain's Transatlantic Slave Trade, 1688–1714." *The William and Mary Quarterly* 64, no. 1 (2007): 3–38. http://www.jstor.org/stable/4491595.

Rugemer, Edward B. "The Development of Mastery and Race in the Comprehensive Slave Codes of the Greater Caribbean during the Seventeenth Century." *The William and Mary Quarterly* 70, no. 3 (2013): 429–58. https://doi.org/10.5309/willmaryquar.70.3.0429.

Alana Edmondson

lying at 13 Degrees and
the bignes of Barbados, —
s by the Lord William —
Maties use. A small
y sent hither by the
ghby, part whereof dyed
of the aire.

t is situate in 26 Degrees
ins about 25 leagues in
e Inhabitants have —
ties Sovereignty by Articles
tween their Cheife Captains,
Lord Willoughby.

ico lyes at 15 Degrees,
leagues long, and not

are very mountainous
of Timber for Shipping,

They

Inhabitants.

They are inhabited by Indians who were 1500 strong in Bowmen, but their number at present is not soe great.

In St Vincents are 600 Negroes which are come thither either out of Ships driven upon the Coast by storme, or else escaped from their Masters in ye neighboring Colonies.

Of late some French Families have setled themselves upon these Islands.

Other Islands.

There are severall other Islands within ye limits of this Goverment, which as they are either possessed by the French, or unfit for inhabitation or any other use are not taken notice of as particularly belonging to his Ma^ty; the Native Inhabitants whereof, and of all other the Charibbee Islands, bear soe great hatred to the English, that as they doe continualy annoy them, even in time of Peace with the Neighbouring Colonies, soe they are, in time of Warr, like to bee most dangerous and pernicious Enemees, in conjunction with any Forreign State.

Entry #7

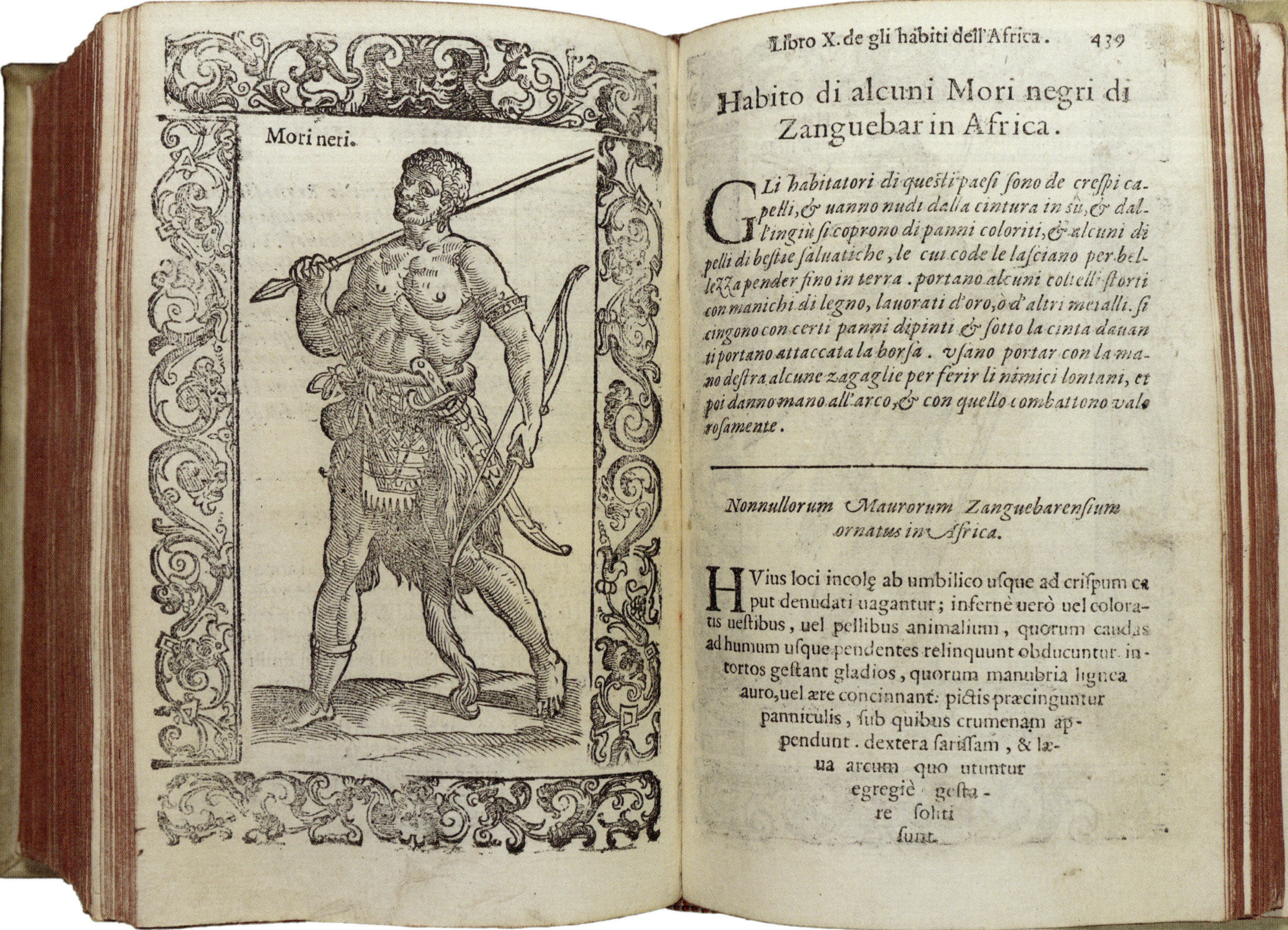

Mori neri.

Libro X. de gli habiti dell'Africa. 439

Habito di alcuni Mori negri di Zanguebar in Africa.

GLi habitatori di questi paesi sono de crespi capelli, & uanno nudi dalla cintura in sù, & dall'ingiù si coprono di panni coloriti, & alcuni di pelli di bestie saluatiche, le cui code le lasciano per bellezza pender fino in terra. portano alcuni coltelli storti con manichi di legno, lauorati d'oro, ò d'altri metalli. si cingono con certi panni dipinti & sotto la cinta dauanti portano attaccata la borsa. vsano portar con la mano destra alcune zagaglie per ferir li nimici lontani, et poi danno mano all'arco, & con quello combattono valorosamente.

Nonnullorum Maurorum Zanguebarensium ornatus in Africa.

HVius loci incolę ab umbilico usque ad crispum caput denudati uagantur; infernè uerò uel coloratis uestibus, uel pellibus animalium, quorum caudas ad humum usque pendentes relinquunt obducuntur. intortos gestant gladios, quorum manubria lignea auro, uel ære concinnant: pictis præcinguntur panniculis, sub quibus crumenam appendunt. dextera sarissam, & læua arcum quo utuntur egregiè gestare soliti sunt.

Entry #8

Case Study #2: Gendering Race (Women, Race, Aesthetics)

ENTRY #8

Cesare Vecellio (approx. 1521–1601), author; Christoph Chrieger (active sixteenth century), artist of woodcuts (based on Vecellio's drawings); Sulstatius Gratilianus (active sixteenth century), translator (Italian texts into Latin)
Habiti antichi et moderni di tutto il mondo—Vestitus antiquorum recentiorumque totius orbis
(Of Costumes, Ancient and Modern, of Different Parts of the World), 1598
(second edition; first edition was published in 1590)
Book with letterpress and woodcuts

Cesare Vecellio's costume book *Habiti antichi e moderni* (1598) offers an encyclopedic and partly historical treatment of dress. The images are organized hierarchically by continent: European dress takes up the bulk of the book, followed by sections on Asian, African, and American dress. Dress was one dimension of "habit," which in the early modern period referred to the web of customs, manners, and morals that distinguished various cultures. However, the wide circulation of Vecellio's costume books across Europe did more than mark cultural difference: his images of dress also helped construct notions of racial difference.

Vecellio's information about European dress came in part from first-hand encounters in cosmopolitan Venice, but most of his information about Asian, African, and American dress was drawn from secondary sources, such as Theodor de Bry's *Les Grands Voyages* (1590). The depiction of an Indigenous Floridian woman in "Clothing of a Queen" was modeled on a similar image from de Bry. Standing decontextualized from her social and natural surroundings, the woman is positioned as an Eve-like figure. Her partial nudity starkly contrasts with the elaborate, historically contextualized dress of Venetian nobility.

In the section on African dress, Vecellio features more images of men than women. His depictions of African men, such as "The Black Moor from Zanzibar," often feature darkly shaded skin and exaggerated facial features, accompanied by negative commentary. In contrast, his few depictions of African women emphasize their dress rather than physiognomic difference. The lack of representation of Black women raises questions about the gendered nature of early modern racial prejudice. Asian cultures occupy a higher position in Vecellio's continental hierarchy: for instance, he accurately included the Persian terms used for their job titles and garments of the Ottoman Sultan's Persian staff bearers. While Vecellio sometimes depicted foreign dress with nuance and cultural sensitivity, *Habiti antichi e moderni* nevertheless helped solidify negative racial stereotypes that were used to justify European colonial projects.

Further Readings

Jones, Ann Rosalind. "Cesare Vecellio's Floridians in the Venetian Book Market: Beautiful Imports." In *The Discovery of the New World in Early Modern Italy: 1492–1750*, edited by Elizabeth Hodorowich and Lia Markey, 248–269. Cambridge: Cambridge University Press, 2017.

Jones, Ann Rosalind, and Margaret F. Rosenthal. *Cesare Vecellio's* Habiti Antichi et Moderni: *The Clothing of the Renaissance World*. London: Thames & Hudson Ltd., 2008.

Paulicelli, Eugenia. "Mapping the World: The Political Geography of Dress in Cesare Vecellio's Costume Books." *The Italianist* 28, no. 1 (2008): 24–53. https://doi.org/10.1179/ita.2008.28.1.24.

Melani Shahin

ENTRY #9

Jan Huygen van Linschoten (1563–1611) and Bernard Paludanus (1550–1663), authors
Johannes van Doetecum (1530–1605), engraver

Sati Ritual in *Itinerario, voyage ofte schipvaert* (*Discourse of Voyages into the East & West Indies*), 1596
Book with letterpress and engravings
VAULT Ayer 124 .D91 L7 1596
*This image is from a 1596 edition at the John Carter Brown Library, R 1-SIZE F596 .L759i

The 1596 publication of Jan Huygen van Linschoten's *Itinerario* was a watershed in the history of European colonialism. The *Itinerario* contained classified information collected during Linschoten's time working for the Portuguese in Goa that allowed the Dutch to disrupt Portuguese domination over trade with East and South-East Asia. Accompanying the text were 36 engraved illustrations of the peoples, customs, and topography of India that Linschoten claimed were drawn from life and could thus be understood by the contemporary audience as empirical content.

One illustration depicts the Hindu ritual of *sati*, in which widows sacrifice themselves through self-immolation. In the center of the image, the widow jumps with arms outstretched into her husband's funeral pyre. Between 1500–1800, Europeans frequently reported on the ritual, but the ethnographic accuracy of these accounts is questionable since *sati* was rarely practiced in early modern India. Moreover, descriptions of *sati* found in sources like the *Itinerario* often followed formulaic narratives.

Of the sati practice, Linschoten provides two explanations: first, that the wives perform this act as a sign of marital devotion; second, that the tradition began as a way to police the "wickedness" of Indian women who allegedly poisoned their husbands. In Linschoten's engraving, the dangerousness of the non-European female body is disciplined by ritualistic death, carefully observed by the audience of men —both inside and outside the image—who surveil her body throughout the sacrifice. The woman is laden with jewelry and clothed only in a loincloth, prominently displaying her breasts and her exotic, sexual, and material excess. Linschoten, who heavily criticized racial miscegenation in his text, subdues the figure of the Indian woman by visually distancing her from European propriety all while flaunting her body to the European readers.

Further Readings

Banerjee, Pompa. *Burning Women: Widows, Witches, and Early Modern European Travelers in India*. New York: Palgrave Macmillan, 2003.

Celso de Castro Alves, José. "Rupture and Continuity in Colonial Discourses: The Racialized Representation of Portuguese Goa in the Sixteenth and Seventeenth Centuries." *Portuguese Studies* 16 (2000): 148–161. https://www.jstor.org/stable/41105143.

van den Boogaart, Ernst. *Civil and Corrupt Asia: Image and Text in the* Itinerario *and the* Icones *of Jan Huygen van Linschoten*. Chicago: University of Chicago Press, 2002.

Arianna Ray and Melani Shahin

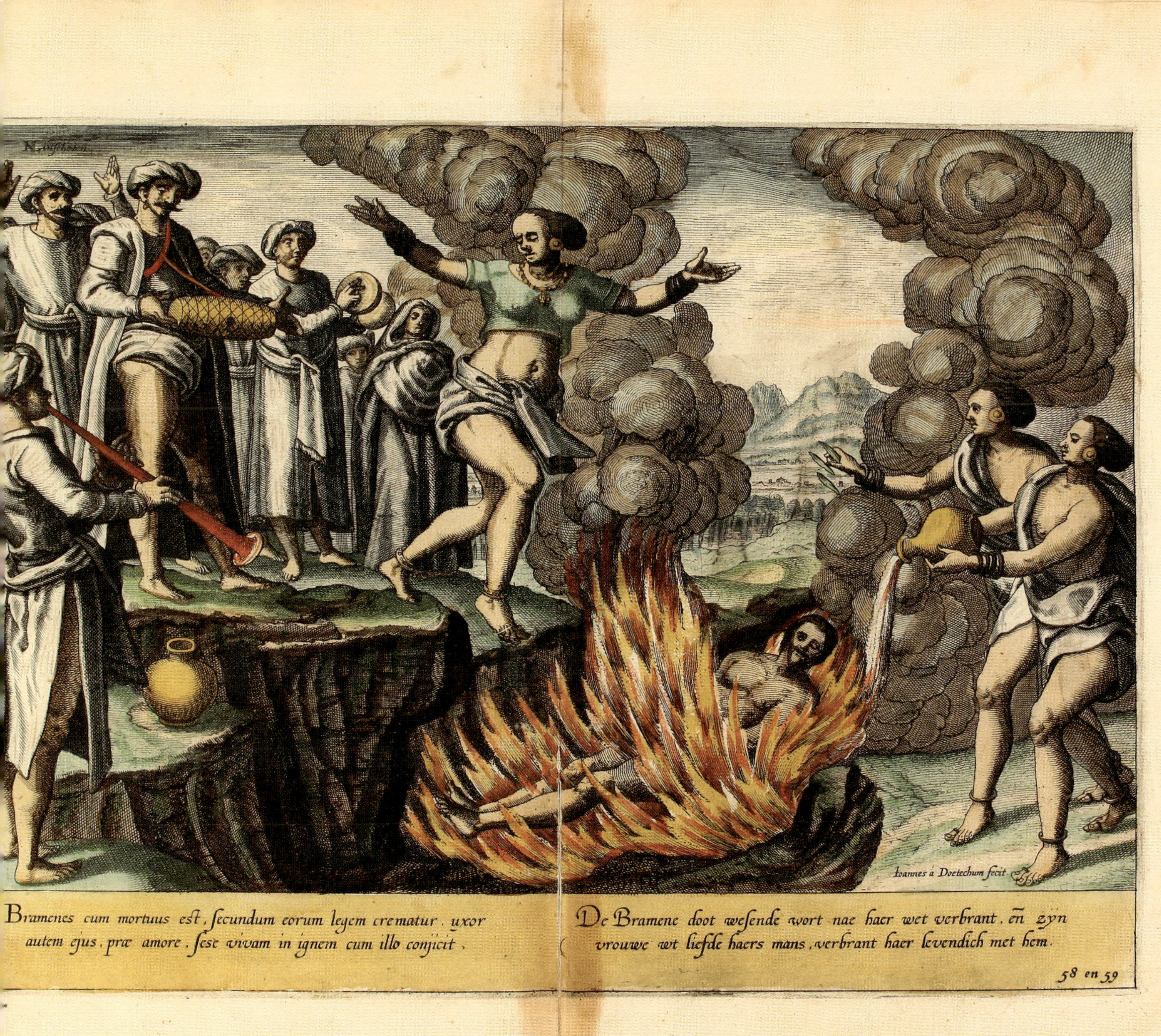
Ioannes à Doetechum fecit
Bramenes cum mortuus est, secundum eorum legem crematur. uxor
autem ejus, præ amore, sese vivam in ignem cum illo conjicit.
De Bramene doot wesende wort nae haer wet verbrant, ēn zyn
vrouwe wt liefde haers mans, verbrant haer levendich met hem.
58 en 59

Entry #9

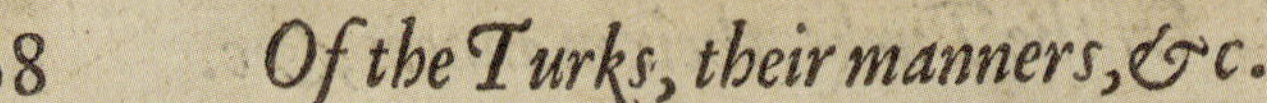

breis, and eye-browes: (the latter by art made high, halfe circular, and to meete, if naturally they do not) so do they the haire of their heads:

Leda fuit nigra conspicienda coma. Ouid. Am. l.2. Eleg.4.

And Leda more faire showing
In blacke haire losely flowing.

as a foyle that maketh the white seeme whiter, and more becomming their other perfections. They part it before in the midst, and pleate it behind, yet sometimes wearing it disheueled. They paint their nailes with a yellowish red. They weare on the top of their heads a cap not vnlike the top of a sugar lofe, yet a little flat, of paist-boord, and couered with cloth of siluer or tisshue. Their vnder-garments (which within doores are their vppermost) do little differ from those that be worne by the men, which we will present to the eye to auoyde repetition.

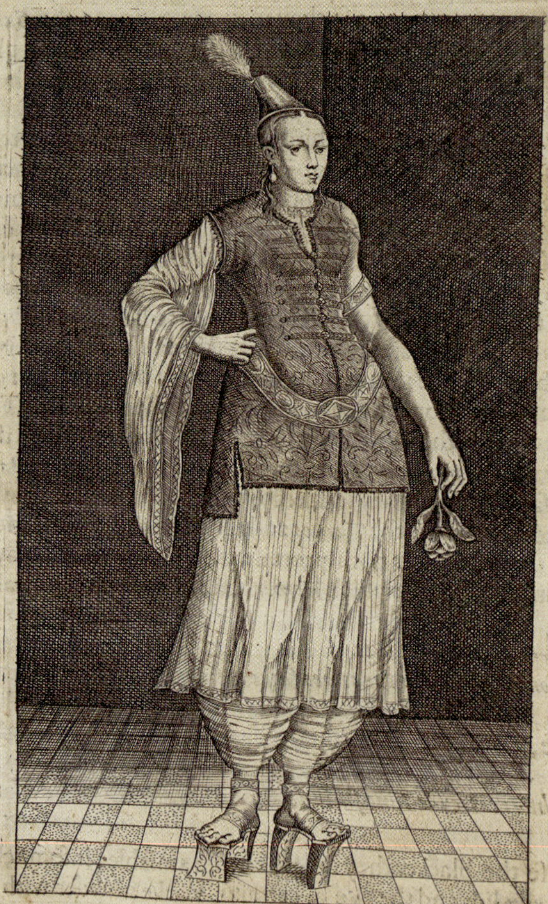

The better sort about the vpper part of their armes, and smalls of their legs weare bracelets, & are elsewhere adorned with iewels. When they go abroad they weare ouer all long gownes of violet cloth, or scarlet, tied close before, the large sleeues hanging

Entry #10

ENTRY #10

Francis Delaram (1590?–1627?), engraver; George Sandys (1578–1644), author
"An Ottoman Lady" in *A relation of a iourney begun an. Dom. 1610: foure bookes, containing a description of the Turkish Empire of Aegypt, of the Holy Land, of the remote parts of Italy and ilands adioyning*, 1615
Book with letterpress and engravings
Case Folio G 29 .777

George Sandys published his influential *Relation of a Journey* in 1615. On p. 68, a relatively large engraving (3.2 × 5.5 inches) offers a full body portrait of an anonymous Ottoman woman, which supplements Sandys's verbal description: "they be women of elegant beauties, for the most part ruddy, cleare and smoothe as polished ivory." Sandys describes cosmetic practices and female hairstyles, as well as the under-garments which "within doors are their uppermost," and which he decides to "present to the eye to avoide repetition." Since neither Sandys nor his readers would have had access to the domestic spaces of Ottoman women, the image constitutes a scene of voyeurism, where readers get to see what they should not.

Mark the lower half of the woman's outfit: while the lines on her skirt seem at first to be textile folds, the diaphanous* quality of her right sleeve orients the reader's gaze, suggesting that her skirt too might be diaphanous, and encouraging us to focus on the slightly bolder lines of that skirt, which actually reveal the shape of the woman's legs through her skirt and fluid trousers. The image rewards an intrusive male gaze, granting English readers access to the Ottoman woman's body and the license to engage in proto-Orientalist erotic fantasies. The juxtaposition of this soft-core erotica with Sandys's description (on the right page) of the veil that Muslim women wear outdoors "that no more is to be seene of theem then their eyes" makes the voyeuristic dimension of the image particularly salient.

Further Readings

Andrea, Bernadette. *Lives of Girls and Women from the Islamic World in Early Modern British Literature and Culture*. Toronto: University of Toronto Press, 2017.

Burton, Jonathan. *Traffic and Turning: Islam and English Drama, 1579–1624*. Newark: University of Delaware Press, 2005.

Said, Edward W. *Orientalism*. New York: Pantheon Books, 1978.

Noémie Ndiaye

ENTRY #11

Lady Mary Wroth (approx. 1587–1561/3)
The Countesse of Mountgomeries Urania, 1621
Book (folio) with letterpress and engraved frontispiece
Case folio Y 155 .W94

Mary Wroth's *The Countess of Montgomery's Urania* (1621) is a romance (proto-novel) with a collection of sonnets appended to the end. The sweeping narrative follows a core group of royal characters — vaguely based on real-life nobles at the British court of King James VI and I — who travel the world seeking adventure, surviving magical enchantments, and navigating complicated erotic entanglements. Its idealized international setting offers a convenient backdrop for exploring fantasies of race and foreign encounter. Indeed, *Urania* appears to respond directly to contemporary travelogues, atlases, and literature in which objects of colonial interest (land, resources, etc.) were conflated with erotically enticing female figures — that is, visibly "foreign" women whose desirability threatened a core element of European women's already limited power.

If European men were advancing white supremacy as justification for colonization, then Wroth's work shows European women had a vested interest in valorizing white femininity to maintain sexual power as their exposure to other cultures increased. *Urania*'s white heroines often encounter dark-featured antagonists whose sexuality endangers their relationships; in the sonnet cycle, Wroth's speaker compares her pale complexion against "Indians scorch'd with the sun" to measure her own erotic devotion — an image that recalls Wroth's documented experience performing at court in blackface as a "Daughter of Niger" who yearns to turn white in Ben Jonson's *Masque of Blackness* (1605). By staging such scenarios repeatedly across the narrative and related poems, Wroth works to reinforce imaginatively the desirability and thus the socio-sexual power of white European women.

Further Readings

Andrea, Bernadette. "The Tartar Girl, the Persian Princess, and Early Modern English Women's Authorship from Elizabeth I to Mary Wroth." In *Women Writing Back/Writing Women Back: Transnational Perspectives from the Late Middle Ages to the Dawn of the Modern Era*, edited by Anke Gilleir, Alicia Montoya, and Suzan van Dijk, 255–281. Amsterdam: Brill, 2010.

Hall, Kim F. *Things of Darkness: Economies of Race and Gender in Early Modern England*. Ithaca, NY: Cornell University Press, 1995.

Rebecca L. Fall

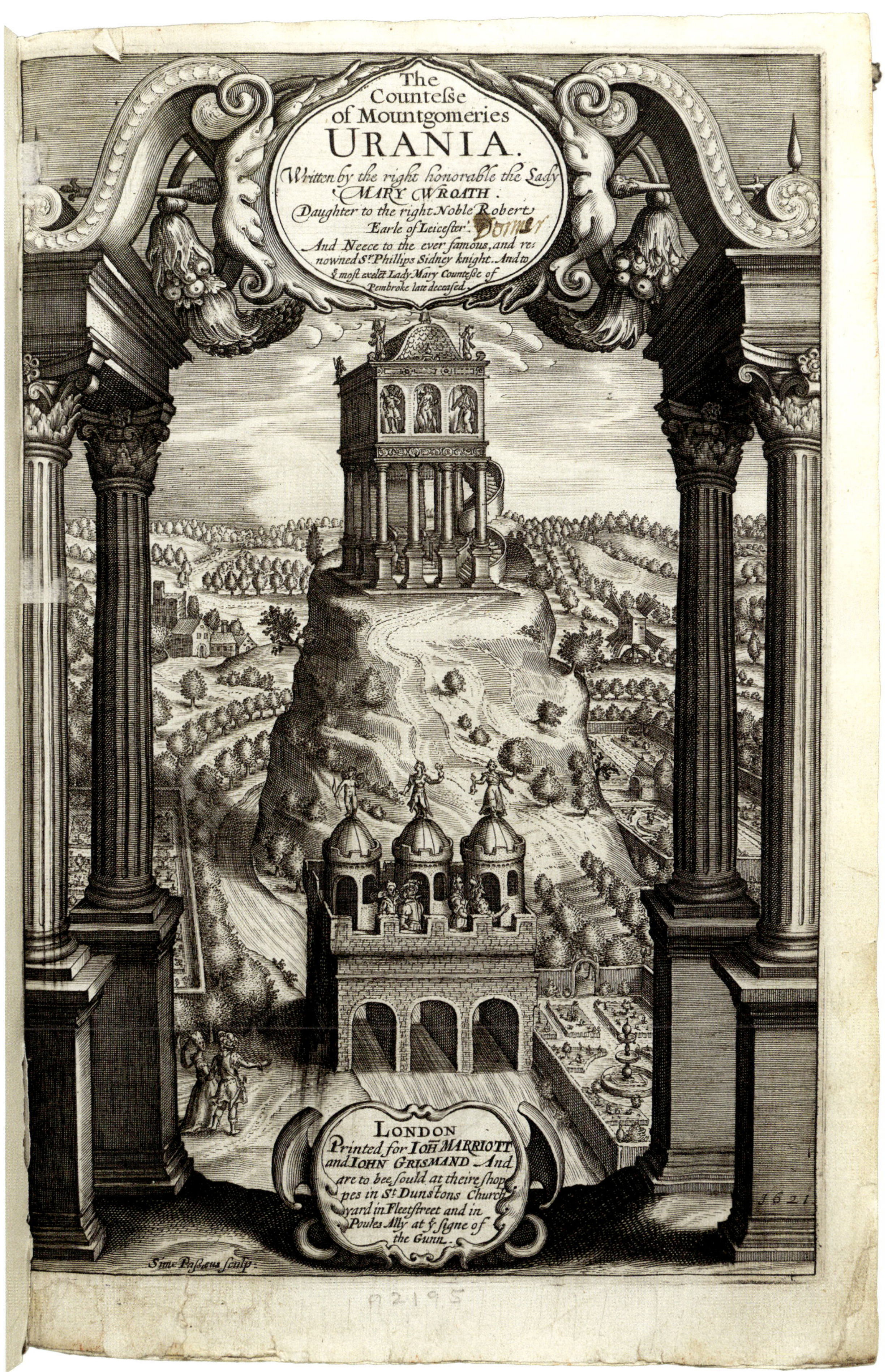
The Countesse of Mountgomeries
URANIA.
Written by the right honorable the Lady MARY WROATH.
Daughter to the right Noble Robert Earle of Leicester.
And Neece to the ever famous, and renowned Sr. Phillips Sidney knight. And to ẏ most exele Lady Mary Countesse of Pembroke late deceased.
LONDON
Printed for IOHN MARRIOTT and IOHN GRISMAND And are to bee sould at theire shoppes in St. Dunstons Church yard in Fleetstreet and in Poules Ally at ẏ signe of the Gunn.
1621
Sime Passaeus sculp:

Entry #11

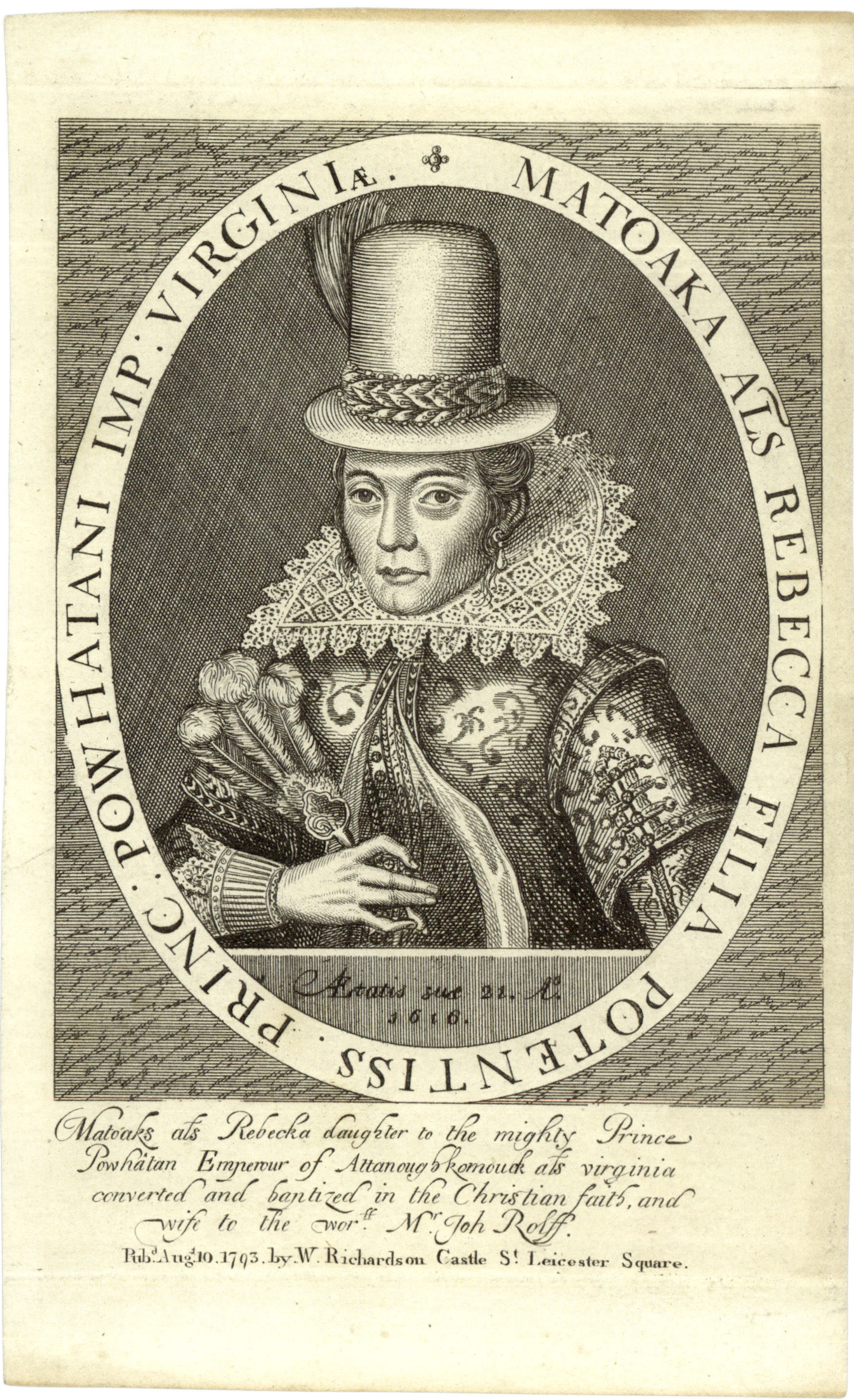
MATOAKA ALS REBECCA FILIA POTENTISS · PRINC · POWHATANI IMP · VIRGINIÆ.
Ætatis suæ 21. A° 1616.
Matoaks als Rebecka daughter to the mighty Prince Powhâtan Emperour of Attanoughkomouck als virginia converted and baptized in the Christian faith, and wife to the wor.ff Mr. Joh Rolff.
Pubd. Augt. 10. 1793, by W. Richardson Castle St. Leicester Square.

Entry #12

ENTRY #12

Portrait of Pocahontas, 1793, reprint after Simon van de Passe (1595–1617), artist;
John Smith (1580–1631), author
Portrait of Pocahontas, from *The Generall Historie of Virginia, New England, and the Summer Isles*, 1624.
Engraving
Ayer E99 .P85 M38 1793

This 1793 reprint after the 1616 engraving is the only known portrait from the life of Pocahontas, alias Matoaka or Rebecca Rolfe. The half-length oval portrait depicts Pocahontas in contemporary English dress: she wears a fitted gown with a high lace collar, an embroidered jacket, and a captain hat. Her jewelry and fan emphasize her noble status as an ambassador. The portrait's Latinate frame names its subject as "Matoaka, alias Rebecca, daughter of the most powerful prince of the Powhatan Empire, in Virginia."

Pocahontas's engraved portrait was commissioned by the Virginia Company to publicize her 1616 goodwill tour of England. Wearing this costume, Pocahontas appeared before King James I alongside her husband, colonist John Rolfe. Her performance at court reassured the Crown of the safety of its investment in the Jamestown colony. Dressed in English fashion and using her Christian name of Rebecca Rolfe, Pocahontas embodied the potential assimilation of the Indigenous Powhatan Confederacy into a white, Christian, colonial society.

In 1624, after Pocahontas's death, Captain John Smith reprinted her portrait in his bestselling memoir, *The Generall Historie of Virginia, New England, and the Summer Isles*. His fictionalized narrative inspired later depictions of a romance between Pocahontas and Smith himself. However, the 1616 portrait demonstrates that the historical Pocahontas appeared to her contemporary audience not as the stereotypical "Indian Princess," whose image was constructed through contemporary travelogues, maps, and costume books, but as a well-dressed English lady. The conventions of her portrait enact the erasure of Pocahontas's American Indian identity, which the Virginia Company replaced with an advertising image of the profitability of colonial investment. This 1793 reprint shows the enduring legacy of Pocahontas's iconography into the late eighteenth century.

Further Readings

Ganteaume, Cécile R. *Officially Indian: Symbols That Define the United States*. Washington, DC: National Museum of the American Indian, Smithsonian Institution, 2017.

Townsend, Camilla. *Pocahontas and the Powhatan Dilemma*. New York: Hill and Wang, 2004.

Julia Marsan

Painting with faire incisions, an old humour of our Auncestors.

History you may find, cut in brasse, where the *Picts* of both Sexes are painted out with their faire incisions, as *Herodian* describeth them. So that you see this humour of painting hath been generall in these parts: There being no cause of mocking, if the Indians have done, and yet do the like. By which things above recited, we may know, that this hither world hath anciently been as much deformed and savage as any of the *Indians*, and may come about to the same point of cuticular bravery.

p.538.

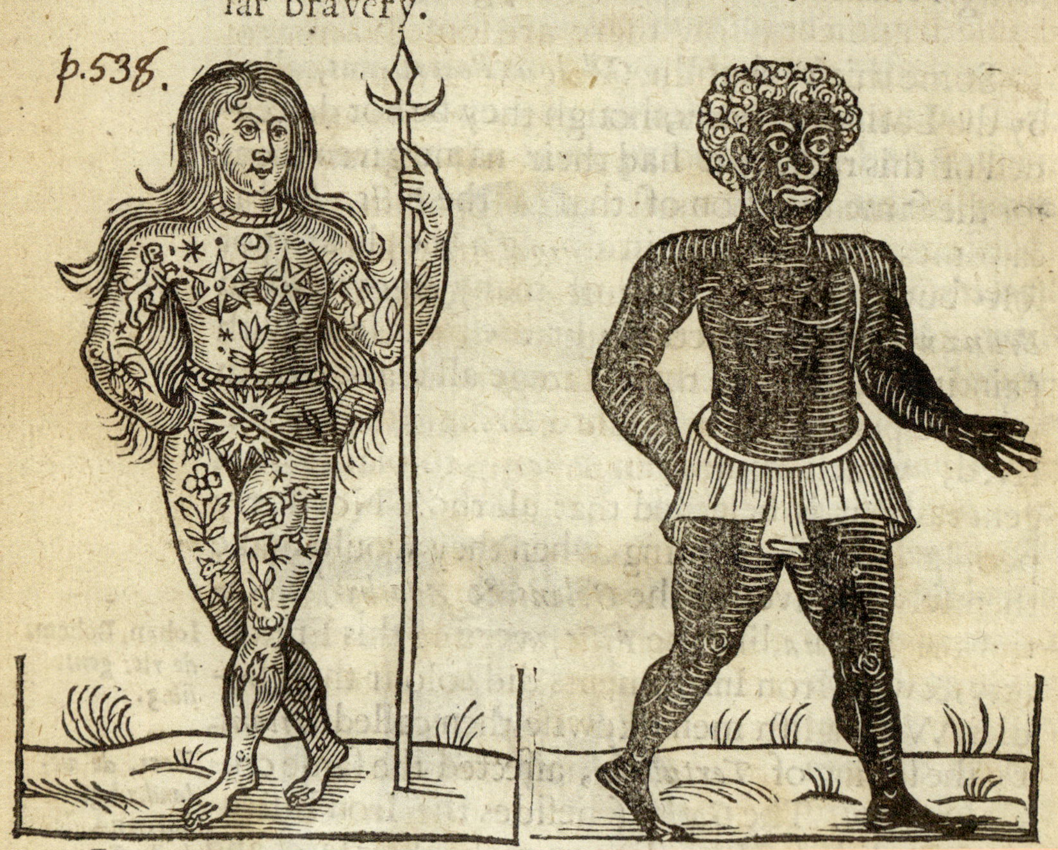

Why some men, and they a mighty and considerablepart of mankind, should first acquire and still retaine the glosse and tincture of blacknesse they,

ENTRY #13

John Bulwer (1606–1656), author; William Hunt (1647–1660), printer
Anthropometamorphosis: man transform'd; or The artificiall changling, 1653
Book with letterpress and woodcuts
Case F 03.13

John Bulwer was an English physician whose encyclopedic *Anthropometamorphosis* (1653), divulges an ethnology* of complicated racial and ethnic markers among various nations. Including woodcuts representing the modification of human body parts, Bulwer identified various artificial transformations among people from all around the world. He believed that all humans were malleable at birth, and that foreign customs involved voluntary transformations whereby men strayed from the image intended by God (on the book's frontispiece, humans with various bodily mutilations face divine judgment while the Devil laughs). Artificial transformations include head shaping, tattoos, scarring, and more. These aligned closely with early modern ideas of monstrosity, as Bulwer features mythological beings (e.g., humans with dog heads from the ancient region of Scythia) alongside recognizable racial and ethnic groups (e.g., Mexicans, Russians, Americans, Turks, etc.). Bulwer often centers the English body as representative of normativity* and Nature, while aligning foreign nations with the unnatural and the monstrous, based on second-hand information derived from travel details and fictional tales.

In Scene 24, Bulwer describes tattoo practices and inquires into how populations "became Black": the passage is accompanied by a woodcut representing a man of dark complexion wearing a white cloth around his loins. Bulwer offers several explanations for why the "seeds of Adam" may have black skin tones, such as the heat from the Sun, a curse of God, or the "inward use of certain waters." Finally, Bulwer suggests that the "Moors" changed their complexions "into a new and more fashionable hue" because they were affected by the "beauty of blacknesse" and saw whiteness as the Devil's hue. Said Black complexion, "first by art acquired," eventually resulted in the reproduction of generations of similar racially identifiable individuals.

Further Readings

Campbell, Mary Baine. "Anthropometamorphosis: Manners, Customs, Fashions, and Monsters." In *Wonder & Science: Imagining Worlds in Early Modern Europe*, 225–256. Ithaca, NY: Cornell University Press, 1999.

Hall, Kim F. *Things of Darkness: Economies of Race and Gender in Early Modern England*. Ithaca, NY: Cornell University Press, 1995.

Poitevin, Kimberly. "Inventing Whiteness: Cosmetics, Race, and Women in Early Modern England." *Journal for Early Modern Cultural Studies* 11, no. 1 (Spring/Summer 2011): 59–89. https://www.jstor.org/stable/23242188.

Aylin Corona

ENTRY #14

Miso-Spilus, seventeenth-century author
A wonder of wonders, or A metamorphosis of fair faces voluntarily transformed into foul visages: or, an invective against black-spotted faces, 1662
Printed pamphlet with engraved title page
Case K 73 .98

A printed pamphlet of 39 pages (including prefatory material and frontispiece), *A Wonder of Wonders* (1662) directly engages debates about cosmetics, female beauty standards, and anxieties about racial purity in seventeenth-century England. Authored under the pseudonym Miso-Spilus, Latin for "I hate spots," the pamphlet sets forth an extensively annotated argument against women's use of cosmetics—black beauty spots in particular.

Cosmetics in general played a key role in establishing racialized beauty standards in England, especially among women, by reinforcing "long standing associations of beauty and whiteness" and solidifying the relationship between those standards and English ethno-cultural supremacy. Yet even while cosmetics enabled women to perform whiteness more conscientiously, they also exposed complexion as an "unreliable marker of race" because it could be altered artificially. Cosmetics therefore became a flashpoint for anxieties about racial purity.

Miso-Spilus's focus on black beauty spots explicitly connects white beauty standards to social prohibitions against interracial sex. The prefatory poem shown here, attributed to E. Westfield, claims beauty spots make women appear mixed-race: "From *Britains* and from *Negroes* sprung." The immediately preceding lines, not shown here, further suggest that these anxieties go deeper than appearance: "Complexion speaks you Mungrels, and your Blood / Part *Europe*, part *America*, mixt brood." These lines suggest that white beauty standards functioned in part as a bulwark against the perceived threat of miscegenation—proof not only of aesthetic superiority but also of blood purity.

Further Readings

Karim-Cooper, Farah. *Cosmetics in Shakespearean and Renaissance Drama*. Edinburgh: Edinburgh University Press, 2006.

Loomba, Ania, and Jonathan Burton, eds. *Race in Early Modern England: A Documentary Companion*. New York: Palgrave MacMillan, 2007.

Poitevin, Kimberly. "Inventing Whiteness: Cosmetics, Race, and Women in Early Modern England." *Journal for Early Modern Cultural Studies* 11.1 (2011): 59–89. https://www.jstor.org/stable/23242188.

Rebecca L. Fall

A WONDER of WONDERS:
OR,
A Metamorphosis of Fair FACES voluntarily transformed into foul VISAGES.

Or, an Invective against Black-spotted Faces:
By a Well-willer to modest Matrons and Virgins,
MISO-SPILUS, i. *Qui maculas odit.*

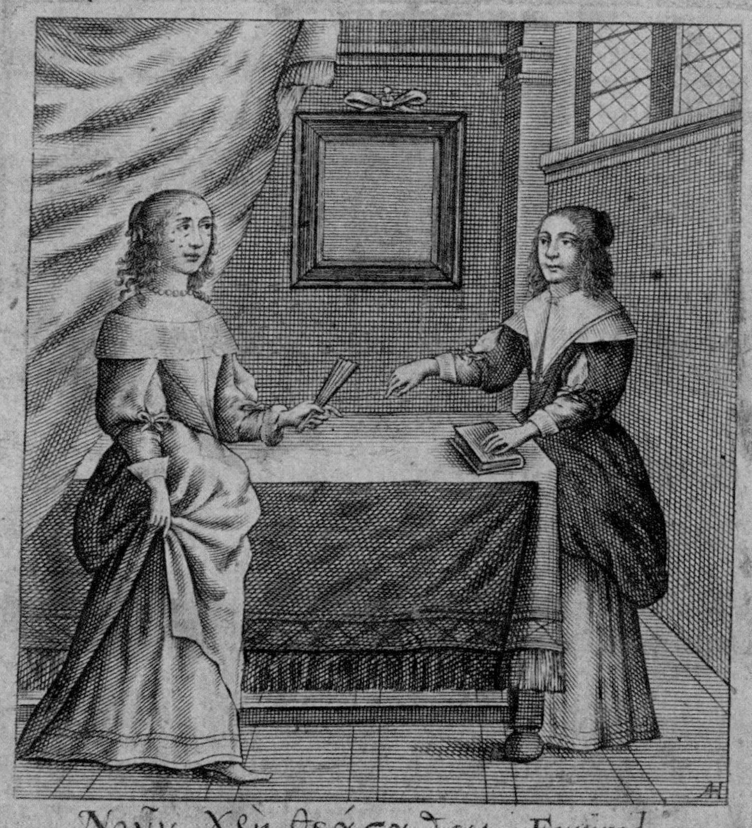

Νοῦν χρὴ θεάσασθαι. Euripid.

Published by *R. SMITH*, Gent.

Non est ornamentum corporis quod corpus *fucata specie adumbrat, sed quod suo* exornat munere, quodque non in voluptatis *lenocinio, sed in virtutis & doctrinae* consistit obsequio. H. Farnesius, de...i cognitione, Quæst. 13.

LONDON, Printed by J. G. for Richard *Royston*, Book-Seller in Ivy-lane. 1662.

Entry #14

PART 2
MAPPING

GEOGRAPHIES OF RACE: CONSTRUCTIONS OF CONSTANTINOPLE / ISTANBUL IN THE WESTERN EUROPEAN IMAGINARY

By Roland Betancourt and Ambereen Dadabhoy

As the only city in the world geographically situated upon two continents — Europe and Asia — Constantinople/Istanbul occupies a special place within the Western and Eastern imaginaries.[1] In fact, the city's geographic location calls into question and puts pressure on notions of East and West precisely because it straddles the geographical and cultural meanings attached to those terms. Positioned at the crossroads, it is both within and without the epistemologies that construct and inform our understanding of cultures based on their affiliations with the terms "Western" and "Eastern." Located in and out of such meaning making practices, Constantinople/Istanbul is a particularly striking case study for an investigation into the processes of premodern racial formation, by which we mean the historical, social, and cultural mechanisms that produce race as difference in order to construct and maintain a system of power and domination over those who occupy that different or Other identity.[2] These mechanisms of race, or discourses, as Stuart Hall labels them, produced race as a "floating signifier," contingent upon

1. We use Constantinople/Istanbul here to signal the dual cultures and empires that we are discussing. When we move to specific Byzantine and Ottoman regimes, we will use Constantinople or Istanbul, as appropriate.

2. We follow the groundbreaking work of Omi and Winant here, with their development and theorizing of the theory of racial formation: "We define racial formation as *the sociohistorical process by which racial identities are created, lived out, transformed, and destroyed*." Michael Omi and Howard Winant, *Racial Formation in the United States*, 3rd ed., (London: Routledge, 2014), 109.

relations within the signifying field and upon structures of power and domination.[3] Thinking about race as a discourse explains the inconsistencies we might encounter in how racialized bodies are fabricated within racial regimes and race-making projects, the way, for example, groups are differently racialized at different historical moments, making transhistorical* racialization untenable. As a discourse, race and racial power often manifest through representation, which holds epistemic power over understanding and apprehending race. Examining the production and maintenance of race within Constantinople/Istanbul discloses the many ways that the assemblage of race in the premodern is deeply connected to the creation of imperial space and geography and to stubborn ideological* investments in strict constructions of East and West, the Orient and the Occident.[4]

Before we explore the contours of race-making within the Byzantine and Ottoman regimes that governed Constantinople/Istanbul, we feel it is both important and necessary to acknowledge the limitations of our study. All critical investigations have their limits, and ours, here, is bound by the archive we are utilizing. The Newberry Library has rich holdings in early modern printed books, many of which display a keen interest in the East and the Ottoman Empire. Therefore, in the early modern period, we have substantially more texts with which to develop our critiques. Archives hold valuable material, yet by virtue of being collections, they also get to determine what is valuable and what constitutes important knowledge. They are by their very nature places that produce knowledge according to the ideologies and biases that have guided and informed the materials in their collection. Archives are exclusive, exclusionary, and deeply implicated in Western discourses of race and empire.[5] Our reliance on the Newberry Library's holdings means that our examination of premodern race in Constantinople/Istanbul is through the ontological* and epistemological frame of Western European writers. Any kind of resistance to those discourses and the cultural supremacy they may support must come from the critical methods we employ. Moreover, our study lacks a dialogic component where we can consider Byzantine and Ottoman racializing practices and views of European cultures. Thus, our work may be seen as supporting projects of European empire and domination, which offers a Eurocentric* view of this geography. We offer these caveats* not to undermine our work or the important scholarship being undertaken in this collection, but rather as a provocation for further research and for archival alliances across cultures and languages which can help us more fully understand and analyze premodern racial formations.

We want to frame our study of Constantinople/Istanbul with the question of how geographies can be racialized. Unlike cartography, wherein physical topography* is rendered legible through mapping technologies which simultaneously impose a visual regime of control (and conquest), our examination of geography is cultural in orientation. We consider space through the human experience of being in, occupying, and experiencing space. The term geography indicates both landscape and the built social environment of a locale, which is "the material setting for social relations — the actual shape of place within which people conduct their lives as individuals."[6] Access to and relations within these "material settings" are determined by identity and forms of marginalization. Exploring geography, then, requires attending to relations of power. As feminist geographer Gillian Rose demonstrates, "these notions of space, location, place, position, mapping and

3. Stuart Hall, "Race, the Floating Signifier: What More Is There to Say about "Race?" eds. Stuart Gilroy and Paul Gilmore, *Selected Writings on Race and Difference* (Durham, NC: Duke University Press, 2021), 359–73.

4. In *Habeas Viscus,* Alexander G. Weheliye notes that racial assemblages are the "conglomerate of sociopolitical relations that discipline humanity into full humans, not-quite-humans, and nonhumans," Alexander G. Weheliye, *Habeas Viscus* (Durham, NC: Duke University Press, 2014), 3.

5. Saidiya Hartman, "Venus in Two Acts," *Small Axe: A Caribbean Journal of Criticism* 12, no. 2 (2008): 1–14, https://doi.org/10.1215/-12-2-1; Kim F. Hall, "I Can't Love This the Way You Want Me To: Archival Blackness," *postmedieval* 11, no. 2 (2020): 171–79 https://doi.org/10.1057/s41280-020-00174-9.

6. Tim Cresswell, "Defining Place," *Place: A Short Introduction* (Malden, MA: Blackwell Ltd, 2004), 7.

landscape imply radically heterogeneous geometries. They are lived, experienced and felt. And they also articulate specific arguments about power and identity."[7] Geography as lived experience, one affected by identity, privilege, and power exposes the ideological underpinnings of spaces in terms of what they are designed to do, for whom they are made, and who they exclude. Cultural Geographer David Delaney argues that "elements of the social (race, gender, and so on) are not simply *reflected* in spatial arrangements; rather, spatialities are regarded as *constituting* and/or *reinforcing* aspects of the social."[8] By focusing on relations of power as inherent to spatial arrangements, we can also observe how spatial relations are racial relations, through their capacity to animate and reinforce social hierarchies and racial difference. In the context of Constantinople/Istanbul we argue that the city's landscape, social and political locale, and its built environment are mobilized by European writers to create and bolster racial difference, often articulated through the division of East and West, thereby imbricating those terms within a racial matrix. In this chapter, we first examine the ambivalent representations of Byzantium and Constantinople and then turn to representations of Ottoman Istanbul. In doing so we seek to understand how Constantinople/Istanbul was variously racialized by Western onlookers, highlighting the ways that the city was either Othered or embraced by the West throughout its medieval and early modern history.

Oscillating Visions of Byzantium and Constantinople

By Roland Betancourt

Scholars have often remarked that the "Byzantine" Empire is a misnomer*, given that the so-called Byzantines only referred to themselves as the "Romans" (ῥωμαῖοι). When they spoke of "Byzantium" or "Byzantines," of which they did often, these terms referred instead to the empire's capital, Constantinople, and its inhabitants. Byzantium (or, Byzantion) had been the city's name before Constantine the Great established his capital for the Roman Empire there. Once a provincial colony and trading port, the city of Byzantion was understood as having a key tactical position at the southern tip of the Bosporus, the strait linking the Black Sea to the Sea of Marmara, and at the juncture of the two main military highways of the empire. Constantine's city was founded in 324 CE and dedicated on 11 May 330 CE.[9] The wearing down of Rome's power and influence across the fifth and sixth centuries marked a consolidation of power for Constantinople as the "New Rome"—a title the Turks would inherit when the Ottomans conquered the city, and which nineteenth-century Russian ideologists would develop into the notion of Moscow as the "Third Rome."[10] Yet, this was a fraught position for the West, which, while recognizing the relocation of the Roman capital, repeatedly sought to contest the religious, political, and cultural authority of Constantinople.[11] It is through this long history of imperial competition, religious cleaving, and processes of Othering that we

7. Gillian Rose, *Feminism and Geography: The Limits of Geographical Knowledge* (Minneapolis, University of Minnesota Press, 1993), 140–41.

8. David Delaney. "The Space that Race Makes." *The Professional Geographer* 54, no. 1 (2002): 7, https://doi.org/10.1111/0033-0124.00309.

9. Cyril Mango, "Constantinople," *Oxford Dictionary of Byzantium*, ed. Alexander Kazhdan (Oxford: Oxford University Press, 1991).

10. On the lands of Rum, see Cemal Kafadar, "A Rome of One's Own: Reflections on Cultural Geography and Identity in the Lands of Rum," *Muqarnas* 24 (2007): 7–26, https://doi.org/10.1163/22118993_02401003. On Third Rome, see Dimitri Strémooukhoff, "Moscow the Third Rome: Sources of the Doctrine," *Speculum* 28, no. 1 (1953): 84–101, https://doi.org/10.2307/2847182; Robert Lee Wolff, "The Three Romes: The Migration of an Ideology and the Making of an Autocrat," *Daedalus* 88 (1959): 291–311, https://www.jstor.org/stable/20026497; Donald Ostrowski, "'Moscow the Third Rome' as Historical Ghost," in *Byzantium: Faith and Power (1261–1557): Perspectives on Late Byzantine Art and Culture*, ed. Sarah T. Brooks (New York: The Metropolitan Museum of Art, 2006), 170–79. On contemporary Russian politics and Byzantium, see Theodore Christou, "The Byzantine History of Putin's Russian Empire," *The Conversation*, March 15, 2018, https://theconversation.com/the-byzantine-history-of-putins-russian-empire-90616.

11. For the most overarching study of Byzantium and the West in the early Middle Ages, see Michael McCormick, "Byzantium and the West, 700–900," chap. 14 in *The New Cambridge Medieval History*, vol. 2, ed. Rosamond McKitterick (Cambridge: Cambridge University Press, 1995), 349–80.

encounter a city that repeatedly presented an uneasy place in Western literature and thought.

In 800 CE, when Charlemagne (c. 742–814) took on the title of emperor, we can witness one of the most critical contestations of the Byzantines' identity as Romans by Western actors. In the *Life of Charlemagne* (c. 830), written by his courtier, Einhard (c. 770–840), we are told that Charlemagne himself begrudged having "accepted the title of emperor and augustus," but that the title also stirred the ire of the Byzantine Empire. There, Einhard praises Charlemagne's character by describing how "he bore the animosity that the assumption of this title caused with great patience, for the Roman emperors were angry over it."[12] In as much as Einhard dismisses the Byzantine emperors' protestations here, he also slips into properly addressing them as the "Roman emperors." It is as much a contestation as it is an attestation of the Byzantines' imperial power and unique claim to the title.

In a sixteenth-century edition of the text, a copy of which is preserved at the Newberry Library, we can find a curious alteration to the Latin text of Einhard's chronicle. There, the line has been changed from the "Roman emperors" to the "Constantinopolitan emperors" so as to negate the "Roman" authority and identity of these emperors.[13] This copy was published in Cologne by the printer Johannes Soter (c. 1519–1538) under the auspices of humanist Graf Hermann von Neuenahr (c. 1492–1530) in 1521.[14] Here, we can appreciate how the tensions regarding the identity of the Byzantines was as hotly contested by medieval European authors as it was by later historiographers and editors responsible for the preservation and transmissions of these texts across the early modern period.

A useful comparison to this case is the depiction of the Byzantines in Notker the Stammerer's (d. 912) own *Deeds of Charlemagne* (883/4). There, depicting the proceedings of the embassy from Charlemagne to Constantinople, the reader is told what occurred when one of the diplomats broke with Byzantine customs at dinner. While it was customary, we are told, to eat only the top of any animal placed on the dinner plate, the Westerner turned over the fish that was covered in spices, which caused the outrage of all the Byzantine nobles at the table who demanded that the emperor put him to death immediately. But, before doing so, the emperor allowed him one petition. The clever envoy therefore asked for anyone who had witnessed him turn over the fish to be blinded. One by one, all the nobles, including the emperor and empress, swore they had seen nothing, thus absolving him of his guilt and death. There, Notker exclaims, "and so the clever Frank beat the empty-headed sons of Hellas in their own land and came home safe and sound."[15] This curious event betrays a notable distaste for the Byzantines, staging their customs as foolish, arcane, and, ultimately, barbaric.[16] Here, the justification for the penalty of death is attributed to "the laws of the Greeks" ("legem Grecorum") speaking of the Constantinopolitans precisely as "Greeks" or the "sons of Hellas," rather than Romans.[17] This event precisely seeks to ostracize and Other the Byzantines as foolish Greeks, against "the clever Frank."

In the Newberry's holdings, we can find this text preserved in the early-nineteenth-century *Monumenta Germaniae Historica* (MGH), an edited series published in Prussia that sought to collect, edit, and publish primary sources from the European Middle

12. "Imperatoris et augusti nomen accepit . . . Invidiam tamen suscepti nominis, Romanis imperatoribus super hoc indignantibus, magna tulit patientia." Einhard, *Vita Karoli*, 28, trans. Paul Edward Dutton, *Charlemagne's Courtier: The Complete Einhard* (Peterborough, ON: Broadview Press, 1998), 33–34.

13. "Constantinopolitanis imperatoribus." *Vita et gesta Karoli Magni*, Chicago, Newberry Library, Case E 5.C37122, p. 33.

14. On this sixteenth-century Humanist, see Charles G. Nauert, Jr., "Graf Hermann von Neuenahr and the Limits of Humanism in Cologne," *Historica Reflections* 15, no. 1 (1988): 65–79. https://www.jstor.org/stable/41298892

15. "Tum sapiens ille Francigena, vanissima Hellade in suis sedibus exsusperata, victor et sanus in patrium suam reversus est." Notker the Stammerer, *De gestis Karoli*, 2.6, trans. David Ganz, *Two Lives of Charlemagne* (New York: Penguin Books, 2008), 152–53.

16. On this event, see Patricia Skinner, *Living with Disfigurement in Early Medieval Europe* (New York: Palgrave Macmillan, 2017), 77.

17. Notker the Stammerer, *De gestis Karoli*, 2.6, trans. Ganz, *Two Lives*, 153.

Ages.[18] This publishing project was largely built on nineteenth-century scholarly Romanticism and the burgeoning nationalisms of the era, which provide us with an interesting glimpse into the imperial dynamics and positionings of the period.[19]

But regarding the flip-flopping animosities toward Byzantium, there is no better embodiment of Western ambivalences than that provided by the mid-tenth century account of Liudprand, Bishop of Cremona (c. 920–972). Liudprand's embassy to Constantinople captures the wonder and anxieties of Western authors. In his texts, Liudprand comments on the ostentatious marvels of the Byzantine court, recounting how he and his fellow envoys were received in the imperial palace by a series of automata, including chirping birds and roaring lions, and even a wondrous throne upon which the emperor sat that could fly up into the air, changing the emperor's garb as it ascended.[20] Similarly, the description of Greek fire is shown as a particular military wonder of the Byzantines, demonstrating its common use and its undefeatable power. Liudprand explicitly describes this technology as a weapon against racialized foes when describing how the Byzantines "quickly burned all the Saracens' ships, having spewed out Greek fire."[21]

The description of these technological marvels and military prowess are nevertheless subverted by a generally dismissive approach to the empire. Repeatedly, for example, Liudprand deploys archaic names for the Byzantines, calling them by names like "the Achaeans" or "the kingdom of the Argives," in order to contest their imperial authority and their identity as the Roman empire.[22] And, they are referred to as "the Greeks," rather than as the "Romans," a title which he instead uses to acclaim his patrons, the Ottonians, as the "august emperors of the Romans."[23] In Liudprand's text, there is a clear understanding of the Byzantines as Greeks, positioned against a Roman Western Europe.

More hostile descriptions of the Byzantines also occur in Liudprand's text, particularly ones that seek to distance them as "monstrous" or as racialized Others. In one instance, describing the "Greek fashion" of the Emperor, Liudprand describes how Westerners perceived him "not [as] a man but some monster," elucidating his distaste for Byzantine customs.[24] In an even more virulent instance, Liudprand describes his encounter with the Emperor Nikephoros II Phokas (c. 912–969), describing him as follows: "he is a quite monstrous man, dwarfish, with a fat head . . . deformed by a short beard that is wide and thick and graying . . . in color quite like the Ethiopian whom you would not like to run into in the middle of the night."[25] The so-called "monstrosity" is associated with vilifying ideations of disability, as he is called a "dwarf" ("pygmaeun"), and with the suggestion that he is ill-formed.

Notably, Liudprand labels him "in color an Ethiopian" ("colore Aethiopem"), while making a reference back to the *Satires* of Juvenal (c. 60–136) about encountering an Ethiopian in the dark.[26] This language not only demonstrates the ways Byzantine rulers could be racialized as Others in the eyes of Western medieval Europeans, but also the long and pernicious history of

18. *Monachi sangallensis De gestis Karoli imperatoris libri duo*, Monumenta Germaniae Historica, vol. 2 (Hanover: Impensis Bibliopolii Hahniani, 1829), 750.

19. See William Miller Thomas Gamble, "The Monumenta Germaniae Historica: Its Antecedents and Motives," *The Catholic Historical Review* 10, n. 2 (1924): 202–33, https://www.jstor.org/stable/25012071.

20. Liudprand of Cremona, *Antapodosis*, 6.4–5, trans. Paolo Squatriti, *The Complete Works of Liudprand of Cremona* (Washington, D.C., The Catholic University of America Press, 2007), 197–98.

21. Liudprand of Cremona, *Antapodosis*, 5.16, trans. Squatriti, *Complete Works*, 181.

22. "Ottones Romanorum invictissimos imperatores augustos." Liudprand of Cremona, *Antapodosis*, 5.16, trans. Squatriti, *Complete Works*, 119 and 123.

23. Liudprand of Cremona, *Embassy*, trans. Squatriti, *Complete Works*, 238.

24. Liudprand of Cremona, *Antapodosis*, 5.16, trans. Squatriti, *Complete Works*, 119.

25. "hominem satis monstruosum, pygmaeum, capite pinguem . . . barba curta, lata, spissa et semicana foedatum . . . colore Aethiopem, cui per mediam nolis occurrere noctem." Liudprand of Cremona, *Embassy*, 3, trans. Squatriti, *Complete Works*, 240.

26. Juvenal, *Satires*, 6, ed. and trans. Susanna Morton Braund, *Juvenal and Persius*, Loeb Classical Library 91 (Cambridge, MA: Harvard University Press, 2004), 290–91.

race-thinking that medieval authors deployed. These racist prejudices had deep roots in the literature and art of antiquity, emerging here as a citation to the well-known Roman poet from the late-first and early-second centuries CE.[27]

The writings of Liudprand of Cremona continued to have an impact in the early modern period. In 1640, for example, they were handsomely transmitted by an edition of Liudprand's collected works that was published in Antwerp by the printer Balthasar I Moretus (1574–1641) and compiled by the Jesuit scholar Jerónimo Román de la Higuera (1538–1611), featuring frontispieces after Peter Paul Rubens (1577–1640), a copy of which is preserved at the Newberry.[28]

The flux that the Byzantine Empire was subjected to meant that it could rapidly be Othered as an antagonist to Western forces or embraced as Christian kin, critical to Western interests. This is made clear in Crusader rhetoric around the Empire, as exemplified in an incunable* printed in Cologne in 1472, which combines two Crusader narratives from the twelfth century: the *History of Jerusalem* of Robert of Reims (c. 1055–1122) and the *History of the Expedition to Jerusalem* (Cat. No. 19) of Fulcher of Chartres (c. 1059–1127).[29] In Robert's chronicle of the First Crusade, the Turks are described as "filthy" ("inmundis") as he ventriloquizes the call of Pope Urban II (r. 1088–1099). Their corruption is articulated precisely through their crimes against Byzantine Christians, even though he constantly vilifies the Byzantines.[30] The city of Constantinople is staged in Robert's account as a mere refuge for Christianity in the East, filled with relics that they "stole" from churches across the old Roman Empire and now serving as a safe house for them.[31] Such texts seamlessly move between oscillating visions of Byzantium, while also coming to validate the irreparable destruction and looting of Constantinople that occurred in the thirteenth-century during the Latin occupation of the city as part of the Fourth Crusade.

As a late-fifteenth-century compilation, this incunable also helps validate the many relics and objects stolen from Constantinople itself, which now filled the treasuries of Western European churches in this period.[32] Not surprisingly, this work was printed less than two decades after the conquest of Constantinople by the Ottoman Turks in 1453. Hence, its title, *History of the Campaign Against the Turks*, places an important emphasis on its attack against the Turks, seeming to collapse the distinction between the First Crusade's attack on the Seljuk Turks and the modern Ottoman Turks.

The fall of Constantinople on 29 May 1453 certainly produced a distinct mark on the Western imaginary, forcing a certain reevaluation of the place of the Byzantine Empire in the West's dealings with the Ottomans and the various Islamic powers that they often monolithically collapsed into one.[33] During this period, we begin to see a shift in how Constantinople is evaluated in the eyes of the West, and while a wholly positive view of the empire is never fully embraced, we begin to see a rosier depiction of history. This history often glosses over the violence committed against Constantinople by Western Europeans, including but not limited to the Fourth Crusade in the thirteenth century,

27. On race in antiquity, see Denise Eileen McCoskey, *Race: Antiquity and its Legacy* (Oxford: Oxford University Press, 2012); Benjamin Isaac, *The Invention of Racism in Classical Antiquity* (Princeton: Princeton University Press, 2004); Frank M. Snowden Jr., *Blacks in Antiquity: Ethiopians in the Greco-Roman Experience* (Cambridge, MA: Harvard University Press, 1970), and *Before Color Prejudice: The Ancient View of Blacks* (Cambridge, MA: Harvard University Press, 1983). See also Martin Bernal, *Black Athena: The Afroasiatic Roots of Classical Civilization*, 3 vols. (New Brunswick, NJ: Rutgers University Press, 1987–2006).

28. *Luitprandi Subdiaconi Toletani Ticinensis Diaconi tandem Cremonensis Episcopi Opera quae extant: Chronicon et adversaria nunc primum in lucem exeunt*, Monumenta Germaniae Historica, vol. 2 (Hanover: Impensis Bibliopolii Hahniani, 1829), 136. On the frontispiece after Rubens, see Nils Büttner, "Rubens's Legacy in Book Design," *Gateways to the Book: Frontispieces and Title Pages in Early Modern Europe* (Leiden: Brill, 2021), 422–48.

29. Robert of Reims, *Hystoria de Itinere [con]tra turchos* (Cologne: Printer of Dares Johannes Solidi, ca. 1472), Chicago, Newberry Library, Inc. 998.

30. See Robert of Reims, *Historia Hierosolymitana*, trans. Carol Sweetenham, *Robert the Monk's History of the First Crusade* (London: Routledge, 2005).

31. Cf. Robert of Reims, *Historia Hierosolymitana*, 20, trans. Sweetenham, *History of the First Crusade*, 101–2.

32. On the loot of Byzantine relics and reliquaries, see Holger A. Klein, "Eastern Objects and Western Desires: Relics and Reliquaries between Byzantium and the West," *Dumbarton Oaks Papers* 58 (2004): 283–314, https://www.jstor.org/stable/3591389.

33. On this matter, see Nancy Bisaha, *Creating East and West: Renaissance Humanists and the Ottoman Turks* (Philadelphia: University of Pennsylvania Press, 2004).

when the city was sacked, looted, and occupied by Latin Crusaders for nearly sixty years.

After 1453, a series of laments composed for the loss of the city also emerges in the Greek-speaking world, staging the brutality of the Turks against the piety, trauma, and destitution of the Greeks. These texts present an apocalyptic vision of the fall, presenting Mehmed II (1432–1481) and the Turks as lawless "dogs," feasting on the corpses of the slaughtered Byzantines, and marking the arrival of the Antichrist.[34] The sensationalist depiction of Constantinople's fall is perhaps best captured in the depiction of the siege in the *Nuremberg Chronicle* (1493) of Hartmann Schedel (1440–1514) (Cat. No. 17) (Figure 3.1), produced just a few decades after the conquest. There, the flowing fluids from the central gate of the city seem to allude to the line in the chronicle's text above, describing how: "So much blood was spilled that it ran through the city in rivulets."[35]

These hyperbolic depictions of the conquest fueled the Western imaginary, joining with other trends in early modern apocalypticism, to engender a particular construction of the fallen Constantinople as a symbol of Islamic and Turkish hegemony in the East. In the Newberry's collection, this fact is best articulated in *On the Future Triumphs of the Christians over the Saracens* (1485) by Giovanni Nanni (1437–1502), dedicated to Pope Sixtus IV (r. 1470–1484).[36] Better known as Annius of Viterbo, Nanni was an Italian Dominican, whose many forgeries of genealogies and etymologies* left a long lasting mark on the humanistic interests of the period.[37] In this commentary on the Apocalypse, Nanni aims to prove the inevitable reconquest of the Holy Land from the so-called "Saracens."[38]

Nanni's commentary attributes the fall of Constantinople to the Byzantines' schism with the Latin Church. He states that the city fell to the Muslims because of a rebellion against the Roman Church, due to "a separation from obedience to the Roman pontiff."[39] The conquest of the city by Christian forces was not only seen as inevitable, but contiguous with the Second Coming of Christ. In the text, the Prophet Mohammad is described as the Antichrist with Islam as the manifestation of the Beast.[40] Nanni is thus able to enfold Constantinople into a Western, Christian history, while still attributing its demise to having turned its back on the Latin church. Nevertheless, we are told that when the Pope manages to institute a Christian emperor in Constantinople, the city will be recovered and along with it all of Asia Minor and even Egypt, culminating in the return of "all the schismatic churches" ("omnes ecclesias schismaticas") to Rome.

34. On the "Lament for Constantinople" (Ανακάλημα της Κωνσταντινόπολης) and for a translation, see Eleni Kefala, *The Conquered: Byzantium and America on the Cusp of Modernity* (Washington, DC: Dumbarton Oaks, 2020), 27–70.

35. "tanta sanguinis effusion facta, ut rivi cruoris per urbem currerent." Hartmann Schedel, *Liber chronicarum* (Augsburg: Johann Schönsperger, 1497), Chicago, Newberry Library, Inc. 1786, plate 249.

36. Giovanni Nanni, *Tractatus de futuris Christianoru[m] triumphis in Sarcenos Magistri Johannis Viterbiensis* (Nuremberg: Peter Wagner, ca. 1485), Chicago, Newberry Library, Inc. 2227.

37. On Giovanni Nanni, see Giuseppe Marcocci, *The Globe on Paper: Writing Histories of the World in Renaissance Europe and the Americas* (Oxford: Oxford University Press, 2020), 31–32. See also Roberto Weiss, "Traccia per una biografia di Annio da Viterbo," *Italia medioevale e umanistica* 5 (1962): 425–41.

38. On the usage of the term, see Shokoofeh Rajabzadeh, "The Depoliticized Saracen and Muslim Erasure," *Literature Compass* 16, no. 9–10 (2019): e12548, https://doi.org/10.1111/lic3.12548.

39. "schismata ab obediential romani pontifices." Nanni, *Tractatus de futuris*, Newberry Library, Inc. 2227.

40. For an overview of the text, see Lynn Thorndike, *A History of Magic and Experimental Science*, vol. 4 (New York: Columbia University Press, 1934), 263–67.

Sexta etas mūdi CCXLIX

De expugnatione constantinopolitane vrbis anno .1453.

Constanstinopolis ciuitas orientis imperij sedes ⁊ vnicū grecie domiciliū sapiētie hoc anno q̄rto kal. iunias a mahumeto turchoꝝ principe p. 50. dies obsessa vi ⁊ armis expugnata diripit̄ ⁊ fedat̄ anno regni mahumeti tercio. q̄ coactis vndiqꝫ copijs mirabili apparatu terra mariqꝫ regiā vrbē aggressus. cuius descriptio in superiorib' habita ē. Ad terciū aūt diē captato vrbis situ machinas innumeras craticulosasqꝫ ex virgultis viminibusqꝫ ꝯtextas qbꝰ pugnātes tegerent̄ fossatis admouit. Erat aūt murus fortis. q̄ tn̄ machine cā horribili cedebat. Bombardaqꝫ ingens turrī iuxta scti romani portā collidit. cuiꝰ ruina anmuralis fossatū replet equatqꝫ vt via hostibus pateret. At cū turchꝰ tribꝰ iā locis ꝯcussis lapidibus muros desperaret. Memoratu cuiusdā inuidi xpiani ex colle biremes intromittere curat. Est em̄ portꝰ ille in lōgū angustūqꝫ ꝓtractꝰ. cuiꝰ orietalē plagā colligate naues ⁊ cathena muniebant. inde hostibꝰ aditus impossibilis erat. quā ob rē vt coangustaret circūuallaretqꝫ magis vrbē iussit in via eq̄re ex colle suppositis leuitis vasis lacertoꝝ vi ad stadia septuagīta trahi biremes. q̄ ascēsu grauiꝰ sublate post hac eo apice in decliuū ad ripā leuissime sinꝰ introrsum vehebāt̄. Inde pōte lōgitudis stadioꝝ circiter. xxx. ex ripa vrbi oppoita q̄ vasis vinarijs colligatis sub constructis ꝯfixisqꝫ lignis q̄ exercitꝰ decurreret ad murū. dyametralisqꝫ cinctio ingressuꝫ transitūue ꝓhibebat. Tandē dato signo vndiqꝫ nō solū ꝯstātinopolis orientis columen. s̄ ipa qꝫ pera ne q̄d auxilij grecis p̄staret oppugnari cepta ē. Turchi rursus subruere murū portasqꝫ q̄tere inniti. Cernit̄ varia pereuntiū forma ⁊ plurima mortis imago. Cūqꝫ defensio remissior fieret turchi aīaduertentes acriꝰ incūbūt. In ingressu demū porte octigēti circiter milites ex latinis grecisqꝫ periere. ⁊ iā hostis supiorē muꝝ tenebat saxa in ciues deuoluens. Cū subito capta vrbe cesis oībꝰ in rapinas itū ē. In huiꝰ aūt vrbis populatiōe cōstātinꝰ paleologus ⁊ ip̄e mr̄e helena genitꝰ orietis impator capite trūcatꝰ regni sil' ⁊ vite finē fecit. datis qꝫ edictis vt a sex annis supra oēs vtriusqꝫ sexꝰ p̄sone necarēt̄. sacerdotes ⁊ vniuersi monachi diuersis tormētoꝝ generibꝰ necati sunt. Reliquū oē vulgus gladio datū. tāta sanguinis effusio vt riui cruoris p vrbeꝫ currerent. Sic nobilissima vrbs p constantinū primū cōdita in manus infideliū venit. Ab eius ꝯditione M.c.xxx. vl' circa. Quibus gestis omnia in predā dedit. sacra templa fedauit. postremo turchi varia nephanda pegerūt

Constantinopolis expugnatio a turchis

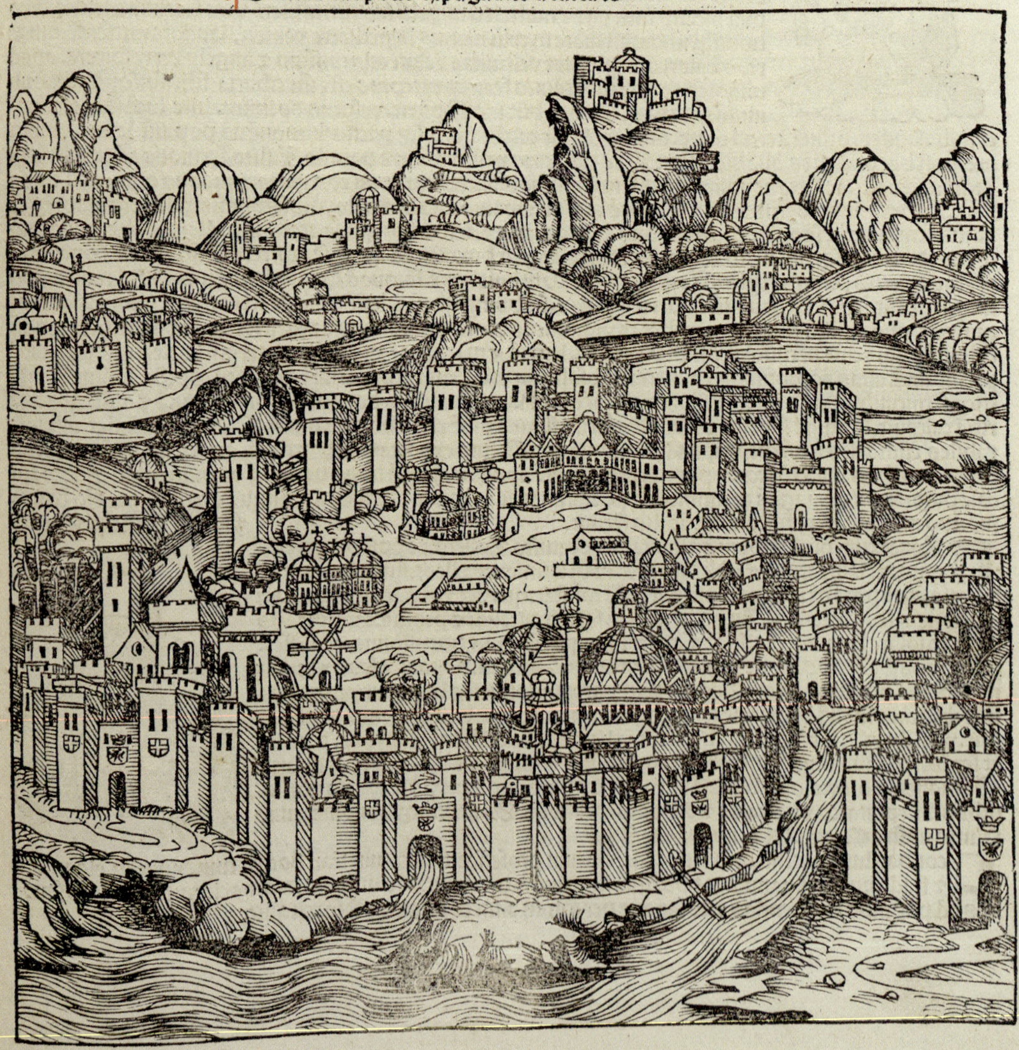

◂ **Figure 3.1**
Hartmann Schedel, "Constantinople" in *Liber chronicarum*. Nuremberg, 1493,
Newberry Library, VAULT oversize Inc. 2084

In other words, what we find in this text is the sense that in the end times, Constantinople will finally, at last, be *properly* Western.

In the centuries after the fall of Constantinople, we see a clear shift from a dismissive yet apocalyptic approach to the conquest, which then fades into a growing desire to historicize* and distinguish the Byzantine Empire as a discrete category. This discrete category of the "Byzantine Empire" is often attributed to Hieronymus Wolf (1516–1580) in the mid-fifteenth century, whose work on Byzantine history helped to popularize the term "Byzantium" through the publication of his *Corpus Historiae Byzantinae* from 1557 to 1562.[41] While the term has a complex history that extends beyond Wolf, this broader moment marks an overall shift in the historiography of the empire, less as a rupture and more as a consolidation of scholarly interest. Critically, Wolf's project was bankrolled by the German merchant Anton Fugger (1493–1560), who saw in Byzantium a stalwart model for defending against the Ottoman Turks. Fugger's investments in Byzantium were motivated by a desire to learn from Byzantine history how to resist the advances of the Ottomans during his own time.[42] Therefore, Byzantium became an object lesson for mediating Western anxieties about their place in the world, their relationship to history, and their international relations with the Ottoman Empire.

During the seventeenth century, we witness this rise in a scholarly interest in Byzantium, which not only came to categorize it as distinct and different from the ancient and Western Roman Empire, but also sought to understand its historical rise and fall. At the Newberry, we can witness elements of this history across various seventeenth-century publications that provide us with early, synthetic summaries of what we might today refer to as Byzantine history. From Venice, we have Giacomo Fiorelli's *The Monarchy of the East* (1679), which traces the history of the Roman empire, beginning with Constantine the Great (r. 306–337) in 330 to the fall of Constantinople in 1453 under the rule of Constantine XI Palaiologos (r. 1449–1453).[43] From Paris, we have the multivolume *History of Constantinople* (1672–1674) by Louis Cousin (1627–1707), which traces the history of the empire from the reign of Justin to "the end of the empire."[44] This work is predominantly a collection of Byzantine sources covering the range of the empire through Byzantine writers, including Procopius of Caesarea (c. 500–565), Anna Komnena (1083- c. 1153/54), Niketas Choniates (c. 1155–1217), and Doukas (c. 1400–1462).

Translations of Byzantine texts into modern languages, however, were even scarcer. One notable exception is the translation into English of Procopius of Caesarea's sixth-century text on Emperor Justinian's wars by Sir Henry Holcroft in 1653, published in London as *The History of the Warres of Emperour Justinian*.[45] There, a detailed etching with engraving by Thomas Cross (active 1642–1682) serves as the frontispiece for the volume (Figure 3.2). At the top of the image, two angels crown a sculpted bust of Justinian with a laurel

41. On Hieronymus Wolf, see Diether Roderich Reinsch, "Hieronymus Wolf as Editor and Translator of Byzantine Texts," in *The Reception of Byzantium in European Culture Since 1500*, eds. Przemysław Marciniak and Dion C. Smythe, 43–53 (Farnham: Ashgate, 2017). See also Anthony Grafton, "Western Humanists and Byzantine Historians," in *The Invention of Byzantium in Early Modern Europe*, eds. Nathanael Aschenbrenner and Jake Ransohoff (Washington, DC: Dumbarton Oaks, 2021), 71–104.

42. See Hans-Georg Beck, "Hieronomus Wolf," in *Ideen und Realitäten in Byzanz: gesammelte Aufsaetze*, 169–93 (London: Variorum, 1972).

43. Giacomo Fiorelli, *La monarchia d'Oriente del padre maestro Giacomo Fiorelli . . . comincia da Costantino 'l Grande nell' anno CCCXXX e termina in Costantino Paleologo nell' anno MCCCCLIII. Alla sacra cesarea maesta' di Leopoldo Avstriaco avgvsto* (Venice: D. Milocco, 1679), Chicago, Newberry Library, folio F 325.301.

44. Louis Cousin, *Histoire de Constantinople, depuis le régne de l'ancien Justin, jusqu'à* la fin de *l'empire* (Paris: Chez Damien Foucault, 1672–1674), Chicago, Newberry Library, F 325.21.

45. Procopius, *The history of the warres of the Emperour Justinian*, trans. Henry Holcroft (London: H. Moseley, 1653), Chicago, Newberry Library, Case Y 642.P82.

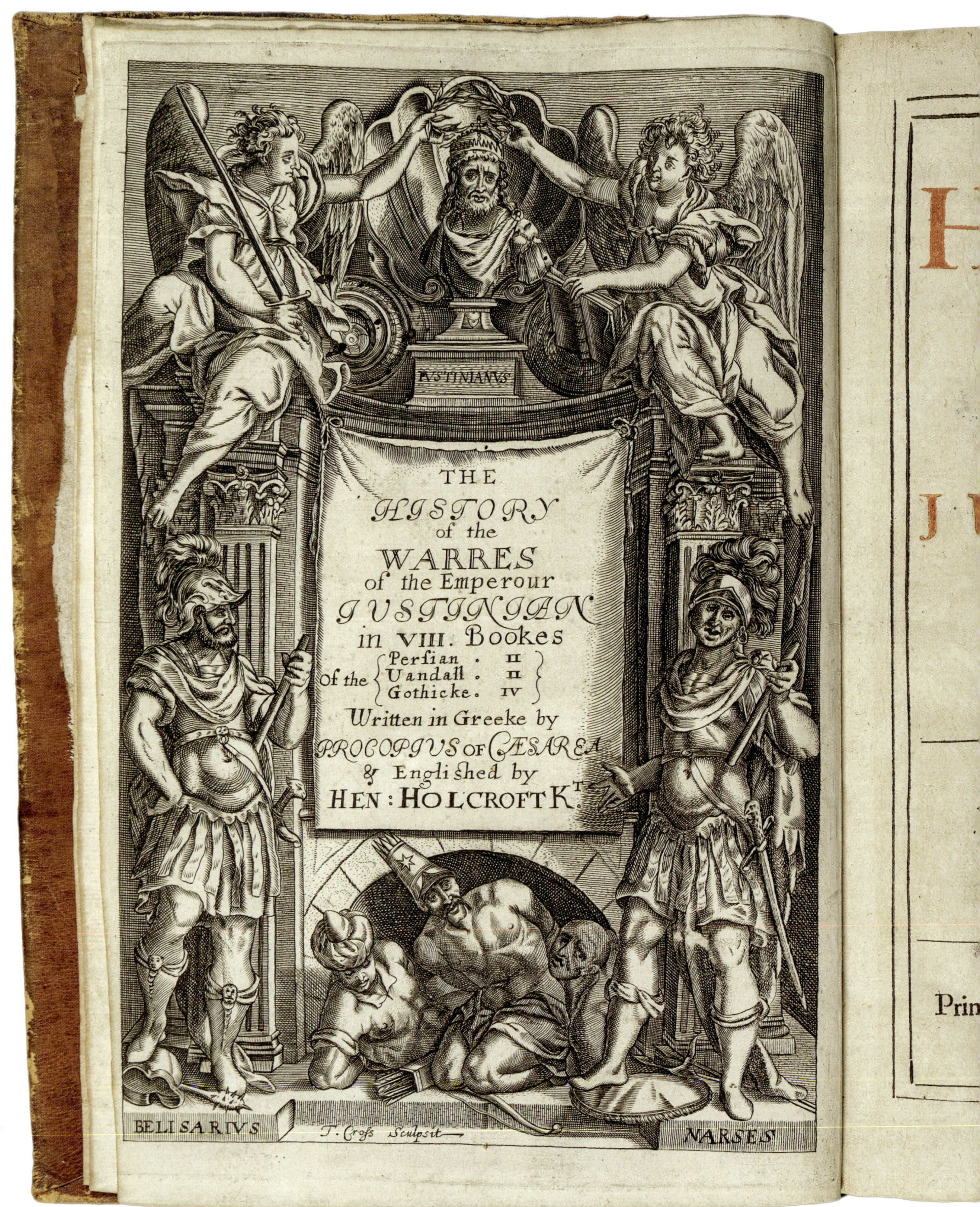
IVSTINIANVS
THE
HISTORY
of the
WARRES
of the Emperour
IUSTINIAN
in VIII. Bookes
Of the Persian . II Uandall . II Gothicke . IV
Written in Greeke by
PROCOPIUS OF CÆSAREA
& Englished by
HEN: HOLCROFT Kt.
BELISARIVS
T. Cross Sculpsit
NARSES
Prin

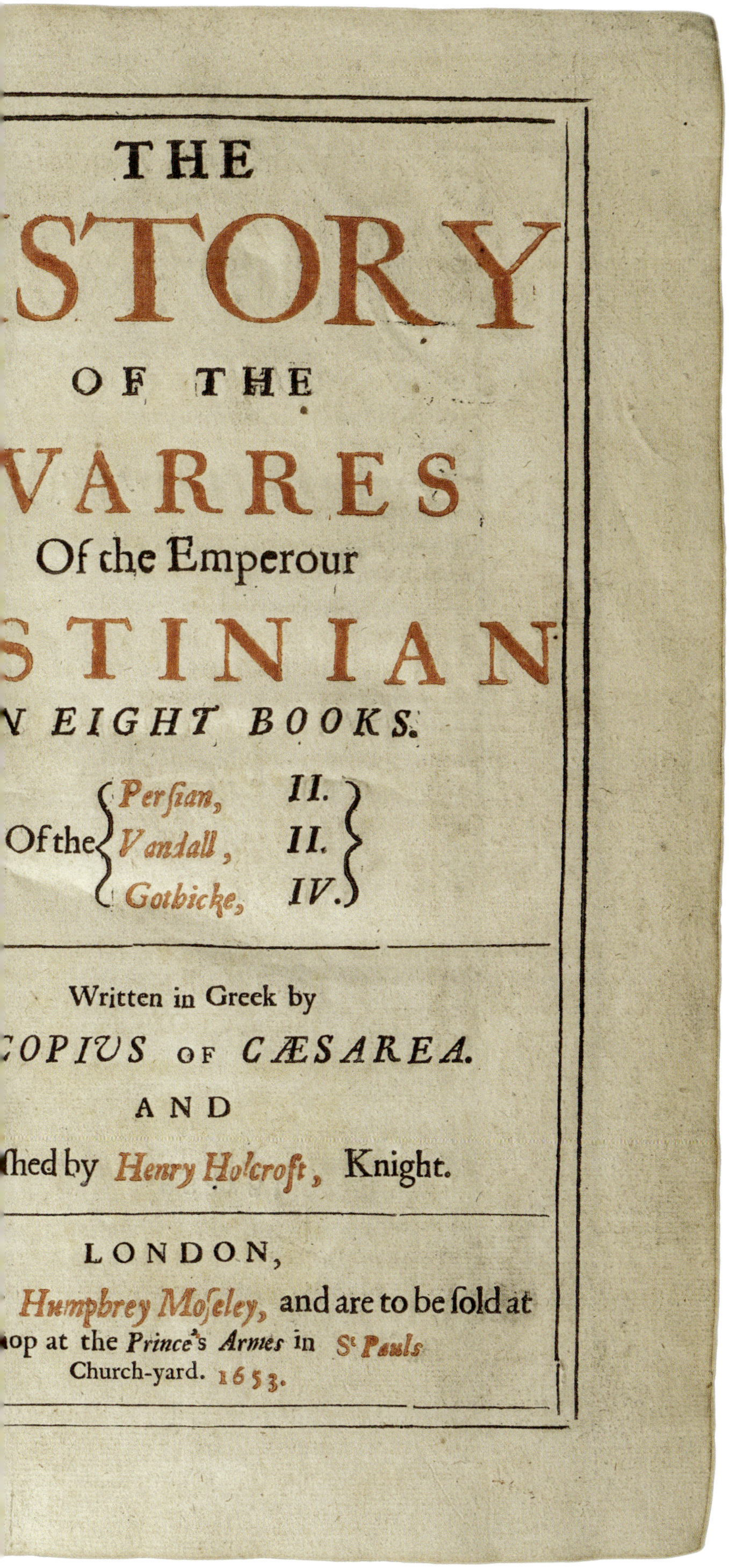

THE
STORY
OF THE
VARRES
Of the Emperour
STINIAN
N EIGHT BOOKS.
Of the Persian, II. Vandall, II. Gothicke, IV.
Written in Greek by
COPIVS OF CÆSAREA.
AND
fhed by Henry Holcroft, Knight.
LONDON,
Humphrey Moseley, and are to be sold at
op at the Prince's Armes in St Pauls
Church-yard. 1653.

crown. Justinian wears a Western crown and vaguely Roman attire, and the inscription of his name on the bust's pedestal is written in Latin. The architecture is similarly Western, depicting a vaguely neo-classical façade, decorated with a draped banner featuring a brief table of contents for the book. The book is here divided into the Persian wars, the Vandal wars, and the Gothic wars. Below this, an apparent depiction of these three foes is shown below, as if coming out of a sewer. The figure on the left, perhaps depicting the Persian enemies, is shown wearing a contemporaneous Ottoman turban and his eyes are downcast. Beside these figures, towering over the scene, is Justinian's military general, Belisarius (c. 505–565), on the far left. He looks across the page to his fellow Byzantine general, Narses (d. 605/6). Both Belisarius and Narses are clearly labeled, and they stand upon the trampled implements of their enemies. The weapons are purposely shown as crude and "primitive," a rustic mace and flimsy shield, to emphasize the subjugation of their enemies. The Byzantines are shown here as resolutely Western; they are illustrated as white Europeans and styled as heroic soldiers with muscular limbs and towering stature.

In Sir Henry Holcroft's frontispiece, we find the clearest iteration of the Byzantine Empire appropriated as fully Western and ecumenically* Christian, a process that appears to have occurred through the act of translation into a modern European language and through the Othering of the Byzantine's enemies. It is in such moments when Islamic adversaries are Othered that

Figure 3.2
Henry Holcroft,
Frontispiece of *The history of the warres of the Emperour Justinian*,
London, 1653,
Nebwerry Library, Case Y 642 .P82

we find the clearest embrace of Byzantium as a Western, European power. The development of this process is hardly linear nor static, demonstrating that Byzantium served as a floating signifier that Western writers used to position themselves against the Islamic world —and, at times, other Christian groups in the East.

As we have seen here, the image of the Byzantine Empire and Constantinople was in flux throughout the medieval and early modern period. The stereotypes about the Empire developed by Western authors during the Middle Ages persisted, yet they were also strategically modified to confront early modern Western anxieties around the Ottoman Turks. The fraught iterations of Byzantium in the early modern period similarly persisted in how Western visitors to Istanbul imagined, Othered, and racialized the Ottoman city itself, contouring how they defined and projected the empires that shared that city as its capital.

Erotic / Exotic Istanbul

By Ambereen Dadabhoy

In the late spring of 1453 the military forces of the Ottoman sultan, Mehmet II (1432–1481), successfully laid siege to and conquered the imperial seat of the Eastern Roman Byzantine Empire, Constantinople. While other Islamicate forces had attempted to capture the city, most notably the Umayyads in the latter part of the seventh century, Constantinople would remain under European, Christian control until the mid-fifteenth century. Mehmet's rousing campaign against the city reverberated across Europe because it signaled the bellicose arrival of the Ottomans into what had hitherto been ambivalently thought of as a European geography. While the conquest made the Ottomans the legitimate rulers of Constantinople, which they renamed Istanbul, it was framed as an existential danger to European powers, since the city offered a portal to further westward Ottoman expansion.[46] The explanations and rationales generated by Europeans for the conquest resorted to forms of racializing, not only of the Ottomans but also of the geography in ways that indicated their Otherness (through religion, ritual, and custom) and the geography's Europeanness. This seeming contradictory and incoherent strategy underscores the shifting and contingent ways that race was being formed in the period and also points to the availability of race as a discourse through which to impose difference. Racial awareness, then, was a commonplace thing, particularly in early modern English and European discourses about Constantinople/Istanbul, the East, and the Ottomans.

The narratives that circulated around Mehmet II's conquest of Constantinople provide the initial racializing material through which subsequent narratives about the empire and its practices would further develop and expand. First-person accounts of the events following the capture of Constantinople fervently remark upon Ottoman "cruelty," "barbarity," "violence," and "venality*." They scrupulously allege the "rapacious" and "savage" nature of the Ottoman forces, from the lowliest soldier to the sultan. As translated and rehearsed in multiple European printed books, the fall of Constantinople portended the fall of Western civilization, with menacing foreign hordes eager to despoil the beauty of the city and its citizens. We find one such narrative in the *History of Mehmed the Conqueror* by Kritovolous (d. 1570), a Greek resident of Imbros who became part of the new Ottoman administration, yet still bemoaned the fall of Constantinople:

> When they had had enough of murder, and the City was reduced to slavery, some of the troops turned to the mansions of the mighty, [. . .] for plunder and spoil. Others went to the robbing

46. Pinar Emiralioğlu points out that the Ottomans commonly slipped between Constantinople and Istanbul when they referred to the city. Pinar Emiralioğlu, *Geographical Knowledge and Imperial Culture in the Early Modern Ottoman Empire* (London: Routledge, 2016), 1.

> of churches, and others dispersed to the simple homes of the common people, stealing, robbing, plundering, killing, insulting, taking and enslaving men, women, and children, old and young, priests, monks—in short, every age and class.[47]

From the European perspective, the fall of the city augured the advent of savagery and barbarism into the heart of European culture and civilization. Indeed, Kritovoulos compares the loss of Constantinople to the loss of other great imperial cities from which Western Europe draws its cultural inheritance including Troy, Babylon, Carthage, Rome, and Jerusalem. Locating Constantinople within this imperial itinerary exposes the cultural and psychic effects of the conquest. It simultaneously highlights Constantinople's elevated position within the European cultural imaginary as vital to European self-fashioning as Europe. Ottoman control of Constantinople endangered not only those living in the confines of the city and its environs, but also it imperiled all of Europe since they now held an imperial seat in that geography.[48]

Kritovoulos's *History* was dedicated to and written for the Sultan; therefore, his lament on the fall of Constantinople, which does agonize over the rapine of the city's fair youth, is mild in its reproach. Other European writers, particularly those far from the action in Constantinople/ Istanbul do not exhibit the same reticence. The early modern discourses I examine below —produced during or after a Western European diplomatic embassy to Istanbul—offer more strident critiques of both the city's capture by Ottoman forces and of Ottoman cultural and imperial practices. These accounts "discover" Ottoman difference through their social, political, and religious Otherness. These differences are further racialized through Ottoman occupation of Constantinople/Istanbul, because the city's prior "European" history renders their control illegitimate. Geography, thus, intersects with the process of race-making, underscoring the claim that "racial formation shape[s] space, give[s] meanings to places, and condition[s] experiences of embodied subjects emplaced in and moving through the material world."[49] In fact, even as the Ottomans are being racialized as non-white and non-European in their relation to Constantinople, the European diplomatic envoys to the imperial capital are being racialized as white and European through their ability to mark the Ottomans as Other to this geography.[50] The physical geography of Constantinople/Istanbul symbolizes endangered white European identity and reflects the whiteness of these writers even as the city and its cultural inheritance are being mobilized by the Ottomans to legitimate their claims to a new identity, to being the new "Caesars of Rome."[51]

The two travelogues* I explore from the Newberry's collection of early printed books on the Ottoman Empire include Nicolas de Nicolay's (1517–1583) *The Navigations, Peregrinations and Voyages Made into Turkie* (1585) and Sir Paul Rycaut's (1629–1700) *The Present State of the Ottoman Empire* (1668).[52] These texts coalesce around their shared European ambassadorial

47. Michael Kritovoulos, *History of Mehmed the Conqueror. By Kritovoulos,* trans. Charles T. Riggs (Princeton: Princeton University Press, 1954), 72.

48. It might seem that we are being quite flexible with our use of Europe and European, but in these premodern texts, we encounter this precise framing of this geography. For example, Kritovoulos points out that when Mehmet travels to Bursa he is going out of Europe (Byzantium) and into Asia. The boundaries between East and West; Europe and Asia are drawn along cultural lines as much as they are geographic.

49. Delaney, "Space that Race Makes," 7.

50. Delaney, 7.

51. Jerry Brotton, *Trading Territories: Mapping the Early Modern World* (Ithaca, NY: Cornell University Press, 1998), 90.

52. Nicolas de Nicolay, *The Navigations, Peregrinations and Voyages, Made into Turky, by Nicholas Nicholay Dualphinois, Lord of Arfeuile, Chamberlain and Geographer in Ordinary to the King of France: Containing Sundry Singularities Which the Author Hath There Seen and Observed: Divided into Four Books, with Divers Fair and Memorable Histories, Which Happend in Our Time* in *Collection of Voyages and Travels*, ed. Thomas Osborne, (T. Osborne, 1747), 10920 v. 7. Paul Rycaut, *The history of the present state of the Ottoman Empire: containing the maxims of the Turkish polity, the most material points of the Mahometan religion, their sects and heresies, their convents and religious votaries: their military discipline, with an exact computation of their forces both by sea and land: illustrated with divers pieces of sculpture representing the variety of habits amongst the Turks: in three books* (London: Printed for R. Clavell, J. Robinson and A. Churchill., 1686), Chicago, Newberry Library. F 59 .764. The editions cited in this essay were accessed from *Early English Books Online*, Nicolas de Nicolay, *The nauigations, peregrinations and voyages, made into turkie by nicholas nicholay daulphinois, lord of arfeuile, chamberlaine and geographer ordinarie to the king of fraunce conteining sundry singularities which the*

missions into the Ottoman Empire and their subsequent knowledge-making projects, which frame the Ottoman Empire, its people, and its culture as totally foreign and Other to their own European Christian cultures and identities. The epistemic power of these texts imposes a racial frame upon the Ottoman Empire and its geographies — including Constantinople/Istanbul — that tidily aligns with the Orientalism undergirding these projects. These texts, the publication of each almost a century apart, attest to the longue durée* of both racial formation and Orientalism and the strategic ways these discourses intersect in order to advance relations of epistemic power in situations where material power is often lacking. Constantinople/Istanbul becomes an important site/sight in these texts precisely because of its imperial history — past and present — and because its physical and cultural geography animates the alterity upon which these texts insist. Indeed, early modern European travel writing itself mandates such forms of difference. It is a discourse that demands the production of Otherness while simultaneously exerting control over that Otherness so that it becomes less threatening and can be domesticated. As Mary Louise Pratt explains in *Imperial Eyes*, such texts "created the imperial order for Europeans 'at home' and gave them their place in it. [. . .] They created a sense of curiosity, excitement, adventure, and even moral fervor about European expansionism. They were, [. . .] a key instrument, in other words, in creating the 'domestic subject' of empire."[53] These travelogues elevated the power of the home audience, allowing them to apprehend the Other while also creating in them a shared white identity crafted through opposition with that Other. Geography plays a crucial role within this calculus because land and territory are central to imperial projects, through physical control and domination and through epistemic domination, as we witness in discourses such as travelogues, which contain various techniques of knowledge production including maps and images of foreign people. These texts bring the Other home, which allows for both the home and the Other to be racialized.

Nicolas de Nicolay's *The Navigations, Peregrinations, and Voyages Made into Turkey* appeared in English translation in 1585, almost twenty years after its publication in French and almost thirty years after the actual embassy into the Ottoman Empire that Nicolay chronicles.[54] Traveling to the Ottoman Empire in order to effect a diplomatic and military alliance between Henry II and Sultan Süleyman, Nicolay (1517–1583) was employed by his monarch in this capacity because of his proven military, cartographic, espionage, and diplomatic skills.[55] His *Navigations* rehearses some of those immediate reasons for the embassy, but its primary interest lies in making Ottoman alterity legible to his domestic audience. Divided into four parts, the *Navigations* relates the voyage to Istanbul via the Eastern Mediterranean, the customs and habits of Ottoman imperial subjects, the administrative bureaucracy of the empire, and Islamic religious practice. Wide and capacious in its investigations, the *Navigations* provides one of the earliest, most comprehensive, and authoritative European accounts of the Ottoman Empire. Its popularity, as exhibited through several print runs and translation into many European languages, identifies the European appetite for material on the Ottoman Empire, while also signaling the text's epistemic authority on the Ottoman Empire. Moreover, the signature feature of the *Navigations* are the woodcuts that accompany Nicolay's

author hath there seene and obserued: Deuided into foure bookes, with threescore figures, naturally set forth as well of men as women, according to the diuersitie of nations, their port, intreatie, apparrell, lawes, religion and maner of liuing, aswel in time of warre as peace: With diuers faire and memorable histories, happened in our time. translated out of the french by T. washington the younger (London, At the cost of John Stell] by Thomas Dawson, 1585), https://www.proquest.com/books/nauigations-peregrinations-voyages-made-into/docview/2240927451/se-2?accountid=10141 (accessed December 10, 2021).

53. Mary Louise Pratt, *Imperial Eyes: Travel Writing and Transculturation* (New York: Routledge, 2007), 3.

54. *The Navigations* provide a rich resource into early modern European construction of cultural, racial, and religious difference beyond that of Christian and Muslim. Kaplan and Katz's essay in this volume, Fashioning Racial Materiality in Nicolas de Nicolay's Representations of Jews (pp.–pp.), explores *The Navigations'* representation of Jewish identity.

55. Marcus Keller, "Nicolas de Nicolay's 'Navigations' and the Domestic Politics of Travel Writing," *L'Esprit Créateur* 48, no. 1 (2008): 18–31, http://www.jstor.org/stable/26289452.

narrative. The images of the manifold subjects under Ottoman dominion display both the empire's alterity and its power to incorporate Others into its imperial body politic. Because travelogues traffic in knowledge and truth claims, the *Navigations'* accompanying images inscribe, stabilize, and render knowable — controllable — Ottoman imperial Otherness. The images operate as an easily digestible shorthand for cultural and human difference, performing important race-work by accessing the visual register upon which race functions and depends. In offering embodied, physical images of the Other, Nicolay's ethnographic* depictions also consolidate white, European, Christian identity — because that difference is easily distinguishable from the subjects on view in his text.

While the entirety of the *Navigations* is of interest to students and scholars of early modern racial formation, I focus on the representation of two geographies designated in these texts as particularly Ottoman: the harem and the hammam. The word harem in Arabic contains a double meaning: that which is sacred and that which is forbidden. As spatially manifested through the architecture of Islamicate geographies, the harem is a restricted and intimate domestic space, separated from other public rooms of the home. In the Ottoman imperial context, the harem was the private quarters of the sultan, where he could remove himself from the public and bureaucratic spaces of the *sarayı* or palace. The double meaning that the word holds is crucial to the spatial logics under which it operates, which is why in Islamicate regimes, the places of intimate, familial, and political relations were labeled as harems. The domestic or imperial harem operates under a similar ontological premise: the harem is the most closed and intimate site within the home or imperial palace, entrance to its domains highly restricted because it is the site of familial or imperial reproduction and longevity. The harem then is simultaneously a geographic locale and an ideological site, wherein the family or dynasty ensures its futurity. The harem was also the women's quarters, occupied by the sultan's mother and his concubines, in addition to the enslaved people such as Black eunuchs meant to patrol and oversee the security and sanctity of this domain.[56]

The harem's gendered and racialized habitus rendered it a particularly exotic geography for European travelers and audiences. It became the site *par excellence* through which to locate Ottoman alterity. No man who was not the sultan or one of the Black eunuchs in charge of the harem could gain access to its environs. No visitors, no matter how important the diplomatic mission that brought them to the empire, would have been able to see the living arrangements of the sultan. The harem's proscribed status transformed it into a site of lurid European fantasy. George Sandys's (1578–1644) *Relation of a Journey* (1610), for example, depicts the women of the harem in semi-pornographic detail (Cat. No. 10). They were a site/sight he could only have accessed in his dreams, yet his account, with its accompanying engraving purports to relate truth.[57] In such an imaginary, the harem was a place where all manner of sexual deviance was thought to be practiced with furious gusto, and where perceived or projected Ottoman sexual liberty further served to differentiate and demonize Ottoman cultural and religious mores from those of Christian Europe. Indeed, the fact that the sultan's concubines were commonly enslaved women from Eastern Europe, the Caucuses, and other such geographies was both a cause of lament, because of the physical and sexual danger posed by the Ottoman Empire, and a source of cultural and ethnic value because the fairness and desirability of these women reflected their own superiority. Whiteness subtended both of these contradictory responses. Similarly, the hammam, or the public bathhouse, aroused related

56. Leslie P. Peirce, *The Imperial Harem: Women and Sovereignty in the Ottoman Empire* (New York: Oxford University Press, 1993); for an analysis of queer and racialized labor within the Ottoman harem, see Abdulhamit Arvas, "Early Modern Eunuchs and the Transing of Gender and Race" *Journal for Early Modern Cultural Studies* 19, no. 4 (2019): 116–36. https://doi.org/10.1353/jem.2019.0040.

57. For more on Sandys' depiction of women in the harem, see George Sandys, Richard Field, and William Barrett, *A Relation of a Iourney Begun an. Dom. 1610: Foure Bookes, Containing a Description of the Turkish Empire of Aegypt, of the Holy Land, of the Remote Parts of Italy and Ilands Adioyning.* (London: Printed for W. Barrett, 1615), Chicago, Newberry Library LC: 20011267.

anxieties and animated parallel prurient interest. The public bath was another sex-segregated space and one of the few locales that Ottoman women could gather outside of their homes. The hammam offered women freedom from patriarchal* surveillance and so became another site/sight in the masculinist European imaginary wherein to fix Ottoman moral laxity and cultural lewdness. Ottoman women, then, functioned as symbols for Ottoman difference. Their social position and the mandates of the sex-segregated spaces they occupied helped the writers of European travelogues exhibit Ottoman tyranny while also ascribing to Ottoman women the empire's gendered and racial Otherness.

When Nicolay turns his attention to the imperial palace and to its many and varied inhabitants, including the women in the harem, he is offering up one of the sites/sights necessary to any discursive representation of the Ottoman Empire. The woodcut of "The great lady and wife vnto the Turk" (Figure 3.3) precedes this chapter, presenting the image of the wife of Sultan Süleyman, Hurrem Sultan or Roxolana as she was popularly called in the West. The portrait offers for popular consumption the figure of a woman who would rarely be seen outside of the imperial family, whose public movements were deliberately curated affairs of state, and whose power resided in guarding and controlling her image. In fact, the semblance of the image of the "The great lady and wife" to the actual Hurrem is quite doubtful; what is not doubtful is the European hunger for such images and knowledge about Ottoman women and their condition. Nicolay's rehearsal of the site/sight of the harem performs the same ideological work as his woodcut. It activates the early modern European appetite for the exotic and erotic East, while also conjuring the discourse of whiteness to racialize the Ottomans as non-white both somatically and culturally. In the citational* manner of Orientalist discourses, Nicolay's harem description relates an already familiar narrative to his readers, of vulnerable white European women and of the boundless material and sexual excess of the Ottoman Empire:

> whithin which do dwell the wiues & concubines of the great Turk, which in number are aboue 200. being the most part daughters of Christians, [. . .] presented vnto the great Turke, who keepeth them within this Sarail, wel apparrelled, nourished & entertained vnder streight keeping of the Eunuches, and euery ten of them haue a Matrone, too instruct, gouerne, and teach them too woorke all sorts of needle woorkes. The captaine of this Sarail called Capiangassi, is also an Eunuch or a gelded man, [. . .] he hath vnder him fortie Eunuches, which supply the common seruice of these Dames, of whiche the great Lorde taketh his pleasure when hee thinketh good: and if it so come too passe that any of them be gotten with childe, he causeth her to be separated from the other.[58]

While Nicolay notes that the harem was a place of instruction for its occupants, where they were educated in various domestic arts, its primary function as the site of dynastic futurity is obscured by his emphasis on the geographic origins of the concubines in the sultan's harem. As Leslie P. Peirce points out, "by the mid-fifteenth century, legal marriage had lapsed" within the Ottoman imperial household as a way to ensure dynastic lineage.[59] In its place was the widespread practice of concubinage and the elevated status granted to the mothers of the sultan's children. The anonymous concubines we encounter in Nicolay's narrative point to this practice, but their situation provokes anxiety in his text because it signals the military and regional power of the Ottoman Empire to acquire and incorporate Others into its imperial political body. In fact, the women's incorporation signals an erasure of their ethnic and racial status since any children

58. Nicolay, *Nauigations*, trans. Washington, 189.

59. Pierce, *Imperial Harem*, 29.

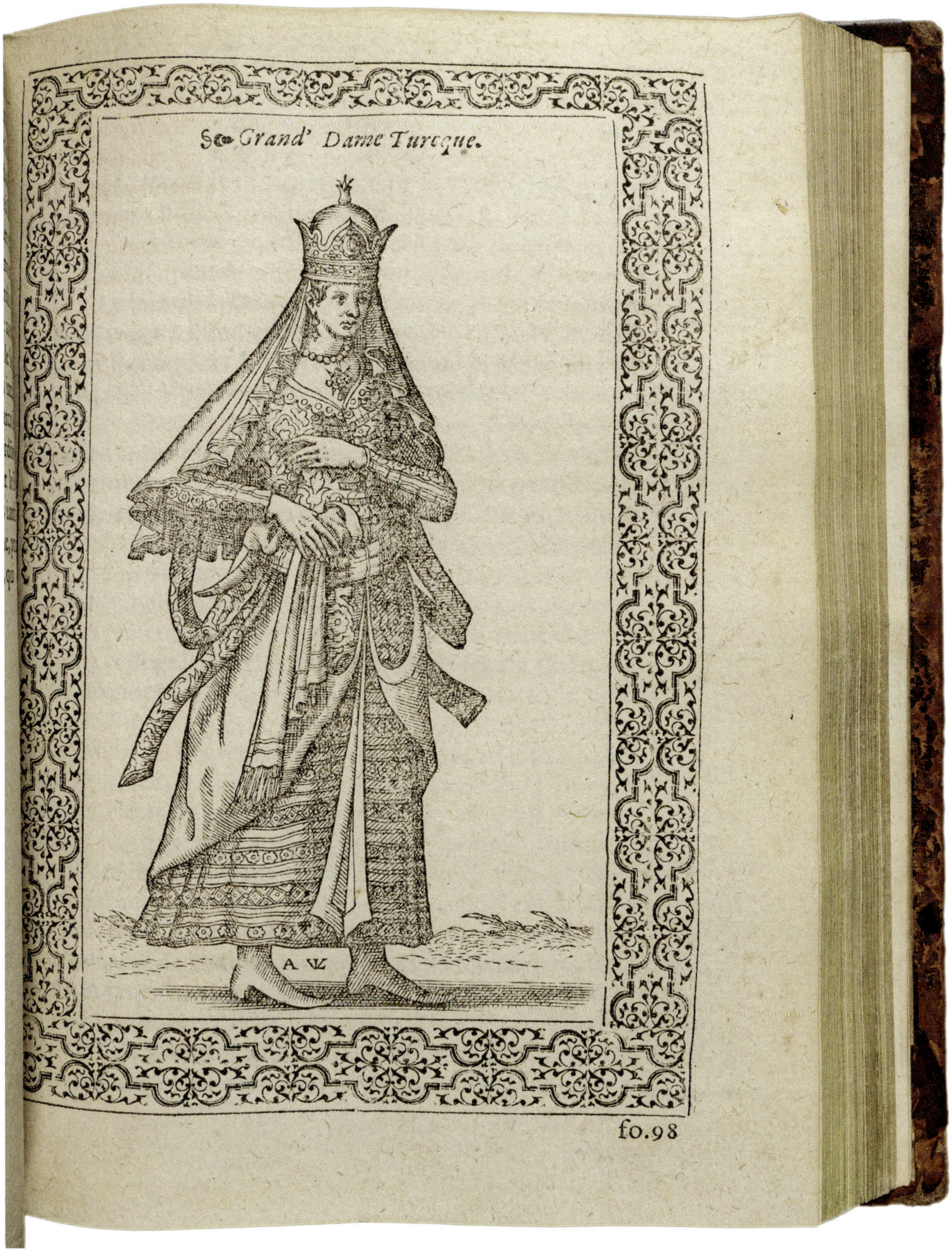

Figure 3.3
Nicolas de Nicolay, "Grand Dame Turque" (98r),
Les navigations pérégrinations et voyages, faicts en la Turquie,
Antwerp, 1576,
Newberry Library, Wing ZP 5465 .S587

they might give birth to will be Ottoman subjects and might one day rule the empire.

The political realities of the harem and its organization are elided; however, in favor of the shocking and spectacularly Other site/sight that the harem offers: a location of sexual excess and a space where one finds the exotic, unusual, and prodigious, such as the eunuchs that patrol its limits and grant access into its erotic domains. The "gelded men" favored by the Ottomans to control sexuality within the harem symbolize the sexual perversion that structures European representations of the Ottoman Empire and its geographies.[60] Near the end of his description, Nicolay admits that he has not himself observed the sites/sights through which he has titillated his audience; however, by befriending a eunuch, Zafer Aga, a "former Ragusan," he is able to have his curiosity appeased and his eye-witness authority confirmed: Zafer Aga "satisfie[d] my mind, caused to be be clothed two publique Turkish women, with very rich apparrell, which hee sent for the Bezestan whereas there is too be solde of all sortes, by the which I made the draughtes and protractes heere represented vnto you."[61] These Turkish sex workers are substitutes for the women in the harem—they are the ones Nicolay can access and through whom his entire description is sanctioned (Figure 3.4).

Whatever discretion Nicolay exhibits in his relation of the harem disappears when his narrative arrives at the sex-segregated space of the hammam. Framed as a religious observance, the Islamic injunction to perform ablutions before prayers, the practice of bathing still manages to find censure with Nicolay because his Christian religious position cannot allow any Islamic practice to have spiritual value: "And principally for, the obseruing of their law which commādeth y • no Muselmans shall enter into their Mosques■ without they be first wel washed and purified, these brutish Barbarians esteeming of the outward washing, and not that which inwardly toucheth the soule."[62] For Nicolay, such cleansing practices are further evidence of Islam's fixation on the body and not the soul: from his perspective, a clean body and an unclean soul is a sign of Islamic spiritual bankruptcy and a racializing discourse which positions Islam as foul and dirty in contrast with the pristine and white truth of Christianity.

Nicolay advances this claim by meticulously detailing the "deviant" sexual practices that he believes Ottoman women indulge in at the hammam. He points out that Ottoman women are usually confined to their homes; therefore, visits to the hammam offer them freedom from the domestic and patriarchal spheres:

> principalest reason is, to haue good occasion and honest excuse too goe abroade out of their houses, within the whiche they are continually closed vppe for the greate ielousie of theyr husbandes, or rather for the obseruing of the ancient custome of their ancetors, whiche after that sorte kepte theyr wiues & daughters closed vp in the backsides of their houses, which they cal Ginaises: so as the Turky women being shut vp without permission to go abroad, nor to appeare in the streets openly, except it be going to the bathes, wherto they ne•erthelesse goe with their faces couered too bring their Ielous husbands out of suspition, which continually so keepe them vnder subiection and closed in.[63]

Ottoman masculine tyranny, provocatively linked here to Greek social practice through Nicolay's reference to the *gynaeceum*, sutures women's confinement to this geography, naturalizing it through patriarchal lineage and custom. Like the sultan who pens up his concubines, Ottoman men, too, exhibit irrational "jealousy and suspicion" of their wives. While the narrative seems sympathetic to Ottoman women

60. Jane Hathaway, *The Chief Eunuch of the Ottoman Harem: From African Slave to Power-Broker* (Cambridge: Cambridge University Press), 2018.

61. Nicolay, *Nauigations,* trans. Washington, 197.

62. Nicolay, *Nauigations,* trans. Washington, 204.

63. Nicolay, *Nauigations,* trans. Washington, *206*.

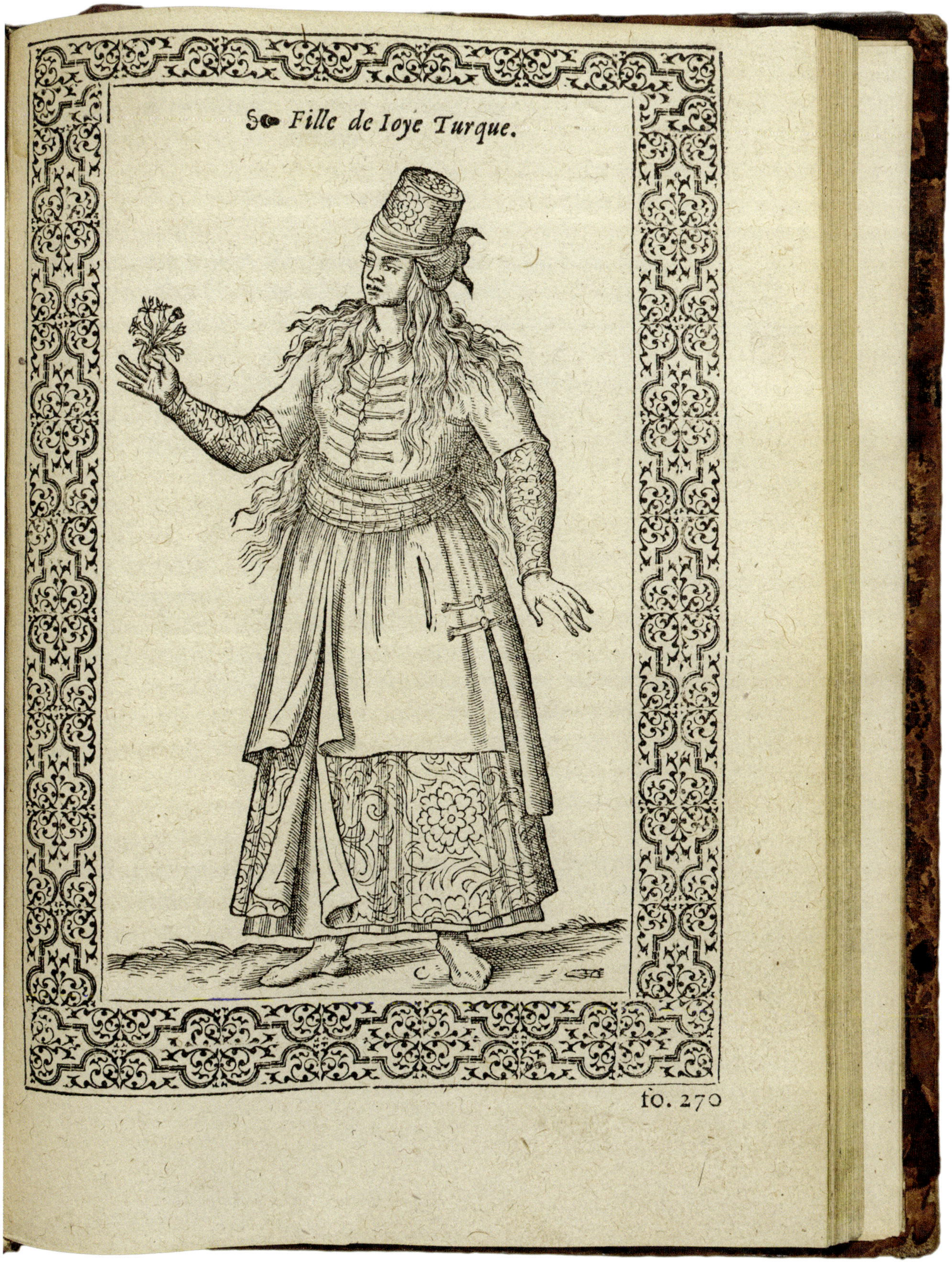

Figure 3.4
Nicolas de Nicolay, "Fille de Ioye Turque" (270r),
Les navigations pérégrinations et voyages, faicts en la Turquie,
Antwerp, 1576,
Newberry Library, Wing ZP 5465 .S587

and their "imprisoned" condition, Nicolay suggests that the fears of Ottoman men are well-founded, since Ottoman women are given to all manner of "unnatural" and "degenerate" sexuality:

> somtimes they do go. 10. or 12. of them together, & somtimes more in a company aswel Turks as Grecians, & do familiarly wash one another, wherby it cōmeth to passe that amōgst the womē of Leuā, ther is very great amity proceding only through the frequentatiō & resort to y • bathes: yea & somtimes become so feruētly in loue the one of the other as if it were with men, in such sort that perceiuing some maidē, or woman■ of excellēt beauty, they wil not ceasse vntil they haue found means to bath with thē, & to handle & gr•pe them euery where at their pleasures, so ful they are of luxuriousnes & feminine wantonnes.[64]

Same-sex desire, presented as "luxuriousnes & feminine wantonnes," is another sign of Ottoman difference, which is particularly gendered. Nicolay presents his readers with aggressive and dangerous Ottoman women who embody irreligious and immoral sexuality. The site/sight of the hammam represents sexual inversion. By appropriating the masculine role and by cuckolding their husbands, Ottoman women usurp their social location within the patriarchal regime. Their hypersexuality destabilizes that regime by effeminizing Ottoman men. Thus, while Ottoman men seek to confine their women to sex-segregated spaces, those same locales endanger the stability of patriarchal rule. The site/sight Nicolay conjures performs race-work by rendering Ottoman women and their (imagined) desires as monstrous Others.[65] Thus, Nicolay's descriptions of the sex-segregated spaces of the harem and the hammam establish Ottoman difference within the imbricating formations of race, gender, and religion. Their alterity resides primarily in cultural practices but simultaneously in Nicolay's ability to fabricate their difference *and* locate it geographically. In this way, the *Navigations* actively participates in Orientalist discourse.

Almost a century later, Sir Paul Rycaut (1629–1700) traveled to the Ottoman Empire as the secretary to the Earl of Winchelsea on an ambassadorial mission from Charles II to Mehmet IV. Rycaut spent five years in Istanbul on that embassy and then more time in the Ottoman Empire as the general consul for the Levant Company.[66] By the time of the publication of *The Present State of the Ottoman Empire* in 1668, Rycaut was quite familiar with the social, cultural, political, and bureaucratic milieu of the Ottoman Empire, yet his text betrays a cultural chauvinism* akin to what we find in Nicolay.[67] Indeed, building on the tradition of writing about the Ottoman Empire from travelogues like Nicolay's and histories like Richard Knolles's (1545–1610) *The Generall Historie of the Turkes* (1603), Rycaut traverses familiar ground. The innovation of his text is in the virulent tropes of difference it harnesses to represent Ottoman Otherness.[68] Rycaut's depictions of the harem illustrate how this site/sight conjures difference by harnessing and establishing racialized tropes of Ottoman identity. His account of the harem differs in significant ways from his predecessor's through its focus on the lives of historical Ottoman women. Writing in the latter half of the

64. Nicolay, *Nauigations*, Trans. Washington, 207.

65. Hall, *Things of Darkness*, 153–60.

66. Linda T. Darling, "Ottoman Politics through British Eyes: Paul Rycaut's *The Present State of the Ottoman Empire*," *Journal of World History* 5, no. 1 (1994): 71–73, https://www.jstor.org/stable/20078582.

67. Rycaut, *History*, Newberry Library 57–290. The edition cited in this essay was accessed from *Early English Books Online*, Sir Paul Rycaut, 1628–1700, *The present state of the ottoman empire containing the maxims of the turkish politie, the most material points of the mahometan religion, their sects and heresies, their convents and religious votaries, their military discipline . . . : Illustrated with divers pieces of sculpture, representing the variety of habits amongst the turks, in three books / by paul rycaut esq . . .* (London, Printed for John Starkey and Henry Brome .., 1668), www.proquest.com/books/present-state-ottoman-empire-containing-maxims/docview/2240924764/se-2?accountid=10141 (accessed December 10, 2021).

68. Richard Knolles, *The Generall Historie of the Turkes, from the First Beginning Ofthat Nation to the Rising of the Othoman Familie: With All the Notable Expeditions of the Christian Princes Against Them* (London: Printed by A. Islip, 1603), Chicago, Newberry Library Case F 59 .463.

seventeenth century, Rycaut narrates the realities of imperial life under the so-called "sultanate of women," a period of political upheaval in the empire when the mothers of the reigning sultan exerted an outsized influence over their sons and therefore over official imperial policy.[69] The shadow rule of women was met with deep criticism in elite Ottoman political circles and led to the murder of the sultan's mother Kösem in 1651 by his concubine, Turhan, and her allies.[70] Rycaut presents this intrigue in his book; however, it operates in service of his larger claims about the misrule practiced by this woman-led shadow government:

> For in the time of Sultan Mahomet, the present Grand Signior, when the whole government of the Empire rested in the hands of one Mulki Kadin, a young audacious woman, by the extraordinary favour and love of the Queen Mother (who, as it was divulged, exercised an unnatural kind of carnality with the said Queen) so that nothing was left to the counsel and order of the Visier and grave Seniors, but was first to receive approbation and authority from her; the black Eunuchs and Negroes gave laws to all, and the cabinet councels were held in the secret appartments of the women; and there were proscriptions made, Officers discharged, or ordained as were most proper to advance the interest of this Feminine Government.[71]

Rycaut's "feminine government" is both gendered and racialized: its deviance lies in the same-sex desire he attributes to the *valide sultan* (queen mother) and the concubine, Mulki. Moreover, the power that the Black eunuchs exert over administrators in the palace serves as another source of agitation for Rycaut. Political power in the hands of women and Black men can only be suspect and illegitimate.[72] Thus, the remedy for this unnatural rule was the restoration of power into appropriately masculine hands. At the same time, however, Rycaut emphasizes how even this action served to undermine the power of the sultan:

> But at length, the souldiery (not used to the tyranny of women) no longer supporting this kind of servitude, in a moment resolved on a remedy, and in great tumults came to the Seraglio, where commanding the Grand Signior himself to the Kiosch, or banquetting-house, demanded without further prologue the heads of the favourite Eunuchs; there was no argument or Rhetorick to be opposed to this unreasonable multitude.[73]

The sultan's power is eroded on all sides: from his mother on the one hand, and from his subordinates on the other. Rycaut's narrative signals the deterioration in the masculine power of the sultan.

The decline of the empire as embodied by the effeminate figure of the sultan is ironically reiterated through Rycaut's relation of the degenerate sexuality to be found in the harem, which includes same-sex desire between men as well as the deeply ritualized sexual escapades between the sultan and his concubines. Taken together, these enslaved people represent the racial and cultural alterity of the empire, particularly as it seeks to incorporate Others into itself, but they are also sites/sights in themselves, spectacles of human difference. Before arriving at the doors of the imperial harem filled with beautiful enslaved Christian women, Rycaut pauses on the other important inhabitants of the harem that includes the beautiful youths also captured and enslaved from the empire's Christian territories, and the dwarves, mutes, and eunuchs who function as oddities and objects of interest for his domestic

69. Pierce, *Imperial Harem,* 65.

70. Pierce, 24.

71. Rycaut, *History*, 10–11.

72. As observed in the catalogue entry in this volume on Jean Racine's 1672 play *Bajazet* (Cat. No. 34), women and Black eunuchs were cause for much sexual and political anxiety in the early modern European imaginary.

73. Rycaut, *History*, 11.

audience. About the enslaved youths, Rycaut points out how the sex-segregated living arrangements of the imperial palace contribute to same- sex desire, which is not confined to desire between the youths only, but also implicates the sultan:

> The Grand Signiors themselves have also been slaves to this inordinate passion. For Sultan Morat became so enamoured of an Armenian Boy called Musa as betrayed him, though otherwise a discreet Prince, to a thousand follies; and at another time preferred a youth for his beauty only from the Novitiate of Galata, to be one of the Pages of his Haz-Oda or Chamber of his Royal Presence, and in a short time made him Silahtar Aga or Sword-bearer, one of the greatest Offices in the Seraglio. And this present Sultan became so enamoured of a Canstantinopolitan youth, one of the Pol, called Kulogli, or Son of a slave, that he made him his chief Favourite, never could content himself without his Company, Clothed him like himself, made him ride by his side, commanded all to present and honour him, in the same manner as if he had made him Companion of the Empire.[74]

Rycaut's account of Ottoman sultans' passion for Christian youth points to the desirability of white men and the depravity of the sultan. The usurpation of rank effected by the sultan's desire indicates disorder within the imperial political body, just as the same-sex desire suggests disorder from heteronormativity*. The sultans' desire, which is not confined to one particular sultan, demonstrates inherited "degeneracy." By politicizing the sexual practices of Islamicate regimes, Rycaut participates in a long Orientalist tradition that accuses Muslims of sodomy and other same-sex acts in an effort to delegitimize their religion as well as their political regimes.[75] In this case, sex acts, religion, and race corroborate Ottoman Otherness.

Rycaut further mobilizes sexual and racial difference when he finally arrives at the site/sight of the women's quarters of the harem. Knowing full well that his exegesis upon the empire and its composition would be incomplete without a rehearsal of the "delights" of the harem, Rycaut, tongue-in-cheek notes that he has brought his readers to "the door," and that it would violate his readers' expectations if he did "not introduce [them] into those apartments, where the Grand Signiors Mistresses are lodged: And though I ingenuously confess my acquaintance there (as all other my conversation with Women in Turky [sic]) is but strange and unfamiliar; yet not to be guilty of this discourtesie."[76] Rycaut admits his ignorance on the matter of Ottoman women and especially on the occupants of the sultan's harem; however, his lack of knowledge does not stop him from contributing to knowledge about the Ottoman Empire and its customs. Indeed, he needs no first-hand knowledge on this subject because, as Edward Said records:

> Every writer on the Orient (and this is true even of Homer) assumes some Oriental precedent, some previous knowledge of the Orient, to which he refers and on which he relies. Additionally, each work on the Orient *affiliates* itself with other works, with audiences, with institutions, with the Orient itself. The ensemble of relationships between works, audiences, and some particular aspects of the Orient therefore constitutes an analyzable formation.[77]

Rycaut depends on the citationality of European discourses on the harem to construct his own narrative.

74. Rycaut, 33

75. Norman Daniel, *Islam and the West: The Making of an Image* (Edinburgh: Edinburgh University Press, 1980), 144. For more on Islamic, Moorish, or Ottoman sexuality, see Ian Smith, "The Queer Moor: Bodies, Borders, and Barbary Inns," in *A Companion to the Global Renaissance: English Literature and Culture in the Era of Expansion,* ed. Jyotsna G. Singh, 190–204, Blackwell Companions to Literature and Culture 60 (Oxford: Wiley–Blackwell, 2009); Abdulhamit Arvas, "Leander in the Ottoman Mediterranean: The Homoerotics of Abduction in the Global Renaissance," *English Literary Renaissance* 51, no. 1 (2021): 31–62, https://doi.org/10.1086/711601.

76. Rycaut, *History*, 38.

77. Edward Said, *Orientalism* (New York: Pantheon Books, 1978), 20.

The harem functions as a necessary trope to articulate the authenticity and veracity of his narrative. Rehearsing this narrative proves Rycaut's epistemic power; therefore, it becomes a requisite trope of European travel and diplomatic writing about the Ottoman Empire.

Rycaut's troped* harem is prefaced with the acknowledgment that these women are enslaved, stolen from their homelands to serve at the erotic pleasure of the sultan. Within this reminder, Rycaut raises the racial dimension of Ottoman concubinage:

> here an army of Virgins make it the only study and business of their life to obtain the single nod of invitation to the Bed of their great Master. The Reader then must know that this Assembly of fair Women (for it is probable there is no other in the Seraglio) are commonly prizes of the Sword, taken at Sea and at Land, as far fetched as the Turk commands, or the wandering Tartar makes his excursions, composed almost of as many Nations as there are Countries of the world; none of which are esteemed worthy of this Preferment, unless beautiful and undoubted Virgins.[78]

As Kim F. Hall argues, "fair" is a racially freighted term, indicating moral and aesthetic qualities that coalesce around whiteness and the desirable body of the white woman. Fairness secures futurity because dynastic discourses demand fair women to ensure the generation of the community. In early modern texts fairness is often made visible through tropes of blackness.[79] We observe this process in the troped harem through its emphasis on the beauty of enslaved white European Christian women and the presence of Black eunuchs. Rycaut's focus here is on the reach of Ottoman sexual tyranny: the women who populate the sultan's seraglio are taken from far and wide "at Sea and a Land," suggesting total Ottoman control of the geography surrounding their empire.

Both Rycaut and Nicolay evoke feminine Ottoman geographies for their readers to satisfy the prurient curiosity about these forbidden spaces, which simultaneously exert discursive control over the subjects and places about which they are writing. These texts display a form of early modern Orientalism by attempting to fix the gendered and racial Otherness of the Ottoman Empire in its sex-segregated spaces. While Nicolay's *Navigations* contains a more neutral or documentary tone, Rycaut's *Present State* makes no such attempts. Difference as demonization marks Rycaut's ideological investment in his ethnographic study of the Ottoman Empire. We might attribute the shift in tone and aim between Nicolay and Rycaut as one of historical contingency and material power. Nicolay's visit to Istanbul was during the reign of Sultan Süleyman, called "the Magnificent" in Europe, while Rycaut was writing during a period when Europeans foresaw (or hoped for) the decline of Ottoman imperial power. Tethered to the many cultural and religious differences of the Ottoman Empire, Rycaut's focus on women and other marginalized identities underscores its imminent demise, while Nicolay's text makes no such claims.

The Istanbul represented in early modern European and English travel writing (itself a problematic generic label, given the diplomatic purposes of the texts I have investigated) produce a geography firmly ensconced in familiar notions of the "East." It exhibits the traits and stereotypes that popularly circulated about Ottoman culture: its violence and barbarism on the one hand, and its luxurious carnality on the other. These texts find the East as they expected to encounter it. In other words, the Istanbul of these texts corroborates their popular belief, and that confirmation supports the epistemological power of their representations. While buttressing the authority of these writers to make knowledge about the Ottoman Other, these discourses also function as racializing projects wherein they construct racial difference in nonwhite Others and racial normativity and hegemony

78. Rycaut, *History*, 38–39.

79. Kim F. Hall, *Things of Darkness: Economies of Race and Gender in Early Modern England* (Ithaca, NY: Cornell University Press, 1995), 3–24.

in their target audiences. Within such processes of racial formation, geography becomes an important arena through which to exert power. Texts about foreign, non-European geographies are always texts that engage in race-making and in promoting the interests of imperial domination. Geography is the ground upon which these discourses construct identity and difference. Because of its own unstable geographic position, straddling both Asia and Europe, Constantinople/Istanbul is a slippery geography, escaping attempts to fix its identity as Western or Eastern. It is precisely because of its fluidity that the discourses charted above perform extraordinary race-work in order to ensure that the city remains Other to the white European self.

RACE, EMPIRE, AND CARTOGRAPHY

By Ricardo Padrón and Risa Puleo

We often think of maps as objective representations of territory but, in actuality, they tend to embody a particular point of view, one that is embedded in the culture and ideology of the mapmaker, not to mention the particular purposes for which the map was made. This essay explores the relationship between maps and race in two very different cartographic projects produced in two very different contexts for very different reasons. The first, a set of maps by the French mapmaker Nicolas de Fer (1646–1720) represents one of many attempts by European intellectuals to make the world and its people visible to their fellow Europeans in ways that were supposed to be objective and scientific but were in fact saturated with the ideology of Eurocentrism that sustained Western colonialism. The second, a map made by an unknown Native inhabitant of colonial Mexico and known as the *Farmers vs. Covarrubias map* (1569), represents one of the many maps produced by Indigenous Americans in their effort to defend a variety of interests from the onslaught of Spanish colonialism. Each of these projects has its own voice, its own politics, its own complex point of view. The de Fer maps allow us to appreciate how Western ideas about race developed in tandem with ideas about global geography; the *Farmers vs. Covarrubias map* allows us to appreciate how maps became tools in the effort to resist racialized notions of property ownership.

The de Fer maps, made in Paris toward the end of the 1690s, depict the four parts of the world, Europe, Asia, Africa, and America, in monumental style

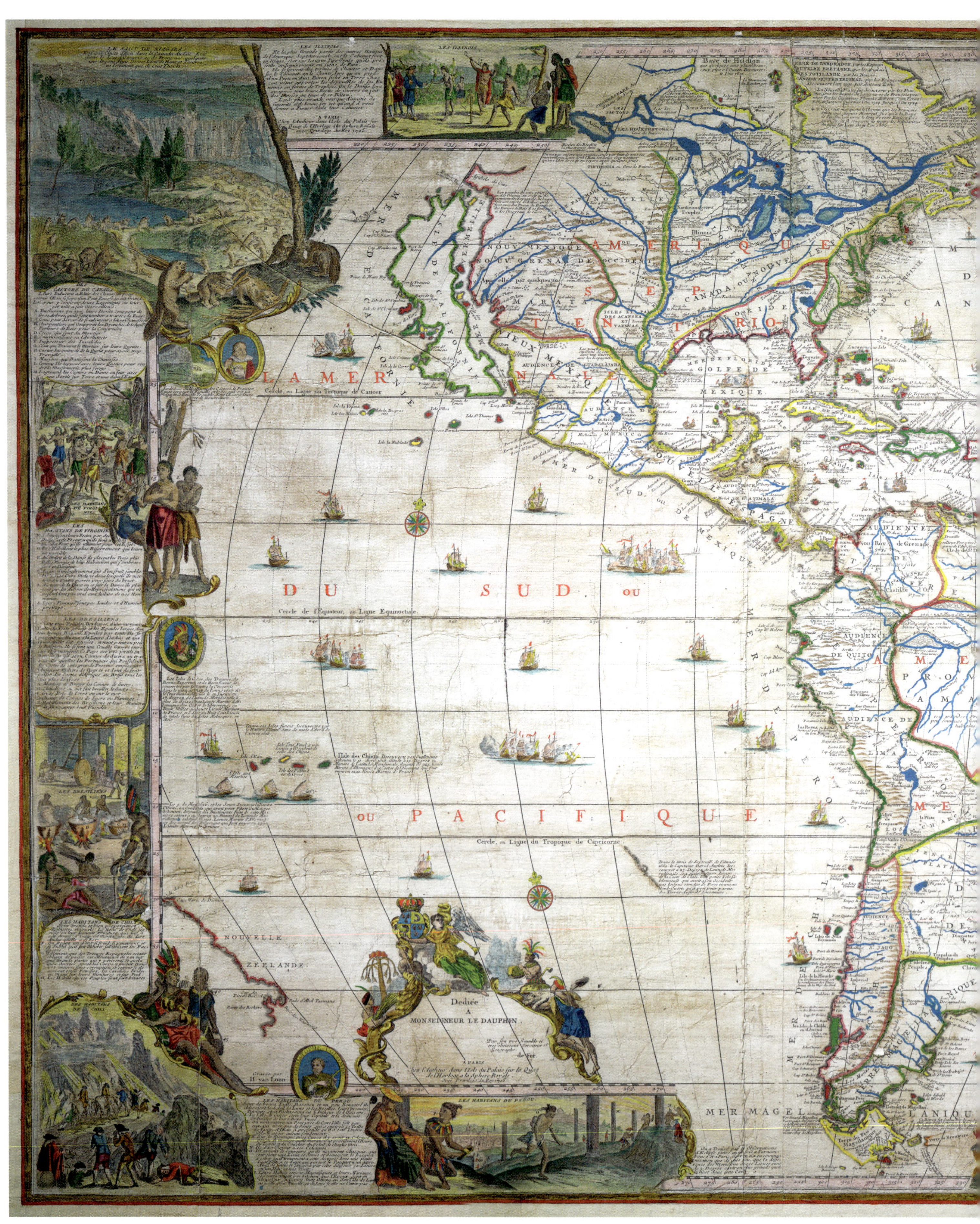
Baye de Hudson
Cercle, ou Ligne du Tropique de Cancer
DU SUD ou
Cercle de l'Equateur, ou Ligne Equinoctiale.
ou PACIFIQUE
Cercle, ou Ligne du Tropique de Capricorne
NOUVELLE
ZEELANDE
Dediée
A
MONSEIGNEUR LE DAUPHIN
MER MAGEL

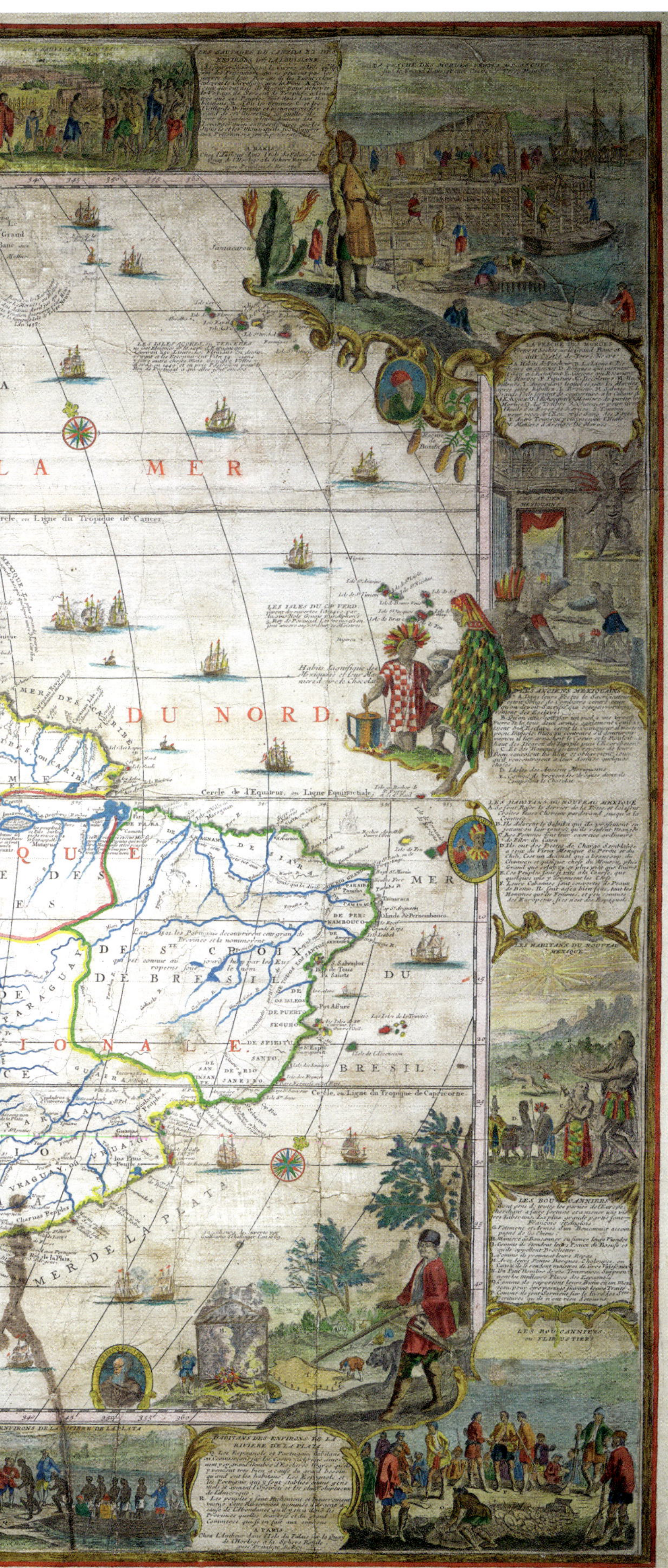

Figure 4.1
Nicolas de Fer, "L'Amérique, Divisée Selon l'etendue Ses Principales Parties," 1698, Newberry Library, Novacco 8F 02 01

(Figure 4.1).[1] These were luxury products produced by a preeminent mapmaker with close ties to the royal family. Each was printed on eight sheets of paper from custom-made copper plates. The pieces were then assembled into a single image roughly 160cm wide and 110cm tall, one so massive that it could only be taken in when mounted on a wall. The maps were not only enormous, but also encyclopedic. They include lengthy verbal descriptions of the continents, as well as numerous captioned illustrations that depict the various human communities that inhabited each continent. We know little about the sources that de Fer used to construct and illustrate his maps, but we can tell that he meant them to be authoritative. In the pages that follow, we read them in the context of the history of European approaches to human difference on a global scale. They capture a moment in the history of European racial thinking when notions of Eurocentrism that were so fundamental to the colonial enterprise of the West had been fully consolidated, yet they also dramatize the ways the human migrations at the heart of that enterprise cried out for a notion of biological race that could consolidate the ongoing construction of white supremacy.

The *Farmers vs. Covarrubias* map, conversely, depicts the local setting of a community of Indigenous people in colonial Mexico. It was painted on paper made from the bark of a mulberry or fig tree, using paper-making traditions practiced in the Americas long before the arrival of the Spanish (Figure 4.2). The pigments used to color the terrain

1. The maps are available as high-resolution images on the website of the Bibliothèque National de France. See http://catalogue.bnf.fr/ark:/12148/cb406741424 (Africa); http://catalogue.bnf.fr/ark:/12148/cb40675711r (America); http://catalogue.bnf.fr/ark:/12148/cb40740247q (Asia); http://catalogue.bnf.fr/ark:/12148/cb40577015h (Europe).

derived from botanicals and minerals found in the landscape. The Indigenous mapmaker who made this map did so with subtle knowledge about the land, not only its topography, but also details about where to find the materials to make the map itself that can only be attained through studied interactions with its flora and fauna across generations. Despite this ancestral relationship to the land, the mapmaker who made this map did so to defend his community's claim to it and right to be on it. *The Farmers vs Covarrubias* gets its name from the 1569 court case in which the two named parties appealed to a colonial court to settle a dispute about the boundaries of property. Made just under fifty years after the Spanish military conquest of the Americas, the *Farmers vs. Covarrubias* map shows us how race was mediated by property lines in the earliest moments of Spanish occupation. Maps produced to support legal claims to territory in court cases demonstrate how Spaniards attempted to control the Indigenous population, *los naturales*, through a system of bureaucracy that was far from natural. As an example of this type of map, *Farmers vs. Covarrubias* shows how an Indigenous mapmaker, who represented the people of Tultepec, made claim to space and navigated a bureaucratic web using a system of picture-writing that was illegible to the Spanish court system.

Though made many decades after the *Farmers vs. Covarrubias* map, the de Fer map is discussed first because of the global nature of the mapping project. We then turn to the more localized issues raised by the *Farmers vs. Covarrubias* map.

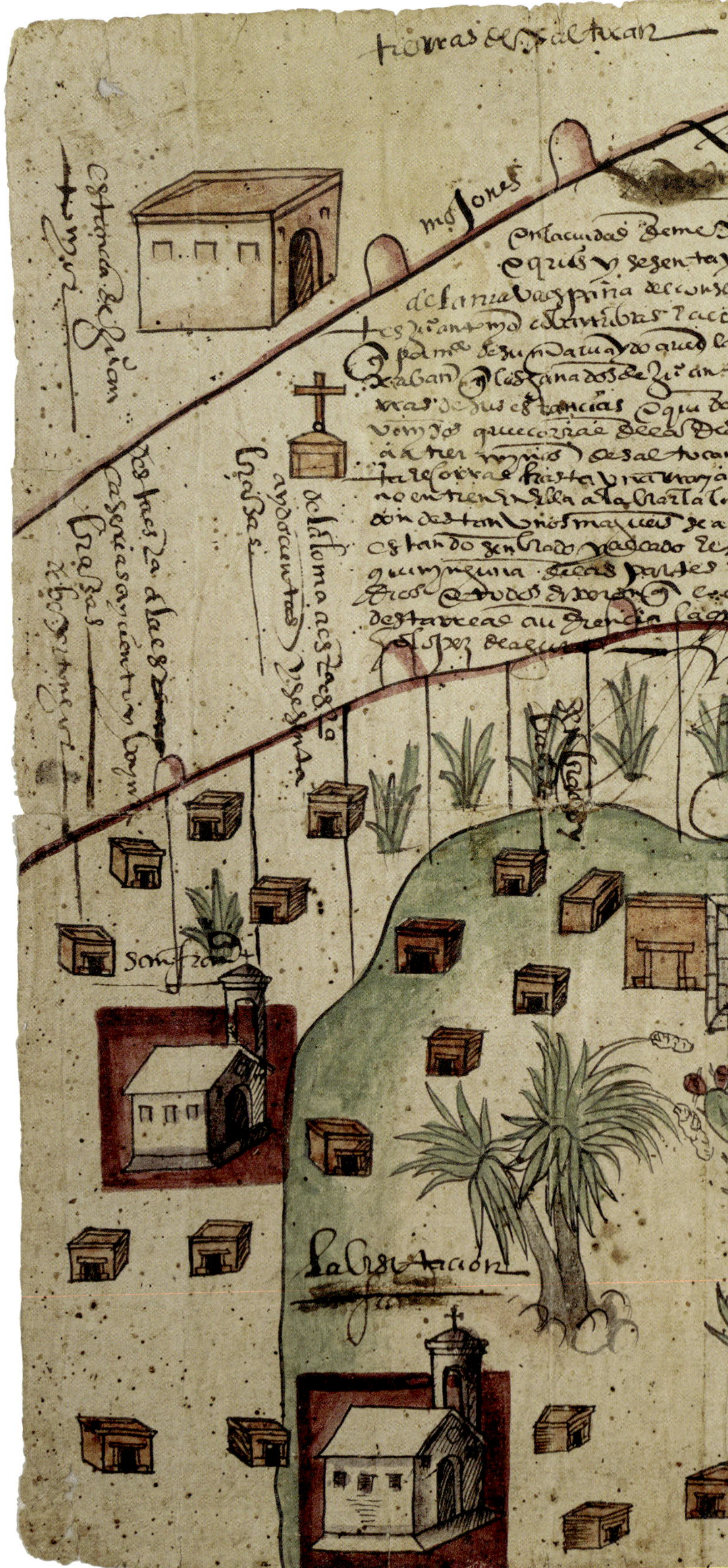

Figure 4.2
Map of lands in the Tultepec and Jaltocán regions adjacent to the Hacienda de Santa Inés (Mexico), 1569, Pen-and-ink and watercolor (red, green, brown, yellow); mounted on amatl paper, Newberry Library, VAULT drawer Ayer MS 1801 map 1

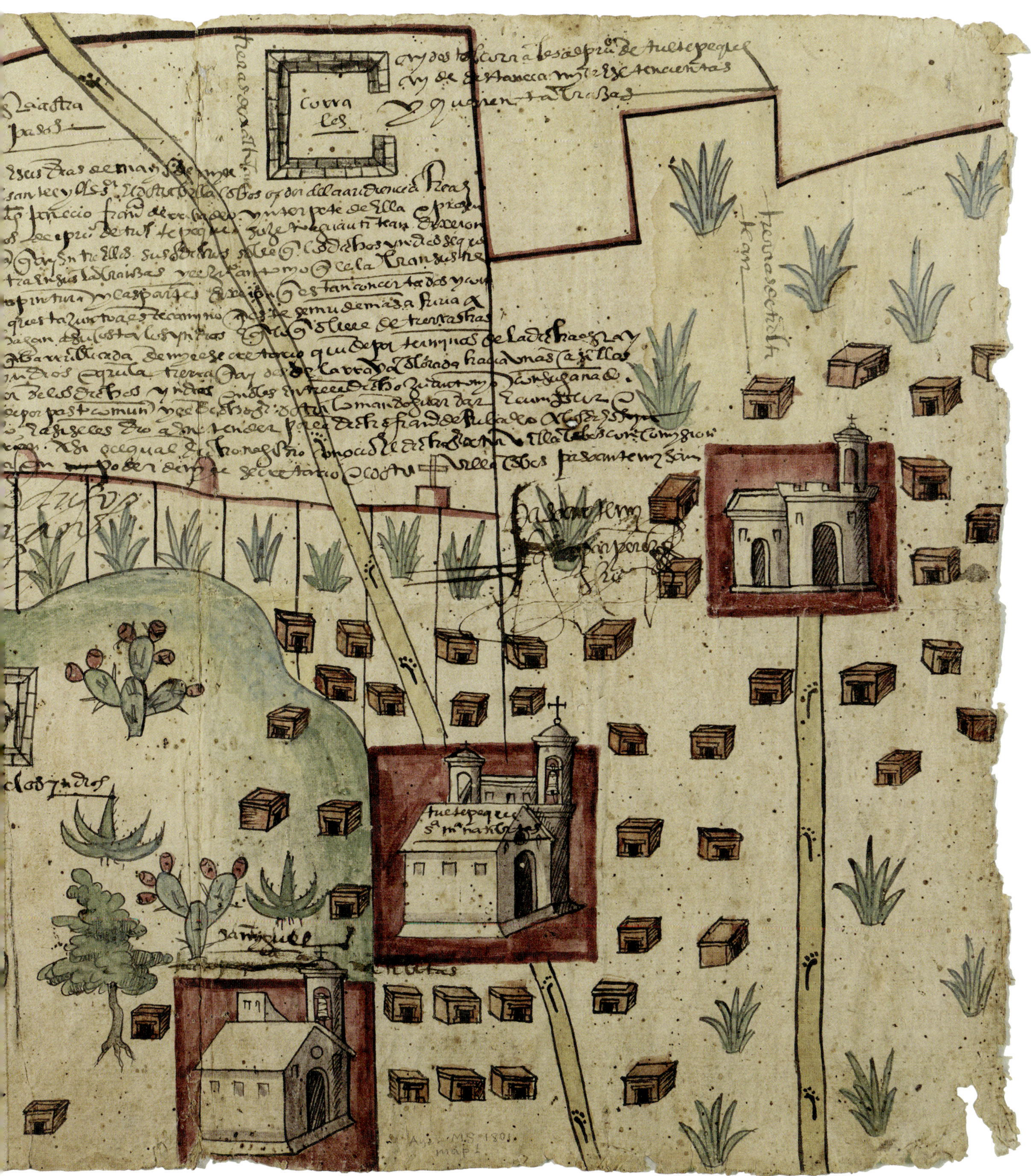

The World Viewed from Paris

by Ricardo Padrón

The division of the world into continents is largely arbitrary and has a lengthy history. The Ancient Greeks were the first to divide the world this way, but they disagreed about whether the world had two or three parts. Some of them even believed that the whole system was ill-conceived and best abandoned.[2] Medieval intellectuals settled on three parts, but the number rose to four when their early modern successors designated the newly-discovered lands in the Atlantic a "fourth part of the world" called "America."[3] Today, English-speakers usually learn that there are seven continents, while Spanish-speakers learn that there are six, thanks to the tendency in Latin America to count the Western hemisphere as a single landmass. Just as there have been disagreements over the number of the world's parts, so there have been disagreements over their boundaries. The same medieval intellectuals who set the number at three also determined that the parts of the world were separated by the Mediterranean Sea, the Nile River, and the Don River. As Europeans began to map Russia's rivers with accuracy, however, it became clear that the Don River did not extend far enough North to serve as a boundary between Europe and Asia. Eventually, a Swedish army officer suggested that the Ural Mountains would work better than any river.

This example illustrates a key idea: the way that we chop the world up into continents goes hand in hand with value judgments about people who live in certain places, and how they size up in comparison with others elsewhere. The decision to identify the Ural Mountains as the true border was controversial, but it was well received among Russian intellectuals who supported Tsar Peter the Great's efforts to Westernize their country, because it identified the Russian heartland as "European" rather than "Asian" or "Oriental."[4] Conveniently, it also consigned Siberia to Asia, converting it into a space ripe for colonization.[5] The question nevertheless remains unsettled. Martin Lewis and Karen Wïgen have gone so far as to argue that Europe should be deprived of continental status, because it is actually no larger or any more diverse than the various subcontinents that comprise Asia. The elevation of Europe to continental status on a par with Asia, in fact, constitutes one of the central gestures of Eurocentrism.[6] The de Fer maps illustrate this perfectly, but they also help us understand why elevating the status of Europe and its people did not in itself suffice as a way of underwriting the project of European colonialism. The fact was that in the early modern world, people moved around, and this made the notion of biological race not only convenient but necessary to sustaining the project of European colonialism on a global level.

From Climates to Continents

In order to understand this, it helps to go back to a time when the continents mattered much less. Before the early modern period (1300–1700), the architecture of the continents did not figure as prominently in global geography as another system, the theory of climate.[7] According to the Ancient Greeks, climate had a

2. Some readers may be aware that the expressions "part of the world" and "continent" are not synonymous and that, in fact, the introduction of the word "continent" into European geography is part and parcel of a significant transformation in geographical thought. In these pages, I will ignore this distinction for simplicity's sake.

3. Edmundo O'Gorman, *The Invention of America: An Inquiry into the Historical Nature of the New World and the Meaning of Its History* (Bloomington: Indiana University Press, 1961).

4. Martin W. Lewis and Kären E. Wigen, *The Myth of the Continents: A Critique of Metageography* (Berkeley: University of California Press, 1997), 27, https://www.jstor.org/stable/10.1525/j.ctt1pnv6t.

5. Valerie Kivelson, *Cartographies of Tsardom: The Land and Its Meanings in Seventeenth-Century Russia* (Ithaca, NY: Cornell University Press, 2006).

6. Lewis and Wigen, *Myth*, 35–46.

7. The discussion of climate theory in this paragraph and the next is based upon Nicolás Wey Gómez, *The Tropics of Empire: Why Columbus Sailed South to the Indies* (Cambridge, MA.: MIT Press, 2008).

powerful influence on human character, and climate was a function of latitude*.[8] Hot, humid places toward the south of the known world, like the Nile Valley or far-off India, produced people who were clever but timid to the point of being servile, with dark skin and coarse hair. When they did not live in savage bands, they cowered under the rule of tyrants. Cold northern places like Germany, by contrast, produced people who were brutish but brave, with fair complexions. Places in the temperate middle, like Greece, combined the best of both extremes, producing people with both the bravery of northern types and the cleverness of southern ones. Only they were truly capable of living lives that counted as rational and civilized, as the Greeks understood those terms. What mattered most in mapping the global distribution of different human difference, therefore, was not the continents but the latitudinal climatic bands or zones into which the Earth was divided.

Such differences — white versus Black, "civilized" versus "barbarian," "masters" versus "slaves" — were not a function of biological inheritance but of environmental influence. In this way, climate theory differed from modern racism, but it nevertheless played the same role, that of articulating and managing human difference in ways that distributed power and privilege asymmetrically among different human groups, favoring the group that invented the theory.[9] This was especially true as the Portuguese and the Spanish began to expand into the Atlantic world, and discovered that the ancients had been wrong about climate in one important respect. Near the equator, where the heat was supposed to become so intense as to make life impossible, according to Aristotle, Iberian explorers encountered lush tropical locales, rich in spices and precious metals, and inhabited by people they deemed uncivilized. All of a sudden, the tropical south loomed large and seemed readily available for exploitation. It was not long before apologists of Spain's empire like Juan López de Palacios Rubios (1450–1524) and Juan Ginés de Sepúlveda (1494–1573) began to argue that the Native inhabitants of what they called "the Indies" were the "natural slaves" that Aristotle described in his *Politics*, a people who desperately needed what they considered to be the civilizing influence of Spain.[10]

The very fact, however, that they had to invoke the theory of natural slavery in order to justify colonialism suggests that climate theory alone was inadequate. In fact, it suffered a key limitation, and by the last quarter of the sixteenth century, intellectuals involved in managing Spain's empire were well aware of it. According to climate theory, Europeans who moved to the tropics would eventually come to resemble the Native inhabitants in body and mind. The change might take generations, but it was inevitable. When a Spanish cosmographer* admitted as much in a description of the Indies he hoped to have published, an official censor struck the passage out of the text.[11] He must have realized how very inconvenient it was to admit that Europeans could degenerate in a tropical environment, losing the qualities that made them "natural masters."

The architecture of the continents began to emerge as a solution to the problem. According to Francisco Bethencourt, it was during the early modern period that Europeans began to assemble stereotypes about the peoples of the world following the logic of the

8. See, for example, Aristotle, *The Politics*, trans. H. Rackham, Loeb Classical Library 264 (Cambridge, MA: Harvard University Press, 1928): 564–65; and Hippocrates of Cos, *Airs, Waters, Places*, ed. and trans. Paul Potter, Loeb Classical Library 147 (Cambridge, MA: Harvard University Press, 2022): 72–73. See also James S. Romm. "Continents, Climates, and Cultures: Greek Theories of Global Structure," in *Geography and Ethnography Perceptions of the World in Pre-Modern Societies*, ed. Kurt Raaflaub (Malden, MA: Wiley-Blackwell, 2010), 215–35.

9. Here I invoke the expansive definition of race set forth by Geraldine Heng, "The Invention of Race in the European Middle Ages II: Locations of Medieval Race," *Literature Compass* 8, no. 5 (2011): 3, https://doi.org/10.1111/j.1741-4113.2011.00795.x.

10. Juan López de Palacios Rubios, *De las Islas del mar Océano* (Fondo de Cultura Económica, 1954); Juan Ginés de Sepúlveda, *Demócrates Segundo, o, De Las Justas Causas de La Guerra Contra Los Indios*, vol. 2a (Madrid: Consejo Superior de Investigaciones Cientáificas, Instituto Francisco de Vitoria, 1984).

11. Juan López de Velasco, *Geografía y Descripción Universal de Las Indias*, ed. Justo Zaragoza (Madrid: Real Academia de la Historia, 1894), 36–37. That influence would be absorbed through local foods as much as through the influence of heavenly bodies. See Rebecca Earle, *The Body of the Conquistador: Food, Race, and the Colonial Experience in Spanish America, 1492–1700* (Cambridge, UK: Cambridge University Press, 2012).

continents rather than the climatic zones.[12] These stereotypes were crystallized in a famous image that appeared on the title page of the first modern atlas, Abraham Ortelius's *Theatrum orbis terrarum* (1570) (Cat. No. 26). It depicts the world as a group of female figures who embody the parts of the world: Europe, Asia, Africa, and America, and has been analyzed time and again.[13] The attributes of the figures and their spatial arrangement on the page suggests a clear cultural and geographical hierarchy. Europe sits at the top, fully dressed and wearing a crown, holding symbols of empire, and surrounded by emblems of culture and knowledge. Asia and Africa stand opposite each other on the next tier down, the one wearing less than the other, both of them holding exotic commodities. America stretches out the bottom, practically nude, holding primitive weapons and brandishing the remains of a cannibalistic feast.

Europe can occupy the top spot precisely because Ortelius has chosen the continents rather than the climatic zones as his basic geographical framework. That choice probably made little difference in the handling of America and Africa, because notions of tropicality dominated European thinking about those parts of the world; these notions made it possible to ignore signs of American or African sophistication, like the cities of the Aztecs and Inca or the glittering wealth of Mali, and depict all Native Americans and Black Africans as "uncivilized" people. Where the choice really mattered was in the treatment of Europe and Asia. Climate theory divided Asia into a temperate north and a tropical south. The north was home to the Chinese and Japanese, who were thought to be white-skinned near-peers of civilized Europeans. The south was home to the dark-skinned, supposedly less civilized people of South and Southeast Asia. The architecture of the continents, however, required Ortelius to depict a single, unified Asia, and therefore allowed him to make a choice between the two. Rather than depict Asia as a learned mandarin*, for example, he depicted it as an eroticized woman holding a censer of myrrh, favoring the exotic sensuality associated with the south while erasing the civility of the north. This allowed Europe to sit at the top of the hierarchy all by herself, white, knowledgeable, and in charge. The problems posed by climate and the threat of tropical degeneracy were simply set aside.

Those problems, however, did not go away. The notion that the tropics exercised a degenerative influence on European bodies and minds continued to vex Westerners, creating fertile circumstances for the development of new theories of difference. The raw materials were already there in notions that the blood of aristocratic elites or white Christians was "pure" of the taint of disbelief that was carried in the blood of Jews and Muslims. These ideas, which made identity a function of biological inheritance rather than environmental influence, migrated to the colonies, where they were adapted to impose order on societies where people of all kinds were mixing in ways that the authorities found alarming. The "impure blood" of Jews became that of the Indigenous Americans.[14] The "pure" blood of French aristocrats became that of all French people.[15] The blood "purity" of Spanish Old Christians became that of the ruling elites of Spanish America.[16] And so forth. Colonial developments of this

12. Francisco Bethencourt, *Racisms: From the Crusades to the Twentieth Century* (Princeton: Princeton University Press, 2013), 63–158, traces the development of stereotypes about the four continents from which Ortelius draws and which he nourishes.

13. The image has been analyzed in print many times. For a recent discussion and bibliography, see Maryanne Cline Horowitz and Louise Arizzoli, *Bodies and Maps: Early Modern Personifications of the Continents* (Leiden: Brill, 2020).

14. María Elena Martínez, *Genealogical Fictions: Limpieza de Sangre, Religion, and Gender in Colonial Mexico* (Stanford: Stanford University Press, 2008); David Nirenberg, "Was There Race before Modernity? The Example of 'Jewish' Blood in Late Medieval Spain," in *The Origins of Racism in the West*, eds. Miriam Eliav-Feldon, Benjamin Isaac, and Joseph Ziegler (Cambridge, UK: Cambridge University Press, 2009): 232–64; Ben Vinson, *Before Mestizaje: The Frontiers of Race and Caste in Colonial Mexico* (Cambridge, UK: Cambridge University Press, 2018).

15. Guillaume Aubert, "'The Blood of France': Race and Purity of Blood in the French Atlantic World," *William and Mary Quarterly* 61, no. 3 (2004): 439–78, https://doi.org/10.2307/3491805.

16. Jorge Canizares Esguerra, "New World, New Stars: Patriotic Astrology and the Invention of Indian and Creole Bodies in Colonial Spanish America, 1600–1650," *American Historical Review* 104, no. 1 (1999): 33, https://doi.org/10.2307/2650180.

kind became the background against which metropolitan intellectuals began to articulate modern theories of biological race, albeit often without acknowledging the colonial precedent.

Some of these theories involved new ways of mapping the world. The French physician François Bernier (1620–1688), for example, proposed "A New Division of the Earth" (1684) according to different "races" organized on the basis of physical appearance according to which the inhabitants of Europe, North Africa, the Middle East, Persia, India, and Thailand constituted a single race, converting these lands into a single region.[17] In general, however, new theories of race mapped their hereditary human groups onto the established continental system, even while recognizing that the fit between races and landmasses was not always perfect. Black Africans came to be imagined as descendants of Noah's son Ham, who had been cursed to a life of servitude by his father.[18] The Chinese and Japanese ceased to be white and became "yellow."[19] The effects of the environment were shifted to the distant past, when each race became what it was and would forever be, in the relative isolation of its own continental setting. As Carl Ritter (1779–1859), one of the most important geographers of the nineteenth century put it, "Each continent is like itself alone . . . each one was so planned and formed as to have its own special function in the progress of human culture." One of these functions was to produce a major racial group. Europe produced the "white" race, Africa the "Black" race, Asia the "yellow," and America the "red."[20] Eventually, the Native inhabitants of the Pacific were identified as another major group, producing the popular nineteenth-century notion that there existed "five races of man." In this new dispensation, white people could still degenerate, but not by moving to tropical climates. The French writer Arthur Gobineau (1816–1882) flatly rejected that the environment could profoundly affect human beings within the short span of historical time.[21] The degeneration of the white race was not the result of life in a tropical climate, but of intermarriage with dark-skinned, "inferior" people.[22] This was a truly convenient racial logic for a globalized world, in which populations migrated, freely or not, in which certain groups ruled over others and believed themselves entitled to do so, and wanted very much to keep hold of their power.

The de Fer Maps

The de Fer maps were made in the midst of all these changes. By the 1690s, Bernier had already published his precocious attempt to divide humanity into racial groups. France was well established as a colonial power, with possessions in the Caribbean, North America, and South Asia. In 1685, the French government had enacted the first of its *Codes Noirs*, or "Black Codes," laws governing the treatment of enslaved populations that were the first to identify subjects of the crown on the basis of skin color. In the meantime, the government was making it possible for enslavers to bring their human property back to the metropolis, upending centuries of tradition that prohibited slavery on the soil of France. Nevertheless, a full-blown theory of biological racism had not yet emerged, much less come to dominate racial thinking. The word *nègre* [Black] enjoyed considerable ambiguity when applied to human beings. It could be used to refer to enslaved people, people of African origin, or dark-skinned people from places other than Africa, such as India.[23] This final ambiguity suggests that the French continued to

17. Pierre Boulle, *Race et Esclavage Dans la France de l'Ancien Régime* (Paris: Perrin, 2007), 49–50.

18. Benjamin Braude, "The Sons of Noah and the Construction of Ethnic and Geographical Identities in the Medieval and Early Modern Periods," *William and Mary Quarterly* 54, no. 1 (1997): 103–42, https://doi.org/10.2307/2953314.

19. D. E. Mungello, *The Great Encounter of China and the West, 1500–1800*, 3rd ed. (Rowman & Littlefield Publishers, 2009), 143–44; Michael Keevak, *Becoming Yellow: A Short History of Racial Thinking* (Princeton: Princeton University Press, 2011).

20. Cited in Lewis and Wigen, *Myth*, 30.

21. Arthur Gobineau, *The Moral and Intellectual Diversity of Races*, trans. Henry Hotze and Josiah Nott (Philadelphia: Lippincott, 1856), 341–43.

22. Gobineau, *Moral*, 149–51.

23. Sue Peabody, *"There Are No Slaves in France": The Political Culture of Race and Slavery in the Ancien* Régime (New York: Oxford University Press, 1996), 60–70.

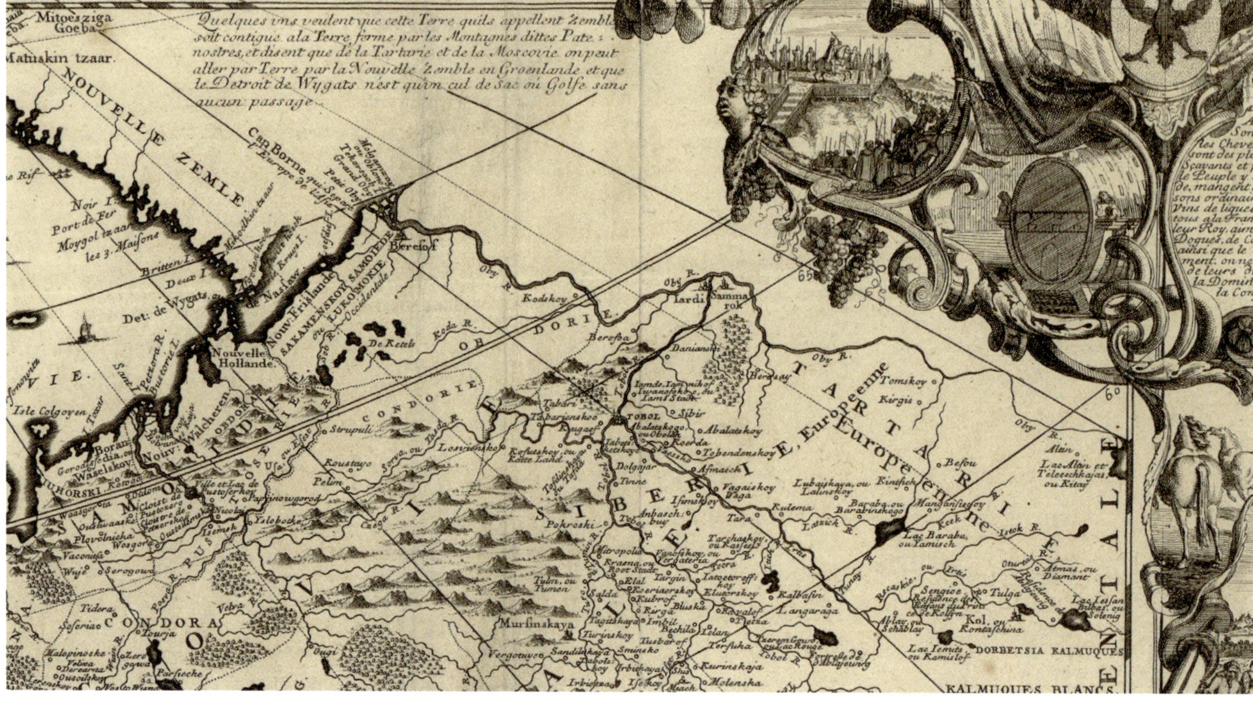

think about human difference in terms of climate theory, conflating the dark-skinned peoples of the tropics into a single category, no matter what their continental origins.

De Fer's maps help the reader abandon the theory of climate for the architecture of the continents. Once again, the arbitrariness of the system is best grasped by observing the treatment of the boundary between Europe and Asia. The maps identify the Don and Oby Rivers as the boundary between the two continents, but one struggles to see why these rivers and not others should serve as the crucial dividing line (Figure 4.3). We come to realize that it is not the rivers at all, but the material separation of the two continents onto two images of similar size, each using a different cartographic scale. The effect is to zoom in on Europe and zoom out on Asia, converting them into separate but equal landmasses, each of them appearing on a large map, rich in detail, that demands to be taken in on its own. It becomes difficult to see similarities and differences along lines of latitude that traverse the continents themselves, and much easier to make those comparisons continent by continent. The reader is thus trained to treat the continents, not the climates, as the fundamental categories of physical and human geography.

The French and the Chinese, who should exhibit similar levels of civility by virtue of their shared location in the northern temperate zone, come out looking quite different from each other. In the vignette depicting the French, one man sculpts while another paints, a fashionable couple chats, while other groups assemble around a large pair of globes or peer through a telescope (Figure 4.4). The other European vignettes feature urban life, martial prowess, technical inventiveness, and commercial success, while making room for the "oriental" sumptuousness of Istanbul and the "barbarity" of Lapland*, but only Paris glows as a center of art and learning. De Fer's human geography is not only Eurocentric: it is Francocentric. It is from Paris that the world is known and represented. Not only does this vignette say so, but so do all the elaborate title cartouches* proclaiming that Paris is the place where the maps were made. The vignette depicting the Chinese, meanwhile, downplays their civility. It depicts an orderly, urbanized world with a rich material culture, and bears a caption acknowledging China's love for the arts and sciences, but the image of two men discussing a piece of writing is lost in the middle ground, while the text itself draws the reader's attention to the sumptuous dress of the two figures in the foreground and to the exotic practice

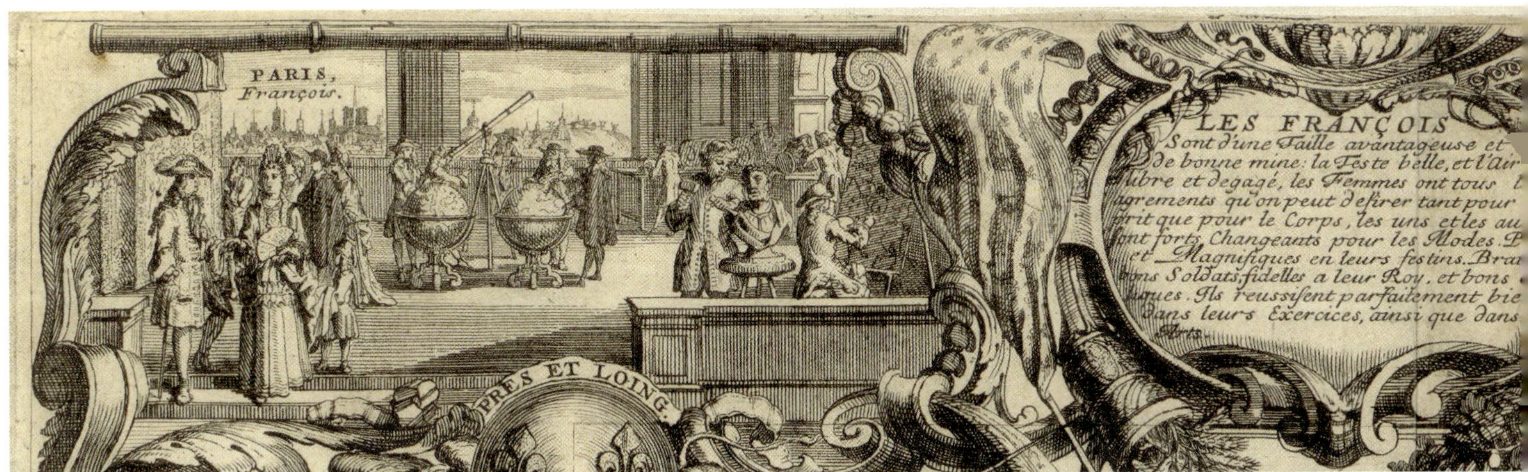

◂ **Figure 4.3**
Detail from Nicolas de Fer, "L'Europe Divisée Selon l'étendue de Ses Principales Parties," Paris, 1696. Bibliothéque Nationale de France.
The mapmaker leaves the "Asian" land beyond the Orby River blank, but one fails to see why this river and not some other should serve as the intercontinental boundary.
https://gallica.bnf.fr/ark:/12148/btv1b53089033c.

Figure 4.4
Detail from Nicolas de Fer, "L'Europe Où Tous Les Points Principaux." Paris, 1695. Bibliothèque Nationale de France.
The French capital is portrayed as the global headquarters of art and science.
https://gallica.bnf.fr/ark:/12148/btv1b530530140.

of foot binding (Figure 4.5). The Japanese fare even worse, appearing primarily as "idolators" and ferocious warriors. Everywhere else on the map of Asia we find images of excess, luxury, and exoticism typical of modern Orientalism. The map of Africa, meanwhile, features people who are clearly black-skinned, who are often engaged in activities that would be deemed "primitive" by the Parisian reader and are frequently described with exceedingly negative language.

In treating Europe, Asia, and Africa in this way, de Fer draws on a representational tradition established roughly one-hundred years earlier, that of the so-called *cartes à figures* (Cat. No. 24). On these maps, the inhabitants of the region depicted — whether it was a locality, a kingdom, a continent, or the world as a whole — appeared along the image margins as stylized, costumed individuals or couples.[24] De Fer replaces the stiff figures of the *carte à figure* with action scenes: animal hunts, musical performances, coronations, mining, divine worship, star gazing, cannibalism, and a myriad of other things. The identity of the people depicted is not just a matter of what they wear, but what they typically or most characteristically do. In each case, however, the people in question seem to be the Native inhabitants of that continent. They exhibit diversity while simultaneously falling into the overall patterns typical of Europeans, Asians, or Africans.

It is here that America begins to look like the odd map out (Figure 4.1). The map is famous for its depiction of beavers busily building a dam, but here I will focus on its treatment of human populations. Like the others, the map of America portrays Native inhabitants of the continent, group by group. It portrays the civilizations of the Mexica and the Inca as having occurred in the past, and tinges them with strong

24. Valerie Traub, "Anatomy, Cartography, and the New World Body, Geographies of Embodiment in Early Modern England," in *Geographies of Embodiment in Early Modern England,* eds. Mary Floyd-Wilson and Garrett A. Sullivan (Oxford: Oxford University Press, 2020), https://doi.org/10.1093/oso/9780198852742.003.0004 ; Valerie Traub, "Mapping the Global Body," in *Early Modern Visual Culture*, eds. Peter Erickson and Clark Hulse, Representation, Race, and Empire in Renaissance England, New Cultural Studies (Philadelphia: University of Pennsylvania Press, 2000), 44–97; Valerie Traub, "History in the Present Tense: Feminist Theories, Spatialized Epistemologies, and Early Modern Embodiment," in *Mapping Gendered Routes and Spaces in the Early Modern World*, ed. Merry E. Wiesner-Hanks (Ashgate Publishing, Ltd., 2015), 15–53; Valerie Traub, "The Nature of Norms in Early Modern England: Anatomy, Cartography, 'King Lear,'" *South Central Review* 26, no. 1/2 (2009): 42–81, https://www.jstor.org/stable/40211291.

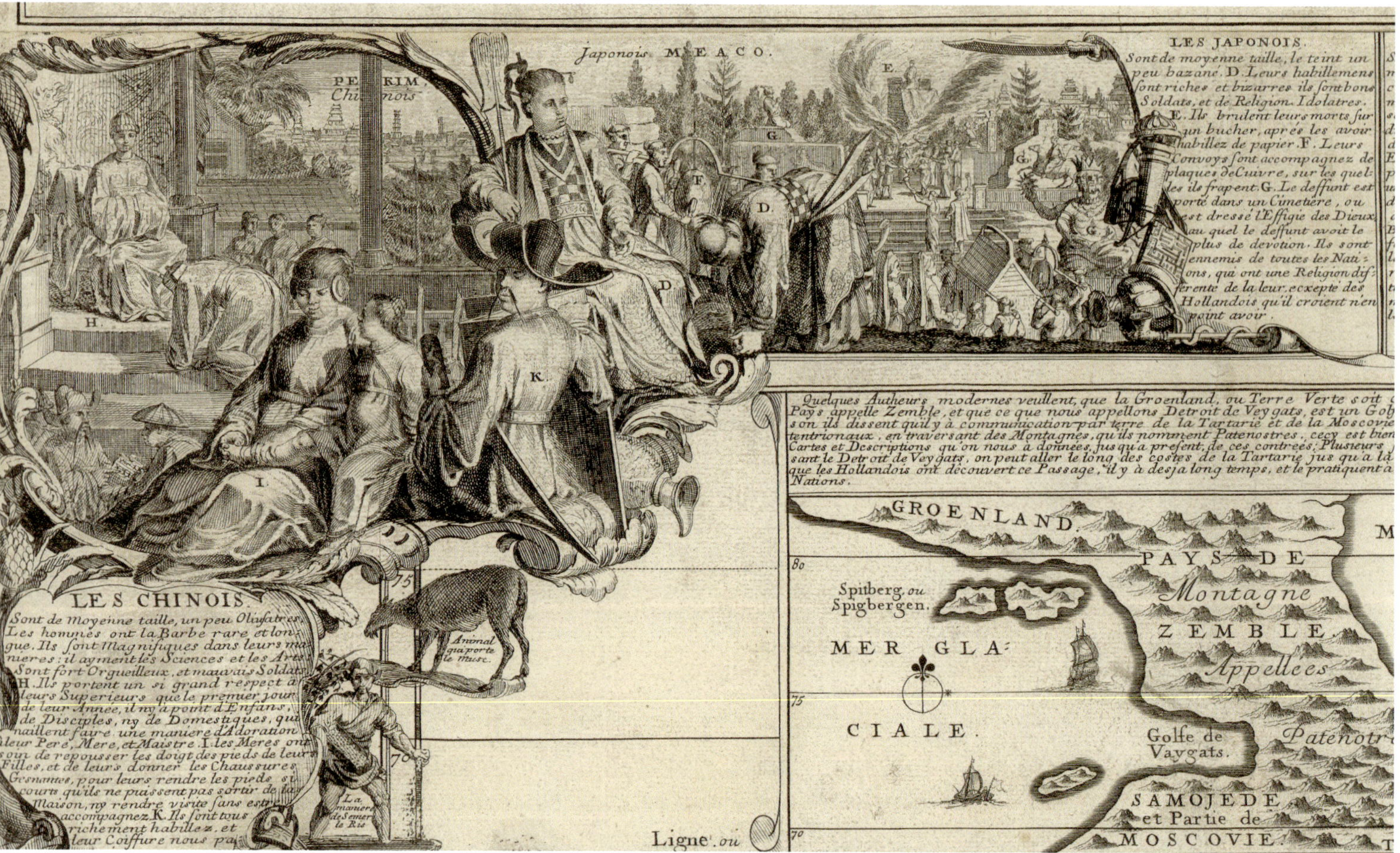

Figure 4.5
Detail from Nicolas de Fer,
"L'Asie Divisée Selon l'étendue de Ses Principales Parties . . .,"
Paris, 1696. Bibliothéque Nationale de France.
The vignette about the Chinese downplays Chinese literacy,
and shines the spotlight on Asian exoticisim. The vignette
about the Japanese emphasizes violence and idolatry.
https://gallica.bnf.fr/ark:/12148/btv1b53089033c

hints of "savagery" and "idolatry." Other Indigenous groups are rendered as either peaceful or warlike but seem to be universally "primitive." In this way, de Fer's map of America participates in the proto-racialization of the Indigenous Americans. Nevertheless, it also forces Native Americans to share the space of representation with Europeans and Africans. European cod fishermen, buccaneers, and Spanish conquistadors* get their own vignettes. Whites sell enslaved Africans to the Indigenous inhabitants of Río de la Plata, while in Brazil, enslaved Black people engage in the grueling work of sugar production. In this way, de Fer's America looks like the home of a "race," just like the other maps, but it also renders visible the key phenomenon that made a notion of biological race so essential to the project of European colonialism: the migration, voluntary or not, of Europeans and Africans to the New World. De Fer's map dramatizes the presence of white and Black communities in places that are not Native to them, inviting the reader to see how they remain the same no matter where they go. It would be left to the intellectuals of the next century to provide the theory of biological race necessary to explain how this could happen.

The World Viewed from Tultepec

By Risa Puleo

Maps help us remember how to get from one place to another. But whose idea of place do they record?

In the *Indigenous Farmers of Tultepec vs. Spanish Rancher Juan Antonio Covarrubias* map in the Newberry's collection, two different interpretations of a site located in the valley of Mexico north of the capital city are present in the same document. Each interpretation is founded on two very different conceptions of what constitutes ownership and governance in this early moment in the Spanish occupation of Mexico (Figure 4.2). The map can be read in two different ways because Nahuatl, the language of the people of the Central Mexican Valley before Spanish Conquest, was written in a complex system of phonetic rebuses*, ideograms*, and pictographs before it was transliterated* into the Latin alphabet. Thus, what a Spaniard understood in the sixteenth century, and perhaps what we, as contemporary viewers of the map, register as an image of a landscape was equally a text written in a series of image-puzzles that can be read and deciphered. Whether we look at the map as an image through European conceptions of space or as a text through Nahuatl picture-writing determines whether we see a map of a newly settled New Spain or of a recently occupied Ānāhuac.[25]

The *Farmers vs. Covarrubias* map is named for the two parties in the 1569 court case that settled their property dispute. Covarrubias's sheep had intruded into the farmers' fields and were eating their crops. The farmers appealed to the Spanish court in Mexico City to intervene and had a *tlacuilo*, a person trained in the arts of mapmaking and record keeping, usually a member of the Native elite, draw up the map as evidence to defend their claims.[26] The sheeps' transgression of property boundaries is described on the map by two *corrales*, or pens, that the animals would return to after grazing in the hilly grasslands surrounding the valley in which Tultepec lies. The one pen within Covarubbias's property line in the top left quadrant* of the map is notably empty. But the pen at the top of the green area in the lower right-hand quadrant of the map contains a horned ram. Beneath this second pen is a handwritten note that demarcates the green area as *"es de los yndios,"* meaning it "belongs" to the Tultepec farmers.

This phrase is written with the same flourished penmanship in which the Spanish judge wrote his verdict atop the Indigenous-made map. It speaks directly to the Spanish readers of the map, including the judge who ruled on the case, Covarrubias, whose actions would be determined by the court, and perhaps the Tultepec farmer who acquired Spanish as a first or second language in this moment nearly five decades after Spain's military conquest of Mexico. "Belongs to," in the Spanish connotation, relates the idea that the Indigenous farmers of Tultepec *own* this area as property. The farmers of Tultepec conceptualized their place in the world, not through European concepts of property, but through ideas of sovereignty related to independent polities in a network of city-states. Terms that the historian Anthony Pagden develops in his study of empire through the ages helps us distinguish between Spanish and Native Mexican concepts of the land, and by association, who can use it, how, and under what circumstances; in other words, governance. Pagden explains how *imperium*, the Roman concept of empire that the Spanish adopted and employed in the Americas, is an authority that is taken by force over foreign territories. He writes, *imperium* assumes "long-term *de facto* occupation to be recognized *de iure* as conferring retrospective rights of

25. Ānāhuac is the Indigenous name for the lands the Spanish declared "New Spain" at conquest that are presently called Mexico. In Nahuatl, the Ānāhuac means "Place Surrounded by Waters," a name that signals the lake that once filled the basin of the Central Mexican Valley and connected life across the Aztec Empire. Barbara Mundy, "Mapping the Aztec Capital: The 1524 Nuremberg Map of Tenochtitlán, Its Sources and Meanings," *Imago Mundi* 50, no. 1 (1998): 15, https://doi.org/10.1080/03085699808592877.

26. The Nahuatl word for "scribe" translates literally to mean equally both "painter" and "writer" and points to the ways in which image and text are interchangeable.

property and jurisdiction, no matter how illicit the original occupation might have been."[27] *Dominium*, or sovereignty, by Roman terms, is the tribal rule of the people in place before occupation and relates to the individual authority held by constituencies under the umbrella of empire. But the farmers of Tultepec did not think in these terms. Rather, the Tultepecan perspective is better understood through the Nahuatl word *tlalticpac*. This term translates to a range of concepts related to earth: from dirt to land and the sphere of human existence, as distinct from the realms of the sky and underworld.[28] The land itself speaks through the map's materiality and in the ways that the Tultepecans conceptualized how they belonged to it. *Tlalticpac* and *Imperium* are at a standoff in the *Farmers vs. Covarrubias* map.

One way that racialized power relations between Natives and settlers manifested in the early colonial period is as property disputes. Conquistadors were given land in the newly established colony, and the indebted service of the Native people living on it. Land was also granted to new settlers and missionaries by the Spanish Crown in efforts to occupy and Christianize the Americas. Much of this property passed to further generations or was sold to other Spaniards, like Covarrubias, who purchased property from the family of a conquistador at an auction.[29] In addition to creating a physical separation from Indigenous Mexicans, property ownership allowed Europeans and their descendants to capitalize upon the land, as well as the indentured servitude of Native people and the forced labor of enslaved Africans who worked it, to generate inheritable wealth. Over time, this accumulated wealth generated a racialized caste system —pictured most notably in eighteenth-century *castas** paintings— in which race, class, and the capacity to own property and generate wealth are inextricably linked. Notably, many of these new residents of Mexico brought sheep with them from Spain.

We can begin to grasp the danger the sheep posed to the farmers and the reason that the farmers took Covarrubias to court by reading the Nahuatl images as a text. Nahuatl maps differ from European territorial maps in that features of a place or in a landscape are often abbreviated. For example, the *Farmers vs. Covarrubias* map represents a twenty-five-mile span between five towns, themselves represented by five churches, as if it were a walkable space. And that one horned ram within the green area marked *es de los yndios*? He is an abbreviation for the 5,000 –20,000 sheep that would have comprised a ranch such as Covarrubias's. Multiplying that number by the thousands of new sheep ranches in the area means that by 1569, when the Farmers took Covarrubias to court, 24% of the highlands surrounding Tultepec were half-pasture, supporting upwards of 700,000 heads of sheep.[30] Within a few years, these grazing lands would become "scrub-covered badlands" when overgrazing sheep ate the prairie beyond its capacity to recover.[31] The Farmers vs. Covarrubias court case is only one of many examples of sheep-related property transgressions at this moment.[32] Across the Central Mexican Valley, Native farmers lobbied to the Spanish court system in defense of their land and their ability to generate and protect their food supply from Spanish sheep.

But Spanish courts did not mediate a universal ideal of truth and justice. Rather they judged one's ability

27. Anthony Pagden, "Fellow Citizens and Imperial Subjects: Conquest and Sovereignty in Europe's Overseas Empires," *History and Theory* 44, no. 4 (2005): 30–31 https://www.jstor.org/stable/3590856.

28. John F. Schwaller, "The Ilhuica of the Nahua: Is Heaven Just a Place?," *The Americas* 62, no. 3 (2006): 391–412, http://www.jstor.org/stable/4491090.

29. *Catalogo, resumen e indices de Protocolos,* 30 April 1574, fol. 695v.; see Shirley Cushing Flint, *No Mere Shadow: Faces of Widowhood in Early Colonial Mexico* (Albuquerque: University of New Mexico Press, 2013), 119n33.

30. Elinor Melville includes the data she collected about the number of sheep per decade found in multiple subregions of the northern area of the Central Mexican Valley over the sixteenth century in a series of charts included in chap. four of *A Plague of Sheep: Environmental Consequences of the Conquest of Mexico* (Cambridge, UK: Cambridge University Press, 1994), 78–115.

31. Melville, *Plague of Sheep*, 100.

32. Melville's *Plague of Sheep* is the best source for all sheep-related lawsuits in colonial Mexico.

to produce evidence in the proper forms and formats. In the early moments of occupation, the bureaucratically-minded Spanish understood pre-Conquest Nahuatl maps as city charters and took them as proof of Indigenous ownership of a territory.[33] Other communities without such documents were dispossessed and indentured to the Spanish owners who claimed their lands.[34] With less experience in producing this kind of paperwork to the standard that was acceptable to the court, Native people often lost their cases as judges defaulted to the party who was most able to uphold the formality of the court, i.e. other Spaniards who were familiar with the court's protocol. Thus, one reason that Nahuatl map-making practices persist after Conquest is so that Native Mexicans could make written claims to the spaces they inhabited, in their moment and ancestrally.

Rather than describe geography spatially, Nahuatl maps are structured according to what art historian and Nahuatl map specialist Barbara Mundy calls "the social layout of the city," meaning Indigenous maps marked political alliances and genealogical lineages rather than territorial borders.[35] Take for examples, Codex Reese, a map made to defend the claims of a Native people in Mexico City in the mid-sixteenth century, and the Codex Mendoza, a compendium* of pre-Conquest Aztec life written after Spanish occupation. The frontispiece of the Codex Mendoza is a map that represents the Aztec capital city Tenochtitlán, which in the moment in which it was written in 1541, was well into the process of becoming the capital of New Spain: Mexico City (Figure 4.6). In the center of this map, an eagle stands atop of the nopal cactus that grows out of a rock. This emblem, recognizable as the design for the contemporary Mexican flag, describes the mythopoetic* divinatory* sign the Mexica looked for to identify the site to build their capital city. Its inclusion on the Codex Mendoza's frontispiece map, then, places it within a longer, ancestral, framework of history. Surrounding this emblem, ten figures are spread across four city districts. Each represents one of the ten founders of Tenochtitlán to which the city's inhabitants could chart their genealogy. Writing about the Codex Reese, also known as the Beineke map, sociologist* Pablo Escalante Gonzalbo describes the seven houses depicted on the map's left edge not as seven literal houses, but rather the seven lineages to which the township could trace their genealogy.[36] Made in 1565, the Codex Reese charts one hundred and twenty-one land claims and Native rulership in Tenochtitlán back to 1538 (Figure 4.7). According to Mary E. Miller, an art historian of the pre-Columbian arts of Mexico, the decision to include a genealogy of governance demonstrates how the "*tlatoque* (Nahuatl *tla'to'que'*; rulers) pictured on the map still had some claim to power."[37] Barbara Mundy expands upon Miller's statement by showing how the *tlatoque* still held positions of power at the time of the Beinecke Map's making. Over time, they would be even though they had been pushed to Native-only zones at the edge of Mexico City where they still held power within their own communities though demoted down Spain's power structure.[38]

No figures that demonstrate the ancestry of the farmers of Tultepec are pictured on the *Farmers vs. Covarrubias* map, but it does communicate the map-

33. Barbara Mundy, *The Mapping of New Spain: Indigenous Cartography and the Maps of the Relaciones Geographias* (Chicago: University of Chicago Press, 1996), 166.

34. Kelly S. McDonough writes of primordial land titles—a narrated version of drawn maps—in the Chaco region of the central Mexican Valley, southwest of present day Mexico City, in "Plotting Indigenous Stories, Land, and People: Primordial Titled and Narrative Mapping in Colonial Mexico," *Journal for Early Modern Cultural Studies* 17, no. 1 (2017): 1–30, https://doi.org/10.1353/jem.2017.0003. See also Stephanie Wood's discussion of primordial titles in *Transcending Conquest: Nahua Views of Spanish Colonial Mexico* (Norman: University of Oklahoma Press, 2003).

35. Mundy, *Mapping of New Spain*, xvi.

36. Pablo Escalante Gonzalbo, "On the Margins of Mexico City: What the Beinecke Map Shows," in eds. Mary Miller and Barbara Mundy, *Painting a Map of Sixteenth-Century Mexico City: Land, Writing, and Native Rule* (New Haven: Yale University Press, 2012), 101–110, 101.

37. Mary E. Miller and Barbara E. Mundy, eds., *Painting a Map of Sixteenth-Century Mexico City: Land, Writing, and Native Rule* (New Haven: Yale University Press, 2012).

38. Barbara Mundy, "Crown and Tlatoque: The Iconography of Rulership in the Beineke Map," in *Painting a Map*, eds. Miller and Mundy, 177–178.

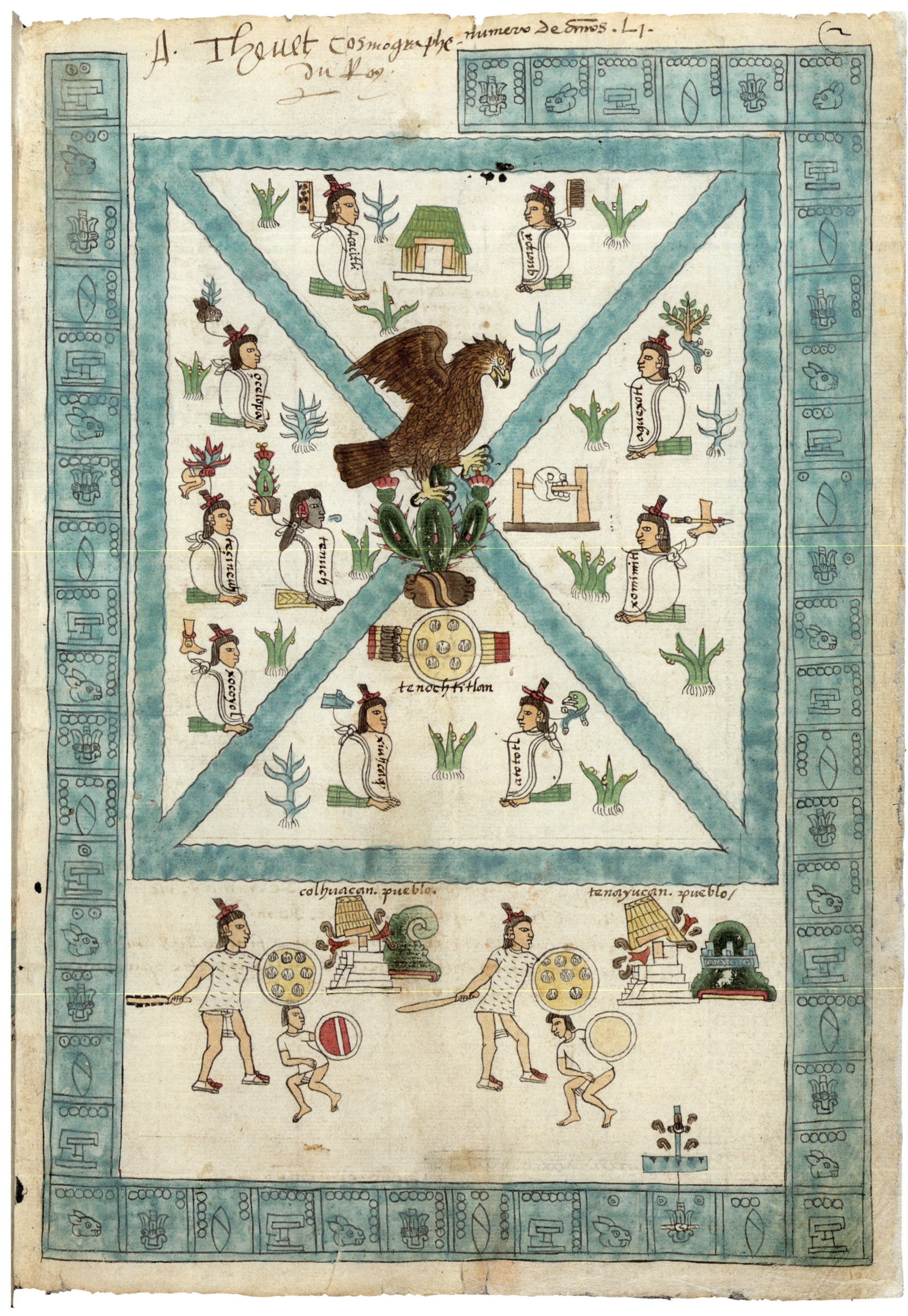
A. Thevet cosmographe du Roy
tenochtitlan
colhuacan. pueblo.
tenayucan. pueblo

◂ **Figure 4.6**
MS. Arch. Selden. A. 1, fol 2r,
Codex Mendoza, Viceroyalty of New Spain,
c. 1541–1542, pigment on paper,
© Bodleian Libraries, University of Oxford

maker's ancestral ties to places in other, rather quiet ways. The mapmaker's embeddedness within *tlalticpac* is found, first in the paper on which the image is written. To make *amantl* paper, the thin, flaky bark of fig and mulberry trees would have been harvested and boiled down. The resulting viscous fibers would have been laid in alternating layers to provide the paper with structure, then pounded flat into sheets. This process dates back before Spanish occupation. The *Farmers vs. Covarrubias* map also shows the mapmaker's knowledge of plants and minerals of the region, specifically, how to process each variety to extract the brightest pigments to paint the map. The map's materiality, however, would not have been legible to the Spanish reader as proof of a deep engagement with the land that the image depicted.

While the Spanish audience of the map read the text *"es de los yndios"* within European frameworks of property ownership, the map's Indigenous audience would have seen the green area in which this phrase is written as an articulation of Native sovereignty as loudly as a representation of a *tlatoque*. I contend that the shape of the green area and its color, so different from the rest of the map, would have communicated that it "belonged" to the Indigenous farmers of Tultepec to the Native readers of the map without the written words *"es de los yndios."* From the Indigenous perspective, the terms of "belonging" have a meaning radically different from the property regimes of *imperium* and relate more closely to the terms of *tlalticpac*.

Before Conquest, the Aztec people represented towns with the *altepetl* glyph on maps and documents. The spoken word "altepetl" is a portmanteau, combining the words *atl* for "water" and tepetl for "hill" to signify these basic necessities of water and land respectively needed to support life.[39] Together, "water" + "hill" move beyond the objects they represent in the world to signify a polity, or governed territory, much like a city-state. Each city-state was represented in writing with the basic form of the *altepetl*: a green hill, occasionally depicted with swirling water issuing from its base or blooming from both sides of its green-pigmented bell-shape. Additional notation on the top or sides of the hill gives that city-state a name. For example, Muchitlan's name translates to "Place of the Mochil" and suggests this was a place where the medicinal plant would have been found. The glyph that represents the town in pictorial Nahuatl is composed of the hill-shaped *altepetl* glyph topped by a representation of a four-petaled flower that resembles the *cuamochil* plant.[40] The name of the plant itself signifies its use: *cua* is the Nahuatl verb "to eat" and mochil, an abbreviation of *xochitl*, the word for "flower." Thus, Muchitlan roughly translates to medicinal flower-town. To write the toponym for Tultepec a *tlacuilo* would place four long pointed green stems with black tips atop the same hill-shaped *altepetl* glyph to represent the tule plant for which Tultepec is named (Figure 4.8). The marks that distinguish Muchitlan from Tultepec each derive from looking at plants in the landscape.

After Conquest, when churches became the most significant architectural and social feature of a town after occupation, the "church" glyph replaced the *altepetl* in written Nahuatl. On the *Farmers vs. Covarrubias* map, five neighboring town are represented by five small drawing of churches. Each has an arched door, much like the doorway of Covarrubias's *hacienda* in the top left corner of this map, as well as steeped roofs. These arches contrast with the pier and lintel door frames used to describe the Native houses that dot the central portion of the map. This difference in architecture also describes the divide between Spanish space and Native space in life. In addition to being the space

39. Elizabeth Boone Hill, "Glorious Imperium: Understanding Land and Community in Moctezuma's Mexico," in *Moctezuma's Mexico*, eds. Pedro Carrasco and Eduardo Matos Moctezuma (Niwot: University Press of Colorado, 1992), 161.

40. Mundy, *Mapping of New Spain*, 146.

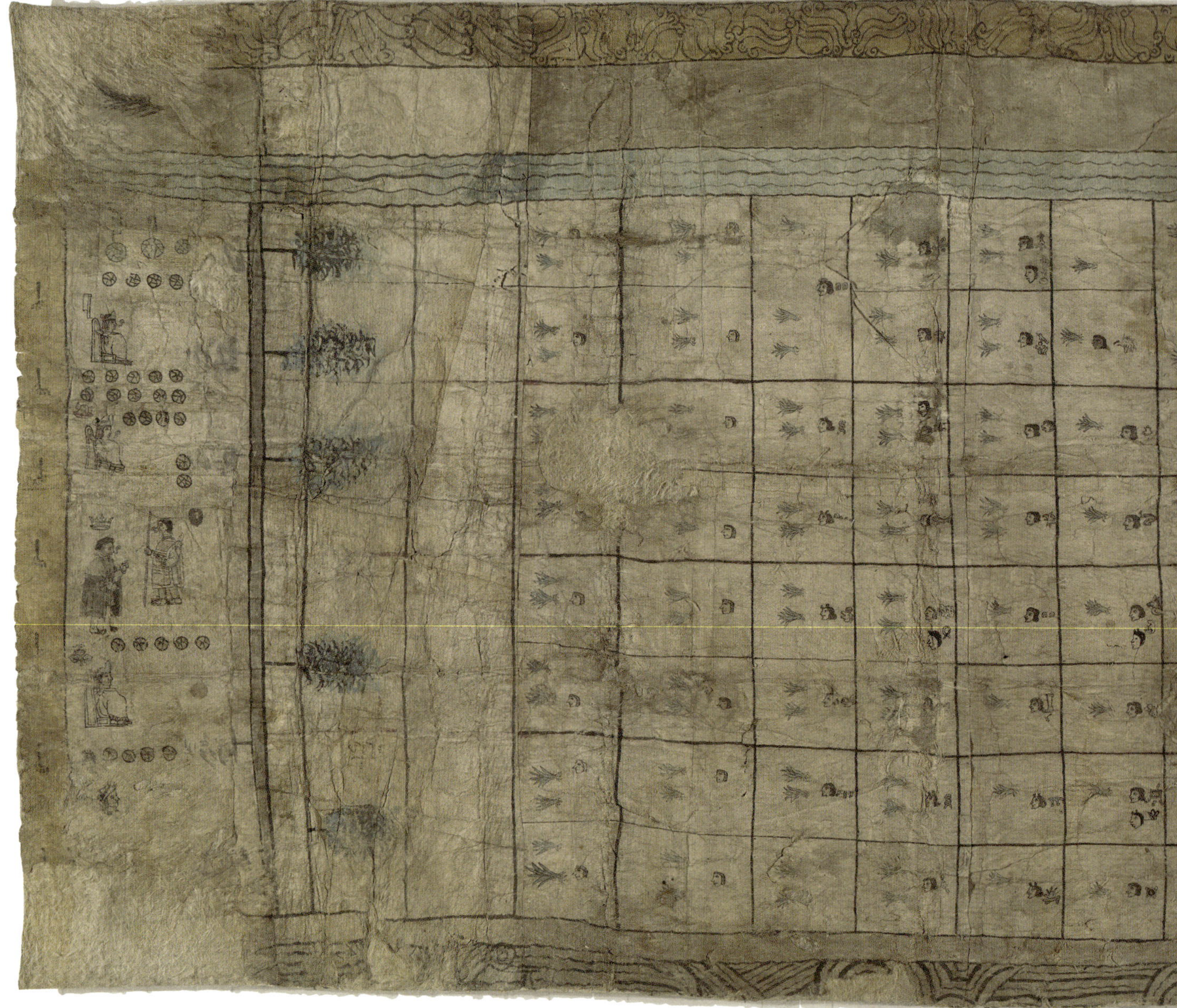

Figure 4.7
Codex Reese, sixteenth-century Mexico, Yale Collection of Western Americana, Beinecke Rare Book & Manuscript Library

in which Indigenous Natives and settlers most often came into contact, churches were often built atop hills and mountains as the Spanish recognized the sacred significance that Aztec and other Indigenous people attached to them. The placement of the Iglesia de Nuestra Señora de Los Remedios upon Tlachihualtepetl, a Nahuatl name that identifies it as a "hand-made mountain," in 1594 is a well-known example of an absorbed and supplanted place of Indigenous worship in the Central Mexican Valley. Yet, despite this shift in language for indicating a township from the altepetl glyph to the church glyph, art historian Barbara Mundy questions the degree to which the church actually supplanted Indigenous conceptions of community in this initial moment of settlement. She argues that churches on Indigenous-made maps in this early colonial period represent a "double-consciousness" because they are painted equally for Spanish patrons

and Indigenous users, in most cases under the direction of Spanish missionaries.[41]

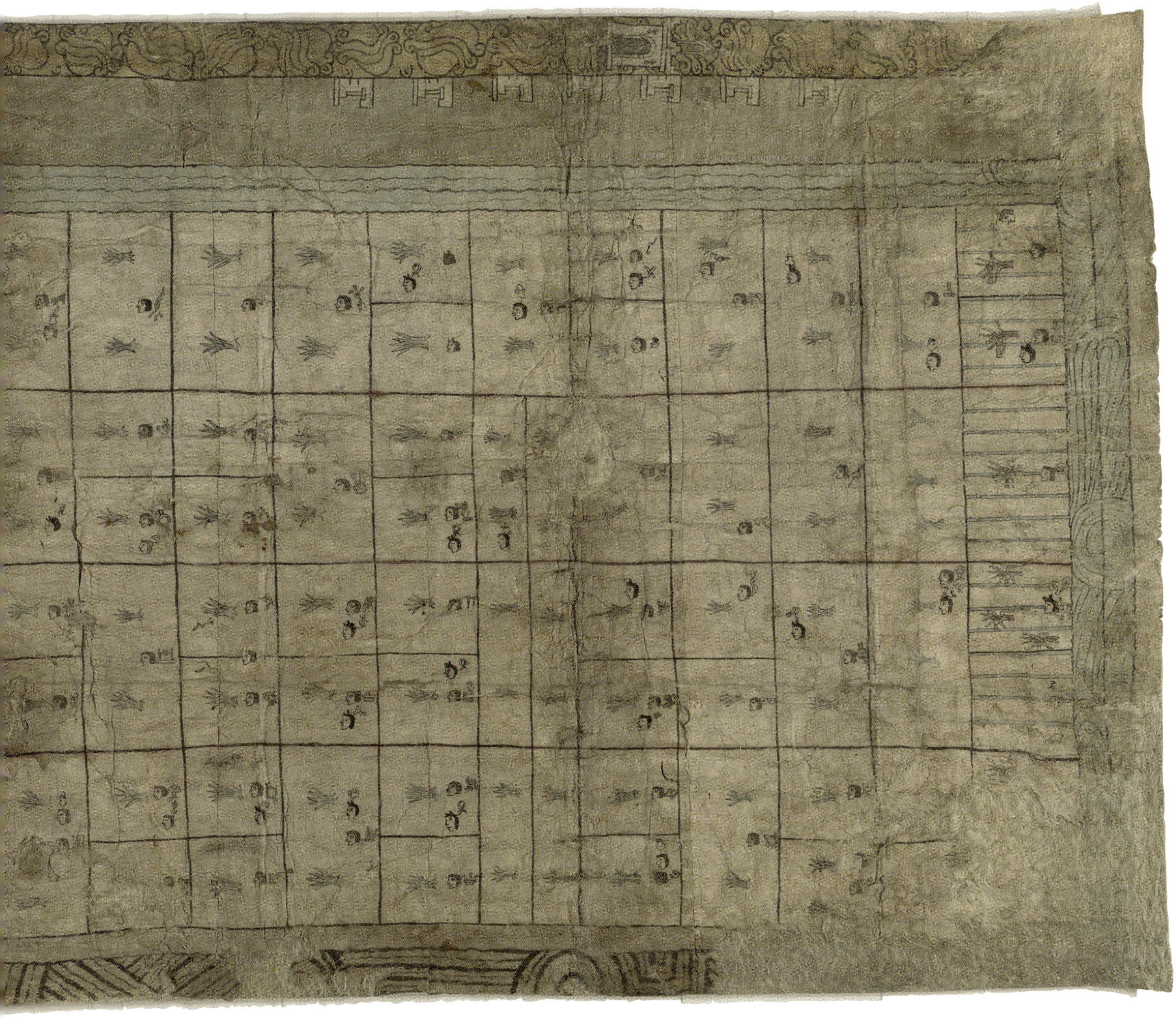

With its distinctive hill-like shape, could the green area on the *Farmers vs. Covarrubias* map be a modification of the *altepetl* glyph? Directly translated into English, the spoken word Tultepec means "hill of Tule." But this translation misses the depth of the written Nahuatl word. "Hill of Tule" identifies a geographic feature. But the "*Altepetl* of tule" relates the governing body and community established in the region where the tule grows. The "*Altepetl* of tule," then, is a sovereign territory and not an owned property.

In 1569, was the meaning of the *altepetl* glyph loaded with the same authority as it had been pre-Conquest? Does the *altepetl* used here function the same way as the *tlatoque* deployed on the Codices Reece and Mendoza? By drawing it on the *Farmers vs. Covarrubias* map, did the *tlacuilo* activate a claim for *tlalticpac*, in both its literal sense as land and its more expansive meaning as the realm of the farmer's existence? Was

41. Mundy, 68–74.

the use of this written word a cultural memory whose full meaning was fading out of use? To what degree did the farmers of Tultepec speak from this position of sovereignty is a question to be explored. The *tlacuilo's* use of the *altepetl* on the *Farmers vs. Covarrubias* map does tell us that the Tultepecans exist in a state of double consciousness, much like the map itself. Rather than the church glyph supplanting the *altepetl* glyph, the *altepetl* glyph hides on the *Farmers vs. Covarrubias* map in plain sight.

Nearly fifty years after the military conquest of the Aztec Empire, the Spanish residents of New Spain were becoming more aware of how Spanish law, ways of life, and animals were affecting the Indigenous people of Mexico and the environment. Perhaps for this reason, Judge Francisco Santiago de Bazán ruled in favor of the farmers of Tultepec. Other Native people who took Spaniards to court were not so lucky. The judge ordered Covarrubias "to move the corral of the said *estancia* [ranch] next to the road, further back behind the Indians of Xaltocán," a neighboring Native village, thus offsetting the Farmer's problem to another group of Indigenous people. Additionally, the Tultepecans were ordered to pay to move Corvarrubias's corral and were also forbidden from entering Corvarrubbia's property. They were authorized to "obtain from the lands" up to the red line "where some magueys are for the work of the said Indians" but "cannot enter . . . the common pasture."[42] The line of maguey agave that define the Farmer's property line would have been inedible to sheep and suggests that other plants at the borderline were utilized to deter the sheep's transgressions.

Judge Bazán and his clerk, Gaspar Peréz, signed directly underneath the red line that delineates Covarrubias property and above the line of maguey agave that defines the limits of the Farmer's altepetl. Within the system of the Spanish court, this signature functions as an official seal that is symbolic of Spanish authority in the region and Covarrubias's right to property. Within the system of Nahuatl writing, the

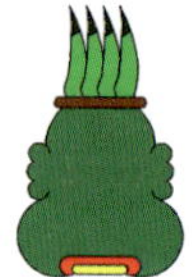

Figure 4.8
Toponyms for Tultepec (Wikipedia)

altepetl holds the same symbolic weight of authority and speaks to the continuation of markers of Native sovereignty, if not the right to self-determine one's own life in the lands to which one belongs outside of colonial control.

From the Spanish perspective, the map defines the division between two communities and two properties based on Spanish concepts of ownership. But we also see an Indigenous village in the process of being deterritorialized by the imposition of property lines. In this way, the green area appears as a space of imprisonment surrounded on all sides by Spanish claims. From the Nahuatl perspective, we can potentially think of the *Farmers vs. Covarrubias* map as a treaty between two nations. Both perspectives of the *Farmers vs. Covarrubias* maps demonstrate how property disputes were race relations in early colonial Mexico.

Conclusion

No map is neutral. No map is entirely objective. Whether it claims to document the physical and human geography of the entire world or define the property rights of different groups in a particular locality, it is always imbued with purpose and saturated with ideology. To put it another way, it always has a point of view. Within the broad context of global colonialism, that point of view often has to do with matters of race. We see how de Fer depicts the entire world from the privileged, white, European perspective of metropolitan France, racializing the world beyond Europe in ways that would prove useful to eighteenth-century thinkers. We see how the farmers involved in the litigation against Covarrubias depict their locality from the perspective of their own

42. Author's translation of the Spanish text written on the map.

embattled Indigenous understanding of land, property, and sovereignty, deploying the language of Western cartography for their own ends, against the impositions of the colonial regime.

Yet we also see that while maps adopt a particular point of view, they also lend themselves to a variety of interpretations. The meaning of the *Farmers vs. Covarrubias map* is clearly in the eye of the beholder, and deliberately so. To the Spanish officials who were its intended audience, it speaks the language of Western property rights, the only language that has authority in a racialized colonial regime. Yet it also speaks the language of traditional Nahuatl conceptions of land and sovereignty, allowing Indigenous readers to glimpse their home in the terms of their traditional worldview. In this way, it tells us something about how the cosmologies of oppressed groups survive in racialized regimes. The de Fer maps, meanwhile, give away something that they may not intend to reveal. By acknowledging that the New World is a place that has been refashioned by colonial-era migrations, it charts the limits of its own attempt to sort the world and its people into neat continental compartments. To an early modern reader, it might speak of the need for a theory of biological race that would explain who people remained the same after moving to new places, but to today's reader, it speaks of the arbitrariness of the project of race itself.

Note From the Field 2

DISPLAYING BLACK ART IN THE MEDIEVAL GALLERIES AT THE MET MUSEUM

Andrea Myers Achi

In 1997, The Met's groundbreaking exhibition, *The Glory of Byzantium*, created a model for museums and cultural institutions to incorporate cross-cultural* narratives about ethnicity and identity into their curatorial programing. It included artworks from regions and communities beyond the center of the Byzantine Empire, such as Egypt and Ethiopia. African art in this significant Byzantine exhibition created a space to decenter established art historical narratives. A year after the exhibition, Helen Evans, Mary and Michael Jaharis Curator of Byzantine Art, and Alisa LaGamma, Cecil and Michael E. Pulitzer Curator-in-Charge of the Michael C. Rockefeller Wing (previously Arts of Africa, Oceania, and the Americas), collaborated on the joint acquisition of an Ethiopian gospel book, which was featured in *The Glory of Byzantium*.[1] This monumental acquisition contrasted with other works in The Met's collection that depicted medieval Africans because the manuscript included representations of Ethiopians painted by Ethiopians.[2] When Evans and LaGamma presented the manuscript

1. Helen Evans, "The Arts of Byzantium," *Metropolitan Museum of Art Bulletin* 58, no. 4 (2001): 63; Helen Evans, ed., *Byzantium: Faith and Power (1261–1557)* (New York: Metropolitan Museum of Art2004), 441.

2. Academic and curatorial focus on representations of Africans in medieval Art usually is directed toward Western European depictions of Africans. For a general survey of these representations in museum collections, see David, Bindman, Henry Louis Gates. Jr., and Karen C. C. Dalton, eds., *The Image of the Black in Western* Art, new ed. (Cambridge, MA: Belknap Press of Harvard University Press, 2010).

to Philippe de Montebello, a previous director of The Met, he asked them why they had presented to him a "folk art" work. While this disparaging view was prevalent at the time, it became clear that the manuscript was a masterpiece for the collection. The manuscript has twenty-four full-page illustrations dating to the late fourteenth and early fifteenth century, and draws from early Christian, Byzantine, Syrian, Armenian, and Copto-Arabic traditions. The decorative borders of the manuscript, for example, represent the strong connections between Ethiopia and Arabia, and the visual paradigms in the illuminations relate to macro-regional* styles prevalent in East African art. The joint acquisition recognized Ethiopian art as medieval art and firmly grounded the manuscript in its African context. Building upon the momentum of the manuscripts' acquisition, Evans eventually acquired an Ethiopian processional* cross and a single Ethiopian manuscript leaf for the Byzantine collection. These works allowed Evans to highlight the importance of Ethiopia in the medieval world; Ethiopia was one of the first Christian nations, and the kingdom remained in close contact with its Byzantine and medieval counterparts for over a thousand years.[3] Most medieval collections only have a few works from the continent of Africa, and it can be difficult for curators to tell complex stories of medieval Africa with only a few objects.[4] Evans and LaGamma were ahead of their time, and these acquisitions prompted the discussion on medieval Africa at The Met.[5]

Like Evans and LaGamma, the focus of my curatorial practice is not on displaying Western European depictions of Black people; rather, when appropriate, I seek to incorporate medieval African art into the medieval galleries at The Met.[6] This incorporation is a complicated endeavor, as the inclusion of African Art in traditionally white spaces (here, The Met's medieval gallery) forces visitors to confront issues related to modern ideas of race and ethnicity. This "Note from the Field" considers the implications of displaying African Art within the medieval galleries at The Met. I developed an approach to the arts of Africa in medieval galleries in my recent co-authored article with Seeta Chaganti, "*Semper Novi Quid ex Africa*, Redrawing the Borders of Medieval Art and Considering its Implications for Medieval Studies."[7] The article considered how African art might be read as Black art in a white space. Here, I present two short notes on permanent collection interventions that engage with this issue and prompt a reflection on stories of medieval Africans within The Met's galleries. I conclude by considering an aspect of curatorial work that is not always appreciated: the development of exhibitions and installations to present diverse narratives to the public. Museums are the first entry point to the medieval world for many people, and these spaces have the opportunity to share the multifaceted perspectives of the medieval period.

3. For a comprehensive discussion on where Ethiopian Studies fits within medieval studies, see Suzanne Conklin Akbari, "Where is Medieval Ethiopia? Mapping Ethiopic Studies with Medieval Studies," in *Toward a Global Middle Ages: Encountering the World through Illuminated Manuscripts*, ed. Bryan Keene, 82–93 (Los Angeles: The J. Paul Getty Museum, 2019).

4. The Walters Museum, with their large Ethiopian Art collection, is an exception.

5. After the acquisition of the Ethiopian works, The Met began a series of installations and educational programming that centered on African Christianity. For example, in 2005, there was a series of lectures that examined the impact of Christianity on African history and culture and considered the continent's contribution to the development of the faith and its art. Speakers included Thelma Thomas, Elizabeth Bolman, Chester Higgins, and Alisa LaGamma.

6. Kristen Collins and Bryan Keene's Balthazar exhibition is a model for curators considering how to engage with the display of medieval European depictions of Black people.

7. Andrea Myers Achi and Seeta Chaganti, "Semper Novi Quid ex Africa': Redrawing the Borders of Medieval African Art and Considering Its Implications for Medieval Studies," in *Disturbing Times: Medieval Pasts, Reimagined Futures,* eds.Catherine E. Karkov, Anna Kłosowska, and Vincent W.J. van Gerven Oei, 73–106 (Brooklyn: punctum books, 2020), https://doi.org/10.21983/P3.0313.1.00.

African Christian Crosses: An Intervention in The Met's Medieval Galleries, Note #1

The Met's Michael C. Rockefeller Wing (MCRW) is beginning their large-scale renovation.[8] Most of that collection will be in storage until 2024. As a means to keep some of the African works on view, Alisa LaGamma and Diana Craig Patch, Lila Acheson Wallace Curator-in-Charge of the Department of Egyptian Art, collaborated on a long-term exhibition that juxtaposed West and Central African art with Ancient Egyptian art.[9] LaGamma also proposed to install small interventions of other African artworks throughout The Met. The proposal to move pre-modern African works from their geographic space to their temporal space made sense. I presented some early thoughts on the movement of African works in an encyclopedic museum in 2019 and 2020 at the Art Gallery Ontario.[10] This project also inspired some brainstorming that went into the article "Redrawing the Borders of Medieval African Art."

To an extent, MCRW's planned installation was a product of the global turn in medieval studies, which coincides with a turn in the curatorial practices in medieval departments.[11]As such, twenty years after the joint acquisition of the Ethiopian Gospel Book, LaGamma suggested that the selection of Ethiopian crosses in her department might find a temporary home in the medieval galleries. This was a natural fit since the medieval department already had a small collection of Ethiopian works. LaGamma asked us to display crosses from Christian Kongo in the medieval galleries as well. Though these works are not medieval, their relationship to the medieval collection is due to their connections to Christianity. While they were featured in LaGamma's exhibition *Kongo Power and Majesty*, this aspect of West African art still surprises and intrigues many visitors. In the sixteenth century, the sovereign Kingdom of Kongo adopted Catholicism as their state's official religion. The tens of thousands of European Christian devotional artifacts imported at that time served as prototypes for early Modern Kongolese artists. While some of these new works retained the naturalism of Portuguese models, others translated the imagery into a highly expressive Kongolese Christ.

Early on, I considered putting the MCRW's African Christian material in The Met's Byzantine Egyptian galleries. However, the dates of the artworks in those galleries are between the fourth to seventh centuries. A more appropriate location, then, would be the Western medieval galleries with our thirteenth- to fifteenth-century artworks. The Byzantine and medieval galleries at The Met are connected by a stunning sightline of two processional crosses, and the end of this sightline is our Byzantine Apse. We display a Byzantine processional cross and a Spanish processional cross on the same plane. On the labels for both crosses, we discuss the objects in their original contexts and what the crosses meant to the Christian communities who used them. Because of their formal connections, I decided to place the Ethiopian and Kongolese crosses on the same plane as the other medieval and Byzantine processional crosses. Working closely with LaGamma, this intervention allowed me to display the African processional crosses compellingly and discuss the crosses' original context. Hence, we brought new cross-cultural narratives into galleries through this installation and didactics.

8. For more information on the transformative renovation, see "Reenvisioning the Michael C. Rockefeller Wing," The Met, https://www.metmuseum.org/about-the-met/collection-areas/the-michael-c-rockefeller-wing/reenvisioning-mcr-wing.

9. "The African Origin of Civilization," The Met, https://www.metmuseum.org/exhibitions/listings/2021/african-origin-of-civilization.

10. Andrea Achi and Adam Levine, "Shape of the Museum," talk, Art Gallery Ontario, September 10, 2020, https://ago.ca/events/shape-museum-andrea-achi-and-adam-levine; Seeta Chaganti, "Seeta Chaganti Talks about a Hand Cross . . .," Art Gallery Ontario, November 5, 2018, on YouTube video, 5:19, https://www.youtube.com/watch?v=C3Sf3T4O84E.

11. Recent exhibitions that have mirrored the global turn in medieval studies include The Getty's *Balthazar,* The Block's *Caravans of Gold*, and The Bode Museum's *Beyond Compare.*

Medieval African Sculpture: An Intervention in The Met's Medieval Galleries, Note #2

The gradual incorporation of Ethiopian Art into the medieval department primed The Met's visitors for more experimental endeavors, such as The Met's 2020 Crossroad's installation, where I juxtaposed The Cloisters' African Magus with a medieval period Dogon Sculpture (Figure 1). The African Magus was part of a group of wooden sculptures representing the Adoration of the Magi; the figure initially stood behind an altar in a German church. According to the Gospel of Matthew, after the birth of Jesus, a group of Magi offered the child and his mother gifts of gold, frankincense, and myrrh. The New Testament does not identify the number in the group or their ethnicities. However, medieval literature and art depict the Magi as three kings from far corners of the known world, including Africa. Trade routes, diplomatic excursions, and increased contact between Europe and Africa in the medieval period led to more depictions of people with African descent in medieval art, particularly in scenes with the Magi.[12] This figure represented an imagined African royal and a reverent, wise man from the ancient world.

The Dogon sculpture is one of the earliest and largest surviving Dogon sculptures from the central plateau region of Mali; this commanding figure depicts a man at prayer. Skillfully carved, the sculpture represented a distinguished elder from his community. Individual characteristics, such as the delicate scars on his face and body and the jewelry on his neck and arms, suggest his significance. His raised hands are a symbol of prayer. For Dogon peoples, wooden sculptures acted as intermediaries between men and the ambiguous supernatural world. These statues could generate abundance or protection for their community. Displayed as altars and in shrines*, the sculptures were so potent and potentially dangerous that after they served their community for some time, a priest would ritually discard them to weaken their power.

It was striking that the "African Magus" and "Male Figure with Raised Arms" were so different but embodied similar responses to devotion and prayer. Out of their original contexts, both figures could evoke negative stereotypes. The presence of an unclothed African body in the medieval galleries caused discomfort, but the image is not unlike that of the stripped Christ in crucifixion scenes. To some, the magus appeared as a caricature of an African, but his elegant pose and attire are reminiscent of a medieval royal courtier. While the Dogon figure signified a real individual and the Magus represented a character from the Bible, together, the pairing represented powerful depictions of medieval Africans.

Black Art in a White Space?

As I consider similar interventions for the future, I recognize that many visitors might view African artworks in the medieval galleries as Black objects in a white space. This is a topic that scholars across fields are thinking about as well. For example, my colleague at the Stanford Classics department, Dr. Sarah Derbew's groundbreaking book includes a discussion on the display of Janiform* vases in museums (Figure 2).[13] She provides a model for curators to rethink descriptions, labels, and object titles. For example, her suggestion of a title for Janiform vases would be "Janiform kantharos with addorsed heads of black and brown figures," rejecting the gendered and ethnic descriptors. By calling the tan figure a brown figure instead of

12. Paul Kaplan is the leading scholar on this topic. His extensive work stems from his dissertation, see Paul H. D. Kaplan, *The Rise of the Black Magus in Western Art*, Studies in the Fine Arts: Iconography, number 9. (Ann Arbor, MI: UMI Research Press, 1985). However, a new generation of scholars is engaging European representations of Africans, such as the African Magus, and pre-modern Critical Race Theory more directly. See, for example, The Met's 2021–22 Jane and Morgan Whitney Fellow, Jacqueline Lombard's forthcoming dissertation on pre-modern conceptions of ethnic and racial identity: "Visual Languages of Race: Representing Blackness in 11th–13th Century Northern Europe," (PhD diss., University of Pittsburgh, 2022).

13. Sarah F. Derbew, *Untangling Blackness in Greek Antiquity* (Cambridge: Cambridge University Press, 2022), 29–65.

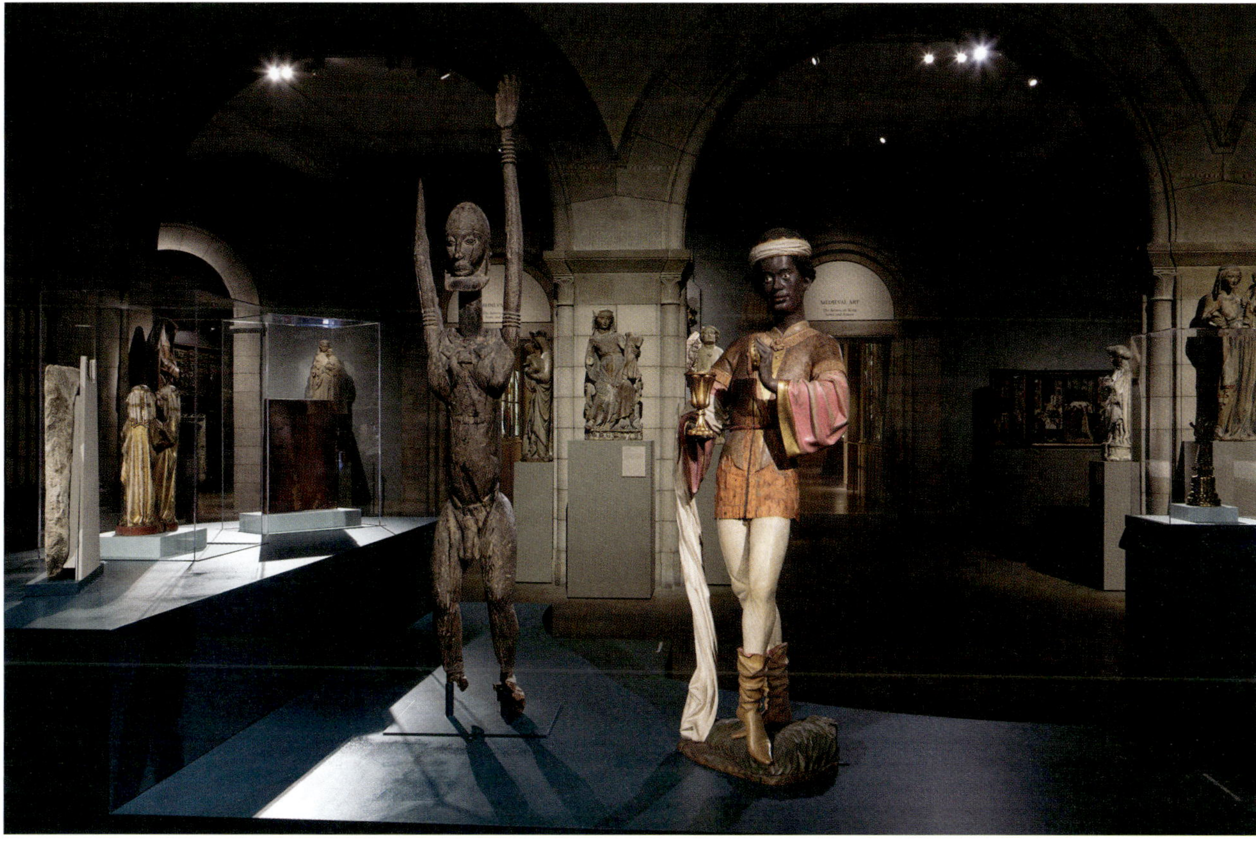

Figure 1
Crossroads Installation 2020
LEFT: *Male Figure with Raised Arms*, 14th–17th Century, Dogon peoples, The Michael C. Rockefeller Memorial Collection, Gift of Nelson A. Rockefeller, 1969 (1978.412.322)

RIGHT: *African Magus, one of the Three Kings from an Adoration Group*, before 1489, German, The Cloisters Collection (1952.52.83.2)

a Greek or white figure, Dr. Derbew forces the viewer to confront their perceptions of race and ethnicity.

Whereas those engaging with Western or Byzantine depictions of Africans might reference Premodern Critical Race Theory directly, my immediate task considers how the modern viewer understands African works in unexpected areas of the museum.[14] Because of these considerations, my next projects include discussing color theory in medieval African Art.[15] For example, in the Ethiopian manuscript acquired in 1998, almost all of the figures are painted with red pigment. Color theory is important in medieval Ethiopian artistic practice: for example, red symbolized fire, and blood, and was the described color of Christ.[16] Here, the Ethiopian figures are red and not "Black". By confronting issues of race and color directly, I hope that visitors will come to have a more nuanced understanding of Ethiopian art, African painting practices, and African Christian connections to the medieval world. This is an exciting task in these

14. Likewise, Elizabeth Williams, Curator of Byzantine Art at Dumbarton Oaks, is considering how the approaches Roland Betancourt put forth might be incorporated into her reinstallation of Dumbarton Oaks' Byzantine galleries. For her early thinking on this topic, see Elizabeth Williams, "Transforming Processes and New Global Narratives: Reimagining the Permanent Byzantine Galleries at Dumbarton Oaks," August 17, 2021, YouTube video, 24:52, https://www.youtube.com/watch?v=0RwzbA92x_U

15. For a comprehensive introduction on color theory and the hierarchy of colors in art history, see Aaron Fine, *Color Theory: A Critical Introduction* (London: Bloomsbury Visual Arts, 2021).

16. For an expansive description of the color red in Ethiopian art, see the entry on color in Siegbert Uhlig and Alessandro Bausi, eds., *Encyclopaedia Aethiopica*, 5 vols. (Wiesbaden: Harrassowitz Verlag, 2003), 1:A–C.

galleries, and I believe we will be able to bring new, cross-cultural narratives through these new installations and our didactics*.

Potential of Museums

The exhibitions and permanent gallery installations mentioned in this note provided training opportunities, such as formal internships, for diverse groups to collaborate on exhibition development, catalogs, and programming. These programs present the opportunity to tell the stories of medieval objects and help students think critically about their relationship to these objects, discuss original contexts, and ponder how the artworks got into the museum. Curators mentor these students and encourage them to take foreign languages and other necessary courses to graduate school. These internship projects are often tied to the development of exhibitions or permanent collection installations. The internships allow students to engage with primary sources and objects in ways that might be challenging to do within typical coursework.

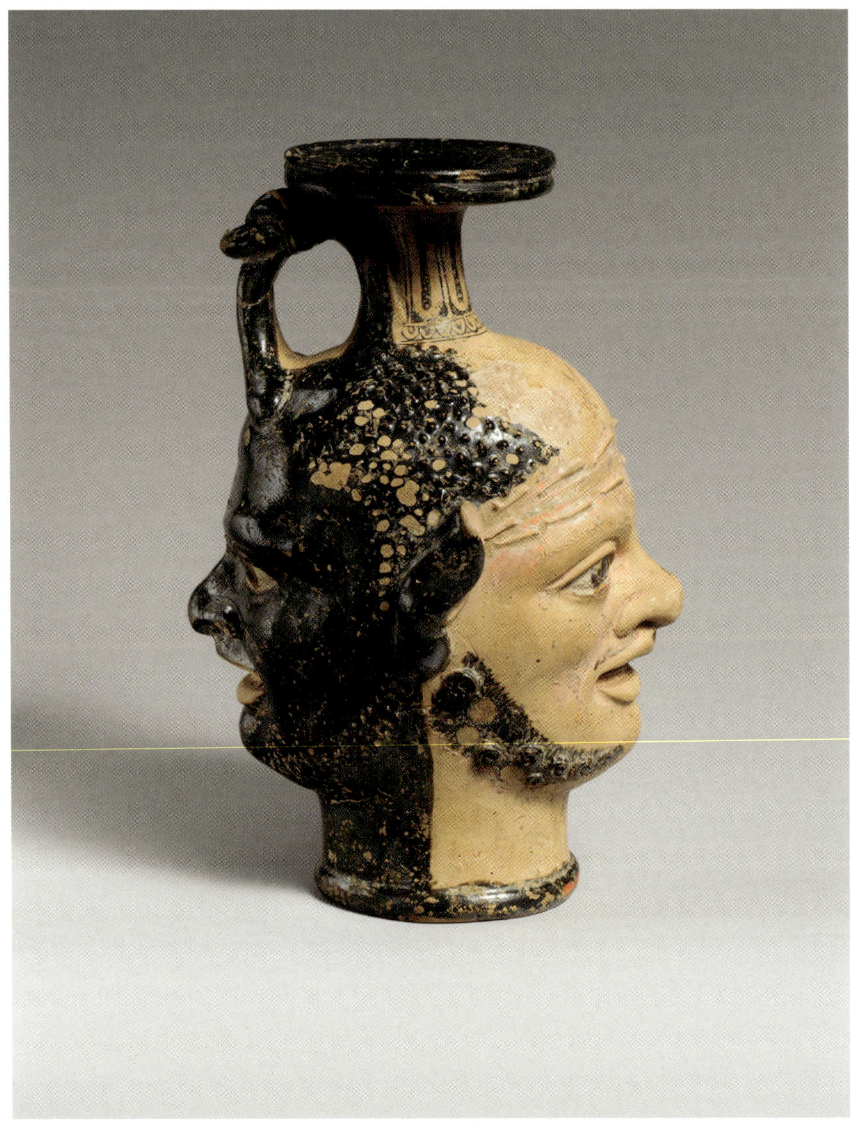

Figure 2
Terracotta vase with janiform heads, Etruscan, 4th century BCE, Metropolitan Museum of Art, Rogers Fund, 1906, 06.1021.204

Each of these opportunities helps with applications to graduate school, resumes for the job market, and so on. In short, exhibitions help to create multiple entry points into our fields. Exhibitions and their development also provide opportunities for historically underrepresented students to enter medieval studies. Indeed, we cannot depend on one or two institutions to do this work of creating an inclusive space to allow historically marginalized students to thrive, but what if keepers of every medieval collection viewed their upcoming exhibitions as an opportunity to diversify our field? What if we worked together — universities, colleges, museums, and libraries — to help students get hands-on training with object-centered research? Our interns do not have to start as medievalists, but we can introduce them to the field.

EXHIBITION CATALOG

PART 2. MAPPING

Case Study #1. Medieval Epistemologies of Race and Geography

ENTRY #15 (NO IMAGE)

Sir John Mandeville, attributed author; Jean d'Outremeuse (1338–approximately 1399), possible author;
Cornelis de Zierikzee, printer
Iohannis de Montevilla Itinerari[us] in partes Iherosolimitanas: et in ulteriores transmarinas
(also known as the *The Book of Sir John Mandeville*), c. 1500.
Book with letterpress
VAULT Inc. 1498

The Book of Sir John Mandeville chronicles Sir John Mandeville's journey from St. Albans, England, eastward to the Terrestrial Paradise. Like many medieval *itineraria**, *The Book* allows its readers to visualize themselves journeying alongside Mandeville. *The Book* further functions mnemonically*, similarly to a T-O *mappa mundi**, depicting wonders of the world in topical groupings and thus reflecting cosmological truths rather than geographical realities. Mandeville populates the East with people considered monstrous such as pygmies, Amazons, dog-headed people (cynocephali), and headless humans (blemyae). These peoples are depicted alongside vast civilizations, including enemy Saracen kingdoms in the Holy Lands, the Great Khan's powerful empire of Cathay (China), and Prester John's marvelous lands in India among the islands near the Terrestrial Paradise. Prester John, a Christian, is particularly notable for simultaneously representing a potential ally against the Saracens and a fearful yet desirable distant realm, filled with both gold and monstrous humans. In its depictions of the world, therefore, *The Book* both reflects and constructs a medieval European discourse of race.

Though Mandeville's identity, possibly a pen name for Jean d'Outremeuse, is contested, *The Book*'s influence is undeniable. Its widespread reproductions have resulted in at least 25 different versions of the text. It was translated from French into nearly 10 languages across the European continent and likely influenced Christopher Columbus on his voyages to the Americas. This edition of *The Book* was printed in 1495 in Cologne, underscoring its longevity since the earliest surviving manuscript was penned in 1371.

Further Readings

Greenlee, John Wyatt, and Anna Fore Waymack. "Thinking Globally: Mandeville, Memory, and Mappaemundi." *The Medieval Globe* 4, no. 2 (2018): 69–106.

Heng, Geraldine. *The Invention of Race in the European Middle Ages*. Cambridge, UK: Cambridge University Press, 2018, 127–38.

Tzanaki, Rosemary. *Mandeville's Medieval Audiences: A Study on the Reception of the Book of Sir John Mandeville (1371–1550)*. Burlington: Ashgate Publishing Company, 2003, 120–22.

Jamie Keener

ENTRY #16 [CONTEXTUAL SUPPLEMENT: RACISM IN ACTION]

Unknown German artist
Judensau (*Jew's Sow*), printed c. 1700
Woodcut on paper from a woodblock carved c. 1470
VAULT oversize fragment Inc. 37.7

The *Judensau* is an obscene antisemitic caricature dating back to at least thirteenth-century Germany. It shows a standing female pig surrounded by male figures depicted as Jews (with specific hats and somewhat large noses). They are caught in the transgressive acts of suckling on and caressing the animal and framed as rabbis ineffectively upholding the Torah's prohibition on touching or consuming pork.

Initially an allegory of greed with no connection to Judaism, the *Judensau* later appeared in church sculptures and then on city gates and private property. Becoming even more widespread through prints, the theme persisted into the nineteenth century. The Newberry's *Judensau* is the first complete printed image to survive, dating to around 1470. This oversized woodcut may have been displayed on walls. All known impressions were however printed about 1700 from the original block, which shows its age and the toll of frequent reprinting in its border losses.

The German caption below reads: "This is why we do not eat roast pork. And thus we are lustful and our breath stinks." These insinuated bodily appetites pair with the stench of a curvaceous pile of porcine filth nearby. The image's large scale further accommodates scurrilous texts implying other incestuous and unclean behaviors. The texts even appear as meaningless pseudo-Hebrew characters woven into the tunic hem of the Jew riding backwards on the sow. He raises her tail so another can inspect beneath it. Martin Luther described this scatological interaction in the still-extant Wittenberg Church's *Judensau* statue in explicit terms in 1543, further cementing the damage of its perversely inverted iconography.

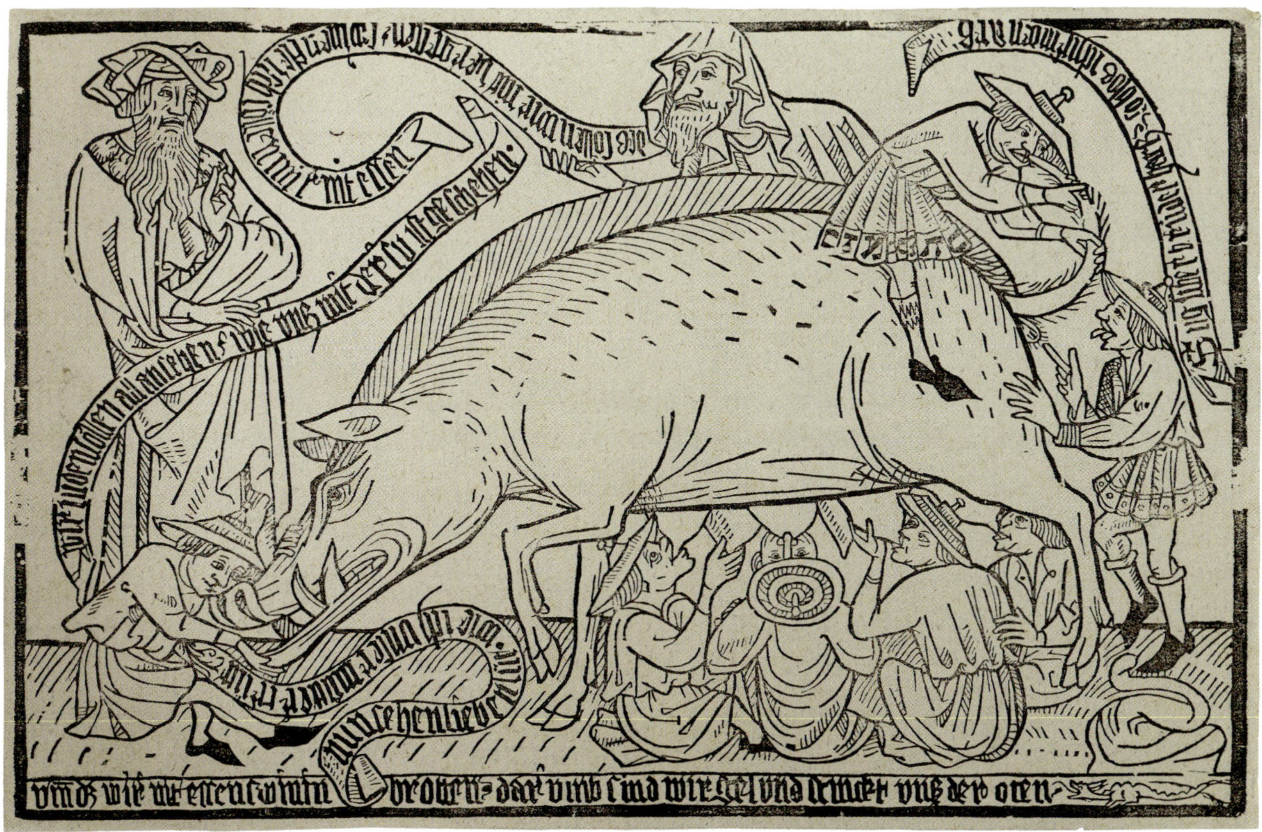

Entry #16

Further Readings

Luther, Martin. *Vom Schem Hamphoras und vom Geschlecht Christi*. Wittenberg: Georg Rhaw, 1543.

Shachar, Isaiah. *The Judensau: A Medieval Anti-Jewish Motif and Its History.* Warburg Institute Surveys, 5. London: Warburg Institute, 1974.

Wiedl, Birgit. "Laughing at the Beast: The *Judensau*." In *Laughter in the Middle Ages and Early Modern Times: Epistemology of a Fundamental Human Behavior, its Meaning, and Consequences*, edited by Albrecht Classen, 325–64. Berlin: De Gruyter, 2010.

Suzanne Karr Schmidt

ENTRY #17

Hartmann Schedel (1440–1514), author;
Michael Wolgemut (1434–1519), Wilhelm Pleydenwurff (1460–1494), and Albrecht Dürer (1471–1528), illustrators;
Anton Koberger (1440–1513), printer
Prince of Savoy (1663–1736), former owner
Map with Monstrous Races, in *Liber chronicarum* (also known as *The Nuremberg Chronicle*), 12 July 1493
Book with letterpress and woodcuts
VAULT oversize Inc. 2084

As detailed on its first page, the 1493 *Nuremberg Chronicle* relates the histories of the world. Drawing from older models such as Ptolemy's world map and Christian cosmography, this incunable, or early printed book, continued the medieval tradition of the *mappa mundi* and made it more accessible through its print format and later publication in a smaller, more economical edition. The *Chronicle* declared the centrality of Europe — particularly Nuremberg — and analogously, the cultural, religious, and moral superiority of the nations and continents at the center.

Folios XIIr–XIIIv depict the Second of the Seven Ages of the World, as per the Christian tradition. Dominating this two-page opening is the *mappa mundi*, held up in three corners by Noah's sons, Japhet, Shem, and Ham. On the left, Africa appears below Europe; Asia reaches across the right side. Lining the left border of the page is a vertical grid exhibiting some of the "Monstrous Races": the Six-Armed Man, Hermaphrodite*, Twelve-Fingered Man, Satyr*, Bearded Woman, Four-Eyed Ethiopian, and long-necked Crane Man. Unlike in medieval precedents, the "monsters" here are presented in a gallery on the border of the page rather than on the edge of the map. Natural landscapes frame the

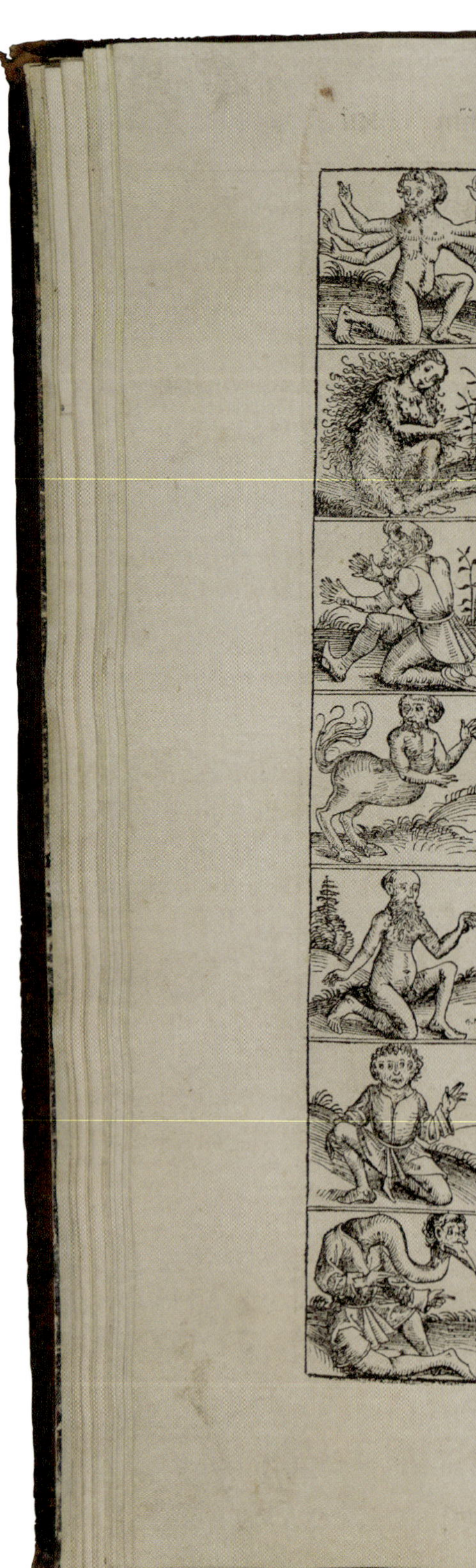

Entry #17

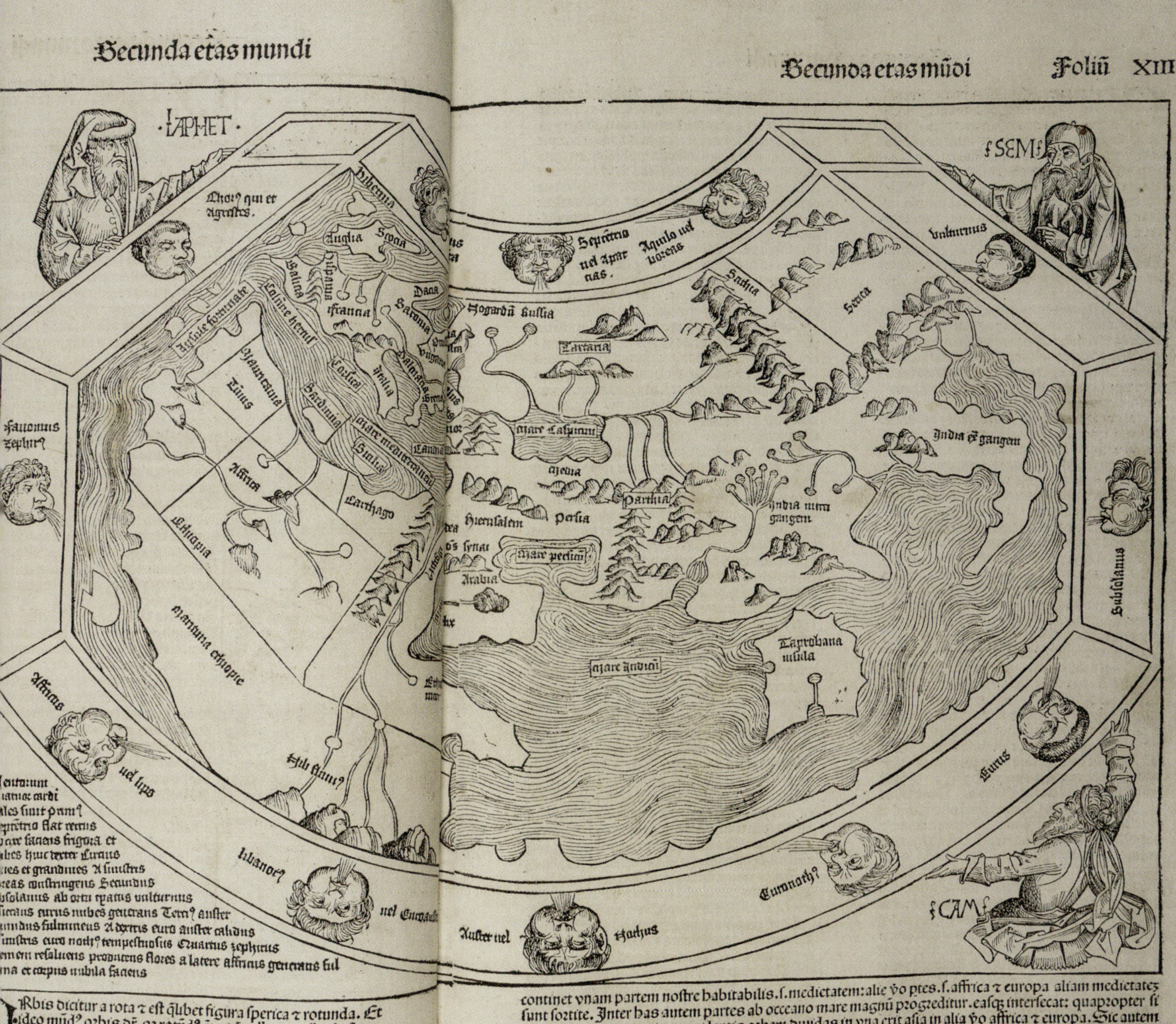

Orbis dicitur a rota ⁊ est qͥlibet figura sperica ⁊ rotunda. Et ideo mũd⁹ orbis dr̃. qꝛ rotũd⁹ ē: ⁊ dr̄ orb terre vl' orbisterrarũ. Dicũt āt fm vincẽ. filij sem obtinuisse asiã. filij chã affri… filij iaphet europã. Ysiđ. in li. Ethy. asserit ꝙ orbis diuisus ē in partes ſ nõ eq̄liter. Nã asia a meridie ꝑ orientem vſqꝫ ad septē… puenit. Europa vo a septētrione vſqꝫ ad occidentẽ ꝑtingit. affrica ad occidentem ꝑ meridiez se extendit. Sola quoqꝫ Asia

continet vnam partem nostre habitabilis. s. medietatem: alie vo ptes. s. affrica ⁊ europa aliam medietatez sunt sortite. Inter has autem partes ab occeano mare magnũ progreditur. easqꝫ intersecat: quapropter si in duas partes orientis ⁊ occidentis orbem diuidas in vna erit asia in alia vo affrica ⁊ europa. Sic autem diuiserunt post diluuiũ filij Noe: inter quos Sem cum posteritate sua asiam. Japhet europam: cham affricam possederunt. vt dicit glo. super Gen. x. ⁊ super libro Paralippo. primo. Idem dicit Crisostomus Isidorus ⁊ Plinius.

figures in contrast to the elaborate cityscapes of European cities throughout the rest of the book. Despite the knowledge and depiction of Ethiopia on the map, a distorted representation of an Ethiopian appears outside of the centrally framed biblical narrative and attendant human lineage. Conveying with assumed authority a division between white and non-white humans, this historicized account provides a widely disseminated model of late medieval race-making. The first edition of this incunable appeared just before Columbus returned to Europe from the Americas.

Further Readings

Green, Jonathan. "Text, Culture, and Print-Media in Early Modern Translation: Notes on the 'Nuremberg Chronicle' (1493)." In *Fifteenth-Century Studies Vol. 33*, edited by Edelgard E. DuBruck, Barbara I. Gusick, and William C. McDonald, 114–32. Woodbridge, UK: Boydell & Brewer, 2008.

Leitch, Stephanie. *Mapping Ethnography in Early Modern Germany: New Worlds in Print Culture*. New York: Palgrave Macmillan, 2010.

Strickland, Debra Higgs. "Foreign Bodies in the Nuremberg Chronicle." *Bulletin of the John Rylands Library* 95, no. 2 (2019): 19–42.

Earnestine Qiu

ENTRY #18

Sebastiao Lopes, sixteenth century
Portolan, 1565
Painted on vellum*
Oversize Ayer MS map 26

A large-scale illuminated atlas on twenty-four pages of vellum in its original late-sixteenth-century binding, the *Lopes portolan* is an atlas designed for Portuguese royalty or the affluent merchant class. Its size, extensive gold leaf, and elaborately painted pages evoke luxury and wealth. Fingerprints in the bottom right corner of most of the pages indicate that it was also a beloved and often-studied manuscript. Portolan charts had been the most common and most accurate map for sea travel in the fifteenth century as they were based on measurements of coastlines and the use of the compass. By the mid-sixteenth century, when this atlas was produced, printed atlases were available and portolan charts were likely not used for the purposes of travel as frequently.

This portolan acts as a showpiece that propagandistically lays claim to Portuguese lands through the use of flags, coats-of-arms, architecture, and bodies. For instance, the pages representing Africa include Portuguese flags, a church, and numerous European townscapes. A central aim of the manuscript was also to demonstrate religious control over regions throughout the world. An enthroned Prester John presides over the east coast of Africa. Prester or Priest John, now a mythical figure, throughout the premodern period was believed to be a Christian ruler of Africa, possibly descendent from Asia and related to the Three Magi. He makes his way on to portolan charts as early as the mid-fourteenth century. Here on the *Lopes portolan*, as in other portolan atlases from the time, he is racialized through the depiction of dark skin.

Further Readings

Cortesão, Armando, and Avelino Teixeira da Moto. *Portugaliae monumenta cartographica*, vol. IV (Lisbon, 1960).

Kaufmann, Miranda. "Prester John," In *Encyclopedia of Blacks in European History and Culture*, edited by Eric Martone, 2 vols. (Westport, CT: Greenwood Press, 2009). II: 423–24.

Lanman, Jonathan T. "On the Origins of Portolan Charts." *The Hermon Dunlap Smith Center for the History of Cartography Occasional Publication*, No. 2 (Chicago: Newberry Library, 1987).

Lia Markey

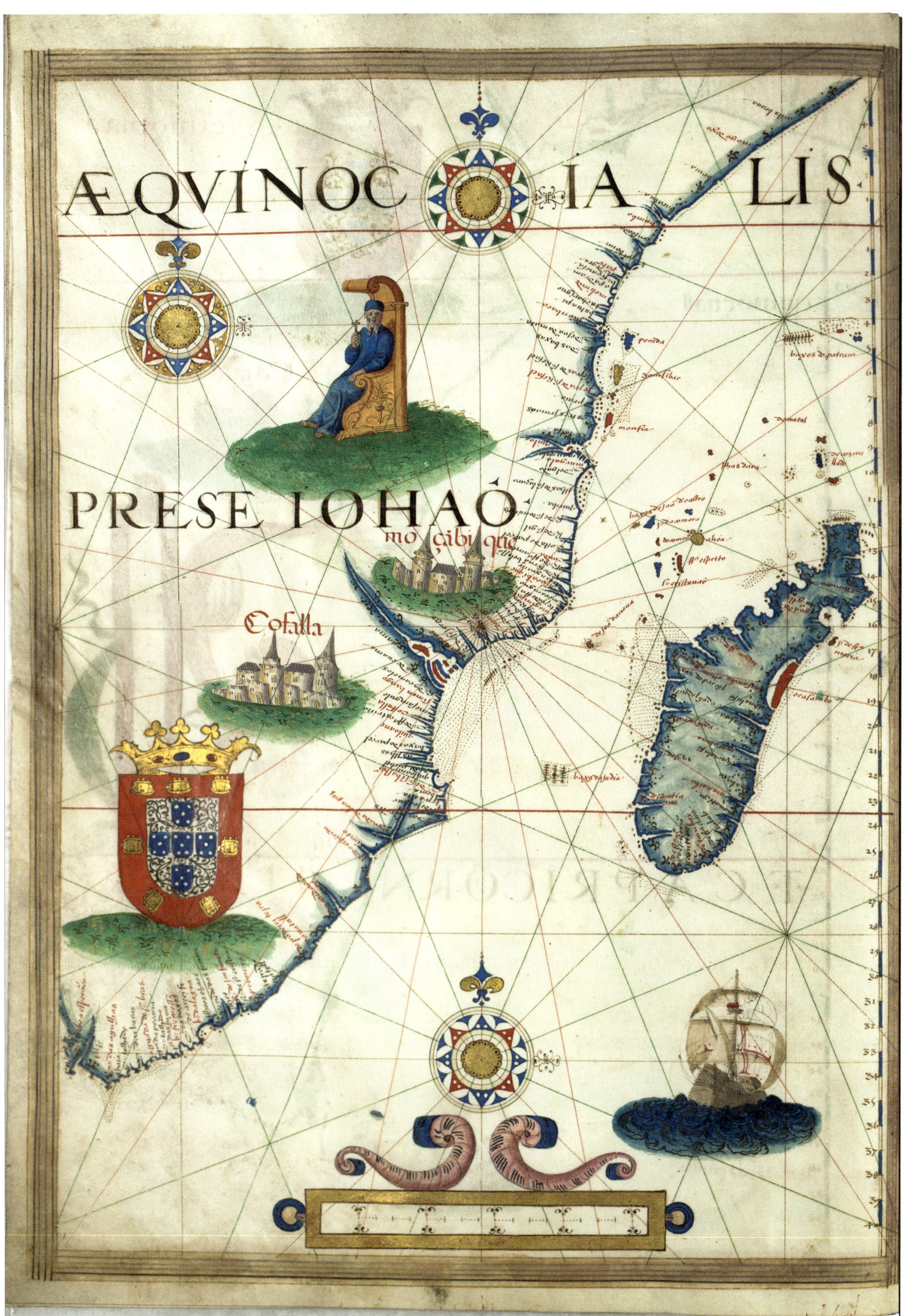

Entry #18 (verso)

Case Study #2.
The Early Modern Turn Towards the Ottomans and the Americas

ENTRY #19 (NO IMAGE)

Robert the Monk and Fulcher of Chartres, authors
Hystoria de Itinere [con]tra turchos (Chronicle of the First Crusade), c. 1472
Book with letterpress
Inc. 998

The Crusades caused a major shift in the medieval understanding of race, as they represented the most extensive interactions between some northern Europeans and non-Christian cultures since Late Antiquity. However, for the majority who never experienced one themselves, the Crusades were primarily a *literary* event. Widely held notions about the nature and purpose of the Crusades and the peoples involved were shaped far more by their depictions in chronicles, romances, liturgy*, and other genres. As such, the conventions and stock characterizations of the vast body of Crusade literature fundamentally shaped how Europeans saw the non-Christian cultures of the Eastern Mediterranean long after the fall of the last Crusader kingdom in 1291. Chronicles of the First Crusade (none of which were true eyewitness accounts), for instance, depicted the Seljuk Turks as an inhuman, menacing force; the widely popular chronicle of Robert the Monk, for instance, described them as "abominable people" who "know nothing of God." Though Crusaders themselves developed a more nuanced understanding of the different Islamic peoples they encountered, Europeans at home clung to these labels for centuries. During the fifteenth century, for example, editions of Crusade chronicles, such as the compilation shown here, were printed to help Europeans understand the ascendancy of the Ottoman Empire. Centuries later, Europeans would still rely on them to, once again, justify military and political attempts to reclaim control of lands in the Levant.

Further Readings

Lapina, Elizabeth. "Crusader Chronicles." *The Cambridge Companion to the Literature of the Crusades*. Edited by Anthony Bale, 11–24. Cambridge, UK: Cambridge University Press, 2019.

Ramey, Lynn. *Christian, Saracen and Genre in Medieval French Literature: Imagination and Cultural Interaction in the French Middle Ages*. 2nd ed. New York: Routledge, 2014.

Christopher Fletcher

ENTRY #20

Attributed to Battista Agnese (1500–1564)
Manuscript portolan atlas of the world, 1550
Painted vellum
VAULT Ayer MS map 12.

Attributed to the prolific Genoese cartographer Battista Agnese, this portolan atlas offers a fascinating view of European expansion, self-(re)conceptualization, and assertion in the mid-sixteenth century. Portolan, or nautical, maps were originally used as navigational tools in late-medieval sea voyages, as evidenced by the network of ruled lines representing various wind directions in this example. By the time of the production of this atlas, however, the map's artistic adornments and inland detail suggest they were becoming objects acquired as much for their decorative value. This degree of sophisticated decoration nevertheless points towards a new function by representing the ever-intensifying nexus between knowledge and power in Europe. On the folio presented, European monarchs emerge as generally standardized representations of sovereignty defined primarily over land rather than peoples. In contrast, every other region throughout the collection (including Africa, the Americas, and much of Asia) lacks human representations. Overall, the collection intimates European territorial control and opens non-European lands to conquest and material exploitation.

The sole non-European figure represented, the Ottoman Sultan Suleiman the Magnificent, also captures the development of a distinct European identity in contrast to the non-European Other. Marked by his distinctive headwear and reclining aspect, Suleiman's westward-facing profile is confronted by a generally united coalition of upright, standardized European sovereigns. This organization of figures carves out the core European territories as a culturally and religiously coherent unit in opposition to the non-European Muslim Sultan, marked out as he is from his counterparts through his dress, posture, and marginal position.

Further Readings

Astengo, Corradino. "The Renaissance Chart Tradition in the Mediterranean." In *Cartography in the European Renaissance*, edited by David Woodward, 174–262. Chicago: University of Chicago Press, 2007.

Campbell, Tony. "Portolan Charts from the Late Thirteenth Century to 1500." In *Cartography in Prehistoric, Ancient and Medieval Europe and the Mediterranean*, edited by J.B. Harley and David Woodward, 371–458. Chicago: University of Chicago Press, 1987.

Edward Johnson

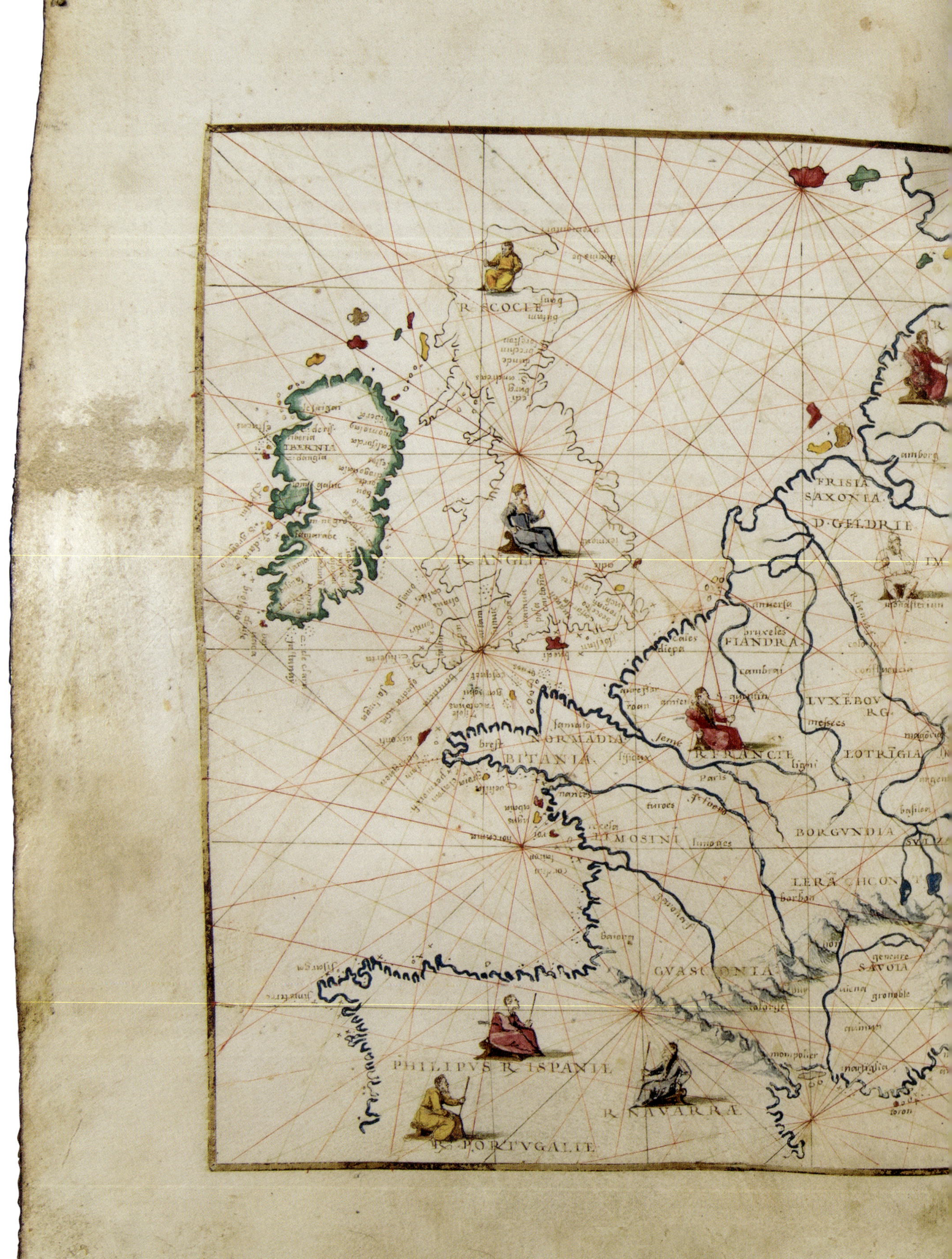

R. SCOCIE
IBERNIA
R. ANGLIE
FRISIA
SAXONIA
D. GELDRIE
FIANDRA
bruxeles
anversa
cales
diepa
cambrai
roan
LUXEBOURG
NORMADIA
brest
sanmalo
BITANIA
R. FRANCIE
Paris
nantes
turoes
LOTRIGIA
LIMOSINI
limoges
BORGUNDIA
borbon
bayona
GUASCONIA
SAVOIA
geneure
gronoble
monpolier
marsiglia
PHILIPUS R. ISPANIE
R. NAVARRAE
R. PORTUGALIE

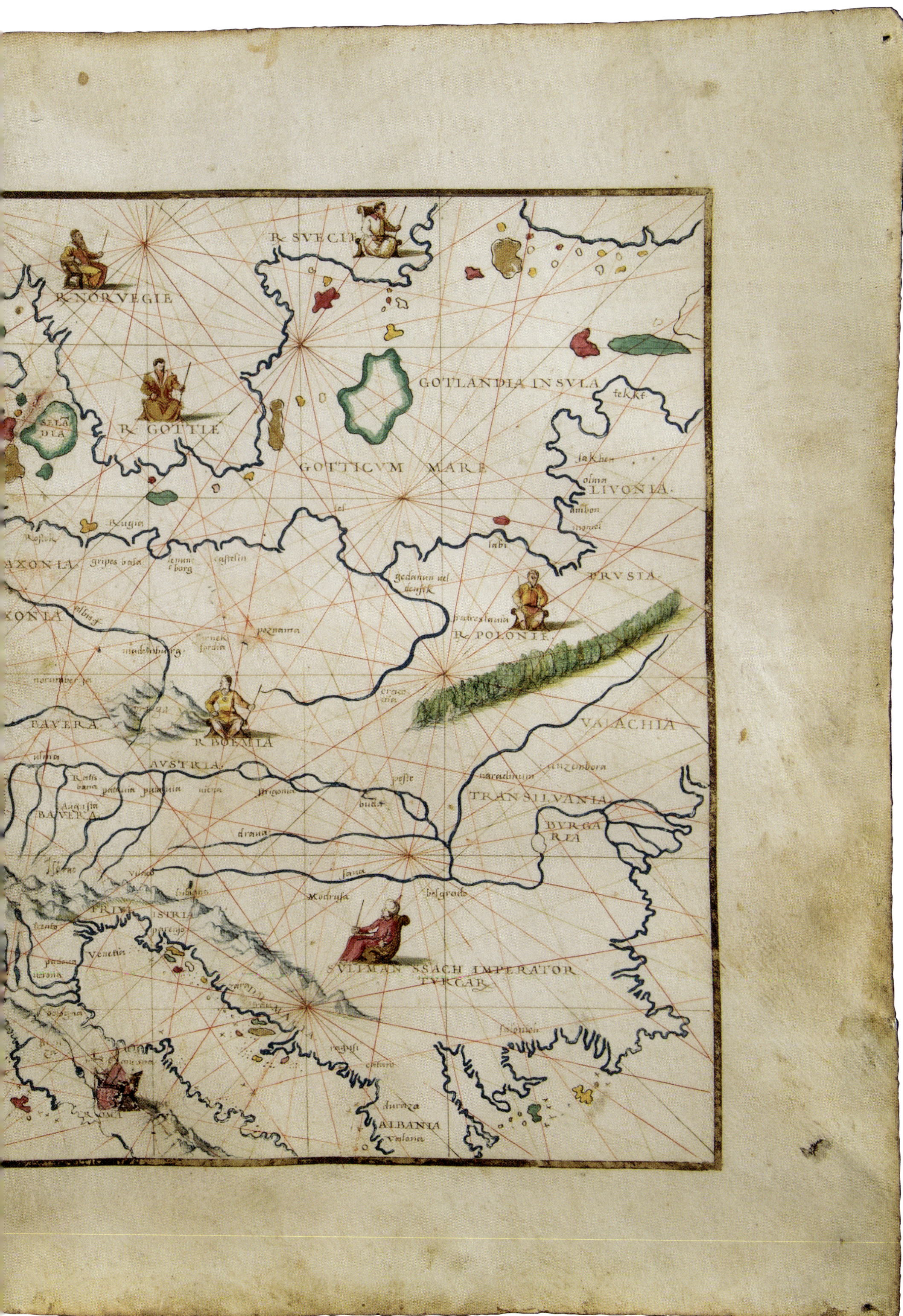
R. SVECIE
R. NORVEGIE
GOTLANDIA INSVLA
R. GOTTIE
GOTTICVM MARE
LIVONIA
PRVSIA
R. POLONIE
VALACHIA
R. BOEMIA
BAVERA
AVSTRIA
TRANSILVANIA
BVRGARIA
buda
pesti
belgrado
ISTRIA
SVLIMAN SSACH IMPERATOR
TVRCAR
durazo
ALBANIA
Valona

ENTRY #21

Author Unknown
Tarih-i Yeni Dünya, el-musemma be hadis-i nev (A History of the India of the West), c. 1600
Painted on glazed paper
VAULT Ayer MS 612

This Ottoman Turkish manuscript fits in the palm of the hand and is composed of 107 pages with 13 images and 3 maps colorfully illuminated with gold and muted tones on a distinctly non-European glazed paper. The renowned manuscript in Turkish Arabic includes handwritten texts, maps, and images about the Americas based primarily on Giovanni Battista Ramusio's third volume of the *Navigazioni et viaggi*, a compilation of travel writing about the world first published in Venice in 1565, as well as other Spanish publications, including Gómara, Oviedo, and Peter Martyr. The Newberry's *Tarih* manuscript is one of 19 in the world that all derive from the same source. The original text was likely presented to Sultan Murad III in the late sixteenth century. The author/chronicler states in the first pages of the Newberry's manuscript that he "collected some responsible truthful books and recent maps containing the. . . information, and after translating and commenting on them in general, a summary was set forth."

Critical analysis of this "summary" in the text in relation to its complex images reveals intertextuality and representations of a changing world economy. For instance, the image of Potosì in the Newberry manuscript is borrowed from an Italian edition of Pedro Cieza de León's 1553 chronicle of Peru, and the abundant use of gold leaf on the page seems to comment on the subject itself, reflecting the role of silver mining in the region. The figures at the bottom of the scene represent people of different races with a white man at left and Black man at right. Does the Black figure reference the enslaved laborers from Africa put to work in the mines in the region? In any case, the figure clearly delineates the distinctions between races described in the texts of illustrated travel accounts from this period but that are often not made apparent in the print medium.

Further Readings

Goodrich, Thomas D. *The Ottoman Turks and the New World: A Study of Tarih-i Hind-i garbi and Sixteenth-century Ottoman Americana*. Wiesbaden: O. Harrassowitz, 1990.

Leibsohn, Dana. "Made in China, Made in Mexico." In *At the Crossroads: The Arts of Spanish America and Early Global Trade*, edited by Donna Pierce and Ronald Otsuka, 11–40. Denver: Denver Art Museum, 2012.

Tezcan, Baki. "The Many Lives of the First Non-Western History of the Americas: From the New Report to the History of the West Indies." *The Journal of Ottoman Studies*, 40 (2012): 1–38.

Lia Markey

Entry #21

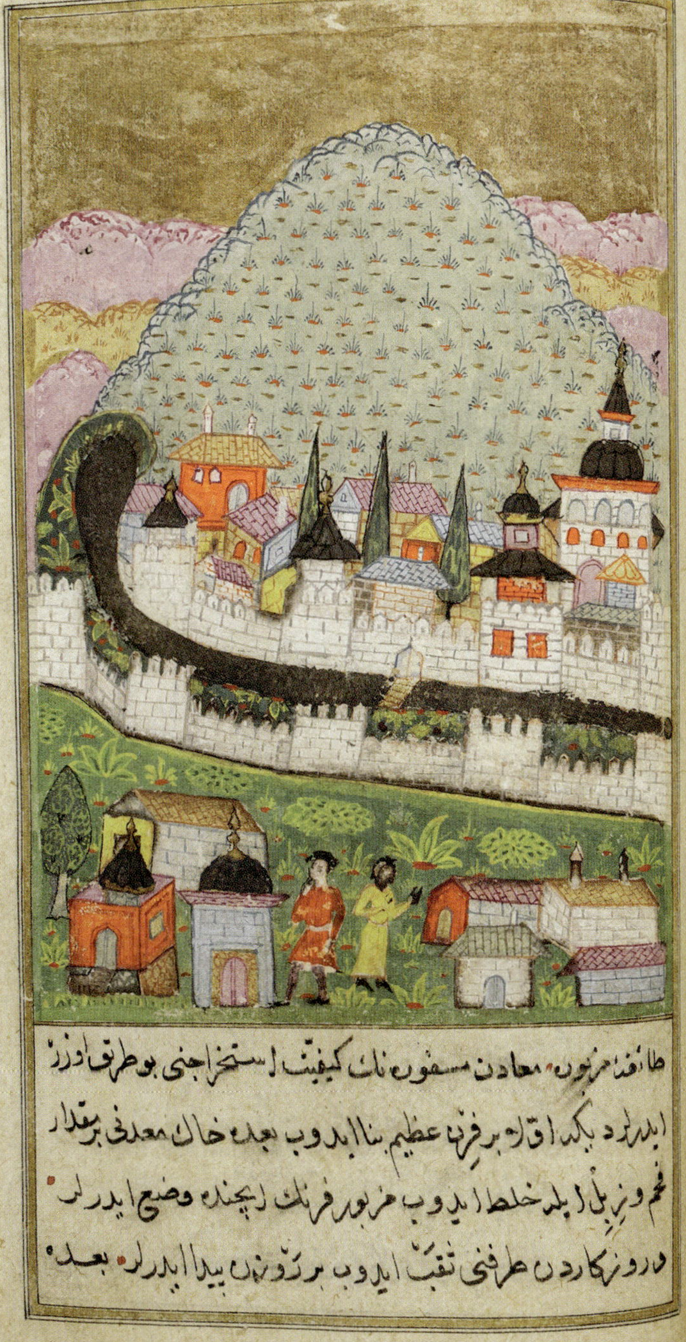

ENTRY #22

Carlo Verardi (1440–1550), author,
In laudem Serenissimi Ferdinandi Hispaniarum regis Bethicae & regni Granatae obsidio, victoria, & triumphus (*In Praise of King Ferdinand*), 1494
Christopher Columbus (1451–1506), author; Leandro di Cosco, translator (Spanish text into Latin);
Anonymous woodcutter
De insulis in Mari Indico nuper inuentis (*Of islands recently discovered in the Indian Ocean*), 1493
Book with letterpress and woodcuts
Vault Ayer 105.56 1493

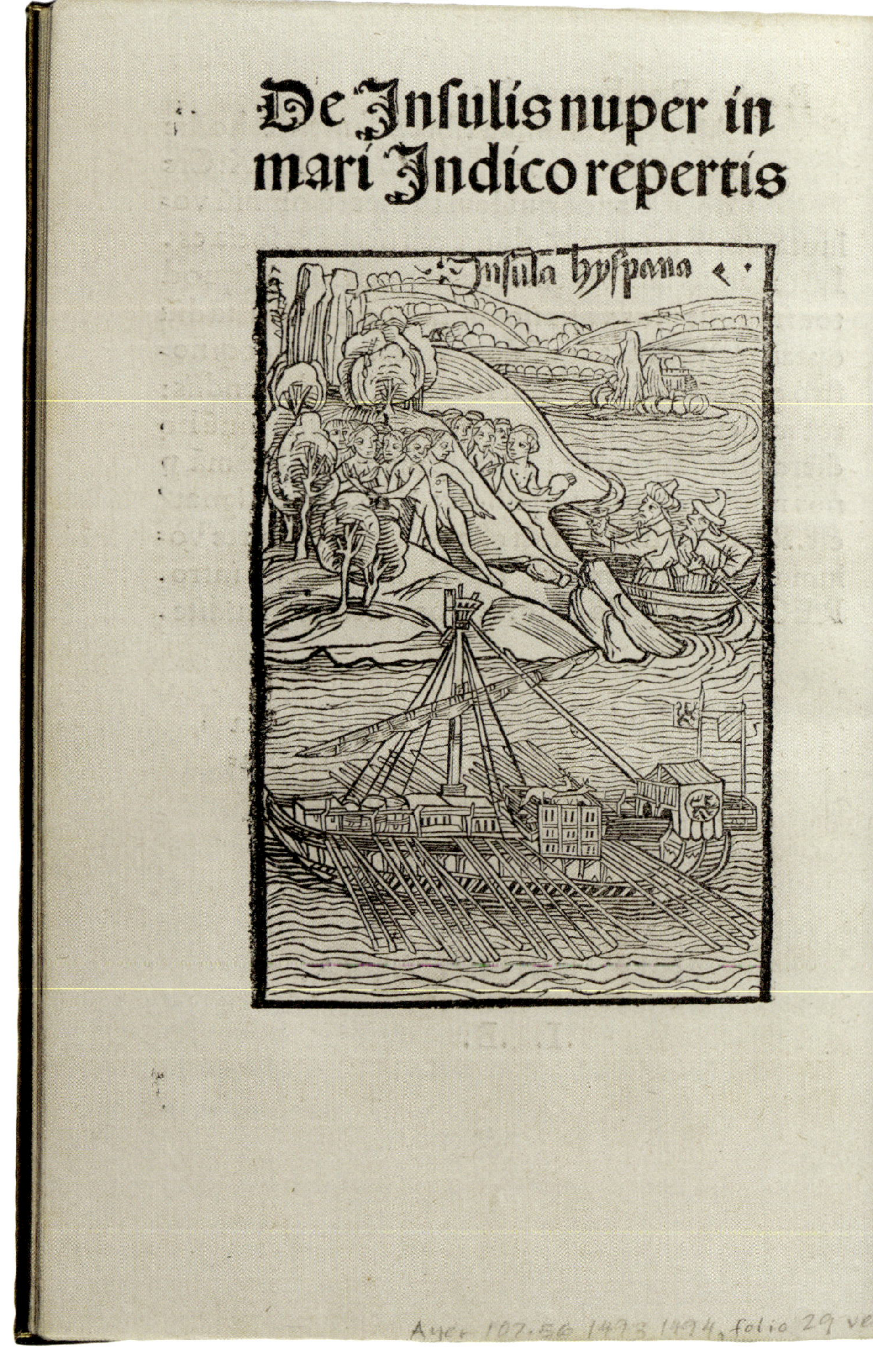
De Insulis nuper in mari Indico repertis

Two books are bound together in this Latin edition: a play entitled *In laudem Serenissimi Ferdinandi Hispaniarum regis Bethicae & regni Granatae obsidio, victoria, & triumphus*, and a Latin translation of a letter sent by Christopher Columbus to the royal treasurer Rafael Sánchez in 1493. Written by the Italian Humanist Carlo Verardi and dedicated to Ferdinand II of Aragon and Isabella I of Castile, the former dramatizes the end of the *Reconquista*, a long period of Christian military campaigns against Muslims in Spain. Granada, Iberia's last Islamic kingdom, would surrender to the forces of the Catholic Kings in January 1492. The frontispiece woodcut shows Ferdinand holding the shields of the two kingdoms, Castile and Leon, and Granada.

The second text is a letter written by Columbus where he describes the geography and natural landscape of the Caribbean islands, as well as the physical aspect, customs, and character of its native population. The letter is accompanied by a renowned woodcut (based on a woodcut in the Pforzheim's edition of Columbus's letter printed in Basel in 1493) depicting the ships arriving at a bountiful but uncultivated land. Columbus is shown approaching a group of nude Indigenous Americans who appear fearful of the encounter. The idea of the Americas as a naturally marvelous land inhabited by uncivilized and simple-minded peoples—the so-called Noble Savages—would spread across Europe, serving to justify future colonial enterprises.

The juxtaposition of the two texts articulates a narrative of Imperial expansion in the name of Christianity. Verardi's play functions as a precedent and justification to Columbus's mission, and consequently, to the oppression of non-Christian bodies. Considered together, these texts offer a racialized vision of religion.

Further Readings

Fuchs, Barbara. *Mimesis and Empire: The New World, Islam, and European Identities*. Cambridge, UK: Cambridge University Press, 2001.

Zamora, Margarita. *Reading Columbus*. Berkeley: University of California Press, 1993.

Daniela Gutiérrez Flores

De Inſulis nuper inuentis

Epiſtola Chriſtoferi Colom (cui etas noſtra multum debet: de Inſulis in mari Indico nuper inuentis: ad quas perquirendas octauo antea menſe: auſpiciis & ęre inuictiſſimi Fernandi Hiſpaniarũ Regis miſſus fuerat) ad Magnificũ dominũ Raphaelem Sanxis: eiuſdem ſereniſſimi Regis Theſaurari um miſſa: quam nobilis ac litteratus vir Aliander de Coſco: ab Hiſpano ideomate: in latinum conuertit: tercio Kalendas Maii. M. cccc. xciij. Pontificatus Alexandri Sexti Anno primo.

QVoniam ſuſceptę prouinciæ rem perfectã me conſecutũ fuiſſe: gratum tibi fore ſcio. has conſtitui exarare: quæ te vniuſcuiuſq; rei in hoc noſtro itinere geſtę inuẽtęq; admoneãt. Triceſimotercio die poſtq̃ Gadibus diſceſſi: in mare Indicũ perueni: vbi plurimas Iuſulas innumeris habitatas hominibus reperi: quarũ omnium ꝓ fœliciſſimo Rege noſtro: præconio celebrato / & vexillis extenſis: cõtradicente nemine poſſeſſionẽ accepi. primęq; earum: diui Saluatoris nomẽ impoſui. cuius fretus auxilio: tam ad hanc q̃ ad cęteras alias ꝑuenimus. Eam vero Indi Guanahanyn vocant. Aliarꝫ etiam vnãquanq; nouo nomine nũcupaui. Quippe aliam Inſulam Sanctę Marię Conceptionis. aliam Fernandinam. aliam Hyſabellam. aliã

ENTRY #23

Philip II, King of Spain (1527–1598), original author; Scribe unknown
Official copy of royal cedulas from the *real cedulario* of the Audiencia de Guatemala, 1559
Manuscript leaves in red morocco* slipcase
VAULT Ayer MS 1917

In September of 1543, the Spanish Crown established a centralized high court in Central America called the *Audiencia de Guatemala* to control *conquistadores* who were severely abusing Indigenous populations and trading them around like private property. The Audiencia began issuing royal *cedulas*, or decrees, addressing a range of matters, that were copied into a royal *cedulario*, a portion of which is presented here. The Newberry manuscript contains leaves 179–190 with cedulas numbered 291–315, dated from 17 January 1556 to 8 September 1559 and directed by King Phillip II. The matters addressed are administrative, legal, and concern the specific management and punishment of racially subjugated populations: Indigenous people, Jews, Lutherans, and Moors. Signs of use on the corners and sections that appear to have been underlined by another hand evidence the standardized referencing of the royal cedulario. Sections are briefly summarized in the margins for quicker navigation.

The royal cedulas and cedulario were crucial to the invention of race in colonial Central America, revealing the legal foundations of the racial distribution of power. These specific cedulas reflect aspects of segregationist policies that controlled how the "*indios*" were to interact with the justice system, pay specific taxes, and even conduct Mass. While some cedulas tried to better conditions for the Indigenous, they also sanctioned *encomienda** labor laws, perpetuating the dehumanization and distribution of Indigenous slave labor. Any new decrees from the Spanish Crown that threatened the power and racial superiority of *encomenderos** were either ignored or fiercely opposed.

Further Readings

Kramer, Wendy. *Encomienda Politics in Early Colonial Guatemala, 1524–1544: Dividing the Spoils*. Boulder: Westview Press, 1994.

Rodríguez Becerra, Salvador. *Encomienda y Conquista: Los inicios de la colonización en Guatemala*. [Sevilla]: Publicaciones de la Universidad de Sevilla, 1977.

Andrés Irigoyen

legitimos y pobres la graçia y md haze se a de procurar se de[n]
de los que la quisieren conseguir todo lo mas que ser pueda segun
el valor de sus yndios ochoa de luyando//

El Rey.

314 Para que sean rigurosamente castigados los lutheranos y demas hereses judios moros — En valld. 13. de julio. 1559.

Muy reverendos y muy xpos padres arçobispos de las çiudades de santo domingo de la ysla española y mexico de la nueva españa y çiudad de los reyes de las provinçias del peru y reverendos y muy xpo padres obispos de las nras yndias yslas e tierra firme del mar oceano y a cada uno y qualquier de vos a quien esta mi çedula fueremos tirada/o su traslado signado de escrivano publico como abreis sabido a permitido nro señor por nros pecados que en estos reinos a avido algunos que an tenido la opinion y heregia de lutero de muchos de los quales se a hecho castigo y se hara de todos los de mas que en esto se hallaren culpados y porque podria ser que como la maldad es tan grande y el demonio tan soliçito para senbrar en la xpiandad heregias ayan pasado o pasen a estas partes algunos luteranos y otros de casta de moros y judios que quieran bibir en su ley y çirimonias y conviene que donde se planta agora nuevamente nra fee catolica aya gran vigilançia para que ninguna heregia se sienbre ni aya en ella y que si alguna se hallare se extirpe y deshaga y se castigue con rigor e ansi os ruego y encargo a todos y a cada uno de vos en vras dioçesis arçobispados y obispados tengais muy gran cuidado y advertençia de os ynformar y saber si alla an pasado algunos que sean luteranos moros judios/o que tengan algunas heregias y hallando alguno o algunos destos lo castigueis exemplarmente que para ello mandamos a los nros viso reyes presidentes e oidores de las nras audiençias reales de esas partes y a qualesquier nros governadores dellas que os den todo el favor e ayuda que les pidieredes y menester ovieredes e ansimismo os ynformareis si an pasado/o pasan o ay en esas dioçesis algunos libros luteranos/o de los prohibidos y si hallaredes algunos los tomeys y recojais todos y los enbieys a estos nros reynos al nro consejo de la santta y general ynquisiçion y proçedereis contra aquellos en cuyo poder los

ENTRY #24

John Speed (1542–1629); Abraham Goos (1590–1643), engraver
America with those known parts in that unknown worlde both people . . ., 1626
Folded engraved map
Ayer 133 S.74 1626

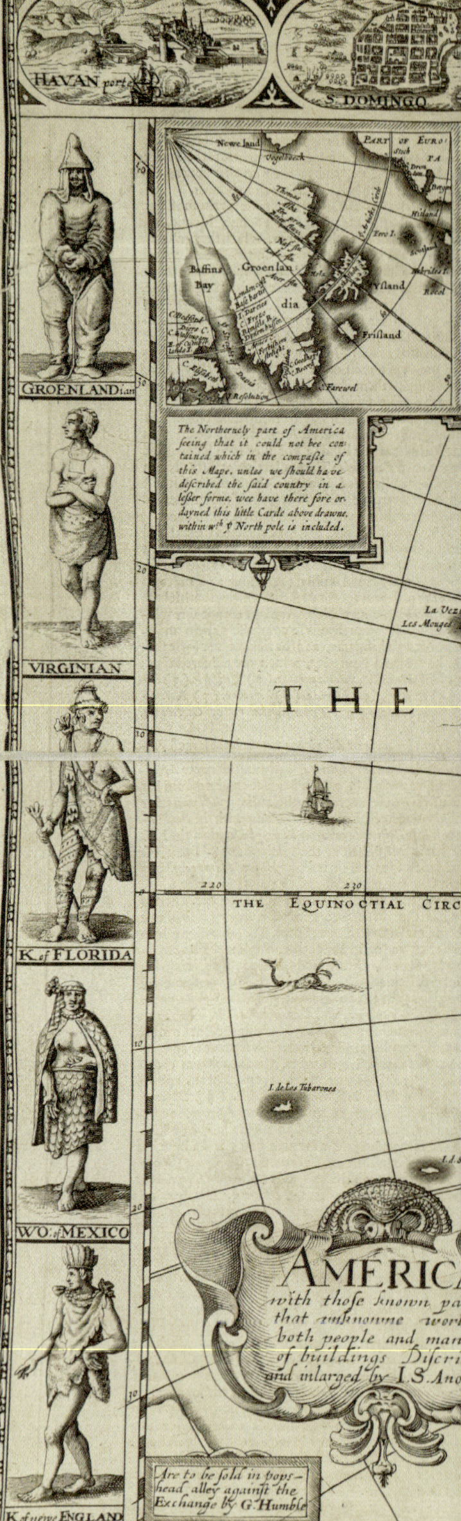

This engraving represents the first edition of John Speed's popular map of the Americas, which was subsequently reprinted in various editions throughout the seventeenth century. A renowned cartographer and historian based in London, Speed produced countless maps of the counties of England as well as world atlases. He worked primarily with the Dutch engraver Abraham Goos, who specialized in producing cartographic prints in Antwerp. This folded engraved map was likely sold as a single sheet print to be collected in an album or hung on a wall. The print can also be found in editions of Speed's *A Prospect of the Most Famous Parts of the World* (1627).

Unlike portolan charts (Cat. Nos. 18 and 20) where bodies are often represented within the map, here the bodies border the map. Yet Speed's representation of vignettes framing the map with depictions of cities and Indigenous figures from different regions is not the first of its kind. Already in 1572 Georg Braun and Franz Hogenburg developed this format in some of their maps in the *Civitates Orbus Terrarum*. In the Speed map, the racial profiling inherent in costume books like Vecellio's *Habiti antichi e moderni* (1590) (Cat. No. 8) merges with the map to produce a new genre of cartography. In fact, many of the men and women represented on this sheet are borrowed from figures in costume books and from de Bry's *Grand Voyages*.

Further Readings

Speed, John. *A Prospect of the Most Famous Parts of the World*. London, 1627.

Tooley, R.V. *The Mapping of America*. London: The Holland Press, 1980.

Traub, Valerie. "Mapping the Global Body." In *Early Modern Visual Culture: Representation, Race, and Empire in Renaissance England*, edited by Peter Erickson and Clark Hulse, 44–97. Philadelphia: University of Pennsylvania Press, 2000.

Lia Markey

CARTAGENA
MEXICO
CUSCO
MOCA
RIAN
EIRO
OLINDA
THE NORTHERNE
PART OF AMERICA
NEWE BRITTAINE
Part of Groenland
PART OF EUROPA
THE ATLANTICKE
THE
OCEAN
NORTH
SEA
THE BAY OF MEXICO
The Tropicke of Cancer
The Fortunate or Canaries Ilands
Westerne Ilands
THE PERUVIANE
SEA
OCEAN
THE PACIFICKE
SEA
GUIANA
BRASIL
SOUTHERNE PART
OF AMERICA
CHICA
The Tropicke of Capricorne
THE UNKNOWNE WORLD
PERUVIANE
BRASILIANE
BRASILIANE
A MOCHAN
MAGELLANICAN
Rio de la Plata dat is the Silver river
The Bermudas now called the Sommer Ilands

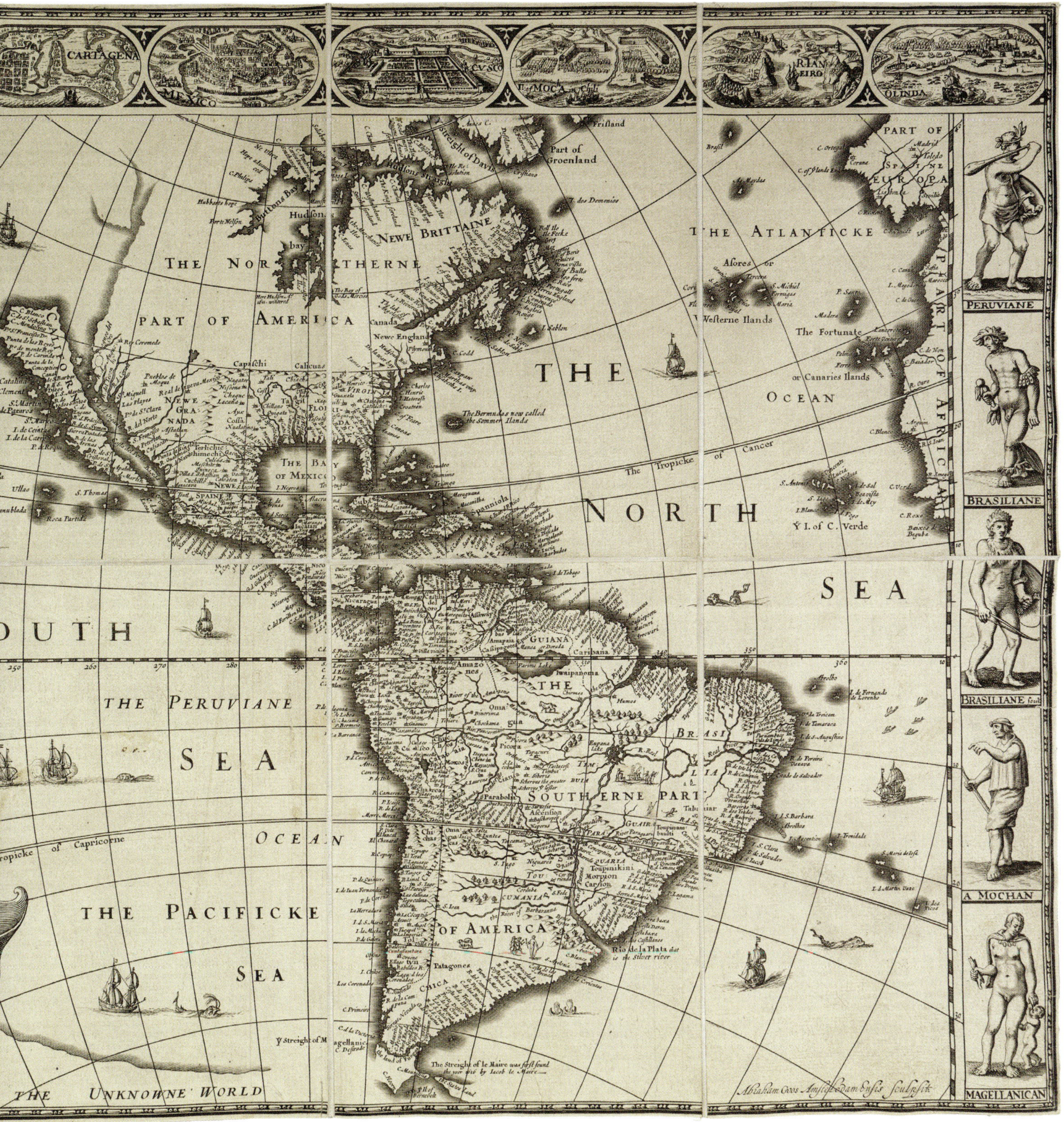

Entry #24

Case Study #3. Further Expansion

ENTRY #25

Joan Blaeu (1596–1673), cartographer
Pecheli, sive Peking Imperii Sinarum provincia prima (Map of Peking), in *Le grand atlas*, 1663
Book with letterpress and engravings

With the publications of cartographer Joan Blaeu, detailed maps of China were for the first time brought under the voracious eye of wealthy Europeans. This map of Peking (now Beijing) published in 1663 initially appeared a decade prior as part of Blaeu's seminal atlas on China, which collated a series of maps translated from Chinese sources by the Jesuit missionary Martino Martini. As the official cartographer of the Dutch East India Company (VOC), Blaeu produced maps that were intimately intertwined with the ambitions of the Dutch global elite attempting to acquire Chinese trading privileges. Though based on Chinese sources, the map was modified to fit a European prototype. The sizeable title is framed by a couple and two servants and topped by two phoenixes (fenghuang) while the scale at upper right is embellished by two Chinese men holding the cartographic tools with which, the image suggests, they made the map upon which the beholder currently gazes. The inclusion of the cartographers appealed to the fascination with Chinese cultural products while also visually asserting the map's non-European origins.

The uneven relationship between Europeans and the Chinese, wherein the latter held greater economic power and the former hungered for Chinese wares, affected the racialization of the map's figures. In terms of their dress, the embroidered birds on the left man's robe, for instance, accurately mark him as a civil official, though his servant's winged hat was reserved for bureaucrats, indicating a lapse of understanding in favor of exoticizing differences. The elegant silk garments allude to their material wealth and status, while the talon-like fingernail guards (another accurate representation of high-class fashion) develop the sensational animalistic imagery of the clawed armchair and phoenixes. These elements denote the figures' corporeal difference and mark a visual boundary between the mapped bodies and the European viewer.

Further Readings

Cams, Mario. "Displacing China: The Martini-Blaeu *Novus Atlas Sinesis* and the Late Renaissance Shift in Representations of East Asia." *Renaissance Quarterly* 73, no. 3 (2020): 953–90. https://doi.org/10.1017/rqx.2020.123.

Finnane, Antonia. "Fashions in Late Imperial China." In *Changing Clothes in China: Fashion, History, Nation*. New York: Columbia University Press, 2008.

Zandvliet, Kees. "Mapping the Dutch World Overseas in the Seventeenth Century." In *The History of Cartography*, vol. 3, part 2, edited by David Woodward, 1433–1462. Chicago: University of Chicago Press, 2007.

Emily Kang and Arianna Ray

ENTRY #26

Ortelius, Abraham (1527–1598), author; Christoffel Plantin (1520–1589), publisher
Theatrum oder Schawbüch des Erdtkreijs: opus nunc denuò ab ipso auctore recognitum, multisquè locis castigatum quamplurimis nouis tabulis atque commentarijs auctum (*Theater of the World*), 1580
Book with letterpress and colored engravings
VAULT Baskes oversize G1006 .T515 1580b

Abraham Ortelius's *Theater of the World* is the earliest printed volume to assemble cartographic knowledge in the format that we would today recognize as an atlas. The volume presents commentary and maps of global geography, assembled from a variety of sources and standardized. As a portal into this constructed world, the volume's frontispiece characterizes the places the reader will explore by reading and provides categories through which to imagine the people that lived there. It asserts a hierarchy that subordinates other lands and their inhabitants to Europe and Europeans.

Personifications of four continents pose around a theater. Europe, at top center, sits enthroned. Her crown and scepter imply her dominion over the continents below. Her Christ-like pose and cross-surmounted globe ground that dominion in Christianity. At left, Asia, richly dressed in robes, holds a smoking censer filled with incense. Africa stands at right, poorly clothed from the waist down. In the Newberry's volume, her skin is painted brown. Although some of the coloring in this volume was likely added after the nineteenth century, later editions of the frontispiece consistently repeat this coloring. America, wearing only an anklet and helmet, carries a cudgel, bow, arrows, and a decapitated human head. These violent attributes argue that the continent is dangerous to Europeans who travel there and apply centuries old tropes regarding cannibals living at the edges of the earth to the inhabitants of the Americas. At the same time, America, lying beautiful and naked on the ground, is presented as ready to be ravished by Europeans.

Further Readings

Binding, Paul. *Imagined Corners: Exploring the World's First Atlas*, 209–20. London: Headline, 2003.

Horowitz, Maryanne Cline. "Rival Interpretations of Continent Personifications." In *Bodies and Maps: Early Modern Personifications of the Continents*, edited by Maryanne Cline Horowitz and Louise Arizzoli, 1–24. Leiden: Brill, 2020.

van den Broecke, Marcel P. R. *Ortelius Atlas Maps: An Illustrated Guide*. Netherlands: Hes & de Graaf Publishers, 2011.

Olivia Dill

Cum privilegio Sacræ Cæsareæ Majestatis, & Ordinum Belgicæ Fœderatæ.
XANSI
PROVINCIÆ
PARS.
HO-
NAN
PRO-
VIN-
CIÆ
PARS.
Occidens.
Paoting
Chinting
Xunte
Quangping
Changte
Gueihoei
Taming
Tungchang
Hokien
XUNTIEN
XAN-
TUNG
PROVIN
Notarum Explicatio.
METROPOLIS.
Vrbs.
Civitas major.
Civitas minor.
Fortalitia.
Signum militare.
Aurifodina.
Cataractæ.
M. mons.
fl. F. fluvius.
A. Amnis.
L. Lacus.

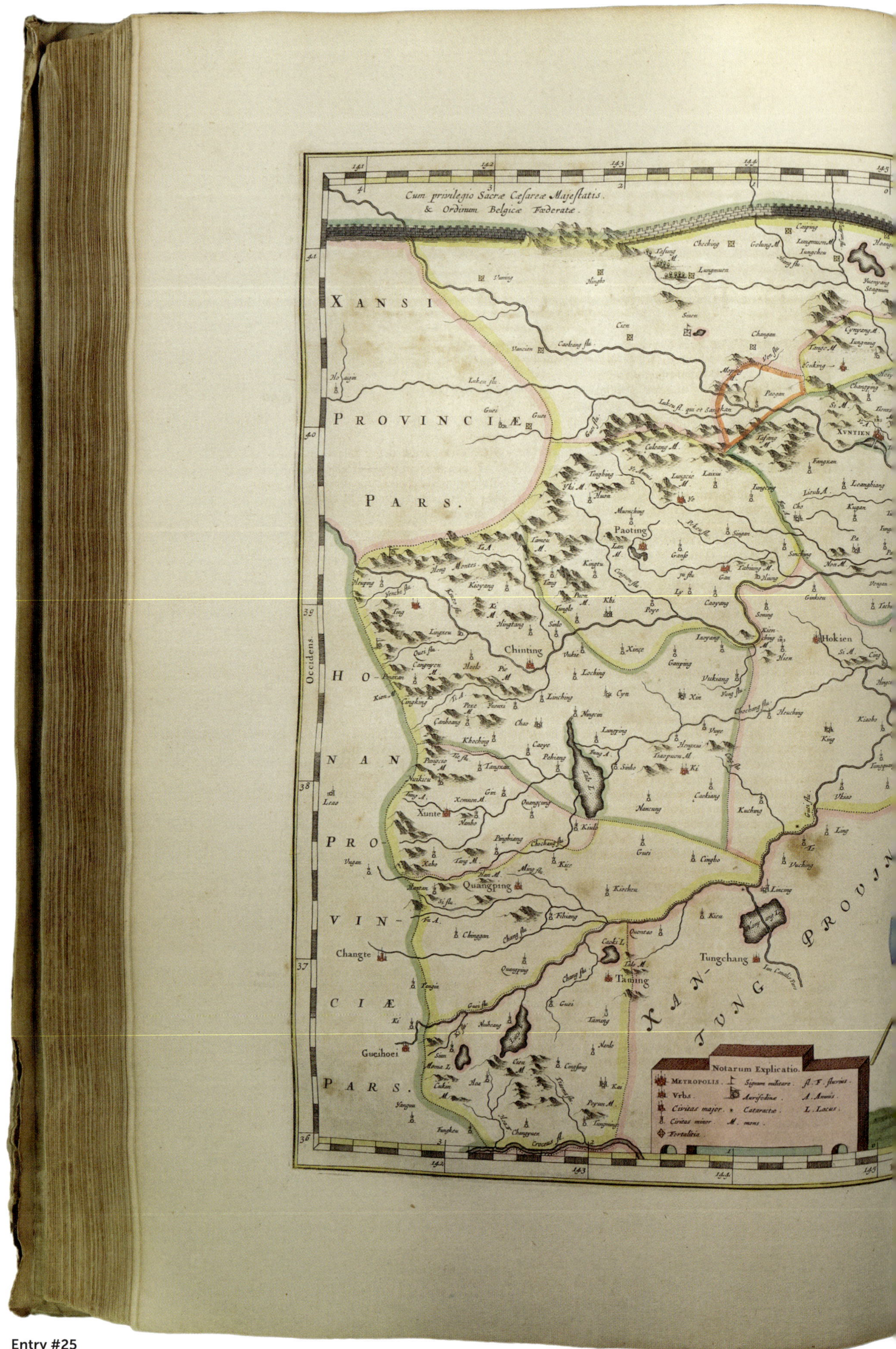

Entry #25

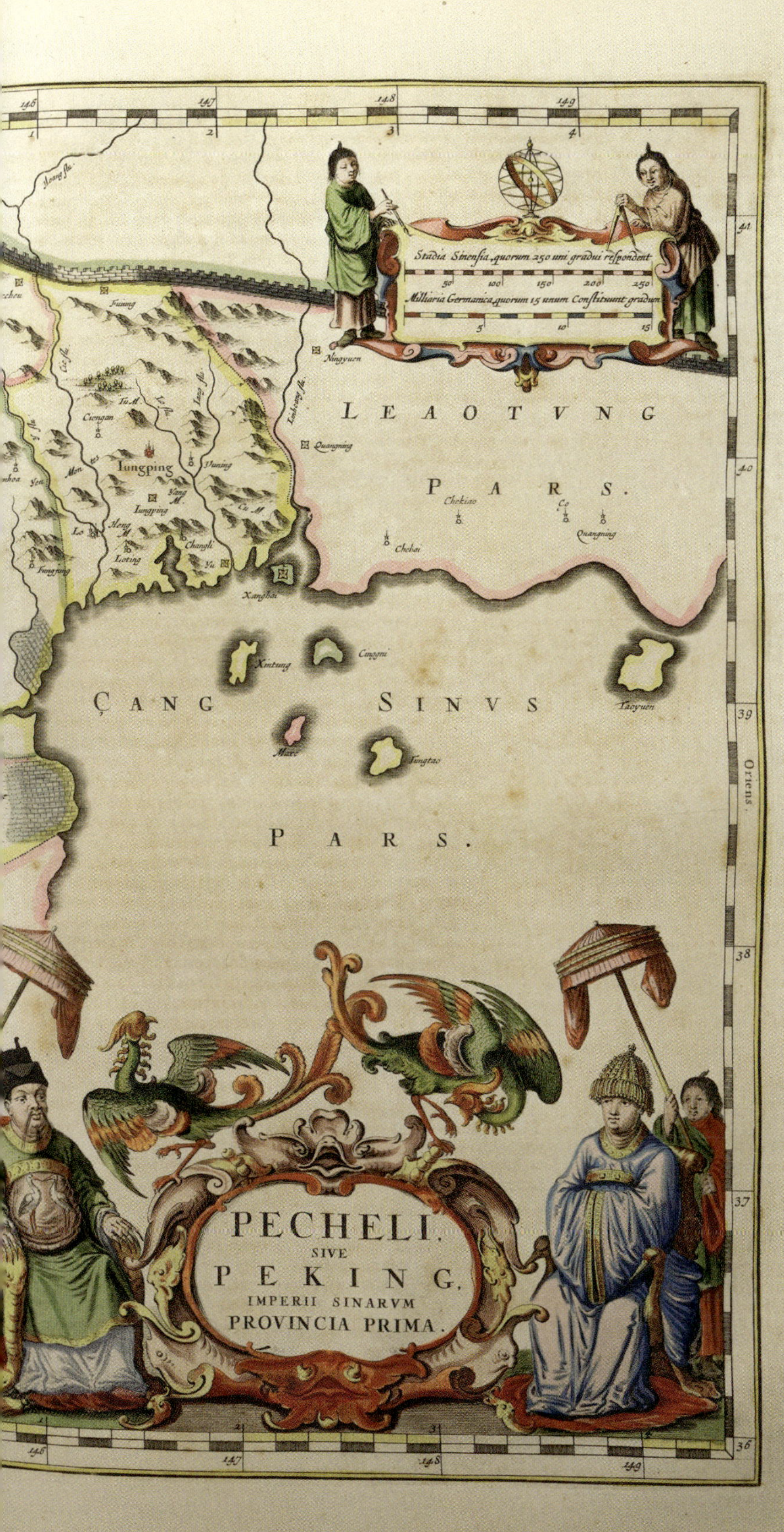

Stadia Sinensia, quorum 250 uni gradui respondent
50 100 150 200 250
Milliaria Germanica quorum 15 unum Constituunt gradum
5 10 15
Ningyuen
Quangning
LEAOTVNG
PARS.
Iungping
Xanghai
ÇANG SINVS
PARS.
Oriens.
PECHELI,
SIVE
PEKING,
IMPERII SINARVM
PROVINCIA PRIMA.

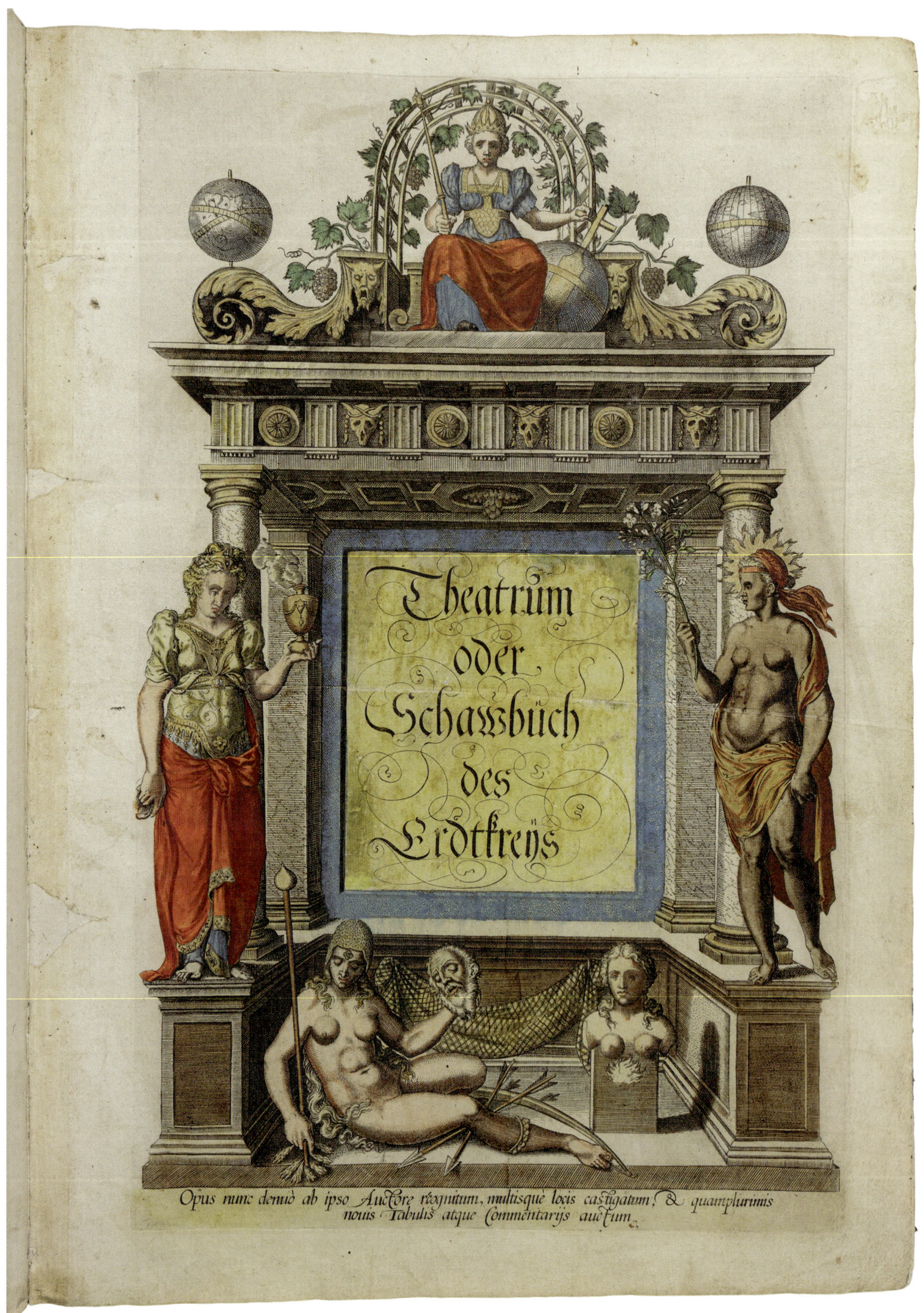
Theatrum
oder
Schawbüch
des
Erdtkreys
Opus nunc denuò ab ipso Auctore recognitum, multisque locis castigatum, & quamplurimis
nouis Tabulis atque Commentarijs auctum.

Entry #26

PART 3
PERFORMING

BACK BENDING LABOR, SAVAGE DANCES, PIOUS STANCES: RACE IN MOTION BETWEEN AFRICA AND THE AMERICAS

By Elena FitzPatrick Sifford and Cécile Fromont[1]

Skin color—its origins, variations, stability across time and generations—has been a pre-eminent locus* for reckonings over racial formation in European visual and material culture of the early modern period, alongside religion and genealogy.[2] Humoralism* inherited from those whom Europeans called the Ancients posited a connection between geography and the nature of human bodies reflected in their complexion, of which skin color formed a most visible part.[3] Another set of distinguishing features, with an equally long history also arching back to European Antiquity and central to early modern understanding of difference and formulation of race, was that of civility and its outward manifestations in

1. The authors would like to thank the editors Lia Markey and Noémie Ndiaye, and the anonymous reviewers for their constructive comments. Elena FitzPatrick Sifford is grateful to Kathryn Santner, Matthew Rarey, Suzanne Stratton-Pruitt. Cécile Fromont acknowledges the support of a Berenson Fellowship from I Tatti, The Harvard University Center for Italian Renaissance studies in the writing of this chapter.

2. Grace Harpster, "The Color of Salvation: The Materiality of Blackness in Alonso de Sandoval's *De Instauranda Aethiopium Salute*," in *Envisioning Others. Race, Color, and the Visual in Iberia and Latin America*, ed. Pamela Anne Patton, 83–110 (Leiden: Brill, 2016); and Larissa Brewer-García, "Imagined Transformations: Color, Beauty, and Black Christian Conversion in Seventeenth-Century Spanish America," *Envisioning Others. Race, Color, and the Visual in Iberia and Latin America*, ed. Pamela Anne Patton, 111–14 (Leiden, Boston: Brill, 2016).

3. See Surekha Davies, "Climate, Culture or Kinship? Explaining Human Diversity c. 1500," chap. 1 in *Renaissance Ethnography and the Invention of the Human: New Worlds, Maps and Monsters* (Cambridge: Cambridge University Press, 2016), 23–46.

comportment. Aristotle (384–322 BCE), Thomas Aquinas (1225–1274 CE), and their early modern era readers, historian Surekha Davies reminds us, saw an observable hierarchy between civilized and uncivilized, which material traces could be observed in mores* and customs at the level of societies, but also in behavior at the level of the individuals.[4] "Strange gestures" were the marks of the savage, the witch, the idolater, and featured in early modern European visual culture as motifs, emblems, and iconographic markers of social, cultural, religious, and eventually racial otherness.[5] Further, in counterpoint to these depictions of heathens and "savages" and their "strange gestures," early modern images of European catechization* around the Atlantic world suggested the success of proselytism* in the representation of converted Africans and Indigenous individuals in bodily attitude suggesting pious demeanor in Europe's visual vocabulary, i.e. kneeling and hands joined in prayer.

This chapter considers a range of images conceived by Europeans in their attempts at making sense of difference and ascribing significance to social and cultural diversity in the context of their ambitions to colonize the Americas and Africa in the early modern period. Foremost in this process was the formulation and systematization of ideas of hierarchized difference that underlie conceptualizations of race. Visually and conceptually, racialization depended on identifying a set of visible markers to which meaning could be ascribed. Skin color, as well as other physical characteristics, would be the foremost signs of difference, but bodily comportment and motion also played an important role. In some examples, gesture, movement, and attitudes of the body could even supersede complexion and physiognomy as indicators of racial taxonomies. Racialized thinking penetrated deeper than outside visible appearance and attached its ideas to the body itself and its motion. The association of physical traits with bodily comportment played a central role in the circular logic of racial construction and its attempts at ascribing social significance to physical difference. Considering gestures and the meanings they encompassed as racial markers in early modern visual culture thus not only sheds light on the complex, multifaceted process of racial construction in European early modern thought, but also brings to the fore its ambiguities and contradictions and points to the centuries-long shadow these notions have cast over the circum-Atlantic world.

Back Bending Labor

Racial ideologies were not only perpetuated socially but became further systematized and normalized in the visual realm. Artists in the early modern Atlantic world utilized pigments, facial features, hairstyles, as well as ethnic clothing and accessories to visually mark figures as European, African, Indigenous, or any mixture thereof.[6] In addition to these details of skin color, dress (as discussed in this volume by Kaplan and Katz), and objects, the position of the body also served as a further racialized marker. Body posture and comportment were particularly important in Europe, a society that viewed the exterior body as revealing inner mind and character. Etiquette books and artists manuals from the period reveal the emphasis placed on bodily attitude.

Early modern scholars of rhetoric and the arts (oratory but also dancing and painting) discussed the connection between bodily temperament and quality of the mind, after Plato (c. 427–347 BCE) and

4. Davies, *Renaissance Ethnography*, 40–41.

5. Thomas Harriot, Briefe and True Report of the New Found Land of Virginia: of the Commodities and of the Nature and Manners of the Naturall Inhabitants . . .. trans. Richard Hakluyt (London, 1590). See Michael Gaudio, *Engraving the Savage: The New World and Techniques of Civilization* (Minneapolis: University of Minnesota Press, 2008), 54–55.

6. Ananda Cohen Suarez [Aponte], "Making Race Visible in the Colonial Andes," in *Envisioning Others: Race, Color, and the Visual in Iberia and Latin America*, ed. Pamela A. Patton, 187–212 (Leiden: Brill, 2015), 188.

Quintilian (c. 35–100 CE): "The temper of the mind can be inferred from the glance and the gait."[7] In turn, sixteenth-century Milanese choreographer Cesare Negri (c.1535–1605) outlined proper posture: "In order to go well above the body with that utmost grace and composure that others can honor means to go well with the body straight and the arms at the sides, moving them a little, and the toes of the feet a little out, so that the legs and the knees remain very straight, and in passing one foot ahead of the other." He describes this posture as "gracious movement and beautiful good manners."[8] In this view, upright positions denoted civility while bending or contorted bodies were considered wayward and lacking in composure.[9] This discourse also extended to social and economic status, the bending body attached to those of modest social and material conditions, of any race.

German artist Christoph Weiditz depicted such a slouched posture in his *Trachtenbuch*, a costume book produced during his 1529 travels in Spain (Figure 5.1). The inscription reads: "Negro slave with a wineskin in Castile: Thus the Moors who have been sold carry wine in goatskins in Castile; if they run away from their masters, they have to work thus and wear chains."[10] The man in tattered clothing has shackles around the ankles, one chained and connected to his waist. Curiously, he wears just one shoe. As expected in a costume book, frayed clothing indicates the laborer's status, but, notably, his bodily posture, paired with the profile view commonly associated with servility in early modern European iconography, equally communicates his servitude. A former runaway, the man is consigned to physically taxing work made all the more laborious by the chains constraining him, the humiliating and burdensome consequence of his foiled escape.

Bowed postures signifying servitude can also be seen crossing the Atlantic in one of the earliest images of New World slavery, an engraving featuring Africans processing sugarcane on the island of Hispañola (Figure 5.2). Though Theodor de Bry (1528–1598), a Protestant originally from the Spanish Netherlands, never set foot in the Americas himself, he executed twenty-seven volumes of woodcut prints based on accounts of various travelers, including three volumes of Milanese merchant-explorer Girolamo Benzoni's (1519–1570) *The History of the New World*. One of the earliest images of African slavery in the Americas, it provides visual evidence of the transition from gold mining to sugar production on the Caribbean Island.[11]

The enslaved in the engraving wear almost no clothes. Yet, rather than an erect classicizing posture of the heroic nude, the expected contemporary European depictions of the unclothed male, the bodies of the enslaved are shown bending, hauling, kneeling, and contorting. The focus of the image is on their toil at every step of the sugar production process. At the top right, figures begin the process by cutting the cane, the sun illustrated above beating down on their exposed backs. The cane is then bundled and carried

7. Quintilian, *Insitutio oratoria*, trans. Harold Edgeworth Butler (Cambridge, MA: Harvard University Press, 1922), 11.6.66, retrieved from Perseus Digital Library, http://www.perseus.tufts.edu/hopper/text?doc=Perseus%3Atext%3A2007.01.0069%3Abook%3D11%3Achapter%3D6%3Asection%3D66. See Leon Battista Alberti, *On Painting and On Sculpture: The Latin Texts of* De pictura *and* De statua, trans, Cecil Grayson (London: Phaidon, 1972), and Marjorie O'Rourke Boyle, "Deaf Signs, Renaissance Texts," in *Perspectives on Early Modern and Modern Intellectual History: Essays in Honor of Nancy S. Struever*, eds. Joseph Marino and Melinda W. Schlitt, 164–92 (Rochester: University of Rochester Press, 2001). About dancing, see Jennifer Nevile, ed., *Dance, Spectacle, and the Body Politick, 1250–1750* (Bloomington: Indiana University Press, 2008), 87. About gait and noble carriage of the body in early modern Italy, see Frances Gage, *Painting as Medicine in Early Modern Rome: Giulio Mancini and the Efficacy of Art* (University Park: The Pennsylvania State University Press, 2016), 76. For the link between movement of the body and movement of the soul since the early Middle Ages, see Stephen Kolsky, "Graceful Performances: The Social and Political Context of Music and Dance in the Cortegiano," *Italian Studies* 53, no. 1 (1998): 14–16, https://doi.org/10.1179/its.1998.53.1.1.

8. As quoted in Sander L. Gilman, *Stand Up Straight!: A History of Posture* (Chicago: University of Chicago Press, 2018), 148.

9. Michiel van Groesen, "The De Bry Collection of Voyages (1590–1634): Early America Reconsidered," *Journal of Early Modern History* 12, no. 1 (2008): 205, https://doi.org/10.1163/138537808X297135. Gage, *Painting*.

10. As quoted in Carmen Fracchia, *'Black but Human': Slavery and Visual Arts in Hapsburg Spain, 1480–1700* (Oxford: Oxford University Press, 2019), 109.

11. K. Dian Kriz, Susan Danforth, and Elena Daniele, eds., *Sugar and the Visual Imagination in the Atlantic World, circa 1600–1860*. Providence: Brown University, published in conjunction with an exhibition of the same title, organized by and presented at the John Carter Brown Library, September 2013–December 2013, https://www.brown.edu/Facilities/John_Carter_Brown_Library/exhibitions/sugar/index.html.

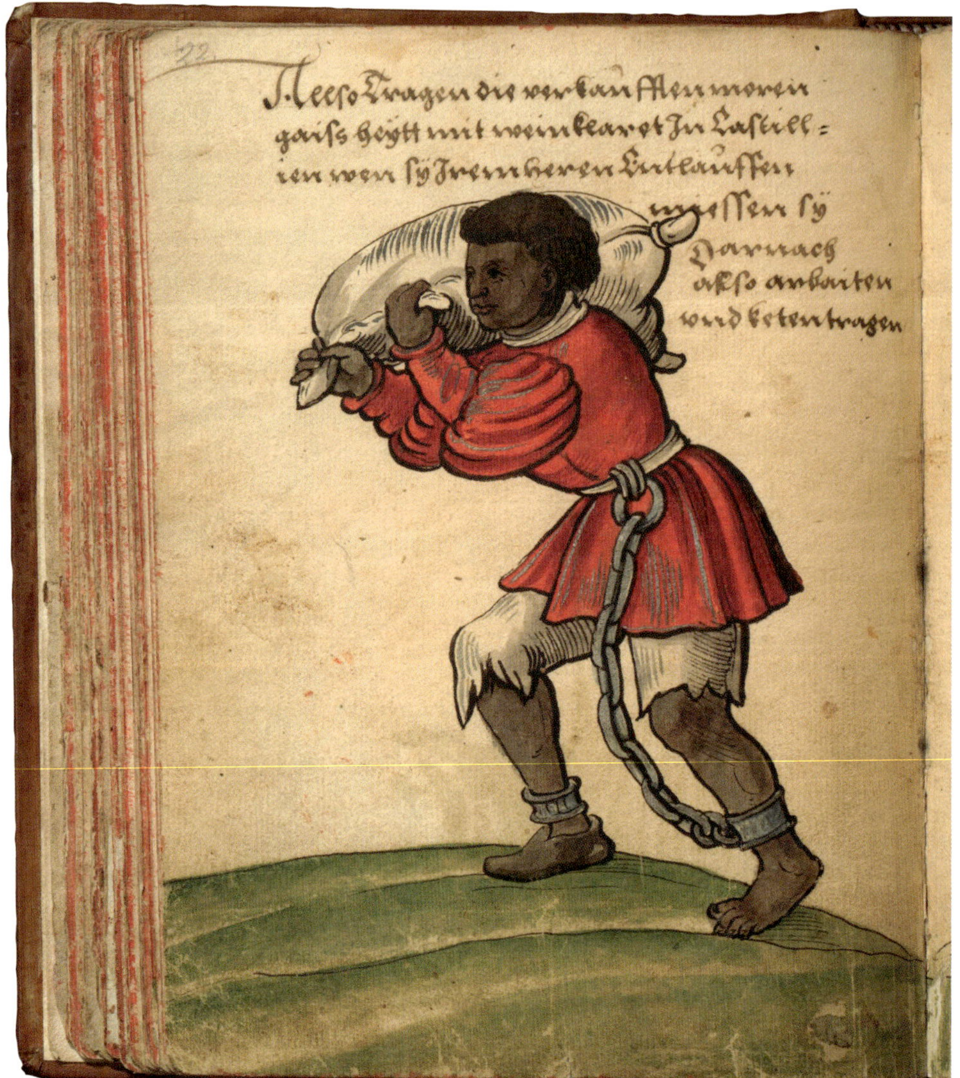

Figure 5.1. Christoph Weiditz, "African with a wineskin" in *Trachtenbuch*, 1529, Germanisches Nationalmuseum, Nuremberg, Germany

from the field to one of the two presses on the plantation, one a water mill in the distance, and the other, in the midground, human powered. These machines crushed the cane to extract their juice for further processing into crystalized sugar or molasses.[12]

Although the figures de Bry depicted are Africans, he represented them in the engraving without the heavy cross-hatching* frequently used to denote dark skin. He did not figure their countenances either with rotund lips or flat noses following typical European stylizations of African features. Instead, the focus is on the figures' bodies and postures to signify their status as laborers. Here the figures' back bending toil within the Caribbean landscape, along with their lack of clothing and hunched postures, serve to identify them as enslaved Black Africans. The bent attitudes are what make clear to early modern viewers that the figures' whole or near nakedness, far from Classical heroic nudity or Renaissance humanist idealization, is a sign of humiliation that marks them as "savage" and therefore suited to enslavement in the physically taxing Caribbean sugar mills.

12. B.W. Higman, "The Sugar Revolution," *The Economic History Review, New Series* 53, no. 2 (2000): 213–36, https://www.jstor.org/stable/2598696; and Theodore De Bry, *Nigritae exhaustis venis metallicis consciendo saccharo operam dare debent. In Americae pars quinta nobilis & admiratione plena Hieronymi Bezoni Mediolanensis secundae setionos Hispanorum . . .*, 1595, image, John Carter Brown Library at Brown University, Providence, Accession no. 34724, https://mypages.unh.edu/hoslac/book/early-sugar-plantation.

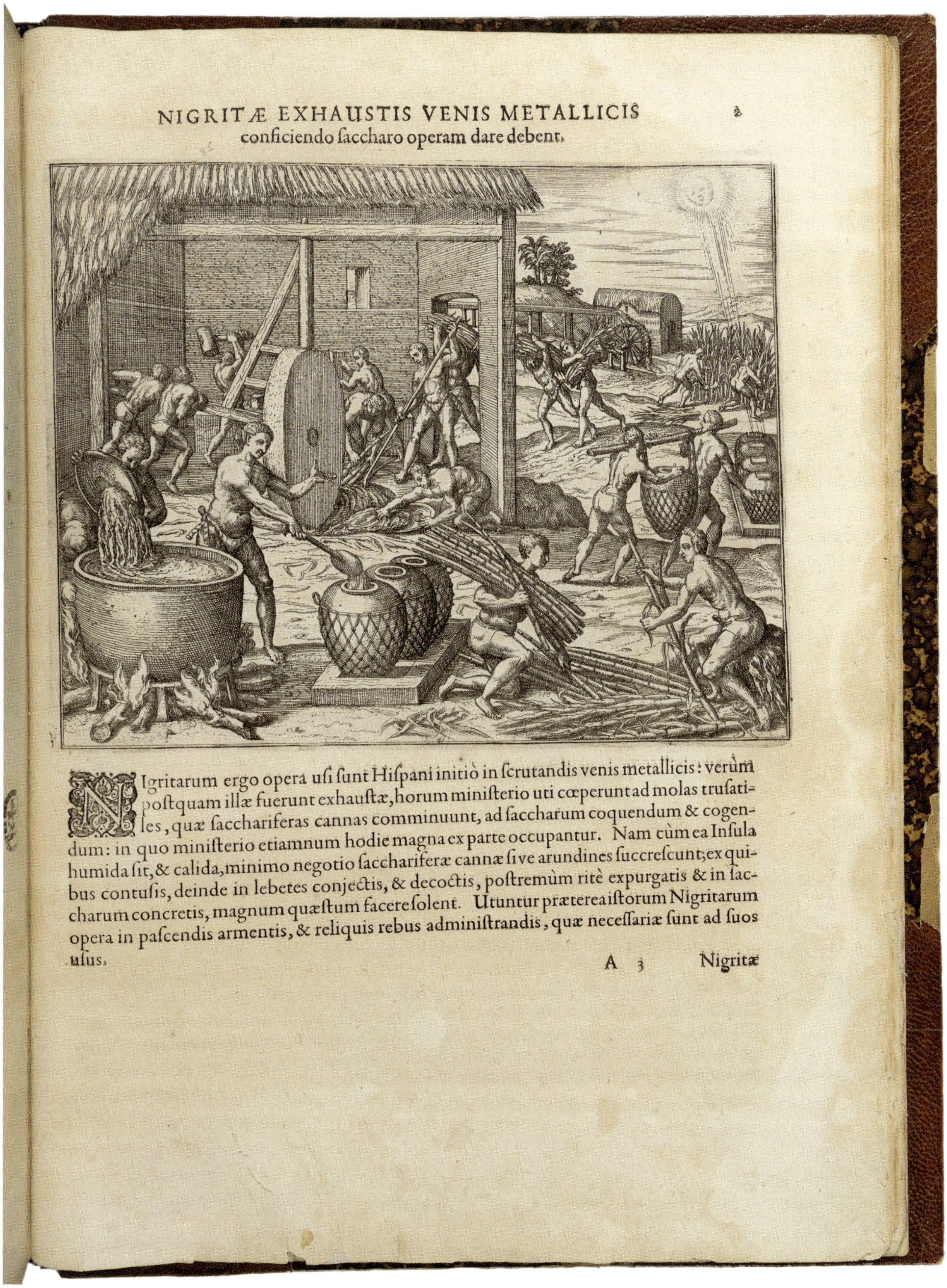

NIGRITÆ EXHAUSTIS VENIS METALLICIS conficiendo ſaccharo operam dare debent.

a

Nigritarum ergo opera uſi ſunt Hiſpani initiò in ſcrutandis venis metallicis: verùm poſtquam illæ fuerunt exhauſtæ, horum miniſterio uti cœperunt ad molas truſatiles, quæ ſacchariferas cannas comminuunt, ad ſaccharum coquendum & cogendum: in quo miniſterio etiamnum hodie magna ex parte occupantur. Nam cùm ea Inſula humida ſit, & calida, minimo negotio ſacchariferæ cannæ ſive arundines ſuccreſcunt, ex quibus contuſis, deinde in lebetes conjectis, & decoctis, poſtremùm ritè expurgatis & in ſaccharum concretis, magnum quæſtum facere ſolent. Utuntur prætereaiſtorum Nigritarum opera in paſcendis armentis, & reliquis rebus adminiſtrandis, quæ neceſſariæ ſunt ad ſuos uſus.

A 3 Nigritæ

Figure 5.2
Theodor de Bry,
"Nigritae exhaustis venis metallicis consiciendo saccharo operam dare debent,"
in *America. Pt. 5,* Frankfurt am Main, 1595,
Newberry Library, VAULT Ayer 110 .B9 1590b v. 5

"Savage" Dances

Dance was an expressive genre equally important to Europeans, Indigenous Americans, and Africans in the early modern period as an activity of spiritual, political, and social significance. As Europeans confronted difference — real or imagined, at home or abroad — they took special note of choreographed, socially significant movement. Records of dance within rituals, entertainment, or pageantry, and often a combination of several of these, became a significant part of the colonial archive that Europeans strove to compile and interpret.[13] However, both documentations and interpretations met with the limitations of cross-cultural misunderstanding, willing or unwilling, and of the ideological nature of European descriptions and judgment of those they considered their "others."[14]

In the early modern period, Europeans staged a range of performances that, through movement, costume, and choreography, both expressed and reinforced the conceptions of Otherness and racial difference they developed in support of their imperial and colonial ambitions. Balls, masks, processions featuring "savage" dress, movements, instruments, and choreographies formed foils against which Europeans systematized notions of racialized but also often religious difference. A foremost example in this regard is the broad tradition of Moors and Christians festival celebrations in which a danced battle featuring Catholics defeating infidels served a number of political purposes across Iberia and the lands in their sphere of direct control or indirect influence.[15] They presented the battle against Muslim opponents as a religious quest in a teleological* narrative of the victory of Spaniards not only in the Reconquista of the Iberian peninsula, but against heathens anywhere. The triumph of Christians over Moors, for instance, became that of Spaniards over the Indigenous populations of the Americas.[16] In turn, the danced festival would find echoes in similar statements of victory and conquest outside of Europe, such as that of the Christian aristocracy of the Kongo who staged mock battles called *sangamentos* that strongly evoked the Moors and Christians dances they witnessed in their interactions with the Portuguese initiated at the end of the fifteenth century. Later, Africans and Afro-descendants living enslaved or free in the Americas and Europe found in the organization of events derived from *sangamentos* occasions to express social identity and exercise power, however limited, over their lived circumstances.[17] Related, non-Iberian early modern European courtly performances called morris, morisca, or moresque staged allegorical scenes including exotic characters, mocked combat, and dancing in circles with high leaps to the sound of percussion instruments.[18] Notably, Portuguese traveler Duarte Lopes (mid/late sixteenth century) and Italian cosmographer Filippo Pigafetta (1533–1604) used the term *moreschа* in their 1591 *Report of the Kingdom of Congo* to

---

13. Paul A. Scolieri, *Dancing the New World: Aztecs, Spaniards, and the Choreography of Conquest* (Austin: University of Texas Press, 2013).

14. Michel de Certeau, *Heterologies: Discourse on the other* (Minneapolis: University of Minnesota Press, 1986).

15. Carolyn Dean, *Inka Bodies and the Body of Christ: Corpus Christi in Colonial Cuzco, Peru* (Durham, NC: Duke University Press, 1999). Cécile Fromont, ed., *Afro-Catholic Festivals in the Americas: Performance, Representation, and the Making of Black Atlantic Tradition*, Africana Religions (University Park: The Pennsylvania State University Press, 2019). Lynn Matluck Brooks, *The Dances of the Processions of Seville in Spain's Golden Age* (Kassel: Reichenberger, 1988).

16. Max Harris, *Aztecs, Moors, and Christians: Festivals of Reconquest in Mexico and Spain* (Austin: University of Texas Press, 2000).

17. Cécile Fromont, "Dancing for the King of Congo from Early Modern Central Africa to Slavery-Era Brazil," *Colonial Latin American Review* 22, no. 2 (2013): 184–208, https://doi.org/10.1080/10609164.2013.808466. Fromont, ed., *Afro-Catholic Festivals*.

18. John Forrest, *The History of Morris Dancing, 1458–1750* (Toronto: University of Toronto Press, 1999), 74. Cf. Eugene McDowell Kenley, "Sixteenth-Century Matachines Dances: Morescas of Mock Combat and Comic Pantomime" (Ph.D. diss., Stanford, 1993), 1–2, 5–8, 11–12, 16–19, 30, 33–36, 53. Katherine Tucker McGinnis, "Moving in High Circles: Courts, Dance, and Dancing Masters in Italy in the Long Sixteenth Century" (PhD diss., University of North Carolina, Chapel Hill, 2001), 170–73. Michael Gaudio, *Sound, Image, Silence: Art and the Aural Imagination in the Atlantic World* (Minneapolis: University of Minnesota Press, 2019), 8–10. Gaudio notes the use of the term *morisque* to describe Tupinamba dances in the 1585 edition of Jean de Léry's report on Brazil. While the first edition of 1578 describes the dances as "rondes," this later version, expanded by the author, specifically uses the term *morisque* as a comparison; see Jean de Léry, *Histoire d'un voyage faict en la terre du Bresil, autrement dite Amerique: contenant la navigation, & choses remarquables, veuës sur mer par l'auteur: le comportement de Villegagnon en ce pays-la: les murs & façons de viure estranges des sauuages bresiliens: auec vn colloque de leur langage* . . ., 3rd ed. ([Geneva]: Pour Antoine Chuppin, 1585), 137.

praise the dances the former had observed at the court of the great Christian king of Kongo.[19]

At a formal level, as already mentioned above, for early modern Europeans, bodies acted socially and their movements betrayed civility or lack thereof. Early modern European dance treaties described how performers "should be measured, moderated, always avoiding the extremes of excessive movement or too little movement."[20] These ideals, expressed in Italian by the term *misura*, defined elegant, noble character, and gave visible form to virtue and ethical behavior. In contrast to the *misura* and civility of the courtly dancer, the late medieval visual and literary genre of the *Dance of Death* offered examples of unrestrained bodies in motion (Figure 5.3).[21] In vignettes from the genre, skeletal allegories of death leap and twirl around their victims in jerky, contorted moves, paying no heed to the dying's social standing, age, or the purported morality of their societal role. Unrestrained gesturing of arms and legs, sardonic allusions to nudity from suggestively draped or tailored clothing revealing nothing but bare bones, give visual and gestural form to the wayward and ever looming threat of death and the social chaos it leaves in its wake. Arms above the head, legs folded and thrown to the back, the skeletal figures model gestures and attitudes unrestrained by social order. They are outrageous, excessive, immoderate, or, in the language of early modern Italian dance treaties, *smisurati* i.e. lacking *misura*. In this context, their excessive and transgressive movements have the purpose of delivering a moralizing message of *memento mori*, reminding all that they will inevitably die. Authors and illustrators of travel literature would turn to the same movements of the body in their depictions of Africans and Indigenous peoples, no longer as motifs of threatening, humorous sarcasm but as literal evocations of projected notions of lack of civility.

Image-makers of the early modern period drew from the iconography of the *Dance of Death* in devising a visual vocabulary to portray dances and rituals among African and Indigenous populations they included as cartouches in maps, illustrations in printed travelogues, and motifs in artworks of all kinds. These representations were not ethnographic in that they did not attempt to record Indigenous or African comportment per se. Rather, they offered conventional representations of bodily movements that were considered to lack civility. In this regard, they ran parallel to the emblematic use of feathers as clothing and adornment to connote American origins in early modern images, regardless of the actual practices of the populations represented.[22] The high-stepping, arms-up stance the skeletons modeled would thus serve to illustrate a full range of peoples and activities that early modern Europeans homogenized as Other. The recourse to the *Dance of Death* not only inscribed ideas of lack of restraint and chaotic behavior unto the represented scenes, but also made a value judgment on the practices as unbound, uncouth, and lacking civility.[23]

Compare the *Dance of Death* skeletons to German artist Hans Burgkmair's (1473–1531) depiction of an African child in his proto-ethnographic 1508 woodblock print of the people of "Gennea" (Figure 5.4). The child clumsily balances on one foot in his flailing imitation the impressive warring gesture of his father whose mastery is rendered, in contrast, in a dynamic

19. Esther J. Terry, "Choreographies of Trans-Atlantic Primitivity: Sub-Saharan Isolation in Black Dance Historiography," *Early Modern Black Diaspora Studies* (Cham, Switzerland: Palgrave Macmillan, 2018), 65–82, 74–76, notes the mention of morescha at Kongo court in Lopes Pigafetta. See Duarte Lopes and Filippo Pigafetta, *Relatione del reame di Congo et delle circonvicini contrade* (Rome: Bartolomeo Grassi, 1591), 69.

20. Jennifer Nevile, *The Eloquent Body: Dance and Humanist Culture in Fifteenth-Century Italy* (Bloomington: Indiana University Press, 2004), 79.

21. Elina Gertsman, *The Dance of Death in the Middle Ages: Image, Text, Performance* (Turnhout: Brepols, 2010), 65–67.

22. William C. Sturtevant, "La tupinambisation des Indiens d'Amérique du Nord," in *Les Figures de l'Indien*, Les cahiers du department d'études littéraires 9, ed. Gilles Thérien, 293–303 (Montréal: Typo, 1988). Elizabeth Hill Boone, "Seeking Indianness: Christoph Weiditz, the Aztecs, and Feathered Amerindians," *Colonial Latin American Review* 26, no. 1 (2017): 39–61, https://doi.org/10.1080/10609164.2017.1287323.

23. Co-editor Noémie Ndiaye discussed a similar use of movement in early modern racecraft in England in Noémie Ndiaye, "'Come Aloft, Jack-little-ape!': Race and Dance in The Spanish Gypsie," *English Literary Renaissance* 51, no. 1 (2021): 121–51, https://doi.org/10.1086/711604.

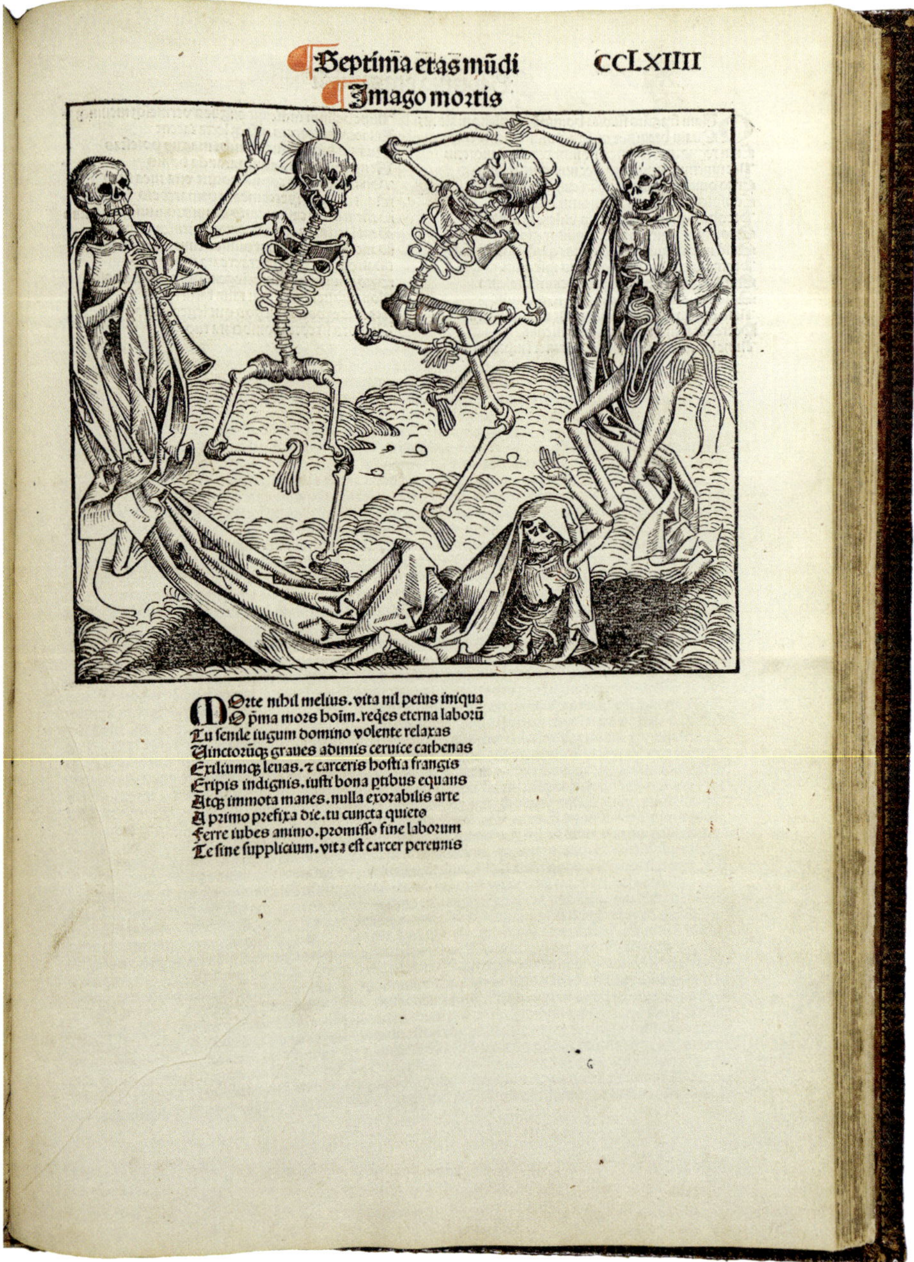

Figure 5.3
Michel Wolgemut, "Dance of Death" in Hartmann Schedel, *Liber chronicarum*. Nuremberg, 1493, Newberry Library, VAULT oversize Inc. 2084

Figure 5.4 ▸
Hans Burgkmair, "Natives of Guinea and Algoa," 1508, handcolored woodcut (28.5 × 42.4 cm). Freiherrlich von Welsersche Familienstiftung, Neunhof (Photo credit: copyright Freiherrlich v. Welsersche Familienstiftung)

but stable contrapposto*. The baby in the arms of the poised mother figure also twists as to wiggle out of the woman's grasp. The attitude of the standing child would evoke to its early modern viewers images of both *moresca* dances and the dance of death.[24] The clumsy gesture and unselfconscious nakedness of the child also conjured ideas of naive innocence that European travelers to Africa and the Americas repeatedly associated in their reports with Indigenous people, who "go around" "naked" "with no shame at all."[25] The juxtaposition of the African man pictured in a classical contrapposto and the African child in an

24. Interest in Italian dance, including the *morescha*, from Nuremberg in the early sixteenth century has been discussed in Ingrid Brainard, "The Art of Courtly Dance in Transition," in *Crossroads of Medieval Civilization: The City of Regensburg and Its Intellectual Milieu: A Collection of Essays*, eds. Edelgard E. DuBruck and Rudolf Holbach, 61–79 (Detroit: Marygrove College, 1984). See also Ingrid Wetzel, "'Hie innen sindt geschriben die wellschen tenntz': le otto danze italiane del manoscritto di Norim-berga," in *Guglielmo Ebreo da Pesaro e la danza nelle corti italiane del XV secolo, Proceedings of the 1987 Pesaro Conference*, ed. Maurizio Padovan, 321–43 (Pisa: Pacini, 1990).

25. See the citations gathered in Jill Burke, "Nakedness and Other Peoples: Rethinking the Italian Renaissance Nude," *Art History* 36, no. 4 (2013): 724–25, https://doi.org/10.1111/1467-8365.12029.

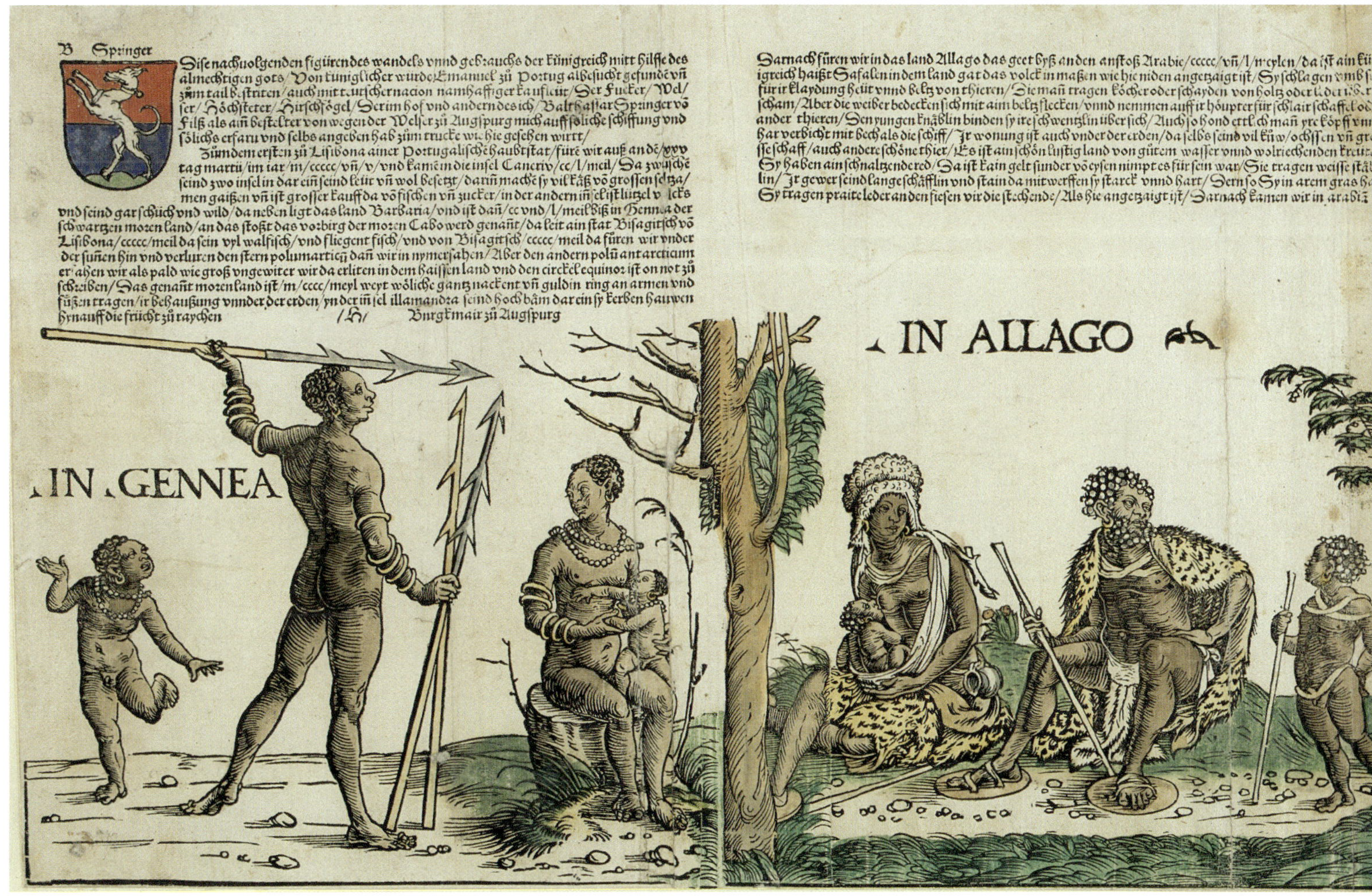

exuberant stance, of the wiggling baby and the African woman seated as a Christian Virgin Mary, also reveals ambivalences and contradictions about the nature, limits, and stability of difference that would remain central to European conception and representations of racialized Others.

Art historian Stephanie Leitch has rightly underlined how the figures testified to Burgkmair's "virtuoso exploration of movement for its own sake" that not only pushed the boundaries of the medium of wood printing, but also explored new possibilities for ethnographic visual representation.[26] Burgkmair's print is part of a multiblock series based on Balthasar Springer's travelogue *The Voyage and Discoveries of New Paths to Many Unknown Islands and Kingdoms* chronicling his 1505–1506 journey along the coast of Africa to India's Malabar Coast. Though not directly the product of eye witnessing on the part of the printmaker, the series is at least partly inspired from sketches executed in situ* by a travel companion of Springer's.[27]

An innovative combination of modes of showing otherness in the medium, from physical features to cultural traits, supports the print's ambition to achieve visual empiricism*. Inked lines bring volume to the curves of the figures and successfully evoke dark skin. Curly hair and rounded noses pinpoint the physical features Europeans most often associated with Africans. Necklaces and bracelets suggest socially meaningful adornment that highlight the absence of clothing, the first and most preeminent means of outward

26. Stephanie Leitch, "Burgkmair's Peoples of Africa and India (1508) and the Origins of Ethnography in Print," *The Art Bulletin* 91, no. 2 (2009): 151, https://doi.org/10.1080/00043079.2009.10786162.

27. Stephanie Leitch, *Mapping Ethnography in Early Modern Germany: New Worlds in Print Culture*. (New York: Palgrave Macmillan, 2010), 64–66.

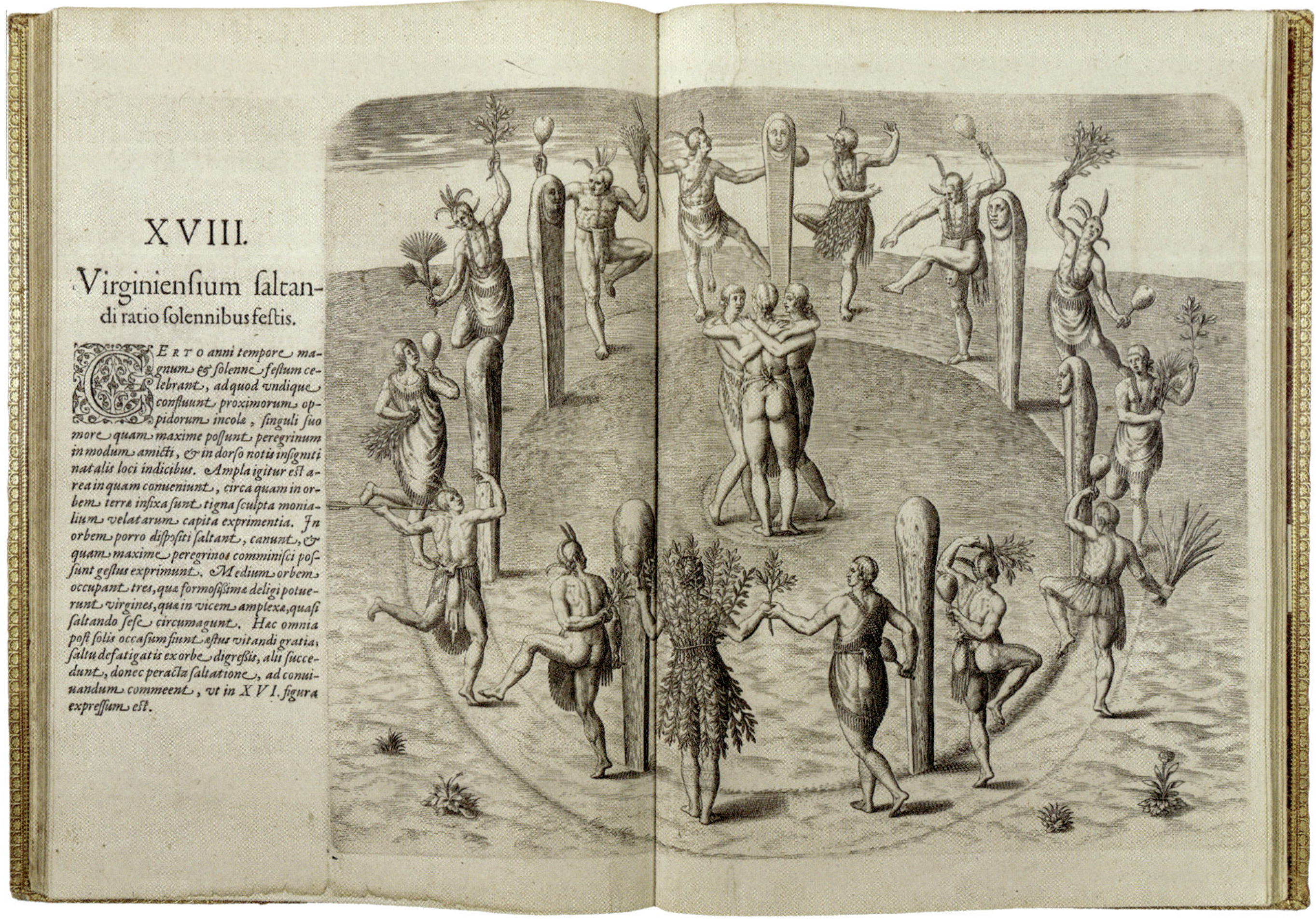

XVIII.

Virginienſium ſaltandi ratio ſolennibus feſtis.

CERTO anni tempore magnum & ſolenne feſtum celebrant, ad quod vndique confluunt proximorum oppidorum incolæ, ſinguli ſuo more quam maxime poſſunt peregrinum in modum amicti, & in dorſo notis inſigniti natalis loci indicibus. Ampla igitur eſt area in quam conueniunt, circa quam in orbem terræ infixa ſunt tigna ſculpta monialium velatarum capita exprimentia. In orbem porro diſpoſiti ſaltant, canunt, & quam maxime peregrinos comminiſci poſſunt geſtus exprimunt. Medium orbem occupant tres, quæ formoſiſſimæ deligi potuerunt virgines, quæ in vicem amplexæ, quaſi ſaltando ſeſe circumagunt. Hæc omnia poſt ſolis occaſum fiunt æſtus vitandi gratia, ſaltu defatigatis ex orbe digreſſis, alii ſuccedunt, donec peracta ſaltatione, ad conuiuandum commeent, vt in XVI. figura expreſſum eſt.

social identification in Europe, the latter a point Kaplan and Katz discuss in this volume. This same idea of imperfect civility that emerges from showing lack of clothing paired with the presence of adornment is taken up in the motif of the half tree trunk on which the woman sits. The trunk highlights the lack of furniture, as the tree to the right highlights the lack of dwelling, but it nonetheless visibly suggests human industry. Its flat top is manufactured, the result of human intervention. Finally, the unbalanced attitudes of the children destabilize the poise of their parents, making their genteel poses seem happenstance rather than stable characteristics of comportment "in Gennea." In presenting this array of visual solutions to the depiction of the other, Burgkmair's print demonstrates the possibility of showing race in the medium but does not give an authoritative statement on the necessary or even the sufficient visual means for this representation. Rather, in addition to physical features, Burgkmair relied on what his European viewers would perceive as unbalanced bodily comportment and imperfect social values to denote racial difference. Already in this early moment, reckonings with the possibility of visual racial representations turns to movement, in conjunction with physical features and clothing, as a powerful marker of difference.

Leaps and flying, bent limbs demonstrating excess and imbalance appeared in the dance of death alongside another feature iconographically* associated with paganism: the ronde.[28] It is a ronde of naked men in dynamic motion suggesting dance that forms, for instance, what is likely the first European painting of Indigenous Americans, executed in 1494 by Pinturicchio (Bernardino di Betto, 1454–1513) in Pope

28. Gaudio, *Sound, Image, Silence*, 6–18.

◂ **Figure 5.5**
Theodor de Bry,
"Virginiensium saltandi ratio solennibus festis,"
in *America. Pt. 1*,
Frankfurt am Main, 1590,
Newberry Library, VAULT Ayer 110 .B9 1590b v. 1

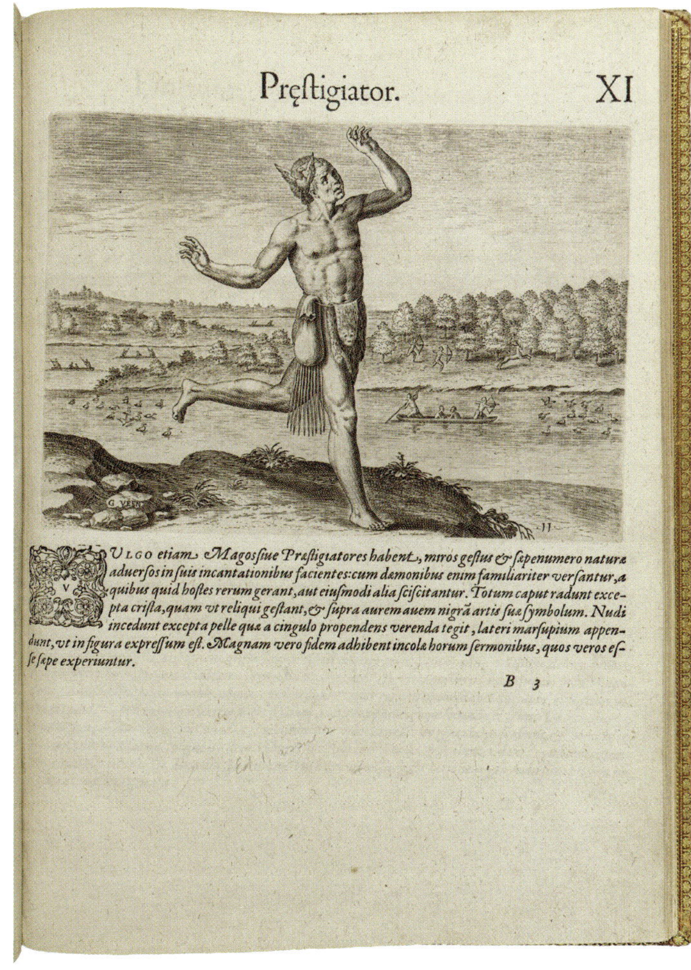

Prǽſtigiator. XI

VULGO etiam Magos ſiue Præſtigiatores habent, miros geſtus & ſæpenumero naturæ aduerſos in ſuis incantationibus facientes: cum dæmonibus enim familiariter verſantur, a quibus quid hoſtes rerum gerant, aut eiuſmodi alia ſciſcitantur. Totum caput radunt excepta criſta, quam vt reliqui geſtant, & ſupra aurem auem nigrā artis ſuæ ſymbolum. Nudi incedunt excepta pelle quæ a cingulo propendens verenda tegit, lateri marſupium appendunt, vt in figura expreſſum eſt. Magnam vero fidem adhibent incolæ horum ſermonibus, quos veros eſſe ſæpe experiuntur.

B 3

Figure 5.6
Theodor de Bry,
"Prestigiator," in *America. Pt. 1*,
Frankfurt am Main, 1590,
Newberry Library, VAULT Ayer 110 .B9 1590b v.1

Alexander VI Borgia's (1431–1503) apartments.[29] At the end of the sixteenth century, the attitude of the high stepping skeletons in the ronde seen in Wolgemut's *dance macabre* appears in cartographers John White's (1539–1593) watercolor* representations of the Indigenous people of Roanoke Island in the emerging English colony of Virginia. The scenes painted from life in 1585 would circulate widely in their engraved versions in an edition of Thomas Harriot's (1560–1621) travelogue edited by Theodor de Bry (Figure 5.5). Stepping high and waving their arms, a group of Indigenous men and women dance around a set of posts and a central group in a ritual scene. In fact, the ronde and dynamic limb movement regularly appeared in European illustrations of otherness, real or imagined, from paganism to witchcraft, and from the Americas to Africa.[30] In another image from the same publication, the twisted body and flailing limbs of a "conjurer" caught mid-trance conveys his overtake by numinous forces (Figure 5.6).

A century after Harriot, a Capuchin missionary in the Kongo turned to the same set of gestures to convey ritual dancing in central Africa in watercolors later published as etchings in Giovanni Antonio Cavazzi's *Historical Description of Three Kingdoms* published in 1687 (Figures 5.7 & 5.8).[31] In what the cleric perceived as an idolatrous funeral ronde, or in "dishonest balls" the same movements continued to mark

29. See Andrés H. Rubiano, "The First Painted Image of America in Europe: A Detail from Pinturicchio's Resurrection in the Sala dei Misteri," *H-ART. Revista de historia, teoría y crítica de arte*, no. 8 (2021): 286–304; Jessica Horton, *Art for an Undivided Earth* (Durham, NC: Duke University Press, 2017), 149–51; Gaudio, *Sound, Image, Silence*, 11–16.

30. Gaudio, *Sound, Image, Silence*, 11–16.

31. Cécile Fromont, *Images on a Mission in Early Modern Kongo and Angola* (University Park, PA: The Pennsylvania State University Press, 2022).

128 LIBRO PRIMO.

ſe vi penſaſte ciò procedere da ſchietta cordialità, ò da incontaminato
affetto; imperoche v'aſſicuro, e lo ſperimentarete quando ſarò morto,
che d'altro non ſi querelano, ſe non che tardando io à morire, tarda la
loro conſolazione. Morì egli frà poche ore, e vidi effettiuamente ve-
rificarſi quanto m'haueua detto; atteſoche mutata faccia à quell'apparente duolo, tutta la facenda ſi riſoluè in ſoddisfare la fame di que'
maſcalzoni, che intanto, ebrij, e ſatolli, mà non giammai appie-
no contenti, intrecciauano ſtupendamente alla meſtizia il ballo, à ſin-
gulti il canto, & à ſoſpiri il ſuono, borbottando rimproueri contro la
tenacità de gli Eredi, quaſi non adempiſſero le parti loro verſo chi
compatiua preſentemente la perdita del Padrone.

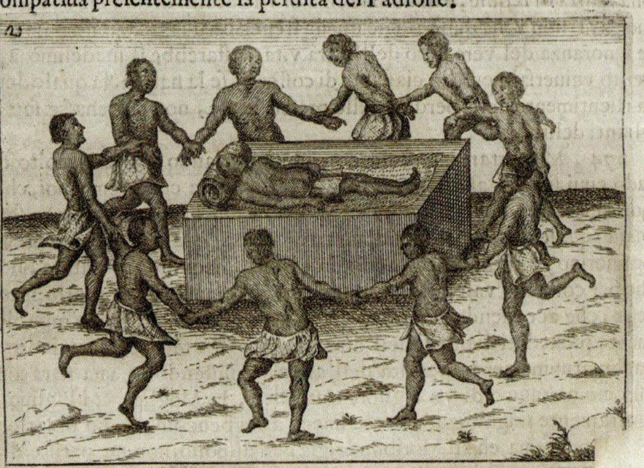

Modo di habitare in queſti Regni.

Habitazioni de Neri, perche ſiano viliſſime.

275 DAlle coſe concernenti alla ſuperſtizioſa Religion
che parmi di hauerne parlato à ſufficienza, & à l
luogo dourò dirne qualche poco) paſſiamo à quelle, che riſguarc
viuere ciuile; ſe pure vn titolo sì honeſto meritano le coſtuma
Barbari. Queſti Neri per naturale viltà di animo totalmente d
to, & alieno dalla induſtria, e dalle fatiche, reſtringendoſi, ſot
teſto di moderazione, à quel tanto, di cui malageuolmente può
farſi la nuda neceſſità, non ſolo traſcurano il luſſo, rimprouerano
ciò gli Europei, mà eziandio quell'arte, che dalle beſtie iſteſſe
no cotidianamente praticarſi con ſingolare applicazione, e m

Figure 5.7
Paolo da Lorena (attr.),
Plate 23 in Giovanni Antonio Cavazzi
and Fortunato Alamandini,
Istorica descrizione de' tre' regni
Congo, Matamba, et Angola,
Bologna, 1687,
Newberry Library,
Ayer 263 .C211 C2 1687

LIBRO PRIMO. 167

nell'Eſercito hanno queſta incombenza, accoppiando à quell'ottuſo,
e formidabile rimbombo altrettanta fierezza di voci, di vrli, e di ſtra-
niſſimi atteggiamenti del Corpo, come ſe daddouero foſſero inuaſati,
ò impazziti. Più picciola, mà ſimile al ſudetto, è la Ndunga, che ſi bat-
te con vn pezzo di legno rotondo, e peſante. I Rè, & i Signori di Pro-
uincie vſano vna ſorte di Tamburetti chiamati Ndembo coperti di pelle da vna parte ſola, e cerchiati con laminette di ferro, ò di ottone, ed
in ſoſtanza poco differenti da que' ruſticali Cembali, che ſuonano talo-
ra le Paſtorelle: coſtumanſi queſti per honorare qualche funzione; mà
ſpecialmente quando il Rè, eſſendo in publico, ſtarnutiſce. Il più go-
dibile ſembrami la Marimba, la quale è ordita di quattordici, ò ſedici
Zucchette diſpoſte in buona conſonanza, e ben collegate frà due aſſi-
celle, con le bocche all'ingiù turate da vna ſottile corteccia, ſi come
all'incontro nella parte oppoſta euui à ciaſcuna di eſſe vna tauoletta di
legno larga circa due oncie, & vn palmo in lunghezza, che percoſſa
dalle dita del Suonatore, mentre ſi alza, e ſi abbaſſa forma vn'armo-
nia, che non è diſpiaceuole: laonde mi dò à credere che ſe queſto inſtru-
mento foſſe adoperato da mano eccellente, eccheggierebbe vn perfet-
tiſſimo concerto. Alcuni in vece delle dita lo percuotono con baſton-
celli noderuti, e peſanti, mà richiederebbeſi artificioſa velocità, e leg-
giadria, conciofiacoſache eſſendo per ſe ſteſſo moderatamente ſonoro,
ſarebbe ancora più guſtoſo.

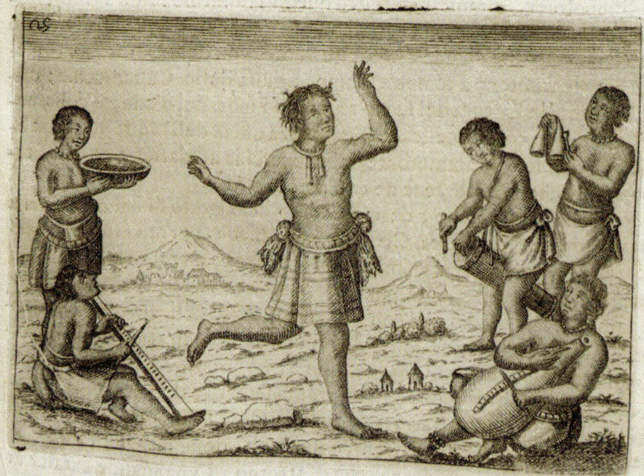

333 I Bal-

Figure 5.8
Paolo da Lorena (attr.),
Plate 25 in Giovanni Antonio Cavazzi
and Fortunato Alamandini,
Istorica descrizione de' tre' regni Congo,
Matamba, et Angola,
Bologna, 1687,
Newberry Library, Ayer 263 .C211 C2 1687

non-European individuals as culturally strange, morally suspicious, and spiritually compromised. Movement, thus, along with dress and skin color, served as a marker that early modern Europeans read as a sign of lack of civility, religion, and social sophistication.[32] It would unsurprisingly feature in the visual vocabulary of idolatry in the early eighteenth-century publication by Bernard Picart, the *Ceremonies and Religious Customs of the World*, whose impact on European perceptions and representations of religions worldwide would be felt for centuries (Cat. No. 38).[33]

Pious Stances

Contrasting with the "savage" comportment evinced in depictions of Africans and Indigenous people ranging from dancers to ritual specialists or vanquished enemies, visual representations of the Other linked to Christian piety displayed them in attitudes with positive connotations. One of the common markers, for example, of Blackness in Spanish Viceregal visual and literary rhetoric was a servile or supplicant position, often rendered in conjunction with a childlike appearance.[34] This trope, already well established in the seventeenth century, can also be seen in the following century, for instance in a 1750 painting of *Saint Luis Beltrán Baptizing an African Slave* (Figure 5.9). Since the mid-sixteen hundreds, Saint Luis Beltrán (1526–1581) had been a patron of New Granada, which encompassed present-day Ecuador, Colombia, Venezuela, and Panama.[35] The Spanish Dominican spent most of his life in Valencia, Spain, but is best remembered for his missionary work in Colombia, Panama, and the Lesser Antilles (1562–68).[36] In 1561 he sailed on a galleon to Cartagena, an important port city that received slave ships. He likely baptized newly arrived Africans in the port of Cartagena before embarking on his missionary work of converting Indigenous groups in the interior of the continent.[37] The painted scene takes place in a tropical setting communicated to the viewer via the palm tree in the right background emblazoned with a cross, alluding to the saint's successful apostolate in the region. It features numerous symbols that refer to the saint's life, including a small crucifix that emerges from the barrel of a rifle, evoking a miracle he performed in Colombia. Under attack by Indigenous Colombian warriors, the Dominican genuflected towards the weapon, which miraculously transformed into a crucifix.

The small African figure wearing a billowing blue robe, a red feathered diadem, a drop pearl earring, and a jeweled, golden armlet is of particular interest. Such finery was a convention used to signal Africans as valuable commodities of those who owned them as slaves, and contrasts sharply with the image of the nearly naked Africans of the sugar mill or the ritual dances. The figure's accoutrement is a fanciful riff based on various sources. It draws from the roughly contemporaneous engraving *St. Francis Xavier Baptizing a Native* produced by the Klauber workshop (Augsburg, Germany).[38] The Quito painter replaced the Old World Jesuit Saint Francis Xavier (1506–1552) with the New World Dominican Saint Luis Beltrán by changing the habit and substituting the emblems that identify each saint.

32. Burke, "Nakedness," 714–39.

33. See for example Bernard Picart, *Le grand sacrifice des Canadiens à Quitchi-Manitou ou le grand esprit de Jean Frédéric Bernard, Cérémonies et coutumes religieuses de tous les peuples du monde* (1723).

34. Brewer-García, "Imagined Transformations: Color, Beauty, and Black Christian Conversion in Seventeenth-Century Spanish America," in *Envisioning Others: Race, Color, and the Visual in Iberia and Latin America*, ed. Pamela A. Patton, 119 (Leiden: Brill, 2015).

35. The region was an Audiencia called the New Kingdom of Granada (1549–1716), until it became a Viceroyalty in 1717.

36. "St. Louis Bertrand," Dominican Friars Foundation, https://dominicanfriars.org/st-louis-bertrand/.

37. Suzanne Stratton-Pruitt, unpublished manuscript (Thoma Foundation).

38. The Klauber print was used as a thesis sheet print, possibly based on an earlier composition by Johann Georg Bergmüller (1688–1762), which may have been the source of the Quito School painting. See PESSCA: Project on the Engraved Sources of Spanish Colonial Art, https://colonialart.org/archives/locations/united-states/state-of-illinois/city-of-chicago/thoma-collection/6006a-6006b

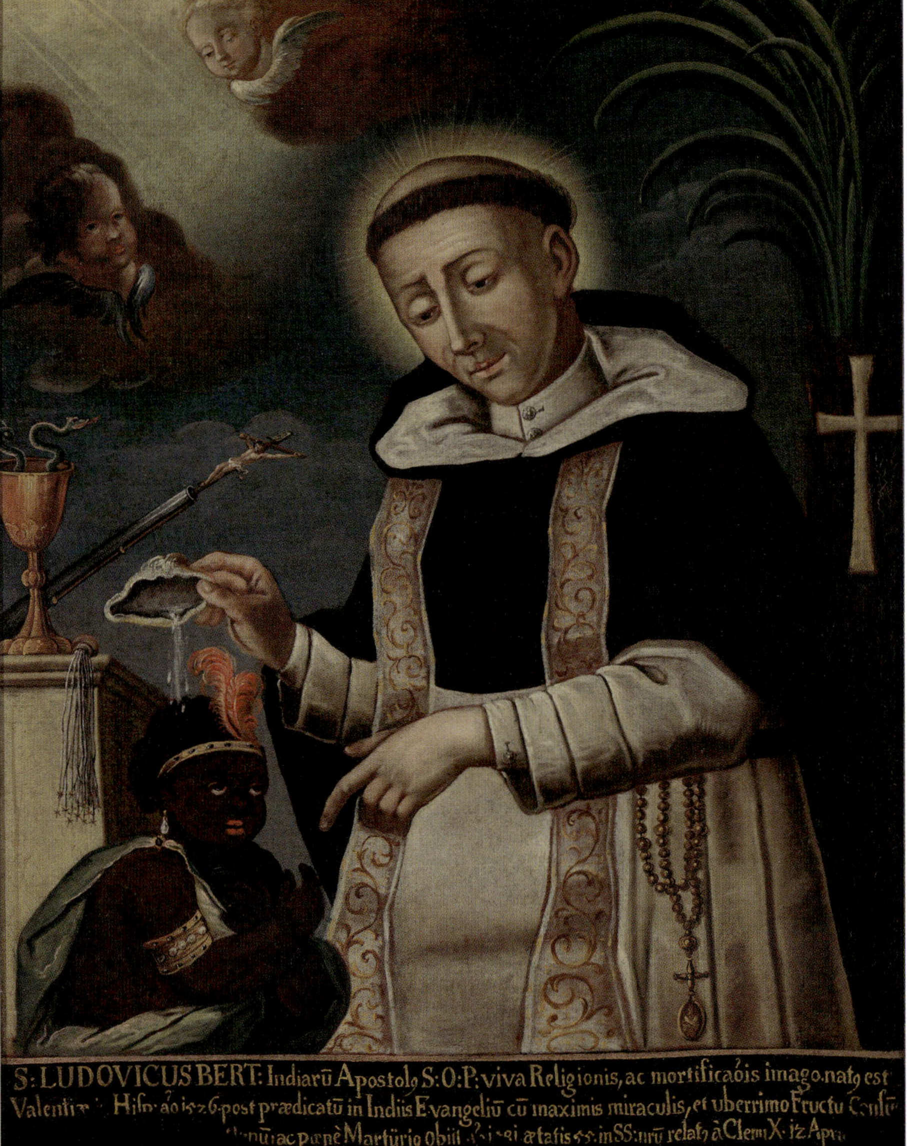

Figure 5.9
Unidentified Artist,
Saint Luis Beltrán Baptizing an African Slave,
39½ x 30⅛ in, oil on canvas,
Ecuador, 1750,
Thoma Foundation

Figure 5.10 ▸
Klauber Workshop.
St. Francis Xavier Baptizing a Native,
engraving, 18th century,
Trento, Museo Diocesano Tridentino

In the print, Saint Francis Xavier wears the black colored and high collared Jesuit clerical robes (Figure 5.10). He holds a crucifix in one hand though he lacks his other symbols including the lily, ship, and flaming heart. That the Quito artist chose Francis Xavier's image as a prototype makes sense considering the great fame of the Jesuit, known as the "Apostle of the Indies," and that both saints were missionaries originally from Spain serving in foreign lands. In his new interpretation, the Quiteño artist collapsed the source engraving's three figures adoring the saint to just one. In the Klauber workshop print, the three figures surrounding the saint allude to his mission in Asia. The two closest to the foreground, including the figure being baptized, have dark skin and wear feathered accessories including an armlet, headpiece, and quilled arrows. Behind them a lighter-skinned turbaned man looks outwards, a typical type that referred in the early modern period to a diffuse European idea of western Asia. The other two figures result from the collapsing of distant lands into the abstract idea of the Indies, a notion rather than a place denoting in early modern European thought an exotic, faraway, Other, elsewhere. In a similar process, the darker skinned figures who likely personify converts in Goa, India, where Francis Xavier spent much of his mission, are

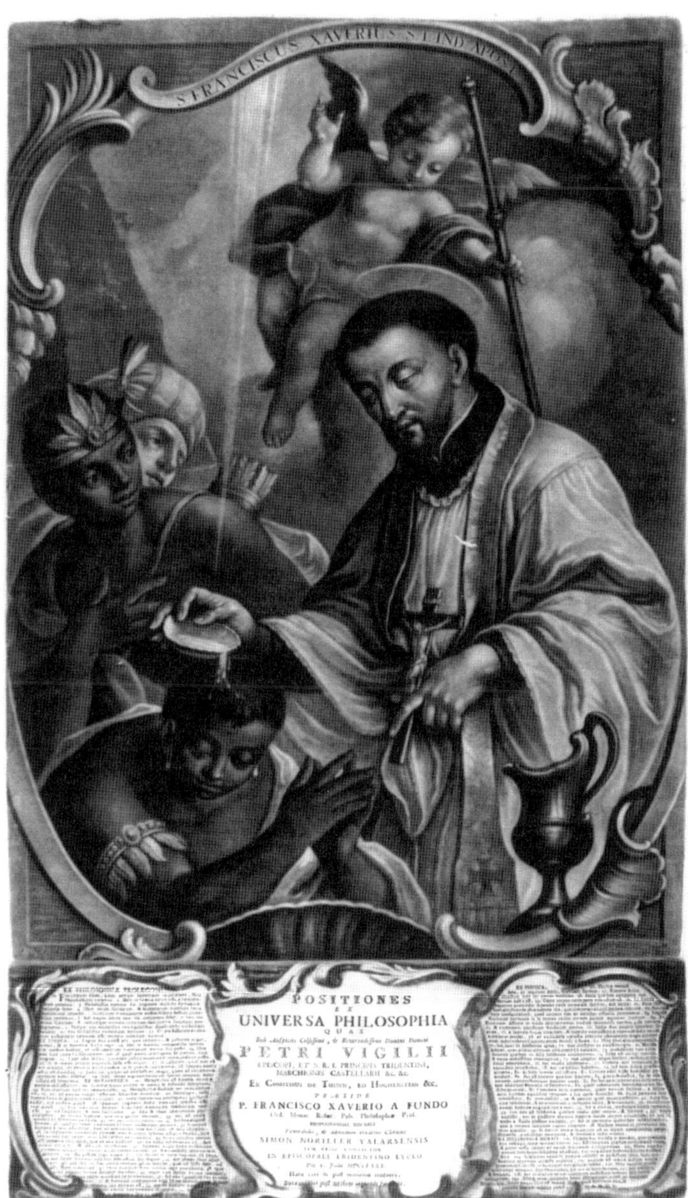

depicted in the befeathered guise of the "savage" and are racialized as Black based on their dark skin color.[39] The Quito painter loses the arrow motif and collapses the feathered armlet and headdress into a singular dark-skinned figure. Here the various exotic types merge into the *bozal* (i.e. recently arrived to the Americas) African baptized by Saint Luis Beltrán.

The tendency to flatten exotic types was common in early modern Europe, and the collapsing of African types with both western Asian and Indigenous tropes frequent. For instance, feathers, while particularly emblematic of Indigenous Americans, also signified savageness in portrayals of individuals far outside of that geography.[40] Reversely, the feathered headdress (or *penacho*) of Motecozuma II was famously labeled a "Moor's Hat" when first recorded in the 1596 inventory of Austrian Archduke Ferdinand II von Tyrol.[41] Similarly, early missionaries in New Spain erroneously called Mexica temples mosques.[42] In the seventeenth-century *Wunderkammern*, or cabinet of wonders, items from Africa and the Americas were often labeled "Moorish" or "Indian." These interchangeable terms not only blurred Black and Indigenous American cultures into a singular foreign category, but also drew illogical equivalencies between simplified and inaccurate geographic, ethnic, religious, and racial signifiers.[43]

Returning to the diminutive African of the Quito School painting, the figure's fanciful fineries are clearly exoticizing tropes, but could also suggest elite status, perhaps as an African noble just arrived in Cartagena.[44] That an African prince could arrive in the slave port in all his finery of course was pure fantasy, as the middle passage inflicted its physical and material wounds to all captives, no matter their former social status. Yet, in his allegorical role, the man communicated through

39. Kathryn Santner, personal communication (Thoma foundation).

40. W. C. Sturtevant, "La tupinambisation," 293–303.

41. Esther Pasztory, *Aztec Art* (Norman: University of Oklahoma Press, 1998), 280; and Khadijah von Zinnenburg Carroll, *The Contested Crown: Repatriation Politics Between Europe and Mexico* (Chicago: University of Chicago Press, 2022), 87.

42. Gauvin Bailey, *Art of Colonial Latin America* (New York: Phaidon Press, 2005).

43. See Elke Bujok, "Ethnographica in the Early *Kunstkammern* and their Perception," *Journal of the History of Collections* 21, no. 1 (2009): 17–32, https://doi.org/10.1093/jhc/fhn031, and Jessica Keating and Lia Markey, "'Indian' objects in Medici and Austrian-Habsburg inventories," *Journal of the History of Collections* 23, no. 2 (2011): 283–300, https://doi.org/10.1093/jhc/fhq030.

44. Suzanne Stratton Pruitt, unpublished manuscript (Thoma foundation).

his small stature and supplicant posture the success of Beltrán in pacifying him and bringing him into the Christian faith. The African crosses his arms over his chest, a gesture that differentiates him from the "natives" of the source engraving, one of whom instead clasps his hands before himself in prayer. A subtle change perhaps, but the adjustment in gesture begs investigating. As art historian and co-editor of this volume Lia Markey describes, "The word 'gesture' derives from the Latin words *gestura*, meaning 'bearing,' 'way of carrying' or 'mode of action,' and *gerere*, the infinitive form, which means 'to carry, to behave, to take on oneself, to take charge of, to perform or to accomplish.'"[45] Various treatises were written about gesture in the early modern period including John Bulwer's 1644 *Chirologia, or the Natural Language of the Hand* (Cat. No. 13), based on the study of gesture in the ancient world, drawing from Cicero's *De oratore* of 55 BCE.[46] If gestures serve as a visual language, one that art historian André Chastel describes as "para-language . . . a rhetoric of non-verbal communication," what, then, does the crossed arm gesture communicate?[47] And how does that gesture differ from the hands in prayer from the engraving?

In the history of European art this attitude is perhaps best known in the pose of the Virgin Annunciate of Jan and Hubert Van Eyck's *Ghent Altarpiece* (c. 1425–1432).[48] Similar to our African figure, the future mother of Christ crosses arms in front of her chest while gazing upwards. The crossed-arm pose was popular in fourteenth- and fifteenth-century Annunciation scenes, where they suggested the "Humiliatio" or submission of the Virgin Mary to divine will.[49] The crossed-arm gesture also has connections to church liturgy. The writings of ninth-century Amalarius of Metz describing the symbolism behind actions performed during mass associated crossed arms with the Passion, and particularly of Christ's submission on the cross.[50] Following the consecration of the host, the crossed arms pose accompanied by a bow became part of Catholic liturgy by the early thirteenth century. Symbolizing Christ's acquiescence to his sacrifice, the gesture held further associations through its use in various Biblical subjects.

The attitude shows up in scenes of the Baptism of Christ, such as in the Limbourg Brothers' illumination for *The Beautiful Hours of Jan, Duke of Berry* (1410–15).[51] There, it foreshadows the Passion, the sacrifice that would redeem the sins that baptism could not wash away.[52] The pose appeared in various saints' images, particularly those of penitential saints. Eventually it would show up in mythological or historical subjects where, as Wilberding describes, "it shear[s] away any theological* references, only the idea of submission and reverence is retained."[53] Submission and reverence is what the crossed-arm pose of the *bozal* baptizand* signifies, emphasizing his conversion and piety.

The pose also has Black Atlantic resonance. Art historian Robert Farris Thompson connects the gesture to the Cuban *rumba yambu* where it signifies communication or a greeting between parties.[54] The gesture's Black Atlantic dimension arches to the early modern

45. Lia Markey, "Gesture," University of Chicago :: Theories of Media :: Keyword Glossary, accessed February 28, 2022. https://csmt.uchicago.edu/glossary2004/gesture.htm. See also Adam Kendon, "The Study of Gesture: Some Observations on Its History," *Recherches Semiotique/Semiotic Inquiry* 2, no.1 (1982): 44–62.

46. Markey, "Gesture," and Kendon, "Study of Gesture."

47. André Chastel, "Gesture in Painting: Problems in Semiology," *Renaissance and Reformation* 1, no. 10 (1986): 9, https://www.jstor.org/stable/43444573.

48. Jan Van Eyck, the Virgin Annunciate from the closed view. Back panels of *Ghent Altarpiece*. San Bavo. See https://commons.wikimedia.org/wiki/File:Ghent_Altarpiece_F_-_Maria_message_2.jpg.

49. Baxandall identifies a sermon by Franciscan Fra Roberto Caracciolo (c. 1425–95) on the five reactions of the Virgin Annunciate. Michael Baxandall, *Painting and Experience in Fifteenth Century Italy: A Primer in the Social History of Pictorial Style* (Oxford: Oxford University Press, 1988), 55.

50. Erick Wilberding, "Embracing the Cross: A Liturgical Gesture," *Notes in the History of Art* 8, no. 2 (1989): 2. https://doi.org/10.1086/sou.8.2.23202528

51. Paul Herman and Jean de Limbourg (Franco-Netherlandish, active in France by 1399–1416). *Belles Heures of Jean de France, duc de Berry*. 1405–1408/9. folio 211v. See "The Art of Illumination," The Metropolitan Museum of Art, https://blog.metmuseum.org/artofillumination/manuscript-pages/folio-211v/.

52. Wilberding, "Embracing the Cross," 3.

53. Wilberding, "Embracing the Cross," 4.

54. Robert Farris Thompson, *Four Moments of the Sun: Kongo Art in Two Worlds* (Washington, DC: National Gallery of Art, 1981), 168.

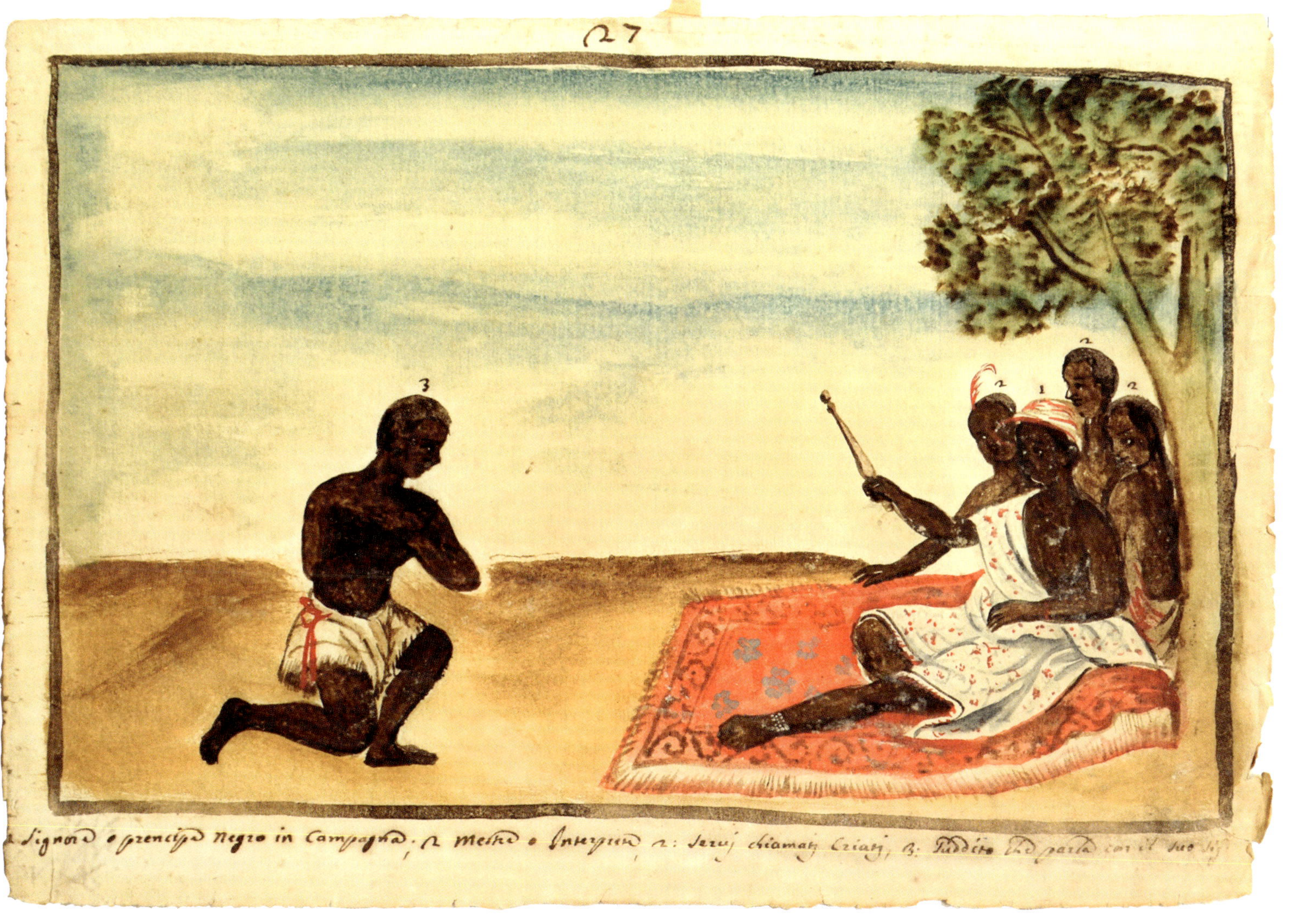

Figure 5.11
Unknown Capuchin artist,
Black Lord or Prince in the Countryside,
watercolor on paper, 34 ×24 cm, late seventeenth century,
Parma Watercolors, folio 27, Virgili Collection,
Photograph: C. Fromont

kingdom of Kongo where it was a local attitude of greeting and respect. In a late seventeenth-century watercolor a vassal approaches his overlord, kneeling and crossing his arm in front of his chest in sign of deference (Figure 5.11). The image, part of an album aimed at instructing missionaries about their work in the Christian kingdom of Kongo, describes with ethnographic detail the mores and customs of the region.[55] It also functions analogically by likening the Kongo ruler in the act of adjudicating to the famed Saint Louis of France (1214–1270) who officiated similarly under a tree. The use of imported textiles and outfitting such as the crimson carpet reflects the cosmopolitan horizons of the aristocrats of the kingdoms, active in the commercial, diplomatic, and religious networks of the early modern Atlantic world. The figure of the Kongo noble and the gesture of the man before him also bring further perspective on the depiction of the African slave in the painting of San Luis Beltrán. The gestures and finery that the hagiographic* painting

55. Fromont, *Images on a Mission*.

strives to naturalize as emblems and attitudes denoting enslavement appear in contrast in the watercolor as symbols and demonstrations of African civility and cosmopolitan sophistication. The comparison underlines the mechanics at play in the creation and interpretation of images such as the Quiteño canvas whose heavy-handed rhetoric contributes to the construction of race. Once relocated within a vaster set of early modern Atlantic visual, material, and gestural vocabularies, the attitude and adornment of the baptizand, which viewers are invited to see as the attribute of the "savage" for whom enslavement brings salvation, rightly become contingent on their ideological context. That early modern Europeans used gesture and movement in addition to skin color and physical features in crafting an early modern discourse of race helps underline the willful and strenuous mechanics that the arduous work of racialization demanded to be put into motion. It also brings attention to the enduring racialized meaning rooted in the early modern period of certain movements and bodily attitudes that are often today willingly or unwillingly overlooked as expressions of racialized discourse and often serve as terrains of resistance to it.

Conclusion

The preceding visual examples highlight some of the ways bodily comportment functioned as a racial marker in the early modern Atlantic world. Specific gestures, postures, and movement of Indigenous Americans as well as Africans and their descendants depicted in these images both further established and reified the European view of racialized people as naturally unruly and in need of pacification. Such views permeated colonial society. Throughout the Spanish Viceroyalties,* for example, legal codes separated Spanish, Indigenous, and Africans and conferred different laws based on these categories (see for example the patent of nobility and cedula in Cat. No. 40 & 23). These rules were made by and for Europeans who placed themselves within the system in a position of superiority, thereby legally enacting white supremacy.

Throughout the independence period, and indeed until the multicultural turn of the 1980s, many Latin American countries embraced what has been called a "monocultural *mestizaje*," where ethno-racial diversity was ignored in favor of an ideological whitening of the population.[56] Often mestizos (mixed Spanish and Indigenous) were celebrated as the prototype of national identity.[57] Through the process of modern nation building in much of Latin America, Indigenous cultures were framed as part of the national past, thereby incorporating aspects of Indigeneity into a modern, whitened (and thus "improved") mestizo nation. Blackness thereby continued to be relegated to the margins, prescribed as existing outside of the national imaginary. Only in approximately the last twenty-five years have many Latin American countries officially recognized their multiculturalism. This occurred in Ecuador, for example, for the first time in 1998, when the rewritten constitution acknowledged both Indigenous peoples and Afro-descendants as "indivisible" parts of the modern Ecuadorian state.[58] Yet still, Afro-Ecuadorians, like many other Afro-descendants in former colonies, continue to face discrimination and poverty.[59]

When we look at early modern images of difference, we can see many of the rooted attitudes of the colonial period that continued into the independence and post-independence periods. The visual record is

56. Jean Muteba Rahier, "From the Transatlantic Slave Trade to Contemporary Ethnoracial Law in Multicultural Ecuador: The 'Changing Same' of Anti-Black Racism as Revealed by Two Lawsuits Filed by Afrodescendants," *Current Anthropology* 61, no. S22 (2020): 248–59, https://doi.org/10.1086/710061.

57. Most famously José Vasconselos (1889–1959), the Mexican reformist minister of education, wrote on the *raza cosmica*, or the cosmic race that inherited the "best" of their Spanish and Indigenous forbearers.

58. Rahier, "Transatlantic," 251.

59. A 2019 United Nations report calls out the poverty in the region of Esmaraldas, a majority Afro-descendant province, as particularly indicative of such disparities. United Nations, "Much Work Needed to 'Target Unacceptable Levels' of Racism in Ecuador: Un Experts, UN News, accessed March 1, 2022, https://news.un.org/en/story/2019/12/1054201.

rife with images that projected the stereotype of an unruly, transgressive Black body that could be controlled only through European intervention. As demonstrated, the trope of the bowing, kneeling, submissive Black figure has a long history, seen in this paper's examples as early as Weiditz and de Bry in the sixteenth century. What is more, this iconography that was once associated with otherness of many kinds would become increasingly associated with Blackness in particular. The kneeling African, for instance, came to be a trope for the "Black slave" type, and featured often in emancipation visual culture, perhaps most famously on the masthead* of William Lloyd Garrison's (1805–1879) abolitionist newspaper *The Liberator*.[60]

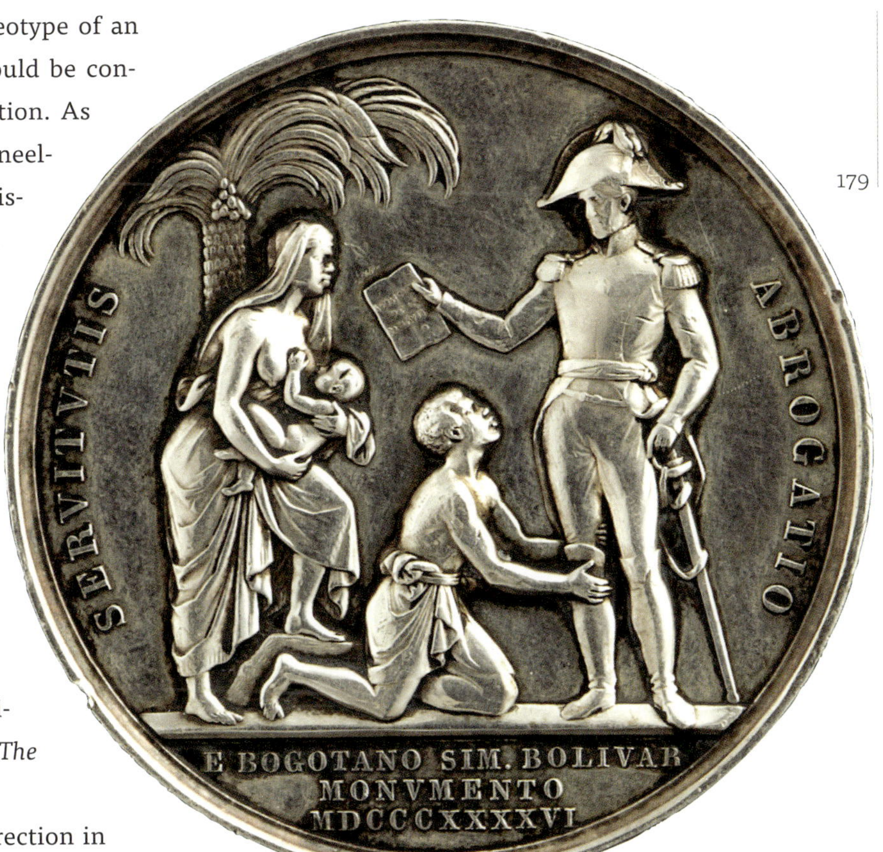

Figure 5.12
Tenerani and Voigt,
Bolivar Freeing the Slaves Statue Inauguration,
silver medal, 48.58 mm.;
57.96 gms, 1846,
Colonial Williamsburg Foundation,
accession #2002–28

An 1846 medal commemorates the erection in Bogotá, Colombia of a statue of Simón Bolívar, known as "*El Libertador*." One side of the medal reproduces a relief at the base of the statue (Figure 5.12). It shows Bolívar (1783–1830) standing at attention in classical contrapposto. He holds a book above a kneeling man behind whom crouches a nursing mother and child. Created by Italian Neoclassical sculptor Pietro Tenerani (1789–1869), the medal and relief celebrate Bolívar as the emancipator of South America's enslaved African population. During his campaigns against Spanish occupation, Bolívar, a *criollo*, received aid from Alexandre Pétion (1770–1818), a man of color and the first president of the Republic of Haiti. In return, Bolívar vowed to free slaves in the areas he liberated from Spain. In the relief we see how the artist portrays Bolívar in contrapposto and with a three-quarter view of his face. In contrast, the African figures are shown in profile, a convention used to convey servitude. They are rendered with full lips and round noses, following European conventions for African phenotypes. The female figure has her hair covered, while the male figure's hair is cropped short. In contrast with Bolívar's tailored military costume, the Africans are in a state of undress, both wearing only draped cloth threatening to come loose on their bottom halves. Here their bodies, though rendered no different in color to that of Bolívar due to the nature of the medium, are nonetheless revealed as Black bodies. They look up to their emancipator in deference and gratitude, almost a secularized version of the saved African alongside Saint Luis Beltrán.

Such images and the racial hierarchies they herald have come under scrutiny in recent years. In December of 2020 the Boston Art Commission voted to remove a statue of Abraham Lincoln (1809–1865)

60. See the digitization of *The Liberator* via the Smithsonian's National Museum of African American History and Culture: https://transcription.si.edu/project/11766.

that includes a Black man at his feet, kneeling with broken chains around his arms (Figure 5.13).[61] The statue, a copy after a Thomas Ball (1819–1911) prototype in Washington, D.C., depicts Lincoln holding the Emancipation Proclamation. It was commissioned by Black freedmen and Union veterans. Of the original statue Frederick Douglas (1818–1895) wrote: "The negro here, though rising, is still on his knees and nude. What I want to see before I die is a monument representing the negro, not couchant on his knees like a four-footed animal, but erect on his feet like a man."[62] Douglas highlights the importance of embodiment in communicating status. Though perhaps rising as Douglas mentions, the figure is subordinate to Lincoln who is couched as the white savior, thereby denying the agency of enslaved people in their own liberation. In more recent years, of course, Black male athletes beginning with Colin Kaepernick (b.1987) have re-signified the kneeling stance from servile to one of empowerment and protest.

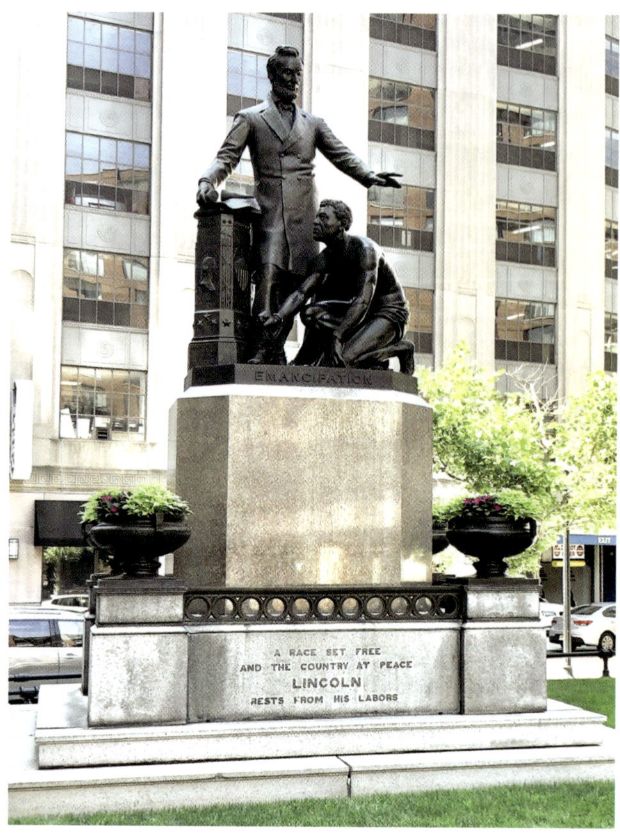

Figure 5.13
Copy of Thomas Ball, *Emancipation Memorial*, bronze, 1876, Boston

Along with pious stances, "savage" dances have a long posterity. The perceptions of Indigenous Americans, and to an even greater extent Africans and Afro-descendants as unrestrained and lacking civility that emerged and stabilized in the early modern period, continued to cast their long shadow in the twentieth and twenty-first centuries. In 1927, French illustrator Paul Colin (1892–1985) published *Le tumulte noir*, a portfolio of hand colored lithographs celebrating the African-American performers who shook the Parisian live stage of the *Années folles*, first among whom featured Josephine Baker (1906–1975).[63] The French visual artist's depictions of the dancers and his written memoirs of his first experience of the *Revue nègre* demonstrate the enduring hold of the visual and textual vocabulary for the representation of non-European dance and movement honed in the early modern period. In "Harlem on the Champs-Elysees," he wrote:

> Harlem with its contortions, its howls, its multicolored feathers against coal Black skin, its banner of trembling or hardened buttocks, its pairs of provocative, yielding, athletic, jolly breasts! Harlem, with its starched shirt fronts, its cotton fabrics, its boaters, its gray bowler hats, its pomaded hairdos, and its odors, exported to Europe for the first time the Charleston.[64]

61. Bill Chappell, "Statue of Lincoln with Formerly Enslaved Man at His Feet is Removed in Boston," *Race* (blog), *NPR*, December 29, 2020, https://www.npr.org/2020/12/29/951206414/statue-of-lincoln-with-freed-slave-at-his-feet-is-removed-in-boston.

62. Jonathan W. White and Scott Sandage, "What Frederick Douglass Had to Say about Monuments," *Smithsonian Magazine*, June 30, 2020, https://www.smithsonianmag.com/history/what-frederick-douglass-had-say-about-monuments-180975225/.

63. Karen CC Dalton and Henry Louis Gates Jr., "Josephine Baker and Paul Colin: African American Dance Seen through Parisian Eyes," *Critical Inquiry* 24, no. 4 (1998): 903–34, https://doi.org/10.1086/448901. See selections from the portfolio at "Le tumulte noir: Paul Colin's Jazz Age Portfolio," National Portrait Gallery, https://npg.si.edu/exh/noir/

64. Paul Colin, *La Croute (Souvenirs)* (Paris, 1957), 74. Translation from Dalton and Gates Jr., "Josephine Baker," 920.

Undress or improper use of clothing, dynamic motions of the limbs and bodily stances, feathers and dark skin are as much a concern for the twentieth-century artist as they were for his early modern predecessors. In a 1930 drawing, Colin surrounds the smiling face of Josephine Baker, radiant in her lacquered hairdo and *accroche-coeur* curls, with four dancing silhouettes capturing her crowd-slaying Charleston (Figure 5.14). The high forward and backward kicks, flying elbows, and hip tilts enhanced by hints of feathers over her naked Black body that shocked and seduced the Parisian public in equal measure are the clear heirs of the early modern European imagery of the "savage dance."

In the sixteenth and seventeenth centuries, the steps and attitudes Colin seized in his images had become under the brush, chisel, and etching needle of image-makers emblematic of European ideas of otherness. They still resonated as such in the primitivist project of Colin where they were no longer put to work to galvanize a contradistinctive European early modernity, but rather served as a provocative call to disband it. Colin saw in the movement of the dancer an otherness that he couched, along with the artistic avant-garde of the time, as a path towards "a new civilization, finally relieved of fetters centuries old."[65] Yet, the celebratory discourse of primitivism was and still is in its twenty-first century iterations steeped in racist ideas of essentialized otherness.

In 2021, Josephine Baker became the first Black woman recognized by a cenotaph* in the Panthéon, the French Mausoleum dedicated to its greatest national heroes. President Emanuel Macron (b. 1977) welcomed her in the monument as "War heroine. Fighter. Dancer. Singer," praising her role in the Resistance against the Nazis during World War II, glossing as universalism her anti-racist activism, and not entirely avoiding the pitfalls of primitivist language in his rightful celebration of her embodied fight against racial prejudice.[66] Macron's speech reframed Baker's resistance and activism as emblematic of French Republican values, where distinctions of race are subsumed under the homogenizing ideal of universalism. In doing so, it detached her struggle from the specificities of Black female experience of and resistance to racism. It also misread her powerful subversions of racialized discourse as a well-deserved, but ultimately gentle hand slap—or rather "hip swing"—brushing away the "clichés" held by an easily and willingly enlightened Parisian public.

The long historical perspective outlined in this essay reveals the deep currents underlying Josephine Baker's provocative moves. Her performance was not an easily achieved correction of superficial prejudice,

Figure 5.14
Paul Colin, *Josephine Baker*, crayon and gouache on paper, 1930, Framed: 44 in. × 32½ in. × 1½ in.), The Collection of Richard H. Driehaus, Chicago, inv. 49.2016.3

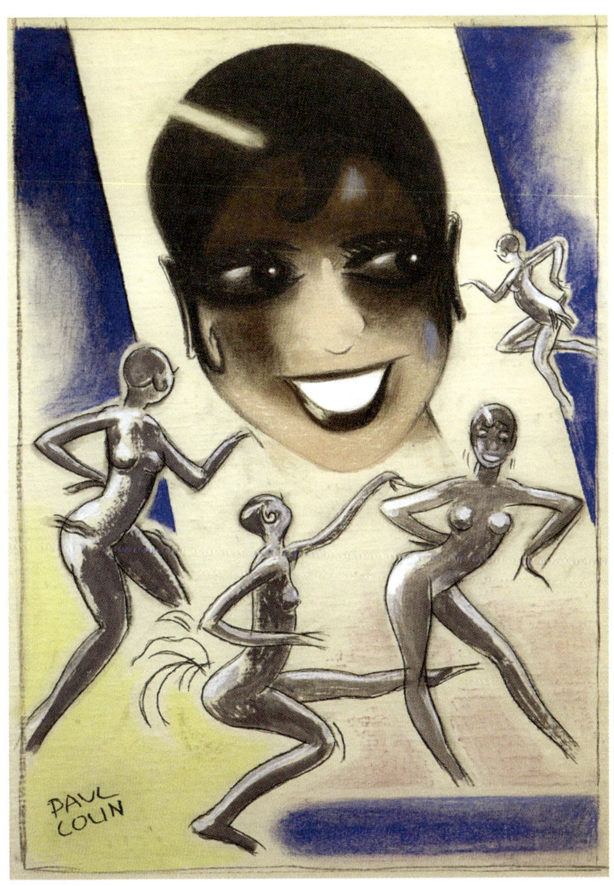

65. Dalton and Gates Jr., 921.

66. "Discours du Président de la République à l'occasion de la cérémonie d'entrée de Joséphine Baker au Panthéon," *Élysée*, 30 novembre, 2021, https://www.elysee.fr/emmanuel-macron/2021/11/30/josephine-baker-entre-au-pantheon.

but intervened on the terrain of centuries-old processes through which Europe created ideas and images of racialized otherness in support of its imperial and colonial projects. Her dance and political moves had more to do with the sardonic, knowing, and ultimately grave jig of the allegory of death than those of the fantasized engraved savage. Grotesque humor was central to her performance. With crossed eyes and grimaces, she both enhanced and threatened to break the spell that her hypersexualized dance moves and nudity held over her public. With the same trenchant edge as her skeletal counterparts, she held her viewers in a powerful headlock, bringing them face-to-face with the image of their flawed social stances. As viewers questioned the civility against which they judged the performance as unacceptably and/or liberatingly "savage," Baker's humorous grimaces and knowingly grotesque moves spelled a counter-text. She drew from a long genealogy of Black women that mobilized power by subverting racialized ideas of their bodies as licentious, sexually available, and commodifiable. As generations of African and Afro-descendant women whose life was waged in slavery and post-emancipation-era on the terrain of the Black Atlantic, her body, in the words of historian Jessica Marie Johnson "enacted a radical opposition to bondage, reinterpreting wickedness as freedom, intimacy as fugitive, and Blackness as diasporic and archipelagic*."[67]

The images of back-breaking labor, "savage" dances, and pious stances, Baker continues to remind us, are not only European projections of ideas of Otherness with enduring power. They are also records of the deep challenges and efficacious resistance that African and Indigenous men and women inflicted on Europe's ability to create and effect a worldview supporting their imperial desires and colonial ambitions.

67. Jessica Marie Johnson, *Wicked Flesh: Black Women, Intimacy, and Freedom in the Atlantic World* (Philadelphia: University of Pennsylvania Press, 2020), 10.

Note From the Field 3

BRINGING PREMODERN CRITICAL RACE CONSCIOUSNESS TO SHAKESPEARE'S GLOBE

Farah Karim-Cooper

I want to begin this essay by declaring that I deployed Premodern Critical Race Studies (PCRS) relatively late in my scholarly practice and career. While studying for my doctorate on cosmetics and early modern drama at the University of London in 1998, I attempted to pursue a critical race interpretation of women, beauty, and ideals of whiteness. Dismayingly, I was actively discouraged from doing so. I was in an academic institution where there were no scholars of color to speak of and no other students of color researching Shakespeare; the methodologies and expertise available were, therefore, limited in this domain. I was emphatically told that if I were to pursue this line of enquiry, I'd fail my Ph.D.; race was not considered a viable topic because it was "anachronistic." As such, I would be engaging in "projecting" my own identity onto the early modern text and analyzing a "fantasy" of racial construction in the period. I was being told that my observations were not to be trusted, that my lens was skewed by my own ethnicity and lived experience in a brown body.

I had just read Kim F. Hall's book, *Things of Darkness: Economies of Race and Gender in Early Modern England*, published two years before I started doing research for my Ph.D. research. She had proven beyond a shadow of a doubt that the discourse of beauty and whiteness were intersecting and that any discussion of cosmetic beauty had to engage with the linguistic and visual articulation of race. Since then, Margo Hendricks has reminded us of the critical genealogy of PCRS, that the study of racial formation and structures of difference had been a topic of discussion for decades by the early 2000s, and that it was a discipline that had been mostly ignored by much of mainstream Shakespeare scholarship. Yet, she observes, this is still an issue: the "problem of race and periodization continues, largely due to academic gatekeeping."[1] During my doctoral study, none of my own instructors were alert to this critical legacy, demonstrating the repeated violence enacted upon scholars of color in particular that is the omission, denial, and consequent relegation of Premodern Critical Race Studies to the margins. My status anxiety as a graduate student, my internalized racism, and my experiential impression that I categorically did *not* belong in British academia made me back down.

By 2017, PCRS and its methodologies finally emerged fully in my scholarship and in my curatorial practice within the public Shakespeare organization where I have worked since 2004. This essay will briefly chart this curatorial process and will remark upon the ways that cultural organizations have the power to integrate scholarly conversations into their programming that can influence and even alter the public discourse in impactful ways.

Shakespeare's Globe and its White History

Shakespeare's Globe has a legacy of Anglo-American privilege, although it was founded by immigrants, the American Sam Wanamaker and New Zealander Theo Crosby, who both were left-wing in their politics and had experienced marginalization in their own histories. The Globe nevertheless became associated with Tudor nostalgia, and with Shakespearean universality, which assumes that white, English exceptionalism is the norm and aspiration. It seems odd to make such a judgment, having spent almost twenty years there as its Head of Research and now one of its Directors of the Education department. But despite the intentions of its artists and educators, Shakespeare was nonetheless presented and received gladly as an icon of white, English identity.

It is undeniable that over the Globe's twenty-five years, it has created a richly varied program of education and artistic work. Casting diversely since the outset, though not consistently, the Globe was an actor's space and through its outreach and international fellowships, aimed to attract actors of all backgrounds. Meanwhile, the organization's research strategy revolved around the theatre buildings — the Globe Theatre and its indoor Jacobean counterpart, the Sam Wanamaker Playhouse — their fabric and construction, the craft and legacy of Tudor joinery, early modern theatre company practices, and the staging of early modern drama. This focus informed the creation and content of the Masters in Shakespeare Studies taught jointly between the Globe and King's College London for twenty years. Analyses of race and racial formation, however, did not figure into this matrix of research inquiries, however.

Despite its celebration of English theater history, the Globe has never been an insular organization. The creation of the Globe-to-Globe projects (international companies performing at the Globe and touring Globe shows into every country in the world), the talks and conferences on Shakespeare and Islam, Shakespeare and the Jews, and intercultural Shakespeare over the years signal that the organization recognized and acknowledged Shakespeare's global appeal and proved England did not "own" the Bard, nor should it. Moreover, its education department's quest to reach hundreds of thousands of school children through its many outreach projects, its Playing Shakespeare with Deutsche Bank program (which gives thousands of London and Birmingham schools free tickets to a play produced specifically for them) and its workshop program focusing on active approaches have introduced

1. Margo Hendricks, "Coloring the Past, Considerations of our Future: RaceB4Race," *New Literary History* 52, no. 3/4 (2021): 366. https://doi.org/10.1353/nlh.2021.0018

Shakespeare to diverse audiences of children for over thirty years. But in spite of this rich history of access, global-facing events, and artistic programming, the critical vocabularies that enable us to consider race and racial thinking did not enter rehearsal rooms, studios, or classrooms. The Globe, like most theatres in Britain, practiced colorblind casting in the interest of diversity. Artistic leaders programmed Shakespeare's "race" plays repeatedly, but without problematizing them, appointing only white directors to direct them. Once in rehearsal, there was no infrastructure enabling actors to unpack the racist and racialized language and characterizations in those plays. Shows continued to be designed, blocked, and lit without consciousness and attention to the effects of staging upon black and brown actors. As film studies academic Richard Dyer has shown, white faces are the norm, the baseline upon which photographic and theatrical technologies have been built, which ultimately have "the effect of privileging the white performer."[2] Indeed, the Globe's two historically informed theatres, particularly the indoor, candlelit Sam Wanamaker Playhouse, has perpetuated unknowingly this "privileging of the white performer." In the Education wing, there were conferences, seminars and lectures programmed every year that did not engage at all with PCRS, and rarely had a BIPOC scholar spoken on any of our platforms. Shakespeare's Globe inadvertently reflected other Shakespearean academic and performance spaces in the UK, which were, and largely still are, white spaces.

Shakespeare and Race in the White Space

"As long as whiteness is felt to be the human condition, then it alone both defines normality and fully inhabits it . . . the equation of being white with being human secures a position of power."[3] This belief in the normativity of whiteness and white experience characterizes the Shakespeare academy and much of the scholarship it produces, as well as performance venues dedicated to the Bard. American sociologist Elijah Anderson notes that a "city's public spaces, workplaces, and neighborhoods may now be conceptualized essentially as a mosaic of white spaces, black spaces, and cosmopolitan spaces," the latter defined as "racially diverse islands of civility."[4] We know that these spaces are not stable; "as demographics change," Anderson suggests, "public spaces are subject to change as well." White people who occupy white spaces often do so unawares: what white people perceive to be rather "diverse" environments, Black, Indigenous, People of Color "may see as homogeneously white and privileged."[5] This misconception characterized Shakespeare's Globe for many years. With its predominantly white directors, creatives and production teams, its white-only leadership (until now) and its mainly white educators at the time, the Globe had work to do not only to diversify its staff and faculty, but also to commit to developing a sense of *belonging*. Moreover, the organization would need to ensure that scholars and artists of color felt empowered to effect change and shape the conversation.

In 2017 I proposed a week-long festival on "Shakespeare and Race," that would focus on Shakespeare studies and theatre performance; it suggested platforming mainly the voices of scholars and theatre artists of color. What felt like an obvious next phase for our research focus, turned out to be much more revolutionary, and I had not grasped the extent of the kind of revolution we could create. None of us anticipated how many people we would be upsetting amongst the community of theatre critics and audiences who had been "fans" of the Globe for many years. I never imagined how many toes we would step on just by asking Black, Asian, and South Asian scholars to take up

2. Richard Dyer, *White* (London & New York: Routledge, 1992), 101.

3. Dyer, *White*, 9.

4. Elijah Anderson, "The White Space," *Sociology of Race and Ethnicity* 1, no. 1. (2014): 11, https://doi.org/10.1177/2332649214561306.

5. Anderson, "White Space," 11.

space and talk about their experience and knowledge of Shakespeare's world and texts.

Shakespeare and Race was more than a festival; it was an inquiry that would become a permanent focus for the academics and artists based at the Globe. It initially revolved around a set of defining questions:

- How does Shakespeare's work engage with race, racism and Black people and those hailing from a minority ethnic background?
- What was the early modern experience of race?
- How do modern productions of Shakespeare tackle race?
- How do theatre artists engage or not engage with it?
- Do actors and creatives of color have access to the same opportunities to pursue a career in theatre and to maintain their careers?
- How does unconscious bias enable white actors to have the advantage when it comes to costume, lighting, and set design?
- What does it mean to be from the global majority and study, teach, perform, produce, or read Shakespeare?
- How does antisemitism and anti-Black racism permeate the reception of Shakespeare?

As an international cultural center with iconic theatre spaces and a global presence, we needed to explore the ways Shakespeare's plays, his theaters, and his moment could be put in dialogue with the present, with our diverse cultures and our diverse bodies. The festival was also a direct response to the 2016 special issue of *Shakespeare Quarterly*, edited by Kim F. Hall and Peter Erickson, in which they set clear objectives for advancing PCRS, which included the call for deeper, more exploratory conversations about race in performance.[6]

The festival consisted of a Folger Library-sponsored performance of *American Moor* by Keith Hamilton Cobb, which dramatizes a Black actor's experience of and response to Shakespeare, a workshop on unconscious bias in lighting and set design, lectures and interviews with Black and South Asian artists and a two-day conference focused on Anglo-American discussions of Shakespeare and Race, opened by Critical Race theorists and legal scholars Kimberlé Crenshaw, Luke Harris, and Devon Carbado. The general public had access to all the events; they read blogs and program notes and listened to an accompanying podcast series, creating the scaffolding necessary to empower them to engage with the conversation in which they were invited to take part. This initiative also enabled participating Black and brown artists in the UK and the US to feel that the Globe was accessible in ways they hadn't imagined. This is not to say that the Globe's doors had not been open to BIPOC artists, but did they feel empowered to have high stakes conversations in the rehearsal room? Did they feel like they had somewhere to report or express concerns about microaggressions on site, in the rehearsal rooms or in reviews? Did they feel as if their bodies could ever be brought to bear upon the roles they were playing or were they asked to erase their race and play Shakespeare as if they were white? The festival stimulated conversations and took the lid off a hot pot that had been bubbling for a long time. Subsequently, in 2019, the Globe's long-standing partnerships and work on drama school training became a subject for an exploration of inclusive practices in actor training and in the industry. That same year, the Globe staged the first all women-of-color production of any Shakespeare play. *Richard II*, conceived of and directed by its star, Adjoa Andoh and co-directed by Lynette Lynton, in the Sam Wanamaker Playhouse was a response to Brexit and the conversations it provoked about English identity: *Who* is English? What does it mean to look back on an English past and see that it was not racially homogenous? What better way to explore such questions than

6. Kim F. Hall and Peter Erickson, eds. *Shakespeare Quarterly*, 67, no. 1 (2016), https://doi.org/10.1353/shq.2016.0002.

with an English history play known for the simultaneous celebration and questioning of "this sceptred Isle" and told entirely by British women of color?

Shakespeare and Race as a method of inquiry explored the many levels of exclusion and white racial privileging that had characterized the Shakespeare industry in the UK and, in large part, the US, but the UK had been leagues behind when it came to having a national conversation about race. The festival left an indelible impression upon the identity of Shakespeare's Globe and has since led to a larger inquiry about the lack of racial diversity in early modern studies in the UK and in the theatre industry. The fact that, as of 2019, there were still no Black Shakespeare or early modern scholars employed by a UK university led me to host a 'Diversity forum' in January of 2020, where I invited early modernists from across the UK to the Globe to discuss this gap and how we could close it as a community of scholars and institutions. It was shocking how many people did *not* reply to the invitation and how many did not show up. But of those who did, many are now crucial allies and change-makers at their institutions. COVID-19 locked down the country, demonstrating how much more vulnerable ethnically diverse people were to its ravages, and in the wake of George Floyd's murder, the global rise of Black Lives Matter shone its light upon the theatre industry and the academy in the UK. If anything, our Shakespeare and Race festival, underpinned as it was by Critical Race questions, had launched a journey of change that took on an even more powerful significance and momentum in the face of the brutal reality of systemic racism.

Antiracist Shakespeare and the "Woke" Wars

One of the most disturbing challenges of conducting conversations about race in a public or cultural organization is the racist backlash, fed by the deliberate misunderstanding and willful ignorance of editorialists, conservative, right-wing press and its army of "anti-woke" followers on social media. In 2021, our inquiry developed a new phase, as we partnered with Cambridge University Press to curate free webinars — *Antiracist Shakespeare* — each one featuring a scholar and artist discussing a Shakespeare play in the Globe's theatre seasons. The webinars are free and easily accessible. Their announcement elicited an ugly response. Letters condemning our scholarship and artistry, editorials undermining the scholars and artists of color participating in the discussions attacked the Globe for its so-called "woke" agenda. Newspapers and social media expressed dismay at the "sideshow," suggesting that approaching Shakespeare in this way was a response only to the "woke drum" and, like the toppling of the statue of slaver Edward Colston in Bristol in 2020, the greatest canon of works would be next. Clearly, the critical lineage of PCRS so clearly articulated by Margo Hendricks was entirely lost on the critics of Antiracist Shakespeare.[7] It was as if academic conversations about race, postcolonialism*, and cultural exchanges had never taken place and were only instigated by the events of 2020. Taking part in a fabricated culture war was those writers' only agenda. The culture war threatens the social justice endeavors not just of scholars but of public institutions that are trying to become more accessible and inclusive. *The Telegraph's* insistence that antiracism work is "nonsense," for example, is dangerous, not to mention, racist:

7. Dominic Cavendish, "The Woke Brigade are Closet to 'Cancelling' Shakespeare," *The Telegraph*, 9 February 2020, https://www.telegraph.co.uk/theatre/what-to-see/woke-brigade-close-cancelling-shakespeare/

> The Globe has form for this sort of nonsense. Its website claims there are "harmful, challenging and uncomfortable moments in Shakespeare." And if you doubt it, you should have paid attention to its "Anti-Racist Shakespeare" project, which ran last summer.[8]

The Telegraph's sentiment is echoed by *The Daily Mail*:

> "There are things in the plays that are really harmful to contemporary audiences," explained one participant, Madeline Sayet of Arizona State University. "They do have these violent colonial implications . . . If you're reading Shakespeare's plays and you're not seeing any sexism or racism, then there's a lot of education that I think, as a human being, you need to be looking at." That last sentence is wonderfully revealing. You're not really allowed to disagree with Ms. Sayet, because if you don't think Shakespeare is sexist and racist, you need a "lot of education."[9]

The article is attacking the new initiatives of the Royal Shakespeare Company's education department to deliver a Shakespeare that is more "relevant," but the Globe's webinars are simultaneously attacked, undermining if not mocking Indigenous scholars/practitioners, like Madeline Sayet for their insights into *The Tempest*.

The "sideshow" is this unbalanced and ill-informed response, not the action. Crucially, the underpinning principles and methodologies of Premodern Critical Race Studies are sustainable within a performing arts venue brave enough to integrate its ideas not only into its public conversations but also its rehearsal rooms, something we have begun at the Globe. Antiracist webinars are only one small feature of a larger infrastructural project, which will take a few years. The project includes the creation of an antiracist taskforce that examines the systemic nature of racism at the Globe; the introduction of training workshops for teachers on antiracist active approaches to Shakespeare in the classroom; a re-tooled auditioning and rehearsal process as well as support structures for its artists; a more studied racial consciousness in approaches to casting; serious attentiveness to design and its impact on artists of color; an attention to the diversification of the student body and faculty in the higher education program; the gradual diversification of leadership, staff, and faculty and a consistent educational journey for all. A crucial initiative is the creation of the Shakespeare Centre London, a research partnership between King's College London and Shakespeare's Globe: a significant strand of the Shakespeare Centre London's work is to develop pipeline strategies and to widen access to Shakespeare Studies for students of color in an endeavor to shift the racial demographic of Shakespearean expertise. Premodern Critical Race Studies is sustained by its clarity of methodology, passionate activism, and by the rigor of its practice. When it underpins the antiracist work of a cultural organization, its expression becomes public, accessible, and potentially change-making. The centering of race in conversations at Shakespeare's Globe upset the status quo and made certain audiences and critics deeply uncomfortable, but it has also opened the doors a bit wider, altered public perception, and brought awareness of the role Shakespeare has played and continues to play in our racial discourse — which is a good start.

8. Dominic Cavendish, "Why 'Problematic' Shakespeare is in Danger of Being Cancelled," *The Sunday Telegraph*, 9 February 2020; Dominic Cavendish, "William Shakespeare Was an Empty Vessel: He Doesn't Need Decolonising," *The Telegraph*, 17 September 2021, https://www.telegraph.co.uk/theatre/what-to-see/shakespeare-empty-vessel-doesnt-need-decolonising/

9. Dominic Sandbrook, "The Royal Shakespeare Company Should be Ashamed of Its Campaign to Tarnish Britain's Greatest Writer with the Woke Obsessions of Our Age," *The Daily Mail*, 9 February 2022, https://www.dailymail.co.uk/debate/article-10491873/DOMINIC-SANDBROOK-Royal-Shakespeare-Company-ashamed-woke-campaign.html

EXHIBITION CATALOG

PART 3. PERFORMING

Case Study #1. Literary Drama

ENTRY #27

William Shakespeare (1564–1616)
"The Tragedy of Othello, the Moore of Venice" in *Mr. William Shakespeares comedies, histories, and tragedies: published according to the true originall copies,* 1632
Book with letterpress, engraving, and woodcuts
Case folio YS .02

Shakespeare's *Othello* (1604) constitutes the most well-known representation of Blackness on the early modern English stage: the play famously follows the trajectory of Othello, a "Moor" and general in service to Venice, and his doomed marriage to Desdemona. The plot is partially derived from a novella by the Italian writer Giovanni Battista Giraldi, also known as Cinthio (1504–1573). The play text, particularly in the speech of Othello who details a personal history that includes a period of enslavement, incorporates language reminiscent of popular early modern travelogues; such travel writings blend personal narrative with fantastical accounts of an exoticized world outside England. *Othello* is often read and taught side by side with the Moorish characters of Vecellio's 1590s costume book *De gli habiti antichi et moderni di diversi parti del* mondo (Cat. No. 8).

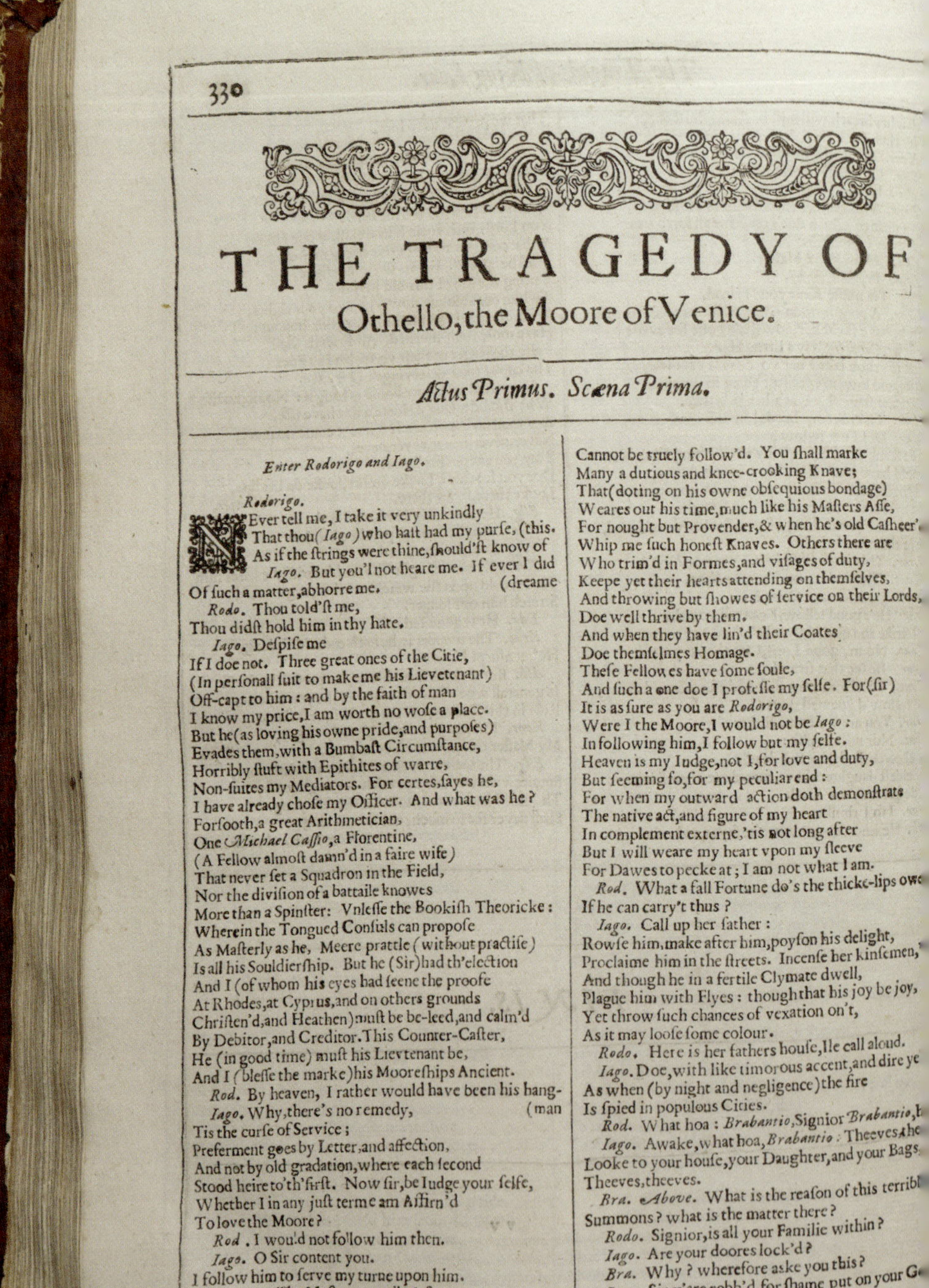

330

THE TRAGEDY OF
Othello, the Moore of Venice.

Actus Primus. Scæna Prima.

Enter Rodorigo and Iago.

Rodorigo.
NEver tell me, I take it very unkindly
That thou (*Iago*) who haſt had my purſe, (this.
As if the ſtrings were thine, ſhould'ſt know of
Iago. But you'l not heare me. If ever I did (dreame
Of ſuch a matter, abhorre me.
Rodo. Thou told'ſt me,
Thou didſt hold him in thy hate.
Iago. Deſpiſe me
If I doe not. Three great ones of the Citie,
(In perſonall ſuit to make me his Lievetenant)
Off-capt to him: and by the faith of man
I know my price, I am worth no wofe a place.
But he (as loving his owne pride, and purpoſes)
Evades them, with a Bumbaſt Circumſtance,
Horribly ſtuft with Epithites of warre,
Non-ſuites my Mediators. For certes, ſayes he,
I have already choſe my Officer. And what was he?
Forſooth, a great Arithmetician,
One *Michael Caſſio*, a Florentine,
(A Fellow almoſt damn'd in a faire wife)
That never ſet a Squadron in the Field,
Nor the diviſion of a battaile knowes
More than a Spinſter: Vnleſſe the Bookiſh Theoricke:
Wherein the Tongued Conſuls can propoſe
As Maſterly as he, Meere prattle (without practiſe)
Is all his Souldierſhip. But he (Sir) had th'election
And I (of whom his eyes had ſeene the proofe
At Rhodes, at Cyprus, and on others grounds
Chriſten'd, and Heathen) muſt be be-leed, and calm'd
By Debitor, and Creditor. This Counter-Caſter,
He (in good time) muſt his Lievtenant be,
And I (bleſſe the marke) his Mooreſhips Ancient.
Rod. By heaven, I rather would have been his hang- (man
Iago. Why, there's no remedy,
Tis the curſe of Service;
Preferment goes by Letter, and affection,
And not by old gradation, where each ſecond
Stood heire to'th'firſt. Now ſir, be Iudge your ſelfe,
Whether I in any juſt terme am Affirn'd
To love the Moore?
Rod. I would not follow him then.
Iago. O Sir content you.
I follow him to ſerve my turne upon him.
We cannot all be Maſters, nor all Maſters
Cannot be truely follow'd. You ſhall marke
Many a dutious and knee-crooking Knave;
That (doting on his owne obſequious bondage)
Weares out his time, much like his Maſters Aſſe,
For nought but Provender, & when he's old Caſheer'
Whip me ſuch honeſt Knaves. Others there are
Who trim'd in Formes, and viſages of duty,
Keepe yet their hearts attending on themſelves,
And throwing but ſhowes of ſervice on their Lords,
Doe well thrive by them.
And when they have lin'd their Coates
Doe themſelmes Homage.
Theſe Fellowes have ſome ſoule,
And ſuch a one doe I profeſſe my ſelfe. For (ſir)
It is as ſure as you are *Rodorigo*,
Were I the Moore, I would not be *Iago*:
In following him, I follow but my ſelfe.
Heaven is my Iudge, not I, for love and duty,
But ſeeming ſo, for my peculiar end:
For when my outward action doth demonſtrate
The native act, and figure of my heart
In complement externe, 'tis not long after
But I will weare my heart vpon my ſleeve
For Dawes to pecke at; I am not what I am.
Rod. What a fall Fortune do's the thicke-lips owe
If he can carry't thus?
Iago. Call up her father:
Rowſe him, make after him, poyſon his delight,
Proclaime him in the ſtreets. Incenſe her kinſemen,
And though he in a fertile Clymate dwell,
Plague him with Flyes: though that his joy be joy,
Yet throw ſuch chances of vexation on't,
As it may looſe ſome colour.
Rodo. Here is her fathers houſe, Ile call aloud.
Iago. Doe, with like timorous accent, and dire ye
As when (by night and negligence) the fire
Is ſpied in populous Cities.
Rod. What hoa: *Brabantio*, Signior *Brabantio*,
Iago. Awake, what hoa, *Brabantio*: Theeves, the
Looke to your houſe, your Daughter, and your Bags,
Theeves, theeves.
Bra. Above. What is the reaſon of this terribl
Summons? what is the matter there?
Rodo. Signior, is all your Familie within?
Iago. Are your doores lock'd?
Bra. Why? wherefore aske you this?
Iago. Sir, y'are robb'd, for ſhame put on your G

Othello was performed widely in the seventeenth century and in a range of settings, including the Stuart Court and the Globe Theatre. Little is known as to the specific

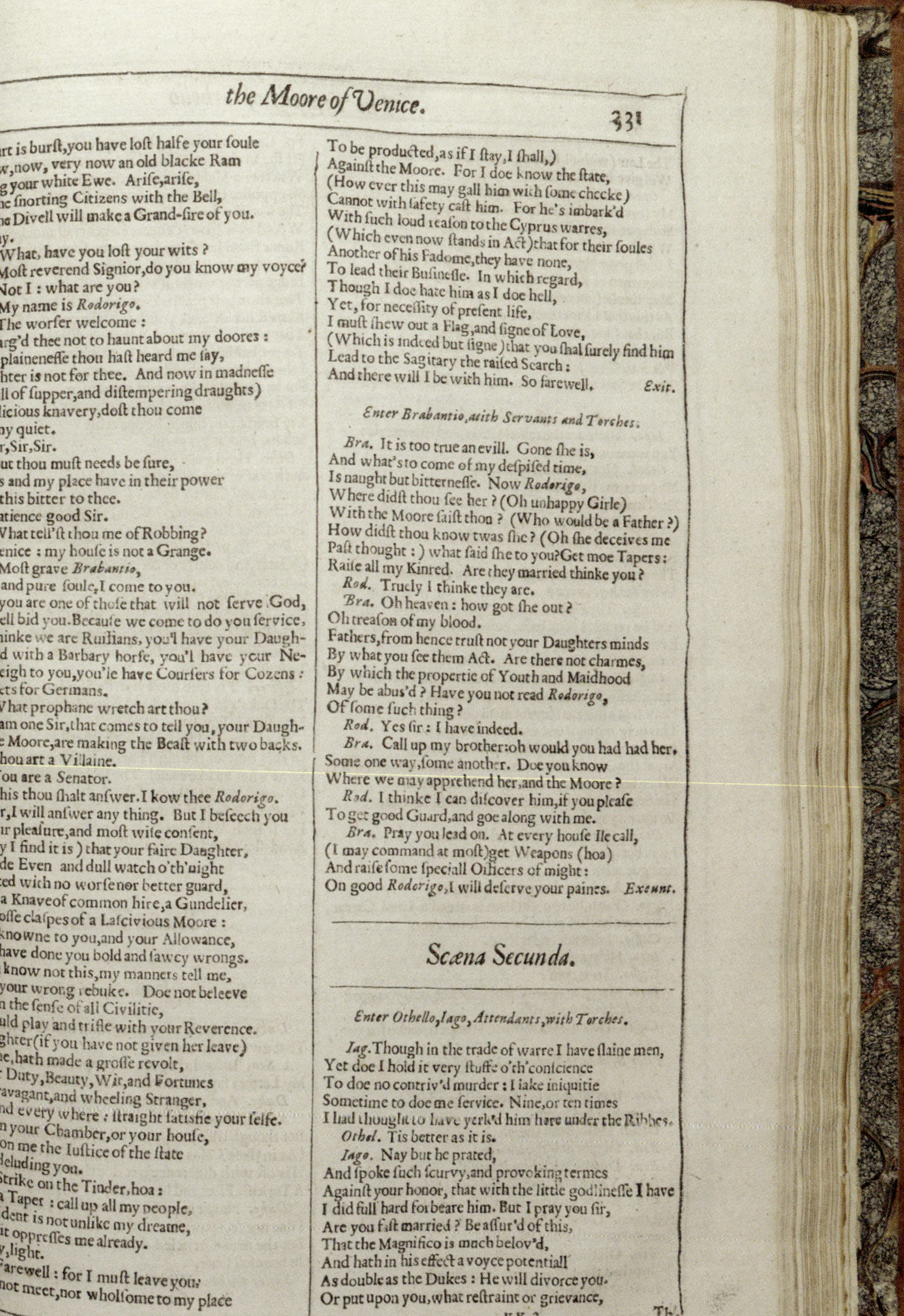

the Moore of Venice. 331

eart is burſt,you have loſt halfe your ſoule
ow,now, very now an old blacke Ram
ing your white Ewe. Ariſe,ariſe,
the ſnorting Citizens with the Bell,
the Divell will make a Grand-ſire of you.
ſay.
. What, have you loſt your wits ?
. Moſt reverend Signior,do you know my voyce?
. Not I : what are you?
. My name is *Rodorigo*.
. The worſer welcome :
harg'd thee not to haunt about my doores :
ſt plaineneſſe thou haſt heard me ſay,
ughter is not for thee. And now in madneſſe
full of ſupper,and diſtempering draughts)
alicious knavery,doſt thou come
t my quiet.
Sir,Sir,Sir.
But thou muſt needs be ſure,
its and my place have in their power
e this bitter to thee.
Patience good Sir.
What tell'ſt thou me of Robbing?
Venice : my houſe is not a Grange.
. Moſt grave *Brabantio*,
le and pure ſoule,I come to you.
ir,you are one of thoſe that will not ſerve God,
ivell bid you.Becauſe we come to do you ſervice,
thinke we are Ruffians, you'l have your Daugh-
er'd with a Barbary horſe, you'l have your Ne-
s neigh to you,you'le have Courſers for Cozens :
nnets for Germans.
What prophane wretch art thou?
I am one Sir,that comes to tell you, your Daugh-
the Moore,are making the Beaſt with two backs.
Thou art a Villaine.
You are a Senator.
This thou ſhalt anſwer.I know thee *Rodorigo*.
Sir,I will anſwer any thing. But I beſeech you
our pleaſure,and moſt wiſe conſent,
rtly I find it is) that your faire Daughter,
odde Even and dull watch o'th'night
orted with no worſe nor better guard,
h a Knave of common hire,a Gundelier,
groſſe claſpes of a Laſcivious Moore :
e knowne to you,and your Allowance,
n have done you bold and ſawcy wrongs.
ou know not this,my manners tell me,
e your wrong rebuke. Doe not beleeve
om the ſenſe of all Civilitie,
would play and trifle with your Reverence.
aughter(if you have not given her leave)
aine,hath made a groſſe revolt,
her Duty,Beauty,Wit,and Fortunes
xtravagant,and wheeling Stranger,
and every where : ſtraight ſatisfie your ſelfe.
e in your Chamber,or your houſe,
ſe on me the Iuſtice of the ſtate
s deluding you.
Strike on the Tinder,hoa :
e a Taper : call up all my people,
ccident is not unlike my dreame,
of it oppreſſes me already.
ſay,light.
Farewell : for I muſt leave you:
es not meet,nor wholſome to my place

To be producted,as if I ſtay,I ſhall,)
Againſt the Moore. For I doe know the ſtate,
(How ever this may gall him with ſome checke)
Cannot with ſafety caſt him. For he's imbark'd
With ſuch loud reaſon to the Cyprus warres,
(Which even now ſtands in Act)that for their ſoules
Another of his Fadome,they have none,
To lead their Buſineſſe. In which regard,
Though I doe hate him as I doe hell,
Yet,for neceſſity of preſent life,
I muſt ſhew out a Flag,and ſigne of Love,
(Which is indeed but ſigne)that you ſhal ſurely find him
Lead to the Sagitary the raiſed Search:
And there will I be with him. So farewell. *Exit.*

Enter Brabantio,with Servants and Torches.

Bra. It is too true an evill. Gone ſhe is,
And what's to come of my deſpiſed time,
Is naught but bitterneſſe. Now *Rodorigo*,
Where didſt thou ſee her ? (Oh unhappy Girle)
With the Moore ſaiſt thou ? (Who would be a Father ?)
How didſt thou know twas ſhe? (Oh ſhe deceives me
Paſt thought :) what ſaid ſhe to you?Get moe Tapers:
Raiſe all my Kinred. Are they married thinke you?
Rod. Truely I thinke they are.
Bra. Oh heaven : how got ſhe out?
Oh treaſon of my blood.
Fathers,from hence truſt not your Daughters minds
By what you ſee them Act. Are there not charmes,
By which the propertie of Youth and Maidhood
May be abus'd? Have you not read *Rodorigo*,
Of ſome ſuch thing?
Rod. Yes ſir : I have indeed.
Bra. Call up my brother:oh would you had had her.
Some one way,ſome another. Doe you know
Where we may apprehend her,and the Moore?
Rod. I thinke I can diſcover him,if you pleaſe
To get good Guard,and goe along with me.
Bra. Pray you lead on. At every houſe Ile call,
(I may command at moſt)get Weapons (hoa)
And raiſe ſome ſpeciall Officers of might:
On good *Roderigo*,I will deſerve your paines. *Exeunt.*

Scæna Secunda.

Enter Othello,Iago,Attendants,with Torches.

*Iag.*Though in the trade of warre I have ſlaine men,
Yet doe I hold it very ſtuffe o'th'conſcience
To doe no contriv'd murder : I lacke iniquitie
Sometime to doe me ſervice. Nine,or ten times
I had thought t'have yerk'd him here under the Ribbes.
Othel. Tis better as it is.
Iago. Nay but he prated,
And ſpoke ſuch ſcurvy,and provoking termes
Againſt your honor, that with the little godlineſſe I have
I did full hard forbeare him. But I pray you ſir,
Are you faſt married? Be aſſur'd of this,
That the Magnifico is much belov'd,
And hath in his effect a voyce potentiall
As double as the Dukes : He will divorce you.
Or put upon you,what reſtraint or grievance,
VV 2 Th

Entry #27

mechanics of its early modern staging of Blackness, but we know that, generally, Blackamoor characters were performed in black-up in early modern English performance culture. The play's popularity and extensive performance history position *Othello* as an enduring race-making object. The play constructs its own self-defined category of "Moor," reinforces medieval and early modern associations of Blackness with the devil, and sensationalizes interracial relationships as inherently dangerous to white femininity for centuries of productions to follow.

Further Readings

Akhimie, Patricia. "*Othello*, Blackness, and the Process of Marking X." Chap. 1 in *Shakespeare and the Cultivation of Difference: Race and Conduct in the Early Modern World*. New York: Routledge, 2018.

Smith, Ian. "White Skin, Black Masks: Racial Cross-Dressing on the Early Modern Stage." *Renaissance Drama* 32 (2003): 33–67. https://doi.org/10.1086/rd.32.41917375.

Thompson, Ayanna. "Introduction." In *Othello*. By William Shakespeare. Edited by E.A.J. Honigmann, 1–116. New York: Bloomsbury Publishing, 2016.

Beatrice Bradley

ENTRY #28 (NO IMAGE)

Thomas Rymer (1641–1713)
A short view of tragedy it's original, excellency and corruption: with some reflections on Shakespear and other practitioners for the stage, 1693
Book with letterpress
Case Y 0278 .77

Thomas Rymer's scholarly work *A short view of tragedy* (1693) glosses over the literary history of tragedy on the European stage, tracing the genre's successes and failures from ancient Greece to seventeenth century England. Embracing neoclassical* views, Rymer believes a tragedy is made up of four essential parts: the fable, the characters, the rhetoric, and the expression. By mobilizing these elements, a tragedy distills the essence of beauty and humanity into literary knowledge that transcends superficial sensory pleasure. Rymer criticizes contemporaries such as Shakespeare on the basis that his plays are "bloody farces" that betray the tragic tradition. Yet, in pointing out contemporary tragedies' deviations from the classical model, he also inadvertently reveals how literary productions are indeed rooted in changing social circumstances. The book's struggle to reconcile tragedy's essence with its history is best reflected in the chapter on *Othello*, as Rymer projects his anxieties onto analyses of Shakespeare's Black general.

Rymer argues that *Othello* is a fable with unconvincing characters that lacks relevance to life. Desdemona defies the expectations attached to aristocratic daughters, while Iago is nothing like a virtuous soldier. Othello's credibility is questioned on the basis of his identity: Rymer does not find it probable that a Black character could possess a name, a reputation, let alone gain trust from Venetians to be a general. Blackness is posited as an essence that cannot be transcended at the very end of the seventeenth century. Rymer's neoclassical dismissal of the play's verisimilitude ironically mirrors the prejudices that Othello experiences in the play.

Further Readings

Cacicedo, Alberto. "Othello, Stranger in a Strange Land." *Interdisciplinary Literary Studies* 18, no. 1 (2016): 7–27. https://doi.org/10.5325/intelitestud.18.1.0007.

Cannan, Paul D. "'A Short View of Tragedy' and Rymer's Proposals for Regulating the English Stage." *The Review of English Studies* 52, no. 206 (2001): 207–26. https://doi.org/10.1093/res/52.206.207.

Nicholson, Catherine. "'Othello' and the Geography of Persuasion." *English Literary Renaissance* 40, no. 1 (2010): 56–87. https://doi.org/10.1111/j.1475-6757.2009.01061.x.

Vivian Lei

ENTRY #29 (NO IMAGE)

Jean-François Ducis (1733–1816)
Othello, ou, Le more de Venise: *Tragédie*
Book with letterpress, 1794
FRC 17779

Jean-François Ducis's adaptation of *Othello* premiered at the Théâtre de la République in November 1792, at the height of French Revolution fever. Ducis had previously adapted several Shakespearean plays, but with superstar François-Joseph Talma as lead, *Othello* would be his greatest success. In the "*avertissement*" (warning), Ducis warns the reader that he had Talma use bronzeface instead of the blackface in vogue on

English stages in order not to "revolt the ladies' eyes" and to let the actor use facial expressions more effectively. Arguing that the most brutal aspects of Shakespeare's play could not please "le caractère de la nation française" (the character of the French nation), Ducis published the play with two alternative endings: in the happy version, allies stop Othello from murdering Desdemona in the nick of time.

Both versions, however, emphasize the role of General Othello as the precious instrument of a State whose Frenchness is palpable in its pervasive revolutionary language. The happy version ends with Othello stating: "Should rebels trouble the Republic / And tear her down, let me save it / Or die trying." The prolonged opposition of Desdemona's father to her wedding leads him to conspire against the State itself, construing racism as a political crime of grave import. It may not be a coincidence that Ducis dedicated his *Othello* to his brother in Saint-Domingue, about half a year after the National Assembly granted political and civil rights to free men of color as a compromise following the start of the Haitian Revolution. At the time, abolitionist plays flourished in Paris.

Further Readings

Carlson, Marvin, trans. *Shakespeare Made French: Four Plays by Jean-François Ducis*. New York: Martin E. Segal Theatre Center Publications, 2013.

Chalaye, Sylvie. *Du Noir au Nègre: L'image du Noir au théâtre (1550–1960)*. Paris: L'Harmattan, 1998.

Monaco, Marion. *Shakespeare On the French Stage in the Eighteenth Century*. Paris: Didier, 1974.

Noémie Ndiaye

ENTRY #30 (NO IMAGE)

Aphra Behn (1640–1689)
Oroonoko, or The Royal Slave (1688),
in *The histories and novels of the late ingenious Mrs Behn: in one volume. Viz. Oroonoko, or The royal slave. . . etc*, 1696
Book with letterpress
Case 3A 483

Aphra Behn's 1688 novella, *Oroonoko*, was reprinted in this posthumous 1696 collection of her works in prose. The title page draws attention to Behn's career-long experimentation with narrative form, as "Histories and Novels" is printed in the largest font on the page. *Oroonoko* is the lead title of this collection, which is fitting as *Oroonoko* is often considered one of the first novels written in the English language. The narrative follows the life of African aristocrats Imoinda and Oroonoko. The story recounts their romance in Coramantien and their separate capture and enslavement by white traders operating in colonial Surinam. In Surinam, Imoinda and Oroonoko are reunited and initiate a slave rebellion that leads to their deaths.

Oroonoko's form and ethics are indeterminate: Is this an early novel? Is this proto-abolitionist fiction? Narrative ambiguity is a hallmark of the novel form —from the unreliable narrator, to the irrepresentability of the spectacular scene of dismemberment befalling the protagonist, to the tenuous relationship between reality and fiction. These novelistic elements produce a complex representation of early plantation relationships between race and gender, properties and persons, enslavement and freedom. While Behn's female narrator appears sympathetic to Oroonoko and Imoinda's plight, her inaction upon their rebellion's dissolution demonstrates the fraught bonds between colonial white women and enslaved Black persons. In doing so, the novel lays bare the complicity of white sentimentality within structures of colonialism and slavery. Behn's passive gaze on Oroonoko's gruesome end parallels the passive white gaze of her novel's audience.

Further Readings

Anderson, Emily Hodgson. "Novelty in Novels: A Look at What's New in Aphra Behn's *Oroonoko*." *Studies in the Novel* 39, no. 1 (2007): 1–16. https://www.jstor.org/stable/29533796.

Ellis, Markman. "'The house of bondage': Sentimentalism and the Problem of Slavery." Chap. 2 in *The Politics of Sensibility: Race, Gender, and Commerce in the Sentimental Novel*. Cambridge, UK: Cambridge University Press, 2004.

Ferguson, Margaret W. "Juggling the Categories of Race, Class and Gender: Aphra Behn's *Oroonoko*." In *Troping Oroonoko from Behn to Bandele*, edited by Susan B. Iwanisziw, 16–34. London: Routledge, 2018.

Sarah-Gray Lesley

ENTRY #31 (NO IMAGE)

Thomas Southerne (1660–1746), author;
Based on the novel by Aphra Behn (1640–1689)
Oroonoko: a tragedy as it is acted at the Theatre-Royal, by His Majesty's servants, 1696
Book with letterpress
Case Y 135 .S7269

The title page of Thomas Southerne's 1696 play, *Oroonoko*, occludes that it is an adaptation of Aphra Behn's 1688 novel by the same name. This omission is prophetic for *Oroonoko*'s eighteenth-century reception history: Southerne's play (first performed in 1695) is referenced far more often than the original in later adaptations. The differences between Southerne's play and Behn's novel reveal what later audiences preferred. Southerne's play is entirely set in Surinam, omitting Imoinda and Oroonoko's love story in Coramantien, which is central to Behn's novel. He replaces it with a romantic-comedy subplot for new characters — the white Welldon sisters. His most striking change, however, is his choice to whiten Imoinda, who is Black in Behn's novel. It is this version of Imoinda that survives into the eighteenth century.

In whitening Imoinda, Southerne puts his story in dialogue with another famous seventeenth-century play featuring a Black protagonist — William Shakespeare's *Othello* (1604). In both Behn's and Southerne's versions, Imoinda dies willingly by her husband's hand, but Southerne's staging of a white woman's death at the will of her Black husband uniquely evokes Desdemona's fate in *Othello*. Southerne thus dramatizes, exaggerates, and tropes the white racial fantasy of the passive white woman and the violent Black man. Made canon by Shakespeare, this fantasy is translated here onto the early plantation setting. In obscuring Behn's place as source author, adding a white romantic-comedy subplot, and whitening Imoinda, Southerne's *Oroonoko* anchors its conception of race in fantasies of white femininity.

Further Readings

MacDonald, Joyce Green. "Race, Women, and the Sentimental in Thomas Southerne's *Oroonoko*." *Criticism* 40, no. 4 (1998): 555–70. http://www.jstor.org/stable/23124316.

———. "The Disappearing African Woman: Imoinda in *Oroonoko* after Behn." Chap. 4 in *Women and Race in Early Modern Texts*. Cambridge, UK: Cambridge University Press, 2009.

Rosenthal, Laura J. "Owning Oroonoko: Behn, Southerne, and the Contingencies of Property." *Renaissance Drama* 23 (1992): 25–58. https://doi.org/10.1086/rd.23.41917283.

Sarah-Gray Lesley

ENTRY #32 (NO IMAGE)

William Shakespeare (1564–1616)
The most lamentable tragedie of Titus Andronicus.
As it hath sundry times beene plaide by the Kings maiesties seruants, 1611
Book with letterpress
VAULT Case 3A 888

William Shakespeare's first tragedy *Titus Andronicus* (1591) orchestrates a revenge plot full of graphic violence and deep-seated racial anxieties. Although the play was long seen as one of Shakespeare's less polished works, it was extremely popular on the early modern English stage. Following general Titus Andronicus' return to Rome with a group of Gothic prisoners, the play's plot unfolds as the imprisoned Gothic queen schemes her revenge against Titus with her black-skinned "Moorish" lover Aaron. The play's gruesome poetics situate flesh as the ground for racial and cultural conceptualizations.

Aaron's flesh is marked differently by his skin color and subaltern* status, resonating with the image of Spanish runaway slaves (*cimarrónes*) in sixteenth-century Europe. Aaron's "fleshiness" is also metaphorized through the play's characterization of him as someone "barbarous," licentious, and driven by physical passion. Yet, Aaron's trickster quality is so overpowering that his words, replete with literary allusions to the humanistic* tradition, become a weapon that indirectly kills many of the characters in the play, turning them into bloody corpses: literal flesh whose identity can no longer be located in a bounded, normative, and cultivated body. Racial boundaries are erased as the audience becomes unable to differentiate the flesh of the Moor from his allegedly more rational and "civilized" white counterparts. Ultimately, the soon-to-be emperor of Rome, Lucius, further blurs the lines by acting as a Barbarian when he feeds Tamora's corpse to beasts, standing in opposition to the values of law, justice, and civility that are often deemed central to the Roman (and to Shakespeare's) culture.

Further Readings

Ndiaye, Noémie. "Aaron's Roots: Spaniards, Englishmen, and Blackamoors in Titus Andronicus." *Early Theatre: A Journal Associated with the Records of Early English Drama* 19, no. 2 (2016): 59–80. https://doi.org/10.12745/et.19.2.2847.

Sale, Carolyn. "Black Aeneas: Race, English Literary History, and the 'Barbarous' Poetics of Titus Andronicus." *Shakespeare Quarterly* 62, no. 1 (2011): 25–52. https://doi.org/10.1353/shq.2011.0001.

Willis, Deborah. "The Gnawing Vulture: Revenge, Trauma Theory, and Titus Andronicus." *Shakespeare Quarterly* 53, no. 1 (2002): 21–52. https://doi.org/10.1353/shq.2002.0017.

Vivian Lei

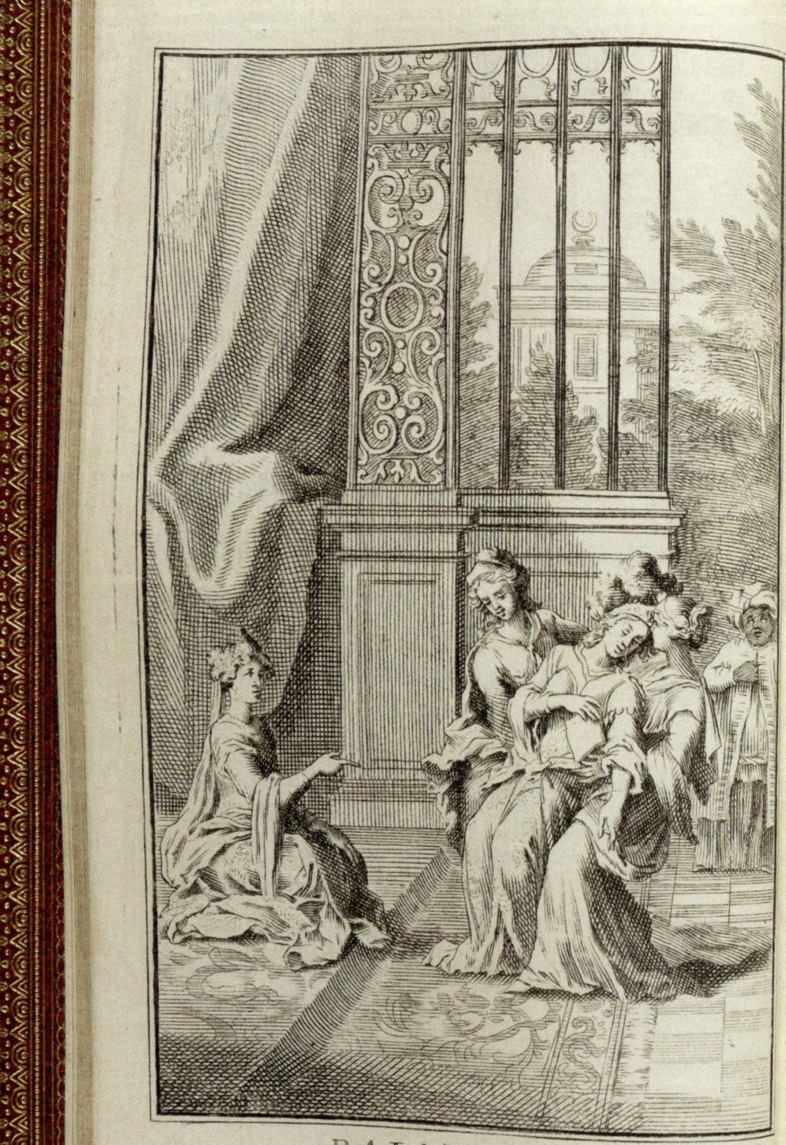
BAIAZET

BAJAZET.
TRAGEDIE.

ACTE I.
SCENE PREMIERE.
ACOMAT, OSMIN.

ACOMAT.

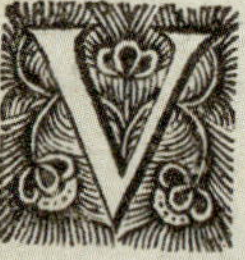
Vien, suy-moy. La Sultane en ce lieu se doit rendre.
Je pourray cependant te parler, & t'entendre.

OSMIN.

Et depuis quãd Seigneur, entre-t-on dans ces lieux,
Dont l'accés estoit même interdit à nos yeux?
Jadis une mort prompte eût suivi cette audace.

ACOMAT.

Quand tu seras instruit de tout ce qui se passe,
Mon entrée en ces lieux ne te surprendra plus.
Mais laissons, cher Osmin, les discours superflus.

Entry #33

ENTRY #33

François Chauveau (1613–1676), engraver
Frontispiece of *Bajazet*, in *Oeuvres de Racine, Tome II*
Book with engravings, 1697
PQ1885 1697

This 1697 edition of Jean Racine's plays copies the engravings that François Chauveau had produced for the original collected edition of 1676. The frontispiece of *Bajazet* (1672) represents Act IV scene 3, when Sultana Roxane shares with a fainting Atalide the letter she received, in which Sultan Murad IV demands that she execute his brother Bayazid, whom Roxane and Atalide both love. The curtain and the view onto the garden of the seraglio, which looks like one of the painted screens used in baroque scenography*, form a theatrical décor for this Orientalist scene. Notice the Black character in Turkish habit upstage left. The juxtaposition between this Black eunuch and the cluster of white women (their outfits touch) draws on the popular trend in late- seventeenth-century portraiture to represent aristocratic women with a Black page as a visual strategy constructing their whiteness.

In the play, this character is Orcan, a high-ranking enslaved African, who has just delivered the Sultan's letter, and whose secret mission is to murder Roxane. The play's resolution hinges on Orcan, yet he never appears on stage. Chauveau, who is notorious for engraving moments not represented on stage, perceived the importance of Orcan, and captured his invisibilization. Indeed, the particular placement of Orcan in the crease of this tiny book (6.5 × 5.5 inches), which the reader will not fully open for fear of breaking the binding, puts him at risk of literal disappearance in the pages of history, and highlights the attention needed to see Blackness in neoclassical French archives.

Further Readings

Hall, Kim F. "'An Object in the Midst of Other Objects': Race, Gender, Material Culture." Chap. 5 in *Things of Darkness: Economies of Race and Gender in Early Modern England*. Ithaca, NY: Cornell University Press, 1995.

Ndiaye, Noémie. "Blackspeak: Acoustic Blackness and the Accents of Race." Chap. 3 in *Scripts of Blackness: Early Modern Performance Culture and the Making of Race*. Philadelphia: University of Pennsylvania Press, 2022.

Picard, Raymond. "Racine and Chauveau." *Journal of the Warburg and Courtauld Institutes* 14, no. 3/4 (1951): 259–74. https://doi.org/10.2307/750342.

Noémie Ndiaye

ENTRY #34

Thomas Kyd (1558 – 1594), author (published anonymously)
The Spanish tragedy, or Hieronimo is mad againe:
containing the lamentable end of Don Horatio and Belimperia, with the pittiful death of Hieronimo
(also known as *Hieronimo is mad againe*), 1623
Book with letterpress and woodcuts
Case Y 135 .K984

A woodcut appears on the title page of Thomas Kyd's *The Spanish Tragedy* in four editions from 1615 to 1633, including the 1623 edition. To the right, Bel-Imperia attempts to fight off abduction by her brother Lorenzo in Act 2. The play text describes Lorenzo as accompanied by multiple men and "disguised" ($D2^r$)—an apparently ineffective disguise, as Bel-Imperia immediately recognizes her kidnappers—but Lorenzo in the woodcut is depicted alone and in blackface. The image suggests that the actor's so-called disguise involved either cosmetic makeup or, perhaps more likely, a mask. As represented in the woodcut, Lorenzo's hands are white, with one gripping his sister and the other a sword. Banderoles (speech ribbons) are attached to the figures of Hieronimo, Bel-Imperia, and Lorenzo, featuring condensed speech from the play.

Lorenzo's appearance in blackface underscores early modern associations of Blackness with wickedness, but it also points to the complicated representation of foreignness in the play. *The Spanish Tragedy* takes place in the midst of Spain's colonial expansion, following its annexation of Portugal. The characters represent an English imagining of Spanish and Portuguese persons, but the markers of cultural difference in the play are not specific to either population. Lorenzo's identity as Spanish intersects with the blackface of the woodcut to perform an over-determined yet mutable racialized other that is above all non-English. The woodcut illustrates how easily categories of identity could be tried on, exchanged, and discarded on the early modern stage, while nonetheless suggesting that racial disguises ultimately result in failure.

Further Readings

Griffin, Eric. "Nationalism, the Black Legend, and the Revised 'Spanish Tragedy.'" *English Literary Renaissance* 39, no. 2 (2009): 336–70. https://doi.org/10.1111/j.1475-6757.2009.01050.x.

Jakacki, Diane K. "'Canst paint a doleful cry?': Promotion and Performance in the 'Spanish Tragedy' Title-Page Illustration." *Early Theatre* 13, no. 1 (2010): 13–36. https://www.jstor.org/stable/43499547.

Mazzio, Carla. "Staging the Vernacular: Language and Nation in Thomas Kyd's *The Spanish Tragedy*." *Studies in English Literature, 1500–1900* 38, no. 2 (1998): 207–32. https://doi.org/10.2307/451034.

Beatrice Bradley

The Spanish Tragedy.

Or,

HIERONIMO is mad againe.

Containing the lamentable end of *Don Horatio,* and *Belimperia*; With the pittifull Death of HIERONIMO.

Newly Corrected, Amended, and Enlarged with new Additions, as it hath of late been diuers times Acted.

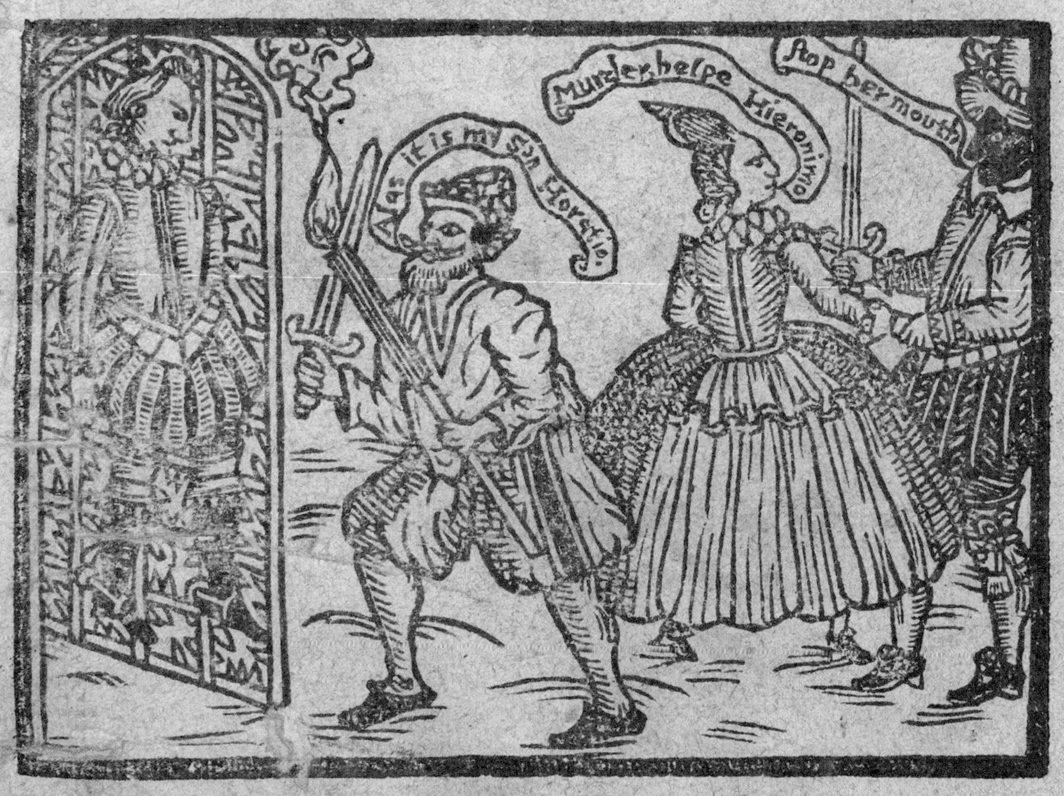

LONDON,

Printed by *Augustine Mathewes*, and are to bee sold by *Iohn Grismand*, at his Shop in Pauls Alley, at the Signe of the Gunne. 1623.

Case Study #2.
Performance Culture: Masques, Carnival, Theatricality

ENTRY #35

Jonson, Benjamin (1573?–1637), author
"[Masque] of Blacknesse" in *The workes of Ben Ionson*, 1616
Book with letterpress, engraving, and woodcuts
Case Y 135 .J735 v. 1

Masque of Blacknesse is the first masque to appear in the 1616 folio of Ben Jonson's collected works. The masques of the Stuart Court combined dramatic action, musical song, and visual spectacular, and Jonson's prefatory notes to *Blacknesse* in the folio illuminate an elaborate scene and stage setting. The masque was first performed in 1605, with a pregnant Queen Anne—wife to King James I—and multiple ladies of the court appearing in cosmetic blackface in the roles of "Ethiopian" nymphs. The short action of the masque follows Euphoris (Anne as fertility nymph) and her sisters in a quest to turn their skin white. Jonson's introductory remarks emphasize the queen's involvement and her professed desire that the masque include "Black-mores" (Ffff3r). *Blacknesse* also serves in support of James' agenda of a unified "Great Britain," with repeated praise of Britannia as a promised land in which the nymphs will achieve their desired whiteness. The fiction of Africa in the masque thus mobilizes a cultural understanding of Britain as an expansive, powerful, white nation that insistently reproduces its own whiteness.

In addition to Jonson's introductory comments on *Blacknesse*, there exists a spectatorial account: Dudley Carleton, who attended the court performance, details in two letters the following year his revulsion in response to Anne's painted face and arms (as opposed to the use of prosthetics such as a mask or gloves). Carleton provides a rare early modern response to the use of cosmetic blackface, and the masque more broadly locates Blackness as a site of spectacle in early modern England.

Further Readings

Hall, Kim F. "Sexual Politics and Cultural Identity in *The Masque of Blackness*." In *The Performance of Power: Theatrical Discourse and Politics*, edited by Sue-Ellen Case and Janelle Reinelt, 3–18. Iowa City: University of Iowa Press, 1991.

Stevens, Andrea. "Mastering Masques of Blackness: Jonson's 'Masque of Blackness,' The Windsor text of 'The Gypsies Metamorphosed,' and Brome's 'The English Moor.'" *English Literary Renaissance* 39, no. 2 (2009): 396–426. https://doi.org/10.1111/j.1475-6757.2009.01052.x.

Thiel, Sara B. T. "Performing Blackface Pregnancy at the Stuart Court: *The Masque of Blackness* and *Love's Mistress, or the Queen's Masque*." *Renaissance Drama* 45, no.2 (2017): 211–36. https://doi.org/10.1086/694326.

Beatrice Bradley

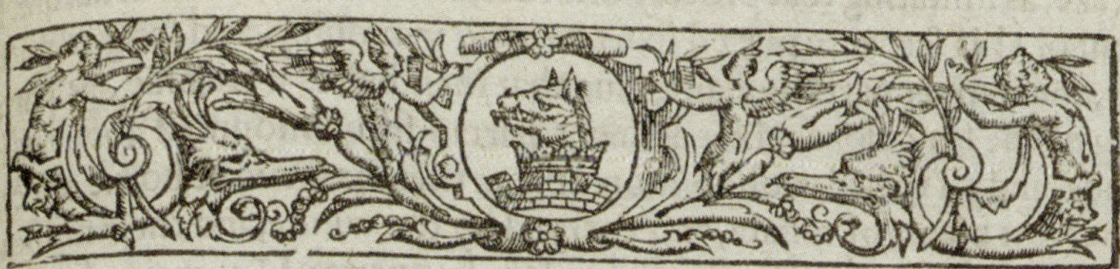

THE QVEENES MASQVES.

The first, OF BLACKNESSE:

Personated at the Court, at WHITE-HALL, *on the Twelu'th night,* 1605.

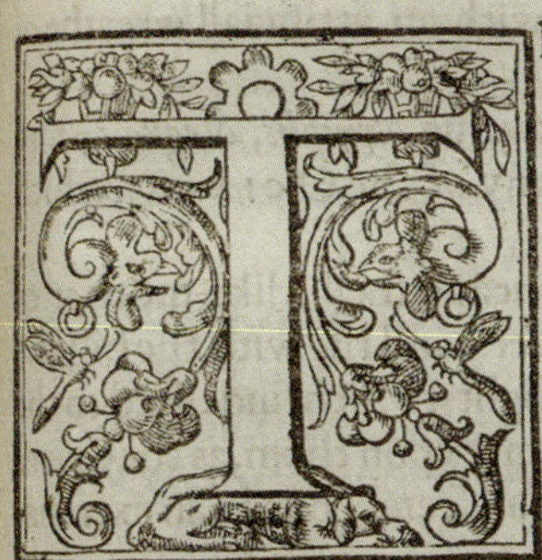

THe honor, and splendor of these *spectacles* was such in the performance, as could those houres haue lasted, this of mine, now, had been a most vnprofitable worke. But (when it is the fate, euen of the greatest, and most absolute births, to need, and borrow a life of posteritie) little had beene done to the studie of *magnificence* in these, if presently with the rage of the people, who (as a part of greatnesse) are priuiledged by custome, to deface their *carkasses*, the *spirits* had also perished. In dutie, therefore, to that *Maiestie*, who gaue them their authoritie, and grace; and, no lesse then the most royall of predecessors, deserues eminent celebration for these solemnities: I adde this later hand, to redeeme them as well from Ignorance, as Enuie, two common euills, the one of *censure*, the other of *obliuion*.

[a] PLINY, [b] SOLINVS, [c] PTOLOMEY, and of late LEO [d] the *African*, remember vnto vs a riuer in *Æthiopia*, famous by the name of *Niger*; of which the people were called *Nigritæ*, now *Negro's*: and are the blackest nation of the world. This [e] riuer taketh spring out of a certaine *lake*, east-ward; and after a long race, falleth into the westerne *Ocean*. Hence (because it was her Maiesties will, to haue them *Black-mores* at first) the inuention was deriued by me, and presented thus.

First, for the *Scene*, was drawne a Landtschap, consisting of small woods, and here and there a void place fill'd with huntings; which falling, an artificiall sea was seene to shoote forth, as if it flowed to the land, rayled with waues, which seemed to moue, and in some places the billow to breake,

a *Natu. Hist. l.* 5 *cap.* 8.

b *Poly. hist. cap.* 40. & 43.

c *Lib* 4. *cap.* 5.

d *Descrip. Afric.*

e Some take it to be the same with *Nilus*, which is by *Lucan* called *Melas*, signifying *Niger*. Howsoeuer, *Plinie*, in the place aboue noted, hath this: *Nigri fluuio eadem natura, quæ Nilo, calamum, papyrum, & casdem gignit animantes*. See *Solin*. aboue mentioned.

Entry #35

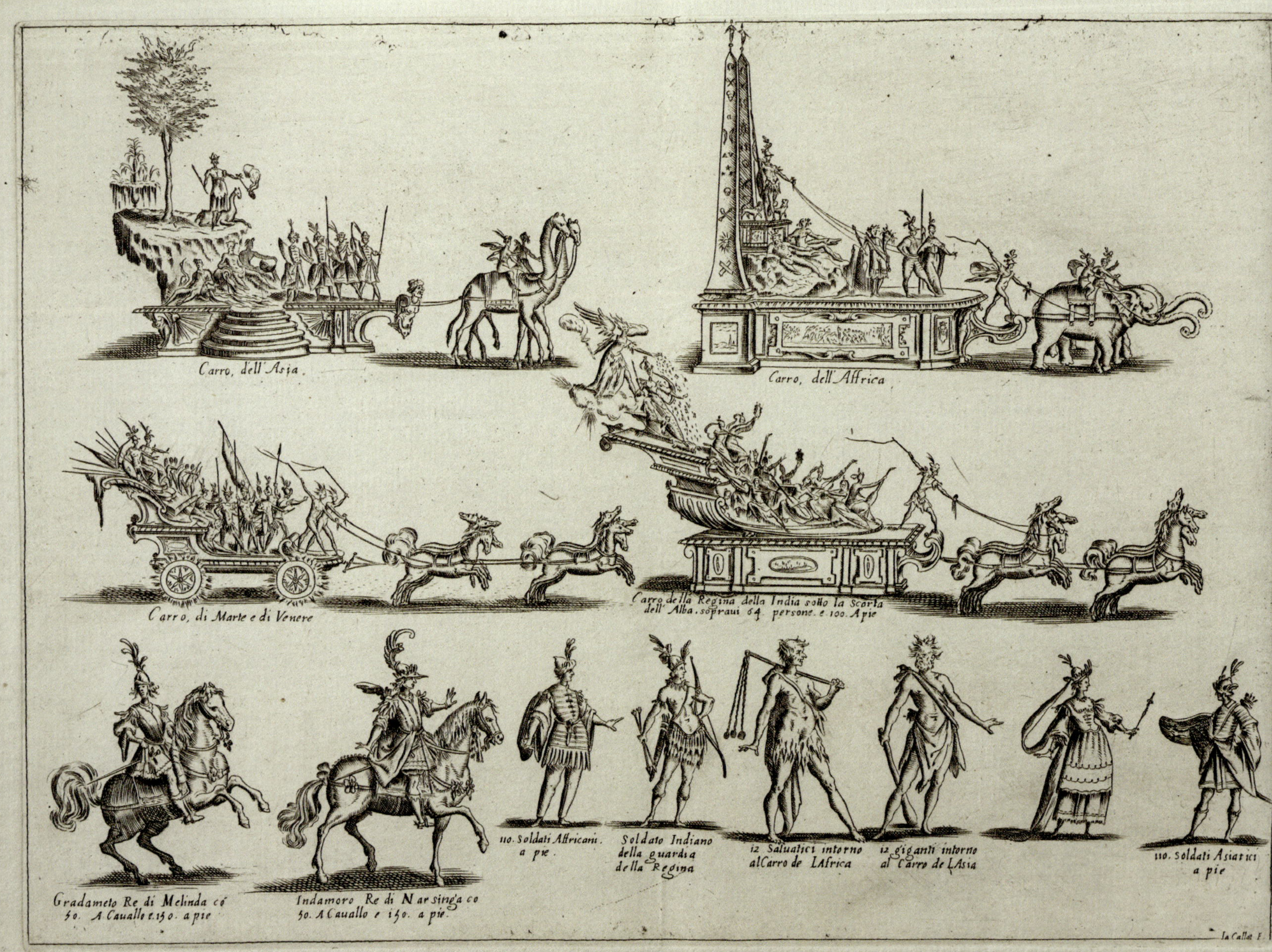
Carro, dell'Asia
Carro, dell'Affrica
Carro, di Marte e di Venere
Carro della Regina della India sotto la Scorta dell'Alba. sopraui 64 persone. e 100. A pie
Gradameto Re di Melinda cō 50. A Cauallo e 150. a pie
Indamoro Re di Narsinga co 50. A Cauallo e 150. a pie
110. Soldati Affricani. a pie.
Soldato Indiano della guardia della Regina
12 Saluatici intorno al Carro de L'Africa
12 giganti intorno al Carro de L'Asia
110. Soldati Asiatici a pie
Ja Callot F.

ENTRY #36

Jacques Callot (1592–1635)
The Chariots and The Characters, from War of Love, 1616
Etching
Case V 461 .6773

The prolific French artist Jacques Callot documented Florentine spectacles in etchings and engravings from 1611 to 1621 during the reign of Grand Duke Cosimo II. This etching is part of a set of prints representing ephemeral events in Florence for carnival festivities in 1616 that included a procession, mock battle, and a horse ballet, entitled *Guerra d'amore* (*War of Love*). The single sheet prints are therefore often found folded and inserted into printed editions of the related libretto* for *Guerra d'amore*. Working closely with other artists involved in Medici productions, Callot likely copied a drawing of an "Indian" by Giulio Parigi that might have functioned as a costume design for this event. *Guerra d'amore* included an elaborate battle between "Africans" and "Indians," with one of the Kings played by the Grand Duke himself.

This sheet likely functions as a record of a procession in which Florentines dressed as "Indians," Asians, and Africans performed race as they made their way through the streets of Florence to the piazza*. The inscriptions on the etching tell us that the upper register of the print depicts the carriage or float for Asia and the carriage of Africa, while the middle register includes the float for Venus and a more elaborate float for the "Queen of India" that could hold "64 people seated and 100 people standing." Finally figures at the base of the sheet reveal more detailed renderings of the figures costumed as soldiers, "savages," kings, and queens of these other lands.

Further Readings

Bertelà, Giovanna Gaeta, and Annamaria Petrioli Tofani. *Feste e apparati medicei: Mostra di disegni e incisioni*. Florence: Olschki, 1969.

Boorsch, Suzanne. "America in Festival Presentations." In *First Images of America: The Impact of the New World on the Old*, edited by Fred Chiappelli, 2 vols., 1:503–15. Berkeley: University of California Press, 1976.

Wilbourne, Emily. "Music, Race, Representation: Three Scenes of Performance at the Medici Court (1608–1616)." *Il Saggiatore Musicale* 27, no. 1 (2020): 5–45.

Lia Markey and
Suzanne Karr Schmidt

ENTRY #37

Diego Valadés (1533–1582), author and engraver
Description of the sacrifices inhumanely made by the Indians of the New World, in particular in Mexico
[TIPVS SACRIFICIORVM QVE IN MANITER INDI FACIEBANT IN NOVO INDIARVM ORBE PRECIPVE IN MEXICO],
in *Rhetorica christiana*, 1579
Book with letterpress and etching
Wing ZP 535 .P447

Fray Diego Valadés' *Rhetorica christiana* (1579), the first book published by an American-born author (who was also the first mestizo to join the Franciscans* in New Spain), illuminates the preaching practices of the Franciscan order in the Americas and argues for increased support from the Church and fellow ecclesiastics* in the conversion of Indigenous peoples. Valadés himself participated in creating the 27 prints that are interspersed throughout the text, primarily constituting didactic tools for other missionaries. The single fold-out image in the Newberry edition, however, instead depicts a pre-Hispanic Indigenous town with a scene of human sacrifice prominently placed in the center.

The etching blends scenes of natural history and Indigenous customs like cooking, harvesting, and fishing. Small figures at work dot a landscape filled with European-style buildings, except for the large Indigenous temple (*teocalli*) at the center, inside of which lies a prone human body on the altar. A priest standing behind him proffers an object, likely the body's heart, to a statue of an Indigenous god. To the right of the temple, an assistant throws the dead bodies of other victims down the stairs.

That Valadés's publication was intended to be of practical use for other missionaries gives this depiction of Indigenous religious ritual a particular weight, which notably includes a dance performance taking place in a large clearing before the temple. The presence of the performance reveals the adaptations and concessions that missionaries were forced to enact in order to better resonate with Indigenous tradition and thus encourage conversions. The particular theatricality of Catholic monasteries (*conventos*) in the Americas reflected Indigenous practice and points to the ways in which Indigenous peoples expressed agency within a system intentionally designed to oppress and subjugate them.

Further Readings

Carrasco, Ronaldo. "El exemplum como estrategia persuasiva en la *Rhetorica christiana* (1579) de fray Diego Valadés." *Annales del Instituto de Investigaciones Estéticas* 22, no. 77 (2000): 33–66. https://doi.org/10.22201/iie.18703062e.2000.77.1939.

Galindo, David Rex. "Shaping Colonial Behaviours: Franciscan Missionary Literature and the Implementation of Religious Normative Knowledge in Colonial Mexico (1530s–1640s)." In *Knowledge of the Pragmatici: Legal and Moral Theological Literature and the Formation of Early Modern Ibero-America*, edited by Thomas Duve and Otto Danwerth, 296–327. Leiden: Brill, 2020.

Leaper, Laura E. "Time, Memory, and Ritual: Deciphering Visual Rhetoric in Diego Valadzés's *Rhetorica Christiana*." Ph.D. diss., New York University Institute of Fine Arts, 2012.

Arianna Ray

TIPVS·SACRIFICIORVM·QVE·IN·MANITER·INDI·FACIEBANT·IN·NOVO·INDIARVM·ORBE·PRECIPVE·IN·MEXICO
BALSA
MAGVEI
FLOR
LIQVID ANBER
CASIA
PLATANO
CACAO
PINNA
TVNA
DIDACVS VALADES FECIT

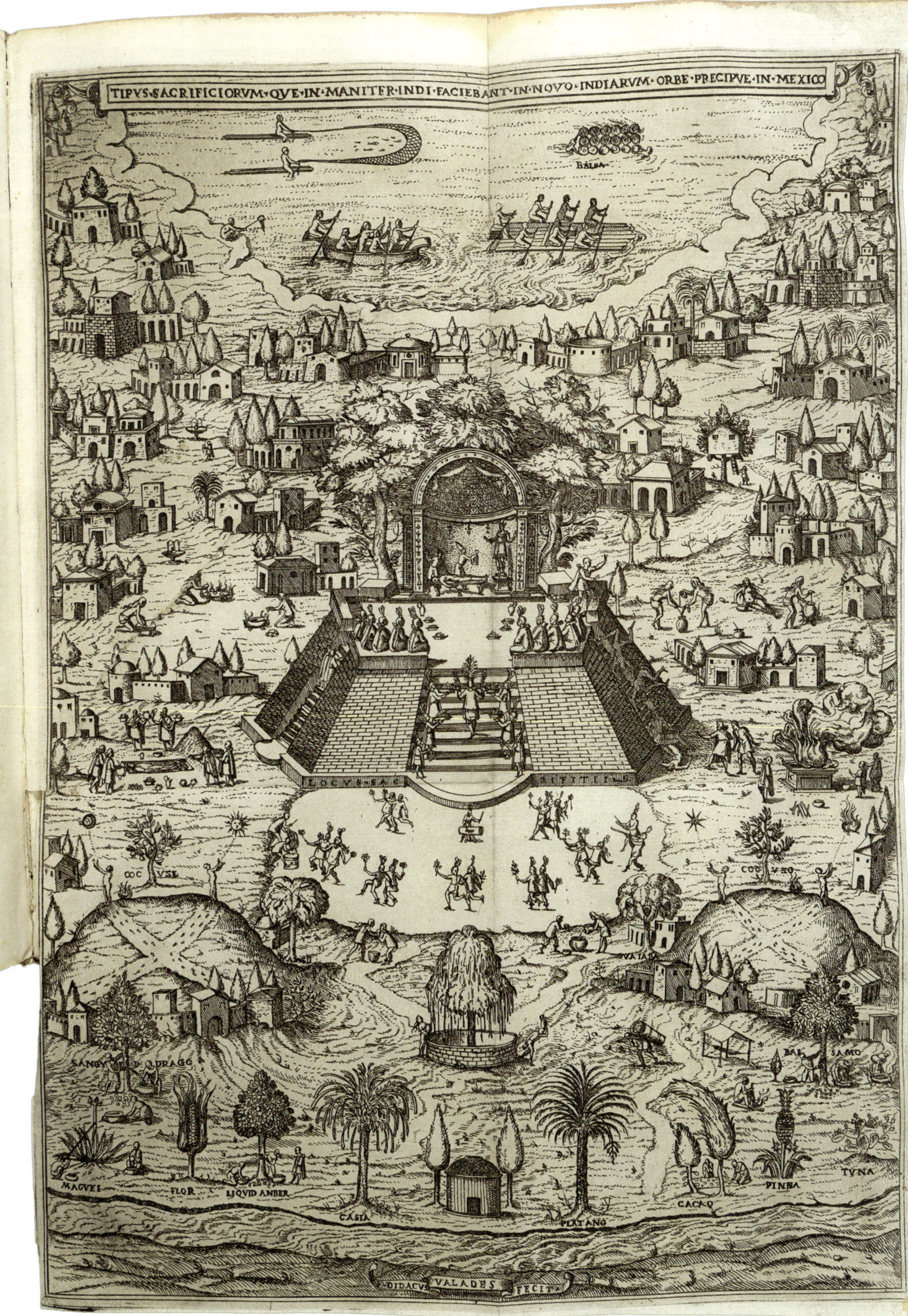

Entry #37

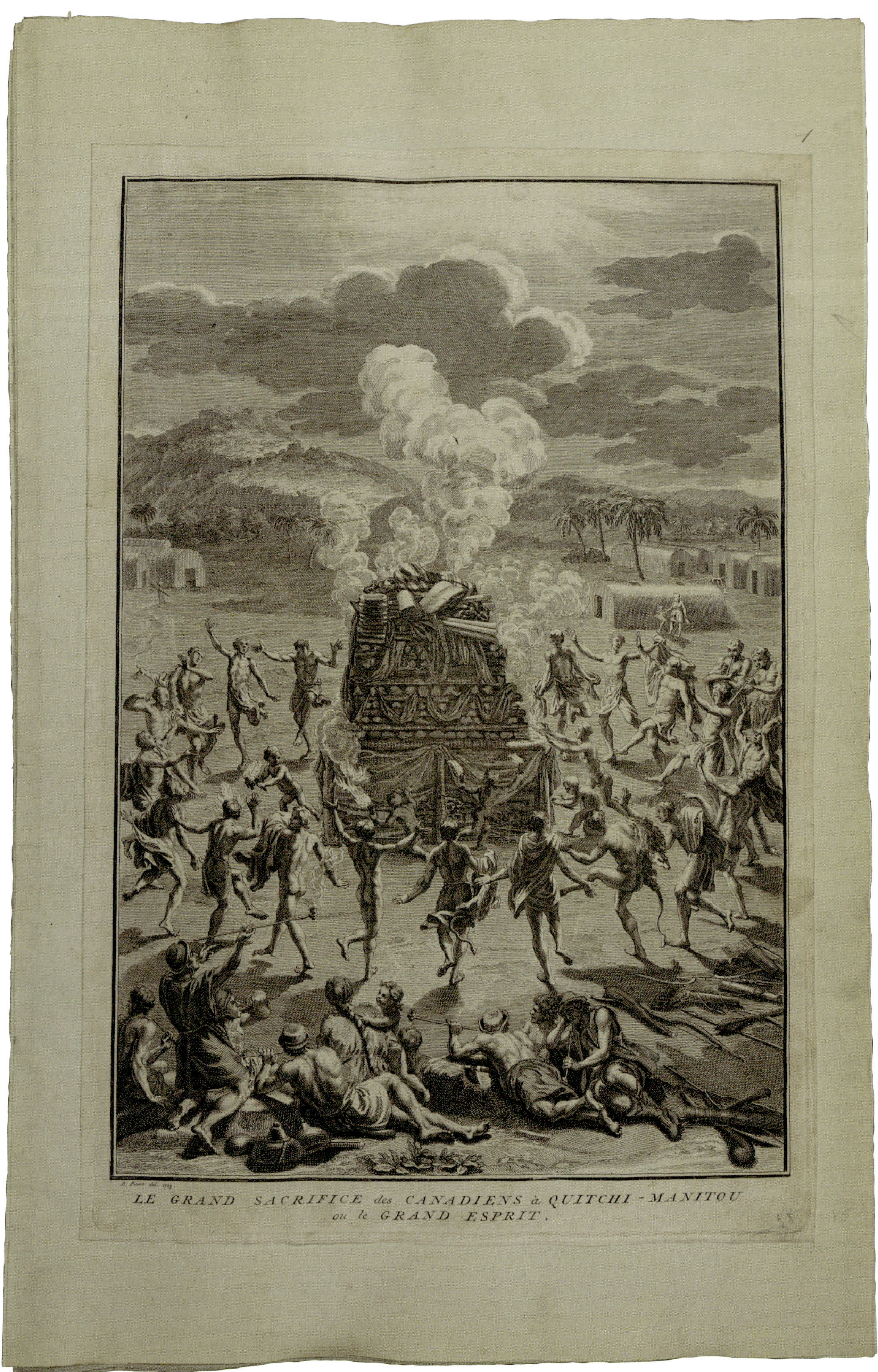

LE GRAND SACRIFICE des CANADIENS à QUITCHI-MANITOU ou le GRAND ESPRIT.

Entry #38

ENTRY #38

Bernard Picart (1673–1733), engraver and etcher; Jean Frédéric Bernard (1680–1744), author
Page from nineteenth-century scrapbook with prints from the French translation, *Cérémonies et coutumes religieuses des peuples idolâtres . . . représentées par des figures dessinées de la main de Bernard Picard, avec une explication historique & quelques dissertations curieuses*, volume 3 (*Religious Customs and Ceremonies of Idolatrous Peoples*), 1723
Ayer 301 .C41 1723

In this print, eighteen partially nude adult bodies are represented mid-leap — arms apart and mouths agape — performing a lively circle dance to the percussive beat of two musicians on the right margin of the page. These figures, identified by the caption as Canadians making a sacrifice to the Quitchi-Manitou (Great Spirit), encircle a pyre of woven textiles, bolts of cloth, and stacked tambourines. These exotic materials of varied geographic origin, often labeled as "Indian" or "Moorish," obfuscate any clear identification of the Indigenous Canadians in favor of collapsing Blackness and Indigeneity into a single foreign category. Published in 1723, this is one of 72 engravings in the third volume of Bernard Picart and Jean Frédéric Bernard's *Cérémonies et coutumes religieuses*, compiled in the late nineteenth or early twentieth century, which endeavored to introduce the people of the Americas to a European audience. Picart's engravings relied on lively compositions of dance and nudity, rather than illustrating darker skin tones through cross-hatching, to construct racial difference on Indigenous bodies. As FitzPatrick and Fromont argue in "Back Bending Labor, Savage Dances, Pious Stances: Race in Motion between Africa and the Americas" in this volume, early modern iconography around the danse macabre and "Moorish" dance served to show animated bodily gestures as markers of lack of civility. Picart's circle dance composition would likely remind viewers of the idolatrous account of Israelites dancing around the golden calf. Here, the early modern audience sees race as a performance, in which various ethnicities are conflated and made legible through choreography.

Further Readings

Gaudio, Michael. "Dancing in Circles: Ethnography and Animation in the *Cérémonies et coutumes religieuses*." Paper presented at The Enlightenment Creation of World Religion: Bernard and Picart's Cérémonies *et coutumes religieuses* Symposium and Research Methods Workshop, Newberry Library, Chicago, March 16, 2018.

Hunt, Lynn Avery, Margaret C. Jacob, and W. W. Mijnhardt. *The Book That Changed Europe: Picart & Bernard's Religious Ceremonies of the World*. Cambridge, MA: Belknap Press, 2010.

Stephanie Lee

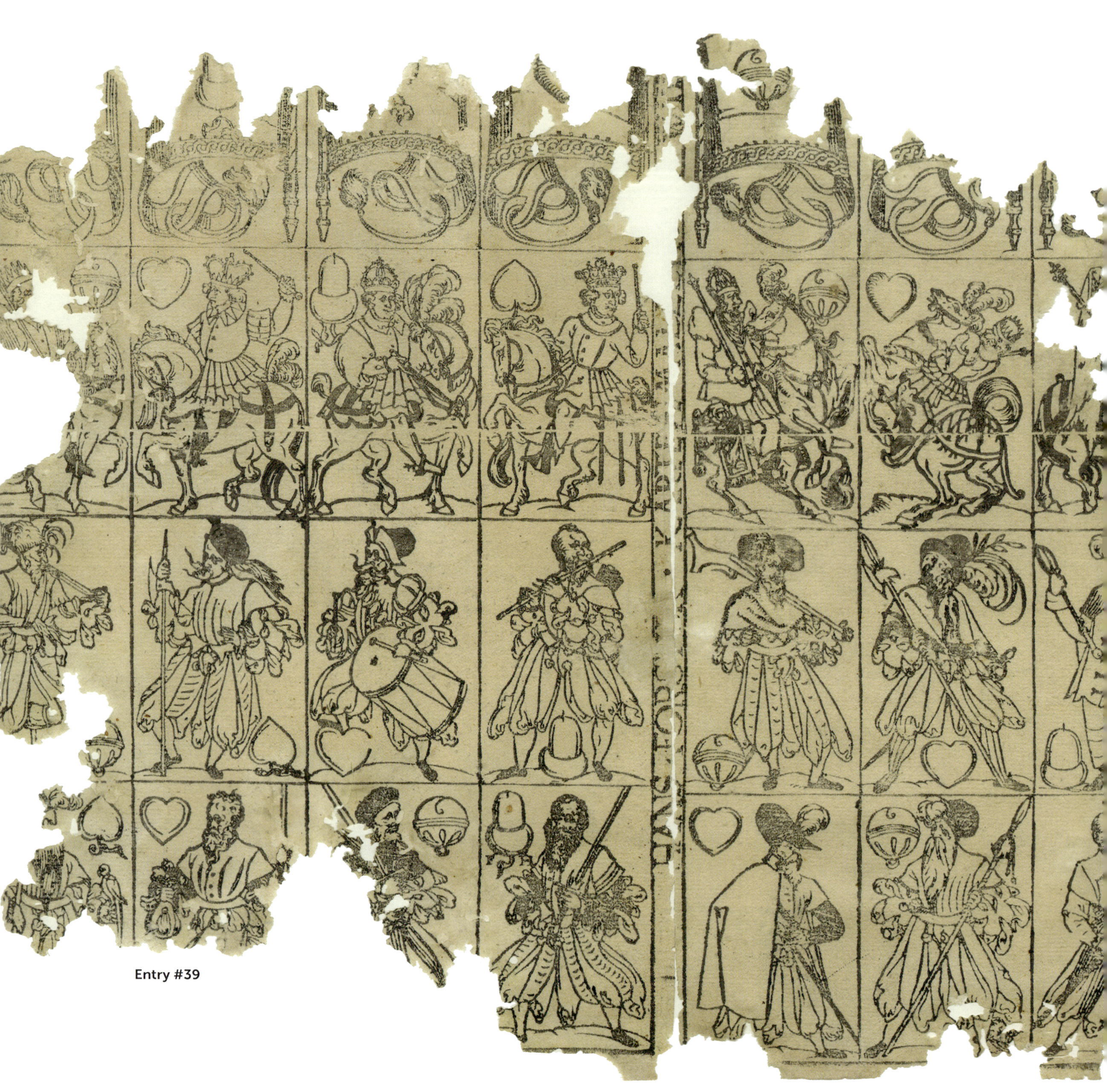

Entry #39

Case Study #3. Performances of the Racial Self

ENTRY #39

Hans Förster (16th century);
block cut possibly by Monogrammist F. H. (active 1543–1553)
Playing Cards for the Game of Landsknecht, 1570s
Woodcut, fragment with two sets
of face cards from three double sheets
Case Wing ZX 547 .F775

Premodern playing cards served many purposes and audiences—from lavish painted and gilded sets for aristocratic recipients to slapdash woodcut sheets with stenciled color for low-brow gambling. Cards came to Europe from the Near East, probably in the fourteenth century, and were often banned, perhaps first in 1367 in Bern, Switzerland. This fragmentary sheet of 32 uncut woodcut cards was made in Vienna around 1570 in the workshop of Hans Förster. His signature describes him as a "Kartenmaler" or card painter, implying that the set was also available in color. While suits and face cards varied by country, the Germanic acorns, leaves, hearts, and bells seen here stayed relatively consistent. German face cards differentiated social status through clothing and appearance as well as the hierarchy of King, Upper Knave, and Lower Knave.

Unusually, Förster's double sheet of face cards depicts the crowned kings on horseback and shows both groups of knaves as mercenary *Landsknecht** soldiers and musicians attired in their famously ostentatious dress. This sheet includes two sets of 16 slightly different face cards, both of which may have been intended for a popular game also called Landsknecht. The Lower Knave of Leaves on the right sheet, who holds a beer stein, seems from his topknot and long, parted beard to exhibit different ethnographic characteristics. He, and the knave of acorns above him with the toggle coat, are intended to appear slightly exotic, as Hungarian rather than German soldiers. They too were recruited as mercenaries for the Holy Roman Emperors. Playing card iconographies set up similar confrontations well into the nineteenth century by including contemporary portraits of rulers for one suit in opposition to unflattering images of non-European peoples for the others. For instance, Nuremberg artist Peter Flötner's famous 1540 deck would pit the Emperor Charles V (King of Leaves) against a Turkish Sultan (King of Hearts), and an "Indian" ruler (King of Bells).

Further Readings

Husband, Timothy B. *The World in Play: Luxury Cards 1430–1540*. New York: Metropolitan Museum of Art, Cloisters, 2016. Exhibition catalog.

Leitch, Stephanie. *Mapping Ethnography in Early Modern Germany: New Worlds in Print Culture*. New York: Palgrave Macmillan, 2010.

Pichler, Gerd. Die Spielkarten des 16. und 17. Jahrhunderts in der Stiftssammlung St. Florian. *Jahrbuch des Oberösterreichischen Musealvereines* 142/1. Linz, 1997.

Suzanne Karr Schmidt

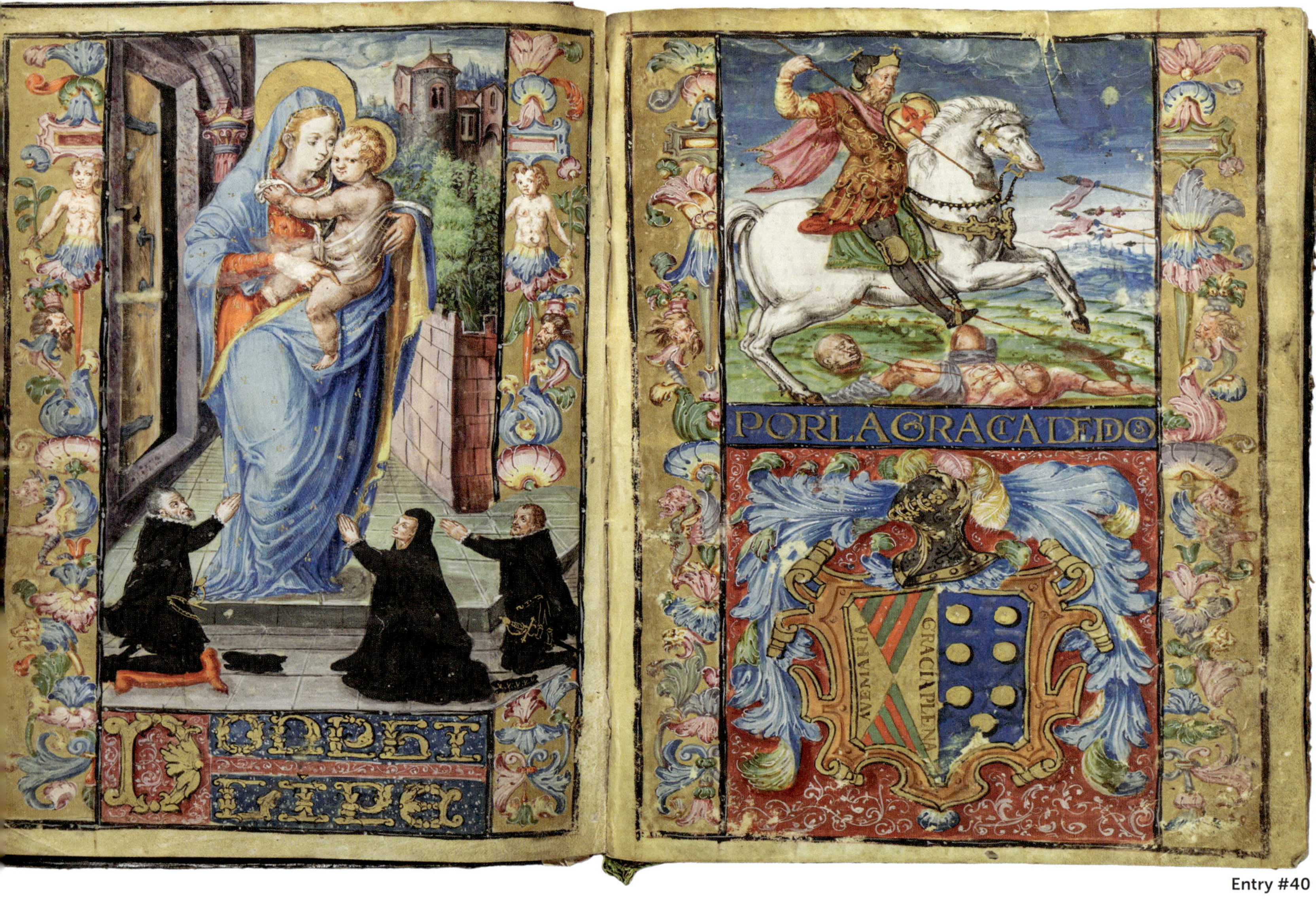

Entry #40

ENTRY #40

Alvar Gonçalez el Moxo (16th century)
Carta executoria in favor of *Alvar Gonçalez* (patent of nobility), 1567
Illustrated manuscript on vellum
VAULT folio CASE MS 5248

This illuminated manuscript is a patent of nobility, a legal document containing the petition for recognition as a *hidalgo* (lowest rank of Spanish nobility) for Alvar Gonçalez el Moxo, resident of Campanario, Spain. The court granted his request on January 27, 1567. These petitions were written and illustrated to demonstrate factors recognized as essential to noble status such as service to the crown, religious devotion, and "purity" of blood. The Blood Purity Statues began in the mid-fifteenth century when civil and ecclesiastical institutions applied discriminatory segregation laws preventing Jewish converts from joining and holding office, the laws were later extended to anyone with Jewish, Muslim, or heretical lineage. If granted, the title of *hidalgo* conferred prestige and tangible privileges, such as exemption from taxes.

This manuscript, with its original gilt brown leather binding, shows the care taken to exemplify status, piety, and loyalty to the crown. The production of these manuscripts reached its peak in the sixteenth and seventeenth centuries. There are two full-page illustrations at the front of the manuscript. The first illustration is a devotional painting of the Virgin of Loreto holding the Christ Child with the much smaller aspiring *hidalgos* kneeling below. On the opposite folio, there is an image of Santiago Matamoros, or Saint James, the patron saint of Spain, known as the "Moor-Slayer." Saint James, astride a white horse and dressed in elaborately adorned armor, rides into battle trampling figures representing the Moorish "Other." This violent iconography reflects the dominant Catholic narrative of the warrior saint defeating the Muslim infidels. Below, there is an illustration of the family's coat of arms. The closeness of these two images is intended to signal the blood purity of the Gonçalez family and their religious fervor.

Further Readings

Domínguez Casas, Rafael. "Ascenso social y visualización simbólica del wwwwwpoder en dos ejecutorias de hidalguía del reinado de Carlos II." *Goya*, no. 363 (2018): 108–25.

Matilla, Jose Manuel. "Símbolos de privilegio y objetos de arte. Los documentos pintados en la sociedad española del Antiguo Régimen." In *El documento pintado: cinco siglos de arte en manuscritos*, 15–21. Madrid: Ministerio de Educación y Cultura, 2000.

Ruiz García, Elisa. "La carta ejecutoria de hidalguía un espacio gráfico privilegiado." *La España medieval*, no. Extra 1 (2006): 251–76.

Elizabeth A. Neary

ENTRY #41

Pietro Ridolfi (active 1710–1723)
Fan-Shaped Diploma for the "University of Big Noses"
(*Noi Macrobio Culaccione visitatore generale dell'Universita de Nasi grossi*), eighteenth century
Hand-colored etching, folded
Case folio NC1529.R48 A7 1710

This satirical etching with anti-Semitic overtones is about "keeping one's nose to the grindstone." It consists of two complementary rectangles with a central gap on a sheet that folded together around a stick into a fashionable fan or *ventole*. Used to cool off attendees at outside festivals or inside church services, their imagery varied greatly. A certificate for the "Universita de Nasi grossi" or University of Big Noses, appears on one side, while the larger caricature on the other reveals the risks of enrolling in such a dubious, unaccredited institution. On the certificate, the university's fictitious general, chancellor, and secretary appear above an extensive intaglio* text explaining the danger of leaving big noses in their natural state. Viewers can fill in blanks with their own name (or of others whose noses they wished to ridicule). The caricature demonstrates the process of whittling down "indecent" noses on a grindstone lubricated with a cascade of feces. While the man whose nose is being reduced appears to struggle, the riveted crowd becomes tempted to undergo the same treatment.

This version of the print etched by Pietro Ridolfo was produced throughout the eighteenth century by the Remondini publishing firm, which offered fan prints in two sizes that were sold by peddlers throughout Italy and beyond. The certificate is dated 1668, suggesting it may have been based on an even earlier version. While the text is not explicitly anti-Semitic, this scatological satire of academia reinforces the undesirability of the oversized or hook noses that were already used to depict Jews in the early modern period. While meant to be a humorous, ephemeral accessory, the way it makes rhinoplasty a prerequisite for an academic education is deeply unsettling, and its racist overtones are unmistakable.

Further Readings

Harrán, Don. "The Jewish nose in early modern art and music." *Renaissance Studies* 28, no. 1 (2014): 50–70. https://doi.org/10.1111/rest.12006.

Infelise, Mario. *I Remondini di Bassano*. Bassano del Grappa: Ghedina & Tassotti, 1990.

Milano, Alberto. "Prints for Fans." *Print Quarterly* 4, no. 1 (1987): 2–19.

———. "'Selling Prints for the Remondini': Italian Pedlars Traveling through Europe during the Eighteenth Century." In *Not Dead Things: The Dissemination of Popular Print in England and Wales, Italy, and the Low Countries, 1500–1820*, edited by Roeland Harms, Joad Raymond, Jeroen Salman, 75–96. Leiden: Brill, 2013.

Suzanne Karr Schmidt

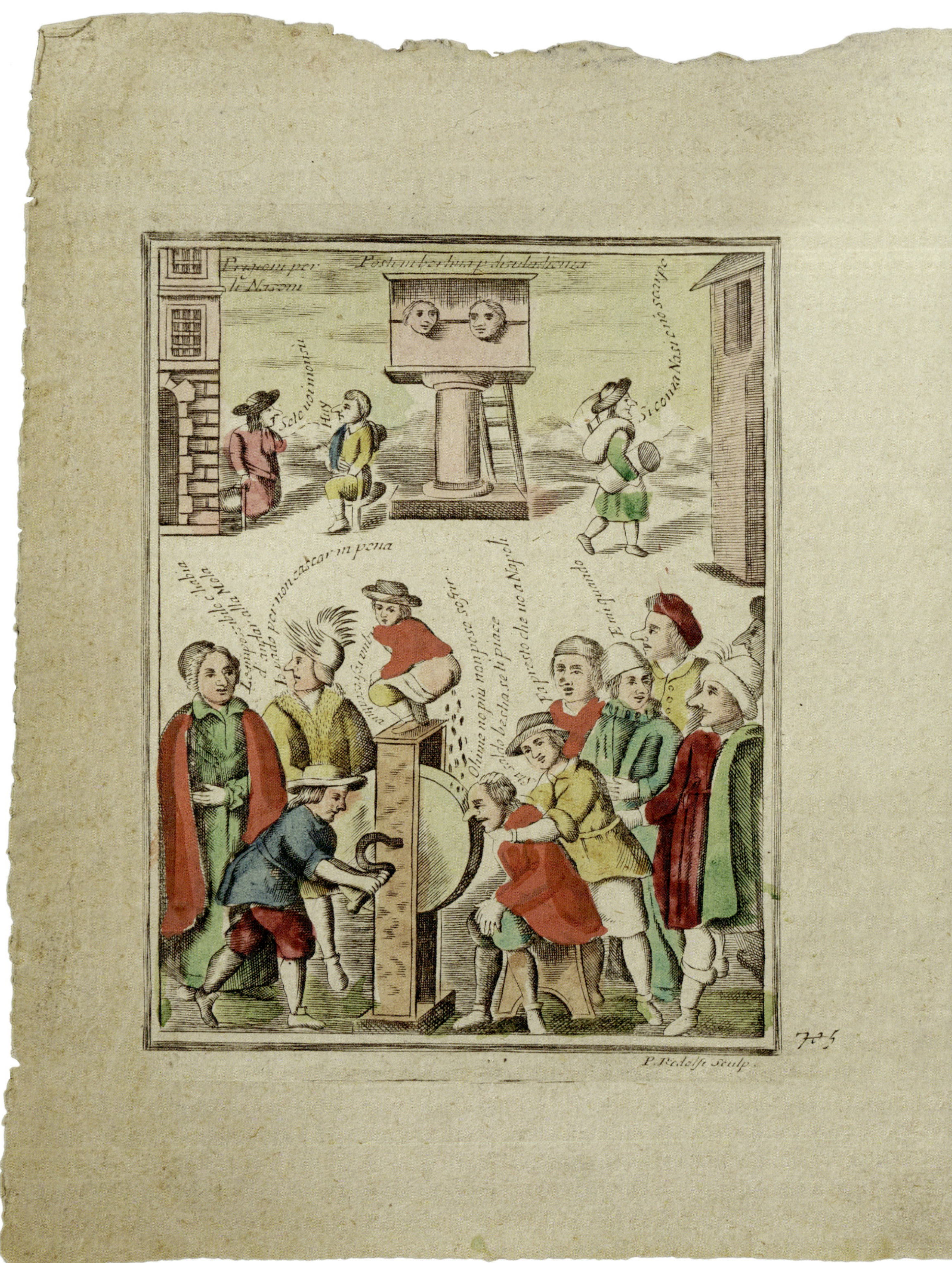

Entry #41 (verso)

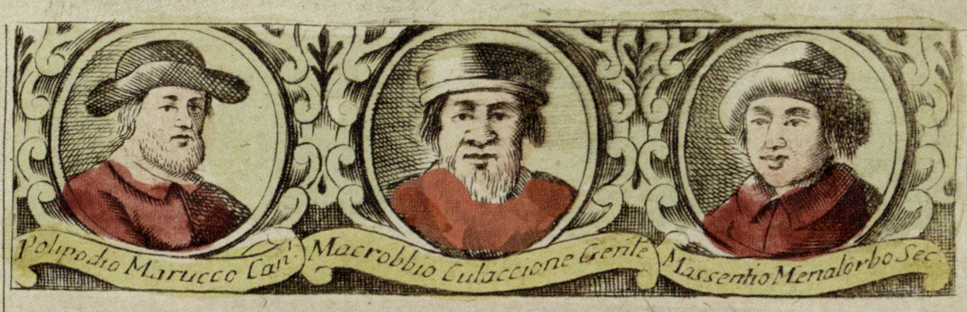

NOI MACROBIO CULACCIONE VISITATORE GENERALE
Dell Universita de Nasi Grossi indecenti Nappioni smisurati disutili difformati e sproportionati Auditore di male lingue e maldicenti Consultore della congregatione de Gossi Protettore de Buffoni magri &c.

Essendo pervenuto all'orecchie nostre come moltis'usurpano il Privilegio di portare senz'altro risguardo publicamente certi Nasi smisurati d'ogni sorte contro le gride di già publicate sotto il di 36 Mag. 1672 dimostrandone apertamente strapazzo, e sprezzo all'autorita nostra, & particolar inobedienza Percio ritrovandosi Voi

particolarmente denontiato, e querelato nell'Officio nostro di tal materia come evidentemente costa nel coperchio della sechietta camerale a punto qto hauendo contravenuto, & trasgredito prosontuosamente anco ai Statuti Napioneschi. Pero

Vi Comandiamo espressamente che nel termine di giorni 3. dobbiate personalmente comparire, e non per sommessa persona, nel nostro Palazzo situato nella Piazza del Taffanario in cui sta la molla piantata per diminuire & agiustare qualunque sorte di Nasazzi prohibiti, e sproportionati accio si possa il vostro scandoloso Moccolone ridure ad honesta e conveniente misura & apparenza per levare le molte mormorationi e scandoli che publicamte cagiona & ha cagionato continuamte e particolarmte in questa Citta di Nasia altrimenti passato il sudetto termine non comparendo come sopra si intenda ipso fatto incorso nella conculcatione del Nasone al meridiano & d'essergli posto in publica Piazza del Chiapponese nella Berlina, si che s'avisa a non mancare & ubidire a questo nostro Preceto e comanto Aliter si procedera con ogni rigore contro di voi irremissibilmente come trasgressore & inobediente in conformita de statuti e sudette nostre gride

Nasia il di 1668.

Macrobio Culaccione Generale.
Polipodio Marrucco Cancelliere. Massentio Menalorbo Secret.o

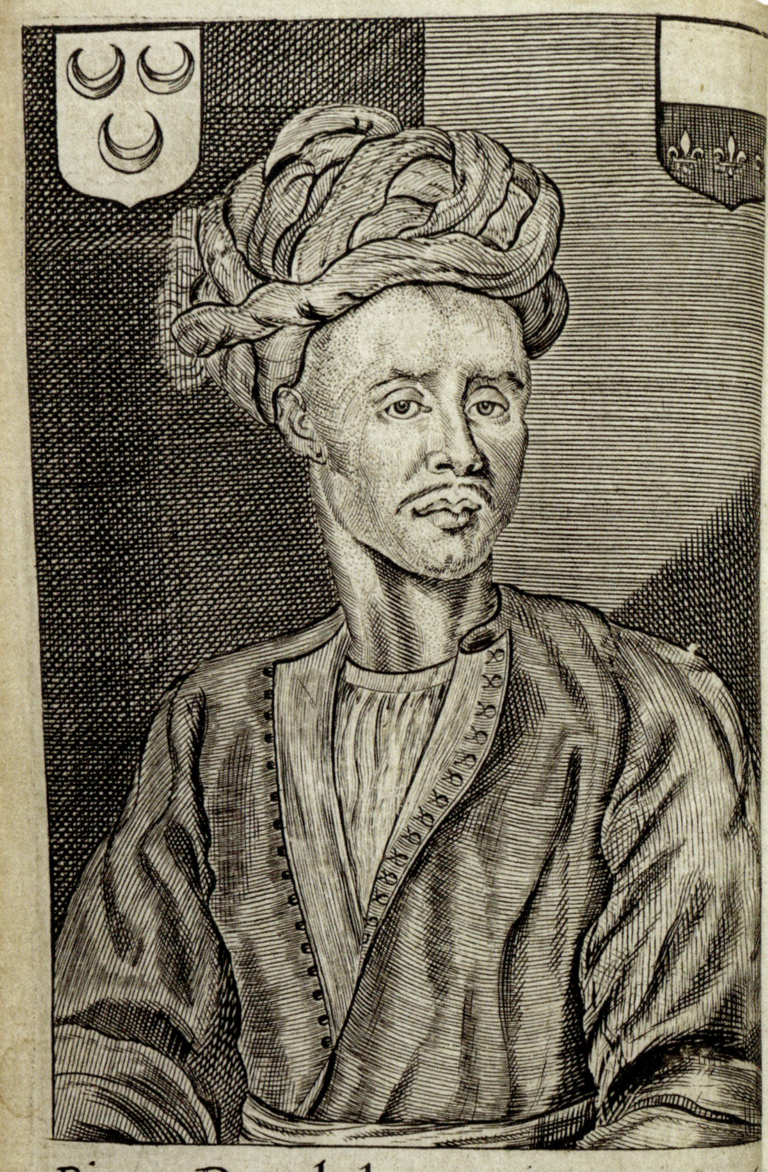

Rigep Dandulo *a Turke by 7. Descents* (c
into England *with* Abde Aga *Agent from ye Illust*
Hamet Basha *of Argier) and was here* Baptiz
ye christian Faith by Mr. GUNNING *at Exeter Chappel in ye St*
November 8th: 1657.

THE Baptized Turk, OR A NARRATIVE

Of the happy Conversion of
Signior *Rigep Dandulo*,
THE
Onely Son of a Silk Merchant in the Isle of Tzio,
from the Delusions of that great
Impostor *Mahomet*, unto the
Christian Religion:
AND
Of his Admission unto Baptism by
Mr. GUNNING at *Excester-house*
Chappel the 8th of *Novemb*. 1657.

Drawn up by *THO. WARMSTRY*, D.D.

Psal. 58. 31. ---*The Morians Land shall soon stretch out her hands to God.*

London, Printed for *J. Williams*, *T. Garthwait* in
St. *Pauls* Church-yard, and *Henry Marsh* at the
Princes Arms at the lower end of *Chancery-lane*
near the inner-Temple-gate in *Fleetstreet*, 1658.

Entry #42

ENTRY #42

Thomas Warmstry (1610–1665), author
The baptized Turk, or, A narrative of the happy conversion of Signior Rigep Dandulo . . . from the delusions of that great impostor Mahomet, unto the Christian religion: happily begun by the author, and effectually prosecuted by the assistance of Mr. Peter Gunning. With the relation of his admission to baptism at Excester-house-chapel. the 8th. of November. 1657, 1658
Book with letterpress and engraving
Case C 6526.9546

The Baptized Turk is Thomas Warmstry's 1657 account of the Anglican* conversion of Rigep Dandulo, "an Islamic Turk." England's relation to the Ottoman Empire in the seventeenth century serves as a backdrop to the written account of Dandulo's conversion and the image on the frontispiece in the Newberry's edition. In early modern Europe, there was a general anxiety about Ottoman empire-building. However, England's geographical location (far from Ottoman borders and oriented towards the Atlantic), political alliances, and shared enemies with the Ottoman assuaged some of those anxieties. Thus, Warmstry's account precedes only by a few years the opening of highly popular Turkish-inspired "coffee shops" in London.

An examination of the frontispiece shows that this vision of Turks could be pressed into service. The portrait of Dandulo depicts him dressed in "traditional" Islamic clothes, an exaggeratedly large and intricate turban atop his head and a kaftan over his shirt. Two coats-of-arms are featured in the top corners of the portrait. While their meaning is unknown, in heraldry, crescents have Islamic origins, and the fleurs-de-lis are frequent symbols of the British monarchy. Therefore, holistically, this image foreshadows Dandulo's conversion and enfoldment into British Protestantism. The broader function of conversion narratives during the seventeenth century was to simultaneously attack Catholicism and define Protestantism as the superior religion. Dandulo is a pawn in this war of religions; his compliance bolsters the power of Protestantism to "enlighten" and "civilize." Therefore, this image is emblematic of race as power management.

Further Readings

Harper, James G. *The Turk and Islam in the Western Eye: 1450–1750: Visual Imagery before Orientalism*. Surrey, England: Ashgate, 2013.

Pearson, Jacqueline. "'One Lot in Sodom': Masculinity and the Gendered Body in Early Modern Narratives of Converted Turks." *Literature and Theology* 21, no. 1 (2007): 29–48. https://doi.org/10.1093/litthe/frl060.

Katherine Chacon

ON CRITICAL INDIGENOUS STUDIES AND EARLY MODERN CRITICAL RACE STUDIES: A TRI-INTERVIEW

By Kim F. Hall, Scott Manning Stevens, and L. Lehua Yim

There has been a rich dialogue between Native Studies/Critical Indigenous Studies (NS/CIS) and Black/Critical Race Studies (B/CRS) in nineteenth-, twentieth-, and twenty-first-century scholarship. But there has been less interaction between those fields in premodern scholarship. The following conversation between Kim F. Hall, Scott Manning Stevens, and L. Lehua Yim tries to get at this problem: in the context of early modern studies, why is it so difficult for NS/CIS work and work that critically analyzes race and anti-Blackness to be in deeper conversation with each other? How does addressing fissures or gaps between our endeavors help us identify epistemological and political issues in early modern studies more broadly? What common political and ideological problems about nineteenth- and twentieth-century narratives defining "the early modern past" can Critical Race Studies and Critical Indigenous Studies interrogate further? This discussion took place on Zoom during Winter 2021 and has been edited by the participants for length and clarity.[1]

1. The co-editors are particularly grateful to L. Lehua Yim for most generously facilitating this tri-interview.

LLY: In my experience, Native Studies continues to be pushed into nineteenth-, twentieth-, and twenty-first-century periodization while early modern studies has continually re-grounded itself in this idea that we can't think about nineteenth-century thought-structures because it's "a-historical." And early modern studies' productions of "the Native" or "the Indigenous" and non-European worldviews and histories prior to the nineteenth century remain caught up in uncritical tropes that replicate settler erasures of Native sovereignty, language archives, ontologies, and epistemologies. Similarly, in North American versions of Native or Indigenous Studies, if I want to talk about "premodern" property and law outside of Europe, I am limited to merely gesturing at Spanish conquest and then Locke with nothing else in between or around those two narrative nodes. And that's singularly unhelpful for looking at the root of our current situation; it's a kind of a-historicism that buttresses certain arguments of modern Native and colonizers' socio-legal and political interactions. But it does nothing to talk about a "before," which I associate with opening up possibilities to make space for past and future Native life that is outside the continual recirculation of "the Native" in settler discourse and knowledge production.

SMS: I've been thinking about these questions a lot and for a long time. And one of the challenges I always have when I'm trying to write something in the context of early modern studies is that each time, I have to reinvent the wheel as to what Indigenous Studies, Indigenous cultures, plural polities, and everything else were and are now. So, I end up with an essay about thirty pages too long from what's wanted. And yet, I've had this experience that if I leave all that out, someone will say, "he's talking about these things that we don't know about." It's an endless frustration for the larger field of Indigenous Studies within the settler colonial* scholarly world. The purposeful impoverishment of U.S. education on Indigenous issues hobbles us as scholars because we're then left with no common ground on which to speak. Even my Native students have difficulty knowing the histories of tribes and nations other than their own. It's this incredibly frustrating space to work in where we've been this blank in U.S. historical discourse, consigned to the past, written off-stage very early on. So, when you start to talk about things like the Doctrine of Discovery* and these things that are vitally important to American Indigenous life today. . .

LLY: And to American life as a whole!

SMS: Right! And I always say, if you think some fifteenth-century papal bull has nothing to do with you living on the Mohawk reserve, you're wrong. In 2005, the U.S. Supreme Court cited the Doctrine of Discovery in the land case between the Oneida and the city of Sherrill, New York. The idea that this fifteenth-century occurrence doesn't live in the present is a misconception. Any expectation that we can somehow make up for an absence of education about the past, which yawns so temporally wide, creates a pressure to privilege modern periods' fields of work. But Indigenous history does not begin at Wounded Knee. It is hard for me as a scholar to write about Native and Indigenous histories and issues while also being responsible to readers who are caught in this social and historical ignorance. It is hard to make sure they are on the same page when that page is two thousand pages long in its absence. And that is what really stymies me. If I were just writing about an early modern English love lyric, I would usually just stick to that standard discourse, those idioms. Because when I try to combine early modern studies and Indigenous Studies, I find it really challenging.

KFH: Scott, so much of what you said resonates with the trajectory of Premodern Critical Race Studies as experienced by Black Shakespeareans. At one point out of frustration after a conference, I told Ian Smith that we needed a manifesto to use every time we present early modern race work and somebody tries to drag us back to "please explain to me the history of race and critical race studies." Fields can't evolve if we're constantly being made to pitch ourselves to the most ignorant. And that is really a demand for us to do their thinking and work for them. I wouldn't engage with other sub-fields and say, "hey, you know what, you can't make your points until you explain to me the entire history of your sub-field." But somehow, those of us who are People of Color, Black, and Indigenous, in particular, get hit with that demand. This ongoing refusal to allow us to use the scholarly tools that we trained in is kind of maddening: it creates writers-block in graduate students and faculty, and it is really stultifying.

SMS: We are forced to backtrack constantly. And I've had the same experience with editors: "You say 'Haudenosaunee,' but then sometimes you say 'Iroquois.'" And I *always* explain why. But if I say "Six Nations," or "Five Nations," "Mohawk," "Kanien'kehá:ka"—heads will explode! Mine doesn't because I can hold these terms; *we can all* hold those terms. And you're absolutely right. We do not go to a talk on the Soviet Union, raise our hand, and say, "Could you explain what Russia was? What do you mean by 'tsar'? I don't know what a 'serf' is." And I see how we are responsible for making scholarly space for everyone else's history, but no one is responsible for ours. And that drives me crazy.

LLY: I am very interested in interrogating what early modern studies thinks a "serf" is because people who claim that as their history are working amidst a discourse deeply conditioned by, made purposeful by the "presentist" needs of white settler colonial societies. Those comfortable versions of English social, political, and legal historical structures need reinvestigation. Akin to Montaigne's appropriation of "Indian" observers of French economic disparities at the end of "Of Cannibals," my interest in a NS/CIS approach to early modern studies appropriates a somewhat anthropological* approach to undoing settled nineteenth- and twentieth-century "understandings" of early modern English life, looking again with concepts and analytical paradigms shaped outside of those canonized in modern European knowledge production. In doing so, I see this work as reclaiming an active power, a sovereign thought-process, to tell people that your ignorance isn't just about my nation and others who live Indigenous ways. It is also about dominant narratives of early modern English society, which have been used to buttress domination and extraction as a mode of modern life. It's a continual frustration to find an unexamined desire, even amongst allies, to erase 'Ōiwi sovereignty and political existences operating outside the paradigm and discourses of the settler state. This is burdensome, because such an erasure speaks in the name of freedom of the individual subject from oppression, while remaining ignorant of its predication upon wiping out all of the socio-political-constructing ways that Native Peoples everywhere live in relation to each other and the places they belong to. For me, that is the biggest reason why we need to have this conversation *now*.

SMS: I hear you. Pointing out the presumption that the early modern European past is all knowable and known to them—because it's not. In fact, what I often have to remind students is the plurality of points of view and traditions within Europe at the time. Because they take weird comfort in the idea that that's just the way people thought back then. Slavery, witch-burning, and other horrifying things get consigned to "that's just how they were 'back then'"—but there were dissenting voices back then that express the horror. Why would Montaigne write an essay like "Of Coaches" and think about the destruction leveled on the Indigenous world for the trade in pearls and pepper? Students have a hard time thinking about these issues because of this historical "pass," which makes these histories appear not worth critiquing. Then you can't even bring Critical Race Studies to that juncture because of this thought that there is nothing in those historical periods to be critical about, and if we do raise a critique, we are being "a-historical." The wrong of slavery remains protected in this kind of "that's just how it was back then" belief.

LLY: I think about those in our Native and Black communities who have fought to learn more about our traditional knowledges, in our languages, and assert the legitimacy of agriculture, water management, familial belonging, and political and social practices pushing against colonial repression. There is common ground between these knowledges in diverse Native communities and diverse Black communities. But our current losses in the pandemic threaten the keeping of those knowledges. We need more spaces in which to be able to say things like "we're not going to let the equivalent of a library burn down when we lose this person in our community."

KFH: Absolutely.

SMS: Yes. And we need other people, so-called "allies" to understand the weight of those losses, that to speak of an individual person as bearing so much importance to a People is not just quaint or folkloric or ethnic — but we are in fact talking about means of knowledge keeping, knowledge production. And the answer isn't just to say, "Well, write everything down or just adopt foreign ways." I've had students say, "Well, you write, you can't think writing is bad." And I reply that I don't think writing is bad, but I think writing is a different kind of knowing than knowing in the way my ancestors or even my elders do. And I always give them the example of my grandmother. When I was a teenager, I got some junior anthropologist notion in my head that I was going to record my grandmother's stories with a tape recorder. And she politely said no — and not for any spooky "you're going to steal my soul" reason. And when I asked why not, she said, because then you won't really have to know them. You'll have them on a tape, which you can put on a shelf and think you always have access. But they won't be a part of you. If you can't recall them to your own children from your own mind, you don't live them, they are not living in you, and they are not part of you. And if you say, "oh let me find that tape — I know it's around here somewhere," that is not knowing them. That had a huge impact on me. Because I realized how much we don't get told when it's to be written down. And all the knowledge that is out there that the anthropologist "missed," as it were, knowledge that "was held back" — whatever we call it — I find my grandmother's stance a really valuable lesson, especially when I think about the value of orality and what histories are for. We have libraries and libraries filled with historic writing and yet phenomenal levels of historical ignorance among the general population. So when someone extols the presumed superiority of European technologies, how has that person been the beneficiary of those technologies given their remarkable historical ignorance? That person is really operating on a kind of folkloric level of this is what happened. How do you know European technologies were superior? Was it due to their own research? No, it's just kind of what that person learned growing up with a disengaged kind of "so it was" history. I noticed recently that in 2019, a group calling themselves the Patriot Front distributed on some college campuses maps of the United States that were just one solid color, with the caption: "Not Stolen. Conquered." This strikes me as a self-explanatory justification. We have so much work to do in the face of that continued declaration. This version of our history is simply a "might makes right," self-legitimizing claim.

KFH: I think what's come out so far shows exactly *why* we need to have more of this Premodern Critical Race Studies (PCRS) and NS/CIS conversation, and why the Newberry Library needs to host it. Because one of the things we're talking about is how Critical Indigenous Studies and Black Studies have been so busy trying to do our work within the protocols of what's considered scholarship that we are hampered by strategies of deflection that have kept us from having rich conversations with each other. Instead, we can take our fields in different, powerful directions. For example, Scott, your thinking about how we listen, what oral histories and traditions mean, pushes back against the notion of "archive" that is built into the Newberry, the Folger, and other institutions. To gain access as a Fellow, you need to identify print documents in this collection that you can speak about. Instead, these institutions need to become spaces for people to share knowledge and make new knowledge that directs us in how to read things differently. And since this volume is about visual representation, this includes thinking more about the visual as a mode of knowledge and knowledge production, rather than it being merely about the decorative. If I am going to put an image in my book, I need to explain that image's interpretive value.

LLY: Your point about the visual, which could be shared between Native communities and Black communities, is that there is an ethics in vision-dominating representations, especially the visual presentations of violence and Native and Black bodies that is also part of the institutional *kuleana* (responsibility) that is not kept by institutions. I've become focused on pushing back against desires to appropriate the Black body and the Native body by scholars in early modern studies work. I think our fields' coming together might engage with the white settler colonial desire to continue to extract cultural-capital value from presentations or mere invocations of "the Black body" or "the Native body." How might our fields come together to address that ethical issue and the power differentials in these extractive visualizations? And why should we take this specific issue up?

SMS: If I think of the way you were both just talking about visual material, which I agree with, as a continuing metaphor, there is a sense in which we are always put in the visual and oral—i.e., the non-alphabetical—documentation of that past. And it's what I call the category of "mere illustration," which is kind of like decorative but also seems to have the authority of "documenting" the past. There are two things that white historians often do with images of any racial import in the past that drive me crazy: they treat the visual representations *as* authoritative—for example, "we can see from this that. . ."—and I'm pointing out that this image is from a European engraver who has never been to the Americas, drawing the fanciful Indigenous people with Greek athletic bodies doing whatever they're illustrated as doing in an imagined context. There's very little to be learned about that Native culture from that visual representation, but there's a lot to be learned about how Europeans think about that Native culture. That's where I find myself looking at the writing, including what I call the tyranny of the document in the discipline of history. There is an over-sized truth value placed by historians in written sources. But is it not possible to write a lie? How about a misperception or misunderstanding? There is something to be gleaned from the Jesuit *Relations of North America*, but you must read extremely critically and engage the text with a very large sense of knowing they exaggerate their understanding of our languages. My own experience in learning other languages makes me suspicious of any claims to learn Mohawk—without any orthography* or known grammars—in three months of hanging out. This emphasis on particular kinds of sources goes to the prejudice in history and our disciplines that historians are doing "something real," and we in literary studies are just studying fairy stories or something. But we are doing something deeply historical and real, and yet that smugness about dealing with historical truth and reality and not "stories" persists, even though the source documents they deal in are forms of stories. That disciplinary divide often explains the sorry state of Indigenous representation amongst the ranks of historians. The discipline pushes us away.

LLY: This makes me think of another challenge. History is not the only discipline that pushes us away. Anthropology has also arisen amidst relationships to white supremacy and imperialism. And anthropology, like history, insists on being the site of *real* knowledge about Natives. Further, scholars working in early modern studies who want to re-engage cultural histories through BS/CRS and NS/CIS are faced with this impression that a touch of the real was enough to tell us all we could need to know about Native and Black lives and imperial and settler colonial cultural formations and encounters in our period.

KFH: I have this sense that the moment of the 1990s let contemporary early modern studies have a kind of complacency, like, "Oh yes. We've done 'the Other.' We've done colonialism."And now we can move on to whatever the next white thing is. This complacency was one of those kinds of clubs used to beat us into submission—"see, so-and-so already said this"

—which attempts to redirect our energies. This gets us back to what Scott started us off with: the forced recursiveness of our early modern work.

SMS: My take on early modern studies' prior turn towards anthropology, especially when it came to Indigenous peoples or non-European peoples was: that's what we get *instead* of history.

LLY: Yes!

SMS: Because it's this whole impression of "no written records, therefore no sources" for Native histories. And the only apparent means of knowing us, absent the records, is through ethnographic records by pre-modern proto-anthropologists.

LLY: As a graduate student in early modern studies, I still felt it incumbent upon me to learn about anthropology, even though I could never see myself joining that discipline, because my entire life was shaped by it. As you say, instead of history, Native people get cultural anthropology.

SMS: Yes, "tell me all about me."

LLY: I worry about our early modern colleagues taking anthropological claims as knowledge without a familiarity with the ethical self-searching some cultural anthropologists have undertaken. I worry about circulating clichés and stereotypes in place of research based on written and oral sources from the periods we work in.

KFH: And part of the struggle of this work is how we talk back to these fields and the history of our own field. My mother and I were listening to a Zoom panel on escape routes for enslaved Blacks. And Cheryl LaRoche said she actually did go and look at the major books on American slavery, and few "credible historians" used the term "underground railroad" before 1998.I was like, "Wait, what??" And learning that licensed her to stop thinking about land as much and to start thinking about water—especially in the eastern U.S., where Black people were using water as a means of escape more than land. So she said that we don't actually have to keep using the term "underground railroad," but that on the other hand, it is the term we're using; so we don't want to get rid of it. Her observation reminds us that you can use that term to track how Black scholars and Black people do push back against a field. So as you are talking, I am thinking about how both of our early modern fields are also pushing back, using our tools in literature and theory to push back against modes of truth or claims to truth that anthropology and history as disciplines tend to make in their worst incarnations.

SMS: I was thinking as we were talking about anthropology, partly because of my generation—especially reading Vine Deloria—that I remember when anthropology was facing its ethical issues in relation to Native peoples. It strikes me that we need the engagement of anthropologists and historians who are deeply invested in the stakes of more ethical versions of those disciplines. Anthropology still has value, still has a lot to teach us that is not getting covered by historical study per se. We need more Indigenous and Black anthropologists; and we need to push back against the idea that you can't write about your own people. Are only white people objective?

LLY: There is a responsibility to push back in early modern studies to help folks find a little wiggle room within the crushing power of so many systems of containment encoding Native and Black peoples in white settler colonial structures of knowledge. The personal is not just political in this work. It also means cultural survival is at stake. So how can we support each other practically and intellectually in this work?

KFH: Yes, and how do we find and support those young people who took a history class thinking, "oh I'm interested in history," and then all of their interests and family traditions get squashed? How do we reach those young people and find a path for them that is not as soul-crushing as the paths that we trod?

SMS: I guess within the academy, I think that it remains vital to support other scholars doing the type of work we're trying to do. And by "support," I mean cite them, invite them, support their tenure, their place of authority within the academy. If we want to reach the students who have made the choice to be within the academy, we have to be there for them. We have to demand a certain level of visibility for them and push back where an administration needs to be moved.

KFH: For me, it's not just about finding students to be academics — although I really want to find students to be academics! But it's also that the knowledge, the tools we offer will be useful to these students, no matter what they do. Administrations primarily invested in STEM would like us in the humanities to forget this, that we actually do offer good tools. And I think this is part of why I am excited about the RaceB4Race goals: if there are ways that we can have public discussion and help students find us, whether they go into academia or not, they have the potential to start catalyzing discussions in a lot of different venues and to push back against this current call for teaching a history of white comfort, amidst claims that any other kind of history can't be taught. There are battles that we can come together around, and *not* in some romanticized version of "Black people and Native peoples have a natural affinity" or that kind of thing — but that there is real struggle here that we need to get on board with. One thing that libraries and institutions with resources could do is make space for learning that is not just about producing a thing — that we could come together and learn about each other's traditions and modes of interpretation and being and survival that aren't in those archives in a transparent kind of way. I'm worried about the conversation because at the same time that Black scholars are chastising our allies, saying, you need to know more about Critical Race Theory, you need to know more about the history of Black studies — I don't want us to come to Native and Critical Indigenous Studies with that same kind of appropriative ignorance. I don't want people out there just using the term "settler colonialism" and not understanding that it has a history. The other thing that I want to learn is how we can think about slowness and nurturing as part of a practice of allyship between Black Studies and Native Studies.

SMS: Right. It's kind of like the cognate to that notion of really knowing an oral story, that it becomes a part of you. But that takes a long time; that *is* a slow process. And it takes a lot of repeating. It takes a lot of reflection, answering questions about the story, etc. And it's a different way of knowing, a more holistic one that we need something cognate to in our exchanges as scholars of Critical Race theory and Indigenous Studies. Because we can't know everything. Each other's fields are capacious enough that it would be a lifetime of learning to know what you know about Black Studies. And so, I think that if we can respect and acknowledge our own ignorance and limitations within our field, and know who to go to, then that would be a great step forward.

LLY: And I think also to help new generations of scholars avoid practices of extraction, which requires them to know who they can send their work to for informed feedback on content and the issues of extractive scholarship. I worry about the job pressures to produce extractive scholarship. A strong place can be held where being ethically responsible and doing good work is possible. But in this highly extractive moment, where demands on Black, Indigenous, and Of Color scholars are very high, this lands really hard on scholars in untenured and precarious, under-resourced positions. And I don't want early career scholars to feel like they have to choose between their career advancement, which may require an appropriative and extractive set of practices, and on the other hand, being ethical and responsible to us as Peoples and communities of knowledge.

KFH: This moment of possibility for both of our fields is also a highly extractive moment. All of us are getting invitations to be part of volumes, to do X, to do Y, and a number of volumes are coming out where a race studies scholar was asked to join in *after* the volume was in process, the SAA seminar had already happened, etc. So again, this is about that time issue. The white scholars had three years to prepare for participating in a volume, to pick their topic and do their research; but then the race scholar is asked, "Hey, can you in two months give us an essay for this?" And sometimes you can. But that's wrong.

SMS: That's exactly an issue. I have lost count of how many things I've been asked to contribute to *after the fact*. I ask, wait, this is due *when*? And the reply is, "well, we've been planning it," but then someone woke up and said we need something by a Native person. Oh really? And then you're caught in a bind, because you ask yourself, do I want *no* representation in that collection that yet again leaves out Indigenous Studies? Or do I want to risk writing a half-baked piece just as a placeholder of Indigeneity in the collection? It's a real bind because you're asked late, and you don't have the time to do what you would like to do, and yet you risk there not being anything in there. And this has been going on like crazy for the last two or three years. Similarly, it's just like being asked by an organization that I'm vaguely connected to, "Can you help us with our land acknowledgment?" As someone said on social media, that's like receiving this message: I have your iPhone. I acknowledge I have your iPhone. Can you help? PS: I am not giving it back. [laughter]

KFH: Oh my gosh! The endless capacity of whiteness to redeem itself and make itself innocent anew forestalls things that people *could* do. So, for example, if we get an invitation, say instead, hey, maybe you and your contributors should all go and read these three essays and include a final essay about how you didn't do that work and what you learned from reading those three essays. But then they'll think, oh, I did my work, and let's go on to the next day. That might be a better option than making us do something quick and half-baked. How about showing your ignorance and your learning, at some point, rather than making our one essay the placeholder for a lot of invisibilizing of work that's been here for years.

LLY: Here's a complication: a lack of sustained, lived engagement with Indigenous Peoples and individuals becomes an excuse for ignorance, for not knowing in fact who are reliable and important thinkers within NS/CIS, let alone who might be linguistically and historically expert or even "knowledge keepers" amidst a person's Native nation or community. This allows for an endless deflection of learning into an excused ignorance. And there is also a shame and fear of valid critique that this ignorance protects. I also worry about how Indigenous lifeways continue to be funneled into and seen erroneously as merely a subset of "race" — which is not to say that "race" is not a structure that Native people are subject to. Rather, as many CIS scholars have noted in their work, "race" also functions as an assimilative tool to eliminate Native nations' political existence and their sovereignty over territory also claimed by the settler state. Similarly, as others writing CIS and feminist critiques have noted, the binary of "Nature vs. Culture" is also a technique of settler colonialism. My concern arises in observing the ease with which work invoking "nature" or "the environment" escapes critique as a tool of white settler colonialism because its ontological categorization and ordering of things is not perceptible as an attack on Indigenous nations and Peoples' sovereignty and self-determination. It looks innocent, speaking of ecologies, of loving the beauty of the natural world, taking better care of the environment. But these ways of thinking and talking about our homelands are used to oppress and eliminate Native Peoples' definitions of and relationships with our places, our lives, and ways. This erasure requires sustained disruption and critique.

SMS: To underline the epistemic difference between our ways of knowledge production, of what is knowing, and what is being is so profound at times that I have to explain to students that this is where Indigenous language scholarship is incredibly useful. It is hard to translate certain concepts typical of Western culture into many Indigenous languages. And then you have to ask why that is the case? For example, the term "wilderness" comes to mind. What would "wilderness" be in Mohawk? What is that space in nature, hostile to humans, where we don't go? We Mohawks understand the woods. We understand the rural places where there are no villages of our people. But there's no "wilderness" — there's certainly no wilderness to be conquered or defeated. There is no errand into that "wilderness." There is no concept like it in Mohawk. And we certainly don't want it. Because that claim on maps of the United States is part of a programmatic way of treating the land, and sovereignty over it, and everything else as a form of Western property dominion. I tell my students, if there is any part of the Christian Bible that you learn, learn Genesis 1:28 about Man having dominion over the world and all of its creatures. That is the least Indigenous way I could think of to be in relationship with "nature." Having been raised Christian, I'm sorry that's part of it. That notion is deadly. It is behind all the crazy "wise use," exploitative, "it's mine to do with as I want" type of thinking. It undergirds greed as an institutional good; it is poison. There is much of the Bible I would excise, but that is the first thing, because it is treated constantly as a justification in our society. The rift between that order to dominate and all of the different ways to be in relation to natural entities in Native societies drives me crazy. I have had similar issues with "ecocriticism"* for these reasons, especially if it does not address the Native critiques of Christian dominion. I was talking with Mohawk-speaking friend of mine, and I said, alright, we can distinguish how "wild" has its own Germanic etymology, and "*wilde tier*" is usually about wild animals. And we distinguish between wild dogs and domesticated dogs. And he says, yeah, but the word for "wild" in Mohawk is the exact word for "free." So if we had to think of a space territorially that is "wild," as you're saying, he said, it would literally break down — because the default pronoun is always "she" in Mohawk, because we're matrilineal — it would be "The-Place-Where-She-Is-Free." And that just does *not* sound so scary.

LLY: So is this actually the beginning of a possible subfield for early modern Critical Race Studies and Critical Indigenous Studies, since we're bringing these efforts together, which might look something like histories of white fear in our period? Similarly, there is room for a sub-field of white settler colonial pleasure studies in early modern studies. This would be interesting to me because my people, Native Hawaiians, get appropriated and defined by the long histories and structures of white settler pleasure.

KFH: Yes! Thinking about white supremacy, remembering past experiences in my career, I remember having conversations when I was presenting work from *Things of Darkness*, where people would ask, do you really mean "white supremacy"? Do you really want to say "white supremacy" — like for years, I would get this. And it was bell hooks' work that gave me the strength to say, no, it *is* white supremacy, and I am going to use this because I have to. Otherwise, it is just contributing to kinds of erasure. And it's disheartening to have been saying this for thirty years, and people are still asking, "Is it white supremacy?"

LLY: This makes me think that what we early modern scholars perhaps need is to define for ourselves — again, following your work Kim — what white supremacy as a term looks like inclusive of the elimination of sovereignty amongst peoples deemed uncivilized?

SMS: I think about the first decades of European conquest in the Americas — those invasions were sanctified by European Christianity, which is able to graft itself onto a sense of "civilization" that is absolute. The papal bulls that make up the Doctrine of Discovery do not explicitly raise color. They are all about Christian doctrine and the supremacy of the civilized. Every horror of the Conquest that is visited on Indigenous Peoples is done in the name of the Church. As racializing discourses develop, this becomes more evident: the *Sublimis Deus* from 1537 announces that Indigenous Americans are fully human. Great. Thank you, Pope. Except a subsequent pope goes on to say ". . .unless they are resistant," which means that then, Europeans can enslave them. These things don't stand like precedent in law; a new pope can change the policy. There is this idea that "white supremacy" means Alabama in 1915 and that I am incorrect in applying it to the Conquest. Yet, in the early moments in the Americas, it's a white supremacy that has yet to fully articulate that whiteness even as it asserts cultural and social superiority over non-European peoples.

KFH: It's locating truth and humanity in a very specific type of body and society.

LLY: At the same time, the moral and epistemological construct of "fairness" operates here as well.

KFH: A defense attorney for the killers of Ahmaud Arbery makes a statement like, "there is no evidence of a soul so blackened as to warrant a life sentence." How many hundreds of years have gone by and are we still doing that?

SMS: Right.

KFH: So I do feel that even if it's not articulated firmly, there is this sense of a moral transcendence that's inherent to Christianity that becomes articulated as whiteness as Europeans seek territory, particularly in the Caribbean. I also wanted to say something about the "expansion" of race studies in the direction of Indigenous Studies. It feels to me that what *I* want, instead of "an expansion into" Critical Indigenous Studies, is for Critical Race Studies to be always changing, adapting, and surviving in part by continuing to learn. I want us to refine our tools, refine our questions, and to teach and learn for transformation and justice. If we look at it as just an expansion of a field, at the possible expense of another field—and it is telling of academic discourse that we don't have better terms for this encounter between race studies and Indigenous Studies—this should be more than allyship. There should be a robust coalescence of these fields at a certain point for how we think about what we do and how we think about the early modern period.

SMS: Yes, I agree—when I hear the word "expansion," I get nervous. [laughter] And it's not a mere issue of semantics. But it may be better to say that Critical Race Studies would not "expand" but instead "*recognize*" this discourse that has been going on between Indigenous Peoples for a very long time. Whether it's going back to Vine Deloria or William Apess, or someone recorded even before that, what should be recognized is that there is an intellectual, resistant tradition among Indigenous Peoples that has its own history; it is its own discourse. And it has been sidelined or marginalized in this other conversation. But if we were to *recognize* it and call on what it has brought to the table, what it is bringing to the table, that would be a way I would be more content with than calling it the next thing that we're going to start now. It's already been happening, for a long time; it just has not been included in the larger Western conversation.

LLY: These are the presets of knowledge production. When I think about what is possible for us, I think in archipelagic terms as a *kanaka*: that we are multiple, and in our episteme, no one gets to claim absolute knowledge of everything. "Not all knowledge is kept in one school." This isn't just a pose; this is respect for limits, a pragmatic* stance. My experience working across different Native nations and communities is that when we get together, we're often very conscious of *where* we gather. Whose house or territory are we in? Who sets the rules? Who is the guest? And then there is a play of languages that becomes a kind of comparative relating. These experiences are paradigmatic for me in how we in our fields might engage with each other. But putting our work in early modern studies in this state requires a rethinking of all the premises that go into knowledge production as *summarizing*, as analyzing and making claims to know more than what one can or should claim to know. Similarly, many questions posed by allies to particular Native nations and communities are unconsciously set in an appropriative framework. The capacity of white settler culture to imagine that it's going to save us and our planet, the repeated refusal to de-center, articulate itself in the most innocent approaches. There are so many issues, including language revitalization and #landback.

SMS: And you'll have a huge portion of people, whether they're hostile to what you say or sympathetic, say to you that it's never gonna happen. "Dream on if you think all these white people are going to step aside and give the country back to Native Americans; it's simply not going to happen." And I would probably agree that it's not going to happen. And so, then, the question is well what do we have to offer beyond the most radical choice, which would be the quickest way to a solution? Either they're not involved or they are — but how? Not everything must be in terms of appropriation. These things have to be teachable to them. Certainly their ways were perniciously teachable to other humans on the planet, through power.

KFH: I want to talk about that "you're never going to get the land back." The kind of unspoken corollaries are: "so you might as well not imagine having your sovereignty, and you might as well not even talk about it." And I say this as someone deeply implicated in this dynamic of talking about a lot of random stuff that won't ever happen. But we can imagine trees, humans, and aliens coming together in space, and we can spend a lot of time talking about that. So white imagination of alternatives is allowed to be capacious and extractive and colonizing of territory, but other forms of imagination — even if you don't talk about it as specific political acts and formations, even if you just think about it as an intellectual and imaginative space — then you somehow are not allowed to have that. Because white people have already decided that that map of conquest is supposed to prevent us from thinking about any other types of histories or response to histories or futures or even the past in a real way.

LLY: The usefulness of North American Indian tribal assertions of #landback, especially First Nations' assertions, as an outsider to that, I can see that phrase's rallying power as settlers treat those nations and communities as foolish or audacious for making that assertion. In my own community, we're in the midst of a climate shift that will cause the oceans to rise, risking the places and lifeways of Pacific Island nations and Native Pacific peoples. With all of that potential loss, #landback only begins to address the urgency of the need to assert our lifeways, which support and enable sustainable life on islands in the middle of the ocean. What will happen when ʻŌiwi are taken from our homeland in these ways?

SMS: That's often what I've wondered as a Haudenosaunee person about those Native nations who were completely removed from their homelands. So like the Trail of Tears and the "Five Civilized Tribes" of the south — I can't imagine what it is to grow up knowing that my traditional homeland is a thousand miles away. And I can't go and visit my people there. It's a big country, and we move around on it, but I know that more people are back in Mohawk land, even though that number is greatly reduced. But I have those feelings about place. I wonder what we can teach non-Indigenous people that will help ameliorate the situation and make them see that Indigenous sovereignty expanded does not mean Indigenous hegemony over them. This tension between a fear of Indigenous hegemony and our aspirations towards the righting of the vessel that's listing — we can say that you need us to steer again. It is our land. It's our place. And we know how to be well in it and with it. There are better ways to live than this. Indigenous Studies can help. You know, I keep going back to the term "recognition" — a recognition of the other for whatever that person's cultural values are, despite any unknownness. This recognition happens all the time between Indigenous nations. There are all sorts of things we need to know about each other's communities and all sorts of wisdoms that we need to share. And I don't think that those are acts of appropriation. Exchange and giving is a big part of our Indigenous cultures. I think we have to acknowledge where that kind of real generosity of spirit lies.

KFH: Maybe this helps me name another part of this, which is what real academic community looks like, and why academia seems to hate it so much. One of the things I hear about RaceB4Race and some of our events is, oh, you guys are just sitting around affirming each other; it's not rigorous. And there's no recognition that sometimes in community, we're letting people present their work and talk about things, and then we have vigorous debates about those things. And we do it in front of them, like we do in other spaces. But we try to do it with an idea that we are a *community*. There's something about the academic world that doesn't want to see this, doesn't want to see this community building as part of what we can do. That's another thing that Black Studies and Indigenous Studies try to give to ourselves and each other and the academy. Community is a real thing, and it's rigorous, powerful, political, and always changing. And it's necessary because it's the only way some of us can actually survive in early modern studies. If I hadn't had other people of color trying to do this work and say, yes, you're not crazy, that was some off-the-wall stuff that was happening—you know, who would get through?

LLY: At RaceB4Race, I can always sense the relief that participants feel that comes with being able to say something that is hard enough to say because of racism in the academy and settler colonialism. And participants don't have to apologize for their work or shield their brilliance.

SMS: The white gaze and white mind has been committed for decades to saying that we didn't have anything of value. And now that we're coming together and saying we actually do value this, and we call it for what it is, they see it as a lack on their part. And so now you have something I don't have, and we want it!

LLY: I am so grateful that you have been willing to share the wealth of your insights. Thank you both for this conversation. You make me think about what it means to be a *kumu*, a teacher and a source. One of my hopes for our continuing work together is to give people an experience of what a *different* way of teaching and learning looks like. So I hope that we can continue these conversations and these learning experiences together. I've learned a lot. Thank you!

SMS: Well, this has been a real delight, so thank you so much!

KFH: Thank you so much, I really appreciate it.

GLOSSARY

Analytic (as a noun): mode or lens chosen to analyze something.

Anglican: observing the religion of the Church of England.

Anthropological: relative to anthropology, the study of humanity at the intersection of biology, cultural studies, archaeology, linguistics, and other social sciences.

Antiquarianism: intense interest in Antiquity, the past, and its remains.

Archipelagic: relative to an archipelago, a group of islands scattered over a body of water.

Atlas: bound collection of maps.

Baptizand: person who receives baptism.

Blazon: genre of poetry that catalogs the physical attributes of a person—usually a woman. The genre was popularized by early Renaissance Italian poet Petrarch.

***Bozal*:** in the Hispanic world, enslaved person of African descent who is not yet acculturated to Hispanic culture and speaks Spanish imperfectly by Castilian standards.

Brocade: silk fabric with raised patterns in gold and silver.

Canon: religious rule approved by the Catholic Pope.

Cartographer: mapmaker.

Cartouche: ornamental frame containing text.

***Castas* painting:** Latin American painting from the eighteenth century representing several patterns of racial mixing in a hierarchical manner.

Catechization: act of bestowing catechism in order to convert people.

Caveat: warning that acknowledges some limitations.

Cedula: official administrative document in the Spanish-speaking world.

Cenotaph: commemorative monument dedicated to a person buried elsewhere.

Chauvinism: undue belief in the superiority of one's own group.

Choreography: art of designing, patterning, or scripting movement.

Citational: citing someone or something else.

***Codex* (plural, *codices*):** bound manuscript often containing ancient texts.

Compendium: abridgement or summary of a longer work.

***Conquistador*:** Spanish colonizer in the Americas, especially in sixteenth century Mexico and Peru.

Contrapposto: position in which one leg holds the full weight of the subject's body.

Copyist: person who copies, imitates, or transcribes documents.

Cosmological: relative to cosmology, which studies the universe as a whole, at the intersection of astronomy and metaphysics.

Cosmographer: person who maps the general features of the celestial and terrestrial worlds.

Critical Indigenous Studies (CIS): field of inquiry centering global Indigenous political, epistemological, and ideological concerns and conditions. It studies the structures and relations of power in a world (including the academic world) dominated by settler colonialism.

Critical Race Theory (CRT): offshoot of what was known since the mid-1980s as Critical Legal Theory, which is premised upon the idea that the law is not neutral and supports the interests of those who make it. CRT highlights the specific role of race in the legal apparatus. It is a movement that started in the 1980s, when law professors of color and allies noticed that the Civil Rights movement had fallen short of its objective in that racial discrimination and inequality had remained in place, and they started investigating the structural enmeshment of racism in law and its institutions. Building upon the pioneering work of Derrick A. Bell, Richard Delgado, and Alan David Freeman, legal scholars such as Kimberlé Crenshaw, Mari Matsuda, Cheryl Harris, Patricia Williams, and others developed a vibrant field of inquiry that is now influencing other disciplines.

Cross-cultural: establishing a conversation between different cultures.

Curatorial: relative to curator, a person in charge of displays and exhibitions in museums and libraries, and, by extension, any manager of cultural content.

Damask: jacquard whose patterns are woven in satin into a different material.

Demographics: quantifiable composition of a human population.

Diaphanous: transparent, see-through.

Didactics: pedagogy, a system for teaching something.

Divinatory: relative to prophecies.

Doctrine of Discovery: in the case *Johnson v. McIntosh* (1823), Chief Justice John Marshall explained the Supreme Court's unanimous view "that the principle of discovery gave European nations an absolute right to New World lands." Based on 1490s papal bulls that allowed Spaniards to "discover" any land one hundred leagues west of the Azores and Cape Verde Islands that was not habited by Christians, the Doctrine of Discovery stripped Indigenous Americans of their land and sovereignty.

Ecclesiastic: clergyman.

Ecocriticism: field of inquiry that studies the environment and the environmental crisis through a humanistic lens that combines literature, culture, history, and ecology.

Ecumenically: in a manner that promotes the unity of the Christian Church across schisms and partitions (such as exist between Catholic, Protestants, and Orthodox Christians, for instance).

Émigré: person who emigrated, leaving their homeland.

Empiricism: method for forming knowledge based on sensory experience.

***Encomendero*:** *encomienda* beneficiary.

Encomienda: patent granting conquistadores the right to colonial lands and to the labor of enslaved Indigenous people on those lands.

Encomium (plural *encomia*): piece of writing written in praise of someone or something.

Engraving: image printed from a metal plate that has been manually engraved.

Epigram: concise and witty poem with a satirical edge.

Episteme: regime of knowledge, system for understanding the world.

Epistemic: relative to knowledge and the different ways knowledge is produced.

Epistemology: theory and study of the systems we use for understanding the world.

Etching: image printed from a metal plate that has been manually and chemically processed.

Ethnographic: relative to ethnography, the study and description of people, societies, and cultures around the world.

Ethnology: cultural anthropology, the methods of which yield ethnographic scholarship.

Etymology: study of the origin and original meaning of words.

Eurocentric: exclusively focused on Europe to the exclusion of the wider world.

Facsimile: exact copy of something.

Folio: large book printed on paper sheets that were folded only once (by contrast with a quarto). Also refers to a single page in such a book.

Franciscan: member of the Order of Friars Minor founded by St. Francis of Assisi in 1209.

Frontispiece: illustration facing a book's title page.

Gentile: person who is not Jewish.

Glyph: symbol that conveys meaning without resorting to language.

Grisaille: technique that uses only one color (gray) to produce an effect of depth.

Hagiographic: relative to the account of saints' lives.

Hatching: technique that uses fine lines in proximity in order to create a shade effect in a drawing or an engraving.

Hermaphrodite: person who has both male and female reproductive organs.

Heteronormativity: worldview that takes heterosexuality as the norm by default.

Heuristic: process or method for problem-solving, and the study of that process.

Hidalgo: person who belongs to the lowest rank of Spanish nobility.

Historicize: to place something in its proper historical context in order to understand it.

Historiography: process of writing history, and the study of that process.

Humanistic: relative to humanism, a European intellectual movement from the fourteenth to the sixteenth century characterized by a renewed interest in classical texts and epistemologies.

Humoralism: ancient medical theory still in vogue during the early modern period, according to which a healthy body had a balanced combination of four liquid humors: blood, phlegm, bile, and melancholy. External factors, including geography and environment, were believed to influence that humoral balance.

Iconographically: by means of iconography.

Iconography: synonym for pictorial representation.

Ideogram: non-verbal symbol used to represent a concept in a system of writing.

Ideological: relative to ideology, the aggregated ideas and sociopolitical values that constitute one's worldview.

Ideologist: someone invested in spreading and imposing a specific ideology.

Illumination: painted embellishment on a manuscript that often includes gold or silver.

In situ: in the very place in question.

Incunable: early book printed before 1501, the design of which is still informed by manuscript culture.

Indentured: subjected to indenture, the contract by which a person bound themselves to serve a master for a limited amount of time in the premodern world.

Intaglio: printed from a plate on which the image is incised or engraved below the surface.

Interpolation: process of inserting additions into a text.

Interregnum: period in English history (1649–1660) when, following a Civil War, England was a republic, between the reigns of Charles I and Charles II.

Intersectionally: in a manner that attends to what Kimberlé Crenshaw has defined as "intersectionality," that is, the ways in which the many features of one's identity, such as race, gender, class, ability, and sexuality, intersect and compound with one another.

Itinerarium (plural, *itineraria*): travelogue.

Jacquard: fabric with intricate patterns woven into it (as opposed to printed or embroidered).

Janiform: in the form of the Latin god Janus, that is, with two faces.

***Landsknecht*:** German mercenary pikeman (a soldier armed with pike).

Lapland: northernmost region of Finland.

Lateran Council: ecclesiastical council of the Catholic Church held in Rome in the Lateran Palace next to the Lateran Basilica in order to rule on questions of doctrine.

Latitude: angular distance of a place North or South from the Earth's equator.

Letterpress: text printed using relief printing.

Levant: (obsolete) stretch of land in the Eastern Mediterranean corresponding to today's Israel, Palestine, Jordan, Lebanon, Syria, and some Turkish regions.

Lexicographical: relative to lexicography, the art or practice of writing dictionaries.

Libretto: text to which an opera or other extended musical composition is set.

Lithograph: image printed from a flat stone through chemical reaction.

Liturgy: form of public worship, especially in the Christian Church.

Locus: place where something happens, in the literal or figurative sense.

Longue durée: term introduced by historian Fernand Braudel and the French Annales School to describe their particular approach to historiography. This French phrase means "long duration."

Macro-regional: specific to a large geographic area.

Mandarin: learned official in the former Chinese Imperial civil service.

Masthead: section in a newspaper (often on the editorial page) giving information such as the owner's name, a list of the editors, the advertising and subscription rates.

***Mestizo*:** person of mixed European and Indigenous American ancestry.

Methodology: body of methods self-consciously used in different disciplines.

Metonymically: in the manner of a metonymy, a figure of speech that consists in mentioning a thing for another thing with which it is somehow associated.

Miscellany: separate pieces of writing collected in one volume.

Misnomer: wrong name or designation.

Misogyny: prejudice against women, male chauvinism.

Mnemonically: in the manner of a device that helps memorize something.

Modicum: small quantity of something.

Morocco: fine flexible leather from goatskin tanned with sumac.

Mores: manners and moral attitudes towards those manners.

Mythopoetic: relative to the creation of myths.

Nadir: opposite of the zenith, lowest point of something.

Neoclassical: European aesthetic movement that advocated for the revival of ancient Greek and Roman aesthetics in domains such as literature, music, art, or architecture.

Normativity: quality of being the norm.

Ontological: relative to ontology, that is, the theory and study of the nature of being.

Orientalism: Edward Said defined "Orientalism" as a body of Western theories and practices that represent the East as fit to be colonized.

Orthography: proper spelling.

Pamphlet: printed publication that is unbound, with no cover.

Paradigm: salient example, typical instance of something.

Parchment: animal skin dressed and prepared for writing, painting, or bookbinding.

Patriarchal: relative to patriarchy, a social organization characterized by the supremacy of fathers in families and the power of men over everyone else.

Patristic: relative to the Christian Church Fathers or their writings.

Peddler: itinerant salesman who sells small items in the street or door to door.

Periodization: established ways of dividing human history into distinct time periods (such as the Middle Ages, the Renaissance, Early Modernity, and the Enlightenment) for the purpose of academic study.

Phenomenological: refers to the dimension of things that we apprehend through experience.

Phenotype: in the scientific context, the observable characteristics of an organism produced by the interaction between its genetic material and its environment. In everyday context, the physical characteristics of an individual used to identify and categorize them.

Philological: relative to philology, the classical study of language and literature.

Physiognomy: facial features and the pseudo-science based on their scrutiny.

Piazza: public square in an Italian city.

Pictography: system of writing that uses non-verbal pictures to represent objects they resemble.

Portolan: nautical map featuring ports and harbors, generally drawn by hand or in manuscript.

Postcolonialism: field of inquiry that grew in the aftermath of Western colonialism: it studies the political, economic, historical, cultural, and social impact of European colonial rule around the world from premodernity to the present. It often centers the conditions, agency, and epistemologies of colonized and formerly colonized people.

Pragmatic: realistic and committed to a concrete approach.

Prefatory: serving as a preface.

Premodern Critical Race Studies (PCRS): term coined by Pr. Margo Hendricks at the RB4R symposium "Race and Periodization" at the Folger Shakespeare Library in 2019 to designate retroactively a field of academic inquiry that was over thirty years old at the time. PCRS extends Hendricks's definition to include the study of race-making informed by Critical Race Theory's methods and ethos in any premodern time period.

Premodernity: era in the history of the Western world that precedes the late-seventeenth-century and eighteenth-century intellectual movement of the Enlightenment.

Processional: designed to be carried and displayed during religious processions.

Proselytism: eagerness to convert others to one's own religion.

Quadrant: quarter divided from other quarters by a rectangular coordinate axis.

Racialization: interpretive process of ascribing racial value to something or a racial identity to someone.

Rebus: riddle representing words or syllables through pictures of objects or through symbols that sound like the intended words or syllables.

Redact: to remove a portion of text from a document by making that text illegible.

***Reconquista*:** series of medieval Catholic campaigns launched to conquer territories that had been under Moorish rule since the eighth century in the Iberian Peninsula. King Ferdinand of Aragon and Isabelle of Castile successfully concluded the Reconquista with the Fall of Granada in 1492.

Romance: genre of marvelous verse or prose narrative popular in premodern Europe, often but not always centered around a knight's quest.

Sartorial: relative to clothing.

Satyr: in Greek and Roman mythology, minor forest deity having both human and goat-like features.

Scenography: stage scenery designed for a theatrical production.

Scribe: someone who copies manuscripts.

Sephardic: refers to the Jewish and Jewish-descended people expelled from Spain and Portugal in the late fifteenth century, and by extension to Mediterranean Jewish culture.

Settler colonialism: defined by historian Patrick Wolfe as a distinct type of colonialism in which colonizers destroy Indigenous peoples and cultures, replace them, and establish themselves as the new rightful inhabitants. Settler colonial discourse normalizes and thus perpetuates in the present the logic of elimination and the mechanisms of dispossession that have animated it over time.

Shrine: holy space containing the relics of a Saint, place of pilgrimage.

Sociologist: scholar studying the development, structure, and functioning of society, social institutions, and social relationships.

Somatic: relative to the body.

Sovereignty: for a state or a people, political independence, and self-determination.

Subaltern: inferior, subordinate.

Supersessionary: bound to replace something else.

Synecdochically: in the manner of a synecdoche, a figure of speech that consists in mentioning a part to refer to the whole, or vice-versa.

T-O *mappa mundi*: medieval map of the world representing the Mediterranean, the Nile, and the Don River conjoined to form a "T" separating Europe, Africa, and Asia, all encircled by the Ocean in the form of an "O."

Taxonomy: detailed and complex system of categorization.

Teleological: moving towards a strategically pre-determined endpoint.

Theological: relative to theology, the knowledge and study of God and religion.

Topography: science or practice of describing a particular location.

Topos: a commonplace, synonym for trope.

Transdisciplinarily: in a manner that applies across academic disciplines (such as history, literature, and art history).

Transhistorical: applying across different historical periods.

Transliterate: to translate a word into a different alphabet (for instance an Arabic word into the Latin alphabet).

Travelogue: travel-focused narrative.

Trope: very commonly used phrase, idea, or device.

Troped: turned into a trope.

Type: block bearing a relief character used with other blocks for printing purposes.

Typesetter: person who arranges the type composing the page for printing purposes.

Typographic: relative to typography, the arrangement of elements on a printed page.

Vellum: parchment of superior quality made from the skin of calves.

Venality: quality of a person who can easily be bribed.

Vernacular: quality of a language or dialect native to the people who speak it (rather than a literate or foreign language).

Versification: process of turning someone or something into the subject of poetry written in verse.

Vestimentary: relative to clothing.

Viceroyalty: colonized territory ruled by a Viceroy in the name of a foreign king.

Watercolor: painting whose paint is made with a water-soluble binder and thinned with water rather than oil.

Western: in premodern times, Europe and its direct sphere of influence in North America.

Woodcut: image printed from a wooden block that has been manually carved.

BIBLIOGRAPHY

Primary Sources

Manuscripts

Anonymous. "A Collection of serious, humorous, and affectionate poems." Chicago, Newberry Library, Case MS Y 184.18.

Anonymous. "An Account of the Indians in Virginia and of some remarkable things in that country." 1698. Chicago, Newberry Library, Ayer MS 9.

Commonplace Book of Jane Pigot. 18th Century. Chicago, Newberry Library, Case MS B 69.188.

Mannyng, Robert. "Handlyng Synne." 14th Century. London, British Library, MS Harley 1701, fol. 59r.

Printed Works

A LETTER from a Merchant at JAMAICA TO A Member of Parliament in LONDON, Touching the AFRICAN TRADE. To which is added, A SPEECH made by a BLACK of Gardaloupe, at the Funeral of a Fellow-Negro. London: Printed for A. Baldwin, 1709.

Cavazzi, Giovanni Antonio. *Istorica descrizione de' tre' regni Congo, Matamba, et Angola situati nell'Etiopia inferiore occidentale e delle missioni apostoliche esercitateui da religiosi Capuccini. . . .* Bologna: Giacomo Monti, 1687.

Cousin, Louis. *Histoire de Constantinople, depuis le régne de l'ancien Justin, jusqu'à la fin de l'empire*. Paris: Chez Damien Foucault, 1672. Chicago, Newberry Library, F 325.21.

Derbew, Sarah F., *Untangling Blackness in Greek Antiquity*. Cambridge: Cambridge University Press, 2022.

Donne, John, et al. *The Harmony of the muses, or The gentlemans and ladies choisest recreation: full of various, pure and transcendent wit: Containing severall excellent poems, some fancies of love, some of disdain, and all the subjects incident to the passionate affections either of men or women / heretofore written by those unimitable masters of learning and invention, dr. joh. donn, dr. hen. king, dr. W. stroad [et al]*, edited by R.C. London: Printed by T.W. for William Gilbertson, 1654.

Einhard. *Vita et gesta Karoli Magni*. Basel, Germany: Johannes Soter, 1521. Chicago, Newberry Library, Case E 5.C37122.

Fiorelli, Giacomo. *La monarchia d'Oriente del padre maestro Giacomo Fiorelli . . . comincia da Costantino "l Grande nell" anno CCCXXX e termina in Costantino Paleologo nell' anno MCCCCLIII. Alla sacra cesarea maesta' di Leopoldo Avstriaco avgvsto*. Venice: D. Milocco, 1679. Chicago, Newberry Library, folio F 325.301.

King, Henry. *Poems, Elegies, Paradoxes, and Sonnets*. London: Printed for Henry Herringman, 1664.

Knolles, Richard. *The Generall Historie of the Turkes, from the First Beginning Of that Nation to the Rising of the Othoman Familie: With All the Notable Expeditions of the Christian Princes against Them*. London: Printed by A. Islip, 1603. Chicago, Newberry Library, Case F 59 .463.

Léry, Jean de. *Histoire d'un voyage faict en la terre du Bresil, autrement dite Amerique: contenant la navigation, & choses remarquables, veuës sur mer par l'auteur: le comportement de Villegagnon en ce pays-la: les murs & façons de viure estranges des sauuages bresiliens : auec vn colloque de leur langage*. Geneva: Antoine Chuppin, 1585.

Liudprand of Cremona. *Luitprandi Subdiaconi Toletani Ticinensis Diaconi tandem Cremonensis Episcopi Opera quae extant.: Chronicon et adversaria nunc primum in lucem exeunt*. Antwerp: Ex Officina Plantiniana Bathasaris Moreti, 1640. Chicago, Newberry Library, folio F 093.517.

Lopes, Duarte, and Filippo Pigafetta. *Relatione del reame di Congo et delle circonvicini contrade*. Rome: Bartolomeo Grassi. 1591.

Luther, Martin. *Vom Schem Hamphoras und vom Geschlecht Christi*. Wittenberg: Georg Rhaw, 1543.

Nanni, Giovanni. *Tractatus de futuris Christianoru[m] triumphis in Sarcenos Magistri Johannis Viterbiensis*. Nuremberg: Peter Wagner, 1485. Chicago, Newberry Library, Inc. 2227.

Nicolay, Nicolas de. *Les navigations pérégrinations et voyages, faicts en la Turquie . . .* Antwerp: G. Silvius, 1576. Chicago, Newberry Library, Wing ZP 5465 .S587.

———. *The nauigations, peregrinations and voyages, made into turkie by nicholas nicholay daulphinois [. . .]With diuers faire and memorable histories, happened in our time. translated out of the french by T. washington the younger*. London: Thomas Dawson, 1585. http://name.umdl.umich.edu/A08239.0001.001.

———. "The Navigations, Peregrinations and Voyages, Made into Turky, by Nicholas Nicholay Daulphinois, [. . .] with Divers Fair and Memorable Histories, Which Happend in Our Time." Translated by T. Washington the Younger. In *A COLLECTION of Voyages and Travel consisting of Authentic WRITERS in our own Tongue, which have not before been collected in English [. . .] Interspersed and Illustrated with NOTES*, vol. 7. 554–708. London: Thomas Osborne, 1747.

Phillips, Edward. *The New World of Words, or A Universal English Dictionary. . . .* London: Printed for J. Phillips and H. Rhodes, 1696.

Procopius of Cæsarea. *The History of the VVarres of the Emperour Justinian in Eight Books. Written in Greek by Procopius of Cæsarea and Englished by Henry Holcroft, Knight*. Translated by Henry Holcroft. London: Humphrey Moseley, 1653. Chicago, Newberry Library, Case Y 642.P82.

Robert of Reims [and Fulcher of Chartres]. *Hystoria de Itinere [con]tra turchos*. Cologne: Dares Johannes Solidi, 1472. Chicago, Newberry Library, Inc. 998.

Rycaut, Paul. *The History of the Present State of the Ottoman Empire containing the maxims of the Turkish politie [. . .] representing the variety of habits amongst the Turks, in three books / by Paul Rycaut Esq*. London: Printed for John Starkey and Henry Brome, 1668. http://name.umdl.umich.edu/A58003.0001.001.

———. *The History of the Present State of the Ottoman Empire containing the Maxims of the Turkish Polity [. . .] In Three Books*. London: Printed for R. Clavell, J. Robinson and A. Churchill, 1686. Chicago, Newberry Library. F 59 .764.

Sandys, George. *A Relation of a Iourney Begun an. Dom. 1610: Foure Bookes, Containing a Description of the Turkish Empire of Aegypt, of the Holy Land, of the Remote Parts of Italy and Ilands Adioyning*. London: Printed for W. Barrett, 1615. Chicago, Newberry Library LC: 20011267.

Schedel, Hartmann. *Liber chronicarum*. Augsburg: Johann Schönsperger, 1497. Chicago, Newberry Library, Inc. 1786.

Speed, John. *A Prospect of the Most Famous Parts of the World*. London, 1627.

Editions and Translations

Alberti, Leon Battista. *On Painting and On Sculpture: The Latin Texts of De pictura and De statua*. Translated by Cecil Grayson. London: Phaidon, 1972.

Andrew of Wyntoun. *The Orygynale Cronykil of Scotland*. Edited by David Laing. 3 vols. Edinburgh: Edmonston and Douglas, 1872–79.

Aristotle. *Aristotle's Politics*. Translated by Benjamin Jowett. Oxford Translation Series. Oxford: Clarendon Press, 1905.

———. *The Politics*. Translated by H. Rackham. Loeb Classical Library 264. Cambridge, MA: Harvard University Press, 1928.

Block, Katherine Salter, ed. *Ludus Coventriæ; or, The Plaie Called Corpus Christi, Cotton Ms. Vespasian D. VIII*. Early English Text Society. Extra series, no. 120. Oxford: Oxford University Press, 1922.

Chaucer, Geoffrey. *The Riverside Chaucer*. Edited by Larry D. Benson. 3rd. ed. Boston: Houghton Mifflin, 1987.

Cramond, William, ed. *The Annals of Banff*. 2 vols. Aberdeen: New Spalding Club, 1891.

Ducis, Jean-François. *Shakespeare Made French: Four Plays by Jean-François Ducis*. Translated by Marvin Carlson. New York: Martin E. Segal Theatre Center Publications, 2013.

Einhard. *Charlemagne's Courtier: The Complete Einhard*. Edited by Paul Edward Dutton. Peterborough, Ontario: Broadview Press, 1998.

——— and Notker the Stammerer. *Two Lives of Charlemagne*. Edited by David Ganz. Harmondsworth: Penguin, 2008.

Ginés de Sepúlveda, Juan. *Demócrates Segundo, o, De Las Justas Causas de La Guerra Contra Los Indios*, vol. 2a. Madrid: Consejo Superior de Investigaciones Científicas, Instituto Francisco de Vitoria, 1984.

Gobineau, Arthur. *The Moral and Intellectual Diversity of Races*. Translated by Henry Hotze and Josiah Nott. Philadelphia: Lippincott, 1856.

Greene, Jack P. "'A Plain and Natural Right to Life and Liberty': An Early Natural Rights Attack on the Excesses of the Slave System in Colonial British America." *The William and Mary Quarterly* 57, no. 4 (2000): 793–808. https://doi.org/10.2307/2674156.

Harriot, Thomas. *A briefe and true report of the new found land of Virginia [. . .] authorised by her Maiesteie and her letters patents*. Frankfurt: Johannis Wechell, 1590.

Herbert, George. *The Works of George Herbert*. Edited by F.E. Hutchinson. Oxford: Clarendon Press, 1972.

Hippocrates of Cos. *Airs, Waters, Places*. Edited and translated by Paul Potter. Loeb Classical Library 147. Cambridge, MA: Harvard University Press, 2022.

Juvenal and Persius. *Juvenal and Persius*. Edited and translated by Susanna Morton Braund. Loeb Classical Library 91. Cambridge, MA: Harvard University Press, 2004.

Kritovoulos. *History of Mehmed the Conqueror*. Translated by Charles T. Riggs. Princeton: Princeton University Press, 1954.

Léry, Jean de. *History of a Voyage to the Land of Brazil, Otherwise Called America*. Translated by Janet Whatley. Berkeley, CA: University of California Press, 1990.

Leslie, John. *The Historie of Scotland, Written First in Latin by the Most Reverend and Worthy Jhone Leslie, Bishop of Rosse, and Translated in Scottish by Father James Dalrymple*. Edited by Rev. Father E.G. Cody and William Murison. 2 vols. Edinburgh: W. Blackwood and Sons for the Scottish Text Society, 1888–95.

Liudprand of Cremona. *The Complete Works of Liudprand of Cremona*. Translated by Paolo Squatriti.

Medieval Texts in Translation. Washington, D.C.: Catholic University of America Press, 2007.

López de Velasco, Juan. *Geografía y Descripción Universal de Las Indias*. Edited by Justo Zaragoza. Madrid: Real Academia de la Historia, 1894.

Mannyng, Robert. *Robert of Brunne's "Handlyng Synne."* Edited by Frederick J. Furnivall. 2 vols. Early English Text Society. Original series, no. 119, 123. Ann Arbor, MI: University of Michigan Library, 2006.

Marwick, J. D., ed. *Extracts from the Records of the Burgh of Edinburgh*. Edinburgh: Scottish Burgh Records Society, 1869. *British History Online*, accessed August 12, 2022, https://www.british-history.ac.uk/edinburgh-burgh-records/1403-1528.

Notker the Stammerer. *Monachi sangallensis De gestis Karoli imperatoris libri duo*. Monumenta Germaniæ Historica, vol. 2. Hanover, 1829. Chicago, Newberry Library, oversize F 47.596 v.2.

Pepys, Samuel. *The Diary of Samuel Pepys*. Edited by Henry B. Wheatley. New York: Crouscup and Sterling Publishers, 1893.

Phillips, Edward. *The new world of words, or, A universal English dictionary*. 5th ed. London: Printed for Richard Bently, J. Phillips, H. Rhodes, and J. Taylor, 1696.

Quintilian. *Instituto Oratoria*. Edited and translated by Harold Edgeworth Butler. Cambridge, MA: Harvard University Press, 1922. Electronic edition via Perseus Digital Library, Tufts University. http://www.perseus.tufts.edu/hopper/text?doc=urn:cts:latinLit:phi1002.phi00111.perseus-eng1:3.

Robert of Reims. *Robert the Monk's History of the First Crusade: Historia Iherosolimitana*. Translated by Carol Sweetenham. Crusade Texts in Translation 11. Aldershot: Ashgate, 2005.

Rolland, John. *The Seven Sages, in Scotish Metre*. Edinburgh: Bannatyne Club, 1837.

Stuart, John, ed. *Extracts from the Presbytery Book of Strathbogie: A. D. M.DC.XXXI.–M.DC.LIV*. Aberdeen: Spaulding Club, 1843.

Vitry, Jacques de. *The History of Jerusalem. A.D. 1180*. Translated by Aubrey Stewart. London: Palestine Pilgrims' Text Society, 1896.

Wever, Richard, and Thomas Ingelend. *The Dramatic Writings of Richard Wever and Thomas Ingelend*. Edited by John S. Farmer. London: Barnes and Noble, 1905.

Secondary Sources

Achi, Andrea Myers, and Adam Levine. "Shape of the Museum." Online talk, Art Gallery of Ontario, Ontario, Canada, September 10, 2020. https://ago.ca/events/shape-museum-andrea-achi-and-adam-levine.

———, and Seeta Chaganti. "'Semper Novi Quid ex Africa': Redrawing the Borders of Medieval African Art and Considering Its Implications for Medieval Studies." In *Disturbing Times: Medieval Pasts, Reimagined Futures*, edited by Catherine E. Karkov, Anna Kłosowska, Vincent W. J. van Gerven Oei, 73–106. Santa Barbara: Punctum Books, 2020.

Akbari, Suzanne Conklin. *Idols in the East: European Representations of Islam and the Orient, 1100–1450*. Ithaca, NY: Cornell University Press, 2009.

———. "Where is Medieval Ethiopia? Mapping Ethiopic Studies with Medieval Studies." In *Toward a Global Middle Ages: Encountering the World Through Illuminated Manuscripts*, edited by Bryan C. Keene, 82–93. Los Angeles: The J. Paul Getty Museum, 2019.

Akhimie, Patricia. *Shakespeare and the Cultivation of Difference: Race and Conduct in the Early Modern World*. New York, NY: Routledge, 2018.

Allerston, Patricia. "Reconstructing the Second-Hand Clothes Trade in Sixteenth- and Seventeenth-Century Venice." *Costume* 33, no.1 (1999): 46–56. https://doi.org/10.1179/cos.1999.33.1.46.

Allewaert, Monique. *Ariel's Ecology: Plantations, Personhood, and Colonialism in the American Tropics*. Minneapolis: University of Minnesota Press, 2013.

American Library Association. "Librarian Ethnicity." Accessed August 14, 2022. https://www.ala.org/tools/librarian-ethnicity.

Anderson, Elijah. "The White Space." *Sociology of Race and Ethnicity* 1, no. 1 (2014): 10–21. https://doi.org/10.1177/2332649214561306.

Anderson, Emily Hodgson. "Novelty in Novels: A Look at What's New in Aphra Behn's Oroonoko." *Studies in the Novel* 39, no. 1 (2007): 1–16. http://www.jstor.org/stable/29533796.

Andrea, Bernadette. *Lives of Girls and Women from the Islamic World in Early Modern British Literature and Culture*. Toronto: University of Toronto Press, 2017.

———. "The Tartar Girl, The Persian Princess, And Early Modern English Women's Authorship from Elizabeth I To Mary Wroth." In *Women Writing Back/Writing Women Back: Transnational Perspectives from the Late Middle Ages to the Dawn of the Modern Era*, edited by Anke Gilleir, Alicia Montoya, and Suzan van Dijk, 255–81. Amsterdam: Brill, 2010.

Arvas, Abdulhamit. "Early Modern Eunuchs and the Transing of Gender and Race." *Journal for Early Modern Cultural Studies* 19, no. 4 (2019): 116–36. https://doi.org/10.1353/jem.2019.0040.

———. "Leander in the Ottoman Mediterranean: The Homoerotics of Abduction in the Global Renaissance." *English Literary Renaissance* 51, no. 1 (January 2021): 31–62. https://doi.org/10.1086/711601.

Astengo, Corradino. "The Renaissance Chart Tradition in the Mediterranean." In *Cartography in the European Renaissance*, edited by David Woodward, 174–262. Chicago: University of Chicago Press, 2007.

Aubert, Guillaume. "'The Blood of France': Race and Purity of Blood in the French Atlantic World." *The William and Mary Quarterly* 61, no. 3 (July 1, 2004): 439–78.

Bailey, Gauvin A. *Art of Colonial Latin America*. London: Phaidon, 2005.

Bailey, Moya. *Misogynoir Transformed: Black Women's Digital Resistance*. New York: New York University Press, 2021.

Banerjee, Pompa. *Burning Women: Widows, Witches, and Early Modern European Travelers in India*. New York: Palgrave Macmillan, 2003.

Baxandall, Michael. *Painting and Experience in Fifteenth Century Italy: A Primer in the Social History of Pictorial Style*. Oxford: Oxford University Press, 1974.

Beck, Hans-Georg. *Ideen Und Realitäten in Byzanz*. Vol. 13. Variorum Collected Studies Series. London: Variorum, 1972.

Bernal, Martin. *Black Athena: The Afroasiatic Roots of Classical Civilization*. Vol. 3, *The Linguistic Evidence*. New Brunswick, NJ: Rutgers University Press, 2006.

Bertelà, Giovanna Gaeta, and Annamaria Petrioli Tofani. *Feste e apparati medicei: mostra di disegni e incisioni*. Florence: Olschki, 1969.

Bethencourt, Francisco. *Racisms: From the Crusades to the Twentieth Century*. Princeton, NJ: Princeton University Press, 2013.

Binding, Paul. *Imagined Corners: Exploring the World's First Atlas*. London: Headline, 2003.

Bindman, David, Henry Louis Gates Jr., and Karen C. Dalton, eds. *The Image of the Black in Western Art*. 5 vol. New ed. Cambridge, MA: Belknap Press of Harvard University Press, 2010.

Bisaha, Nancy. *Creating East and West: Renaissance Humanists and the Ottoman Turks*. Philadelphia: University of Pennsylvania Press, 2004.

Bland, Mark. "The Appearance of the Text in Early Modern England." *Text* 11 (1998): 91–154. https://www.jstor.org/stable/30227734.

Blough, Karen. "The Lance of St Maurice as a Component of the Early Ottonian Campaign against Paganism." *Early Medieval Europe* 24, no. 3 (2016): 338–61. https://doi.org/10.1111/emed.12155.

Boone Hill, Elizabeth. "Glorious Imperium: Understanding Land and Community in Moctezuma's Mexico." In *Moctezuma's Mexico*, edited by Pedro Carrasco and Eduardo Matos Moctezuma, 159–73. Niwot, CO: University Press of Colorado, 1992.

———. "Seeking Indianness: Christoph Weiditz, the Aztecs, and Feathered Amerindians." *Colonial Latin American Review* 26, no. 1 (2017): 39–61. https://doi.org/10.1080/10609164.2017.1287323.

Boorsch, Suzanne. "America in Festival Presentations." In *First Images of America: The Impact of the New World on the Old*, vol. 1, edited by Fred Chiappelli, 503–15. Berkeley: University of California Press, 1976.

Boulle, Pierre. *Race et Esclavage Dans la France de l'Ancien Régime*. Paris: Perrin, 2007.

Bradford, Hannah, and Anna Hevrdejs. "Harrison High Protests of 1968: Demanding Better Education." Digital Chicago, Lake Forest College. 2016. Accessed August 14, 2022. https://digitalchicagohistory.org/exhibits/show/harrison-high-protests-1968/home.

Brafman, David. "Facing East: The Western View of Islam in Nicolas de Nicolay's Travels in Turkey." *Getty Research Journal* 1 (2009): 153–60. https://doi.org/10.1086/grj.1.23005372.

———. "Les quatre premiers livres des navigations et pérégrinations Orientales." In *Christian-Muslim Relations: A Bibliographical History*, vol. 6: *Western Europe (1500–1600)*, edited by David Thomas and John Chesworth, 754–63. Leiden: Brill, 2015. http://dx.doi.org/10.1163/2451-9537_cmrii_COM_26242.

Braganza, V. M. "The Shadow Casts a Body: Racial Dialogue in Two Neo-Latin Lyrics Attributed to George Herbert." *Studies in Philology* 117, no. 1 (2020): 108–28. https://doi.org/10.1353/sip.2020.0003.

Brainard, Ingrid. "The Art of Courtly Dance in Transition." In *Crossroads of Medieval Civilization: The City of Regensberg and its Intellectual Milieu*, edited by Edelgard E. Dubruck and Karl Heinz Göller, 61–79. Detroit: Michigan Consortium for Medieval and Early Modern Studies, 1984.

Braude, Benjamin. "The Sons of Noah and the Construction of Ethnic and Geographical Identities in the Medieval and Early Modern Periods." *The William and Mary Quarterly* 54, no. 1 (1997): 103–42. https://www.jstor.org/stable/2953314.

Brayboy, Bryan McKinley Jones. "Toward a Tribal Critical Race Theory in Education." *The Urban Review* 37, no. 5 (2005): 425–446. https://doi.org/10.1007/s11256-005-0018-y.

Brewer-Garcia, Larissa. "Imagined Transformations: Color, Beauty, and Black Christian Conversion in Seventeenth-Century Spanish America." In *Envisioning Others: Race, Color, and the Visual in Iberia and Latin America*, edited by Pamela Patton, 111–41. Leiden: Brill, 2015.

Britton, Dennis Austin. *Becoming Christian: Race, Reformation, and Early Modern English Romance*. New York: Fordham University Press, 2014.

Broecke, Marcel P. R. van den. *Ortelius Atlas Maps: An Illustrated Guide*. Westrenen, Netherlands: Hes & de Graaf Publishers, 2011.

Brooks, Lynn Matluck. *The Dances of the Processions of Seville in Spain's Golden Age*. Kassel: Edition Reichenberger, 1988.

Brotton, Jerry. *Trading Territories: Mapping the Early Modern World*. Ithaca, NY: Cornell University Press, 1998.

Bujok, Elke. "Ethnographica in Early Modern Kunstkammern and Their Perception." *Journal of The History of Collections* 21, no. 1 (2009): 17–32. https://doi.org/10.1093/jhc/fhn031.

Burke, Jill. "Nakedness and Other Peoples: Rethinking the Italian Renaissance Nude." *Art History* 36, no. 4 (2013): 714–39. https://doi.org/10.1111/1467-8365.12029.

Burton, Jonathan. *Traffic and Turning: Islam and English Drama, 1579–1624*. Newark, DE: University of Delaware Press, 2005.

Büttner, Nils. "Rubens's Legacy in Book Design." In *Gateways to the Book: Frontispieces and Title Pages in Early Modern Europe*, edited by Gitta Bertram, Nils Büttner, and Claus Zittel, 422–48. Leiden: Brill, 2021. https://doi.org/10.1163/9789004464520_012.

Cacicedo, Alberto. "Othello, Stranger in a Strange Land." *Interdisciplinary Literary Studies* 18, no. 1 (2016): 7–27. https://doi.org/10.5325/intelitestud.18.1.0007.

Campbell, Mary Baine. "Anthropometamorphosis: Manners, Customs, Fashions, and Monsters." Chap. 7 in *Wonder & Science: Imagining Worlds in Early Modern Europe*, 225–56. Ithaca, NY: Cornell University Press, 1999.

Campbell, Tony. "Portolan Charts from the Late Thirteenth Century to 1500." In *Cartography in Prehistoric, Ancient and Medieval Europe and the Mediterranean*, edited by J.B. Harley and David Woodward, 371–458. Chicago: University of Chicago Press, 1987.

Cams, Mario. "Displacing China: The Martini-Blaeu Novus Atlas Sinesis and the Late Renaissance Shift in Representations of East Asia." *Renaissance Quarterly* 73, no. 3 (2020): 953–90. https://doi.org/10.1017/rqx.2020.123.

Canizares Esguerra, Jorge. "New World, New Stars: Patriotic Astrology and the Invention of Indian and Creole Bodies in Colonial Spanish America, 1600–1650." *American Historical Review* 104, no. 1 (1999): 33–68. https://doi.org/10.1086/ahr/104.1.33.

Cannan, Paul D. "'A Short View of Tragedy' and Rymer's Proposals for Regulating the English Stage." *The Review of English Studies* 52, no. 206 (2001): 207–26. https://doi.org/10.1093/res/52.206.207.

Carrasco, Ronaldo. "El exemplum como estrategia persuasiva en la *Rhetorica christiana* (1579) de fray Diego Valadés." *Annales del Instituto de Investigaciones Estéticas* 22, no. 77 (2000): 33–66.

Carroll, Khadija von Zinnenburg. *The Contested Crown: Repatriation Politics between Europe and Mexico*. Chicago: University of Chicago Press, 2022.

Cassen, Flora. *Marking the Jew in Renaissance Italy: Politics, Religion, and the Power of Symbols*. Cambridge: Cambridge University Press, 2017.

Cavendish, Dominic. "The Woke Brigade are Close to 'Cancelling' Shakespeare." *The Telegraph*, February 9, 2020. https://www.telegraph.co.uk/theatre/what-to-see/woke-brigade-close-cancelling-shakespeare/.

———. "William Shakespeare Was an Empty Vessel: He Doesn't Need Decolonising." *The Daily Telegraph*, September 17, 2021. https://www.telegraph.co.uk/theatre/what-to-see/shakespeare-empty-vessel-doesnt-need-decolonising/.

Celso de Castro Alves, José. "Rupture and Continuity in Colonial Discourses: The Racialized Representation of Portuguese Goa in the Sixteenth and Seventeenth Centuries." *Portuguese Studies* 16 (2000): 148–161. https://www.jstor.org/stable/41105143.

Certeau, Michel de. *Heterologies: Discourse on the Other*. Minneapolis: University of Minnesota Press, 1986.

Chaganti, Seeta, and Andrea Myers Achi. "Ethiopian Art, 1400–1900 Art Gallery of Ontario exhibit." Online talk, Art Gallery of Ontario, Ontario, Canada, November 5, 2018. https://youtu.be/C3Sf3T4O84E.

Chalaye, Sylvie. *Du Noir au Nègre: L'image du Noir au théâtre (1550–1960)*. Paris: L'Harmattan, 1998.

Chappell, Bill. "Statue of Lincoln with Formerly Enslaved Man at His Feet Is Removed in Boston." NPR, December 29, 2020. https://www.npr.org/2020/12/29/951206414/statue-of-lincoln-with-freed-slave-at-his-feet-is-removed-in-boston.

Chastel, André. "Gesture in Painting: Problems in Semiology." *Renaissance and Reformation / Renaissance et Réforme* 10, no. 1 (1986): 1–22. https://www.jstor.org/stable/43444573.

Christensen, Peter. "'As If She Were Jerusalem': Placemaking in Sephardic Salonica," *Muqarnas* 30 no. 1 (2013): 141–69. https://doi.org/10.1163/22118993-0301P0007a.

Christou, Theodore. "The Byzantine History of Putin's Russian Empire." *The Conversation*, March 15, 2018. http://theconversation.com/the-byzantine-history-of-putins-russian-empire-90616.

Clayton, Mary L. "Evidence for a Native-Speaking Nahuatl Author in the Ayer Vocabulario Trilingüe." *International Journal of Lexicography* 16, no. 2 (2003): 99–119. https://doi.org/10.1093/ijl/16.2.99.

Cohen, Jeremy. *Living Letters of the Law: Ideas of the Jew in Medieval Christianity*. Berkeley: University of California Press, 1999.

Cohen-Aponte, Ananda. "Making Race Visible in the Colonial Andes." In *Envisioning Others: Race, Color, and the Visual in Iberia and Latin America*, edited by Pamela Patton, 187–212. Leiden: Brill, 2015.

Colin, Paul. *La Croûte (Souvenirs)*. Paris: Table Ronde, 1957.

Cooley, Mackenzie. *The Perfection of Nature: Animals, Breeding, and Race in the Renaissance*. Chicago: University of Chicago Press, 2022.

Cortesâo, Armando, and Avelino Teixeira da Moto. *Portugaliae monumenta cartographica*. Vol. 4. Lisbon: Coimbra, 1960.

Craigie, William Alexander. *A Dictionary of the Older Scottish Tongue: From the Twelfth Century to the End of the Seventeenth*. Vol. 4, M–N. Chicago: University of Chicago Press, 1973.

Crenshaw, Kimberlé. "Unmasking Colorblindness in the Law: Lessons from the Formation of Critical Race Theory." In *Seeing Race Again: Countering Colorblindness Across the Disciplines*, edited by Kimberlé Crenshaw, Luke Charles Harris, Daniel HoSang, and George Lipsitz, 52–84. Oakland, CA: University of California Press, 2019.

———, Luke Charles Harris, Daniel HoSang, and George Lipsitz, eds. *Seeing Race Again: Countering Colorblindness Across the Disciplines*. Oakland, CA: University of California Press, 2019.

Cresswell, Tim. *Place: A Short Introduction*. Short Introductions to Geography. Malden, MA: Blackwell, 2005.

Crewe, Jonathan. "Drawn in Color: Aethiopika in European Painting." *Word & Image* 25, no. 2 (2009): 129–42. https://doi.org/10.1080/02666280802047729.

Cummins, Thomas B. F. "Three Gentlemen from Esmeraldas: A Portrait for a King." In *Slave Portraiture in the Atlantic World*, edited by Agnes Lugo-Ortiz and Angela Rosenthal, 118–45. Cambridge: Cambridge University Press, 2013.

Dadzie, Stella. *A Kick in the Belly: Women, Slavery and Resistance*. Londo: Verso, 2020.

Dalton, Karen C., and Henry Louis Gates, Jr. "Josephine Baker and Paul Colin: African American Dance Seen through Parisian Eyes." *Critical Inquiry* 24, no. 4 (1998): 903–34. https://doi.org/10.1086/448901.

Daly, Peter M. *The Emblem in Early Modern Europe: Contributions to the Theory of the Emblem*. New York: Routledge, 2014.

Daniel, Norman. *Islam and the West: The Making of an Image*. Edinburgh: Edinburgh University Press, 1980.

Darling, Linda T. "Ottoman Politics through British Eyes: Paul Rycaut's 'The Present State of the Ottoman Empire.'" *Journal of World History* 5, no. 1 (1994): 71–97. https://www.jstor.org/stable/20078582.

Davies, Surekha. *Renaissance Ethnography and the Invention of the Human: New Worlds, Maps and Monsters*. Cambridge: Cambridge University Press, 2016.

De Grazia, Margreta, Maureen Quilligan, and Peter Stallybrass, eds. *Subject and Object in Renaissance Culture*. Cambridge Studies in Renaissance Literature and Culture 8. Cambridge: Cambridge University Press, 1996.

De Weever, Jacqueline. *Sheba's Daughters: Whitening and Demonizing the Saracen Woman in Medieval French Epic*. New York: Garland, 1998.

Dean, Carolyn. *Inka Bodies and the Body of Christ: Corpus Christi in Colonial Cuzco, Peru*. Durham, NC: Duke University Press, 1999.

Delaney, David. "The Space That Race Makes." *The Professional Geographer* 54, no. 1 (2002): 6–14. https://doi.org/10.1111/0033-0124.00309.

Delgado, Richard, and Jean Stefancic, eds. *Critical Race Theory: An Introduction*. 2nd ed. Critical America. New York University Press, 2012.

Dictionary of Old English: A to I. Edited by Angus Cameron, Ashley Crandell Amos, Antonette DiPaolo Healey et al. Toronto: University of Toronto, 2018. https://tapor.library.utoronto.ca/doe/.

Dilworth, Leah, ed. *Acts of Possession: Collecting in America*. New Brunswick, N.J: Rutgers University Press, 2003.

Dominican Friars Foundation. "St. Louis Bertrand." November 23, 2020. https://dominicanfriars.org/st-louis-bertrand/.

Domínguez Casas, Rafael. "Ascenso social y visualización simbólica del poder en dos ejecutorias de hidalguía del reinado de Carlos II." *Goya*, no. 363 (2018): 108–25.

Duits, Rembrandt. *Gold Brocade and Renaissance Painting: A Study in Material Culture*. London: Pindar Press, 2008.

Dyer, Richard. *White*. London: Routledge, 1992.

Earle, Rebecca. *The Body of the Conquistador: Food, Race, and the Colonial Experience in Spanish America, 1492–1700*. New York: Cambridge University Press, 2012.

Earle, T. F., and K. J. P. Lowe, eds. *Black Africans in Renaissance Europe*. New York: Cambridge University Press, 2005.

Ellis, Markman. "'The house of bondage': Sentimentalism and the Problem of Slavery." In *The Politics of Sensibility: Race, Gender, and Commerce in the*

Sentimental Novel, 49–86. Cambridge: Cambridge University Press, 2004.

Emiralioğlu, M. Pinar. *Geographical Knowledge and Imperial Culture in the Early Modern Ottoman Empire*. Transculturalisms, 1400–1700. Farnham: Ashgate, 2014.

Enlace Chicago. Public Advocacy Organization. https://www.enlacechicago.org.

Erickson, Peter. "Invisibility Speaks: Servants and Portraits in Early Modern Visual Culture." *Journal for Early Modern Cultural Studies* 9, no. 1 (2009): 23–61. https://www.jstor.org/stable/40339610.

———, and Kim F. Hall. "'A New Scholarly Song': Rereading Early Modern Race." *Shakespeare Quarterly* 67, no. 1 (2016): 1–13. https://doi.org/10.1353/shq.2016.0002.

Erickson, Peter, and Clark Hulse, eds. *Early Modern Visual Culture: Representation, Race, Empire in Renaissance England*. New Cultural Studies. Philadelphia: University of Pennsylvania Press, 2000.

Escalante Gonzalbo, Pablo. "On the Margins of Mexico City: What the Beinecke Map Shows." In *Painting a Map of Sixteenth-Century Mexico City: Land, Writing, and Native Rule*, edited by Mary Miller and Barbara Mundy, 101–10. New Haven: Yale University Press, 2013.

Evans, Helen C., ed. *Byzantium: Faith and Power (1261–1557)*. New Haven: Yale University Press, 2004. Published in conjunction with the exhibition of the same name, shown at the Metropolitan Museum of Art.

———, Melanie Holocomb, and Robert Hallman. "The Arts of Byzantium." *Metropolitan Museum of Art Bulletin* 58, no. 4 (2001): 1, 4–68.

Ferguson, Margaret W. "Juggling the Categories of Race, Class and Gender: Aphra Behn's Oroonoko." In *Troping Oroonoko from Behn to Bandele*, edited by Susan B. Iwanisziw, 16–34. London: Routledge, 2018.

Fine, Aaron. *Color Theory: A Critical Introduction*. London: Bloomsbury Visual Arts, 2021.

Finnane, Antonia. "Fashions in Late Imperial China." Chap. 3 in *Changing Clothes in China: Fashion, History, Nation*, 43–68. New York: Columbia University Press, 2008.

Flint, Shirley Cushing. *No Mere Shadow: Faces of Widowhood in Early Colonial Mexico*. Albuquerque: University of New Mexico Press, 2013.

Forrest, John. *The History of Morris Dancing, 1458–1750*. Toronto: University of Toronto Press, 1999.

Fox, Violet B, ed. *Disorientation Guide to Librarianship* (zine). 2021. http://violetbfox.info/disorientation/.

Fracchia, Carmen. *'Black but Human': Slavery and Visual Arts in Hapsburg Spain, 1480–1700*. Oxford: Oxford University Press, 2019.

Freidenreich, David M. "Jews, Pagans, and Heretics in Early Medieval Canon Law." In *Jews in Early Christian Law: Byzantium and the Latin West, 6th–11th Centuries*, edited by John V. Tolan, Nicholas de Lange, Laurence Foschia, and Capucine Nemo-Pekelman, 73–91. Turnhout, Belgium: Brepols, 2014.

———. "Muslims in Western Canon Law, 1000–1500." In *Christian- Muslim Relations: A Bibliographical History*. Vol. 3, *1050–1200*, edited by David Thomas and Alex Mallett, 42–68. Leiden: Brill, 2011.

Fromont, Cécile. "Dancing for the King of Congo from Early Modern Central Africa to Slavery-Era Brazil." *Colonial Latin America Review* 22, no. 2 (2013): 184–208. https://doi.org/10.1080/10609164.2013.808466.

———. *Images on a Mission in Early Modern Kongo and Angola*. University Park: Pennsylvania State University Press, 2022.

———. *The Art of Conversion: Christian Visual Culture in the Kingdom of Kongo*. Chapel Hill: University of North Carolina Press, 2014.

———, ed. *Afro-Catholic Festivals in the Americas: Performance, Representation, and the Making of Black Atlantic Tradition*. University Park: Pennsylvania State University Press, 2019.

Fuchs, Barbara. *Mimesis and Empire: The New World, Islam, and European Identities*. Cambridge: Cambridge University Press, 2001.

Fuentes, Marisa J. *Dispossessed Lives: Enslaved Women, Violence, and the Archive*. Philadelphia: University of Pennsylvania Press, 2016.

Gage, Frances. *Painting as Medicine in Early Modern Rome: Giulio Mancini and the Efficacy of Art.*

University Park: Pennsylvania State University Press, 2016.

Galindo, David Rex. "Shaping Colonial Behaviours: Franciscan Missionary Literature and the Implementation of Religious Normative Knowledge in Colonial Mexico (1530s–1640s)." In *Knowledge of the Pragmatici: Legal and Moral Theological Literature and the Formation of Early Modern Ibero-America*, edited by Thomas Duve and Otto Danwerth, 296–327. Leiden: Brill, 2020.

Gamble, William Miller Thomas. "The Monumenta Germaniae Historica: Its Antecedents and Motives." *The Catholic Historical Review* 10, no. 2 (1924): 202–33. https://www.jstor.org/stable/25012071.

Ganteaume, Cécile R. *Officially Indian: Symbols That Define the United States*. Washington, D.C.: National Museum of the American Indian, Smithsonian Institution, 2017.

Gaudio, Michael. "Dancing in Circles: Ethnography and Animation in the Cérémonies et coutumes religieuses." Paper presented at The Enlightenment Creation of World Religion: Bernard and Picart's *Cérémonies et coutumes religieuses* Symposium and Research Methods Workshop, Newberry Library, Chicago, March 16, 2018.

———. *Engraving the Savage: The New World and Techniques of Civilization*. Minneapolis: University of Minnesota Press, 2008.

———. *Sound, Image, Silence: Art and the Aural Imagination in the Atlantic World*. Minneapolis: University of Minnesota Press, 2019.

Gertsman, Elina. *The Dance of Death in the Middle Ages: Image, Text, Performance*. Turnhout: Brepols, 2010.

Gilman, Sander L. *Stand up Straight!: A History of Posture*. Chicago: University of Chicago Press, 2018.

Gilmore, John T. "Æthiopissæ: The Classical Tradition, Neo-Latin Verse and Images of Race in George Herbert and Vincent Bourne1." *Classical Receptions Journal* 1, no. 1 (2009): 73–86. https://doi.org/10.1093/crj/clp007.

Gomez-Géraud, Marie-Christine, and Stefanos Yerasimos. *Dans l'empire de Soliman le Magnifique*. Paris: Presses du CNRS, 1989.

Goodrich, Thomas D. *The Ottoman Turks and the New World: A Study of Tarih-i Hind-i garbi and Sixteenth-century Ottoman Americana*. Wiesbaden: O. Harrassowitz, 1990.

Gowing, Laura. *Domestic Dangers: Women, Words, and Sex in Early Modern London*. Oxford: Oxford University Press, 1996.

Grafton, Anthony. "Some Uses of Eclipses in Early Modern Chronology." *Journal of the History of Ideas* 64, no. 2 (2003): 213–29. https://doi.org/10.1353/jhi.2003.0024.

———. "Western Humanists and Byzantine Historians." In *The Invention of Byzantium in Early Modern Europe*, edited by Nathanael Aschenbrenner and Jake Ransohoff, 71–104. Washington, DC: Dumbarton Oaks Research Library and Collection, 2021.

Grayzel, Solomon. *The Church and the Jews in the XIIIth Century*, vol. 1. 1196–1254. Rev. 2nd ed. New York: Hermon Press, 1966.

———, and Kenneth R. Stow. *The Church and the Jews in the XIIIth Century*. Vol 2. New York: Jewish Theological Seminary in America, 1989.

Green, Jonathan. "Text, Culture, and Print-Media in Early Modern Translation: Notes on the 'Nuremberg Chronicle' (1493)." In *Fifteenth-Century Studies*. Vol. 33, edited by Edelgard E. DuBruck, Barbara I. Gusick, and William C. McDonald, 114–32. Woodbridge, UK: Boydell & Brewer, 2008.

Greenlee, John Wyatt, and Anna Fore Waymack. "Thinking Globally: Mandeville, Memory, and Mappaemundi." *The Medieval Globe* 4, no. 2 (2018): 69–106.

Grier, Miles Parks. "Inkface: The Slave Stigma in England's Early Imperial Imagination." In *Scripturalizing the Human: The Written as the Political*, edited by Vincent L. Wimpish, 193–218. New York: Routledge, 2015.

Griffin, Eric. "Nationalism, the Black Legend, and the Revised 'Spanish Tragedy.'" *English Literary Renaissance* 39, no. 2 (2009): 336–70. https://doi.org/10.1111/j.1475-6757.2009.01050.x.

Groesen, Michiel van. "The De Bry Collection of Voyages (1590–1634): Early America Reconsidered." *Journal of Early Modern History* 12, no. 1 (2008): 1–24. https://doi.org/10.1163/138537808X297135.

Habib, Imtiaz H. *Black Lives in the English Archives, 1500–1677: Imprints of the Invisible*. Aldershot: Ashgate, 2008.

Hacker, Joseph. "The Sephardi Diaspora in Muslim Lands from the 16th to 18th Century." In *Odyssey of the Exiles: The Sephardi Jews 1492–1992*, edited by Ruth Porter and Sarah Harel-Hoshen, 95–123, 201–4. Tel Aviv: Beth Hatefutsoth, Nahum Goldmann Museum of the Jewish Diaspora, 1992.

Hahn, Thomas, ed. "Race and Ethnicity in the Middle Ages." Special issue, *Journal of Medieval and Early Modern Studies* 31, no. 1 (2001).

Hall, Kim F. "I Can't Love This the Way You Want Me To: Archival Blackness." *postmedieval* 11, no. 2 (2020): 171–79. https://doi.org/10.1057/s41280-020-00174-9.

———. "Sexual Politics and Cultural Identity in The Masque of Blackness." In *The Performance of Power: Theatrical Discourse and Politics*, edited by Sue-Ellen Case and Janelle Reinelt, 3–18. Iowa City: University of Iowa Press, 1991.

———. *Things of Darkness: Economies of Race and Gender in Early Modern England*. Ithaca, NY: Cornell University Press, 1995.

———. "'Troubling Doubles': Apes, Africans and Blackface in Mr. Moore's Revels." In *Race, Ethnicity, and Power in the Renaissance*, edited by Joyce Green MacDonald, 120–44. Madison, NJ: Fairleigh Dickinson University Press, 1997.

———, and Peter Erickson, eds. "Rereading Early Modern Race." Special issue, *Shakespeare Quarterly* 67, no. 1 (2016).

———, and Noémie Ndiaye. "Race in Dialogue: Kim Hall and Noémie Ndiaye." Newberry Center for Renaissance Studies. November 13, 2020. Interview streamed on YouTube. https://youtu.be/Ys2VBTgpyNs.

Hall, Stuart. "Race, the Floating Signifier: What More Is There to Say about Race?" In *Selected Writings on Race and Difference*, edited by Ruth Wilson Gilmore and Paul Gilroy, 359–73. Durham, NC: Duke University Press, 2021.

———. "Subjects in History: Making Diasporic Identities." In *The House that Race Built*, edited by Wahneema Lubiano, 289–300. New York: Pantheon Books, 1997.

Hannaford, Ivan. *Race: The history of an Idea in the West*. Washington, DC: Woodrow Wilson Center Press, 1996.

Harper, James G. *The Turk and Islam in the Western Eye: 1450–1750: Visual Imagery before Orientalism*. Surrey, England: Ashgate, 2013.

Harpster, Grace. "The Color of Salvation: The Materiality of Blackness in Alonso de Sandoval's De Instauranda Aethiopium Salute." In *Envisioning Others: Race, Color, and the Visual in Iberia and Latin America*, edited by Pamela Patton, 83–110. Leiden: Brill, 2015.

Harrán, Don. "The Jewish Nose in Early Modern Art and Music." *Renaissance Studies* 28, no. 1 (2014): 50–70. https://doi.org/10.1111/rest.12006.

Harris, Carissa M. "A History of the Wench." Electric Literature. June 3, 2019. https://electricliterature.com/a-history-of-the-wench/.

———. "Chaucer's Wenches." *Studies in the Age of Chaucer* 45 (2023), forthcoming.

———. *Obscene Pedagogies: Transgressive Talk and Sexual Education in Late Medieval Britain*. Ithaca, NY: Cornell University Press, 2018.

Harris, Max. *Aztecs, Moors, and Christians: Festivals of Reconquest in Mexico and Spain*. Austin: University of Texas Press, 2000.

Hartman, Saidiya V. *Scenes of Subjection: Terror, Slavery, and Self-Making in Nineteenth-Century America*. Oxford: Oxford University Press, 1997.

———. "Venus in Two Acts." *Small Axe* 12, no. 2 (2008): 1–14.

Hathaway, Jane. *The Chief Eunuch of the Ottoman Harem: From African Slave to Power-Broker*. Cambridge: Cambridge University Press, 2018.

Hatzfeld, Adolphe, et al. *Dictionnaire général de la langue Française du commencement du XVIIe siècle à nos jours: précédé d'un traité de la formation de la langue*. Paris: Librairie Charles Delagrave, 1926.

Heffernan, Megan. *Making the Miscellany: Poetry, Print, and the History of the Book in Early Modern England*. Philadelphia: University of Pennsylvania Press, 2021.

Hendricks, Margo. "Coloring the Past, Considerations of Our Future: RaceB4Race." *New Literary History* 52, no. 3/4 (2021): 365–84. https://doi.org/10.1353/nlh.2021.0018.

———. "Coloring the Past, Rewriting Our Future: Race-b4race." Folger Shakespeare Library, July 8, 2020. https://www.folger.edu/institute/scholarly-programs/race-periodization/margo-hendricks.

———. *Race and Romance: Coloring the Past*. Tempe, AZ: ACMRS Press, 2022.

Heng, Geraldine. *The Invention of Race in the European Middle Ages*. Cambridge: Cambridge University Press, 2018.

———. "The Invention of Race in the European Middle Ages II: Locations of Medieval Race." *Literature Compass* 8, no. 5 (2011): 332–50. https://doi.org/10.1111/j.1741-4113.2011.00795.x.

Higman, B. W. "The Sugar Revolution." *The Economic History Review, New Series* 53, no. 2 (2000): 213–36. https://mypages.unh.edu/hoslac/book/early-sugar-plantation.

Hitzel, Frédéric. "Les ambassades occidentales à Constantinople et la diffusion d'une certaine image de l'Orient." *Comptes rendus des séances de l'Académie des Inscriptions et Belles-Lettres* 154, no. 1 (2010): 277–92.

Hobbs, Mary. "An Edition of the Stoughton Manuscript (an Early Seventeenth-Century Poetry Collection in Private Hands, Connected with Henry King and Oxford) Seen in Relation to Other Contemporary Poetry and Song Collections." Ph.D. diss, London University, 1973.

Horowitz, Maryanne Cline. "Rival Interpretations of Continent Personifications." In *Bodies and Maps: Early Modern Personifications of the Continents*, edited by Maryanne Cline Horowitz and Louise Arizzoli, 1–24. Leiden: Brill, 2020.

———, and Louise Arizzoli. *Bodies and Maps: Early Modern Personifications of the Continents*. Leiden: Brill, 2020.

Horton, Jessica L. *Art for an Undivided Earth: The American Indian Movement Generation*. Durham, NC: Duke University Press, 2017.

Howard, Tanner. "Fifty Years Ago, 35,000 Chicago Students Walked out of Their Classrooms in Protest. They Changed CPS Forever." *Chicago Reader*, October 4, 2018. https://www.chicagoreader.com/chicago/student-protests-1968-chicago-public-schools/Content?oid=59097994.

Hoxie, Frederick E. "Businessman, Bibliophile, and Patron: Edward E. Ayer and His Collection of American Indian Art." *Great Plains Quarterly* 9, no. 2 (1989): 78–88. https://digitalcommons.unl.edu/greatplainsquarterly/402.

Hughes, Charles, ed. *Shakespeare's Europe: A Survey of the Condition of Europe at the End of the 16th Century*, 2nd ed. New York: B. Blom, 1967.

Hunt, Lynn Avery, Margaret C. Jacob, and W. W. Mijnhardt. *The Book That Changed Europe: Picart & Bernard's Religious Ceremonies of the World*. Cambridge, MA: Belknap Press of Harvard University Press, 2010.

Husband, Timothy B., ed. *The World in Play: Luxury Cards 1430–1540*, edited by New York: Metropolitan Museum of Art, Cloisters, 2016. Published in conjunction with the exhibition of the same name, shown at the Metropolitan Museum of Art.

Infelise, Mario. *I Remondini di Bassano*. Bassano del Grappa: Ghedina & Tassotti, 1990.

Isaac, Benjamin H. *The Invention of Racism in Classical Antiquity.* Princeton: Princeton University Press, 2004.

Jakacki, Diane K. "'Canst paint a doleful cry?': Promotion and Performance in the 'Spanish Tragedy' Title-Page Illustration." *Early Theatre* 13, no. 1 (2010): 13–36. https://www.jstor.org/stable/43499547.

Jestice, Phyllis. "A Great Jewish Conspiracy? Worsening Jewish-Christian Relations and the Destruction of the Holy Sepulcher." In *Christian Attitudes Toward the Jews in the Middle Age: A Casebook*, edited by Michael Frassetto, 25–42. New York: Routledge, 2007.

Johnson, Jessica Marie. *Wicked Flesh: Black Women, Intimacy, and Freedom in the Atlantic World. Early American Studies*. Philadelphia: University of Pennsylvania Press, 2020.

Jones, Ann Rosalind. "Cesare Vecellio's Floridians in the Venetian Book Market: Beautiful Imports." In *The Discovery of the New World in Early Modern Italy: 1492–1750*, edited by Elizabeth Hodorowich and Lia Markey, 248–69. Cambridge: Cambridge University Press, 2017.

———, and Margaret F. Rosenthal. *Cesare Vecellio's Habiti Antichi et Moderni: The Clothing of the Renaissance World*. London: Thames & Hudson Ltd., 2008.

———, and Peter Stallybrass. *Renaissance Clothing and the Materials of Memory*. Cambridge: Cambridge University Press, 2000.

Kafadar, Cemal. "A Rome of One's Own: Reflections on Cultural Geography and Identity in the Lands of Rum." *Muqarnas* 24 (2007): 7–25. https://doi.org/10.1163/22118993_02401003.

Kaplan, M. Lindsay. *Figuring Racism in Medieval Christianity*. New York: Oxford University Press, 2019.

Kaplan, Paul H. D. "The Calenberg Altarpiece: Black African Christians in Renaissance Germany." In *Germany and the Black Diaspora: Points of Contact, 1250–1914*, edited by Mischa Honeck, Martin Klimke, and Anne Kuhlmann-Smirnov, 21–37. Studies in German History. New York: Berghahn Books, 2013.

———. *The Rise of the Black Magus in Western Art*. Ann Arbor: UMI Research Press, 1985.

Karim-Cooper, Farah. *Cosmetics in Shakespearean and Renaissance Drama*. Edinburgh: Edinburgh University Press, 2006.

Kastner, Carolyn. "Collecting Mr. Ayer's Narrative." In *Acts of Possession: Collecting in America*, edited by Leah Dilworth, 138–62. New Brunswick, NJ: Rutgers University Press, 2003.

Kaufmann, Miranda. "Prester John." In *Encyclopedia of Blacks in European History and Culture*. Vol 2, edited by Eric Martone, 423–24. Westport, CT: Greenwood Press, 2009.

Keating, Jessica. *Animating Empire: Automata, the Holy Roman Empire, and the Early Modern World*. University Park: Pennsylvania State University Press, 2018.

———, and Lia Markey. "'Indian' Objects in Medici and Austrian-Habsburg Inventories: A Case-Study of the Sixteenth-Century Term." *Journal of the History of Collections* 23, no. 2 (November 1, 2011): 283–300. https://doi.org/10.1093/jhc/fhq030.

———. "Response: Medievalists and Early Modernists —A World Divided?" In *Re-Assessing the Global Turn in Medieval Art History*, edited by Christina Normore, 203–17. Baltimore: Johns Hopkins University Press, 2018.

Keene, Bryan, and Kristen Collins, eds. *Balthazar: A Black African King in Medieval and Renaissance Art*. Los Angeles: J. Paul Getty Museum, forthcoming. Published in conjunction with the exhibition of the same name, shown at the J. Paul Getty Museum.

Keevak, Michael. *Becoming Yellow: A Short History of Racial Thinking*. Princeton: Princeton University Press, 2011.

Kefala, Eleni. *The Conquered: Byzantium and America on the Cusp of Modernity*. Washington, DC: Dumbarton Oaks, 2020.

Keller, Marcus, "Nicolas de Nicolay's Navigations and the Domestic Politics of Travel Writing." *L'Esprit Créateur* 48, no. 1 (2008): 18–31.

———. "The Turk of Early Modern France." *L'Esprit Créateur* 53, no. 4 (2013): 1–8.

Kendon, Adam. *The Study of Gesture: Some Observations on Its History*. Toronto: Canadian Semiotic Association, 1982.

Kenley, Eugene McDowell. "Sixteenth-Century Matachines Dances: Morescas of Mock Combat and Comic Pantomime." PhD diss. Stanford University, 1993.

Kim, Dorothy. "White Supremacists Have Weaponized an Imaginary Viking Past. It's Time to Reclaim the Real History." *Time*, April 12, 2019. https://time.com/5569399/viking-history-white-nationalists/.

Kinoshita, Sharon, "'Pagans are Wrong and Christians are Right': Alterity, Gender, and Nation in the Chanson de Roland." *Journal of Medieval and Early Modern Studies* 31 (2001): 79–111. https://doi.org/10.1215/10829636-31-1-79.

Kivelson, Valerie. *Cartographies of Tsardom: The Land and Its Meanings in Seventeenth-Century Russia*. Ithaca, NY: Cornell University Press, 2006.

Klaus, Maurice, and Otto Mayr, eds. *The Clockwork Universe: German Clocks and Automata, 1550–1650*. New York: N. Watson Academic Publications, 1980.

Klein, Holger A. "Eastern Objects and Western Desires: Relics and Reliquaries between Byzantium and the West." *Dumbarton Oaks Papers* 58 (2004): 283–314. https://doi.org/10.2307/3591389.

Koeppe, Wolfram. *Making Marvels: Science and Splendor at the Courts of Europe*. New York: Metropolitan Museum of Art, 2019.

Koerner, Leo Joseph. "The Epiphany of the Black Magus circa 1500." In *The Image of the Black in Western Art*. Vol. 3, edited by David Bindman and Henry Louis Gates, 7–92. Cambridge, MA: Belknap Press of Harvard University Press, 2010.

Kolsky, Stephen. "Graceful Performances: The Social and Political Context of Music and Dance in the Cortegiano." *Italian Studies* 53, no. 1 (1998): 1–19. https://doi.org/10.1179/its.1998.53.1.1.

Kramer, Wendy. *Encomienda Politics in Early Colonial Guatemala, 1524–1544: Dividing the Spoils*. Boulder, CO: Westview Press, 1994.

Kriz, K. Dian, et al. "Sugar and the Visual Imagination in the Atlantic World, circa 1600–1860." John Carter Brown Library. Accessed February 29, 2022. https://www.brown.edu/Facilities/John_Carter_Brown_Library/exhibitions/sugar/pages/plantation.html.

Lanman, Jonathan T. *On the Origins of Portolan Charts*. The Hermon Dunlap Smith Center for the History of Cartography Occasional Publication 2. Chicago: The Newberry Library, 1987.

Lapina, Elizabeth. "Crusader Chronicles." *The Cambridge Companion to the Literature of the Crusades*, edited by Anthony Bale, 11–24. Cambridge: Cambridge University Press, 2019.

Leaper, Laura E. "Time, Memory, and Ritual: Deciphering Visual Rhetoric in Diego Valadzés's Rhetorica Christiana." Ph.D. diss., New York University Institute of Fine Arts, 2012.

Leibsohn, Dana. "Made in China, Made in Mexico." In *At the Crossroads: The Arts of Spanish America and Early Global Trade*, edited by Donna Pierce and Ronald Otsuka, 11–40. Denver: Denver Art Museum, 2012.

Leitch, Stephanie. "Burgkmair's Peoples of Africa and India (1508) and the Origins of Ethnography in Print." *The Art Bulletin* 91, no. 2 (June 1, 2009): 134–59. https://doi.org/10.1080/00043079.2009.10786162.

———, Gary Taylor, François Dupuigrenet Desroussilles, and Elizabeth Spiller. *Mapping Ethnography in Early Modern Germany: New Worlds in Print Culture*. New York: Palgrave Macmillan, 2010.

Lewis, Dallin. "Domesticating the Plantation: The Politics and Tragedy of Slave Kinship in the British Atlantic World." *The Eighteenth Century* 60, no. 3 (2019): 311–30. https://doi.org/10.1353/ecy.2019.0020.

Lewis, Martin W., and Karen E. Wigen. *The Myth of the Continents: A Critique of Metageography*. Berkeley: University of California Press, 1997.

Lewis, Robert E., Mary Jane Williams, and Marilyn S. Miller, eds. *Middle English Dictionary. Plan and Bibliography*. 2nd ed. Ann Arbor: University of Michigan Press, 2007.

Lichtenstadter, Ilse. "The Distinctive Dress of Non-Muslims in Islamic Countries." *Historia Judaica* 5, no. 1 (1943): 35–52.

Light, Laura. "The Thirteenth Century and the Paris Bible." *The New Cambridge History of the Bible: From 600 to 1450*, edited by Richard Marsden and E. Ann Matter, 380–91. Cambridge: Cambridge University Press, 2012.

Lipton, Sara. *Dark Mirror: The Medieval Origins of Anti-Semitic Iconography*. New York: Metropolitan Books, 2014.

Loewenstein, Joseph F. "*Idem*: Italics and the Genetics of Authorship." *Journal of Medieval and Renaissance Studies* 20, no. 2 (1990): 205–24.

Lombard, Jacqueline. "Race and the Romanesque: Visualizing Blackness Between Northern Europe and the Mediterranean, 1000–1250." PhD diss., University of Pittsburgh, 2022.

Loomba, Ania, "Race and the Possibilities of Comparative Critique." *New Literary History* 40, no. 3 (2009): 501–22. https://www.jstor.org/stable/27760273.

———, and Jonathan Burton, eds. *Race in Early Modern England: A Documentary Companion*. New York: Palgrave Macmillan, 2007.

López de Palacios Rubios, Juan. *De las Islas del mar Océano*. Mexico City: Fondo de Cultura Económica, 1954.

Love, Harold. *The Culture and Commerce of Texts: Scribal Publication in Seventeenth-Century England*. Amherst: University of Massachusetts Press, 1998.

Loyer, Jessie. "Collections Are Our Relatives: Disrupting the Singular, White Man's Joy that Shaped Collections." In *The Collector and the Collected: Decolonizing Area Studies Librarianship*, edited by Megan Browndorf, Erin Pappas, and Anna Arays, 3–19. Sacramento, CA: Library Juice Press, 2021.

Lubiano, Wahneema H., ed. *The House That Race Built: Black Americans, U.S. Terrain*. New York: Pantheon Books, 1997.

Lubrich, Naomi. "The Wandering Hat: Iterations of the Medieval Jewish Pointed Cap." *Jewish History* 29, no. 3/4 (2015): 203–44. https://doi.org/10.1007/s10835-015-9250-5.

Lugo-Ortiz, Agnes I., and Angela Rosenthal. *Slave Portraiture in the Atlantic World*. Cambridge: Cambridge University Press, 2013.

MacDonald, Joyce Green. "Race, Women, and the Sentimental in Thomas Southerne's Oroonoko." *Criticism* 40, no. 4 (1998): 555–70.

———. "The Disappearing African Woman: Imoinda in Oroonoko after Behn." Chap. 4 in *Women and Race in Early Modern Texts*, 87–107. Cambridge: Cambridge University Press, 2002.

———. *Women and Race in Early Modern Texts*. Cambridge: Cambridge University Press, 2002.

———, ed. *Race, Ethnicity, and Power in the Renaissance*. Madison, NJ: Fairleigh Dickinson University Press, 1997.

Macron, Emmanuel. "Discours du Président de la République à l'occasion de la cérémonie d'entrée de Joséphine Baker au Panthéon." November 30, 2021. https://www.elysee.fr/emmanuel-macron/2021/11/30/josephine-baker-entre-au-pantheon.

Mango, Cyril. "Constantinople." In *The Oxford Dictionary of Byzantium*, edited by Alexander P. Kazhdan, Alice-Mary Maffry Talbot, Anthony Cutler, et al. 3 vols. New York: Oxford University Press, 1991.

Manning, John. *The Emblem*. London: Reaktion, 2002.

Marcocci, Giuseppe. *The Globe on Paper: Writing Histories of the World in Renaissance Europe and the Americas*. Oxford: Oxford University Press, 2020.

Markey, Lia. "Gesture." In *Theories of Media Keywords Glossary*, University of Chicago. Accessed February 28, 2022. https://csmt.uchicago.edu/glossary2004/gesture.htm.

Marotti, Arthur F. *Manuscript, Print, and the English Renaissance Lyric*. Ithaca, NY: Cornell University Press, 1995.

Martínez, María Elena. *Genealogical Fictions: Limpieza de Sangre, Religion, and Gender in Colonial Mexico*. Stanford: Stanford University Press, 2008.

Matilla, Jose Manuel. "Símbolos de privilegio y objetos de arte. Los documentos pintados en la sociedad española del Antiguo Régimen." In *El documento pintado: cinco siglos de arte en manuscritos*, edited by Rufino Díaz and Mayte Garrido, 15–21. Madrid: Ministerio de Educación y Cultura, 2000.

Mazower, Mark. *Salonica, City of Ghosts: Christians, Muslims and Jews, 1430–1950*. New York: Alfred A. Knopf, 2005.

Mazzio, Carla. "Staging the Vernacular: Language and Nation in Thomas Kyd's The Spanish Tragedy." *Studies in English Literature, 1500–1900* 38, no. 2 (1998): 207–32. https://doi.org/10.2307/451034.

McCormick, Michael. "Byzantium and the West, 700–900." In *The New Cambridge Medieval History*, vol. 2. *c.700–c. 900*, edited by Rosamond McKitterick, 349–80. Cambridge: Cambridge University Press, 1995.

McCoskey, Denise Eileen. *Race: Antiquity and Its Legacy*. Ancients and Moderns Series. London: I. B. Tauris, 2012.

McDonough, Kelly S. "Plotting Indigenous Stories, Land, and People: Primordial Titled and Narrative Mapping in Colonial Mexico." *Journal for Early Modern Cultural Studies* 17, no. 1 (2017): 1–30. https://doi.org/10.1353/jem.2017.0003.

McGinnis, Katherine Tucker. "Moving in High Circles; Courts, Dance, and Dancing Masters in Italy in the Long Sixteenth Century." PhD diss., University of North Carolina, Chapel Hill, 2001.

Melville, Elinor. *A Plague of Sheep: Environmental Consequences of the Conquest of Mexico*. Cambridge: Cambridge University Press, 1994.

Metropolitan Museum of Art. "The African Origin of Civilization." Accessed August 2, 2022. https://www.metmuseum.org/exhibitions/listings/2021/african-origin-of-civilization

———. "Reenvisioning the Michael C. Rockefeller Wing." Accessed August 2, 2022. https://www.metmuseum.org/about-the-met/collection-areas/the-michael-c-rockefeller-wing/reenvisioning-mcr-wing.

Meyer, Gerard Previn. "The Blackamoor and Her Love." *Philological Quarterly* 17 (1938): 371–76.

Milano, Alberto. "Prints for Fans." *Print Quarterly* 4, no. 1 (1987): 2–19.

———. "'Selling Prints for the Remondini': Italian Pedlars Traveling through Europe during the Eighteenth Century." In *Not Dead Things: The Dissemination of Popular Print in England and Wales, Italy, and the Low Countries, 1500–1820*, edited by Roeland Harms, Joad Raymond, Jeroen Salman, 75–96. Leiden: Brill, 2013.

Miller, Mary E., and Barbara E. Mundy, eds. *Painting a Map of Sixteenth-Century Mexico City: Land, Writing, and Native Rule*. New Haven: Yale University Press, 2013.

Mills, Charles W. *The Racial Contract*. Ithaca, NY: Cornell University Press, 1997.

Mirrer, Louise. *Women, Jews, and Muslims in the Texts of Reconquest Castile*. Ann Arbor: University of Michigan Press, 1996.

Monaco, Marion. *Shakespeare On the French Stage in the Eighteenth Century*. Paris: Didier, 1974.

Morgan, Jennifer Lyle. *Laboring Women: Reproduction and Gender in New World Slavery*. Philadelphia: University of Pennsylvania Press, 2004.

Mukerji, Chandra. "Costume and Character in the Ottoman Empire: Dress as Social Agent in Nicolay's Navigations." In *Early Modern Things: Objects and Their Histories, 1500–1800*, edited by Paula Findlen, 151–69. London: Routledge, 2013.

Mundy, Barbara. "Crown and Tlatoque: The Iconography of Rulership in the Beineke Map." In *Painting a Map of Sixteenth-Century Mexico City: Land, Writing, and Native Rule*, edited by Mary E. Miller and Barbara E. Mundy, 177–78. New Haven: Yale University Press, 2012.

———. "Mapping the Aztec Capital: The 1524 Nuremberg Map of Tenochtitlán, Its Sources And Meanings." *Imago Mundi* 50, no. 1 (1998): 11–33. https://doi.org/10.1080/03085699808592877.

———. *The Mapping of New Spain: Indigenous Cartography and the Maps of the Relaciones Geographias*. Chicago: University of Chicago Press, 1996.

Mungello, D. E. *The Great Encounter of China and the West, 1500–1800*. 3rd ed. Rowman & Littlefield Publishers, 2009.

Muzzarelli, Maria Giuseppina. "Reconciling the Privilege of a Few with the Common Good: Sumptuary Laws in Medieval and Early Modern Europe." *Journal of Medieval and Early Modern Studies* 39, no. 3 (2009): 597–617. https://doi.org/10.1215/10829636-2009-006.

Nauert, Charles G. "Graf Hermann von Neuenahr and the Limits of Humanism in Cologne." *Historical Reflections / Réflexions Historiques* 15, no. 1 (1988): 65–79. https://www.jstor.org/stable/41298892.

Ndiaye, Noémie. "Aaron's Roots: Spaniards, Englishmen, and Blackamoors in Titus Andronicus." *Early Theatre: A Journal Associated with the Records of Early English Drama* 19, no. 2 (2016): 59–80. https://doi.org/10.12745/et.19.2.2847.

———. "'Come Aloft, Jack-little-ape!': Race and Dance in the Spanish Gypsie." *English Literary Renaissance* 51, no. 1 (2021): 121–51. https://doi.org/10.1086/711604.

———. "'Everyone Breeds in His Own Image': Staging the Aethiopica across the Channel," *Renaissance Drama* 44, no. 2 (2016): 157–86. https://doi.org/10.1086/688684.

———. "Rewriting the *Grand Siècle*: Blackface in Early Modern France and the Historiography of Race." *Literature Compass* 18, no. 10 (2021): 3, e12603. https://doi.org/10.1111/lic3.12603.

———. *Scripts of Blackness: Early Modern Performance Culture and the Making of Race*. Philadelphia: University of Pennsylvania Press, 2022.

———. "The African Ambassadors' Travels: Playing Black in Late Seventeenth Century France and

Spain." In *Transnational Connections in Early Modern Theatre*, edited by M. A. Katritzky and Pavel Drábek, 73–85. Manchester: Manchester University Press, 2020.

Nevile, Jennifer, ed. *Dance, Spectacle, and the Body Politick, 1250–1750*. Bloomington: Indiana University Press, 2008.

———. *The Eloquent Body: Dance and Humanist Culture in Fifteenth-Century Italy*. Bloomington: Indiana University Press, 2004.

Nicholson, Catherine. "'Othello' and the Geography of Persuasion." *English Literary Renaissance* 40, no. 1 (2010): 56–87. https://doi.org/10.1111/j.1475-6757.2009.01061.x.

Nirenberg, David. "Was There Race before Modernity? The Example of 'Jewish' Blood in Late Medieval Spain." In *The Origins of Racism in the West*, edited by Miriam Eliav-Feldon, Benjamin Isaac, and Joseph Ziegler, 232–64. Cambridge: Cambridge University Press, 2009.

Normore, Christina, ed. *Re-Assessing the Global Turn in Medieval Art History*. Vol. 3. *The Medieval Globe*. Leeds: ARC Humanities Press, 2018.

O'Gorman, Edmundo. *The Invention of America: An Inquiry into the Historical Nature of the New World and the Meaning of Its History*. Bloomington: Indiana University Press, 1961.

Omi, Michael, and Howard Winant. *Racial Formation in the United States: From the 1960s to the 1990s*. New York: Routledge, 1994.

O'Rourke Boyle, Marjorie. "Deaf Signs, Renaissance Texts." In *Perspectives on Early Modern and Modern Intellectual History: Essays in Honor of Nancy S. Struever*, edited by Joseph Marino and Melinda W. Schlitt, 164–92. Rochester, NY: University of Rochester Press, 2001.

Orsini, Carolina, Sara Rizzo, and Luca Tosi, eds. *La voce delle ombre: Presenze africane nell'arte dell'Italia settrionale (XVI–XIX)*. Milan: Silvana editoriale, 2022. Published in conjunction with the exhibition of the same name, shown at the Museo delle Culture di Milano.

Ostrowski, Donald. "'Moscow the Third Rome' as Historical Ghost." In *Byzantium, Faith, and Power (1261–1557): Perspectives on Late Byzantine Art and Culture*, edited by Sarah T. Brooks, 170–79. New Haven: Yale University Press, 2006.

Owen Hughes, Diane. "Distinguishing Signs: Ear-Rings, Jews and Franciscan Rhetoric in the Italian Renaissance City." *Past & Present* 112 (1986): 3–59. https://doi.org/10.1093/past/112.1.3.

Pagden, Anthony. "Fellow Citizens and Imperial Subjects: Conquest and Sovereignty in Europe's Overseas Empires." *History and Theory* 44, no. 4 (2005): 28–46. https://doi.org/10.1111/j.1468-2303.2005.00341.x.

Paley, Ruth, Cristina Malcolmson, and Michael Hunter. "Parliament and Slavery, 1660–c.1710." *Slavery & Abolition* 31, no. 2 (2010): 257–81. https://doi.org/10.1080/01440391003711107.

Pasztory, Esther. *Aztec Art*. New York: Abrams, 1983.

Patton, Pamela Anne, ed. *Envisioning Others: Race, Color, and the Visual in Iberia and Latin America*. The Medieval and Early Modern Iberian World (Formerly Medieval Iberian Peninsula) 62. Leiden: Brill, 2015.

Paulicelli, Eugenia. "Mapping the world: The political geography of dress in Cesare Vecellio's costume books." *The Italianist* 28, no.1 (2008): 24–53. https://doi.org/10.1179/ita.2008.28.1.24

Păun, Radu G. "Sur quelques 'modeles' livresques: Les 'Navigations et pérégrinations' de Nicolas de Nicolay." *Revue des Études Sud-Est Européennes* 33, no. 1/2 (1995): 171–80.

Peabody, Sue. *"There Are No Slaves in France": The Political Culture of Race and Slavery in the Ancien Régime*. New York: Oxford University Press, 1996.

Pearson, Jacqueline. "'One Lot in Sodom': Masculinity and the Gendered Body in Early Modern Narratives of Converted Turks." *Literature and Theology* 21, no. 1 (2007): 29–48. https://doi.org/10.1093/litthe/frl060.

Peirce, Leslie Penn. *The Imperial Harem: Women and Sovereignty in the Ottoman Empire*. Studies in Middle Eastern History. New York: Oxford University Press, 1993.

Perry, Imani. *Vexy Thing: On Gender and Liberation*. Durham, NC: Duke University Press, 2018.

Pettigrew, William A. "Free to Enslave: Politics and the Escalation of Britain's Transatlantic Slave

Trade, 1688–1714." *The William and Mary Quarterly* 64, no. 1 (2007): 3–38. http://www.jstor.org/stable/4491595.

Picard, Raymond. "Racine and Chauveau." *Journal of the Warburg and Courtauld Institutes* 14, no. 3/4 (1951): 259–74. https://doi.org/10.2307/750342.

Pichler, Gerd. "Die Spielkarten des 16. Und 17. Jahrhunderts in der Stiftssammlung St. Florian." *Jahrbuch des Oberösterreichischen Musealvereines* 142, no. 1 (1997): 173–98.

Poitevin, Kimberly. "Inventing Whiteness: Cosmetics, Race, and Women in Early Modern England." *Journal for Early Modern Cultural Studies* 11, no. 1 (2011): 59–89. https://www.jstor.org/stable/23242188.

Pratt, Mary Louise. *Imperial Eyes: Travel Writing and Transculturation*. London: Routledge, 1992.

Project on the Engraved Sources of Colonial Art. "Colonial Art." Accessed February 28, 2022. https://colonialart.org/archives/locations/united-states/state-of-illinois/city-of-chicago/thoma-collection/6006a-6006b.

Radburn, Nicholas. "'[M]anaged at First as If They Were Beasts': The Seasoning of Enslaved Africans in Eighteenth-Century Jamaica." *Journal of Global Slavery* 6, no. 1 (2021): 11–30. https://doi.org/10.1163/2405836X-00601008.

Rahier, Jean Muteba. "From the Transatlantic Slave Trade to Contemporary Ethnoracial Law in Multicultural Ecuador: The 'Changing Same' of Anti-Black Racism as Revealed by Two Lawsuits Filed by Afrodescendants." *Current Anthropology* 61, no. S22 (2020): S248–59. https://doi.org/10.1086/710061.

Rajabzadeh, Shokoofeh. "The Depoliticized Saracen and Muslim Erasure." *Literature Compass* 16, no. 9–10 (2019): e12548. https://doi.org/10.1111/lic3.12548.

Ramey, Lynn. *Christian, Saracen and Genre in Medieval French Literature: Imagination and Cultural Interaction in the French Middle Ages*. 2nd ed. New York: Routledge, 2014.

Ray, Jonathan. "Christian (Re)Encounters with Jews in the Sixteenth-Century Mediterranean." *Jewish History* 30, no. 3/4 (2017): 183–206. https://doi.org/10.1007/s10835-017-9266-0.

Reinsch, Dieether Roderich. "Hieronymus Wolf as Editor and Translator of Byzantine Texts." In *The Reception of Byzantium in European Culture since 1500*, edited by Przemysław Marciniak and Dion Smythe, 43–53. Farnham: Ashgate, 2015.

Riello, Giorgio. "The World in a Book: The Creation of the Global in Sixteenth-Century European Costume Books." *Past and Present* 242, Supplement 14 (2019): 281–317. https://doi.org/10.1093/pastj/gtz047.

Roberts, Justin. "The Whip and the Hoe: Violence, Work and Productivity on Anglo-American Plantations." *Journal of Global Slavery* 6, no. 1 (2021): 108–30. https://doi.org/10.1163/2405836X-00601005.

Rodríguez Becerra, Salvador. *Encomienda y Conquista: Los inicios de la colonización en Guatemala*. Seville: Publicaciones de la Universidad de Sevilla, 1977.

Romm, James S. "Continents, Climates, and Cultures: Greek Theories of Global Structure." In *Geography and Ethnography: Perceptions of the World in Pre-Modern Societies*, edited by Kurt Raaflaub, 215–35. Malden, MA: Wiley-Blackwell, 2010.

Rose, Gillian. *Feminism and Geography: The Limits of Geographical Knowledge*. Minneapolis: University of Minnesota Press, 1993.

Rosenthal, Laura J. "Owning Oroonoko: Behn, Southerne, and the Contingencies of Property." *Renaissance Drama* 23 (1992): 25–58. https://doi.org/10.1086/rd.23.41917283.

Rosenthal, Margaret F. "Cultures of Clothing in Later Medieval and Early Modern Europe." *Journal of Medieval and Early Modern Studies* 39, no. 3 (2009): 459–81. https://doi.org/10.1215/10829636-2009-001.

Rowe, Erin Kathleen. *Black Saints in Early Modern Global Catholicism*. Cambridge: Cambridge University Press, 2019.

Rozen, Minna. *A History of the Jewish Community in Istanbul: The Formative Years, 1453–1566*. Leiden: Brill, 2002.

Rubiano, Andrés H. "The First Painted Image of America in Europe: A Detail from Pinturicchio's Resurrection in the Sala Dei Misteri." *H-ART. Revista de historia, teoría y crítica de arte*, no. 8 (2021): 286–304. https://doi.org/10.25025/hart08.2021.13.

Rublack, Ulinka. *Dressing Up: Cultural Identity in Renaissance Europe*. Oxford: Oxford University Press, 2010.

Rugemer, Edward B. "The Development of Mastery and Race in the Comprehensive Slave Codes of the Greater Caribbean during the Seventeenth Century." *The William and Mary Quarterly* 70, no. 3 (2013): 429–58. https://doi.org/10.5309/willmaryquar.70.3.0429.

Ruiz García, Elisa. "La carta ejecutoria de hidalguía un espacio gráfico privilegiado." *La España medieval*, no. Extra 1 (2006): 251–76.

Said, Edward W. *Orientalism*. New York: Pantheon Books, 1978.

Sale, Carolyn. "Black Aeneas: Race, English Literary History, and the 'Barbarous' Poetics of Titus Andronicus." *Shakespeare Quarterly* 62, no. 1 (2011): 25–52. https://doi.org/10.1353/shq.2011.0001.

Samuels, Joel L. "The John M. Wing Foundation on the History of Printing at the Newberry Library." *The Library Quarterly: Information, Community, Policy* 58, no. 2 (1988): 164–89. https://doi.org/10.1086/601988.

Sandbrook, Dominic. "The Royal Shakespeare Company Should Be Ashamed." *The Daily Mail*, February 9, 2022. https://www.dailymail.co.uk/debate/article-10491873/DOMINIC-SANDBROOK-Royal-Shakespeare-Company-ashamed-woke-campaign.html.

Sanders, Larry (photographer). "Figure Clock with an African Man." *Collection: Milwaukee Art Museum*. 2015, accessed March 31, 2022. https://collection.mam.org/details.php?id=7927.

Schwaller, John F. "The Ilhuica of the Nahua: Is Heaven Just a Place?" *The Americas* 62, no. 3 (2006): 391–412. https://doi.org/10.1353/tam.2006.0044.

Scolieri, Paul A. *Dancing the New World: Aztecs, Spaniards, and the Choreography of Conquest*. Austin: University of Texas Press, 2013.

Shachar, Isaiah. *The Judensau: A Medieval Anti-Jewish Motif and Its History*. Warburg Institute Surveys 5. London: Warburg Institute, 1974.

Sharpe, Kevin, and Steven N. Zwicker, eds. *Reading, Society, and Politics in Early Modern England*. Cambridge: Cambridge University Press, 2003.

Shohat, Ella. "The Specter of the Blackamoor: Figuring Africa and the Orient." *The Comparatist* 42, no. 1 (2018): 158–88. https://doi.org/10.1353/com.2018.0008.

Skinner, Patricia. *Living with Disfigurement in Early Medieval Europe*. New York: Palgrave Macmillan, 2017.

Smith, Ian. "Othello's Black Handkerchief." *Shakespeare Quarterly* 64, no. 1 (2013): 1–25. https://doi.org/10.1353/shq.2013.0017.

———. "The Queer Moor: Bodies, Borders, and Barbary Inns." In *A Companion to the Global Renaissance: English Literature and Culture in the Era of Expansion*, edited by Jyotsna G. Singh, 190–204. Blackwell Companions to Literature and Culture 60. Chichester, U.K: Wiley-Blackwell, 2009.

———. "The Textile Black Body: Race and 'Shadowed Livery' in The Merchant of Venice." In *The Oxford Handbook of Shakespeare and Embodiment: Gender, Sexuality, and Race*, edited by Valerie Traub, 170–85. Oxford: Oxford University Press, 2016.

———. "White Skin, Black Masks: Racial Cross-Dressing on the Early Modern Stage." *Renaissance Drama* 32 (2003): 33–67. https://doi.org/10.1086/rd.32.41917375.

Smith, Jeffrey Chipps. *Dürer*. London: Phaidon Press, 2012.

Smithsonian Institution. "What Frederick Douglass Had to Say about Monuments." *Smithsonian Magazine*, June 30, 2020. https://www.smithsonianmag.com/history/what-frederick-douglass-had-say-about-monuments-180975225/.

Snowden, Frank M. *Before Color Prejudice: The Ancient View of Blacks*. Cambridge, MA: Harvard University Press, 1983.

———. *Blacks in Antiquity: Ethiopians in the Greco-Roman Experience*. Cambridge, MA: Belknap Press of Harvard University Press, 1970.

Sollors, Werner, ed. *An Anthology of Interracial Literature: Black-White Contacts in the Old World and the New*. New York: New York University Press, 2004.

Soyer, François. "Antisemitism, Islamophobia and the Conspiracy Theory of Medical Murder in Early Modern Spain and Portugal." In *Antisemitism and Islamophobia in Europe: A Shared Story?*, edited by

James Renton and Ben Gidley, 51–75. London: Palgrave Macmillan, 2017.

Spicer, Joaneath A., ed. *Revealing the African Presence in Renaissance Europe*. Baltimore: Walters Art Museum, 2012. Published in conjunction with the exhibition of the same name, shown at the Walters Art Museum and Princeton University Art Museum.

Staples, Kate Kelsey. "The Significance of the Secondhand Trade in Europe, 1200–1600." *History Compass* 13, no. 6 (2015): 297–309. https://doi.org/10.1111/hic3.12240.

Stavreva, Kirilka. *Words like Daggers: Violent Female Speech in Early Modern England*. Lincoln: University of Nebraska Press, 2015.

Stevens, Andrea. "Mastering Masques of Blackness: Jonson's 'Masque of Blackness,' The Windsor Text of 'The Gypsies Metamorphosed,' and Brome's 'The English Moor.'" *English Literary Renaissance* 39, no. 2 (2009): 396–426. https://doi.org/10.1111/j.1475-6757.2009.01052.x.

Stratton-Pruitt, Suzanne. Unpublished manuscript, n.d. Thoma Foundation.

Strémooukhoff, Dimitri. "Moscow the Third Rome: Sources of the Doctrine." *Speculum* 28, no. 1 (1953): 84–101. https://doi.org/10.2307/2847182.

Strickland, Debra Higgs. "Foreign Bodies in the Nuremberg Chronicle." *Bulletin of the John Rylands Library* 95, no. 2 (2019): 19–42. https://doi.org/10.7227/BJRL.95.2.2.

———. *Saracens, Demons and Jews: Making Monsters in Medieval Art*. Princeton, NJ: Princeton University Press, 2003.

Sturtevant, William C. "La tupinambisation des Indiens d'Amérique du Nord." In *Les cahiers du department d'études littéraires* 9: *Les figures de l'Indien*, edited by Gilles Thérien, 293–303. Montreal: Typo, 1988.

Tavim, José Alberto Rodrigues da Silva. "The Grão-Turco and the Jews: Translation to the West of Two Oriental 'Powers' (XVI–XVII Centuries)." *Mediterranean Historical Review* 28, no. 2 (2013): 167–90. http://dx.doi.org/10.1080/09518967.2013.837645.

Terry, Esther J. "Choreographies of Trans-Atlantic Primitivity: Sub-Saharan Isolation in Black Dance Historiography." In *Early Modern Black Diaspora Studies*, edited by Cassander L. Smith, Nicholas R. Jones, and Miles P. Grier, 65–82. Cham, Switzerland: Palgrave Macmillan, 2018.

Tezcan, Baki. "The Many Lives of the First Non-Western History of the Americas: From the New Report to the History of the West Indies." *The Journal of Ottoman Studies* 40 (2012): 1–38.

The Indigenization Project. "Decolonization and Indigenization." University of British Columbia. Accessed August 14, 2022. https://opentextbc.ca/indigenizationfrontlineworkers/chapter/decolonization-and-indigenization/.

The Newberry Library. "Newberry Library Will Collaborate with Native Communities to Expand Access to Indigenous Studies Collection." June 2020. https://www.newberry.org/newberry-library-will-collaborate-native-communities-expand-access-indigenous-studies-collection.

Thiel, Sara B. T. "Performing Blackface Pregnancy at the Stuart Court: The Masque of Blackness and Love's Mistress, or the Queen's Masque." *Renaissance Drama* 45, no. 2 (2017): 211–36. https://doi.org/10.1086/694326.

Thompson, Ayanna. "Introduction" in *Othello*, edited by E.A.J. Honigmann, 1–116. New York: Bloomsbury Publishing, 2016.

Thompson, Justin Randolph. *Black Presence: Uffizi Galleries*. Video Series. Galerie degli Uffizi, Accessed March 31, 2022. https://www.uffizi.it/en/video-stories/black-presence.

Thompson, Robert Farris. *The Four Moments of the Sun: Kongo Art in Two Worlds*. Washington, D.C.: National Gallery of Art, 1981.

Thorndike, Lynn. *A History of Magic and Experimental Science*. Vol. 4. *Fourteenth and Fifteenth Centuries*. New York: Columbia University Press, 1934.

Tolan, John Victor. *Saracens: Islam in the Medieval European Imagination*. New York: Columbia University Press, 2002.

Toner, Anne. *Ellipsis in English Literature: Signs of Omission*. Cambridge: Cambridge University Press, 2015.

Tooley, R.V. *The Mapping of America*. London: The Holland Press, 1980.

Townsend, Camilla. *Pocahontas and the Powhatan Dilemma*. New York: Hill and Wang, 2004.

Traub, Valerie. "Anatomy, Cartography, and the New World Body, Geographies of Embodiment in Early Modern England." In *Geographies of Embodiment in Early Modern England*, edited by Mary Floyd-Wilson and Garrett A. Sullivan, 64–112. Oxford: Oxford University Press, 2020. https://doi.org/10.1093/oso/9780198852742.003.0004.

———. "History in the Present Tense: Feminist Theories, Spatialized Epistemologies, and Early Modern Embodiment." In *Mapping Gendered Routes and Spaces in the Early Modern World*, edited by Merry E. Wiesner-Hanks, 15–53. Farnham: Ashgate, 2015.

———. "Mapping the Global Body." In *Early Modern Visual Culture: Representation, Race, Empire in Renaissance England*, edited by Peter Erickson and Clark Hulse, 44–97. Philadelphia: University of Pennsylvania Press, 2000.

———. "The Nature of Norms in Early Modern England: Anatomy, Cartography, 'King Lear.'" *South Central Review* 26, no. 1/2 (2009): 42–81. https://www.jstor.org/stable/40211291.

Tuck, Eve, and K. Wayne Yang. "Decolonization is not a metaphor." *Decolonization: Indigeneity, Education & Society* 1, no. 1 (2012): 1–40. https://jps.library.utoronto.ca/index.php/des/article/view/18630/15554.

Tzanaki, Rosemary. *Mandeville's Medieval Audiences: A Study on the Reception of the Book of Sir John Mandeville (1371–1550)*. Burlington: Ashgate, 2003.

Uhlig, Siegbert, et al., eds. *Encyclopaedia Aethiopica*. Vol. 1, *A–C*. Wiesbaden: Harrassowitz Verlag, 2003.

Uluç, Lale. "Images of Jews in Ottoman Court Manuscripts." In *A History of Jewish-Muslim Relations: From the Origins to the Present Day*, edited by Abdelwahab Meddeb and Benjamin Stora, 902–10. Princeton, NJ: Princeton University Press, 2013.

United Nations. "Much Work Needed to 'Target Unacceptable Levels' of Racism in Ecuador: Un Experts | | UN News." Accessed March 1, 2022. https://news.un.org/en/story/2019/12/1054201.

van den Boogaart, E. *Civil and Corrupt Asia: Image and Text in the* Itinerario *and the* Icones *of Jan Huygen van Linschoten*. Chicago: University of Chicago Press, 2002.

Van Engen, John. *Sisters and Brothers of the Common Life: The Devotio Moderna and the World of the Later Middle Ages*. Philadelphia: University of Pennsylvania Press, 2008.

Veinstein, Gilles. "The Ottoman Jews: Between Distorted Realities and Legal Fictions." *Mediterranean Historical Review* 25, no. 1 (2010): 53–65. https://doi.org/10.1080/09518967.2010.494100.

Vincent, Nicholas. "Two Papal Letters on the Wearing of the Jewish Badge, 1221 and 1229." *Jewish Historical Studies* 34 (1994–1996): 209–24. https://www.jstor.org/stable/29779960.

Vinson, Ben. *Before Mestizaje: The Frontiers of Race and Caste in Colonial Mexico*. Cambridge: Cambridge University Press, 2018.

Weheliye, Alexander G. *Habeas Viscus: Racializing Assemblages, Biopolitics, and Black Feminist Theories of the Human*. Durham, NC: Duke University Press, 2014.

Weiss, Roberto. "Traccia per una biografia di Annio da Viterbo." *Italia medioevale e umanistica* 5 (1962, published 1963): 425–41.

Wendorf, Richard. "Abandoning the Capital in Eighteenth-Century London." In *Reading, Society and Politics in Early Modern England*, edited by Kevin Sharpe and Steven N. Zwicker, 72–98. Cambridge: Cambridge University Press, 2003.

West, Jessamyn Charity. "Segregation in Library Associations." In *Disorientation Guide to Librarianship*, edited by Violet B. Fox. Downloadable zine. 2023. http://violetbfox.info/disorientation/.

Wetzel, Ingrid. "'Hie innen sindt geschriben die wellschen tenntz': le otto danze italiane del manoscritto di Norim-berga." In *Guglielmo Ebreoda Pesaro e la danza nelle corti italiane del XV secolo*, Proceedings of the 1987 Pesaro Conference, edited by Maurizio Padovan, 321–43. Pisa: Pacini, 1990.

Wey Gómez, Nicolás. *The Tropics of Empire: Why Columbus Sailed South to the Indies*. Cambridge, MA: MIT Press, 2008.

Whitaker, Cord J. *Black Metaphors: How Modern Racism Emerged from Medieval Race-Thinking*. Philadelphia: University of Pennsylvania Press, 2019.

Wiedl, Birgit. "Laughing at the Beast: The Judensau." In *Laughter in the Middle Ages and Early Modern Times: Epistemology of a Fundamental Human Behavior, its Meaning, and Consequences*, edited by Albrecht Classen, 325–64. Berlin: De Gruyter, 2010.

Wilberding, Erick. "Embracing the Cross: A Liturgical Gesture." *Notes in the History of Art* 8, no. 2 (1989): 1–5. https://www.jstor.org/stable/23202528.

Wilbourne, Emily. "Music, Race, Representation: Three Scenes of Performance at the Medici Court (1608–1616)." *Il Saggiatore Musicale* 27, no. 1 (2020): 5–45.

Williams, Elizabeth Dospěl. "Transformative Processes and New Global Narratives." Paper presented at the Delaware Valley Medieval Association meeting, "Curating Art of the Global Middle Ages, Fall 2021."

Williams Boyarin, Adrienne. *The Christian Jew and the Unmarked Jewess: The Polemics of Sameness in Medieval English Anti-Judaism*. Philadelphia: University of Pennsylvania Press, 2021.

Willis, Deborah. "The Gnawing Vulture: Revenge, Trauma Theory, and Titus Andronicus." *Shakespeare Quarterly* 53, no. 1 (2002): 21–52. https://doi.org/10.1353/shq.2002.0017

Wilson, Adrian, and Joyce Lancaster Wilson. *A Medieval Mirror: Speculum Humanae Salvationis 1324–1500*. Berkeley: University of California Press, 1984.

Wilson, Bronwen. "*Foggie diverse di vestire de' Turchi*: Turkish Costume Illustration and Cultural Translation." *Journal of Medieval and Early Modern Studies* 37, no. 1 (2007): 97–139. https://doi.org/10.1215/10829636-2006-012.

Wilson, Fred. *Mining the Museum: An Installation*. Baltimore: The New Press / The Contemporary, 1994.

———, and Howard Halle. "Mining the Museum." *Grand Street*, no. 44 (1993): 151–72. https://doi.org/10.2307/25007622.

Wimbush, Vincent L. *Scripturalizing the Human*. London: Taylor and Francis, 2015.

Wolff, Robert Lee. "The Three Romes: The Migration of an Ideology and the Making of an Autocrat." *Daedalus* 88, no. 2 (1959): 291–311. https://www.jstor.org/stable/20026497.

Wood, Stephanie. *Transcending Conquest: Nahua Views of Spanish Colonial Mexico*. Norman: University of Oklahoma Press, 2003.

Wunder, Amanda. "Western Travelers, Eastern Antiquities, and the Image of the Turk in Early Modern Europe." *Journal of Early Modern History* 7, no. 1/2 (2003): 89–119. https://doi.org/10.1163/157006503322487368.

Wynter, Sylvia. "1492: A New World View." In *Race, Discourse, and the Origin of the Americas: A New World View*, edited by Rex Nettleford and Vera Lawrence Hyatt, 5–57. Washington, D.C.: Smithsonian Institution, 1995.

Zamora, Margarita. *Reading Columbus*. Berkeley: University of California Press, 1993.

Zandvliet, Kees. "Mapping the Dutch World Overseas in the Seventeenth Century." In *The History of Cartography*, Vol. 3: *Cartography in the European Renaissance*, edited by David Woodward, Part 2, 1433–62. Chicago: University of Chicago Press, 2007.

ACKNOWLEDGMENTS

First thing first, we the co-editors, Lia Markey and Noémie Ndiaye, wish to thank, from the bottom of our hearts, the staff members of the Center for Renaissance Studies (CRS) at the Newberry Library: Rebecca L. Fall and Christopher Fletcher, without whose ideas, energy, dedication, and good humor not a single part of this multifaceted collaboration would have happened. In fact, it was Becky Fall who planted the seed for this collaboration between the Newberry's CRS and RaceB4Race® back in fall 2019. Similarly, George Amos Poole III Curator of Rare Books and Manuscripts, Suzanne Karr Schmidt, has been invaluable in searching the Newberry's archives for many of the items discussed in this book and Yasmine Hachimi's invaluable input as the Public Humanities Postdoctoral Fellow has helped us propel forward the related exhibition, digital resources, and public programming. The Newberry #DreamTeam made this project possible.

We owe an infinite debt of gratitude to the many contributors to this volume (do read their awing biographies!) who all accepted our invitation enthusiastically and kindly welcomed the productive challenges of co-writing essays across disciplinary lines (for long-form essay writers), intimately discussing the role of PCRS in their personal itineraries (for notes from the field), or embracing a whole new genre (for the interview and the catalog entries). Let us thank them all once again here for their fierceness, determination, promptness, and critical generosity as they keep paving new ways for PCRS. We could not have wished for a better home for this book than ACMRS Press (spearheaded by Ayanna Thompson, Roy Rukkila, and Geoff

Way) whose unwavering commitment to accessibility aligned beautifully with our project. A Samuel H. Kress Foundation grant provided the financial support for the publication, and we are grateful to the Newberry Library's Office of Development, particularly to grant writer Caroline Carter, for supporting this endeavor. Catherine Gass provided the excellent photography of Newberry items for the book and Juan Molina Hernández, Leith Calcote, Natalia Maliga, Patrick Kepley, and Christopher Cialdella were all instrumental in the process. Todd Halvorsen and his team at ACMRS Press, as well as Andrea Villasenor and Mary Kennedy at the Newberry Library worked together to design the book's striking cover while Todd produced the beautiful interior composition. Extra thanks go to Analú María López and Jill Gage for their input on collection items. Finally, we are grateful to the Art Institute of Chicago, Thoma Foundation, and Adler Planetarium curators and staff who were instrumental in shaping this project through discussions about collection items and loans. While these materials are not included in this book, they are represented in the exhibition and were essential for our conception of the volume.

We were most fortunate to have Bryan Keene and Risham Majeed graciously agree to serve as shepherds/peer reviewers for this book manuscript: their positive, constructive, and grounded feedback has truly enabled this volume to reach its full critical potential. Editing a book with so many moving pieces is hard work, and we could not have done it alone. We are particularly grateful to University of Chicago graduate student and Newberry UChicago research associate Vivian Lei, who not only contributed original pieces to this volume but also provided vital help in formatting and editing essays and compiling its bibliography, and to Northwestern University graduate student Emily Wood, who gave this book's bibliography the final big push it needed. And finally, heartfelt thanks go to the marvelous Kavita Mudan Finn who designed the beautiful index and copyedited the proofs for this volume.

This collaboration between the CRS and RaceB4Race® solidified when Noémie and Lia had a cup of coffee at Dollop in March 2020, just before the world shut down, and Noémie wishes to thank Lia for this adventure. You may not know this, Lia, but when I started my doctoral dissertation, I told my advisor that I wanted to study the racializing representation of Blackness in theatre *and* in visual culture. (My advisor had the good sense to point out that this was too much for one book, and I went on to write *Scripts of Blackness*.) Thank you for giving me the opportunity to fulfill the second half of that old dream. Collaborating on an exhibition, the present edited volume, and cultural programming around Premodern Critical Race Studies over the last three years has been a wild ride, and I could not have wished for a better partner in crime. Thank goodness for your brilliance, your vision, your cool, and your patience, Lia.

Lia wishes to thank Noémie for *her* patience and fierce determination to produce an incredible book, even while a pandemic was raging. Most importantly, I am grateful to have had Noémie as an encouraging partner, guide, and mentor in the field of PCRS. Like you, Noémie, I had felt frustrated with my inability to tackle race and visual culture and as an art historian working on the colonial period, this was particularly troubling. You have allowed me to think deeply on the topic and I hope we have invited others to do the same in the process of this collaboration.

CONTRIBUTORS

Andrea Achi. Trained as a Byzantinist, Dr. Achi's scholarship focuses on late antique and Byzantine art of the Mediterranean Basin and Northeast Africa. She specializes in the art and archaeology of Late Antiquity with a particular interest in illuminated manuscripts and ceramics. She has brought this expertise to bear on exhibitions like *Art and Peoples of the Kharga Oasis* (2017), *Crossroads: Power and Piety* (2020), and *The Good Life* (2021) at The Met Museum and in numerous presentations and publications. She holds a BA from Barnard College and a Ph.D. from New York University.

Brandi K. Adams is Assistant Professor of English at Arizona State University. Her research interests include the history of reading, the history of the book, premodern critical race theory of early modern England, and editorial practices of early modern English drama. She has recently published on 'unbookishness' in *Othello* and Keith Hamilton Cobb's *American Moor* in the journal *Shakespeare* and has contributed a chapter in *Shakespeare/Text* edited by Claire M.L. Bourne for *Contemporary Readings in Textual Studies, Editing and Performance*. She has begun working on her first monograph tentatively titled *Representations of Books and Readers in Early Modern English Drama*.

Roland Betancourt is Professor of Art History at the University of California, Irvine. He works on the Byzantine Empire, including its art, liturgy, and theology, with an interest in issues of sexuality, gender variance, and race. Betancourt is the author of *Byzantine Intersectionality: Sexuality, Gender, and Race in the Middle Ages* (Princeton University Press, 2020), *Performing* *the Gospels in Byzantium: Sight, Sound, and Space in the Divine Liturgy* (Cambridge University Press, 2021), and *Sight, Touch, and Imagination in Byzantium* (Cambridge University Press, 2018), as well as several edited volumes.

Beatrice Bradley is Assistant Professor of English at Muhlenberg College. Her research and teaching bring together early modern literature, health humanities, and critical theory, with a focus on the materiality and psychology of embodiment. She is currently working on a book project that examines the literary aftermath of the plague known as the Sweating Sickness, and she has published articles in *English Literary Renaissance* and *Milton Studies*.

Katherine Chacon is an undergraduate student at the University of Chicago, working towards a Bachelor of Arts in Art History and a Bachelor of Arts in Economics. Her primary research interests concern pre-modern visual depictions of race, the intersections of media, technology, and art throughout the twentieth and twenty-first century, and the role of influence and historicity in late nineteenth-century artworks.

Cecilio M. Cooper is currently a Forsyth Postdoctoral Research Fellow with University of Michigan's History of Art Department. Via black critical theory, they address scholarly debates around occult iconography, cartography, political theology, science studies, and gender. Cooper's first book manuscript, *South of Heaven: Surface, Territory + the Black Chthonic*, examines the occulted role blackness plays in cosmological constitutions of subsurface space by engaging the visual cultures of alchemy and demonology. Their research has been supported by the National Endowment for the Humanities, American Antiquarian Society, John Carter Brown Library, and Yale Center for British Art. Visit ceciliocooper.com for more information.

Aylin Corona graduated from the University of Chicago with a master's in Social Sciences, concentrating in History. Her thesis explored the lives of female court dwarves in early modern Europe, specifically within their roles as caretakers/companions and their enforced reproduction by patrons. Aylin is a Ronald E. McNair Scholar and was a fellow at UNC-Chapel Hill, presenting her research on disability representation in HBO's *Game of Thrones*.

Ambereen Dadabhoy is an Associate Professor of Literature at Harvey Mudd College. Her research focuses on cross-cultural encounters in the early modern Mediterranean and race and religion in early modern English drama. She investigates the various discourses that construct and reinforce human difference and in how they are mobilized in the global imperial projects that characterize much of the early modern period. Ambereen is co-author with Dr. Nedda Mehdizadeh of *Anti-Racist Shakespeare* (Cambridge Elements 2023). Currently, she is working on a project that explores the representation of Islam in Shakespeare.

Olivia Dill is a doctoral candidate in the Department of Art History at Northwestern University. She uses archival and technical art historical methods to study seventeenth-century Dutch and British Natural History prints and drawings. Dill's dissertation investigates the function of materials, and aesthetics of sheen in the procurement, observation, and depiction of insects in the early modern Atlantic world.

Caitlin Irene DiMartino is a PhD candidate in the Department of Art History at Northwestern University, where she researches the intersection of race, materiality, and religious identity. She is writing a dissertation on the early-modern phenomenon of Black Madonnas in France, Spain, and the Viceroyalty of Peru, looking specifically at the way these twelfth-century statues, which were reimagined through the application of black pigment, reflect regional preoccupations with dark skin, holiness, and the development of racial capitalism during the seventeenth and eighteenth centuries.

Alana Edmondson is a PhD student in English at Yale University. Her research focuses on histories of adaptation and performance of early modern drama–in particular, how these histories contributed to cultural constructions of Shakespeare and race between the sixteenth- and nineteenth- centuries. Grounded in studies of Shakespeare in performance, classical reception studies, manuscript studies and the history of race, her doctoral research aims to illuminate novel connections and unseat commonplace assumptions by exploring the commodity of blackness on the pre-modern European stage alongside the stakes of Black self-authorization in participating in the construction of Shakespearean cultural identity.

Rebecca L. Fall is Program Manager for the Center for Renaissance Studies at the Newberry Library and co-curator of the *Seeing Race Before Race* exhibition. Her doctoral dissertation was awarded the J. Leeds Barroll Prize by the Shakespeare Association of America, and her public engagement work has been supported by a Mellon/ACLS Public Fellowship. Beyond her work at the Newberry, Rebecca serves as a Pre-Amble Scholar at Chicago Shakespeare Theater and is completing a scholarly book that traces the surprising social functions of nonsense writing in early modern England.

Christopher D. Fletcher is the Assistant Director of the Center for Renaissance Studies at the Newberry Library in Chicago. He earned his PhD in Medieval History from the University of Chicago in 2015. His research and teaching focus primarily on religion and public engagement before 1800. He has published peer reviewed articles on the history of public engagement in medieval and early modern Europe and the digital humanities. He is a co-curator of the *Seeing Race Before Race* exhibition (on view Fall 2023) and has often brought medieval history to the public through in-person collection presentations, exhibitions, social media, and digital resources.

Elena FitzPatrick Sifford is Associate Professor of Art History and Director of Latin American and Caribbean Studies at Muhlenberg College. Her research centers on race, representation, and cross-cultural exchange in the Early Modern period with particular focus on the depicting of Africans and Afro descendants in the Spanish Viceroyalties of New Spain and Peru. She has recently published in *Ethnohistory*, *Art Journal*, *Latin American and Latinx Visual Culture*, and various edited volumes.

Cécile Fromont is Professor of the History of Art at Yale University. Her writing and teaching focus on the visual, material, and religious culture of Africa and Latin America with a special emphasis on the early modern period (ca 1500-1800) and on the Portuguese-speaking Atlantic World. Her publications include *The Art of Conversion: Christian Visual Culture in the Kingdom of Kongo* (2014; French translation 2018), *Afro-Catholic Festivals in the Americas: Performance, Representation, and the Making of Black Atlantic Tradition*, and *Images on a Mission in Early Modern Kongo and Angola* (2022).

Daniela Gutiérrez Flores is Visiting Assistant Professor of Spanish at the University of California, Davis. Her research focuses on the relations between texts, food, and culinary practices in the early modern Spanish Atlantic. Her current project explores cooking as a practice that allowed subjects to engage with lettered culture, shape new identities, and challenge class, gender and racial structures. She received her PhD from the University of Chicago in 2022.

Kim F. Hall is Lucyle Hook Professor of English and Professor of Africana Studies at Barnard College where she teaches courses in Premodern Critical Race Studies, Black Feminist Studies and Food Studies. She is the author of *Things of Darkness: Economies of Race and Gender in Early Modern England* (Cornell University Press 1995), *Othello: Texts and Contexts* (Bedford/St. Martin's 2007), and *The Sweet Taste of Empire: Sugar, Gender and Material Culture in Seventeenth Century England* (under contract with UPenn Press). She was the 2018 Wanamaker Fellow at Shakespeare's Globe and is currently working on the project: "'Othello Was My Grandfather': Shakespeare and Race in the African Diaspora."

Carissa M. Harris is Associate Professor of English at Temple University in Philadelphia, where she teaches courses on medieval sexualities, Chaucer, premodern rape and consent, and wenches. She is the author of *Obscene Pedagogies: Transgressive Talk and Sexual Education in Late Medieval Britain* (Cornell University Press, 2018) and the co-editor, with Sarah Baechle and Elizaveta Strakhov, of *Rape Culture and Female Resistance in Late Medieval Literature: With an Edition of Sixteen Middle English and Middle Scots Pastourelles* (Penn State University Press, 2022).

Andrés Irigoyen is a PhD Candidate in English at the University of Chicago. His research focuses primarily on Early Modern Literature and Philosophy, particularly on how contemporary philosophical and scientific texts inform literary articulations of the phenomenology of embodiment with close attention to various descriptions of its limits, that is, the experiences of labor, fatigue, and illness.

Edward Johnson is a PhD candidate in the Art History and History departments at the University of Chicago. His research focuses primarily on the architecture and urban culture of late-medieval and early modern Italy. He is particularly interested in exploring the role played by the urban environment in the social, political, and cultural construction of premodern Italian city-states.

Emily Kang graduated from the University of Chicago in 2021 with degrees in Art History and English Literature. After teaching English in Lyon, France for the 2021-2022 school year, Emily is now a History of Art Ph.D. student at the University of California, Berkeley. Her research focuses on early American visual culture with a particular interest in the built environment and a thematic focus on race, class, and nation-building.

M. Lindsay Kaplan is Professor of English at Georgetown University where she teaches and writes on the intersection of race, religion, and gender in medieval and early modern theology and literature. Her essays have appeared in *Philological Quarterly, Shakespeare Survey, Shakespeare Quarterly, Renaissance Drama,* and *Early Modern France,* in addition to edited collections. Most recently, she has published a monograph, *Figuring Racism in Medieval Christianity* (Oxford UP 2019) and an edited volume, *The Merchant of Venice: The State of Play* (London: The Arden Shakespeare, Bloomsbury, 2020). Her next book project traces the persistence of medieval theological racism in early modern English dramatic representations of Jews and Muslims.

Farah Karim-Cooper is Co-Director of Education at Shakespeare's Globe, Professor of Shakespeare Studies at King's College London, and Globe Director of the Shakespeare Centre London. She has published five essay collections and two monographs, *Cosmetics in Shakespearean and Renaissance Drama* (Edinburgh University Press 2006) and *The Hand on the Shakespearean Stage: Gesture, Touch and the Spectacle of Dismemberment* (Bloomsbury 2016). Her third book, *The Great White Bard: Shakespeare and Race, Then and Now*, is due out in 2023. Karim-Cooper's work on antiracist approaches to theater and pedagogy has led to the founding of the Early Modern Scholars of Colour Network in the UK.

Suzanne Karr Schmidt is the George Amos Poole III Curator of Rare Books and Manuscripts at Chicago's Newberry Library. She works on the materiality and use of prints and books, notably her monograph *Interactive and Sculptural Printmaking in the Renaissance* (2018), and exhibition catalogue *Altered and Adorned: Using Renaissance Prints in Daily Life* (Art Institute of Chicago, 2011). Recent and forthcoming exhibitions at the Newberry that engaged with her interest in the history of science and in paper engineering respectively include *Renaissance Invention: Stradanus's* Nova Reperta, co-curated with Lia Markey in 2020, and *Pop-Up Books Through the Ages* in 2023.

Dana E. Katz is Joshua C. Taylor Professor of Art History and Humanities at Reed College. Her research explores representations of religious difference in early modern European art. She is the author of *The Jew in the Art of the Italian Renaissance* (University of

Pennsylvania Press, 2008) and *The Jewish Ghetto and the Visual Imagination of Early Modern Venice* (Cambridge University Press, 2017). Her current book project, "Materials of Islam in Premodern Europe," studies the material effect of Christian and Muslim encounters.

Jamie Keener is a PhD student in English literature at the University of Illinois, Urbana-Champaign. Her primary research interests lie in the Global Middle Ages and the intersection between Premodern Critical Race Studies in late medieval England and fairy literature.

Stephanie S.E. Lee (李承恩) is a PhD Candidate in the Department of Art History at Northwestern University. Her research focuses on early modern and modern art, with an emphasis on works-on-paper, photography, Orientalism, and the role of transmediality in colonial visual culture. Her dissertation examines itinerant Japanese and Korean artists at the intersection of race-making, pan-Asianism, and gendered labor in the Japanese Empire.

Vivian Lei is a second-year master's student at the University of Chicago. She graduated in 2022 with an honors bachelor's degree in English Language and Literature. Her research interests include theories of race and ethnicity, contemporary multiethnic literature, medical humanities, and cultural/aesthetic production in late capitalism.

Sarah-Gray Lesley is a PhD candidate in English Literature at the University of Chicago. Her research interests include early modern racemaking, gender and sexuality, and the relationship between domestic and mercantile economies. Her dissertation project argues that early modern English literary writers arrived at a systemic category of white womanhood through depictions of reproduction and consumption.

Analú María López (Guachichil/Xi'iui) is the Ayer Librarian and Assistant Curator of American Indian and Indigenous Studies at the Newberry Library. As the librarian and Assistant Curator, she helps steward the Indigenous studies collection while guiding library users through, connecting them with, and interpreting materials linked to the collection. She is interested in historically underrepresented Indigenous narratives dealing with identity, language, and decolonization, intentional community collaborations for access to materials within colonial institutions, and the preservation, revitalization, and instruction of Indigenous languages. She holds a Master of Library and Information Sciences with a certificate in Archives and Cultural Heritage Resources and Services from Dominican University and a Bachelor of Arts in Photography with a minor in Latin-American Studies from Columbia College Chicago. Mrs. López began her career with the Newberry in 2004. After working for other libraries and museums in Chicago for 13 years, Mrs. López returned to the library in her current role in September 2017.

Lia Markey is the Director of the Center for Renaissance Studies at the Newberry Library. Her publications include a monograph, *Imagining the Americas in Medici Florence* (2016), and two edited volumes, *The New World in Early Modern Italy, 1492-1750* (2017) with Liz Horodowich, and *Renaissance Invention: Stradanus's "Nova Reperta"* (2020). She teaches at the University of Chicago and Northwestern University and has held fellowships at the Folger Library, the Warburg Institute, the Villa I Tatti, the Metropolitan Museum of Art, and the Herzog August Bibliothek. Currently, Lia participates in the Getty Connecting Art Histories Research Group, "Spanish Italy and the Iberian New World."

Julia Marsan is a PhD Candidate in the University of Chicago's Department of Comparative Literature. Her research focuses on Indigenous North American languages and literatures in the nineteenth and early twentieth centuries, with particular emphasis on interactions and collaborations between Indigenous writers and colonial anthropologists.

Noémie Ndiaye is the Randy L. and Melvin R. Berlin Assistant Professor of Renaissance and Early Modern English Literature at the University of Chicago. She works on early modern English, French, and Spanish theater with a critical focus on race. Her monograph *Scripts of Blackness: Early Modern Performance Culture and the Making of Race* (University of Pennsylvania Press, 2022) shows how performance culture helped strategically turn blackness into a racial category across early modern Western Europe. She has published articles in *Shakespeare Quarterly, Renaissance Quarterly, Renaissance Drama, Early Theatre, English Literary Renaissance, Literature Compass, Thaêtre*, and in various edited collections.

Elizabeth Neary is a Ph.D. Candidate in the Department of Spanish & Portuguese at UW–Madison. She specializes in cultural exchanges between Christians and Muslims on the Iberian Peninsula during the sixteenth and seventeenth centuries. Her dissertation project, "Significant Others Mixed Marriage in Early Modern Spanish Literature," examines marriage between Moriscos and Old Christians as represented in both literary and archival sources in early modern Spain.

Ricardo Padrón is Professor of Spanish at the University of Virginia, where he teaches courses about the literature and culture of the early modern Hispanic world, and conducts research on the geopolitical imagination of the Spanish empire as manifested in maps and writing. He is the author of two monographs, *The Spacious Word: Cartography, Literature and Empire in Early Modern Spain* (Chicago, 2004) and *The Indies of the Setting Sun: How Early Modern Spain Mapped the Far East as the Transpacific West* (Chicago, 2020). He has also collaborated with Christina Lee on a collection of primary sources for the study of the early modern Spanish Pacific, *The Spanish Pacific, 1523-1815: A Reader of Primary Sources in English Translation* (Amsterdam UP, 2020).

Risa Puleo is an independent curator and a doctoral candidate in Northwestern University's Art History department, where she studies the history of museums and colonial collecting of Native American, Oceanic, and African art. Her dissertation follows the Iberian Churra —the Spanish sheep discussed in her contribution to this volume — into sixteenth century Mexico, the American Southwest in the nineteenth century, and New York's Museum of Modern Art in the twentieth. The Churra's path makes apparent the disciplinary boundaries placed on Native objects as they moved from ethnographic museums and the discipline of anthropology and into modern art museums and the purview of art history.

Earnestine Qiu is a PhD student in Art and Archaeology at Princeton University. She studies Byzantine art, with a focus on late-medieval Anatolia and the artistic and theological exchanges between Byzantium and Armenia. She is particularly interested in depictions of topography and magic.

Arianna Ray is a PhD candidate in Art History at Northwestern University. She specializes in the study of works on paper in the early modern Atlantic world. Her dissertation examines the printed depiction of West Africans and their diasporic descendants in the Dutch Republic, Brazil, and Suriname in order to analyze the role of art, materiality, and medicine in the epidermalization of race.

Melani Shahin is a PhD Student in Music History and Theory at the University of Chicago. Her research interests include the history of music theory and its intersection with sixteenth-century Christian Hebraist scholarship, early modern historiographies of music, and book history.

Scott Manning Stevens (Akwesasne Mohawk) is Associate Professor of Native American and Indigenous Studies and English and the director of the Native American and Indigenous Studies Program at Syracuse University. Dr. Stevens' areas of interests also include the political and aesthetic issues that surround museums and the Indigenous cultures they put on display. He is a co-editor and contributing author for *Why You Can't Teach United States History without American Indians* and *Home Front: Daily Life in the Civil War North*. As a recent Radcliffe Institute fellow, he worked on completing a monograph titled, "Indian Collectibles: Appropriations and Resistance in the Haudenosaunee Homelands."

L. Lehua Yim is an independent scholar with a Ph.D. from Brandeis University and a J.D. from the University of San Francisco. Her research focuses on freshwater law and "nationalism" in the late Elizabethan period as a means to re-understand prose chorographies, Shakespeare's history plays, and Spenser's poetry. She also works on Native/Indigenous political and legal issues, especially those arising out of Hawai'i, and advocates for more substantial engagement with the twinned fields of Native Studies/Critical Indigenous Studies within early modern studies. Her work has been supported by awards from the Folger Shakespeare Library, the Newberry Library, and other institutions.

INDEX

Note: *Italicized* page numbers refer to images. Artworks discussed in detail are listed under the artist's name, where available, and title, where the artist is unknown.

A

Africa(n) xiv, xix, xx, 162, 166, 167, 170, 178, 182, 234
- **African-American** 42, 43, 44, 180
- **art exhibitions on** xxi, xxvi, 129–33
- **English representations of** 6, 59, *59*, 193, 200
- **European slave trade** 14, 17, 120, 146, *146–47*, 163, 164, 179
- **French representations of** xxv, 53, *58*, 107, 114, 115, 117, 118, 196
- **German representations of** *xv*, 60–61, *60–61*, 138, 155, *158*, *164*, 168–69, *169*
- **Italian representations of** *66*, 67, 143, 203
- **Portuguese representation of** 140, *141*
- **racialization of** 10
- **Spanish representations** 61, 173–77, *174*, *175*, *177*, 229

'African Magus' (sculpture, 15th C) 132, *133*; *see also* Metropolitan Museum of Art, The (New York)

African(a) Studies (discipline) xvi, xxvii

Agnese, Battista
- ***Manuscript portolan atlas of the world* (map, 1550)** 143, *144–45*

Alciato, Andrea 57–59, *57–59*

American Indian xxiv, 42, 43, 45, 75, 227; *see also* Indigenous; Native

America(n)(s) xxi, xxii, xxv–xxvii, 41–44, 75, 77, *106–7*, 107, 110, 129, 146, 166, 167, 168, 180, 218, 222, 226, 227, 234
- **Central** 150
- **colonization of** 119, 120, 149, 162, 230, 232
- **English representations of** 78, 152, *152–53*, *170*, 171

European (Anglo) 46, 184, 186
French representations of 115, 117–18, *206*, 207, 221
German representation of 114, 136, 140, 155
Italian representations of *66*, 67, 143, 163, 170, 224
Latin xx, 49, 112, 178, 179, 229
Spanish representation of *174*, 175, 204, *205*
anthropology xvi, xxvii, 221–22, 229, 231
antiblack(ness) xxvi, xxvii, 186, 217
antiracis(m)(t) xxiii, 181, 187, 188
antisemit(ic)(ism) xiv, xxiv, xxviii, 137, 186, 211
Arabic (language) 97, 130, 146, 234
archive(s)(al) xvi, xviii, xxiv, xxvii, 44, 45, 46, 47, 48, 84, 166, 197, 218, 220, 223
Newberry xxi, xxii, xxiii, xxvi, xxviii
art history (discipline) xi, xvi, xxiv, xxv, xxvi, 169, 234
Indigenous 121, 124
race studies and xviii–xx, 129, 176
Asia(n) xxv, 83, 88, 95n48, 106, 107, 112, 174, 185–86
European maps of 114, 115, 116–17, 138, 143, 234
European stereotypes of 67, 68, *68–69*, 140, 155, 175, 203
Atlantic xiv, xvi, 19, 112, 113, 162, 163, 176, 177, 178, 182, 215
Augsburg xiii, xiv, 173
Ayer, Edward E. xxi–xxii, xxiv, 43, 45n9, 49n25, 62; *see also* librar(y)(ies); Newberry Library (Chicago)

B

Baker, Josephine 180–82, *181*
Ball, Thomas
Emancipation Memorial (bronze, 1876) 180, *180*
Barbados xxiv, 64, *64*
Behn, Aphra
Oroonoko (book, 1696) xxviii, 193–94; *see also* Southerne, Thomas
Benzoni, Girolamo
History of the New World, The (book, 1590) 163–64; *see also* Bry, Theodor de; print/print culture; woodcut(s)
Bible xxiv, 52, 53, 132, 225
blackface xxiii, 10, 72, 192, 198, 200; *see also* cosmetics; Jonson, Ben; Kyd, Thomas; Shakespeare, William
Blackness xiv, xviii, xix, xxviii, 77, 105, 182, 207
poetic representations of 7–12
stage representations of 190–91, 192, 197, 198, *199*, 200, *201*
visual representations of xxiv, 58, *58*, *59*, *76*, 77, 173, 178–79
Black women 181, 182
representation of xxiii, 3–20, 67
Blaeu, Joan xxviii
Pecheli, sive Peking Imperii Sinarum (map, 1663) 154, *156–57*
Blathwayt, William
The Short State of Barbados (1638) 64–65, *64–65*
Blood purity (*limpieza di sangre*) 78, 210–11
book history (discipline) xi, xvii, xxiii, 3, 5, 20
British West Indies xxiii, 3, 14; *see also* Barbados; Caribbean; Haïti; Jamaica
Bry, Theodor de 179
Les Grands Voyages (book, 1590) 67, 152, 163–64, *165*, *170*, 171, *171*
Bulwer, John 176
Anthropometamorphosis (book, 1653) *76*, 77
Burgkmair, Hans 167–70, *169*
Byzanti(um)(ne) xxv, 84–94, *90*, 129, 130, 131, 133; *see also* Constantinople; Istanbul; Ottoman Empire

C

Callot, Jacques xiv
The Chariots (etching, 1616) 202–3, *202–3*
cannibal(s)(ism) 114, 117, 155
Caribbean 7, 18n65, 115, 148, 163, 164, 226; *see also* Barbados; Haïti; Jamaica
cartograph(er)(y)(ic) xxv, xxvi, 84, 96, 106, 116, 127, 143, 152, 155, 171, 229
books xvii, 154
Catholic(ism) xiv, 131, 148, 166, 176, 204, 210, 215, 229, 230, 232, 233
Cavazzi, Giovanni Antonio
Historical Description of Three Kingdoms (book, 1687) 171, *172*
Cedulario (manuscript, 1559) 150, *151*; *see also* Philip II Hapsburg, King of Spain; Spain
censor(ing) 14, 15, 16, 17, 18, 113

Chauveau, François
  Oeuvres de Racine (book, 1697) 196, 197
China 116, 136, 154, 156–57
Christian(ity) 232, 233
  African xxvii, 130, 131, 133, 169, 177
    fictitious rulers 136, 140, 141
  colonialism and xxii, 62, 75, 120, 148–49, 173, 176, 204, 230
  conversion to xvi, 214, 215
  Eastern xxv, 88–89, 90, 92–93, 93–94, 98
  scripture 21, 52
  Western xiv, 53, 62, 96, 97, 142
    clothing as signifier of religious difference 22, 25–26, 31–39, 38–39
    cosmography 138, 138–39
    literary allusion 56
    Native critiques of 225–26
    racialization of Jews xxiv, 26–40
    white supremacy and 22–24, 100, 103–4, 114, 155, 166–67; *see also* blood purity
climate theory xxv, 113, 114, 116; *see also* colonial(ism)
clock xiii–iv, *xv*; *see also* Augsburg
clothing xxiv, 12, 67, 162, 167, 209, 233, 234
  absence of 163, 164, 169, 170, 181
  as sign of otherness 21–22, 24–29, 33
  see also costume
colonial(ism) xx, xxv–xxvi, 10, 12, 43, 46, 48, 49, 59, 107–11, 127, 218, 232
  administration xxviii, 8, 56, 120, 124, 126, 150, 151, 230
  justification for 67, 68, 75, 112–15, 118, 149, 166, 178, 182
  literary responses to 72, 188, 193, 198
  religion and xxvii
  settler *see* settler colonialism
  slavery and 13
color theory 133
Columbus, Christopher 136, 140
  Of islands recently discovered in the Indian Ocean (book, 1493) xxii, 148–49, 148–49
Constantinople xxv, 32, 83–96, 90, 106; *see also* Istanbul, Ottoman Empire
continents xxv, 83, 109, 112–14, 116, 138, 138–39
  personification of 155, 158
conversion xxviii
  to Christianity xvii, xxvii, 24, 176, 204, 214, 215
Cosimo II Medici, Grand Duke of Florence 203
cosmetics xxviii, 78, 183
costume 27, 28n44, 75, 117, 166, 179, 186, 202–3, 203
  books xiv, xviii, xxiv, xxvi, xxviii, 152, 163
    Nicolay 22, 25, 26
    Vecellio 66, 67, 190
  see also clothing
Crenshaw, Kimberlé xix*n*22, 186, 230, 232
Critical Indigenous Studies (CIS) *see* Indigenous Studies (discipline)
Critical Race Studies (CRS) xvi, xvii, xviii, 21, 133, 217–29
Critical Race Theory (CRT) xviii–xix, xx, xxvi, 47, 133, 223, 230, 233
Crusade(s) xxv, xxviii, 88–89
  First Crusade 142
cultural anthropology 222, 230

D

dance xxvi–xxvii, 166–73, 168, 169, 170, 171, 172, 180–82, 204, 205, 206, 207
dance of death (*danse macabre*) xxvi, 167–68, 168, 170
D'Arcy McNickle Center for American Indian and Indigenous Studies 43; *see also* Ayer, Edward E.; Indigenous; Native; Newberry Library (Chicago)
Doctrine of Discovery (1452) 218, 225
Dogon 132, 133; *see also* 'Male Figure with Raised Arms'; Mali; sculpture
Dominican (religious order) 52, 89, 173
dress *see* clothing; costume
Ducis, Jean-François
  Othello (translation, 1794) 192–93
Dürer, Albrecht xiv, 138
  Les Qvatre livres d'Albret Dvrer (1557) 60–61, 60–61
Dutch (language) xxi, 26n36, 27n42

E

Egypt 89, 129, 131
emblem(s) xxviii, 16, 114, 121, 162, 167, 173, 178
  books of 57–59

England xviii, xxvi, 6–8, 13, 14 ,15, 59, 64, 75, 78, 136, *214*, 215, 229, 231
mapmaking in 152
theatrical culture in 184, 190, 192, 200
engraving xxii, 27, 27n42, 68, 71, 75, 91, 97, 163–64, *165*, 173–76, *174*, *202–3*, 203, *206*, 207, 231
frontispiece *196*, 197
map 152, *152–53*
environment 113, 115, 126, 185, 224, 230, 231, 233
built 84, 85
Eschenbach, Wolfram von
Parsival (romance, 13th C) xviii, 56
Ethiopia(n) xxvi, 52, 129–33
European stereotypes of 22, 58, 59, 87, 138, 140
literary representation of 8, 200
Europe(an) xvi, xviii, xix, xxviii, 6, 11, 43, 47, 57, 62, 83, 84, 88, 120, 123, 136, 140, 167, 174, 175, 176, 178, 192, 209, 223
colonialism 225–26, 230
humoralism 161–62
perceived centrality of 112, 116, 117, 138–40, *138–39*, 155, *158*, 219, 220, 231, 234
racialization of Africans xiv, 8, 58–59, *58*, *59*, 60, *60–61*, 78, *79*, 166, 168–69, 179, 180–82
as laborers 163, 164
in art exhibitions 130, 131, 132
in romance 56
in theatre 195
in theology 52, 53, *54–55*
racialization of Byzantines 86, 87
racialization of East Asians 154, *156–57*
racialization of Indigenous peoples xxvi, *66*, 67, 107, 109, 113–19, 126, *148–49*, 149, 204, *205*, 221, 232
through dance 166–73, *170*, *171*, *172*, *206*, 207
racialization of Jews xxiv, xxv, 29, 32, 85
sartorial legislation 25, 26
racialization of Muslims xxiv, xxv, 104–6, 142, 143, *144–45*, 215
Istanbul 85, *92–93*, 93, 94–101, *99*, *101*
racialization of South Asians 68, *68–69*
women 72
see also Christian(ity); whiteness
extractive scholarship xxvii, 48, 223, 227

F

Farmers vs. Covarrubias Map (1569) xxv, xxvi, 107, 109–11, *111*, 119–21, 123–27; *see also* cartograph(er)(y)(ic); Indigenous; maps; Mexico
feminis(m)(t) xxiii, 15, 85, 224
Fer, Nicolas de xxv, xxvi, 107–9, *108–9*, 110, 112, 115–18, 126–27; *see also* cartograph(er)(y)(ic); maps
Field Museum (Chicago) xxii, 42
First Nations 42, 45n9, 227; *see also* Indigenous; Native
Flanders 53
Florence xiv, xxi, 203
Förster, Hans
Playing Cards for the Game of Landsknecht (woodcut, 1570s) 208–9, *208–9*
France xxvi, 59, 115, 126, 177
Franciscan (religious order) xxiv, 52, 176n49, 204, 231
French (language) xxviii, 36, 61, 136, 192–93, 197, 207, 232
Nicolay 22n2, 26n36, 27n42, 31n54, 96
Fulcher of Chartres *see Hystoria de Itinere [con]tra turchos* (book, 1472)

G

gender xviii, xx, xxii, xxiv, 3, 14–20, 24, 25, 26, 27, 34, 67, 85, 97, 98, 102–3, 105, 132, 193, 232
gender studies (discipline) xxviii
geography xxv, 100, 107, 112, 121, 126, 148, 161, 175, 231
cultural 84, 85, 96
Eurocentrism 94, 95, 97, 105–6, 116, 155
German (language) 26n36, 27n42, 61, 137
gesture xiv, 162, 167–68, 171, 176–78, 207
Goa 68, *68–69*, 174
Gonçalez el Moxo, Alvar
Carta executorial (manuscript, 1567) 210, *210*
see also blood purity; Catholic(ism); Spain
Goos, Abraham 152, *152–53*; *see also* Speed, John
Granada 148, 233
Greece/Greek (people) xxv, 31, 33, 86–87, 89, 94, 100, 132, 192, 221
ancient 112, 113, 232, 233

H

habit(s) xxv, 24–25, 67, 96, 173, 197
hairstyle 71, 162; *see also* clothing; costume

Haïti xxviii, 179, 193
Hall, Kim F. xviii, xxvii, xxix, 186
Things of Darkness **(1995)** 6, 7–8, 11, 21, 105, 183–84
Hall, Stuart xvii, 83–84
harem xxv, 97–105; *see also* Istanbul; Ottoman Empire
Hawaiians (Native) 225
Hendricks, Margo xvii, xix, 184, 187, 233; *see also* Premodern Critical Race Studies
Heng, Geraldine xvii, 25n26
History of the India of the West **(manuscript, c. 1600)** 146–47, *146–47*; *see also* Arabic (language); Ottoman Empire; Turk(ey)(ish)
historiography 91, 231, 232
Huygen van Linschoten, Jan xxviii
Itinerario, voyage ofte schipvaert **(book, 1596)** 68, *68–69*
Hystoria de Itinere [con]tra turchos **(book, 1472)** 88–89, 142; *see also* Crusade(s)

I

Iberia(n) 23, 29, 113, 148, 166, 233; *see also* Granada; Portugal; Spain
India 68, 113, 115, 169, 174
European representation of *68–69*, 136, *202–3*, 203, 209
Indigenous xvi, xviii, xxi, xxii, 41–43, 64, 166, 182, 185, 188, 218, 219, 222, 224–28, 230, 232
European representation of 20, 114, 162, 167, 168, *169*, 180, 221
books *66*, 67, *74*, 75, *148–49*, 149, *170*, 170–71, *171*, *172*, 204, *205*, *206*, 207
maps 118, 152
painting 173, 175, *175*
language 62, *63*
legal status of 150, *151*, 178, 230, 232
librarianship xxiv, 43–49
mapmaking xxv, xxvi, 48, 107, 109–10, *110–11*, 119, 120, 121, *122*, 123–27, *124–25*; *see also* American Indian; Indigenous Studies (discipline); Mexico; Native
Indigenous Studies (discipline) xxii, xxiv, 43–46, 218, 224, 227, 228
Critical Indigenous Studies (CIS) xxiii, xxvii, 217, 220, 223, 225, 226, 230
intersectional(ity) xx, xxi, xxiii, 5, 15, 19, 20, 21, 232
intersectional material philology xxiii, 15, 19
Islam xvii, 22, 27, 28, 88, 94, 96, 97, 148, 184
stereotyping of 23–24, 26, 29, 40, 89, *92–93*, 93, 100, 104, 142, *214*, 215
Islamic Studies (discipline) xxviii
Istanbul xxv, 27, 83–84, 94–96, 102, 105, 106, 116; *see also* Constantinople; Ottoman Empire
Italian (language) 26n36, 61, 67, 146, 167

J

Jamaica xxiii, 3, *4*, 13–14
James VI/I Stuart, King of Scotland and England 72, 75, 200
Jew(s) 22–26, 114, 184, 231, 233
French representation of 53
in Nicolay xxiv, 26–40, *30*, *33*, *35*, *38*
German representation of 137, *137*
Iberia(n) 150, 210
Italian representation of 211, *212–13*
see also antisemit(ic)(ism); Judaism, stereotyping of
Jewish Studies (discipline) xxviii
Jonson, Ben 12
Masque of Blacknesse, The **(play, 1616)** xxviii, 72, 200, *201*
see also Africa(n); blackface; gender
Judaism, stereotyping of xvii, 24, 137

K

King, Henry 8
'The Boy's Answer' (poem, 17th C) xxiii, 3, 5, 6, 7, 9–12, 19
see also Rainolds, Henry
Klauber Workshop
St. Francis Xavier Baptizing a Native **(engraving, 18th C)** 173–75, *175*
knowledge production 96, 218, 219, 220–21, 224, 226
Kongo 131, 166–67, 171, *172*, 176–78, *177*; *see also* Africa(n); Christian(ity); processional cross (object)
Kyd, Thomas
The Spanish Tragedy **(1589)** xxviii, 198, *199*; *see also* blackface; woodcut(s)

L

Latin (language) 7–8, 9, 24–25, 53, 62, *63*, 75, 78, 86, 93, 119, 148, 176

***Letter from a Merchant at Jamaica* (pamphlet, 1709)** xxiii 3, *4*, 13–20

librarian(s) xxi, xxii, xxiv, 43, 44–45, 47

librar(y)(ies) xiv, xxiii, xxiv, xxviii, 6, 42, 43–45, 46, 47, 48, 220, 223, 230

Liudprand of Cremona 87–88, 215
  see also Byzanti(um)(ne); historiography

London 8, 12, 18, 19, 152
  print culture in xxiii, 3, 13, 14, 90
  Shakespeare's Globe Theatre 183, 184, 188

Lopes, Sebastiao
  ***Portolan* (map, 1565)** 140, *141*

Ludolphus de Saxonia
  ***Mirror of Human Salvation* (manuscript, 1455)** 53, *54–55*

Luther, Martin 137

M

'Male Figure with Raised Arms' (sculpture, 14th–17th C) 132, *133*; *see also* Dogon; sculpture

Mali 114, 132–33, *133*; *see also* Africa(n); sculpture

Mandeville, John xxviii
  ***Iohannis de Montevilla Itinerari* (translation, c. 1500)** 136

manuscript(s)/manuscript culture xviii, xxi, xxiii, 3, 5–8, 10, 12, 13, 18, 48, 56, 230, 231, 233
  Ayer collection xxii, 20, 49n25, 62, *63*, 64, *64–65*, 140, *141*, 146, *146–47*, 150, *151*
  Ethiopian 129–30, 132
  French 53, *54–55*, 136
  Spanish 210, *210*

maps xviii, xxi, xxii, xxiv, xxv–xxvi, xxviii, 75, 96, 107, 112–15, 146, 220, 225, 227, 229, 230
  Dutch 154, *156–57*
  English 152, *152–53*
  French 107–9, *108–9*, 115–18, *116*, *117*, *118*
  human figures in 24, 155, 167
  Indigenous 44, 48, *49*, 109–10, *110–11*, 119–27, *122*, *124–25*
  mappa mundi 136, 138–40, *138–39*, 234
  portolan 140, *141*, 143, *144–45*, 233

Mehmet II, Sultan of the Ottoman Empire 94, 95n48; *see also* Istanbul; Ottoman Empire

Mesoamerican studies (discipline) 47

Metropolitan Museum of Art (New York) xiii, xxi, xxvi, 129–34, *132*, *134*

Mexico xxii, xxiv, xxvi, 42, 43, 62, 107, 109, 204, *205*, 230
  Tenochtitlán 44, 48, *49*, 121
  Tultepec xxvi, 110, *110–11*, 119–20, 121, 123, 125–26

Miso-Spilus
  ***A wonder of wonders* (pamphlet, 1662)** 78, *79*
  see also cosmetics; gender; whiteness

Mohawk 218, 219, 227
  language 221, 224–25

monster(s)/monstrosity xxviii, 5, 6, 77, 87, 102, 136, 138, *138–39*

Montaigne, Michel de 219

Murad III, Sultan of the Ottoman Empire 146

Murad IV, Sultan of the Ottoman Empire 197

Muslim(s) xxv, 27, 84, 143, 148, 166
  racialization of 114, 210
  representation of 22–24, 25–26, 40, 104
    visual xxiv, xxvii, 28–29, 31, 32, 34, 36, *68*, 69
  see also blood purity; Islam; Ottoman Empire; Turk(ey)(ish)

N

Nahua 41, 43, 44, 47, 48, *49*, 62; *see also* Indigenous; Mexico

Nahuatl (language) xxvi, xxviii, 47, 48, 62, *63*, 119–27

Nanni, Giovanni 89

Native xxvii, 41–42, 43, 45–47, 48–49, 107, 113, 114, 115, 117–24, 126, 218, 219, 220, 221, 222–27; *see also* Indigenous; Indigenous Studies (discipline); Native Studies (NS)

Native Studies (NS) xxvii, 217, 218, 223

Nebrija, Antonio de
  ***Vocabulario trilingüe* (book, 1540)** xxviii, 62, *63*; *see also* Latin (language); Nahuatl (language); Spanish (language)

neoclassical 179, 192, 197, 232

Newberry Library (Chicago) xi–xii, xvi, xviii, xx, xxi–xxiii, xxvii, xxviii, 3, 14, 20, 42, 137, 221
  Indigenous collections in xxiv, xxvi, 43–46, 48, 49

manuscripts 5, 6, 7, 62, 146, 150
maps 119
printed books 61, 84, 86, 88, 89, 91, 95, 155, 204, 215
Nicolay, Nicolas de xxiv, xxv, *37*, *39*, 95, 97–102, 105
representation of Jews 22–23, 26–40, *30*, *33*, *35*, *38*

O

oral(ity) 45, 220, 221, 222, 223
Orientalism xxv, 10, 96, 105, 117, 232
Ortelius, Abraham
Theater of the World (book, 1580) 114, 155
Ottoman Empire 27, 84, 91, 142, 215
representation of 31, 32, 95–96, 97, 98, 100, 102, 104–5

P

Pacific 115, 227
periodization xvii, xviii, xxii, 184, 218, 233
Perry, Imani 3, 14, 15
Persia(n) 67, 93
Philip II Hapsburg, King of Spain 150, *151*
see also *Cedulario* (manuscript, 1559); Spain
physiognomy xvi, xxvi, 60, 162, 233
Picart, Bernard
Cérémonies et coutumes religieuses des peoples idolâtres (book, 1723) 173, *206*, 207
playing cards xviii, xxviii, *208–9*, 209
portolan (map) xxvi, xxviii, 140, *141*, 143, *144–45*, 152, 233; *see also* Agnese, Battista; Lopes, Sebastiao; maps
Portugal/Portuguese (people) 68, 113, 140, 166, 198, 233; *see also* Iberia(n); Spain
Premodern Critical Race Studies (PCRS) xix, xxi, xxii, 3, 6, 183, 184, 188, 218, 220, 233
see also Hall, Kim F.; Hendricks, Margo; Indigenous Studies (discipline)
Prester John 136, 140, *141*
print/print culture xiii, xiv, xxi, 5, 7, 12, 56, 137, 169, 232, 234, 137, 231, 232, 234
atlas 140, 155
books 25, 28, 56, 62, 75, 84, 88, 94, 95, 136, 138, 142
maps 109
miscellanies 11
pamphlets 3, 78
typography 14, 15, 20, 193
processional cross (object) 130, 131, 233

Q

Quito 173, 174, 175

R

Race Before Race (RaceB4Race) xi–xii, xvi, xvii*n*12, xviii, xxiii, xxvi, 223, 227, 228
racial materiality 21, 24
Rainolds, Henry
'A Black-moor Maid wooing a fair Boy' (poem, 17th C) xxiii, 3, 5, 6, 7, 9–13
see also King, Henry
Ridolfi, Pietro
Fan-shaped Diploma (engraving, 18th C) 211, *212*, *213*
Robert of Reims *see Hystoria de Itinere [con]tra turchos* (book, 1472)
romance xxviii, 53, 56, 72, 75, 142, 193, 233
Rome 85, 89, 95, 195, 232
Royal Shakespeare Company (UK) 188
Rugendas, Nikolaus xiii, xiv, *xv*, xxix
Russia(n) 77, 85, 112, 219
Rymer, Thomas
Short view of tragedy, A (1693) 192

S

Saint Luis Beltrán Baptizing an African Slave (painting, 1750) 173–77, *174*, 179
Sandys, George
Relation of a iourney, A (book, 1615) *70*, 71, 97
Sayet, Madeline 188
Schedel, Hartmann
Nuremberg Chronicle (book, 1493) xxviii, 89, *90*, 138, *138–39*, 168, *168*
sculpture 53, 132, 137
settler colonial(ism) xxvii, 218, 219, 221, 222, 223, 224, 225, 228
sexuality xvi, xx, 9, 14, 15, 16–18, 19, 72, 100, 102, 103, 232
Shakespeare, William 183–88, 192–93, 218
Othello (play, 1604) xxviii, 190–91, *190–91*, 192–93, 194
Titus Andronicus (play, 1591) 195
Shakespeare's Globe (London) xxvii, 183–88

slave trade xix, 14, 19, 20
slavery xvi, xix, xx, xxii, 15, 19, 94, 163, 182, 193, 222
as institution 64, *65*, 115
justification for 113, 219
reform xxiii 13, 14
Southerne, Thomas
Oroonoko **(play, 1696)** 194
see also Behn, Aphra; Shakespeare, William
sovereignty xxvi, 46, 119, 120, 122, 126–27, 143, 218, 219, 224, 225, 227, 230, 234; *see also* Critical Indigenous Studies (CIS); Indigenous
Spain xvii, xx, xxii, 45, 113, 119, 120, 121, 148, 150, *151*, 163, 173, 174, 179, 198, 210, *210*, 233
Spanish (language) 43, 48, 49, 62, *63*, 112, 146, 229, 230
Speed, John
America with those known parts **(map, 1626)** 152, *152–53*
see also Goos, Abraham
Suleiman the Magnificent, Sultan of the Ottoman Empire xxxviii, 143, *145*

T

Tarih-i Yeni Dünya, el-musemma be hadis-i nev **(manuscript, c. 1600)** *see History of India in the West* (manuscript, c. 1600)
Tenerani, Pietro
Bolívar Freeing the Slaves Statue Inauguration **(medal, 1846)** 179, *179*
Tenochtitlán *see* Mexico
theatre 184–87, 190, 192
translation xxviii, 8, 9, 18, 26, 91, 93, 96, 148
Nahuatl 47, 48, 62, 125
travelogue xxvi, 72, 75, 95, 96, 97, 98, 102, 167, 169, 171, 190, 232, 234
TribalCrit 47; *see also* Critical Race Theory (CRT); Indigenous; Native
Tultepec *see* Mexico
Turk(ey)(ish) xiv, xxv, 77, 85, 88–911, 94, 146, *146–47*, 232
representation of 31, 32, 36, 142, 197, 209
Nicolay *90*, 98, *99*, 100, *101*, 104, 105
Warmstry *214*, 215
see also Istanbul; Ottoman Empire
Turkish (language) 27n40
typography 5, 234
typology 53; *see also* Bible; Christian(ity); Ludolphus de Saxonia

V

Valadés, Diego
Rhetorica christiana **(book, 1579)** 204, *205*
see also Catholic(ism); colonial(ism); Indigenous; Mexico
Van de Passe, Simon
The Generall Historie of Virginia **(book, 1624)** *74*, 75
Vecellio, Cesare
Habiti antichi et moderni di tutto il mondo **(book, 1598)** *66*, 67, 152, 190
Verardi, Carlo
In Praise of King Ferdinand **(play, 1494)** 148–49

W

Warmstry, Thomas
The baptized Turk **(book, 1658)** *214*, 215
Weiditz, Christoph 179
Trachtenbuch **(book, 1529)** 163, *164*
White, John 171; *see also* Bry, Theodor de; engraving; Harriot, Thomas
white supremacy xvi, xxiv, xxvi, 42, 45, 72, 109, 178, 221, 225–26
whiteness xx, xxvii, 10, 11, 45, 47, 53, 77, 78, 95, 97, 98, 105, 183, 185, 197, 200, 224, 226
Whitney, George
Choice of Emblemes **(1586)** 57, *59*
Wolgemut, Michael 138 *138–39*, 168, 171
woodcut(s) xiv, xxiv, 27, 36, 77, 96, 98, 137, 148–49, 163, 198, 209
Wroth, Mary
Urania **(1621)** xxviii, 72, *73*